Inflation in Emerging and Developing Economies

Evolution, Drivers, and Policies

Editors

Jongrim Ha, M. Ayhan Kose, and Franziska Ohnsorge

WORLD BANK GROUP

1 2 3 4 22 21 20 19

ISBN (paper): 978-1-4648-1375-7
ISBN (electronic): 978-1-4648-1376-4
DOI: 10.1596/978-1-4648-1375-7

Cover design: Lauren Kaley Johnson, World Bank Group.

Library of Congress Cataloging-in-Publication Data has been requested.

Advance Praise for *Inflation in Emerging and Developing Economies*

Many emerging market economies experienced a remarkable decline in inflation rates over the last two decades, after years of seemingly intractable high inflation. Ha, Kose, and Ohnsorge offer the first book-length analysis of this remarkable achievement, asking how it happened, what it tells us about best policy frameworks, and whether it will endure. At a time when global financial conditions pose a challenge to emerging-market currencies and monetary policies, this book is an essential guide to the road ahead. All students of the global economy will want to read it carefully.

Maurice Obstfeld
Economic Counsellor and Director of Research
International Monetary Fund

A remarkable resource for anyone interested in inflation in the modern world, clear and easy to follow. This book is an order of magnitude more comprehensive than anything else out there, not only in its country coverage, but in its exploration of all the major issues and debates surrounding inflation. Curiously, most of the existing academic literature has focused on advanced economies—which are also thoroughly covered here—yet there is so much to be learned from the dramatic inflation decline in emerging markets and low-income economies, including for design of advanced economy institutions. Any student, academic researcher or policy economist who wants to understand the big picture on world inflation, and when and where it might surprise in the future, will find this book fascinating.

Kenneth Rogoff
Thomas D. Cabot Professor of Public Policy
and Professor of Economics
Harvard University

This is an important and timely contribution to our understanding of inflation and the causes of the synchronized decline in the second half of the 1990s around the world. Compared to previous research, it distinguishes specific features of the inflation process in advanced economies, emerging market and developing economies, and low-income countries. It provides many policy insights such as discussions on anchoring inflation expectations and the determinants of exchange rate pass-through, two central issues for price stability. The book reminds us that achieving low inflation does not imply that the risks of high inflation have disappeared and presents policy lessons to achieve and maintain price stability. I am certain that this would be a valuable reference for scholars and policy makers.

José De Gregorio
Dean of the School of Business and Economics, Universidad de Chile
Former Governor of the Central Bank of Chile

Advance Praise for *Inflation in Emerging and Developing Economies*

This book tackles important issues that have received far less attention than they deserve—what drives inflation in emerging and developing economies, what effects it has on the populations of these economies, and how the scourge of high inflation can be conquered. The book is rich in data, analysis, and useful policy prescriptions, all of which are woven together in a masterful and thoughtful way that makes the book a very useful reference source for academics and policy makers alike.

Eswar Prasad
Tolani Senior Professor of Trade Policy
Cornell University

This is a truly monumental work, incorporating pathbreaking data collection, a comprehensive survey of the literature, all viewed through the lens of new empirical methods. The volume represents a much-needed compilation of the research on inflation dynamics and broader economic effects, with special reference to emerging market and low-income country experiences that have heretofore been largely neglected. This will be *the* reference on the phenomenon of inflation for years to come.

Menzie Chinn
Professor of Public Affairs and Economics
University of Wisconsin at Madison

Summary of Contents

Table of Contents

Figures

Tables

Acknowledgments

Although only three names appear on its cover, it has taken the proverbial village to produce this book. We are extremely fortunate to have worked with many outstanding colleagues and are grateful for their generous and insightful contributions. The seven chapters of this book are the product of dedicated efforts by our tireless co-authors: Anna Ivanova, David Laborde, Csilla Lakatos, Will Martin, Hideaki Matsuoka, Peter Montiel, Ugo Panizza, Peter Pedroni, Marc Stocker, Filiz Unsal, Dana Vorisek, and Hakan Yilmazkuday. We are also thankful to Sergiy Kasyanenko, Atsushi Kawamoto, Seong Tae Kim, Wee Chian Koh, Peter Nagle, Yohei Okawa, and Naotaka Sugawara for their contributions to annexes, boxes, and background literature reviews.

We owe a debt of gratitude to colleagues who provided detailed comments, discussed our findings, and patiently answered our many questions: Carlos Arteta, John Baffes, John Beghin, Eduardo Borensztein, Sinem Kilic Celik, Menzie Chinn, Matteo Ciccarelli, Kevin Clinton, Andrew Dabalen, Zsolt Darvas, Jose De Gregorio, Selva Demiralp, Shantayanan Devarajan, Alistair Dieppe, Erik Feyen, Norbert Fiess, Hans Genberg, Stefan Gerlach, Graham Hacche, Raju Huidrom, Ergys Islamaj, Andy Jobst, Alain Kabundi, Gerard Kambou, Gene Kindberg-Hanlon, Patrick Kirby, Stephen O'Connell, Tatsuyoshi Okimoto, Christopher Otrok, David Papell, Franz Ruch, Yirbehogre Modeste Some, Christopher Towe, Kozo Ueda, Mark Watson, Collette M. Wheeler, Lei Sandy Ye, and Kamil Yilmaz. We also would like to thank the participants of many internal seminars for useful suggestions on the preliminary chapters, and numerous scholars and central bank officials for conversations on topics covered here.

We are deeply grateful to Xinyue Wang and Heqing Zhao for shouldering the lion's share of the research assistance burden. We are thankful to Cristhian Javier Vera Avellan, Zhuo Chen, Ishita Dugar, Hao Jiang, Julia Renee Roseman, and Xueliang Wang for excellent research assistance.

We are indebted to our colleagues who worked on the production process. Graeme Littler produced the online publication. Mark Felsenthal, Patricia Katayama, Jewel McFadden, Koichi Omori, and Tomoko Hirai managed media relations and dissemination. Mark Felsenthal and Graeme Littler provided editorial support, with contributions from Betty Dow, Adriana Maximiliano, and Quinn Sutton. Naotaka Sugawara and Maria Hazel Macadangdang produced the index. Lauren Kaley Johnson designed the cover. We truly appreciate the herculean efforts of Adriana Maximiliano, Quinn Sutton, and Maria Hazel Macadangdang in assembling the print publication.

The production of this book was managed by the Prospects Group of the Development Economics Vice Presidency of the World Bank Group. The Prospects Group gratefully acknowledges financial support from the Policy and Human Resources Development (PHRD) Fund provided by the Government of Japan.

Abbreviations

A	annual data
AE	advanced economy
ADF	augmented Dickey-Fuller unit-root test
AIC	Akaike information criterion
AREAER	Annual Report on Exchange Arrangements and Exchange Restrictions
BCB	Central Bank of Brazil
BCC	Central Bank of Chile
BVAR	Bayesian vector autoregression
CB	central bank
CBI	central bank independence and transparency index
CEMAC	Central African Economic and Monetary Community
CES	constant elasticity of substitution
CGE	computable general equilibrium model
CMA	commodity-importing EMDEs
CORE	core consumer price index
CPI	consumer price index
CXA	commodity-exporting EMDEs
DD	domestic demand
DEF	gross domestic product deflator
DOLS	dynamic ordinary least squares
DS	domestic supply
DSGE	dynamic stochastic general equilibrium model
EAP	East Asia and Pacific
ECA	Europe and Central Asia
ECB	European Central Bank
ECM	error correction model
ECCU	Eastern Caribbean Currency Union
EMDEs	emerging market and developing economies
ER	exchange rate
ERPTR	exchange rate pass-through ratio
EX	exchange rate
FAO	Food and Agriculture Organization
FAVAR	factor-augmented vector autoregression model
FE	fixed effects
FIRE	full-information rational expectations
FMOLS	fully modified ordinary least squares
G7	Group of Seven
GDP	gross domestic product
GNI	gross national income
GTAP	Global Trade Analysis Project
GVAR	global vector autoregression
GVC	global value chains
IFAD	International Fund for Agricultural Development
IFPRI	International Food Policy Research Institute
IFS	International Financial Statistics
IMF	International Monetary Fund
IMP	import prices
IRF	impulse response function
IT	inflation targeting

LAC	Latin America and the Caribbean
LICs	low-income countries
MNA	Middle East and North Africa
MP	monetary policy
MPC	Monetary Policy Council
mt	metric ton
NBP	National Bank of Poland
NEER	nominal effective exchange rate
OECD	Organisation for Economic Co-operation and Development
OLS	ordinary least squares
OPEC	Organization of the Petroleum Exporting Countries
PIM	Policies, Institutions, and Markets
PP	Phillips-Perron unit-root test
PPI	producer price index
RHS	right-hand side
Q	quarterly data
SAR	South Asia
SDGs	Sustainable Development Goals
SIC	Schwarz information criterion
SITC	Standard International Trade Classification
SSA	Sub-Saharan Africa
SVAR	structural vector autoregression model
TiVA	Trade in Value Added
UNCTAD	United Nations Conference on Trade and Development
VAR	vector autoregression
VECM	vector error correction model
WAEMU	West African Economic and Monetary Union
WFP	World Food Programme
WHO	World Health Organization
WITS	World Integrated Trade Solution
WPI	wholesale price index
WTI	West Texas Intermediate
WTO	World Trade Organization
XR	exchange rate

Chapter Authors

Jongrim Ha, Economist, Development Prospects Group, World Bank

Anna Ivanova, Deputy Division Chief, Western Hemisphere Department, International Monetary Fund

M. Ayhan Kose, Director, Development Prospects Group, World Bank

David Laborde, Senior Research Fellow, International Food Policy Research Institute

Csilla Lakatos, Senior Economist, Development Prospects Group, World Bank

Will Martin, Senior Research Fellow, International Food Policy Research Institute

Hideaki Matsuoka, Economist, Development Prospects Group, World Bank

Peter J. Montiel, Professor of Economics, Williams College

Franziska Ohnsorge, Manager, Development Prospects Group, World Bank

Ugo Panizza, Professor of Economics, Graduate Institute of International and Development Studies

Peter Pedroni, Professor of Economics, Williams College

Marc Stocker, Senior Economist, Development Prospects Group, World Bank

Filiz D. Unsal, Economist, Research Department, International Monetary Fund

Dana Vorisek, Senior Economist, Development Prospects Group, World Bank

Hakan Yilmazkuday, Associate Professor of Economics, Florida International University

In the 1970s inflation became a severe problem of global dimensions. Following remarkable stability in the 1960s, prices rose sharply in 1973 and 1974.... The inflationary surge helped provoke the global recession of 1974-75.... The developing countries did not pass through these economic disruptions unscathed. Global inflation swept them along, even regions with traditions of price stability experienced high domestic inflation rates.

Bruce K. MacLaury (1981)

There are forces in the global economy today that are conspiring to hold inflation down. Those forces might cause inflation to return more slowly to our objective. But there is no reason why they should lead to a permanently lower inflation rate.

Mario Draghi (2016)

INTRODUCTION

Inflation in Emerging and Developing Economies: Evolution, Drivers, and Policies

Motivation

The global economy has witnessed a remarkable decline in inflation over the past four to five decades. Inflation has fallen around the world, with median annual national consumer price inflation down from a peak of nearly 17 percent in 1974 to about 1.7 percent in 2015—the lowest level in almost half a century (Figure 1). Among advanced economies, median inflation has similarly dropped to its lowest level—0.3 percent—from its highest—15 percent—over the same period.

Encouragingly, emerging market and developing economies (EMDEs) have also experienced an extraordinary decline in inflation over the same time frame: after peaking in 1974 at 17.3 percent, inflation in these economies declined to 3.5 percent in 2017—only marginally up from its lowest level in the period, 2.7 percent, reached in 2015. Despite a checkered history of managing inflation among many EMDEs, disinflation occurred across all regions, including those with a history of persistently high inflation, such as Latin America and Sub-Saharan Africa. Even among low-income countries (LICs), inflation has fallen by two-thirds since the mid-1970s, to 5 percent in 2017.

Although the "near-universal" character of the decline in inflation since the mid-1970s was recognized at an early stage by Rogoff (2003), research has almost exclusively focused on low inflation in advanced economies. Many studies have analyzed the sources of low inflation, its highly synchronized nature, and its policy implications for these economies. To date, however, no comprehensive study has explored the evolving dynamics of inflation in EMDEs. This book fills that critical gap with the following contributions:

- **A comprehensive analysis of inflation in EMDEs and LICs.** Seven chapters analyze the recent history of inflation among EMDEs, including its evolution, its synchronization across countries, the global and domestic sources of inflation, and the roles of expectations and exchange rate pass-through. In addition, the book presents a detailed examination of inflation and monetary policy–related challenges in LICs and assesses their implications for development outcomes.

- **A truly global data set.** By assembling a database that includes the largest sample of countries of any major inflation study, this research is enriched by information that is considerably more representative of "global inflation"

Note: This chapter was prepared by Jongrim Ha, M. Ayhan Kose, and Franziska Ohnsorge.

FIGURE 1 Evolution of inflation

Global inflation declined from a peak of nearly 17 percent (annual average) in 1974 to 2.6 percent in 2017. The decline was broad-based, across country groups and inflation measures, but began somewhat earlier in advanced economies than in EMDEs and LICs. The recent low and stable global inflation environment resembles those of the Bretton Woods fixed exchange rate system in the post-war period up to the early 1970s, and the gold standard of the early 1900s.

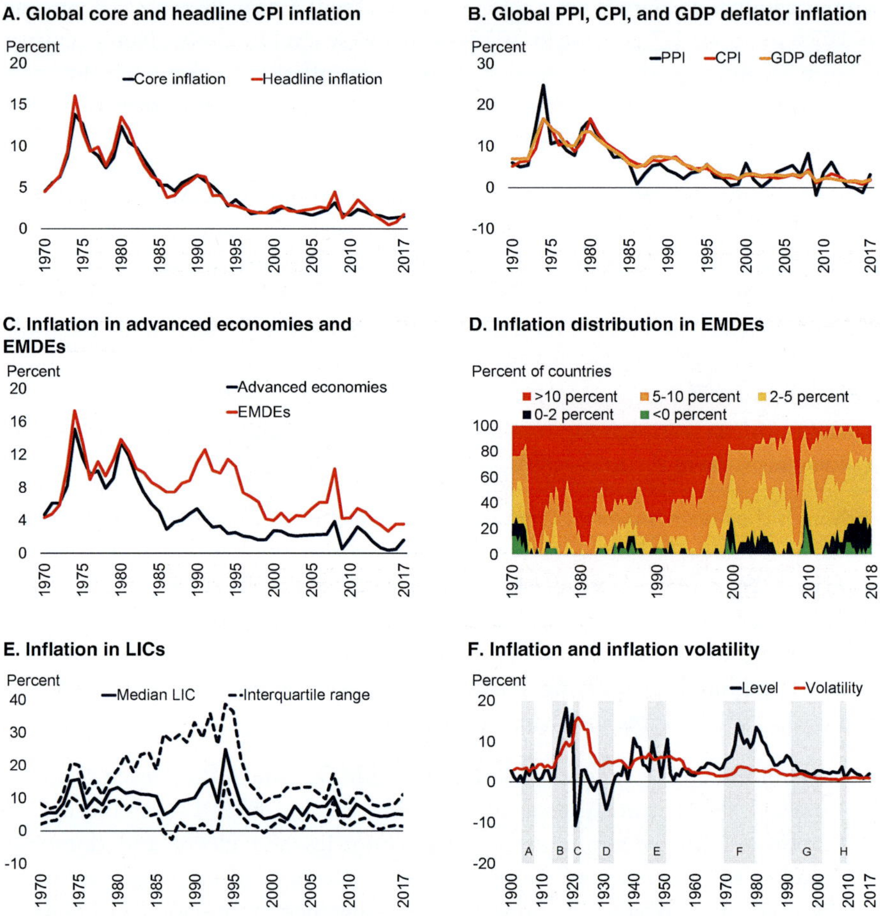

Source: Haver Analytics; ILOSTAT; International Monetary Fund International Financial Statistics and World Economic Outlook databases; OECDstat; UNdata; World Bank.

Note: CPI = consumer price index; EMDEs = emerging market and developing economies; GDP = gross domestic product; LICs = low-income countries; PPI = producer price index.

A. Median headline and core year-on-year inflation for 41 economies, including 16 EMDEs (see details in the Appendix).

B. Median PPI, CPI, and GDP deflator year-on-year inflation for 39 economies, including 22 EMDEs.

C. Median year-on-year consumer price inflation for 29 advanced economies and 123 EMDEs (including 28 LICs).

D. Sample includes 27 advanced economies and 50 EMDEs. Refers to year-on-year inflation.

E. The solid line shows median year-on-year headline inflation; dashed lines refer to the interquartile range, based on 28 LICs.

F. Median of annual average inflation in 24 countries where data are available across the full period. A = gold standard and stability (1880-1913); B = World War I and high inflation (1914-18); C = post–World War I depression and deflation (1920-22); D = Great Depression (1929-33); E = World War II, monetary controls and post-war inflation (1945-49); E to F = Bretton Woods system of fixed exchange rates (1944-71); F = floating exchange rates and oil shocks (Organization of the Petroleum Exporting Countries, 1971-79); G = introduction of inflation targeting (1990-2000); H = global financial crisis.

than earlier work, which relied predominantly on advanced economy data. The database further covers multiple measures of inflation and macroeconomic and structural country features over almost five decades.

- **Use of cutting-edge methodologies.** The study examines EMDE inflation using cutting-edge empirical methodologies that have thus far mostly been employed in studies of inflation in advanced economies. A variety of time-series and panel econometric models are complemented by event studies, case studies, and historical comparisons that shed additional light on the topics under consideration.

Why does inflation matter?

High inflation is often associated with lower growth and financial crises (IMF 2001; Mishkin 2008). Rising price levels are further linked to weaker investor confidence, undercut incentives to save, and erode financial and public sector balance sheets. Moreover, the damage of high inflation can fall disproportionately on the poor, since poorer households are more reliant on wage income, have less access to interest-bearing accounts, and are unlikely to have significant holdings of financial or real assets apart from cash. For these reasons, low and stable inflation has been associated with better growth and development outcomes, financial stability, and poverty reduction.[1]

Key findings and policy messages

The book offers a range of analytical findings and policy messages. A recurring theme is the benefits of stability-oriented and resilient monetary policy frameworks, including central bank transparency and independence. Such policy frameworks need to be complemented by strong macroeconomic and institutional arrangements. For many EMDEs, measures to strengthen monetary policy frameworks, and macroeconomic policy frameworks more broadly, are particularly urgent. The book documents that inflation expectations are more weakly anchored in EMDEs than in advanced economies and, in EMDEs that do not operate inflation targeting frameworks, exchange rate movements tend to have larger and more persistent effects on inflation.

---

[1] Extremely low inflation, however, such as has prevailed in many advanced economies over the past decade, can also be problematic: it may make it difficult for central banks to lower real short-term interest rates sufficiently to provide the requisite stimulus to demand, given the lower bound on nominal interest rates; and it may tip into deflation—a sustained decline in prices—which can exacerbate recessionary tendencies (Blanchard, Dell'Ariccia, and Mauro 2010; Arteta et al. 2018).

Low inflation: Here to stay?

Disinflation over recent decades has been broad-based across country groups and is evident in multiple measures of inflation, including headline and core consumer prices, energy and food prices, producer prices, and the gross domestic product (GDP) deflator.[2] Disinflation began in advanced economies in the mid-1980s and in EMDEs in the mid-1990s. By 2000, global inflation had stabilized at historically low levels. Inflation in EMDEs fell from stubbornly persistent double digits during the 1970s, 1980s, and most of the 1990s to 3.5 percent in 2017. By 2017, inflation was within or below central bank target ranges in three-quarters of EMDEs that had adopted inflation targeting. As the level of inflation has fallen, its volatility has also declined, most sharply in the transition economies of the former Soviet Union and in Sub-Saharan Africa.

Is low inflation here to stay? A reason for optimism is that the confluence of structural and policy-related factors that have fostered global disinflation is unlikely to be reversed. Foremost among these has been unprecedented international trade and financial market integration. In the median EMDE, as in the median advanced economy, trade has increased by half since 1970, to 75 percent of GDP in 2017, and international assets and liabilities have more than tripled (although they remain only one-quarter the level of advanced economies). Technological changes have also transformed production processes in ways that affect the formation of prices (Draghi 2016; Lowe 2017; Yellen 2017).

On the policy front, the adoption of more resilient monetary, exchange rate, and fiscal policy frameworks by some EMDEs has facilitated more effective control of inflation (Hammond, Kanbur, and Prasad 2009; Taylor 2014; Fischer 2015). Twenty-four EMDEs have introduced inflation targeting monetary policy frameworks since the late 1990s. In some EMDEs, structural reforms of labor and product markets have also supported disinflation by making markets more flexible and strengthening competition.

However, there are reasons to worry that factors that have held inflation at bay over the past decades may lose momentum or be rolled back. In his seminal essay, Rogoff (2003) concludes that "the greatest threat to today's low inflation, of course, would be a reversal of the modern trend toward enhanced central bank independence, particularly if trend economic growth were to slow, owing, say, to a retreat in globalization and economic liberalization." The rising protectionist sentiment of recent years and reform fatigue in some economies may slow the pace of globalization and structural policy improvements.

[2] Disinflation is a decline in inflation rates, regardless of inflation being negative (deflation) or positive.

Mounting public and private debt in many countries could weaken commitment to strong fiscal and monetary frameworks. These reversals, especially if they were to coincide with tight labor markets or commodity price volatility, could reignite inflation.

The current period of low and stable inflation resembles those of the Bretton Woods fixed exchange rate system of the post-war period up to 1971 and the gold standard of the early 1900s. All three episodes are characterized by inflation below 5 percent for an extended period. It is notable, however, that the two earlier episodes were followed by sharply rising inflation, illustrating that maintaining low inflation can be as great a challenge as achieving low inflation.[3]

The achievement of low inflation over the course of the past four to five decades may be by no means permanent (Rogoff 2014; Draghi 2016; Carstens 2018). If unwanted inflation makes a comeback, many EMDEs would be particularly vulnerable to the undesirable economic outcomes associated with high inflation: their inflation expectations are less well anchored, and the absence of strong monetary policy frameworks in many of these economies means that inflation is more sensitive to exchange rate movements. In addition, as debt loads have risen in recent years, EMDE fiscal positions have become increasingly vulnerable to shifts in market sentiment and rising borrowing costs. Central banks may struggle to contain inflationary pressures and may not receive much support from stabilizing fiscal policy.

Global inflation cycle: Learning to live with it

A critical feature of the international inflation experience of the past four to five decades has been the rising importance of a "global inflation cycle" (captured in a common global factor) in explaining inflation at the country level (Carney 2015). Since 2001, this global factor has accounted for one-quarter of the inflation variation in the median advanced economy and almost one-fifth in the median EMDE. The role of the global inflation cycle has been most prominent in countries that are more developed and more integrated into the global economy.

The emergence of a global inflation cycle was likely driven by multiple structural and cyclical forces, including globalization, technological progress, changes in

[3] In the 1970s, inflation became a serious global problem after a remarkable period of price stability in the 1960s. The sharp increase in oil prices in 1973-74 led to a rapid acceleration in inflation and sharp decline in growth in many countries. This major oil price shock also triggered the 1975 global recession that in turn marked the beginning of a prolonged period of stagflation (Kose and Terrones 2015). Global inflationary pressures also led to a significant increase in domestic inflation in developing economies, including those that experienced relatively low and stable inflation in the late 1960s and early 1970s (Cline 1981; Bordo and Orphanides 2013).

policy frameworks, and a variety of cyclical global shocks. For example, global demand shocks and oil price shocks have each accounted for 40 percent of the variation in global inflation since 1970. In the median country, three global shocks—global demand shocks, supply shocks, and oil price shocks—have accounted for about one-quarter of domestic inflation variation since 2001. Of these, the most important were global demand (especially the global recession of 2008-09) and oil price shocks (especially the plunge of 2014-16). Nonetheless, domestic shocks—especially domestic supply shocks—have remained the main source of domestic inflation variation.

A strengthening global inflation cycle raises concerns that central banks' control over domestic inflation may have weakened. Inflation synchronization in and of itself need not warrant policy intervention (IMF 2018). However, heads of major advanced economy central banks have acknowledged the need to consider the global environment in setting monetary policy in light of the highly synchronized nature of global inflation (Bernanke 2007a; Draghi 2015; Carney 2015). The increased synchronicity of global inflation could increase the risk of policy errors when the appropriate response to undesirably low or high inflation differs depending on the origin (domestic versus foreign) of the underlying inflation shock (Hartmann and McAdam 2018). In addition, a weakening of monetary policy influence over domestic inflation could raise the stakes for fiscal policy to respond to excessive or insufficient domestic demand.

For policy makers, these observations suggest an increasing urgency to build resilience to global and domestic shocks and develop a keener understanding of their underlying sources. This is particularly the case for EMDEs with deep or rapidly growing integration into the global economy or ones with weak monetary policy frameworks. Options to help insulate economies from the impact of global shocks include the active use of countercyclical policies; strengthening institutions, including through greater central bank independence; and establishing a fiscal environment that is resilient enough to contribute effectively to macroeconomic stabilization.

The global inflation cycle could also strengthen the case for coordinated monetary policy action to respond to undesirably low or high global inflation. Coordinated action could amplify the impact of policies implemented by individual countries.

Anchoring inflation expectations: Better but not enough

Long-term inflation expectations have declined and become more firmly anchored in the past two decades in both advanced economies and EMDEs. However, expectations are more weakly anchored in EMDEs in general than in advanced economies. The introduction of inflation targeting regimes and increased central bank transparency has been associated with the firmer mooring of long-term expectations. Among EMDEs, lower public debt ratios and greater trade openness have also been associated with stronger anchoring of expectations.

Exchange rate pass-through: Amplification mechanism

Exchange rate pass-through to inflation varies widely among EMDEs, depending on the sources of shocks and country characteristics. Exchange rate movements that stem from domestic monetary policy shocks are often accompanied by above-average pass-throughs to inflation in EMDEs. The impact on inflation of exchange rate movements resulting from domestic demand shocks typically produces negative or insignificant pass-through ratios, reflecting the offsetting effects of the growth and exchange rate channels. Global shocks account for a relatively smaller proportion of exchange rate movements, and their pass-through depends on country characteristics and the source of the shock. Greater central bank independence and the adoption of credible inflation targets are associated with significantly lower average pass-throughs.

These findings underscore the importance of understanding the underlying sources of exchange rate movements in the formulation of appropriate monetary policy responses. Moreover, a credible commitment to maintaining low and stable inflation can play a key role in dampening the pass-through of even sizable currency depreciations to prices in EMDEs.

Inflation in LICs: Challenges abound

Global factors have been an important driver of the decline in LIC inflation since 1990. What sets LICs apart from other country groups may be not so much that they differ in country characteristics, but that these characteristics appear to operate differently in the LIC environment. For example, although LICs with fixed exchange rates seem to succeed in anchoring inflation expectations about as well as other EMDEs with fixed rates, LICs with floating exchange rates have had a much more difficult time anchoring inflation expectations than other countries with floating rates. In part because of poorly anchored inflation expectations, any temporary shocks to inflation, such as those arising from food price spikes, can trigger higher inflation than LIC central banks can contain. Separately, the transmission of global food price spikes to domestic LIC inflation (combined with unintended consequences of other policies) can materially raise poverty, as observed during the global food price spikes in 2007-08 and 2010-11.

The sizable role that global factors have played in driving inflation in LICs points to the need to improve LIC central bank control over domestic inflation.

For example, central banks could strengthen their efforts to convince the public of the primacy of the low-inflation objective by committing to an inflation target. However, this strategy may not yet be appropriate for LICs, many of which have weak and uncertain channels of monetary policy transmission, data deficiencies, and limited analytical capacity at their central banks. Beyond monetary policy, the judicious use of budgetary levers that are consistent with macroeconomic stability is critical for LICs. In addition, LICs need to undertake structural reforms that reduce their vulnerability to shocks, strengthen automatic fiscal stabilizers, improve the effectiveness of discretionary fiscal policy, and increase the flexibility of labor markets.

A nuanced policy approach is necessary to mitigate the impact of global food price shocks on poverty without adverse side effects. The use of trade policies (such as changes in export and import restrictions) to insulate domestic markets from food price shocks may compound the volatility of international prices and ultimately be counterproductive in protecting the most vulnerable people. Instead, storage policies and targeted safety net interventions, such as cash, food, and in-kind transfers, can mitigate the negative impact of food price shocks while avoiding the economywide distortionary impacts of trade policies. Measures such as crop and weather insurance, warehouse receipt systems, commodity exchanges, and futures markets could also be used to manage risks.

Synopsis

The remainder of this introduction presents a summary of each chapter. After presenting the motivation of the chapter, each summary explains the main questions, contributions to the literature, and analytical findings. After the summaries, a brief discussion of future research directions is presented.

Part A. Global and Domestic Drivers

Part A first analyzes the evolution of inflation and its correlates and consequences. It then turns to the extent of global inflation synchronization and the roles of global and group-specific factors in driving inflation in EMDEs. It concludes with an analysis of the global and domestic sources of inflation in these economies.

Chapter 1. Inflation: Concepts, Evolution, and Correlates

In Chapter 1, Ha, Ivanova, Ohnsorge, and Unsal analyze the impact of inflation on activity, provide a comprehensive analysis of the evolution of inflation over time, and document the main factors that have contributed to disinflation in recent decades across the world. They address the following questions:

- How does inflation support or hinder economic activity?
- How has global inflation evolved over the past four to five decades?
- What factors have contributed to these trends in global inflation?

The chapter's contributions to the literature are threefold. First, it documents the broad-based nature of disinflation over almost half a century using a sample of countries that is much larger than that of earlier studies, and so provides a truly global picture. Second, in contrast to earlier studies, the chapter identifies stylized facts that are robust across different measures of inflation and extend to various groups of countries. Third, it provides a systematic analysis of the structural factors that have been credited with helping to lower inflation over the past four to five decades, including increased global economic integration and strengthened macroeconomic policy frameworks.

Before delving into the evolution of inflation and its determinants, the authors review the literature on the impact of inflation on activity, poverty, and inequality. Previous studies show that low and stable inflation has often been associated with more stable output and employment and more rapid output growth and investment (Khan and Senhadji 2001; Woodford 2003; Mishkin 2008). Although the evidence regarding the effect of inflation on poverty is mixed when assessed at the economywide level, the negative effects of inflation are more established when examined at the household level.

The empirical exercise conducted in the chapter leads to three major findings.

First, inflation has fallen around the world, reaching historically low levels by 2000 (Figure 1). The decline has been evident among advanced economies and EMDEs, although it began earlier in advanced economies (in the mid-1980s) and started in EMDEs in the mid-1990s. Lower inflation was also accompanied by lower inflation volatility, especially in advanced economies.

Second, this global disinflation has been supported by a wide range of structural changes. The most significant of these have been globalization—increased international economic integration—and the adoption of more effective and more resilient monetary, exchange rate, and fiscal policy frameworks (Figure 2).[4]

Third, although it features lower inflation volatility, the current period of low and stable inflation is similar to two historical episodes: the Bretton Woods fixed

[4] Rogoff (2003) anticipates the discussion here, with an overview of the main factors supporting lower inflation, including globalization and broad-based changes in monetary policy regimes. Cecchetti and Krause (2002) document that lower average inflation has been associated with greater central bank credibility and, to a lesser extent, transparency in 24 advanced economies. Shambaugh (2004) examines the role of the external environment in monetary policy for different types of exchange rate regimes.

exchange rate system of the post-war period up to 1971 and the gold standard of the early 1900s. These two earlier episodes were followed by sharply rising inflation as soon as the two fixed exchange rate regimes were abandoned (Cline 1981; Bordo 1999).

After documenting inflation trends over almost half a century, Chapters 2 and 3 turn to the global synchronization of inflation and underlying drivers of inflation movements.

Chapter 2. Understanding Global Inflation Synchronization

In Chapter 2, Ha, Kose, Ohnsorge, and Unsal motivate their study with a well-known observation: inflation has recently appeared to move in tandem among countries around the globe. They then explore the extent to which global and group-specific factors have driven national inflation rates that led to highly synchronized movements in inflation. In this context, they ask three questions:

- How has inflation synchronization among countries around the world evolved over the past four to five decades?
- Which goods and price indexes have been associated with greater inflation synchronization?
- What country characteristics have been associated with greater inflation synchronization?

The chapter makes several contributions to the rapidly growing literature on global inflation. First, the authors employ one of the largest samples of countries among existing studies—a sample that is considerably more representative of "global inflation" than those used in most earlier studies that relied predominantly on data from advanced economies.[5] In their global sample, the evidence of growing global inflation synchronization during the 2000s is unambiguous, whereas some earlier studies based on advanced economy samples have found no such increase. Second, the authors employ a dynamic factor model to examine the extent of inflation synchronization around the world. In recognition of structural differences between EMDEs and advanced economies, their model explicitly allows for distinct roles for an EMDE factor and an advanced economy factor, whereas the focus of the literature thus far has been on global factors only. Third, the chapter systematically explores commonalities

[5] Ciccarelli and Mojon (2010), Neely and Rapach (2011), Mumtaz and Surico (2012), and Auer, Levchenko, and Sauré (2017) examine the extent of global inflation synchronization and its drivers.

FIGURE 2 Inflation and country characteristics

Greater trade and financial account openness, deeper supply chain integration, and greater central bank independence and transparency have been associated with lower and more stable inflation.

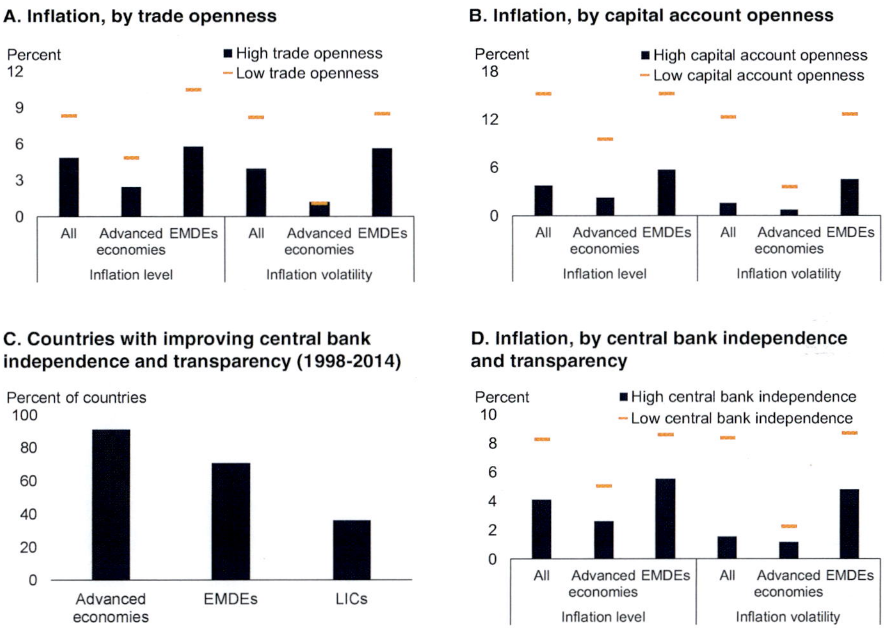

Source: Chinn and Ito 2006; Dincer and Eichengreen 2014; International Monetary Fund; World Bank.

Note: Inflation volatility is defined as volatility in cyclical inflation, detrended using Stock and Watson's (2016) methodology. EMDEs = emerging market and developing economies; GDP = gross domestic product; LICs = low-income countries.

A. Columns indicate median inflation in countries with trade-to-GDP ratios in the top quartile, during 1970-2017. Horizontal bars indicate countries with trade-to-GDP ratios in the bottom quartile. See the Appendix for detailed descriptions on the measures of country characteristics. The difference in inflation levels and volatility (except for volatility in advanced economies) between high and low trade openness is statistically significant at the 1 percent level.

B. Columns indicate median inflation rates and inflation volatility in country-year pairs with the Chinn-Ito index in the top quartile over 173 economies during 1970-2017. Horizontal bars indicate countries in the bottom quartile. The difference in inflation levels and volatility between high and low capital account openness is statistically significant at the 1 percent level.

C.D. The central bank independence and transparency index is taken from Dincer and Eichengreen (2014), extrapolated as described in the Appendix. The index ranges from 0 (least independent and transparent) to 15 (most independent and transparent). The difference in inflation levels and volatility between high and low central bank independence and transparency is statistically significant at the 1 percent level.

D. Columns indicate median inflation rates and inflation volatility in country-year pairs with a central bank independence and transparency index in the top quartile of the sample. Bars denote medians for country-year pairs in the bottom quartile.

and differences in inflation synchronization among a wide range of inflation measures based on price indexes that differ in their tradables content. This permits a more precise interpretation of the global factor and broadens the evidence for increased inflation synchronization. Fourth, the authors systematically study a wider range of country characteristics that are conducive to high inflation synchronization than has been examined in earlier studies.

The analysis yields the following main results.

First, inflation has become increasingly globally synchronized (Figure 3). The role of the global factor has grown, and, since 2001, it explains about one-fifth and one-quarter of EMDE and advanced economy inflation variation, respectively. But over the past four decades, an EMDE-specific factor has also become increasingly important, and since 2001 it has explained nearly a tenth of EMDE inflation variation. With the rising importance of these global and group-specific factors, inflation synchronization has also become more broad-based over time.

Second, international synchronization of inflation has tended to be higher than that of output growth over the past four to five decades. Differences in the degree of synchronization in output growth and inflation may reflect differences in the nature and frequency of global shocks and structural factors, including the evolution of policy frameworks, that influence these two variables. However, the degree of synchronization of output growth has increased over time to become comparable to that of inflation.

Third, global inflation synchronization has broadened—across different types of goods and countries. In 1970-85, the extent of inflation synchronization was pronounced only for inflation measures with large portions of tradable goods; it has more recently become sizable across all inflation measures. During 1970-2017, it was most pronounced for the inflation measures with the largest share of tradables. Since 2001, the contribution of a global factor to inflation variation has grown to one-third even for the core consumer price index (CPI) inflation and GDP deflator.

Fourth, countries differ widely in the degree to which global factors and, to a lesser extent, group factors, account for domestic inflation variation. The global factor has accounted for a larger share of domestic inflation variation in countries that were more open to global trade, participated more in global value chains, relied on commodity imports, and were more developed. In general, the global factor has explained a greater share of inflation variability in EMDEs that were commodity importing or open to trade. It has also been larger in countries with more resilient monetary policy frameworks. That said, over the past four to five decades, this heterogeneity has narrowed such that, since 2001, no country characteristic appears to account systematically for greater contributions of global or group factors.

The analysis in Chapter 2 identifies a global inflation cycle and documents the emergence of group-specific factors in explaining national inflation rates. However, it does not quantify the fundamental sources of global and national inflation, and, beyond providing suggestive evidence of a relationship with

FIGURE 3 Global inflation synchronization

Inflation has become increasingly globally synchronized. The global factor accounted for a higher share of the inflation variance in advanced economies than in EMDEs. A greater tradable goods and services content of the price basket was associated with a higher share of the global factor in inflation variance. Inflation synchronization has been stronger than the synchronization of output growth, especially in EMDEs.

A. Contributions of global and group factors to inflation variation

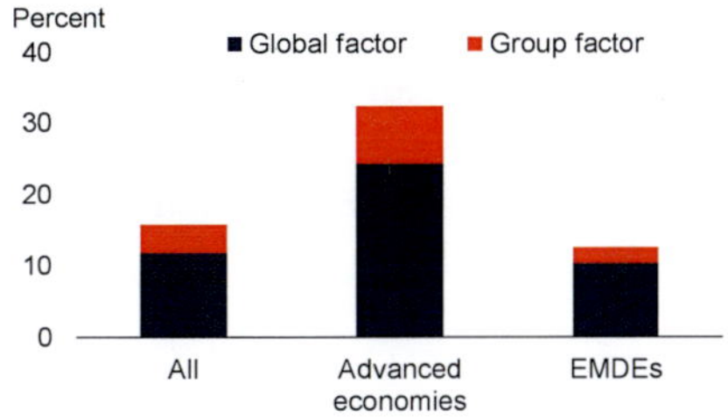

B. Contribution of global factor to inflation variation, by income group

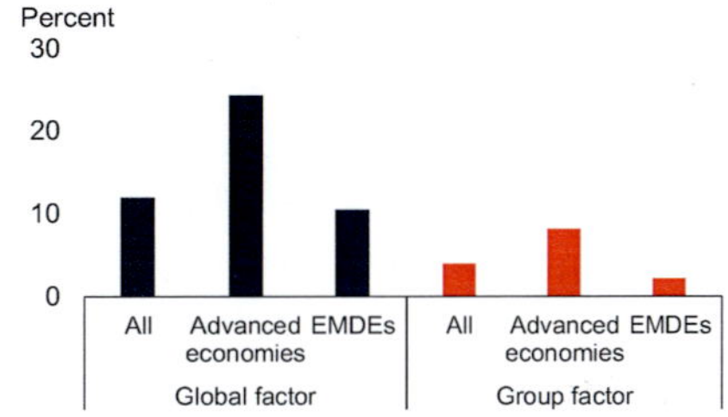

C. Contribution of global factor to inflation variation, over time

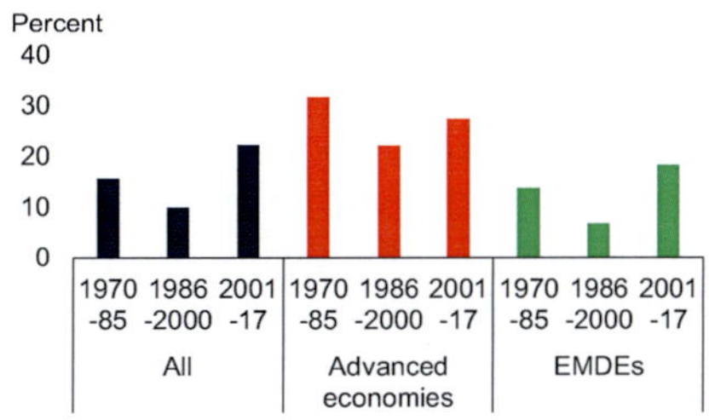

D. Contribution of global and group factors to inflation measures

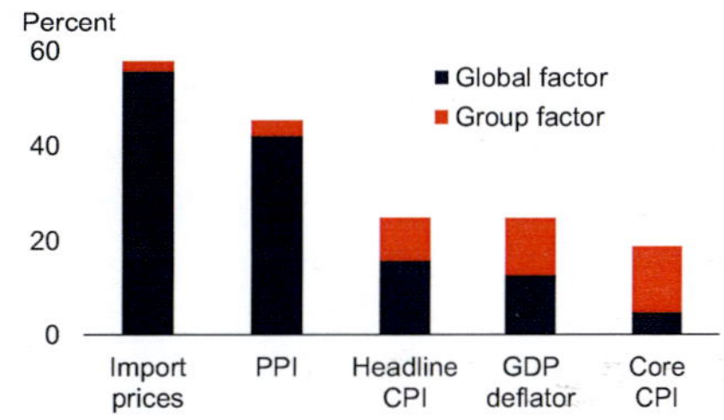

E. Contribution of global and group factors to inflation variation

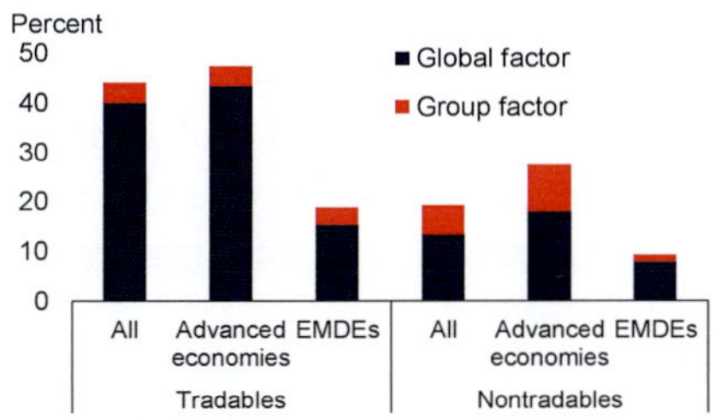

F. Contribution of global factor to output growth and inflation variation

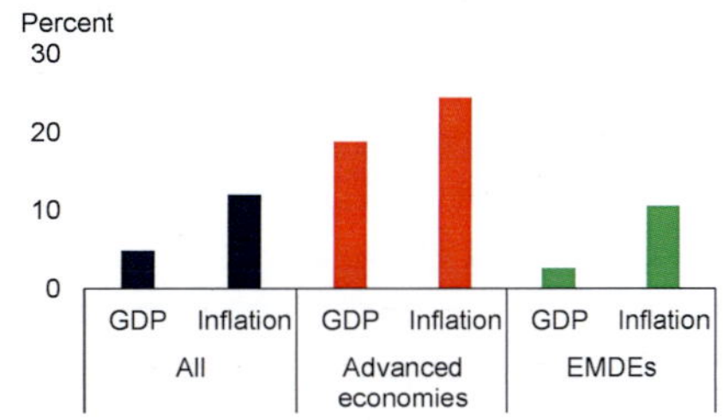

Source: World Bank.

Note: CPI = consumer price index; EMDEs = emerging market and developing economies; GDP = gross domestic product; PPI = producer price index.

A.-C. The results are based on a dynamic factor model with inflation in 99 countries (25 advanced economies and 74 EMDEs). The model includes global and group inflation factors. All numbers refer to median variance shares of total inflation variance counted by the global or group factors.

D.E. The global and group inflation factors are estimated with a two-factor dynamic factor model for annual inflation in 38 countries (25 advanced economies and 13 EMDEs) for the period 1970-2016, the size of the sample being constrained by data availability.

E. Median variance share of global factor in inflation variation. The common factor from three measures for domestic inflation (import prices, producer prices, and headline consumer prices) is used as a proxy variable for the common component for tradable goods. Similarly, common factors for headline consumer prices, core consumer prices, and the GDP deflator are extracted as a proxy for the global inflation factor for nontradable goods.

F. Median contribution of the global and group factor to the variance of real GDP growth and to inflation in 99 countries, based on a two-factor dynamic factor model.

certain country characteristics, the chapter does not interpret these global or group-specific factors. These issues are taken up in the next chapter.

Chapter 3. Sources of Inflation: Global and Domestic Drivers

Ha, Kose, Ohnsorge, and Yilmazkuday begin their analysis in Chapter 3 with a summary of the main movements in global inflation over almost half a century: since 1970, global inflation has undergone considerable swings around a pronounced downward trend. These swings in inflation have generally been associated with cyclical fluctuations in the global economy or sharp movements in oil prices. They then build on the work of Chapter 2 by analyzing the underlying drivers of global and national inflation. Specifically, they address the following questions:

- What have been the main drivers of global inflation?
- What have been the main drivers of domestic inflation?
- How have the main drivers of domestic inflation differed by country characteristics?

The chapter expands the literature in several dimensions. First, it systematically examines the sources of variation in global inflation in a unified econometric model that also serves to explain domestic inflation for a more diverse sample of countries than existing studies.[6] Unlike previous studies that have focused on subsets of the possible drivers of inflation, this chapter examines the contributions of global shocks (global demand, global supply, and global oil price shocks) to global inflation movements, and then quantifies the drivers (domestic demand, supply, monetary policy, and exchange rate shocks) of domestic inflation while controlling for the influence of global shocks. Second, in contrast to previous studies, the chapter employs a global sample of countries, allowing an analysis of inflation dynamics in advanced economies and EMDEs over a long period. Third, the chapter employs an event study to analyze the movements in global and domestic inflation rates during major economic events since 1970. By putting the recent low-inflation episode in historical context, the chapter highlights the exceptional severity of inflation weakness over the past decade. Fourth, the chapter investigates a wide range of country characteristics

[6] Charnavoki and Dolado (2014), Conti, Neri, and Nobili (2015), and Forbes, Hjoertsoe, and Nenova (2017, 2018) also analyze the role of different types of factors in explaining domestic inflation, but they focus on narrower subsets of drivers of inflation in the context of mostly advanced economy samples. Another branch of the literature relies on more traditional Phillips curve models to quantify the response of inflation to changes in domestic and global output gaps or cost factors (Borio and Filardo 2007; Gerlach et al. 2008; Ihrig et al. 2010; Eickmeier and Pijnenburg 2013; Auer, Borio, and Filardo 2017). However, this literature reports mixed findings about the importance of global drivers of domestic inflation.

to see which are associated with a particularly high contribution of global (or domestic) shocks to domestic inflation variability.

The authors report the following findings.

First, rapid changes in global inflation have generally occurred near turning points of the global business cycle or in the wake of sharp movements in global oil prices. In particular, following the global financial crisis and subsequent recession, the past decade witnessed a pronounced and broad-based disinflation that took global inflation well below its downward trend. Exceptionally large fractions of advanced economies (more than three-quarters) and EMDEs (more than one-half) were in outright deflation at some point during 2014-17.

Second, global demand and oil price shocks have accounted for 40 percent, each, of the variation in global inflation since 1970 (Figure 4). Negative global demand shocks were associated with three global recessions and slowdowns, but large positive global demand shocks often coincided with the year before the global economy slid into a recession or slowdown. Positive oil price shocks were generally associated with oil supply disruptions, often coinciding with armed conflict or civil unrest (for example, the Iran-Iraq War, the Iranian Revolution, and the Persian Gulf War) or militant attacks on pipelines (for example, in Iraq and Nigeria). Negative oil price shocks were associated with major decisions of the Organization of the Petroleum Exporting Countries to end production restraint amid discoveries of new sources of oil supply (1986, 2014-16) or price normalization after spikes. The relative importance of global demand shocks has increased since 2001, to account for 60 percent of global inflation variation. However, the 2014-16 oil price plunge was a major source of post-crisis global disinflation.

Third, during the past four to five decades, domestic shocks accounted for about three-quarters of domestic inflation variation, the most important being domestic supply shocks. Since 2001, however, the role of domestic supply shocks has declined. During this period, in part as a result of the global financial crisis and the 2014-16 oil price plunge, the contributions to domestic inflation variation of global demand and oil price shocks have increased to 22 and 17 percent, respectively.

Finally, the contribution of global shocks to domestic inflation variation was larger in advanced economies and countries with higher trade and financial openness, fixed exchange rate regimes, and greater reliance on commodity imports. Domestic shocks contributed more to domestic inflation variation in countries that were less open to global trade and finance and had inflation targeting monetary policy regimes with flexible exchange rates.

FIGURE 4 Drivers of inflation

Global recessions and oil price plunges were typically associated with slowing global inflation. Reflecting this, the estimation results indicate that, since the 1970s, global demand and oil price shocks have accounted for a growing share of the variation in global inflation and domestic inflation. That said, domestic shocks have continued to account for about three-quarters of domestic inflation variation, with domestic supply shocks being most important.

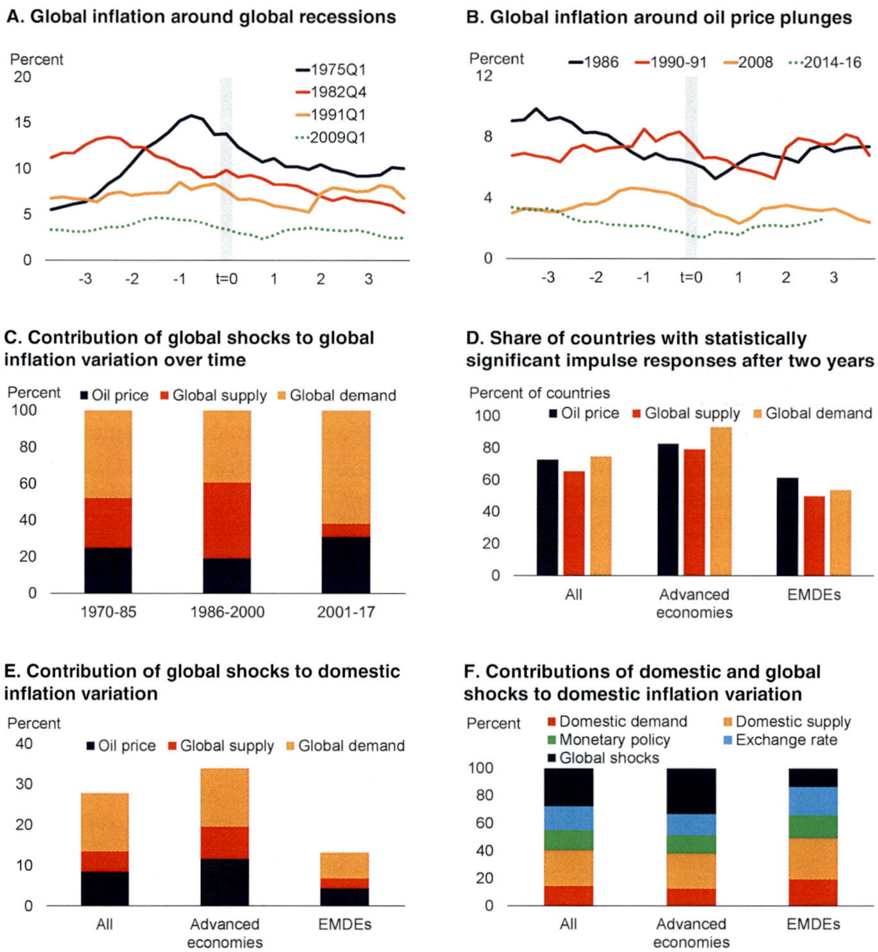

Source: World Bank.

Note: EMDEs = emerging market and developing economies; GDP = gross domestic product.

A.B. The horizontal axis indicates years before and after the troughs of global recessions or local troughs of short-term oil price cycles (t=0). Global inflation is defined as median trend inflation (nine-quarter moving average) across 65 countries.

A. Troughs of global recessions are identified using global per capita GDP and the algorithm in Harding and Pagan (2002) and are consistent with the results in Kose and Terrones (2015).

B. There were six oil price plunges of more than 30 percent (1986, 1990-91, 1997-98, 2001, 2008, and 2014-16) (Baffes et al. 2015). The four episodes with the largest oil price plunges are presented.

C.-F. The results are based on the country-specific factor-augmented vector autoregression estimation, as discussed in Chapter 3.

C.E.F. All numbers refer to median shares of variance.

C.E. Share of global inflation variance (C) or domestic inflation variance (E) accounted for by global shocks.

D. Based on cumulative impulse response of domestic inflation to global shocks after two years.

PART B. Expectations and Pass-Through

Part B delves deeper into two key challenges that confront EMDE central banks. Burdened by a history of high inflation, many EMDE central banks struggle to build credibility, leaving inflation sensitive to shocks and inflation expectations unanchored. Additionally, EMDE exchange rates can be subject to severe swings, amplifying the impact of exchange rate movements on inflation.

Chapter 4. Inflation Expectations: Review and Evidence

In Chapter 4, Kose, Matsuoka, Panizza, and Vorisek argue that, since EMDEs tend to experience more pronounced business and financial cycles than advanced economies, they face greater challenges in anchoring expectations. This makes understanding how inflation expectations are affected by different types of shocks especially critical for policy makers in these economies.[7]

Since robust measurement is key to evaluating inflation expectations, they first examine the pros and cons of survey-based and market-based measures.[8] Due to the breadth of country coverage and the availability of long time series, they employ survey-based inflation expectations in their empirical work. They then present a survey of the literature on inflation expectations. Theoretical studies have examined how public and private information is used by economic agents in formulating inflation expectations.[9] A large body of empirical work has tested the predictions of theoretical models and assessed how firmly inflation expectations are anchored, by measuring the sensitivity of expectations to various shocks. This literature, while extensive, has mainly focused on advanced economies.

The chapter, therefore, represents the first comprehensive analysis of the evolution and determinants of inflation expectations in EMDEs. Specifically, it addresses three key questions:

- How does the degree of anchoring of inflation expectations differ between advanced economies and EMDEs?
- How sensitive are inflation expectations to global and domestic shocks?
- What are the main determinants of the degree of anchoring of inflation expectations?

[7] Bernanke (2007b) explains the importance of inflation expectations for the design of monetary policy.

[8] For background on market- and survey-based measures of inflation expectations, see Coibion et al. (2018) and Grothe and Meyler (2018) for the United States and the Euro Area, and Sousa and Yetman (2016) for EMDEs.

[9] Coibion, Gorodnichenko, and Kamdar (forthcoming) and Mankiw and Reis (2018) survey the literature on the formation of expectations.

The chapter studies these issues by taking novel approaches in several dimensions. First, it employs data for a large and diverse sample of countries (24 advanced economies and 23 EMDEs) for a period of close to three decades.[10] Second, it analyzes the degree of anchoring of inflation expectations by employing two empirical strategies: a panel regression model and a time-varying coefficients model. The former approach provides an overview of how well expectations are anchored in different country groups and time periods; the latter is useful for tracking how country-specific and time-varying measures of the degree of anchoring have evolved. Third, the chapter examines the determinants of the degree of anchoring of expectations, using a dynamic panel regression framework. Fourth, it complements these empirical exercises with case studies that examine the role of inflation targeting in stabilizing inflation expectations in three EMDEs.

This strategy yields the following major results.

First, long-term inflation expectations have declined and become more firmly anchored in the past two decades in advanced economies and EMDEs (Figure 5). However, anchoring in EMDEs remains notably weaker than in advanced economies. This finding is consistent with the view that monetary policy remains less credible in EMDEs than in advanced economies.

Second, long-term inflation expectations in EMDEs are more sensitive to global and domestic shocks than are expectations in advanced economies. However, the sensitivity of EMDE inflation expectations to domestic shocks gradually fell between 2005 and 2012 and has since been mostly stable while their sensitivity to global shocks has fallen slightly since 2000. This contrasts with the experience of advanced economies, where a large drop in the sensitivity of inflation expectations to global shocks in the wake of the global financial crisis followed a steady decline from the late 1990s to the late 2000s, and there was a less pronounced downward trend in sensitivity to domestic shocks.

Third, the institutional and monetary policy environment matters for anchoring inflation expectations, as do the general macroeconomic environment and structural characteristics of the economy. The authors report that the presence of an inflation targeting regime and a rise in central bank transparency are associated with better anchoring of long-term inflation expectations. For EMDEs, lower public debt ratios and greater trade openness are also associated with better anchoring of expectations.

---

[10] IMF (2016, 2018) and Mehrotra and Yetman (forthcoming) also study inflation expectations in advanced economies and EMDEs.

Fourth, case studies of Brazil, Chile, and Poland provide examples of how these factors have worked to anchor inflation expectations. In Brazil, for instance, accommodative fiscal policy and backtracking on central bank transparency for a period may have held back progress on improving the anchoring of inflation expectations. In Chile, a highly transparent central bank, together with a credible macroeconomic framework, appear to have contributed to the central bank's success in anchoring inflation expectations. And in Poland, the simultaneous adoption of inflation targeting and exchange rate flexibility seems to have helped anchor expectations.

Chapter 5 focuses on the role of another channel for monetary policy transmission that is especially important for EMDEs—the pass-through of changes in the exchange rate to domestic prices. It takes the novel approach of quantifying, in a large sample, the extent to which exchange rate pass-through varies according to the different types of shocks that lead to movements in exchange rates.

Chapter 5. Inflation and Exchange Rate Pass-Through

Ha, Stocker, and Yilmazkuday motivate their study with a basic observation: monetary policy authorities in EMDEs have long been worried that significant exchange rate fluctuations can jeopardize price stability and force disruptive policy adjustments. As a result, some EMDEs have adopted managed currency arrangements or employ aggressive policy responses to dampen undesirable currency movements—practices motivated by what has been dubbed the "fear of floating" (Calvo and Reinhart 2002). However, the resulting lack of exchange rate flexibility can amplify the impact of external shocks and make it more difficult for a central bank to anchor inflation expectations credibly.

Although large depreciations have become less frequent in EMDEs, they continue to be associated with large increases in inflation. To formulate the appropriate monetary policy response to exchange rate movements, it is essential to assess correctly their impact on inflation. But pass-through ratios—the percentage increase in consumer prices associated with a 1 percent depreciation of the nominal effective exchange rate—are found to vary considerably across countries and over time. Two fundamental factors help to account for these variations: the nature of the shock triggering the currency movement and country characteristics.

To explore these issues in detail, the authors build on the econometric framework developed in Chapter 3, but they focus on the relative responses of inflation and exchange rates to domestic and global shocks. They address three questions:

FIGURE 5 Inflation expectations

After declining in the 1990s, inflation expectations in advanced economies have remained stable at around 2 percent since the mid-2000s. Inflation expectations in EMDEs declined in the second half of the 1990s, but have risen somewhat since 2005, and remain higher than in advanced economies. The sensitivity of inflation expectations to inflation surprises has fallen in the past decade in advanced economies and EMDEs but remains comparatively higher in EMDEs. Inflation expectations in EMDEs are better anchored in the presence of an inflation targeting regime, and when central bank transparency is high.

A. Inflation expectations, advanced economies

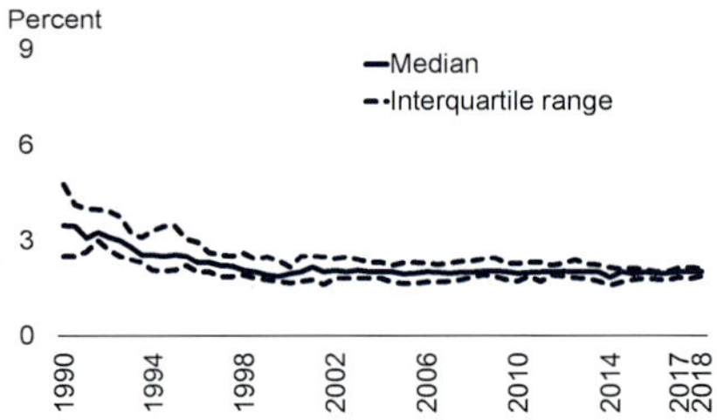

B. Inflation expectations, EMDEs

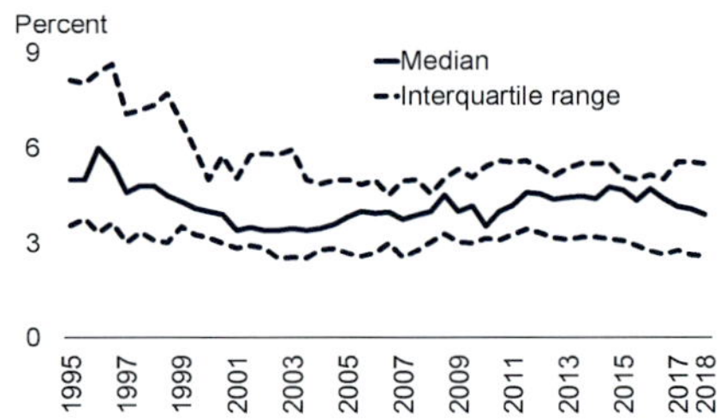

C. Sensitivity of inflation expectations to inflation shocks, advanced economies

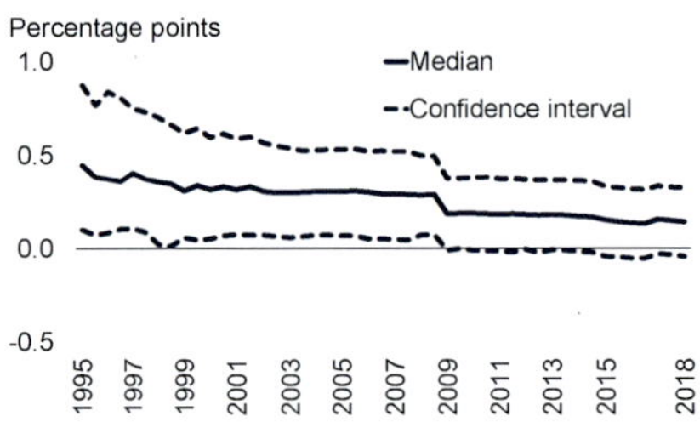

D. Sensitivity of inflation expectations to inflation shocks, EMDEs

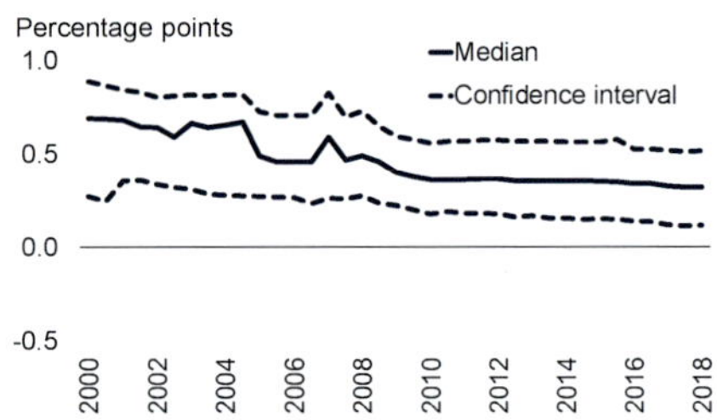

E. Impact of an inflation targeting regime on the sensitivity of expectations

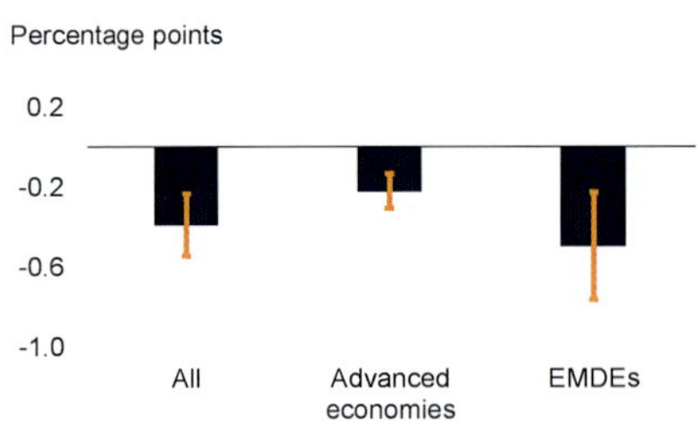

F. Impact of a one-unit increase in central bank transparency on the sensitivity of expectations

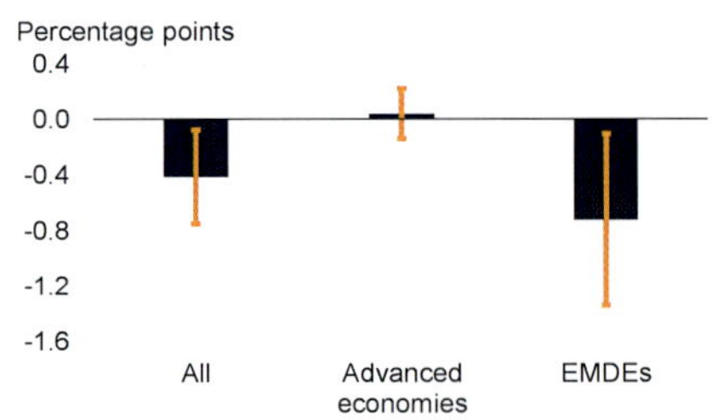

Source: Consensus Economics; International Monetary Fund; World Bank.

Note: Inflation expectations are long-term (five-year-ahead) expectations of annual inflation, measured at biannual frequency. EMDEs = emerging market and developing economies.

A.-D. Sample includes 24 advanced economies (1990H1-2018H1 for panel A; 1995H1-2018H1 for panel C) and 23 EMDEs (1995H1-2018H1 for panel B; 2000H1-2018H1 for panel D).

C.D. Inflation shocks are defined as the difference between realized inflation and short-term inflation expectations in the previous period. Time-varying sensitivity is estimated by regressing the change in five-year-ahead inflation expectations on inflation shocks. The model is described in Chapter 4. Solid lines indicate medians of estimates; dashed lines indicate 68 percent confidence intervals.

E.F. Bars represent coefficients in panel regressions of 24 advanced economies, 23 EMDEs, and all 47 economies, using annual data for 1995-2016. The model is described in Chapter 4. Vertical lines denote 90 percent confidence intervals.

- How have exchange rate movements affected consumer price inflation over time?
- How does the pass-through to inflation depend on the underlying shock triggering the exchange rate movement?
- What country characteristics are associated with lower pass-throughs?

Their analysis is novel in several dimensions. First, they draw on event studies of large currency movements and analyze shifts in the relationship between exchange rates and inflation. This leads to empirical results that shed new light on the heterogeneity of pass-through estimates across countries and over time. Second, the chapter supplements a growing empirical literature linking the exchange rate pass-through to underlying shocks, contrasting with traditional reduced-form approaches that estimate an "average" pass-through based on the assumption of an exogenously determined exchange rate. Third, compared with earlier studies that have derived state-dependent pass-through estimates, their work investigates a greater menu of shocks, uses a larger sample of countries, and employs a state-of-the-art econometric framework that combines domestic and global shocks.[11] Finally, the chapter explores the role of some EMDE-specific characteristics, including monetary policy frameworks, participation in global value chains, and foreign currency invoicing.

This approach yields estimates of exchange rate pass-throughs that differ widely by the source of shocks and country characteristics. The approach produces the following results.

First, domestic shocks were the main driver of exchange rate fluctuations across most countries but resulted in significantly different pass-throughs to inflation, depending on the nature of the shocks (Figure 6). The pass-through associated with domestic monetary policy shocks was generally higher, especially in EMDEs without inflation targeting central banks.[12] In contrast, domestic demand shocks were typically accompanied by negative and mostly insignificant pass-throughs, reflecting the offsetting effects of growth and exchange rate channels (that is, weakening domestic demand giving rise to currency depreciation and declining inflation).

---

[11] Past empirical studies disentangling the impacts of different types of shocks on estimated pass-throughs include Forbes, Hjortsoe, and Nenova (2017, 2018) and Shambaugh (2008).

[12] The link between the adoption of inflation targets by central banks and declining exchange rate pass-throughs has been investigated in some other studies, including Gagnon and Ihrig (2004), Mishkin and Schmidt-Hebbel (2007), and Coulibaly and Kempf (2010).

Global shocks accounted for a smaller proportion of exchange rate movements and their pass-through ratios varied widely, depending on country characteristics and the type of shock. For instance, although global demand shocks were linked to positive pass-throughs in many EMDEs, in some cases pass-throughs were negative or insignificant. The pass-through for oil price shocks was mostly positive for energy exporters, but widely divergent for energy importers.

Second, greater central bank independence was associated with significantly lower pass-through ratios, highlighting a self-reinforcing feedback between central bank credibility and price stability (Carriere-Swallow et al. 2016). The insulation provided by central bank independence was evident in weaker pass-throughs following domestic monetary policy, global demand, and oil price shocks.

Third, evidence of a downward trend in average exchange rate pass-through ratios over the past two decades is consistent with a broader movement toward improved central bank policies and a more solid anchoring of inflation expectations, as reported in Chapter 4. Other structural factors, including growing integration in global value chains, may have played a role as well, but cannot account for substantial cross-country differences in pass-through ratios.[13]

The authors argue that differences in shock-specific pass-through ratios could have important implications for monetary policy. For example, the exchange rate pass-through during an initial economic recovery phase could be low, reflecting the predominance of domestic demand shocks. However, grounding subsequent monetary policy tightening decisions on the assumption of a similarly low pass-through could be misleading, since monetary policy shocks are typically associated with much higher pass-through ratios. Failing to take these factors into account may lead central banks to overshoot their objective, creating unnecessary fluctuations in inflation and real economic activity.

PART C. Low-Income Country Considerations

Part C focuses on inflation and monetary policy–related challenges faced by LICs. Chapter 6 delves into the problem of identifying drivers of inflation in LICs. This is followed in Chapter 7 by an analysis of vulnerability to large food price swings in LICs and the poverty implications.

[13] Some studies have found that global value chain participation can reduce the response of import and export prices to exchange rate movements in advanced economies and EMDEs (Amiti, Itskhoki, and Konings 2014; de Soyres et al. 2018; Georgiadis, Gräb, and Khalil 2017). However, these effects were not detectable in the estimated pass-throughs to consumer price inflation across countries.

FIGURE 6 Inflation and exchange rate pass-through

The frequency and severity of EMDE currency depreciations has declined since the 1990s. Domestic shocks remain the dominant driver of exchange rate fluctuations but are associated with different pass-throughs, from significantly positive for monetary policy shocks to negative for domestic demand shocks. Global shocks accounted for a smaller proportion of exchange rate movements and were associated with considerable heterogeneity of estimated pass-through ratios. Greater central bank independence tends to be linked to lower exchange rate pass-throughs, across countries and over time.

A. Frequency of EMDE currency depreciations

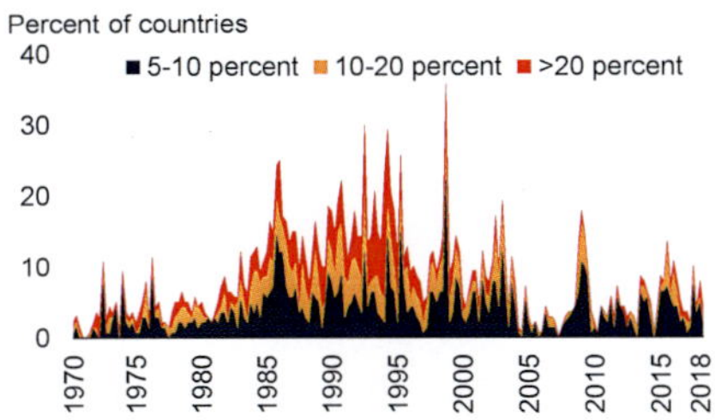

B. Variance decomposition of exchange rate movements

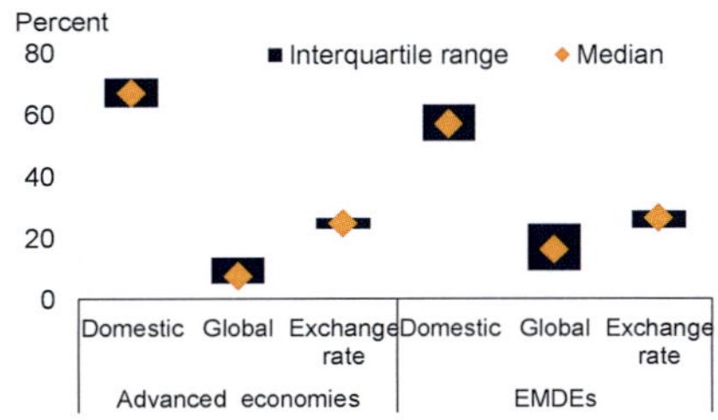

C. Pass-through: domestic shocks

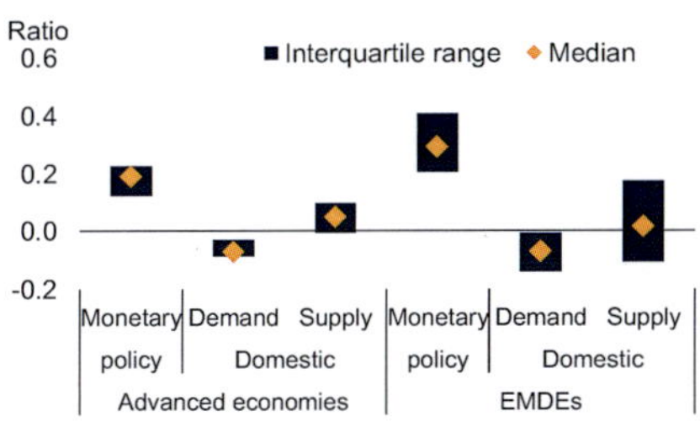

D. Pass-through: Global shocks

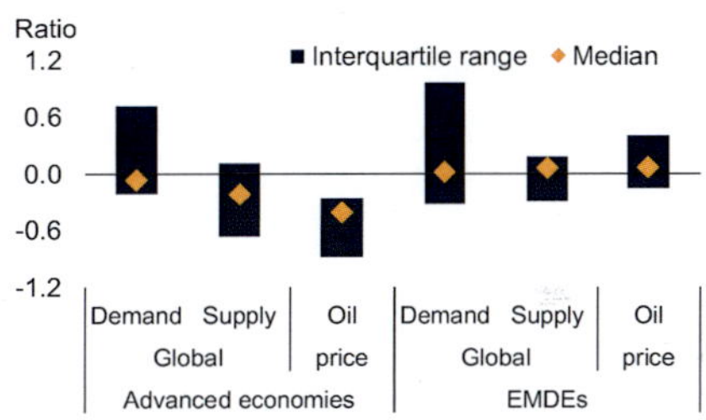

E. Central bank independence and pass-through from monetary policy shocks

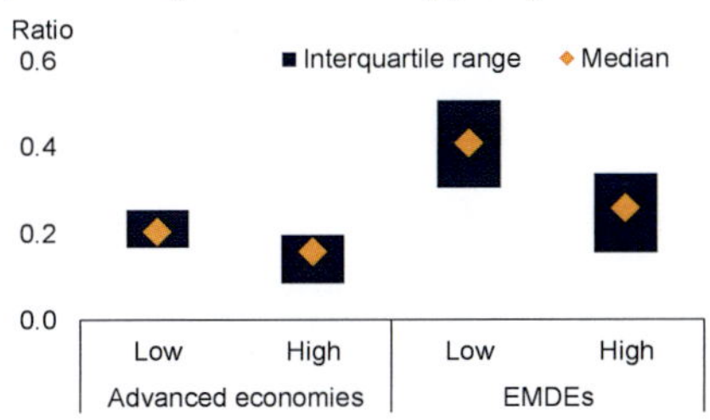

F. Average pass-through

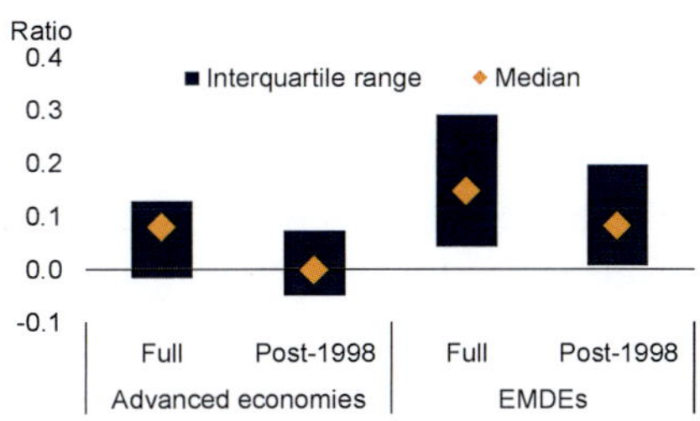

Source: World Bank.

Note: EMDEs = emerging market and developing economies.

A. Depreciations are defined as negative quarterly changes in the nominal effective exchange rate.

B. Median share of country-specific exchange rate variance accounted for by domestic, global, and exchange rate shocks.

C.-F. Pass-throughs are defined as the ratio between the one-year cumulative impulse response of consumer price inflation and the one-year cumulative impulse response of the exchange rate change estimated from factor-augmented vector autoregression models for 29 advanced economies and 26 EMDEs over 1998-2017. A positive pass-through means that a currency depreciation is associated with higher inflation. Bars show the interquartile range and markers show the cross-country median.

E. The central bank independence index is computed by Dincer and Eichengreen (2014). Low and high central bank independence are defined as below and above the sample average.

F. Shock-specific pass-throughs are aggregated using shares of currency movements accounted for by each type of shock as weights. This summary measure reflects the average sensitivity of inflation to exchange rate movements over the entire estimation period. Full sample estimations are over 1971-2017 but can vary at the individual country level.

Chapter 6. Inflation in Low-Income Countries

Ha, Ivanova, Montiel, and Pedroni start their study of inflation in LICs with the observation that, in recent decades, there has been a remarkable degree of convergence in academic and policy circles in views about the principles to which monetary policy should adhere to yield the low and stable medium-term inflation that is conducive to healthy economic growth. Nevertheless, central banks in LICs face significant challenges in achieving low and stable inflation and anchoring inflation expectations (Mishra, Montiel, and Spilimbergo 2012). Meanwhile, globalization has proceeded apace in LICs, as it has elsewhere, magnifying, through several channels, the challenges confronted by LICs in achieving these objectives.

Inflation rates in LICs over the past two decades have declined from exceptionally high levels in many cases and converged closer to those of advanced economies and other EMDEs, despite the special challenges faced by LICs. The challenges include being susceptible to relatively large domestic as well as external shocks. At the same time, global inflation has stabilized at low rates.

These observations lead the authors to study to what extent the improvement in LIC inflation performance over the past two decades reflects improved domestic policies, as opposed to having been imported. The chapter also examines the extent to which core inflation in LICs has remained stable in the face of a variety of external shocks, including shocks to global core, energy, and food price inflation, and other shocks transmitted to domestic economies through exchange rate fluctuations. The authors address the following questions:

- How has inflation in LICs evolved?
- How well anchored are inflation expectations in LICs?
- What country characteristics have been associated with stronger anchoring?

The chapter extends the existing literature in several ways. First, it presents the results of the first-ever investigation of the sensitivity of core inflation to various inflation shocks, domestic and global, in a large group of countries over a long period. The authors estimate a novel econometric model that helps identify the global component of core inflation endogenously and produces a parsimonious representation of the common and idiosyncratic components of core inflation (Pedroni 2013). Second, the chapter is unique in its specific focus on LICs. Third, the chapter reports findings on which country characteristics help explain differences in the responses of core inflation to different types of shocks.

The authors report the following main results.

First, although LIC inflation has declined sharply from the mid-1990s, the level and volatility of headline inflation have remained above those in advanced economies (Figure 7).

Second, core inflation in LICs was more susceptible to external shocks—in particular, to global core and food prices—than in the other country groups. Around three-quarters of the variation in core inflation rates among LICs was due to global shocks, compared with one-quarter in advanced economies. Global food and energy price shocks accounted for 12 percent of core inflation variation in LICs, half more than in advanced economies and one-fifth more than in non-LIC EMDEs.

Third, domestic characteristics appear to matter for determining the responsiveness of inflation to external shocks. Notably, LICs with fixed exchange rates seem to succeed in anchoring inflation expectations as much as other EMDEs with fixed exchange rates, whereas LICs with floating exchange rates have had a much more difficult time.

This suggests that LIC central banks have not been able to secure low and stable medium-term inflation rates on their own, and their improved inflation performance may therefore have been largely imported. Therefore, if global inflation were to rise, LICs would face the risk of their own inflation rising in tandem, unless steps can be taken to improve their homegrown anti-inflation credibility.

The next chapter extends the examination of the sensitivity of LIC inflation to global shocks by considering the effects of global food prices on domestic food prices and poverty.

Chapter 7. Poverty Impacts of Food Price Shocks and Policies

In August 2011, international food prices hit an all-time high. This followed the 2007-08 food price spike, which pushed an estimated 105 million people into extreme poverty and prompted widespread concerns about the food security of the poorest. Although food prices have been lower in recent years, they are still significantly above their lows in 2000 (Figure 8). In Chapter 7, Laborde, Lakatos and Martin ask three questions:

- How do food price shocks affect EMDEs and LICs?
- How do countries intervene to reduce the impact of food price shocks?
- What was the impact of the 2010-11 food price shock on poverty?

The study adds to the literature by quantifying the degree to which countries intervened during this episode. The chapter also estimates the impact of the

FIGURE 7 Drivers of core inflation in low-income countries

Core inflation in LICs was more sensitive to global shocks than elsewhere. Around three-quarters of the variation in core inflation rates among LICs was due to global shocks, compared with one-quarter in advanced economies. Global food and energy price shocks accounted for 12 percent of core inflation variation in LICs, half more than in advanced economies and one-fifth more than in non-LIC EMDEs. Higher central bank transparency and pegged exchange rate regimes have been associated with greater resilience of domestic core inflation in LICs to global core inflation shocks.

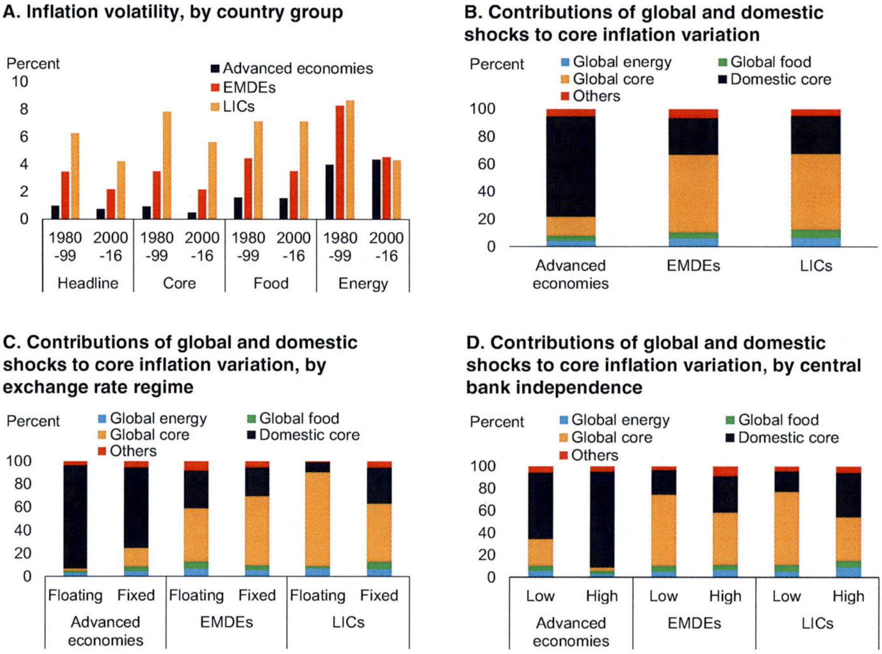

Source: Dincer and Eichengreen 2014; Shambaugh 2004; World Bank.

Note: EMDEs refer to non-LIC EMDEs. EMDEs = emerging market and developing economies; LICs = low-income countries.

A. Inflation volatility is measured as the standard deviation of annual inflation rates for the past 10 years.

B.-D. The results are based on a heterogeneous panel structural vector autoregression model with 104 countries (25 advanced economies, 61 EMDEs, and 18 LICs) between 1970M2 and 2016M12. The forecast error variance decomposition of core inflation is based on the median across countries within each group. The forecasting horizon is 18 months.

C. Exchange rate regimes are based on the classification by Shambaugh (2004).

D. Central bank independence is based on the central bank transparency index of Dincer and Eichengreen (2014). A higher value of the index indicates a more transparent and independent central bank. "High" and "low" indicate countries with above- and below-median central bank independence, respectively.

2010-11 food price spike and associated trade policy interventions on poverty using a general equilibrium model complemented with data from household surveys (Laborde, Robichaud, and Tokgoz 2013).

In some respects, the last two food price spikes (2007-08 and 2010-11) resembled earlier, similar episodes: world prices rose rapidly, whereas domestic prices increased only gradually. . In other respects, however, the 2010-11 spike was different from previous episodes. The 2007-08 increase in food prices came after a long period of stability in food prices (Ivanic and Martin 2008). In 2007-08, world prices of all staple foods increased steeply, led by a strong increase in the world price of rice. Most countries reacted strongly, by introducing insulating policies.[14] In contrast, the 2010-11 episode occurred when world markets and policies were still normalizing after the 2007-08 episode. Government interventions differed considerably across countries and commodities, and insulating policies actually dampened the increase in world rice prices.[15]

The analysis by Laborde, Lakatos, and Martin yields several major findings.

First, food prices can affect poverty through multiple channels, and the effects depend on country characteristics.

- At the macroeconomic level, high shares of agriculture and food in total output, consumption, employment, trade, and government revenues heighten countries' vulnerability to volatility in international food prices. LICs are particularly susceptible, as agriculture in these countries accounts, on average, for close to one-third of value added and two-thirds of total employment, nearly three times their shares in other EMDEs. Additionally, more than three-quarters of LICs are net food importers compared to only half of other EMDEs. During the 2010-11 event, the increase in food prices accounted disproportionately for the rise in inflation—about two-thirds of the change in inflation in LICs and a little more than half in other EMDEs.
- At the microeconomic level, food price spikes are felt most severely by the poor, since they are net buyers of food and a disproportionate share of their income (two-thirds in LICs) is spent on food. Through these channels, food price spikes raise poverty, reduce nutrition, and cut the provision of essential services such as education and health care (World Bank 2011).

Second, the authors show that governments in EMDEs tend to respond particularly strongly to sharp changes in world prices for staple foods—such as rice, wheat, and maize—to smooth volatility. Domestic food prices are considerably less volatile than world food prices in the short run. However, the

[14] During the 2007-08 food price spike, close to three-quarters of EMDEs took policy action to insulate their domestic markets from the sharp increase in world prices (World Bank 2009).

[15] Important net rice exporters, such as India, Pakistan, and the Republic of Yemen, implemented policy interventions that raised domestic rice prices more than the increase in the world price. In India, for example, the abolition of export quotas in September 2011 (in place since 2007) coincided with the agricultural marketing season and resulted in a surge of exports and a rise in domestic prices.

FIGURE 8 Poverty impact of food price shocks

High shares of agriculture and food in total output and consumption, employment, trade, and government revenues heighten countries' vulnerability to volatility in international food prices. Insulating policies introduced during the 2010-11 food price spike accounted for 40 percent of the increase in the world price of wheat and one-quarter of the increase in the world price of maize. Combined with government policy responses, the 2010-11 food price spike increased global poverty by 1 percent, or 8.3 million.

A. Global food prices

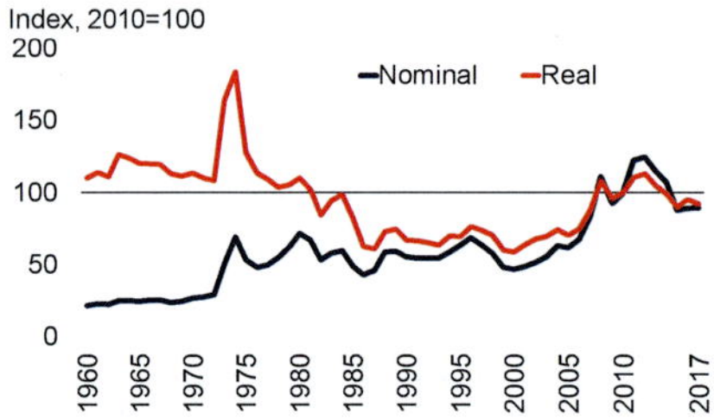

B. Share of food in total consumption expenditure

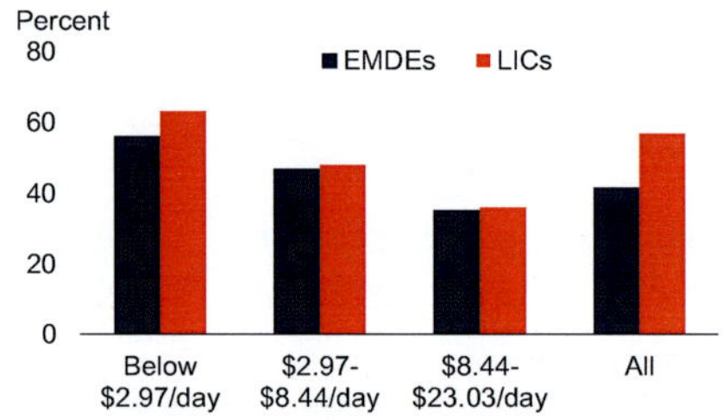

C. Inflation in LICs

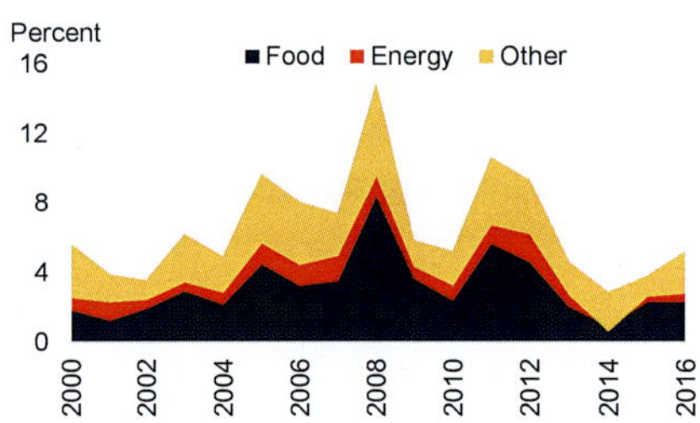

D. Increase in world prices, 2010-11

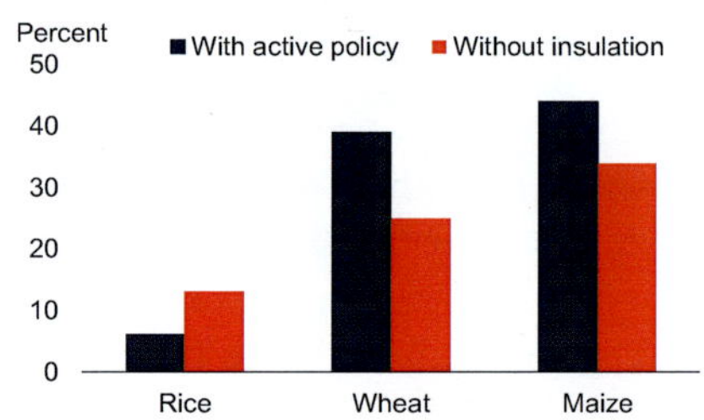

E. Impact of the 2010-11 food price spike on the number of extreme poor, by region

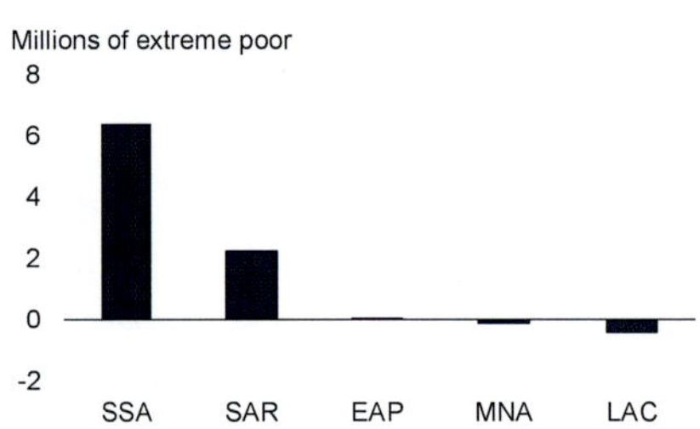

F. Impact of the 2010-11 food price shock on the number of extreme poor, by policies

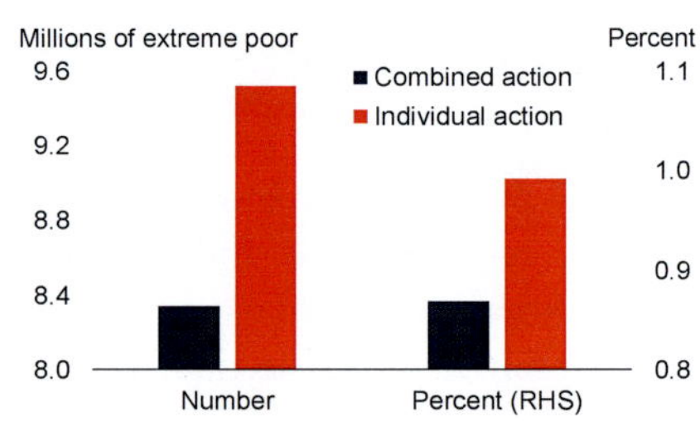

Source: Ag-Incentives Database, World Bank.

Note: EAP = East Asia and Pacific; EMDEs = emerging market and developing economies; LAC = Latin America and the Caribbean; LICs = low-income countries; MNA = Middle East and North Africa; SAR = South Asia; SSA = Sub-Saharan Africa.

A. Based on annual commodity price indexes, deflated using the World Bank manufactures unit value index.

B. Based on household survey data for 2010 on the share of food in total consumption expenditure of households.

C. Average inflation based on a sample of 12 LICs.

D.-F. Based on estimates using the computable general equilibrium model MIRAGRODEP, described in detail in Chapter 7.

E.F. Assuming increases in the price of maize, rice, and wheat, as represented in panel D and based on a poverty line of $1.90/day purchasing power parity.

dampening effect of policies dissipates over time, and domestic prices tend to match world prices in the long term.

Third, although individual countries can insulate their domestic markets from short-term fluctuations in global food prices, these interventions can have the perverse effect of making global food prices more volatile (Anderson, Martin, and Ivanic 2017). Indeed, these policy interventions accounted for 40 percent of the increase in the world price of wheat and one-quarter of the increase in the world price of maize during the 2010-11 food price spike. In contrast, government interventions in rice markets (in part, to reverse restrictions imposed after the 2007-08 food price shocks) dampened the shock to world prices by about 50 percent.

Fourth, overall, the 2010-11 food price spike may have increased the number of poor by 1 percent, or 8.3 million, despite—and in part, because of—widespread government intervention. The increase in world food prices, combined with government intervention, was most strongly felt in countries such as Bangladesh, India, and Uganda, where the extreme poor tend to be net food buyers whose real incomes declined. Countries like Ethiopia and Nigeria implemented insulation policies that reduced poverty.

Future research directions

The analysis in this book not only presents original analytical work on inflation in EMDEs, but also suggests several new research avenues to be explored.

Decline in inflation. The discussion of long-term trend disinflation over almost half a century invites future research in two directions. First, the relative contributions of long-term structural changes—including technological advances, globalization of trade and finance, and others—to global disinflation over the past four to five decades could be more formally quantified. This could be done in a general equilibrium framework, since most empirical models are not well suited to uncovering the relationships between such slow-moving variables. Second, future work could examine more formally the degree of global comovement in long-term inflation trends, as Chapters 2 and 3 do for comovement in short-term inflation movements. This could be set in the context of a more sophisticated measure of trend inflation by extracting cycles at different frequencies.

Global inflation and other sources of domestic inflation. Research on global and EMDE inflation synchronization could be taken further in two directions. First, rather than simply focusing on levels of development, the implications of more granular country characteristics for synchronization could be explored, such as commodity exporter status, regional trade links, and size of the tradables versus nontradables sectors. Second, it would be useful to explore the extent to which synchronization is driven by common shocks that affect all countries, or by country-specific shocks that spill over between countries.

Inflation expectations. This book's study of inflation expectations points to several avenues for future research to explore. First, research could examine the determinants of a wider range of measures of inflation expectations in EMDEs, if data availability improved—for example, with the development of domestic financial markets to provide market-based measures of expectations. Second, it would be useful to consider nonlinearities between institutional factors and the anchoring of inflation expectations. Additionally, there is a need to investigate how complementarities between institutional factors and fiscal and monetary policy frameworks help improve the anchoring of inflation expectations.

Exchange rate pass-through. Future work on this topic could more formally investigate the relationship between estimated exchange rate pass-through and structural factors, such as the degree of value chain participation and foreign currency invoicing practices in EMDEs. This could take the form of event studies around significant policy or other structural changes. The analysis of shock-specific pass-through rates could also be extended to different inflation measures, for example, import prices, producer prices, GDP deflator, and core consumer prices. This could shed light on the source of incomplete pass-through to consumer price inflation and help guide monetary policy decisions that are robust to more volatile price components, including energy and food. Finally, nonlinearities in exchange rate pass-through could be further investigated, looking at the direction and size of the various shocks under consideration.

Inflation in LICs. The implications for the inflation outcomes of country-specific characteristics in LICs remain to be explored. There is also a need to understand which specific reforms to the operations of LIC central banks would be most effective in achieving homegrown credibility. The latter topic has been covered extensively for the advanced economies, but, given the particular challenges faced by LICs, these priorities may well differ from those that have worked elsewhere.

Despite the growing body of literature on food price stabilization policies, several questions remain outstanding. Chapter 7 cautions about the unintended consequences of government policies and highlights the need for a more formal analysis of the effectiveness and development impact of targeted and untargeted policy interventions. Since trade policy interventions are likely to continue to be used, it would be useful to explore how policies—especially those coordinated at the multilateral level—could be designed to reduce their negative effects.

References

Amiti, M., O. Itskhoki, and J. Konings. 2014. "Importers, Exporters, and Exchange Rate Disconnect." *American Economic Review* 104 (7): 1942-78.

Anderson, K., W. Martin, and M. Ivanic. 2017. "Food Price Changes, Domestic Price Insulation and Poverty (When All Policy Makers Want to Be Above-Average)." In *Agriculture and Rural Development in a Transforming World,* edited by P. Pingali and G. Feder. London: Routledge.

Arteta, C., M. A. Kose, M. Stocker, and T. Taskin. 2018. "Implications of Negative Interest Rate Policies: An Early Assessment." *Pacific Economic Review* 23 (1): 8-26.

Auer, R. A., C. Borio, and A. Filardo. 2017. "The Globalisation of Inflation: The Growing Importance of Global Value Chains." BIS Working Paper 602, Bank for International Settlements, Basel.

Auer, R. A., A. Levchenko, and P. Sauré. 2017. "International Inflation Spillovers through Input Linkages." NBER Working Paper 23246, National Bureau of Economic Research, Cambridge, MA.

Baffes, J., M. A. Kose, F. Ohnsorge, and M. Stocker. 2015. "The Great Plunge in Oil Prices: Causes, Consequences, and Policy Responses." Policy Research Note 15/01, World Bank, Washington, DC.

Bernanke, B. S. 2007a. "Globalization and Monetary Policy." Speech at the Fourth Economic Summit, Stanford Institute for Economic Policy Research, Stanford, CA.

———. 2007b. "Inflation Expectations and Inflation Forecasting." Speech at the Monetary Economics Workshop of the National Bureau of Economic Research Summer Institute, Cambridge, MA, July 10.

Blanchard, O. J., G. Dell'Ariccia, and P. Mauro. 2010. "Rethinking Macroeconomic Policy." *Journal of Money, Credit, and Banking* 42 (s1): 199-215.

Bordo, M. 1999. *The Gold Standard and Related Regimes*. New York: Cambridge University Press.

———, and A. Orphanides. 2013. *The Great Inflation: The Rebirth of Modern Central Banking.* Chicago: University of Chicago Press.

Borio, C. E. V., and A. Filardo. 2007. "Globalisation and Inflation: New Cross-Country Evidence on the Global Determinants of Domestic Inflation." BIS Working Paper 227, Bank for International Settlements, Basel.

Calvo, G., and C. Reinhart. 2002. "Fear of Floating." *Quarterly Journal of Economics* 107 (2): 379-408.

Carney, M. 2015. "Inflation in a Globalised World." Remarks at the Economic Policy Symposium, Federal Reserve Bank of Kansas City, Jackson Hole, WY, August 29.

Carrière-Swallow, Y., G. Bertrand, E. Magud, and F. Valencia. 2016. "Monetary Policy Credibility and Exchange Rate Pass-Through." IMF Working Paper 16/240, International Monetary Fund, Washington, DC.

Carstens, A. 2018. Interview with Börsen-Zeitung, May 22, 2018.

Cecchetti, S. G., and S. Krause. 2002. "Central Bank Structure, Policy Efficiency, and Macroeconomic Performance: Exploring Empirical Relationships." *Federal Reserve Bank of St. Louis Review* 84 (4): 47-60.

Charnavoki, V., and J. J. Dolado. 2014. "The Effects of Global Shocks on Small Commodity-Exporting Economies: Lessons from Canada." *American Economic Journal: Macroeconomics* 6 (2): 207-37.

Chinn, M. D., and H. Ito. 2006. "What Matters for Financial Development? Capital Controls, Institutions, and Interactions." *Journal of Development Economics* 81 (1): 163-92.

Ciccarelli, M., and B. Mojon. 2010. "Global Inflation." *Review of Economics and Statistics* 92 (3): 524-35.

Cline, W. R. 1981. *World Inflation and the Developing Countries.* Washington, DC: Brookings Institution.

Coibion, O., Y. Gorodnichenko, and R. Kamdar. Forthcoming. "The Formation of Expectations, Inflation, and the Phillips Curve." *Journal of Economic Literature.*

———, and M. Pedemonte. 2018. "Inflation Expectations as a Policy Tool?" NBER Working Paper 24788, National Bureau of Economic Research, Cambridge, MA.

Conti, A. M., S. Neri, and A. Nobili. 2015. "Why Is Inflation So Low in the Euro Area? Economic Working Papers 1019, Bank of Italy, Rome.

Coulibaly, D., and H. Kempf. 2010. "Does Inflation Targeting Decrease Exchange Rate Pass-Through in Emerging Countries?" Working Paper 303, Banque de France, Paris.

de Soyres, F., E. Frohm, V. Gunnella, and E. Pavlova. 2018. "Bought, Sold and Bought Again." Policy Research Working Paper 8535, World Bank, Washington, DC.

Dincer, N. N., and B. Eichengreen. 2014. "Central Bank Transparency and Independence: Updates and New Measures." *International Journal of Central Banking* 10 (1): 189-259.

Draghi, M. 2015. "Global and Domestic Inflation." Speech at the Economic Club of New York, December 4.

———. 2016. "How Central Banks Meet the Challenge of Low Inflation." Speech at the SUERF (European Money and Finance Forum) conference, February 4, Frankfurt.

Eickmeier, S., and K. Pijnenburg. 2013. "The Global Dimension of Inflation: Evidence from Factor-Augmented Phillips Curves." *Oxford Bulletin of Economics and Statistics* 75 (1): 103-22.

Fischer, S. 2015. "Global and Domestic Inflation." Speech at Crockett Governors' Roundtable 2015 for African Central Bankers, University of Oxford, June 30.

Forbes, K., I. Hjortsoe, and T. Nenova. 2017. "Shocks versus Structure: Explaining Differences in Exchange Rate Pass-Through across Countries and Time." External Monetary Policy Committee Unit Discussion Paper 50, Bank of England, London.

———. 2018. "The Shocks Matter: Improving Our Estimates of Exchange Rate Pass-Through." *Journal of International Economics* 114 (September): 255-75.

Gagnon, J. E., and J. Ihrig. 2004. "Monetary Policy and Exchange Rate Pass-Through." *International Journal of Finance and Economics* 9 (4): 315-38.

Georgiadis, G., J. Gräb, and M. Khalil. 2017. "Global Value Chain Participation and Exchange Rate Pass-Through." European Central Bank, Frankfurt, Germany.

Gerlach, S., A. Giovannini, C. Tille, and J. Vinals. 2008. "Low Inflation: Testing Times for Central Banks." ICMB Geneva Report on the World Economy 10, International Center for Monetary and Banking Studies, Geneva.

Grothe, M., and A. Meyler. 2018. "Inflation Forecasts: Are Market-Based and Survey-Based Measures Informative?" *International Journal of Financial Research* 9 (1): 171-88.

Hammond, G., R. Kanbur, and E. Prasad. 2009. "Monetary Policy Challenges for Emerging Market Economies." In *New Monetary Policy Frameworks for Emerging Markets: Coping with the Challenges of Financial Globalization*, edited by G. Hammond, R. Kanbur, and E. Prasad. Cheltenham, UK: Edward Elgar Publishing.

Harding, D., and A. Pagan. 2002. "Dissecting the Cycle: A Methodological Investigation." *Journal of Monetary Economics* 49 (2): 365-381.

Hartmann, P., and P. McAdam. 2018. "Price and Wage-Setting in Advanced Economies: Take-Aways from the ECB's 2018 Sintra Forum." European Central Bank, Frankfurt, Germany.

Ihrig, J., S. B. Kamin, D. Lindner, and J. Marquez. 2010. "Some Simple Tests of the Globalization and Inflation Hypothesis." *International Finance* 13 (3): 343-75.

IMF (International Monetary Fund). 2001. "The Decline of Inflation in Emerging Markets: Can It Be Maintained?" In *World Economic Outlook*. Washington, DC: IMF.

———. 2016. "Global Disinflation in an Era of Constrained Monetary Policy." In *World Economic Outlook*. Washington, DC: IMF.

———. 2018. "Challenges for Monetary Policy in Emerging Markets as Global Financial Conditions Normalize." In *World Economic Outlook*. Washington, DC: IMF.

Ivanic, M., and W. Martin. 2008. "Implications of Higher Global Food Prices for Poverty in Low-Income Countries." Policy Research Working Paper 4594, World Bank, Washington, DC.

Khan, M., and A. Senhadji. 2001. "Threshold Effects in the Relationship between Inflation and Growth." *IMF Staff Papers* 48 (1): 1-21.

Kose, M. A., and M. Terrones. 2015. *Collapse and Revival: Understanding Global Recessions and Recoveries*. Washington, DC: International Monetary Fund.

Laborde, D., V. Robichaud, and S. Tokgoz. 2013. "MIRAGRODEP 1.0: Documentation." AGRODEP Technical Note, International Food Policy Research Institute, Washington, DC.

Lowe, P. 2017. "Some Evolving Questions." Address to the Australian Business Economists Annual Dinner, Sydney, Australia, November 21.

Mankiw, N. G., and R. Reis. 2018. "Friedman's Presidential Address in the Evolution of Macroeconomic Thought." *Journal of Economic Perspectives* 32 (1): 81-96.

Mehrotra, A., and J. Yetman. Forthcoming. "Decaying Expectations: What Inflation Forecasts Tell Us about the Anchoring of Inflation Expectations." *International Journal of Central Banking.*

Mishkin, F. 2008. "Does Stabilizing Inflation Contribute to Stabilizing Economic Activity?" NBER Working Paper 13970, National Bureau of Economic Research, Cambridge, MA.

———, and K. Schmidt-Hebbel. 2007. "Does Inflation Targeting Make a Difference?" NBER Working Paper 12876, National Bureau of Economic Research, Cambridge, MA.

Mishra, P., P. J. Montiel, and A. Spilimbergo. 2012. "Monetary Transmission in Low-Income Countries: Effectiveness and Policy Implications." *IMF Economic Review* 60 (2): 270-302.

Mumtaz, H., and P. Surico. 2012. "Evolving International Inflation Dynamics: World and Country-Specific Factors." *Journal of the European Economic Association* 10 (4): 716-34.

Neely, C. J., and D. E. Rapach. 2011. "International Comovements in Inflation Rates and Country Characteristics." *Journal of International Money and Finance* 30 (7): 1471-90.

Pedroni, P. 2013. "Structural Panel VARs." *Econometrics* 1 (2): 180-206.

Rogoff, K. 2003. "Globalization and Global Disinflation." *Federal Reserve Bank of Kansas City Economic Review* 88 (4): 45-78.

———. 2014. "The Exaggerated Death of Inflation." *Project Syndicate,* September 2.

Shambaugh, J. C. 2004. "The Effect of Fixed Exchange Rates on Monetary Policy." *Quarterly Journal of Economics* 119 (1): 301-52.

———. 2008. "A New Look at Pass-Through." *Journal of International Money and Finance* 27 (4): 560-91.

Sousa, R., and J. Yetman. 2016. "Inflation Expectations and Monetary Policy." BIS Paper 89d, Bank for International Settlements, Basel, Switzerland.

Stock, J. H., and M. W. Watson. 2016. "Core Inflation and Trend Inflation." *Review of Economics and Statistics* 98 (4): 770-84.

Taylor, J. B. 2014. "Inflation Targeting in Emerging Markets: The Global Experience." Speech at the Conference on Fourteen Years of Inflation Targeting in South Africa and the Challenge of a Changing Mandate, South African Reserve Bank, Pretoria, December 19.

Woodford, M. 2003. *Interest and Prices: Foundations of a Theory of Monetary Policy.* Princeton, NZ: Princeton University Press.

World Bank. 2009. *Global Economic Prospects: Commodities at the Crossroads.* January. Washington, DC: World Bank.

———. 2011. "Responding to Global Food Price Volatility and Its Impact on Food Security." World Bank, Washington, DC.

Yellen, J. 2017. "The U.S. Economy and Monetary Policy." Speech at the Group of 30 International Banking Seminar, October 15, Washington, DC.

In this era of hyperglobalisation, are central banks still masters of their domestic monetary destinies? Or have they become slaves to global factors? … [t]here's evidence of global inflationary cycles that correspond with an intensifying globalisation that propagates common shocks via commodity, trade and financial channels.

Mark Carney (2015)

Over the last decade there has been a growing interest in the concept of "global inflation". This is the notion that, in a globalised world, inflation is becoming less responsive to domestic economic conditions, and is instead increasingly determined by global factors.

Mario Draghi (2015)

PART A

INFLATION

Global and Domestic Drivers

CHAPTER 1

Inflation: Concepts, Evolution, and Correlates

In the past four to five decades, inflation has fallen around the world, with median annual global consumer price inflation down from a peak of 16.6 percent in 1974 to 2.6 percent in 2017. This decline began in advanced economies in the mid-1980s and in emerging market and developing economies in the mid-1990s. By 2000, global inflation had stabilized at historically low levels. Lower inflation has been accompanied by reduced inflation volatility, especially in advanced economies. This improvement in inflation outcomes has stemmed in large part from structural economic changes, including improved monetary and fiscal policy frameworks as well as international trade and financial liberalization. Lower and more stable inflation has often been associated with better growth and development outcomes, partly by reducing uncertainty, fostering a more efficient allocation of resources, and helping preserve financial stability.

Introduction

Inflation has declined sharply around the world since the global financial crisis. Global inflation—defined as median consumer price inflation among all countries—fell from 9.2 percent (year-on-year) in the second quarter of 2008 to 2.3 percent in the second quarter of 2018. In 80 percent of emerging market and developing economies (EMDEs), inflation in the second quarter of 2018 ranged between 0.9 and 7.5 percent (year-on-year), compared with a range of 4.8 to 25.3 percent in the second quarter of 2008. Among EMDEs, this has created room for monetary policy to support activity. In advanced economies, however, persistent below-target inflation since the crisis has increased risks of de-anchoring inflation expectations and led central banks to resort to unconventional monetary policy instruments to support demand.

The recent easing of inflation continues a trend that spans nearly 50 years. After a rapid rise during the 1960s, global inflation peaked in 1974 at 16.6 percent (annual average), four times the global inflation in 2017 (Figure 1.1). Similarly, inflation in EMDEs declined from a peak of 17.3 percent (annual average) in 1974 to 3.5 percent in 2017. The disinflation over the past four to five decades has been the result of a confluence of factors, including the adoption of new monetary and fiscal policy frameworks, severe global shocks, and structural changes in national economies and the global economy.

Note: This chapter was prepared by Jongrim Ha, Anna Ivanova, Franziska Ohnsorge, and Filiz Unsal. Annex 1.1 was prepared by Peter Nagle.

FIGURE 1.1 Global inflation

Global inflation fell sharply between 1970 and 2000. It has been low since then, a trend shared by all measures of inflation. The post-crisis period of globally low inflation has helped bring inflation into target ranges in the majority of EMDEs but has raised concerns about deflation in advanced economies.

A. Global inflation

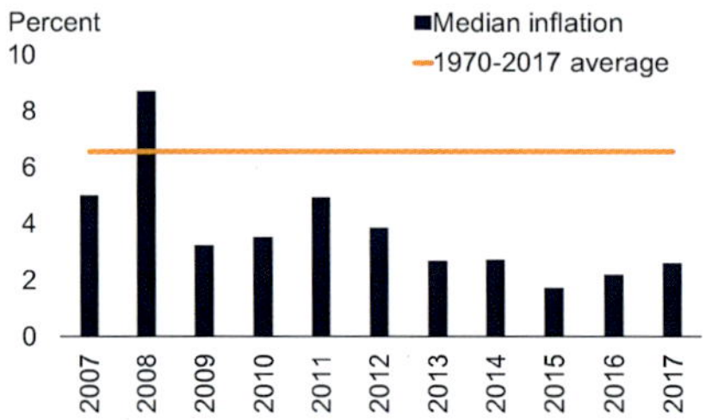

B. Inflation in advanced economies and EMDEs

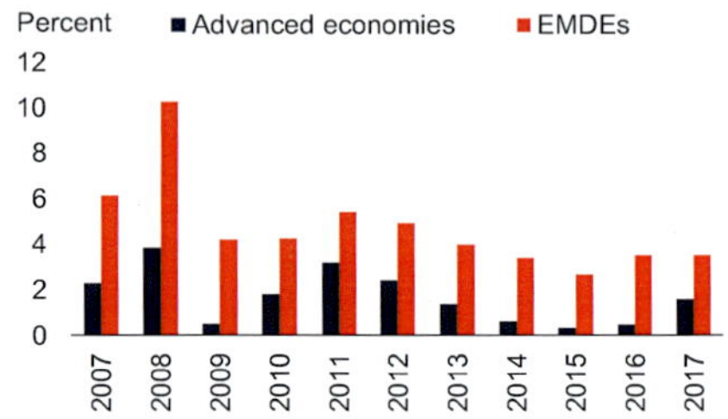

C. Share of advanced economies and EMDEs with inflation below or within target range

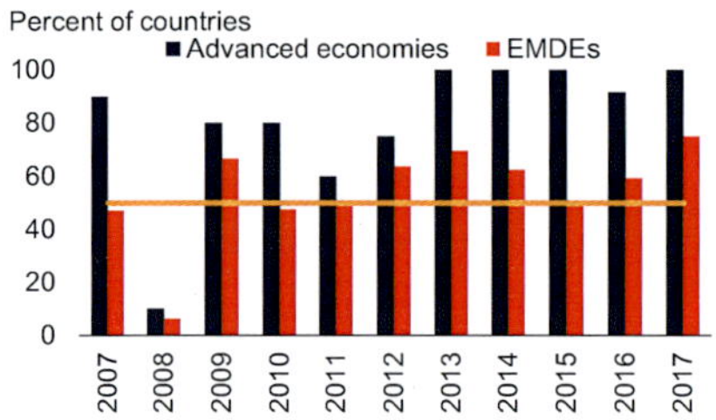

D. Share of advanced economies with low inflation

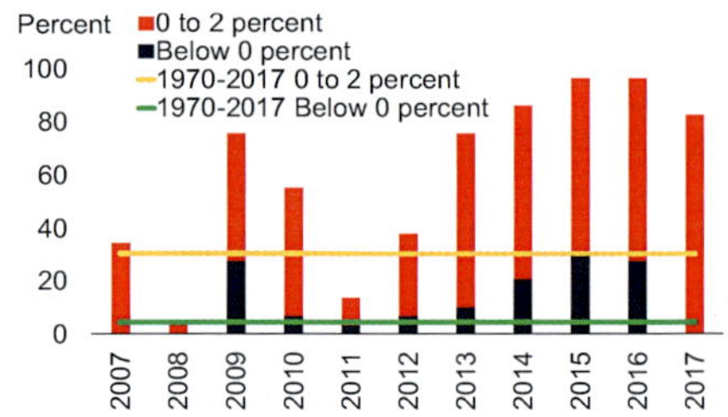

E. Global core and headline inflation

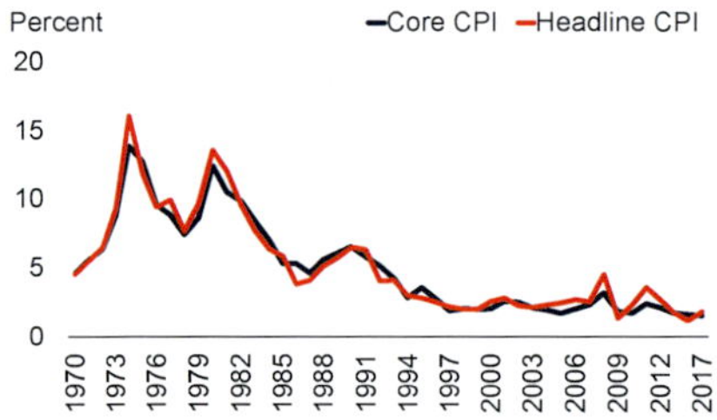

F. Global PPI, CPI, and GDP deflator inflation

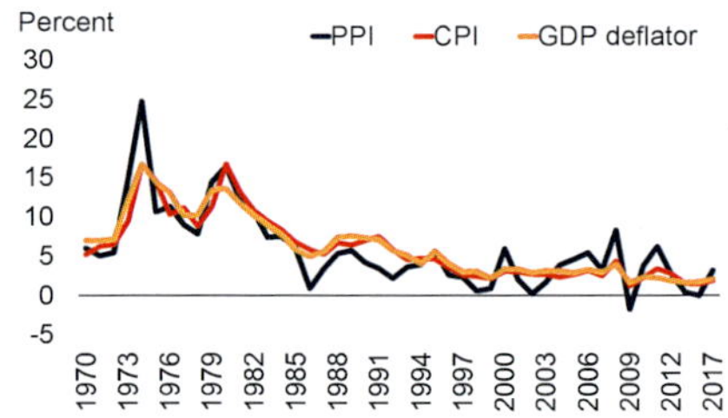

Source: World Bank.

Note: All inflation rates refer to year-on-year inflation. CPI = consumer price index; EMDEs = emerging market and developing economies; GDP = gross domestic product; PPI = producer price index.

A. Median consumer price inflation among 153 economies.

B. Median consumer price inflation of 29 advanced economies and 124 EMDEs.

C. Share of 11 advanced economies and 24 EMDEs with consumer price inflation below target or within target range. The horizontal line indicates 50 percent.

D. Percent of 29 advanced economies with consumer price inflation below zero and between 0 and 2 percent. Horizontal lines indicate 1970-2017 averages.

E. Median for 41 economies.

F. Median for 39 economies.

Low and stable inflation has often been associated with more stable output and employment and more rapid output growth and investment. Low and stable inflation increases the transparency of relative price changes, provides confidence for long-term savers and investors, protects the purchasing power of household income and wealth, and enhances financial stability (Annex 1.1; Box 1.1). By contrast, economies that have experienced high inflation have suffered significantly lower growth (Kremer, Bick, and Nautz 2013). Extended periods of chronically high inflation, often in Latin America, have frequently ended in large output losses during stabilization programs, or even balance of payments crises.

Extremely low inflation, however, such as has prevailed in many advanced economies over the past decade, may make it difficult for central banks to lower real short-term interest rates sufficiently to provide the requisite stimulus to demand, given that the lower bound on nominal rates is close to zero. Extremely low inflation may therefore limit the room for maneuver of conventional monetary policy and lead central banks to use unconventional measures, including large-scale purchases of longer-term financial assets, to reduce longer-term rates. Such difficulties in implementing expansionary monetary policy, in turn, increase the risk of sliding into a self-reinforcing period of deflation that raises debt burdens and further depresses activity. Extremely low inflation may also hinder the adjustment of absolute and relative real wages, because of the general downward rigidity of nominal wages.

Focus. This chapter focuses on the factors that have supported long-term disinflation across the world. It also discusses the benefits from such long-term disinflation. This complements the analysis of the drivers of short-term inflation movements in Chapters 2 to 5. This chapter discusses the following questions:

- How does inflation support or hinder economic activity?
- How has global inflation evolved over the past four to five decades?
- What factors have contributed to these trends in global inflation?

Contribution to the literature. This chapter's contributions are threefold.

First, it documents the broad-based disinflation over the past four to five decades using a rich database of countries and inflation measures. The analysis is based on a comprehensive data set for a virtually global sample of countries over almost half a century (141 EMDEs and 34 advanced economies for 1970-2018). Earlier studies have documented the broad-based global disinflation, but with data sets that covered a narrower set of countries or a shorter time period. These studies have been mostly restricted to advanced economies and have not taken account of either the drop in the price of oil in 2014 or the period of unusually depressed post-crisis inflation.

BOX 1.1 Benefits and costs of inflation: A review

Estimates of the optimal inflation rate lie in a wide range, depending on country characteristics. Excessively high or low inflation can trigger self-perpetuating output losses. Particular policy challenges arise in exiting from high inflation and navigating very low inflation.

A large literature has documented the challenges posed by high inflation for advanced economies and emerging market and developing economies (EMDEs). In the 1970s and 1980s in advanced economies and until the early 1990s in EMDEs, the perils of high inflation were the main macroeconomic policy concern. By the early 2000s, at least for advanced economies, the focus had shifted to the causes and consequences of very low inflation, including deflation (that is, negative inflation). This literature enjoyed a renaissance after the global financial crisis, as fears about deflation mounted.

Against this backdrop, this box addresses the following questions:

- What output losses have been associated with high inflation?
- Why is high inflation associated with weak activity?
- What policy challenges does excessively low inflation pose?

What output losses have been associated with high inflation?

Adverse effects of high inflation on output have been studied extensively since the 1990s.[1] Early studies found that inflation above 40 percent was associated with slower economic growth in large samples of countries from the 1960s to the mid-1990s (Fischer 1993; Bruno and Easterly 1998; Temple 2002). In most (31 of 41) episodes of inflation above 40 percent, output losses were sharp (2.4 percent, on average), but they were not significant at lower inflation levels (Bruno and Easterly 1998). Lower inflation thresholds, typically below 20 percent, for a negative relationship between inflation and growth were also reported by several subsequent studies based on large samples of countries stretching over multiple decades.[2]

[1] The focus here is on the challenges of persistently high inflation. Bohl and Siklos (2018) review hyperinflation episodes, when month-on-month inflation exceeded 50 percent.

[2] See Espinoza, Leon, and Prasad (2012) for a literature review of thresholds in the relationship between inflation and growth. Threshold effects are also estimated by Judson and Orphanides (1999), Omay and Öznur Kan (2010), Bick (2010), and Lopez-Villavicencio and Mignon (2011).

BOX 1.1 Benefits and costs of inflation: A review (*continued*)

There is growing evidence that the threshold for a negative relationship between inflation and growth depends on country characteristics. Some of the earliest studies in this literature documented that the threshold tends to be lower in advanced economies—below 10 percent, and typically around 2-3 percent—than in EMDEs, where inflation thresholds have been estimated at around 20 percent.[3] The range of estimates varies widely, however. Some studies have estimated inflation thresholds at around 5-8 percent for Asian EMDEs and 7-9 percent for Sub-Saharan African EMDEs.[4] Country features that have been associated with a more negative link between inflation and growth include greater financial development and trade openness, larger government, weaker institutions, and greater political risk.[5]

Why is high inflation associated with weak activity?

High inflation is likely to weaken activity by obscuring and distorting relative prices, creating uncertainty that undermines long-term decision making and discourages savings; redistributing incomes and thereby weakening consumption; and eroding financial stability. Activity is also likely to be weakened by the policies needed to reduce inflation from high levels, including tighter monetary policies.[6]

Transparency of relative price changes. High inflation is likely to require frequent price adjustments by firms to maintain their profitability. If price adjustments for different goods and services are asynchronous ("staggered price setting"), relative price distortions will result (Woodford 2003; Fischer 1993). Even if temporary, these will tend to undermine the efficient allocation of resources and productivity growth. In particular,

[3] Khan and Senhadji (2001); Drukker, Gomis-Porqueras, and Hernandez-Verme (2005); Vaona and Schiavo (2007).

[4] Ndoricimpa (2017); Thanh (2015); Vinayagathasan (2013).

[5] In a large sample for 1950-2009 or 1960-2009, Ibarra and Trupkin (2011, 2016) and Eggoh and Khan (2014) find that, on average, inflation above thresholds of 19 and 12 percent, respectively, are associated with lower growth. However, the negative association between inflation and growth is stronger in countries with greater financial depth, broader trade openness, higher investment, and larger government expenditures. The threshold is in the single digits for EMDEs with the highest quality political institutions and most favorable International Country Risk Guide ratings of political risk.

[6] See Mishkin (2008b); Camba-Mendez, Garcia, and Rodriguez-Palenzuela (2003); and Briault (1995) for more detailed literature reviews.

BOX 1.1 Benefits and costs of inflation: A review (*continued*)

inflation may encourage investment in property rather than more productive investments (White 2006). If high inflation obscures relative price changes, it also creates a need for costly information search (Aksoy et al. 2017).

Uncertainty. High inflation may make it difficult for households and firms to disentangle relative from absolute price changes (Lucas 1972). High inflation is also typically associated with more volatile inflation (Logue and Willet 1976; Andersen and Gruen 1995; IMF 2001). Finally, high and volatile inflation signals an inability of government policies to ensure macroeconomic stability (Fischer 1993). These factors increase uncertainty about the future value of assets and hence discourage investment that requires solid long-term returns to ensure profitability (Woodford 2003). Such investment can be an important source of productivity growth, especially when it embodies new technologies (Greenwood, Hercowitz, and Krusell 1997).

Erosion of after-tax and real incomes. High inflation may reduce saving through two channels. First, it lifts nominal income growth and, thus, accelerates tax progression when rising nominal incomes are measured against fixed nominal income tax brackets (Greville and Reddell 1990; Feldstein 1997, 1999). This squeezes post-tax incomes, which will tend to depress household saving. Second, high inflation reduces the real value of debt—which serves as an investment vehicle for household savings—and any income derived from it (Briault 1995). The erosion of after-tax incomes and income derived from debt discourages savings and, hence, the funding envelope for productive investment.

Risks to financial sector stability. With high inflation, households will tend to shun financial instruments carrying fixed nominal returns and thus withdraw from bank-intermediated savings. Such disintermediation may force banks to rely on non-deposit liabilities, which will tend to raise the (short-term) cost of financing their (long-term) investment portfolios. This will raise the maturity risks inherent in the balance sheets of financial intermediaries that hold long-term assets, often at fixed interest rates, against short-term liabilities (Schwartz 1995). Furthermore, high inflation will raise the term premia and maturity risks embodied in long-term interest rates that compensate investors for long-term inflation risks. The

BOX 1.1 Benefits and costs of inflation: A review (*continued*)

resulting higher borrowing costs increase rollover or default risk and the cost of financing long-term investments (Wright 2011).[7]

Income redistribution that weakens consumption. Low-income households tend to rely on wages, pensions, and social benefits as their main sources of income and hold a larger share of their savings in cash (Erosa and Ventura 2002). Wages, pensions, and social benefits tend to respond less and with longer lags to inflation than nonwage income, and the real value of cash savings, being unremunerated, is eroded by inflation (Kahn 1997). As a result, poor households' real incomes tend to decline more than those of higher-income households in high-inflation environments (Romer and Romer 1997; Albanesi 2007).[8] Since poor households have a higher marginal propensity to consume—for example, as shown by Dynan, Skinner, and Zeldes (2004) for the United States—this tends to weaken consumption.

Exiting high-inflation episodes. The detrimental effect on growth of high inflation is well established in the literature, although precise thresholds vary. Additional damage to output is done when the necessary measures are taken to exit high inflation. Indexation of wages and other prices can make large output losses necessary to achieve disinflation, especially when central banks lack credibility (Blanchard and Gali 2007). (See Annex 1.3 for U.S. experience with disinflation.)

What policy challenges does excessively low inflation pose?

The low inflation of the early 2000s raised concerns about the ability of central banks in advanced economies to support demand when policy rates are near the zero lower bound (Reifschneider and Williams 2000; Eggertsson and Woodford 2003). An extended period of low inflation ("lowflation") can distort resource allocation, present policy challenges in

---

[7] The long-term interest rates can be decomposed into (i) expected inflation, (ii) expectations about the future path of real short-term interest rates, and (iii) a term premium that reflects changes in the perceived riskiness of longer-term securities and their liquidity. Term premiums on longer-term securities will be higher when investors are more risk-averse and/or the perceived risk of holding those securities is high. Historically, the most important risk for long-term bondholders has been the risk of unexpected inflation. Uncertainty about the near-term outlook for the economy or monetary policy also raises the riskiness of bonds.

[8] In addition, poor households often lack access to financial technologies that allow hedging against inflation (Mulligan and Sala-i-Martin 2000). Conversely, those poor households that do have access to credit may benefit from inflation because it erodes the real value of nominal claims such as loans (Doepke and Schneider 2006).

BOX 1.1 Benefits and costs of inflation: A review (*continued*)

responding to recessions, and undermine the credibility of central banks.[9] Once entrenched, deflation can trigger a spiral of self-reinforcing output losses.

Lowflation. When inflation is extremely low—meaning significantly below the target—relative price declines may require negative inflation in categories of goods and services with excess supply. This presents a challenge when rigidities prevent nominal price cuts of goods and services (Taylor 2000). When nominal prices cannot be reduced, low inflation can lead to distorted relative prices and inefficient allocation of resources across the economy.

Low inflation also poses monetary and fiscal policy challenges. Low inflation is typically associated with low nominal monetary policy rates. In such an environment, monetary policy may be unable to respond with conventional tools to negative shocks that reduce economic activity and inflation, since the interest rate cuts that are needed to support activity would imply negative nominal monetary policy rates. Two decades ago, it was thought that monetary policy rates could not fall below zero—the so-called "zero lower bound"—because of the incentive this would create for moving out of financial instruments into cash (Svensson 2003). The resulting disintermediation could undermine monetary policy effectiveness and capital markets. Since 2010, however, the experiences of Denmark, the Euro Area, Japan, Sweden, and Switzerland indicate that mildly negative interest rates can be sustained for extended periods without causing large-scale financial disintermediation (Arteta et al. 2016; Rogoff 2015).

However, the limited room for monetary policy action amid very low inflation and short-term interest rates implies that fiscal policy has to shoulder more of the responsibility for macroeconomic stabilization (Feldstein 2002). Such proactive fiscal policy may be difficult when government debt is high, because, all else equal, the real burden of debt is likely to remain persistently higher in a lowflation environment than in an inflationary environment where nominal incomes are rising (Contessi, Li, and De Pace 2014).

Deflation. Outright deflation, if sustained over an extended period, can reduce output by dampening investment and consumption and distorting resource allocation (Fisher 1933; Friedman and Schwartz 1963). Deflation

[9] Ciccarelli and Osbat (2017); Moghadam, Teja, and Berkmen (2014).

BOX 1.1 Benefits and costs of inflation: A review (*continued*)

increases the real burden of debt and debt service and depresses collateral values, thus straining financial systems ("debt deflation") (Bernanke and James 1991; End et al. 2015; Baig et al. 2003). It compresses price dispersion and dulls the signals of relative price changes that are critical for an efficient allocation of resources (Benabou 1992). Once deflation becomes entrenched in expectations, it may become self-reinforcing (Branch and Evans 2017; Banerjee and Mehrotra 2018). By raising real interest rates, negative inflation tightens monetary conditions and depresses activity further (Bernanke, Reinhart, and Sack 2004). Although these mechanisms suggest that theoretically deflation could impose heavy costs, empirical evidence suggests that these costs are modest in practice (Borio et al. 2015).

The optimal inflation rate

The jury is still out on the optimal inflation rate. Theoretical models offer a wide range of optimal inflation rates, negative and positive, depending on the assumptions. Diercks (2017) analyzed 100 studies that provided quantitative estimates for optimal inflation. Of these, about 80 recommended inflation targets at or below zero. Negative inflation would ensure that real interest rates are positive even when nominal interest rates are zero, such that there is no cost for holding money. However, these models typically assume perfect price flexibility. Models with sticky prices generate temporary deviations in relative prices and, hence, give rise to allocative inefficiencies and welfare cost from inflation or deflation. These models typically suggest an optimal inflation rate of zero. In models that incorporate additional constraints that arguably add realism—such as sticky wages, a zero lower bound on nominal interest rates, distortionary taxation, financial frictions, and price indexation—a low positive inflation rate becomes optimal.

The empirical literature suggests that optimal inflation rates lie in a wide range, depending on country characteristics (Anand, Prasad, and Zhang 2015; Mankiw and Reis 2002). "Too high" inflation and deflation are associated with output losses, and "too low" inflation carries the risk of slipping into deflation in the next recession. The threshold for considering inflation to be "too high" varies widely with country characteristics, and the threshold for "too low" depends on the size and frequency of adverse shocks, fiscal policy flexibility, and the effectiveness of monetary policy transmission.

BOX 1.1 Benefits and costs of inflation: A review (*continued*)

Given these trade-offs and risks, some studies (Blanchard, Dell'Arricia, and Mauro 2010; Ball 2014; Krugman 2014; Kiley and Roberts 2017; Andrade et al. 2018) recommend raising central banks' inflation targets to 4 percent, which is double the median inflation target of advanced economy inflation targeting central banks (2 percent). However, other authors (Coibion and Gorodnichenko 2012; Coibion, Gorodnichenko, and Wieland 2012; Mishkin 2018; Dorich et al. 2018; Schmitt-Grohe and Uribe 2010) caution that raising the inflation target is too blunt a solution for addressing risks around the zero lower bound: a higher inflation target imposes higher economic cost most of the time, but it lowers the cost of hitting the zero lower bound only in rare circumstances.

Second, in contrast to earlier studies, this chapter identifies a rich set of stylized facts that are robust across different measures of inflation. Trend disinflation over the past four to five decades manifested in all measures of inflation (headline and core consumer prices, producer prices, import prices, and the gross domestic product (GDP) deflator).

Third, the chapter provides a uniquely comprehensive and systematic analysis of the structural factors that have been credited with lowering inflation over the past four to five decades. The literature has identified many structural changes that have supported the long-term trend toward lower and more stable inflation. These include increased global economic integration and strengthened macroeconomic policy frameworks. However, no study to date has presented a systematic analysis of the role of these factors. This chapter provides such an analysis as well as a preliminary quantification of their associations with the trend decline in inflation.

Findings. The chapter documents the following findings:

- Inflation has fallen around the world. Median consumer price inflation declined from a peak of 16.6 percent (annual average) in 1974 to 2.6 percent in 2017. Similarly, median inflation in EMDEs declined from a peak of 17.3 percent (annual average) in 1974 to 3.5 percent in 2017, and, in low-income countries (LICs) it declined from a peak of 24.9 percent (annual average) in 1994 to 5.0 percent in 2017. The decline began in advanced economies in the mid-1980s and in EMDEs in the mid-1990s. By 2000, global inflation had stabilized at historically low levels. Lower inflation was accompanied by lower inflation volatility, especially in advanced economies.

- Structural economic changes have supported global disinflation. The most significant drivers of global disinflation have included globalization—increased international economic integration—and a shift toward more effective and more resilient monetary and fiscal policy frameworks and exchange rate regimes. On average, inflation has declined faster in countries with greater trade and capital account openness, more transparent central banks, and a switch to inflation targeting regimes.

- The current low and stable inflation environment resembles those of the Bretton Woods fixed exchange rate system from the post-war period to 1971 and of the gold standard of the early 1900s. All three episodes are characterized by inflation below 5 percent for an extended period (7-19 years), but the current environment differs from the two earlier episodes in its lower inflation volatility.

- The gains of the past four to five decades in terms of inflation are by no means guaranteed. Inflation can easily make a comeback if the fundamental structural and policy changes that have compressed inflation over the past four to five decades lose momentum or even reverse. However, as long as strong monetary policy frameworks are supported by sound fiscal policies and institutional structures, it would be possible to keep in check the inflationary implications of fluctuations in business and financial cycles, and movements in commodity prices.

Conceptual considerations

Before exploring the longer-term drivers of inflation, several conceptual issues require clarification. These include the relationship between inflation and relative price changes, the interpretation of different measures of inflation, the appropriate rate of inflation as a policy objective, and the implications of inflation volatility and persistence.

Inflation versus relative price changes. *Inflation* refers to a sustained and broad-based increase in the overall price level.[1] This is distinct from changes in *relative prices*, which measure the price of one good or service relative to the price of another (or a weighted average of all other goods and services) and signal information about relative surpluses or shortages in different product markets. A rising *relative* price of a certain good or service indicates that the demand for it outstrips supply and encourages production while discouraging consumption. Hence, in contrast to inflation, relative price movements are critical for the

[1] When the word "inflation" was first used in economic contexts in the early- to mid-19th century, it referred to growth of the money supply. In the 1930s, it began to be associated with rising prices, which were attributed to growing money supply (Bryan 1997, 2002).

efficient allocation of resources. If goods, services, and factor markets were fully flexible, inflation (which in principle involves no change in relative prices) would not affect the allocation of resources and relative price changes would occur without inflation. However, if nominal rigidities limit the scope for downward price adjustments, then broad-based inflation can facilitate relative price adjustments by allowing above-average price increases for goods, services, or factors of production that are in high demand (Taylor 2000). This is particularly relevant to the market for labor because of the general downward rigidity of nominal wages.

Disinflation versus deflation. Deflation refers to negative inflation—that is, a decline in price levels—whereas disinflation refers to a decline in inflation rates that are still positive (Federal Reserve Bank of San Francisco 1999). Disinflation has been widespread since the mid-1970s, whereas outright deflation has been rare.

Headline versus core inflation. *Headline* inflation usually refers to changes in the prices of all goods and services in a basket of goods and services that is representative of consumer expenditures. *Core* inflation measures are intended to capture the underlying, common trend in all prices, regardless of relative price changes. In practice, core inflation is often measured by excluding from the calculation movements in the prices of goods and services that are most volatile, in particular food and energy. For example, swings in food and energy prices tend to be changes in relative prices that shift consumption and production patterns. Alternatively, core inflation is sometimes calculated as the common component of price movements of all goods and services (Stock and Watson 2007, 2010; Schembri 2017).

Consumer prices, producer prices, and GDP deflators. The most common measure of inflation is the percentage change in the headline consumer price index (CPI), which captures the cost of living of the average consumer. The CPI includes domestically produced and imported consumer goods. The producer price index (PPI), in contrast, reflects the prices charged by domestic producers of goods and services.[2] Domestically produced goods and services can have several purposes, including domestic consumption, domestic investment, and exports. When the composition of consumption differs from that of production, for example, because of large consumer goods imports or extensive production of investment goods, CPI and PPI inflation can diverge materially. Finally, the

[2] The wholesale price index (WPI) is closely related to the PPI but, in principle, refers to sales in the wholesale market, whereas the PPI refers to all sales. In the United States, for example, the WPI was renamed the PPI in 1978 (Bureau of Labor Statistics). In contrast, the personal consumption expenditure index is closely related to the CPI but, in contrast to the CPI, includes services not directly paid for by consumers, for example, employer-paid services such as medical insurance.

GDP deflator measures the average price of the economy's output, broadly defined. It differs from the CPI by excluding import prices but including prices of exports, investment, and government consumption. It differs from the PPI by including taxes net of subsidies. The emphasis in this chapter is on the CPI, because it offers the largest possible cross-country sample, especially at monthly and quarterly data frequencies, and it is the measure targeted by the largest number of central banks.

Contemporaneous quarterly movements in quarter-on-quarter CPI and PPI inflation tend to be correlated (about 70 percent). The correlations for the CPI and PPI with the GDP deflator are considerably lower (below 50 percent). In more closed EMDEs, the correlation between the CPI and PPI is almost complete (95 percent). In contrast, in more open economies, exports and imports drive a wedge between consumption and production such that the correlation of CPI and PPI is only 62 percent. Similarly, in advanced economies more than in EMDEs, taxes and subsidies drive a wedge between the PPI and the GDP deflator; as a result, the correlation between the PPI and the GDP deflator in advanced economies is two-thirds that in EMDEs (Figure 1.2).

Inflation rates and volatility. In the absence of large commodity price or exchange rate shocks, high and accelerating inflation rates signal an economy in which aggregate demand outpaces aggregate supply. High inflation *volatility* is often associated with macroeconomic instability and uncertainty about the future path of prices. High inflation *persistence* near target levels—a tendency of inflation to stay near its recent values, absent economic forces that move it away from the current level—indicates that monetary policy has helped anchor inflation expectations and reflects structural features of the economy such as wage or price indexation (Fuhrer 2009).

Inflation and economic activity

Historically, low and stable inflation, combined with well-anchored inflation expectations, has been associated with greater short-term stability of output and employment and higher long-term growth.

Lower inflation has tended to be accompanied by lower inflation volatility and higher output growth. Lower inflation volatility, in turn, has typically been accompanied by lower output growth volatility and higher investment and savings (Figure 1.3). Several channels account for the beneficial effects of low and stable inflation on economic activity. These include greater predictability for investors and households, greater transparency of relative price changes, and greater financial stability. The large literature documenting these channels is summarized in Box 1.1. The following provides a short summary:

FIGURE 1.2 Correlation between inflation measures

Movements in CPI and PPI inflation tend to be highly correlated, especially in more closed EMDEs. In advanced economies especially, taxes and subsidies drive a wedge between CPI and PPI inflation and GDP deflator inflation, such that their correlations are lower than in EMDEs.

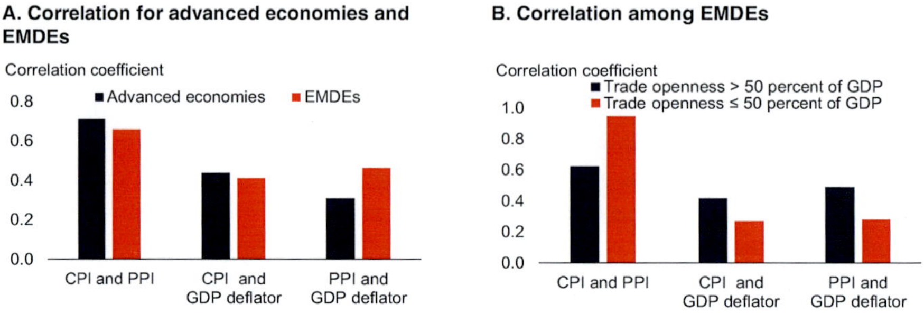

Source: World Bank.

Note: Correlation coefficients for quarter-on-quarter seasonally adjusted (not annualized) inflation among 53 economies (of which 23 are EMDEs) for which CPI, PPI, and GDP deflator data are available. CPI = consumer price index; EMDEs = emerging market and developing economies; GDP = gross domestic product; PPI = producer price index.

B. Trade openness measured as the sum of exports and imports as a percentage of GDP.

- *First,* low inflation reduces uncertainty. By inspiring confidence in the future real value of nominal assets and reducing the uncertainty surrounding future returns on productive investment, low and stable inflation fosters long-term investment. Such investment can be an important source of productivity and income growth, especially when new technologies are embodied in investment.

- *Second,* low and stable—but positive—inflation makes relative price changes more transparent. This reduces the need for costly search for information that would be required when high inflation obscures relative price changes.

- *Third,* low and stable inflation helps preserve the real value of after-tax incomes, especially when tax brackets are fixed in nominal terms, and savings (Box 1.1). This encourages investment and saving.

- *Fourth,* low and stable inflation tends to be associated with greater financial sector stability. This, in turn, supports macroeconomic stability. Stable inflation is usually associated with lower long-term nominal interest rates. This can help reduce rollover or default risk and the cost of financing for long-term investments. Stable inflation also reduces the risks faced by financial intermediaries that hold long-term nominal assets.

FIGURE 1.3 Inflation and economic activity in EMDEs

Low and stable inflation has been associated with higher and more stable output growth, and investment and savings.

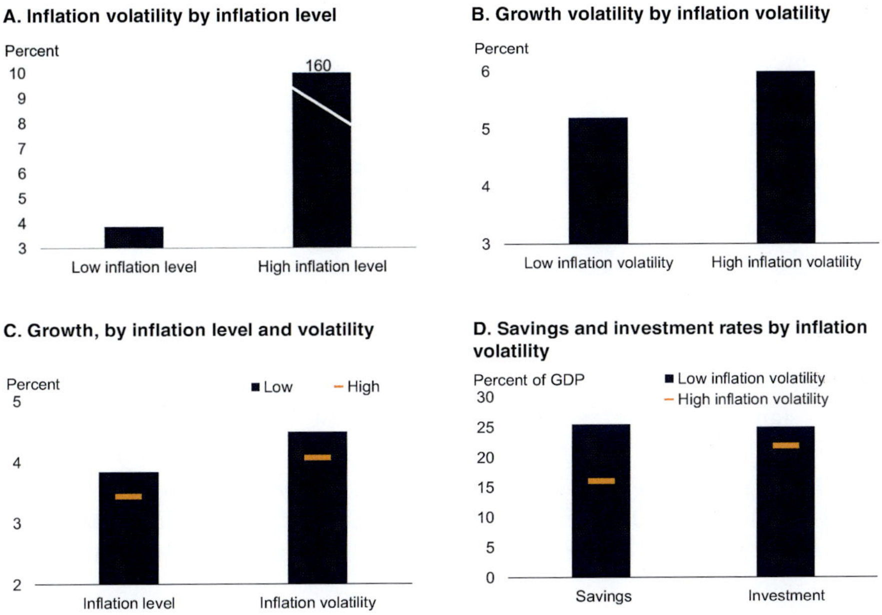

Source: World Bank.

Note: The sample includes 84 EMDEs, including 20 low-income countries. Inflation volatility is defined as the standard deviation. Inflation refers to year-on-year inflation. EMDEs = emerging market and developing economies; GDP = gross domestic product.

A, Average inflation volatility from 1980 to 2016 for countries with average inflation in the top quartile and average inflation in the bottom quartile.

B. Average real GDP growth volatility from 1980 to 2016 for country-year pairs with inflation volatility in the top quartile and average inflation volatility in the bottom quartile.

C. Average real GDP growth from 1980 to 2016 for countries with average inflation (left column and bar) or standard deviation of inflation (right column and bar) in the top quartile and average inflation in the bottom quartile.

D. Average savings and investment from 1980 to 2016 for countries with a standard deviation of inflation in the top quartile and standard deviation of inflation in the bottom quartile.

Evolution of global inflation

Globally, inflation fell sharply from its 1974 peak of 16.6 percent, to 2.6 percent in 2017. This decline began in advanced economies in the mid-1980s and in EMDEs in the mid-1990s. By 2000, global inflation had stabilized at historically low levels. Lower inflation has been accompanied by lower inflation volatility, especially among advanced economies. The current environment of low and stable inflation resembles that during the Bretton Woods fixed exchange system in the post-war period up to 1971 and the gold standard of the early 1900s. This section discusses the developments in detail.

Data. The analysis rests on a comprehensive database of inflation measures and the key drivers of inflation. Data on headline, core, energy, and food CPI inflation; PPI inflation; and GDP deflators, as well as their components, are available for up to 175 countries for 1970-2017 (34 advanced economies and 141 EMDEs, of which 27 are LICs). The data were assembled from a wide range of sources, including ILOSTAT, UNdata, OECDstat, International Financial Statistics, Haver Analytics, internal World Bank databases, and various editions of the International Monetary Fund (IMF) *World Economic Outlook* database. These inflation series are complemented with data on inflation targets, central bank independence, exchange rate regime, inflation expectations, and international trade and financial openness. Global inflation is defined as median CPI inflation, unless otherwise specified. The details of the database can be found in the Appendix.

Trend disinflation, 1970-2017. Since its peak in the mid-1970s, global inflation has been on a declining trend. Global inflation fell from a peak of 16.6 percent (annual average) in 1974 to 2.6 percent in 2017 (Figure 1.4). In EMDEs, inflation declined from a peak of 17.3 percent (annual average) in 1974 to 3.5 percent in 2017; in LICs, it fell from a peak of 24.9 percent (annual average) in 1994 to 5.0 percent in 2017. The trend decline started earlier (in the mid-1980s) in advanced economies than in EMDEs and LICs (in the mid-1990s) (Box 1.2).

In EMDEs, this disinflation process cut across all regions, including those with a history of persistently high inflation, such as Latin America and the Caribbean and Sub-Saharan Africa. The downward trend has manifested in all inflation measures, including headline CPI, core CPI, PPI, and GDP deflator inflation. By the early 2000s, the disinflation was largely completed, although it resumed after the global financial crisis at a milder pace.

The "near-universal" character of disinflation since the mid-1970s was already recognized by Rogoff (2003), but most other studies have focused on advanced economies. The widely shared disinflation in advanced economies has been attributed partly to common terms-of-trade shocks, such as oil price swings (Rogoff 2003). Among Group of Seven economies, it may also have reflected changes in monetary policy regimes, including the increased focus on price stability, which also occurred during the early 1980s and early 1990s (Cecchetti et al. 2007; Levin and Piger 2006).

Other factors may have included sounder fiscal policies, deregulation, globalization, and, in the 1990s, accelerating productivity growth in parts of the world (Rogoff 2003; IMF 2006). Studies of disinflation in EMDEs have focused on specific policy experiments in individual countries, such as the introduction of inflation targeting, greater exchange rate flexibility, or macroeconomic

FIGURE 1.4 Global inflation trends

Since its peak in the mid-1970s, global inflation has been on a decline. The decline began in the mid-1980s among advanced economies before moving to EMDEs and low-income countries in the mid-1990s. This disinflation process cut across all EMDE regions and manifested in all inflation measures. By the early 2000s, the disinflation was largely completed and resumed only after the global financial crisis, albeit at a more modest pace.

A. Global CPI inflation

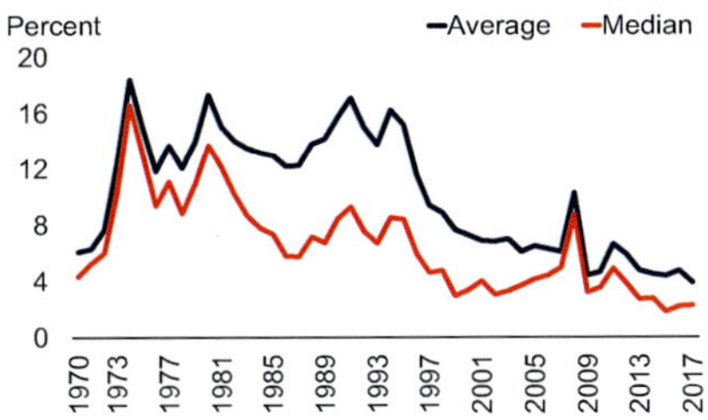

B. Global CPI trend inflation

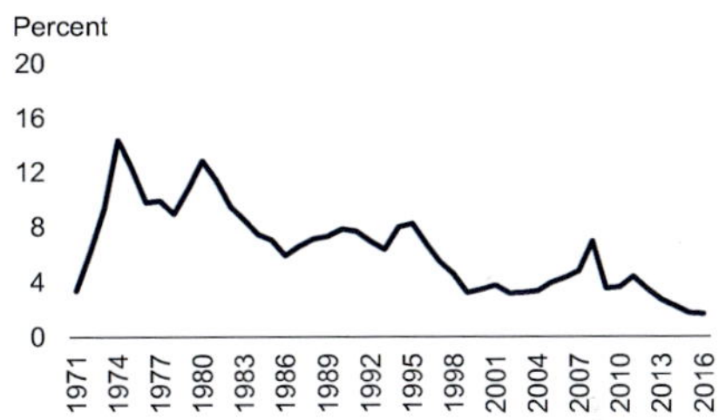

C. Median CPI headline inflation, by region

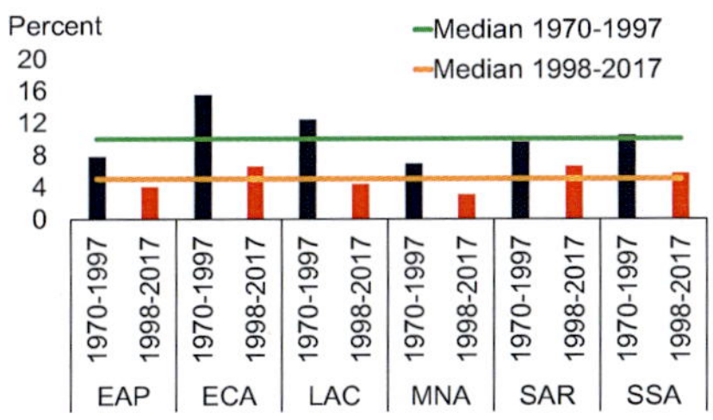

D. Median CPI headline inflation, by country group

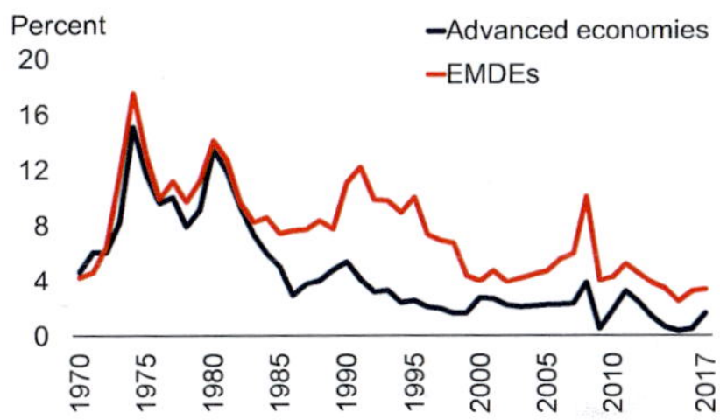

E. Median CPI, PPI headline inflation, and the GDP deflator

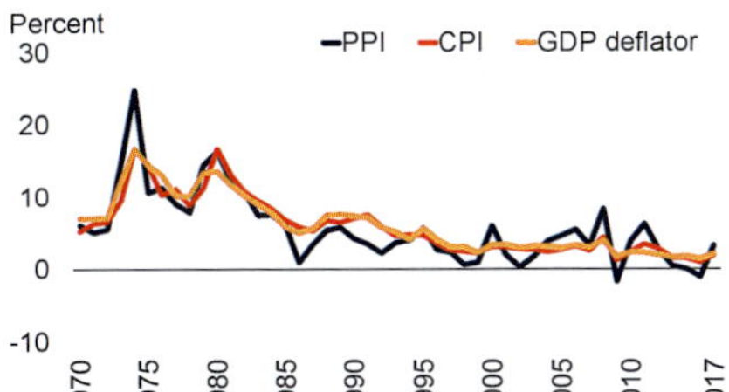

F. Median core, food, and energy CPI inflation

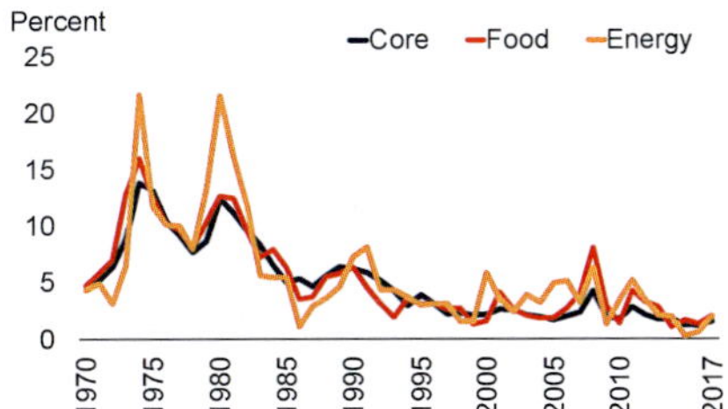

Source: World Bank.

Note: All inflation rates refer to year-on-year inflation. CPI = consumer price index; EMDEs = emerging market and developing economies; GDP = gross domestic product; LICs = low-income countries; PPI = producer price index.

A. Based on 153 countries. The last observation is 2017. The values show headline inflation.

B. Based on 77 countries, including 50 EMDEs. The values show median trend inflation, as defined in Stock and Watson (2016).

C. The horizontal lines reflect median inflation across all EMDEs over 1970-97 and 1998-2017. EAP = East Asia and Pacific; ECA = Europe and Central Asia; LAC = Latin America and the Caribbean; MNA = Middle East and North Africa; SAR = South Asia; SSA = Sub-Saharan Africa.

D. Median of inflation trend of 25 advanced economies, 97 EMDEs (excluding LICs), and 27 LICs. The last observation is 2017:1.

E. Based on data for inflation in 39 countries, including 15 EMDEs.

F. Based on data for inflation in 47 countries, including 18 EMDEs.

BOX 1.2 Inflation in low-income countries

Inflation in low-income countries has declined sharply over the past three decades, to a median of 5.0 percent in 2017 from a peak of 24.2 percent in 1994. This decline in inflation was broadly shared. It has been supported by the move to more flexible exchange rate regimes, greater central bank independence, lower government debt, and a more benign external environment.

The number of low-income countries (LICs) has almost halved since 1994. As of 2018, 34 countries were classified as "low income" according to the World Bank definition, down from 64 in 1994, following the graduation of 31 mostly metals-exporting and transition economies to middle-income status (Annex 1.2). Today, LICs are predominantly agriculture-based, small, and fragile, and they tend to have weak institutions (World Bank 2015). All but seven of them are in Sub-Saharan Africa.

Today's LICs have made large strides in stabilizing their economies over the past five decades, with sharp declines in inflation and inflation volatility. This box documents the achievements in terms of inflation. Chapter 6 delves into the features of LIC inflation and quantifies its drivers in depth. Against this backdrop, this box discusses the following questions:

- How has inflation evolved in LICs?
- What factors have supported inflation developments in LICs?

Evolution of inflation

Among LICs, median inflation has fallen by two-thirds since 1970, to 5.0 percent in 2017—broadly in line with inflation developments in other emerging market and developing economies (EMDEs). The inflation decline has been broad-based across countries as well as inflation components. As a result, the wide heterogeneity of inflation among LICs in the 1990s has narrowed sharply, to a range of 6-18 percent in 2017.

1970s to 1990s. Throughout these three decades, median inflation among LICs was 9-10 percent. Although this was broadly in line with inflation in other EMDEs, LIC inflation underwent bouts of sharp spikes (to 25 percent), especially in the early 1990s, amid exchange rate crises. In half the years between 1970 and 2000, the majority of LICs had double-digit inflation.

BOX 1.2 Inflation in low-income countries (*continued*)

FIGURE 1.2.1 Inflation in low-income countries

Inflation and inflation volatility in LICs have declined since 1970, broadly in line with other EMDEs. The decline has been broad-based across countries and components of inflation.

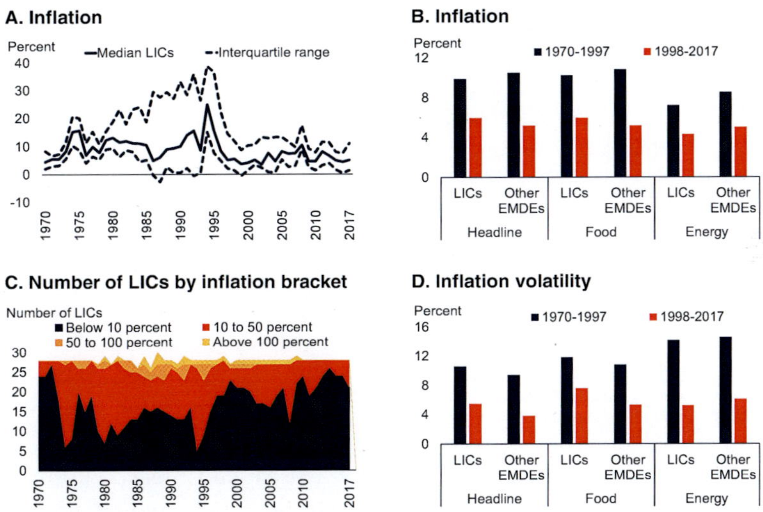

Source: Haver Analytics; International Monetary Fund; World Bank.

Note: Data for 29 low-income countries and 83 other EMDEs. Inflation refers to year-on-year inflation. EMDEs = emerging market and developing economies; LICs = low-income countries.

A. Blue lines are cross-country medians of inflation; dashed lines indicate the interquartile range across 28 LICs.

B. Cross-country medians.

C. Number of LICs in which inflation was in the bracket indicated. Data for 2017 not yet available for some LICs.

D. Cross-country medians over rolling standard deviations.

2000s. During the 2000s, median inflation in LICs fell rapidly, to 5.0 percent in 2017 from a peak of 24.2 percent in 1994 (Figure 1.2.1). This decline was broad-based and narrowed some of the wide heterogeneity in inflation among LICs. In one-third of LICs, inflation in 2017 was less than one-third its level in 1970. In an even larger number (58 percent) of LICs, inflation in 2017 was less than one-third of its 1994 level. By 2008, the two hyperinflation episodes in LICs (with inflation in excess of 1,000 percent) had also subsided. In 2017, inflation was in the single digits in more than three-quarters of LICs, compared with less than one-fifth in 1994. Since 1970, core, food price, and energy price inflation have also declined, as has inflation volatility (although it remains well above inflation volatility in other EMDEs).

BOX 1.2 Inflation in low-income countries (*continued*)

Factors supporting inflation developments

In every year since 2000, except 2002 and 2017, LIC inflation has exceeded inflation in other EMDEs. This difference has been attributed to several factors, of which three have been particularly closely examined: fiscal policy, supply shocks, and uncertainty about monetary policy transmission.

Fiscal policy. For LIC governments with weak revenue-raising capabilities and an absence of well-functioning capital markets, inflation may become an important source of financing fiscal deficits (Baldacci, Hillman, and Kojo 2004). The presence of large fiscal deficits or high government debt in LICs can cause fiscal dominance—with fiscal policy relying on accommodative monetary policy to ensure fiscal sustainability (Baldini and Poplawski-Ribeiro 2011; Weidmann 2013). In almost every year between 1992 and 2002, two-thirds of LICs had higher debt-to-GDP ratios than the one-third of non-LIC EMDEs with the highest debt levels. In half the years between 1995 and 2017, the median fiscal deficit in LICs was above that in non-LIC EMDEs. Weak institutions (Bleaney, Morozumi, and Mumuni 2016) and political instability (Aisen and Veiga 2006) may reinforce the negative association between budget deficits and inflation.

Supply shocks. LIC economies are particularly vulnerable to frequent supply shocks, especially weather-related ones. Agriculture sectors tend to be large; poor transport links prevent risk sharing; and food forms a larger share of household consumption (Bleaney and Francisco 2018; Cachia 2014; Chapter 6). As a result, for example, rainfall appears to have a significant effect on economic growth in EMDEs in Sub-Saharan Africa but not elsewhere (Barrios, Bertinelli, and Strobl 2010).

Uncertainty about monetary policy transmission. In LICs, credit and other financial markets tend to be shallow; contract enforceability is limited; and information asymmetries are pervasive, and many LICs retain elements of financial repression in the form of interest rate controls (Mishra, Montiel, and Spilimbergo 2012). This can impair monetary policy transmission (IMF 2015; Mishra and Montiel 2013).

Since 2000, improvements in LIC policies and a benign global macroeconomic environment have supported the decline in LIC inflation. That said, policy frameworks in the median LIC remain generally weaker than those in other EMDEs.

BOX 1.2 Inflation in low-income countries (*continued*)

Improved policies. Inflation has tended to be lower in LICs with lower public debt ratios, fixed exchange rate regimes, and higher degrees of central bank independence and transparency (Figure 1.2.2). Since 1970, monetary policy frameworks have strengthened in LICs. The index of central bank independence (available for 10 LICs) doubled between 1998, when the series starts, and 2014, when the series ends. In 1970, all but two LICs had pegged exchange rates whereas, in 2017, only half the LICs (14 of 29 with available data) had fixed exchange rate regimes, as defined in Shambaugh (2004). Fiscal pressures on monetary policy also appear to have eased. Government debt has declined from a peak of 123 percent of GDP, on average, in 2003 to 52 percent of GDP, on average, in 2017—broadly in line with the average non-LIC EMDE. In addition, the relationship between fiscal position and inflation appears to be nonlinear: in a low-inflation environment, fiscal deficits tend to be less inflationary (Catao and Terrones 2005; Lin and Chu 2013). As a result, the current low-inflation environment may help further mute the pressures from fiscal dominance on inflation in LICs.

More benign external environment. LIC economies, on average, have become more open to trade and finance since the 1970s, although they remain less open than other EMDEs (IMF 2011a).[1] Higher capital account openness, in particular, has been associated with lower inflation, whereas there has been little difference between LICs that have been highly open to trade and those that have not. Despite a growing number of LICs switching to floating exchange rate regimes, exchange rates have been considerably more stable since 1998 than in the preceding two decades. This has helped lower LIC inflation volatility and inflation.

Conclusion

LIC inflation and inflation volatility have fallen sharply during the past three decades, broadly in line with other EMDEs. The decline has been broad-based across countries, as well as across components of inflation. Both better policies—such as greater central bank independence and transparency, a shift away from pegged exchange rate regimes, and lower government debt burdens—and a more benign global macroeconomic environment have supported the inflation decline in LICs.

---

[1] In the average LIC, trade (exports plus imports) has amounted to 58 percent of GDP since 1970, whereas in the average non-LIC EMDE, it has amounted to 83 percent of GDP; international financial assets and liabilities amounted to 114 percent of GDP in the average LIC compared with 256 percent of GDP in the average non-LIC EMDE.

BOX 1.2 Inflation in low-income countries (*continued*)

FIGURE 1.2.2 Factors supporting falling inflation in LICs

The decline in LIC inflation has been supported by improved policies, greater openness to trade and finance, and a more benign macroeconomic environment.

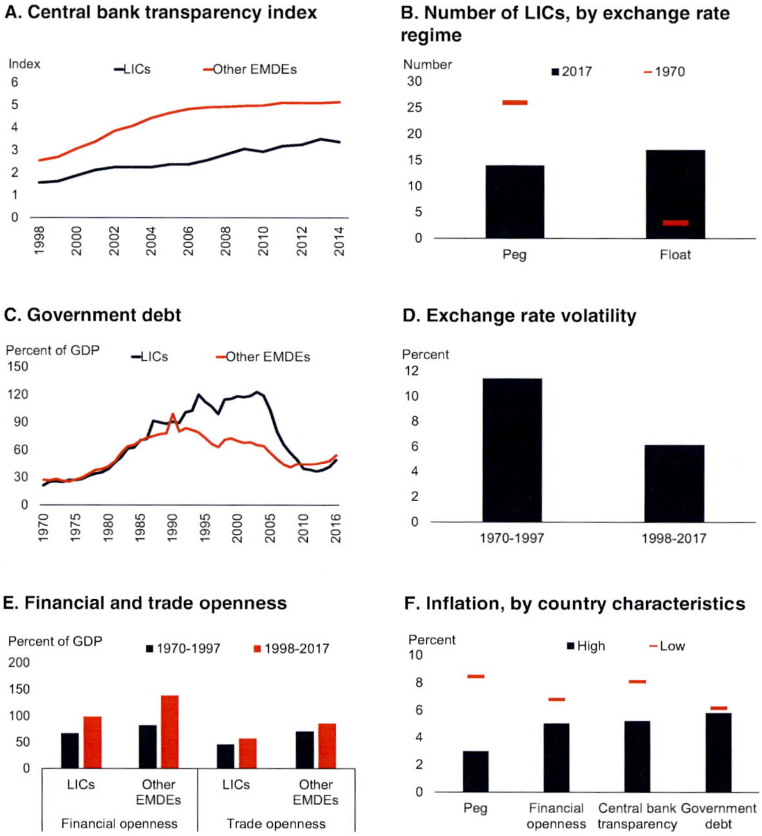

Source: World Bank; Haver Analytics; International Monetary Fund; Shambaugh 2004.

Note: Data for 29 low-income countries and 83 other EMDEs. EMDEs = emerging markets and developing economies; GDP = gross domestic product; LICs = low-income countries.

A.C. Unweighted averages.

B. Exchange rate regime as defined as in Shambaugh (2004).

D. Exchange rate volatility is the cross-country average of the standard deviation of nominal effective appreciation during each time period.

F. Median year-on-year inflation in LICs during 1998-2017, by country characteristics. "High" indicates pegged exchange rate regimes (peg) or above-median financial openness, central bank transparency, and government debt. "Low" indicates floating exchange rate regimes (peg) or below-median financial openness, central bank transparency, and government debt.

stabilization programs (Mishkin 2000; Bernanke et al. 2001; Mishkin and Schmidt-Hebbel 2007; Aizenmann, Chinn, and Ito 2011).

1970s. In the wake of two major oil crises—the quadrupling of oil prices in 1973 and the doubling of oil prices in 1979-80—global median inflation tripled from 4.4 percent in 1970 to 13.7 percent in 1980.[3] Some advanced economy central banks, freed in 1971 from the constraints of the Bretton Woods system of fixed exchange rates, aimed to support economic activity with monetary expansion. The elimination of the nominal anchor of fixed exchange rates set off an inflationary wage-price spiral with weak economic growth (often termed "stagflation"). Among EMDEs, accommodative monetary policy facilitated a spillover of inflation from advanced economies (IMF 2011b).

1980s. In advanced economies, monetary policy tightening in the late 1970s and early 1980s helped rein in inflation, to a median of 3 percent by 1986 from its peak of 15 percent in 1974, and establish central bank credibility, although often at the cost of deep recessions. In the United States, for example, short-term interest rates almost quadrupled between the end of 1976 and mid-1981 (Annex 1.4). In the wake of these interest rate increases, U.S. output contracted by more than 2 percent between early 1981 and mid-1982. In parts of advanced economy Europe, central banks responded more strongly and earlier to rising inflation. In several countries, disinflation was less pronounced than in the United States, but it was also accompanied by output losses in the early 1980s.

In EMDEs, disinflation was delayed by persistent large fiscal and current account deficits, often in conjunction with fixed exchange rate regimes, deteriorating terms of trade for commodity exporters, and political disruptions (Dornbusch 1986; Edwards 1989). For example, for several decades, Argentina, Brazil, Chile, Israel, Mexico, Peru, and Uruguay had chronically high inflation of more than 20 percent for five or more consecutive years. Multiple stabilization programs were attempted, typically resulting in recessions (Calvo and Végh 1994).

1990s. In the second half of the 1980s and during the 1990s, many EMDEs implemented macroeconomic stabilization programs and structural reforms to improve economic efficiency. These initiatives often included the removal or easing of foreign exchange market controls, trade liberalization, tighter fiscal policy, and stronger fiscal and monetary policy frameworks. In EMDEs across Europe, Central Asia, and South Asia, inflation soared, as previously centrally planned economies collapsed, and the accompanying price and exchange rate liberalization released pent-up demand pressures. Subsequent stabilization efforts

[3] During the Arab-Israeli War in 1973, global oil prices quadrupled to about $12 per barrel. Around the time of the Iranian Revolution, oil prices more than doubled in 1979-80 to about $36 per barrel.

were associated with deep output losses. As transition economies exited high inflation and even hyperinflation during 1989-94, output declined sharply—for example, cumulatively by 16 percent in Uzbekistan and 75 percent in Georgia—often amid civil wars and trade embargoes (Fischer, Sahay, and Végh 1996). Within two years, on average, these economies started growing again. In Latin America and the Caribbean, renewed stabilization programs that centered around sound fiscal discipline and greater central bank independence gained traction and inflation declined (Figure 1.5).

2000s. The disinflation of the 1980s and 1990s paused in the early 2000s in the run-up to the global financial crisis, partly as a result of rapidly rising energy and food prices. However, the global financial crisis ushered in a renewed period of mild disinflation and, in many advanced economies, spells of negative inflation. Post-crisis, deflation or low inflation was unusually pervasive across advanced economies: in 2015, inflation was negative in more than half of the advanced economies and, in 2016, inflation was in the low single digits in three-quarters of the advanced economies (Figure 1.6). This raised concerns about low inflation, or possibly even deflation, becoming entrenched in inflation expectations. To reduce the risk of falling into a deflationary environment, advanced economy central banks implemented exceptionally accommodative monetary policy after the global financial crisis, including through unconventional measures. Chapter 4 explores the interaction between inflation expectations and inflation in detail. In EMDEs, inflation fell within or below target ranges in 60 percent of inflation targeting economies (from less than 50 percent in 2007), making room for monetary policy rate cuts to support economic activity. In 80 percent of EMDEs, inflation in the second quarter 2018 ranged between 0.8 and 6.7 percent (year-on-year), compared with a range of 3.9 to 23.9 percent in the second quarter of 2008.

Broad-based disinflation. The disinflation over the past three to five decades has been broad-based across country groups and reflected in headline inflation, core inflation, and energy and food price inflation. Domestic food and energy prices constitute a large share of domestic consumption price baskets. Food prices have been an important contributor to the persistent and steady decline in global inflation over the past four to five decades, whereas energy prices mainly have contributed to declining inflation during major oil price plunges.

- Food prices contributed about 5.5 percentage points to the almost 14 percentage point decline in global headline inflation between 1974 and 2017. This was in addition to food prices' important role in cyclical swings in headline inflation around this general disinflationary trend. Yet, food CPI has reflected global food commodity price developments only to a limited degree. Especially in advanced economies, the estimated pass-through from international food prices to domestic food prices has been modest (Furceri et al. 2015) (Figure 1.7).

FIGURE 1.5 Inflation in Latin America and Europe and Central Asia

Median inflation was 14 percent in Latin America during the 1980s and 128 percent in Eastern Europe and Central Asia during the first half of the 1990s. Eventually, a combination of macroeconomic stabilization and liberalization policies, against the backdrop of global disinflation, helped rein in high inflation in these regions.

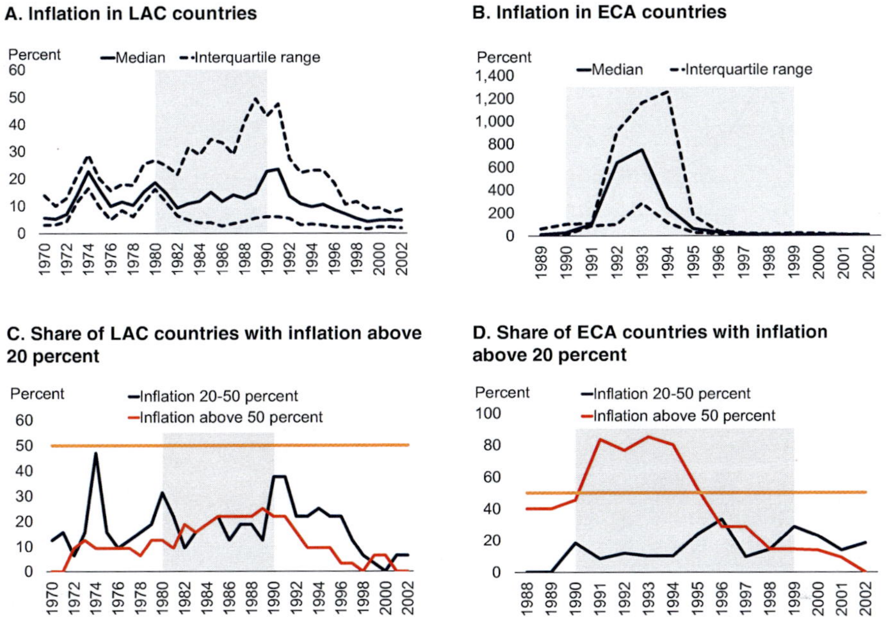

Source: World Bank.

Note: Inflation refers to year-on-year inflation. ECA = Europe and Central Asia; LAC = Latin America and the Caribbean.

A.C. The grey area denotes the 1980s. LAC includes 32 countries in the region. The orange line in panel C indicates 50 percent of the countries.

B.D. The grey area denotes the 1990s. ECA includes 22 countries in the region. The orange line indicates 50 percent of the countries.

- Energy prices have contributed to global disinflation only in episodes of major oil price plunges, most recently in 2014-16. Cumulatively, energy prices contributed 3.2 percentage points to the almost 14 percentage point decline in headline global inflation between 1974 and 2017. Energy price inflation has clearly fallen from its 1970s peaks, and it was broadly stable throughout the 1990s and 2000s.

Subsidies, offsetting exchange rate fluctuations, and a growing domestic services content of cost drove a wedge between domestic food and energy prices and global commodity prices. Domestic energy price inflation was even less homogeneous across EMDEs than domestic food inflation, possibly reflecting a wide variety of fuel subsidy schemes. Domestic food and energy prices have a sizable tradable component, because many countries import energy and food products, but the share of nontradable domestic services (such as logistics and

FIGURE 1.6 Distribution of inflation

Post-crisis inflation has been unusually homogeneous and low in advanced economies and EMDEs.

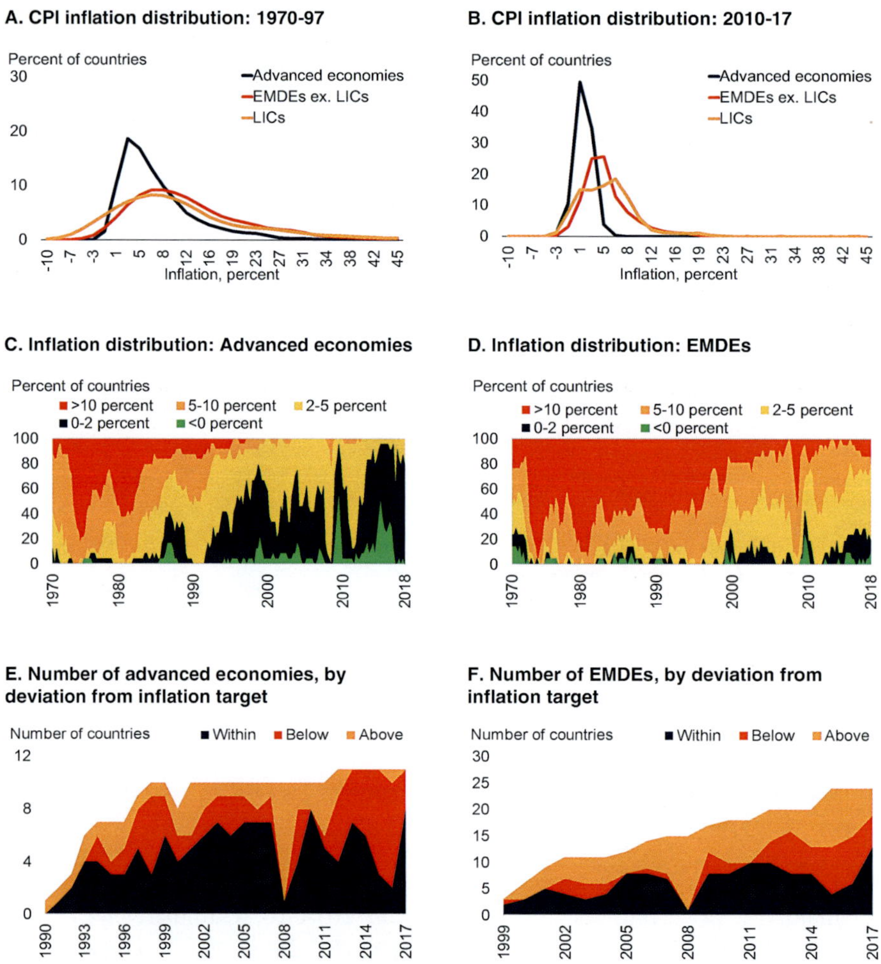

Source: World Bank.

Note: CPI = consumer price index; EMDEs = emerging market and developing economies; LICs = low-income countries.

A.-D. Inflation refers to quarter-on-quarter annualized inflation.

C.D. Sample includes 27 advanced economies and 50 EMDEs.

E.F. Sample includes 17 advanced economies and 27 EMDEs. "Within" indicates the number of countries with inflation within target ranges or within ±1 percentage point of the inflation target for those countries that do not announce a range or below the inflation target for those countries that announce an inflation target ceiling.

FIGURE 1.7 Components of inflation

The disinflation over the past three decades was broad-based in its components, reflected in headline inflation, core inflation, and food price inflation, and cutting across advanced economies and EMDEs.

A. Median food inflation in EMDEs, by region

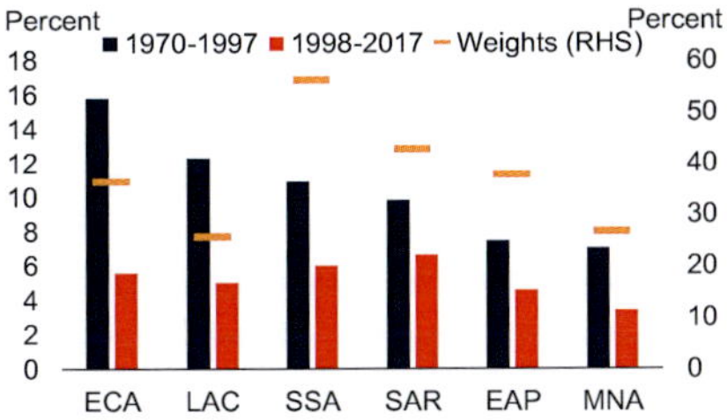

B. Median energy inflation in EMDEs, by region

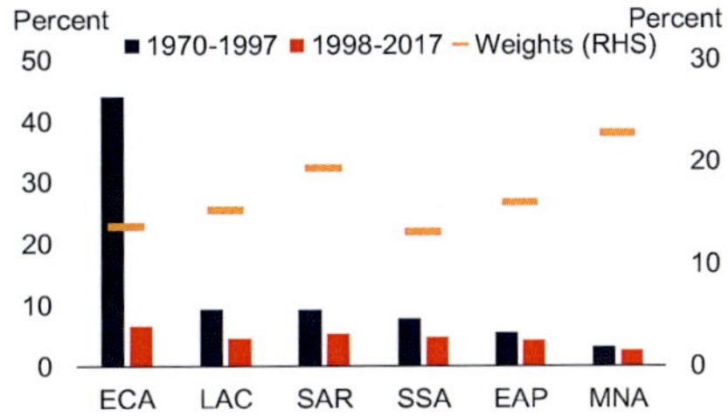

C. Median food price inflation and global food commodity price inflation

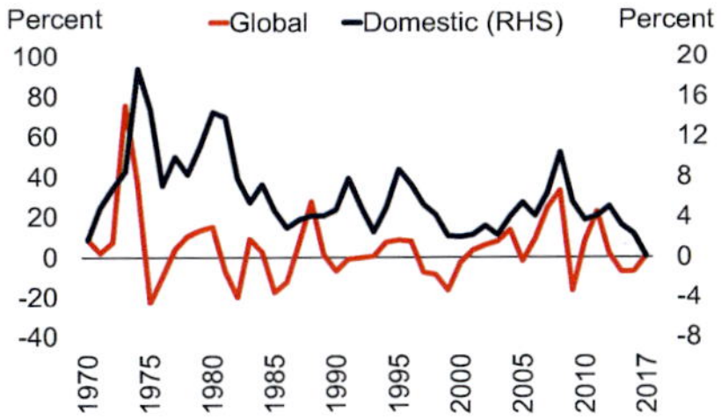

D. Median energy price inflation and global energy commodity price inflation

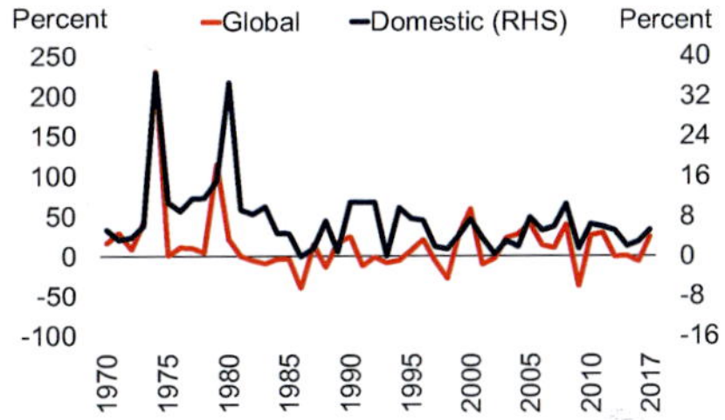

E. Correlation of domestic inflation cycle with global commodity price cycle

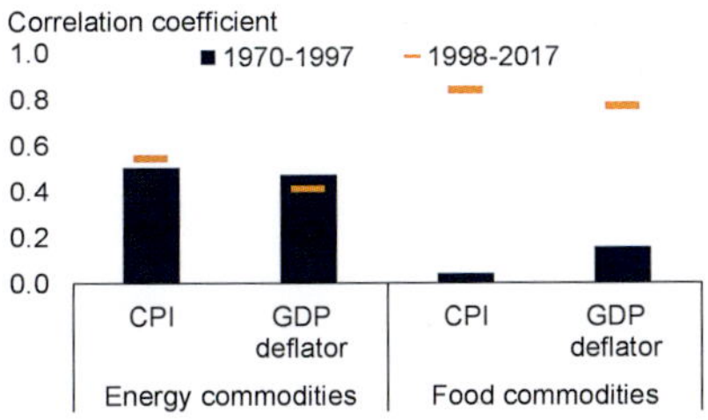

F. Correlation of inflation cycle with global commodity price cycle

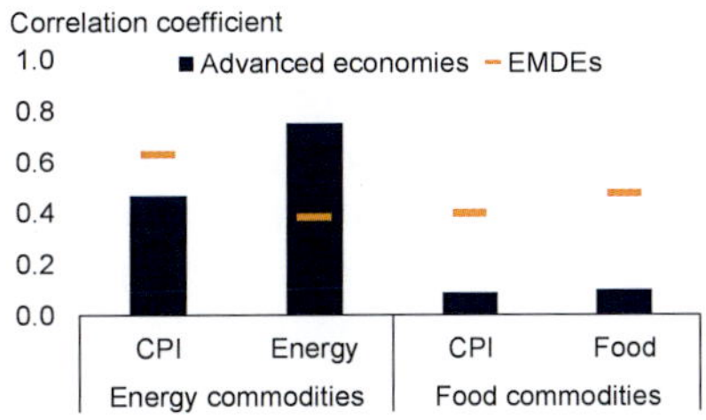

Source: *Pink Sheet*, World Bank.

Note: CPI = consumer price index; EMDEs = emerging market and developing economies; GDP = gross domestic product.

A.B. Weights are food and energy weights used to calculate CPI. Weights are weights of food (A) and energy (B) in CPI baskets.

Inflation refers to year-on- year inflation. EAP = East Asia and Pacific; ECA = Europe and Central Asia; LAC = Latin America and the Caribbean; MNA = Middle East and North Africa; SAR = South Asia; SSA = Sub-Saharan Africa.

C.D. Energy and food commodity price inflation from the World Bank's Pink Sheet of commodity prices.

Correlation of detrended headline CPI and GDP deflator with detrended global energy and food price inflation. Detrended using the Hodrick-Prescott filter.

Correlation between detrended domestic headline, energy, and food price inflation with detrended global energy and food price inflation. Detrended using the Hodrick-Prescott filter.

retail) in domestic food and energy prices is growing. As a result, the correlation of domestic food and energy prices with domestic headline inflation has increased (Furceri et al. 2015). Chapter 6 examines in greater depth the contribution of policies to food prices.

Declining inflation volatility. Trend disinflation has been accompanied by a trend decline in inflation volatility across all EMDE regions, measures of inflation, and inflation components. Inflation volatility is measured as the time-varying volatility of trend and cyclical inflation (Stock and Watson 2016). CPI inflation volatility has fallen in advanced economies and EMDEs (Figure 1.8). Although most of the volatility decline has reflected declining volatility of the trend component of inflation, which approximates the volatility of core inflation, declining cyclical inflation, which captures temporary shocks, has also contributed. Declining trend inflation volatility in part reflects the lower volatility of structural economic shocks. The significant decline in macroeconomic volatility in advanced economies between the mid-1980s and the global financial crisis has been labeled the "Great Moderation."[4]

Differences in inflation volatility among the major groups of economies persist but have narrowed somewhat. EMDEs, especially LICs, have continued to experience higher inflation volatility than advanced economies. Partly because of the inflation swings around economic liberalization in the early 1990s and partly because of domestic conflict, inflation volatility in Europe and Central Asia, South Asia, and Sub-Saharan Africa was high until 1997, but since then it has declined sharply in Europe and Central Asia and Sub-Saharan Africa. In South Asia, it remains elevated because of the high volatility of food prices, which account for a large share of the region's CPI basket (46 percent).

Declining inflation expectations. Well-anchored inflation expectations can ensure that trend inflation remains unaffected by temporary shocks. In both advanced economies and EMDEs, long-term (five-year-ahead) inflation expectations have declined over the past three decades. In advanced economies, inflation expectations have remained stable at about 2 percent per year since 2000, after declining rapidly in the 1990s, with little cross-country variation (Figure 1.9). In EMDEs, inflation expectations decreased markedly in the second half of the 1990s, but then trended up during 2005-14 before retreating somewhat over the following three years. The increase in inflation expectations during 2005-14 was somewhat more pronounced in countries with low central bank transparency than in those with high transparency. Throughout the past

---

[4] Stock and Watson (2003); Bernanke (2004); Clark (2009). In the United States, the Great Moderation has been attributed to smaller variance of shocks and positive and stable technological shocks ("good luck"), new inventory processes and labor supply shocks that reduced wage and marginal cost pressures ("structural change"), and more stabilizing monetary policy ("good policies") (Fernández-Villaverde, Guerrón-Quintana, and Rubio-Ramírez 2010).

FIGURE 1.8 Global inflation volatility

Trend disinflation was accompanied by a trend decline in inflation volatility that cut across EMDE regions, measures of inflation, and inflation components.

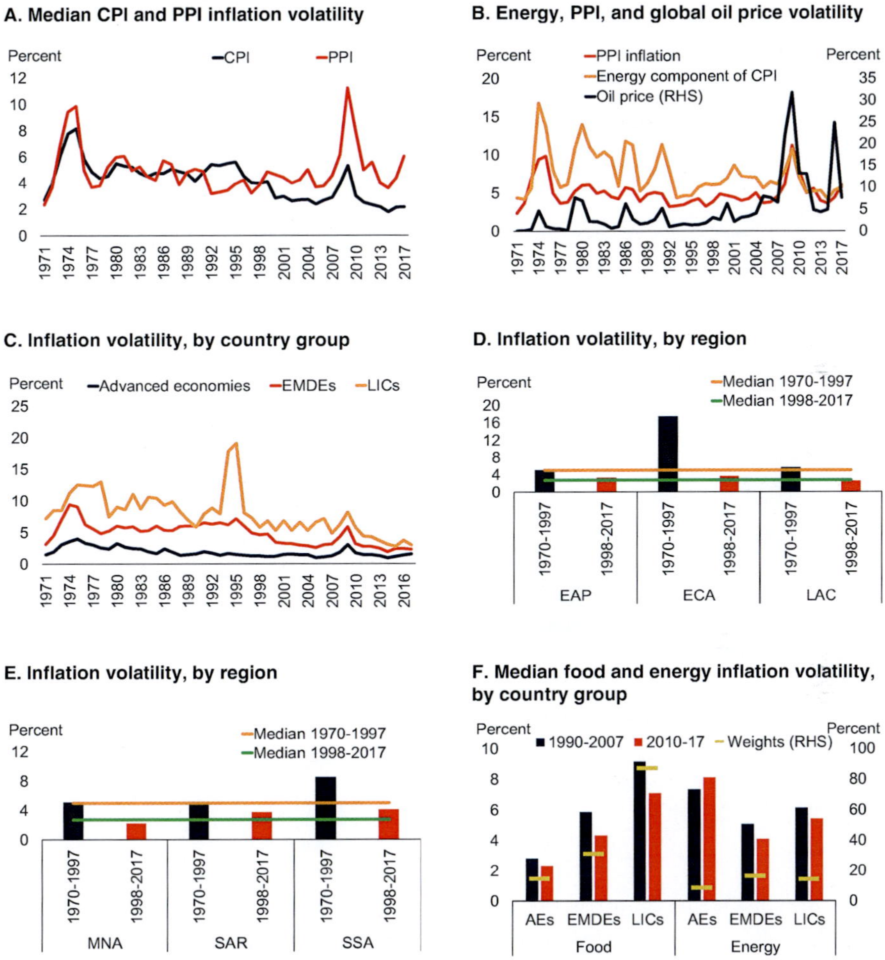

Source: *Pink Sheet*, World Bank.

Note: Volatility of cyclical components of inflation, as estimated by Stock and Watson (2016). Trend inflation is defined as the part of inflation that follows a permanent stochastic trend; cyclical inflation is a serially uncorrelated transitory component of inflation. Inflation refers to year-on-year inflation. AEs = advanced economies; CPI = consumer price index; EMDEs = emerging market and developing economies; GDP = gross domestic product; LICs = low-income countries; PPI = producer price index.

A. Balanced sample of 28 countries. The latest data point is 2017:1.

C. The sample includes 27 advanced economies, 44 EMDEs, and 10 LICs.

D.E. EAP = East Asia and Pacific; ECA = Europe and Central Asia; LAC = Latin America and the Caribbean; MNA = Middle East and North Africa; SAR = South Asia; SSA = Sub-Saharan Africa.

F. Volatility defined as the cross-country median of the standard deviation. Weights are the weight of food and energy in CPI consumption baskets.

FIGURE 1.9 Global inflation expectations

In advanced economies, inflation expectations have been broadly stable since the mid-2000s, following a decline during the 1990s. In EMDEs, inflation expectations fell markedly during the late 1990s but then rose during 2005-14 before retreating again.

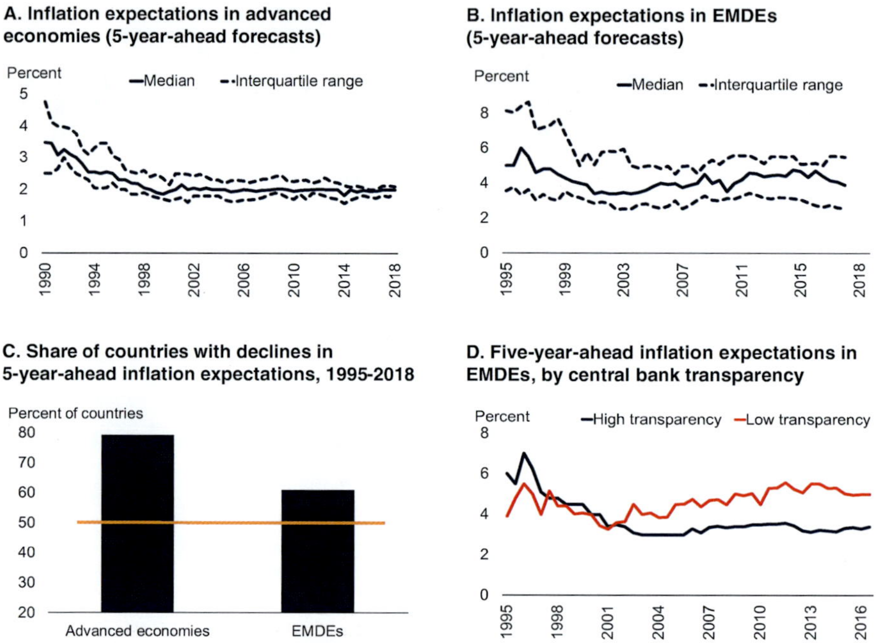

Source: Consensus Economics, International Monetary Fund, Dincer and Eichengreen 2014, World Bank.

Note: EMDEs = emerging market and developing economies.

A.B. Solid lines indicate the median and dotted lines indicate the interquartile range.

C. The orange line indicates 50 percent of the countries.

D. High (low) transparency countries are defined as those with central bank transparency above the 75th (below the 25th) percentile of EMDEs.

three decades, cross-country variation in inflation expectations across EMDEs exceeded the variation across advanced economies. Chapter 4 discusses the drivers of inflation expectations in detail.

Historical precedent. The current low and stable global inflation environment resembles inflation during the Bretton Woods fixed exchange rate system in the post-war period until 1971 and during the gold standard of the early 1900s—both of which provided nominal anchors to countries across the globe (Figure 1.10). In all three periods, global inflation was below 5 percent for an extended time span (7-19 years). The loss of a nominal anchor at the end of the earlier regimes was followed by a period of high inflation until the widespread implementation of inflation targeting and strengthening central bank credibility helped anchor expectations again (Bernanke et al. 2001; Rose 2007; Beyer et al.

2009). However, the post-crisis period of extremely low global inflation differs from the Bretton Woods fixed exchange rate regimes and the gold standard in its lower inflation volatility.

Long-term correlates of inflation

Several structural changes have accompanied global disinflation over the past four to five decades. On average, inflation has declined more in countries that have participated more in global value chains, have moved to inflation targeting regimes, have more independent and transparent central banks, and have more open capital accounts.

Inflation is often affected by unexpected short-term shocks. But, over time, wages and prices adjust and inflation reverts to its long-term trend. This trend is determined by the monetary and fiscal policies, institutional frameworks, and structural features of an economy.[5]

The Phillips curve summarizes the response of inflation to unexpected short-term shocks. Demand-side inflationary pressures include monetary and fiscal policy as well as asset price swings that can affect consumption through wealth effects. Supply-side factors include raw material (energy and food) price shocks, wage growth, and currency depreciation. The role of these drivers of short-term fluctuations in inflation is discussed in detail in Chapters 2 and 3.

Empirically, variants of the Phillips curve have been used to model inflation dynamics.[6] *Wage* Phillips curve models link wage growth to labor market slack (or broader economic slack) and wage bargaining power (Phillips 1958; Gali 2010; Kahn 1980). *Price* Phillips curve models link price inflation to unit labor cost or, more generally, labor market slack and material cost (Bhattarai 2016; Blanchard and Gali 2008). *Open economy* Phillips curve models include external cost-push factors such as foreign inflation, commodity prices, import prices, and exchange rates, and external demand-pull factors represented by global output gaps (Draghi 2015; Abbas, Bhattacharya, and Pasquale 2016).

Long-term structural factors can affect how inflation and inflation expectations respond to short-term shocks and the level at which inflation settles absent such

[5] Monetary policy can cause changes in real activity if inflation expectations are unchanged or adapt with a lag to monetary policy changes (Taylor 1980; Rotemberg 1982; Calvo 1983) or if the wage and price settings adapt with a lag to monetary policy changes (Sims and Zha 1998).

[6] Evidence for a Phillips curve relationship is found by Batini, Jackson, and Nickell (2005); Rumler (2007); Osorio and Unsal (2013); Ciccarelli and Mojon (2010); Eickmeier and Pijnenburg (2013); Gamber and Hung (2001); Guerrieri, Gust, and López-Salido (2010); Bianchi and Civelli (2015); Ihrig et al. (2010); Milani (2012); Zhang (2015); and Nguyen et. al. (2017). Evidence that the link between inflation and output gaps has declined is found by Roberts (2006); Mishkin (2007); and Szafranek (2017).

FIGURE 1.10 Historical perspective

The current period of low and stable inflation resembles inflation during the Bretton Woods system of fixed exchange rates in the 1950s and 1960s and during the gold standard in the early 1900s—both systems provided nominal anchors.

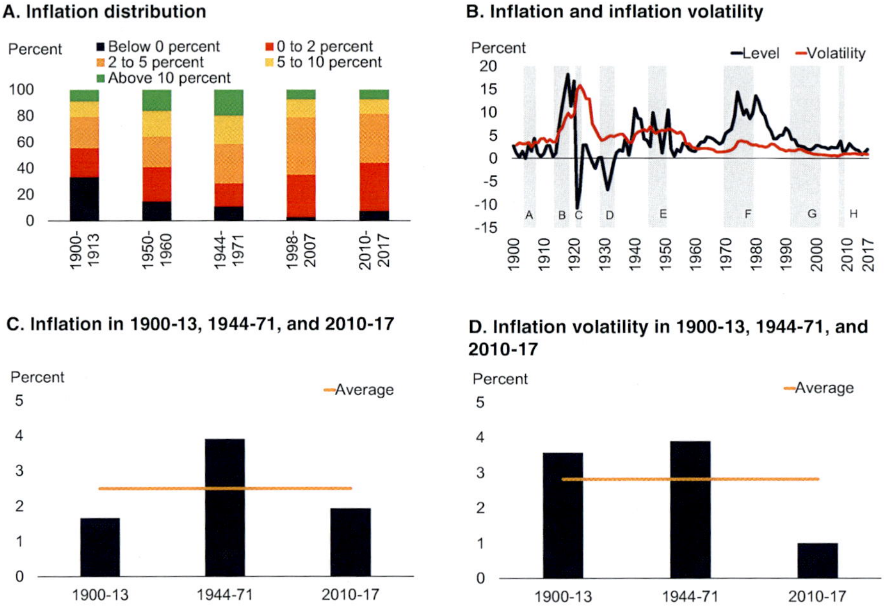

Source: World Bank.

Note: OPEC = Organization of the Petroleum Exporting Countries

A.B. Based on a sample of 26 countries.

B. A = gold standard and stability (1880-1913); B = World War I and high inflation (1914-18); C = post–World War I depression and deflation (1920-22); D = Great Depression (1929-33); E = World War II, monetary controls and post-war inflation (1945-49); E and F = Bretton Woods system of fixed exchange rates (1944-71); F = floating exchange rates and oil shocks (OPEC, 1971-79); G = introduction of inflation targeting (1990-2000); H = global financial crisis.

B.D. Volatility is defined as the rolling standard deviation.

C.D. Cross-country average and standard deviation of annual average inflation. Orange lines denote 1900-2017 average.

shocks. Chapter 4 documents how the presence of inflation targeting regimes has helped better anchor inflation expectations. Among EMDEs, other supporting factors have included greater central bank credibility, greater trade openness, and lower government debt.

These long-term correlates of inflation are the focus of the remainder of this chapter. They have changed significantly over the past four to five decades. Global trade and financial flows have more than doubled since 1970, as many economies have liberalized trade regimes and capital accounts. Many economies have adopted inflation targeting and moved away from fixed exchange rate regimes while strengthening fiscal frameworks and liberalizing labor markets.

In EMDEs, similar structural changes have taken place as in advanced economies, although somewhat later and, in some respects, to a lesser degree.

For example, by 1998, when Poland became the first EMDE to adopt a full inflation targeting regime, more than one-quarter of advanced economies had already switched to inflation targeting. During 2000-14, central bank independence and transparency improved in the median advanced economy and EMDE, but the increase was considerably more pronounced (2.25 index points) in advanced economies than in EMDEs (1 index point). And central bank independence and transparency in the median EMDE remains at only one-third the level in the median advanced economy. Similarly, whereas the increase in trade openness in EMDEs occurred broadly in step with advanced economies, the increase in financial integration during the 1980s and 1990s was considerably more pronounced in advanced economies than in EMDEs.

Trends in long-term drivers have contributed to global disinflation. On average, inflation has been lower and declined by more in countries that have been more open to trade, had (or switched to) inflation targeting regimes, had more independent and transparent central banks, and had more open capital accounts. This section presents these correlations in descriptive statistics and, more formally, in regression analysis and frames them in the context of the literature.

Trade integration

Literature. Trade integration—increased openness to international trade—is typically accompanied by higher shares of imports in consumption and production and lower prices (compared with a closed economy), owing to competitive pressures from foreign producers.[7] Increasing trade integration may also account for the rising international comovement in inflation, as discussed in Chapter 2. The impact on the responsiveness of inflation to domestic economic slack (that is, the slope of the Phillips curve) is ambiguous: greater foreign competition reduces firms' ability to raise prices and wages in response to domestic demand pressures, hence flattening the Phillips curve; alternatively, if greater foreign participation in domestic markets increases competitive pressures, it could encourage a faster response to demand pressures, hence steepening the Phillips curve.[8] Greater trade openness appears to be associated with lower inflation volatility.[9]

---

[7] Yellen (2006); Romer (1993); Terra (1998); Lane (1997); Al Naseer, Sachsida, and Mário (2009); Vuletin and Zhu (2011). In particular, the increased trade integration of China into the global trading system, since its World Trade Organization accession in 2001, may have reduced inflation globally (Frankel 2007; IMF 2016; Eickmeier and Kühnlenz 2013). Meanwhile, the rising role of services, which are less subject to external shocks, may have helped reduce inflation volatility, but the increasing productivity gap between tradables and nontradables with relatively subdued wage growth might have lifted inflation rates (Roncaglia de Carvalho 2014; Lünnemann and Mathä 2005).

[8] Borio and Filardo (2007), Iakova (2007), Kohn (2006), Razîn and Binyamini (2007), and Yellen (2006) argue for flattening Phillips curves; Sbordone (2007) and Benigno and Faia (2016) argue for steepening Phillips curves.

[9] Granato, Lo, and Wong (2006); Bowdler and Malik (2005).

Trade in intermediate goods—a proxy for integration into global value chains—may be more informative about international competitive pressures on inflation than trade in final goods (Lombardo and Ravenna 2014; Burstein, Kurz, and Tesar 2008). Global value chain integration has facilitated the adoption of "just-in-time" inventory practices and associated with lower inflation volatility (Hakkio 2013). It has also been associated with a greater role of global factors in domestic inflation and greater international synchronization of inflation (Auer, Borio, and Filardo 2017).

Trends in trade integration. Over the past four to five decades, global trade openness (the sum of exports and imports relative to GDP) has increased by more than half—to 74 percent of global GDP in 2016, from almost 50 percent of global GDP in 1970. In the median EMDE, trade openness increased from almost 50 percent of GDP in 1970 to 72 percent of GDP in 2016. Similarly, in the median advanced economy, trade openness increased from 47 percent of GDP in 1970 to 80 percent of GDP in 2016. The expansion of trade by EMDEs has been accompanied by rapidly rising trade integration *among* EMDEs, with China becoming the largest trading partner for one-fifth of the countries in this group (World Bank 2016). The most rapid expansion of trade occurred in the 1990s and early 2000s (Figure 1.11).

Since the 1990s, trade integration has fostered the creation and expansion of global value chains, especially among advanced economies. As a result, the share of foreign value added embodied in exports in advanced economies (backward integration) increased from 10 percent in the 1970s to about 30 percent on average during 2000-16. Although less rapidly and somewhat later, the share of foreign value added in domestic exports in EMDEs also increased in the 1990s and 2000s, to 10 percent in 2016, from 1.5 percent in 1990.

Correlation with inflation. Inflation levels and volatility have typically been lower in economies and time periods with greater trade openness. The full sample was split into country-year pairs in the bottom and top quartiles of trade-to-GDP ratios and shares of foreign value added in exports. Median inflation was 4 percentage points lower and half as volatile in the top quartile than in the bottom quartile of trade-to-GDP ratios. Inflation was also more than 3 percentage points lower and one-fifth as volatile in the top quartile than in the bottom quartile of global value chain participation.

A bivariate panel regression suggests that, in countries where trade openness increased by 10 percentage points of GDP over the past four decades—about the median in the sample—inflation declined (although insignificantly) by 0.2 percentage point more than average over the same period. This relationship was even weaker among EMDEs (Tables A.1.3.1 and A.1.3.2, Annex 1.3).

FIGURE 1.11 Trade integration and inflation

Since the 1970s, global trade and global value chain integration has deepened significantly. Greater trade openness and deeper supply chain integration have been associated with lower inflation and inflation volatility and a sharper decline in inflation since the 1970s, especially in EMDEs.

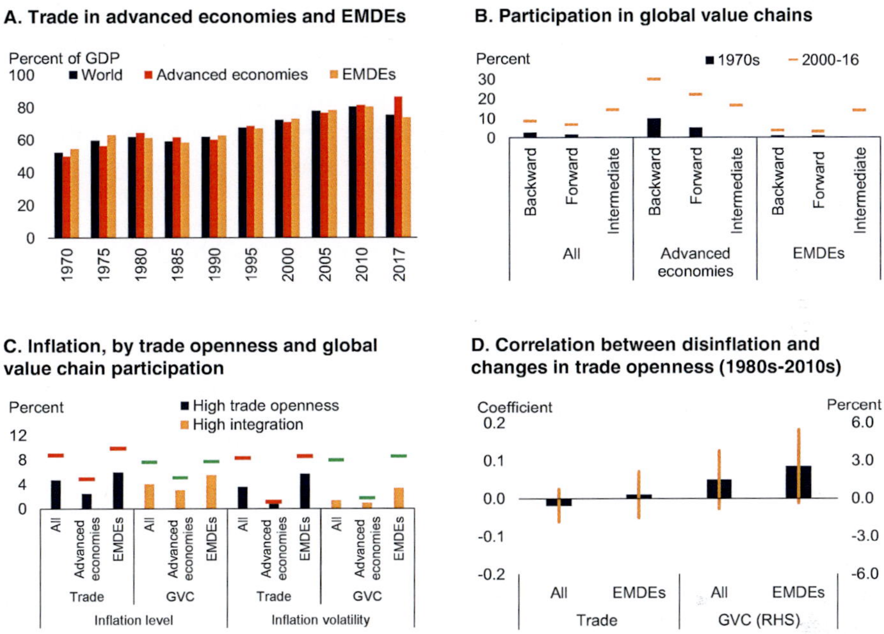

Source: IMF Direction of Trade Statistics; OECD; World Bank World Development Indicators; WTO.

Note: Inflation volatility is defined as volatility in cyclical inflation, detrended using Stock and Watson's (2016) methodology. Inflation refers to year-on-year inflation. EMDEs = emerging market and developing economies; GDP = gross domestic product; GVC = global value chain.

A. Median trade-to-GDP ratio in EMDEs, advanced economies, and globally.

B.C.D. Backward participation in global value chains is a measure of how much foreign value added is embodied in a country's exports, as a percentage of total gross exports. Data are available for 59 countries for 1995, 2000, 2005, and 2008-11. Forward participation in global value chains is a measure of how much a country's value added is embodied in foreign exports, as a percentage of total gross exports. Data are available for 59 countries for 1995, 2000, 2005, and 2008-11. Data are available for a maximum of 166 countries, but with uneven coverage; the data are available for 1988-2016 for 137 countries (World Bank 2017a, 2017b).

C. Columns indicate median inflation in countries with global value chain integration and trade openness in the top quartile. Horizontal bars indicate median inflation in countries with trade openness and global value chain integration in the bottom quartile. The difference in inflation levels and volatility (except for volatility in advanced economies) between high and low trade openness and GVC participation is statistically significant at the 1 percent level.

D. Blue bars show the coefficient estimates from bivariate panel regressions of changes (between the decadal averages of the 1980s and 2010s) in inflation on changes in trade openness over the same period (see Tables A.1.3.1. and A.1.3.2, Annex 1.3). Vertical lines are ±1.64 standard errors of the coefficient estimate

Financial openness

Literature. In theory, financial openness could raise or depress inflation volatility. If capital flows help smooth fluctuations in consumption in a financially open economy, they can moderate domestic demand swings that might otherwise generate inflationary or disinflationary pressures. This would reduce inflation volatility. Conversely, procyclical capital inflows could themselves generate larger domestic demand swings and cause greater volatility in output and inflation.

Empirically, greater capital account openness has been associated with lower inflation. Multiple studies have found in large cross-sections of countries that greater capital account openness has been accompanied by lower average inflation (Badinger 2009; Gruben and McLeod 2002; Aizenman, Chinn, and Ito 2008). This pattern has been attributed to a stronger anti-inflation bias of central banks amid sharper trade-offs between output growth and inflation (Badinger 2009), or to a greater interest rate elasticity of money demand (Gruben and McLeod 2002).

Trends in financial openness. Advanced economies liberalized their capital accounts almost fully between 1970 and 2000, whereas capital account liberalization in EMDEs has proceeded at a more guarded pace (Figure 1.12). In the median advanced economy, the Chinn and Ito (2017) index of capital account openness, which ranges between 0 and 1, increased to 0.9 in 2017 from 0.4 in 1970. In the median EMDE, this index temporarily increased from 0.2 to 0.4 in the mid-1990s, but then declined again as restrictions were reimposed in the aftermath of the Asian crisis. Similarly, capital account openness in EMDEs increased again in the mid-2000s until the global financial crisis but narrowed again thereafter. Since 1970, financial integration has surged: in the median EMDE, as in the median advanced economy, the share of international assets and liabilities has more than tripled, to 121 percent of GDP in 2017 (although they remain only one-quarter the level in advanced economies).

Correlation with inflation. Capital account openness has been associated with lower inflation and inflation volatility. The country-year pairs with the top quartile of most open capital accounts had, on average, 12 percentage points (10 percentage points for EMDEs) lower inflation, and lower volatility, than the bottom quartile of country-year pairs with the least open capital accounts. Similarly, in countries and years with international assets and liabilities relative to GDP in the top quartile of the sample, inflation was less than half (and volatility was one-fifth) its level in those in the bottom quartile. The difference in inflation levels may reflect the disinflation in advanced economies after their capital accounts were largely liberalized. In EMDEs, capital account openness has also been associated with lower inflation, but this relationship has been less pronounced than in advanced economies.

Again, the panel regression suggests that an increase of 0.5 point in the capital account openness index over the past four decades was associated, on average globally, with a 4.7 percentage point stronger disinflation and, among EMDEs, a 4.0 percentage point stronger disinflation (Tables A.1.3.1 and A.1.3.2, Annex

FIGURE 1.12 Capital account openness and inflation

Over the past five decades, advanced economies have liberalized their capital accounts and, at a slower pace, EMDEs have partially liberalized their capital accounts. Greater capital account openness has been associated with lower and more stable inflation.

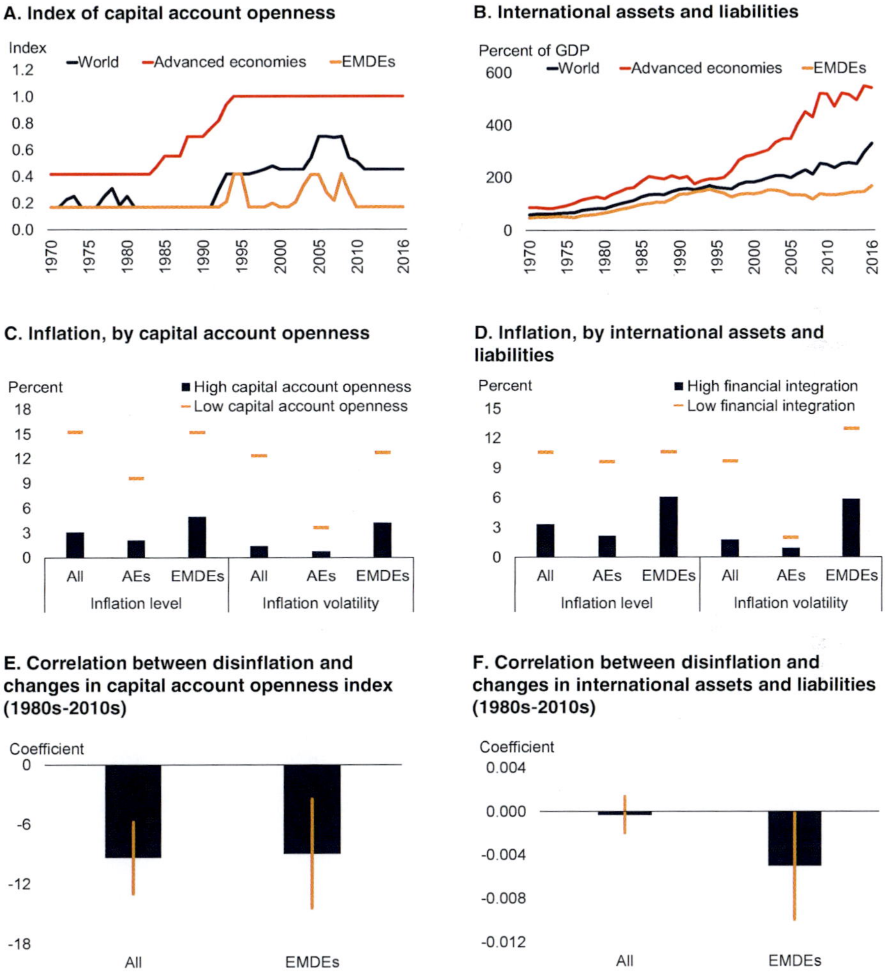

Source: IMF Direction of Trade Statistics; World Bank *World Development Indicators*.

Note: Capital account openness is defined as in Chinn and Ito (2006). The index ranges from 0 (closed capital account) to 1 (open capital account). Inflation refers to year-on-year inflation. AEs = advanced economies; EMDEs = emerging market and developing economies; GDP = gross domestic product.

A.B. Medians (A) or unweighted averages (B).

C.D. Columns indicate the median inflation levels and inflation volatility in country-year pairs with a Chinn-Ito Index (C) or a sum of international assets and liabilities relative to GDP (D) in the top quartile over 173 economies (C) or 175 economies (D) during 1970-2017. Horizontal bars indicate countries in the bottom quartile. Financial integration is defined as the sum of international assets and liabilities as a percentage of GDP. The difference in inflation levels and volatility between high and low capital account openness and financial assets and liabilities is statistically significant at the 1 percent level.

E.F. Blue bars show the coefficient estimates from bivariate panel regressions of change in average annual inflation between the 1980s and the 2010s and the change in the decadal average Chinn-Ito index (E) or the change in the sum of international assets and liabilities relative to GDP (F) over the same period (Tables A.1.3.1 and A.1.3.2, Annex 1.3). Vertical lines are ±1.64 standard errors of the coefficient estimate.

1.3). Such an increase in capital account openness would be approximately in line with the top quartile for advanced economies (0.58 point increase) and the top decile in EMDEs (0.53 point increase) over the past four decades. Similarly, in EMDEs, an increase in international assets and liabilities of 30 percentage points of GDP—the median increase between the 1980s and 2010s—was associated with a statistically significant 1.5 percentage point stronger disinflation over the past four decades (Tables A.1.3.1 and A.1.3.2, Annex 1.3).

Monetary policy frameworks and exchange rate regimes

Literature. Pegged exchange rate regimes and inflation targeting monetary policy regimes—if supported by other policies—can provide the nominal anchor for inflation expectations that can help ensure low and stable inflation (Bernanke and Mishkin 1997; Fischer 2001; Mussa et al. 2000). Particularly for countries with weak institutions, a formal pegged exchange rate regime can signal a commitment to monetary and fiscal policy discipline. Implementation of such a strategy may not be straightforward, however. The level of the exchange rate at which the domestic currency is pegged is especially important if domestic inflation exceeds inflation in the country whose currency forms the peg: the domestic economy will then continue losing international competitiveness until the inflation rates converge. Even after the inflation rates have converged, the domestic economy may be burdened by the loss of competitiveness that has occurred since the peg was established. These issues may give rise to pressures that test the viability of the peg.

For countries with sufficiently strong institutions to implement credible inflation targeting regimes, this can anchor expectations at the inflation target. Thus, a pegged exchange rate or inflation targeting monetary policy regime can ensure that temporary shocks to inflation—caused, for example, by exchange rate swings or food price spikes—remain temporary, without being passed through to trend or core inflation.

Pegged exchange rate regimes have been associated with lower inflation than have other exchange rate regimes (Bleaney and Fielding 2002; Ghosh et al. 1997). In transition economies during the 1990s and 2000s, the switch to a pegged exchange rate regime was associated with disinflation (Domaç and Yuzefovichî 2003). In some EMDEs, the lower inflation achieved by pegging the exchange rate has been at the cost of higher volatility of output growth and inflation (Bleaney and Fielding 2002), whereas in broader samples during an earlier period, pegged exchange rate regimes were associated with more stable inflation (Ghosh et al. 1997; Moreno 2001). That said, any difference between inflation and its volatility in pegged and more flexible exchange rate regimes may partly reflect the highly diverse nature of more flexible regimes, which include countries with a wide range of institutional arrangements (Rose 2011).

In advanced economies, *inflation targeting regimes* have been associated with limited lasting effects on inflation levels and volatility but with lower inflation persistence. In seven advanced economies, the shift to inflation targeting in the 1990s was not always accompanied by significantly lower inflation rates or inflation volatility (Ball and Sheridan 2005; Bernanke et al. 2001; Lin and Ye 2007). Among a broader and more recent sample of advanced economies, the adoption of inflation targeting was associated with lower inflation within two years but at the cost of higher inflation volatility (Fang, Miller, and Lee 2012; Levin, Natalucci, and Piger 2004). In addition, inflation targeting was accompanied by a more modest response of inflation to exchange rate and oil price shocks (Mishkin and Schmidt-Hebbel 2007). Several studies have attributed declining inflation persistence in advanced economies in the early 2000s to inflation targeting or its introduction (Benati 2008; Canarella and Miller 2017). Widespread adoption of inflation targeting regimes has been shown to help promote global economic stability (Rose 2007; Taylor 2014).

In EMDEs, in contrast to advanced economies, inflation targeting regimes have been associated with significantly lower and more stable inflation (Fang, Miller, and Lee 2012). The introduction of such regimes has been associated with significantly larger drops in inflation than in other EMDEs (Gonçalves and Salles 2008). This reduction of inflation has partly been attributed to better anchoring of inflation expectations and, in some EMDEs, lower inflation persistence (Batini and Laxton 2007; Canarella and Miller 2017; Gerlach and Tillmann 2012). That said, some studies have found that the effectiveness of inflation targeting in lowering inflation in EMDEs varies widely by country characteristics, including fiscal positions and the length of time since the adoption of inflation targeting (Mishkin 2000, 2008a; Lin and Ye 2009).

Trends in exchange rate and inflation targeting regimes. Over the past four to five decades, inflation targeting monetary policy regimes have become widespread, while pegged exchange rate regimes, which were predominant up to the 1970s, have receded. In 1990, New Zealand was the only economy implementing inflation targeting. A growing number of advanced economies and EMDEs have subsequently adopted inflation targeting regimes, in an effort to replace the nominal anchor offered by pegged exchange rates. The number of inflation targeting central banks increased to 14 by 2000 and 35 by 2017 (Figures 1.6 and 1.13), and the share of EMDEs relying on pegged exchange rate regimes fell by one-third between 1970 (84 percent of countries) and 2017 (54 percent). Many inflation targeting central banks, especially in EMDEs, have brought inflation within target ranges while also lowering the midpoints of target ranges (Figures 1.6 and 1.13). The transition from fixed to floating exchange rate regimes was smoother in some countries (for example, Chile) than in others (for example, Brazil) where it was followed by exchange rate crises (Annex 4.5).

Correlation with inflation. Among countries with pegged exchange rate regimes or inflation targeting monetary policy frameworks, inflation was, on average, 3-4 percentage points lower than under other exchange rate and monetary policy regimes (Figure 1.14). This was most evident among EMDEs: fixed exchange rate regimes and inflation targeting regimes were associated with 3-4 percentage points lower inflation, whereas in advanced economies, the difference was less than 2 percentage points. Compared with other exchange rate and monetary policy regimes, inflation targeting regimes were also associated with lower inflation volatility, while pegged exchange rate regimes were not.

A panel regression suggests that, over the past four decades, a switch to an inflation targeting regime tended to be accompanied by 6.5 percentage points more disinflation (9.1 percentage points more for EMDEs) than average (Table A.1.3.1, Annex 1.3). One-quarter of the advanced economies and one-tenth of the EMDEs in the sample made the switch to an inflation targeting regime over this period. A switch to a pegged exchange rate regime had no statistically significant impact among EMDEs.

Central bank independence and transparency

Literature. A stability-oriented monetary policy and exchange rate regime can be bolstered by central bank independence and transparency. A more independent central bank is in a more credible position to achieve monetary policy targets, even at the expense of other economic policy targets. More transparent central bank operations, strategy, and communications can safeguard the legitimacy of the central bank, enhance public understanding of and confidence in sound monetary policy, promote informed discussion among market participants and the broader public, and more effectively guide and stabilize inflation expectations.

Empirically, central bank transparency has been found to help anchor inflation expectations in advanced economies (van der Cruijsen and Demertzis 2007; Demertzis and Hallett 2007). In these economies, central bank transparency has reduced inflation expectations and, therefore, inflation and inflation uncertainty (Weber 2016; Siklos 2003; Demertzis and Hallett 2007). More More narrowly, among 87 advanced and emerging market economies, greater detail in central bank forecasts has been accompanied by lower inflation, except in countries with exchange rate targeting regimes (Chortareas, Stasavage, and Sterne 2001). That said, Cecchetti and Krause (2002) find that in 63 advanced and emerging market economies, a long history of low inflation is more important for macroeconomic stability than any particular institutional arrangement. The impact on inflation persistence remains ambiguous (Dincer and Eichengreen 2010).

FIGURE 1.13 Inflation targeting regime and inflation

Over the past five decades, inflation targeting monetary policy regimes have become widespread, while pegged exchange rate regimes, which were predominant in the 1970s, have receded.

A. Share of countries with pegged exchange rate regimes

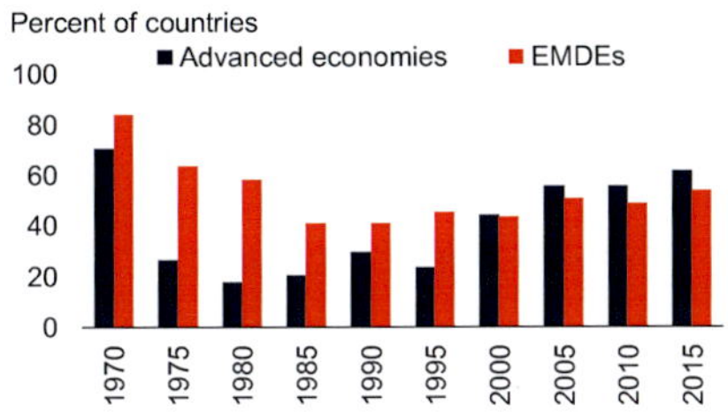

B. Countries with inflation targeting regimes

C. Inflation targets

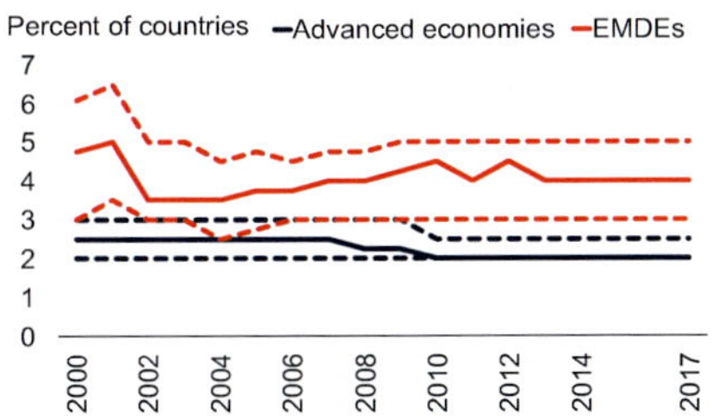

D. Number of advanced economies and EMDEs meeting inflation targets

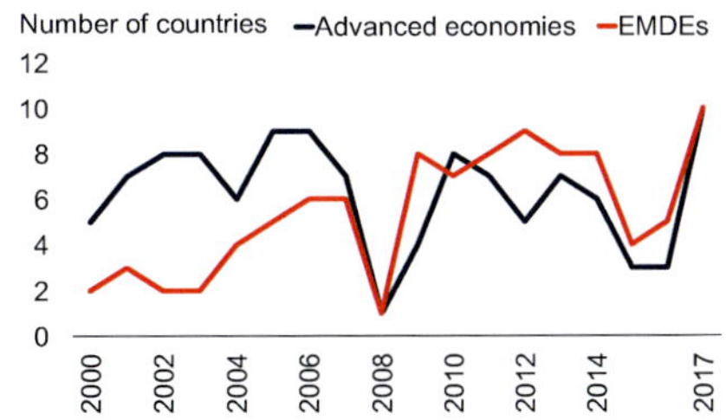

Source: Caceres, Carrière-Swallow, and Gruss 2016; International Monetary Fund; Shambaugh 2004; World Bank.

Note: Pegged exchange rates are defined, based on a de facto classification, as exchange rates fluctuating within a +/-2 percent band or at most, one one-time devaluation over the preceding 11-month period relative to a country-specific reference currency (Shambaugh 2004). Inflation targeting regimes are defined as in Caceres, Carrière-Swallow, and Gruss (2016) and the IMF *Annual Report on Exchange Arrangements and Exchange Restrictions*. EMDEs = emerging market and developing economies.

B. Bars indicate the number of countries with inflation targeting regimes in which inflation is within or below the target range or below the point target ("Within or below target") or above the target range or point target ("Above target").

C. Median inflation target among 34 advanced economies and 141 EMDEs. Dashed lines represent interquartile ranges of upper and lower bounds.

D. Number of advanced economies and EMDEs meeting their inflation targets, 2000-17.

Trends in central bank independence and transparency. Central bank independence and transparency have increased considerably over the past two decades, especially in EMDEs (Figure 1.15). In the median EMDE, the index of central bank independence and transparency increased more than one-and-a-half-fold since 1990, to 5.4 in 2014. Notably, the turnover rate of heads of central banks fell by one-third among EMDEs between 1990 and 2016, with the most widespread improvements in East Asia and Pacific and Europe and Central Asia.[10]

[10] For sources and definitions of data on turnover rates, see the Appendix.

FIGURE 1.14 Monetary framework, exchange rate regime, and inflation

Among countries with pegged exchange rate regimes or inflation targeting monetary policy frameworks, inflation was lower and less volatile and has declined more strongly since the 1970s than under other exchange rate and monetary policy regimes.

A. Inflation, by monetary policy and exchange rate regime

B. Difference in disinflation associated with switch in exchange rate regime and monetary policy regime (1980s-2010s)

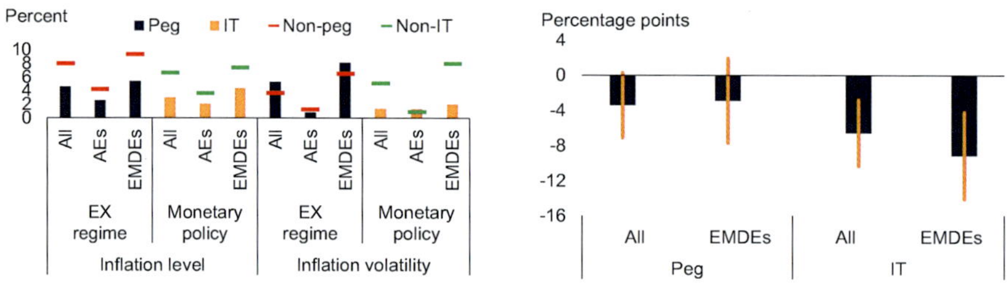

Source: Caceres, Carrière-Swallow, and Gruss 2016; Shambaugh 2016; World Bank World Development Indicators; World Bank.

Note: Pegged exchange rates are defined, based on a de facto classification, as exchange rates fluctuating within a ±2 percent band or at most one one-time devaluation over the preceding 11-month period relative to a country-specific reference currency (Shambaugh 2004). Inflation targeting regimes ("IT") are defined as in Caceres, Carrière-Swallow, and Gruss (2016) and the IMF *Annual Report on Exchange Arrangements and Exchange Restrictions*. Inflation refers to year-on-year inflation. AEs = advanced economies; EMDEs = emerging market and developing economies; EX = exchange rate regime; IT = inflation targeting regime.

A. Columns show median inflation in countries with pegged or inflation targeting monetary policy regimes during 1970-2017. Horizontal bars indicate median inflation in countries without pegged or inflation targeting monetary policy regimes during the same period. The difference in inflation levels and volatility between inflation targeting and other regimes is statistically significant at the 1 percent level.

B. Blue bars show the coefficient estimates from bivariate panel regressions of changes (between 1980-89 and 2010-17) in inflation on a switch (over the same period) to an inflation targeting regime or pegged exchange rate regime (Tables A.1.3.1 and A.1.3.2, Annex 1.3). Vertical lines are ±1.64 standard errors of the coefficient estimate. The difference in inflation levels and volatility between high and low central bank independence and transparency is statistically significant at the 1 percent level.

Correlation with inflation. On average, country-year pairs ranking in the top quartile of the index of central bank independence and transparency have had 4 percentage points lower inflation (3 percentage points for EMDEs) and one-half to one-fifth of the inflation volatility of country-year pairs ranked in the bottom quartile of the sample. These differences are most pronounced in EMDEs. A panel regression suggests that a one point improvement in the Dincer and Eichengreen (2014) central bank independence and transparency index—the median improvement in EMDEs and advanced economies over the past four decades—was accompanied by 1-1.2 percentage points stronger than average disinflation over the same period.

Fiscal frameworks

Literature. When options for private domestic and foreign borrowing by governments are limited or costly, central banks may be compelled to finance fiscal deficits. Unless such deficit financing is accompanied by crowding out of private credit, money supply and inflation will rise, exchange rate pressures will build, and the central bank's room to achieve monetary policy goals will be restricted (Sargent and Wallace 1981).

Empirically, the evidence for such a link between fiscal deficits and inflation has been inconclusive, but it appears to be stronger for countries with preexisting high inflation or during high-inflation episodes. In a large sample of countries, wider fiscal deficits have been associated with higher inflation, especially in countries in which inflation was high to begin with (Fischer, Sahay, and Végh 2002) or where money supply was large relative to GDP (Catao and Terrones 2001). Similarly, rising debt has been associated with higher inflation in countries with already-high initial debt levels (Kwon, McFarlane, and Robinson 2009; Bleaney 1999). Turkey in the late 1980s is an example of a country in which the monetization of large fiscal deficits resulted in high inflation (Rodrik 1990).

Trends in fiscal frameworks. Over the past four to five decades, trends in government debt have diverged between advanced economies and EMDEs (Figure 1.16). Government debt steadily increased in advanced economies to 68 percent of GDP, on average, in 2017. In contrast, in EMDEs, government debt fell to 49 percent of GDP in 2017, well below its peak of 72 percent in 1994, despite a post-crisis reversal of the earlier decline. In EMDEs, lower government debt may have been associated with reduced financing needs, including from central banks. Meanwhile, the number of countries with fiscal rules increased to 88 (including 49 EMDEs) in 2017, from six in 1985 (including two EMDEs) when the data series starts.

Correlation with inflation. There has been little difference, on average, between inflation in countries with government debt-to-GDP ratios in the top and bottom quartiles of the sample. However, countries with government debt in the lowest quartile have had considerably lower inflation volatility. Reflecting the wide range of correlations between inflation and government debt, the panel regression also finds no statistically significant relationship between the initial level of government debt and disinflation over the past four decades (Table A.1.3.1, Annex 1.3). Although low government debt per se was not unambiguously associated with stronger disinflation, inflation has been lower in countries with fiscal rules than in those without them (Figure 1.16).

Labor and product markets

Literature. In 40 advanced and emerging market countries during the 1970s, *wage indexation* was associated with a greater impact of shocks on inflation (Fischer 1983). Such wage indexing also affects inflation persistence: widespread

FIGURE 1.15 Central bank transparency and inflation

Over the past three decades, central banks have become more independent and transparent. Greater central bank independence and transparency has been associated with lower and more stable inflation.

A. Countries with improving central bank independence and transparency, by region (1998-2014)

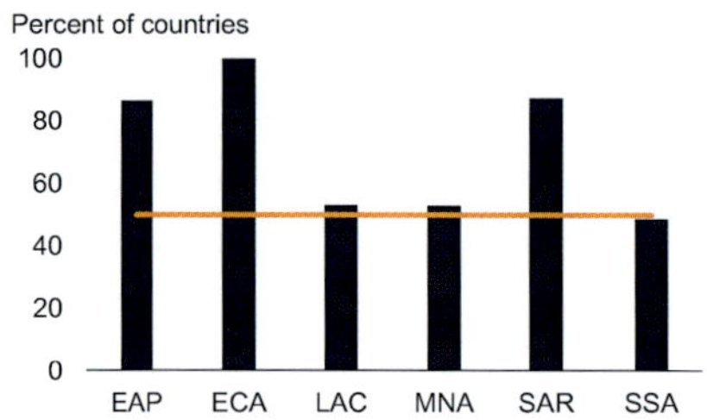

B. Countries with improving central bank independence and transparency, by country group (1998-2014)

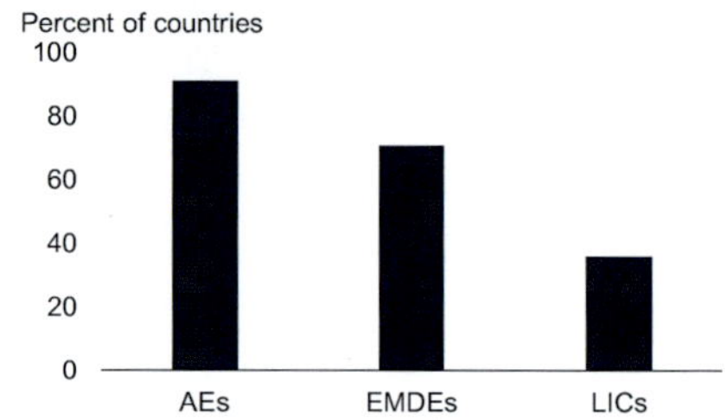

C. Inflation, by central bank independence and transparency

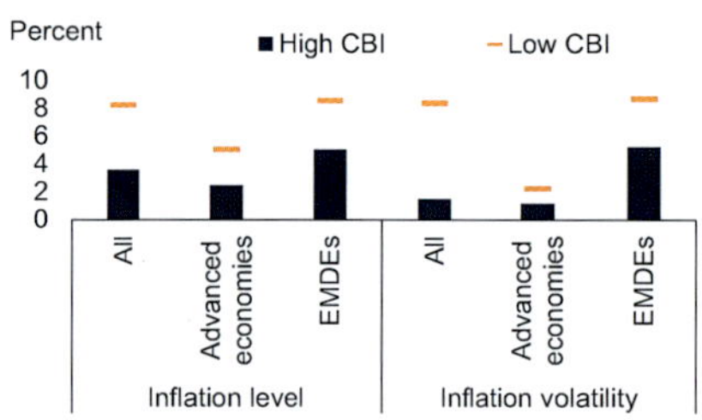

D. Correlation between disinflation (1980s-2010s) and changes in central bank independence and transparency

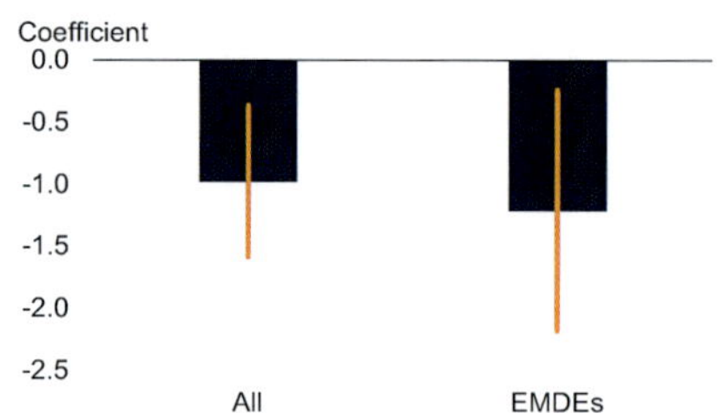

Source: Dincer and Eichengreen 2014; World Bank World Development Indicators.

Note: The CBI is defined as in Dincer and Eichengreen (2014), extrapolated as described in the Appendix. The index ranges from 0 (least independent and transparent) to 15 (most independent and transparent). Inflation refers to year-on-year inflation. AEs = advanced economies; CBI = central bank independence and transparency index; EAP = East Asia and Pacific; ECA = Europe and Central Asia; EMDEs = emerging market and developing economies; LAC = Latin America and the Caribbean; LICs = low-income countries; MNA = Middle East and North Africa; SAR = South Asia; SSA = Sub-Saharan Africa.

C. Columns indicate the median inflation levels and inflation volatility in country-year pairs with a CBI in the top quartile of the sample. Bars denote medians for country-year pairs in the bottom quartile. The difference in inflation levels and volatility between high and low CBI is statistically significant at the 1 percent level.

D. Blue bars show the coefficient estimates from bivariate panel regressions of changes in average inflation between the 1980s and the 2010s on the change in average CBI over the same period (Tables A.1.3.1 and A.1.3.2, Annex 1.3). Vertical lines are ±1.64 standard errors of the coefficient estimate.

wage indexing, possibly enforced by highly collectivized wage bargaining, can entrench short-term inflation shocks into longer-term inflation trends and inflation expectations (Taylor 1979).

Beyond wage indexation, *labor market deregulation* has been associated with lower inflation persistence (Biroli, Mourre, and Turrini 2010). In the Euro Area, in particular, arrangements that facilitate labor market flexibility—such as lower

FIGURE 1.16 Government debt and inflation

Over the past five decades, government debt has grown in advanced economies, especially after the global financial crisis. In EMDEs, it has fallen below early 1990s peaks. Higher government debt has been associated with higher inflation volatility in EMDEs.

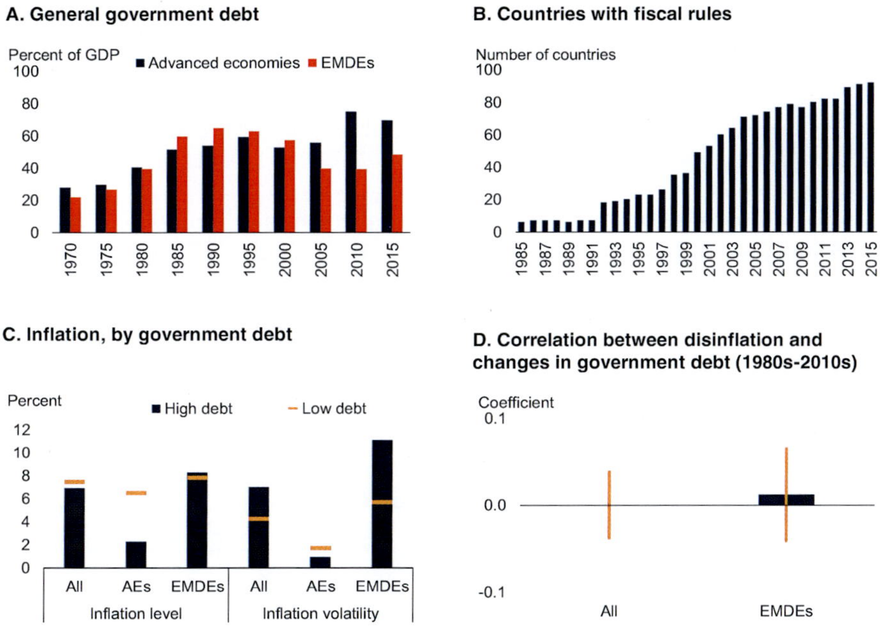

Source: IMF Fiscal Rules Dataset; IMF World Economic Outlook database; World Bank World Development Indicators.
Note: Inflation refers to year-on-year inflation. AEs = advanced economies; EMDEs = emerging market and developing economies; GDP = gross domestic product.

A. Median across countries.

C. Columns indicate the median inflation levels and inflation volatility in country-year pairs with government debt in the top quartile of the sample. Horizontal bars denote medians for country-year pairs in the bottom quartile.

D. Blue bars show the coefficient estimates from bivariate panel regressions of changes (between 1980-89 and 2010-17) in inflation on average government debt as percentage of GDP in the 1980s. Vertical lines are ±1.64 standard errors of the coefficient estimate.

employment protection, less union density, and more limited collective bargaining—have been found to reduce inflation persistence (Jaumotte and Morsy 2012). A similar result was found for a broader sample of countries in the Organisation for Economic Co-operation and Development (OECD) (Geronikolaou, Spyromitros, and Tsintzos 2016).

Greater *product market flexibility* can enhance competition and vice versa. By making wages and prices more flexible, including by deregulating administrative prices, it reduces and makes more transitory the real effects of monetary policy and, hence, reduces the incentive for central banks to use stimulus to boost growth and employment (Rogoff 2003). As a result, inflation expectations and inflation could be lower. Empirically, there is some tentative evidence of lower inflation persistence among advanced economies with greater product market flexibility (Biroli, Mourre, and Turrini 2010).

Trends in labor and product markets. Since 2000, labor market flexibility has increased in advanced economies and EMDEs (Figure 1.17). For example, in EMDEs, union membership declined sharply to 5-15 percent of the labor force in 2013, well below the 2000 level (15-35 percent). In some EMDEs with already-elevated wage bargaining coverage, union membership has expanded, but it remains well below the levels in advanced economies, where it has receded somewhat since 2008.

Correlation with inflation. Lower union membership has been associated with lower inflation and inflation volatility in EMDEs (Figure 1.17). In EMDEs in the bottom third of the sample for union membership, inflation was about 1 percentage point lower, on average, and inflation volatility was less than half that in the top third of the sample.[11] For advanced economies, in contrast, the difference was modest.

Economic structure

Literature. Unless commodity-reliant economies can fully stabilize output growth and exchange rate swings, they may face greater macroeconomic volatility, including inflation volatility, as a result of volatile commodity prices (Bayoumi and Ostry 1997). Conversely, countries that rely heavily on food imports may be subject to greater global food price volatility. However, the consequences of resource reliance for macroeconomic stability depend on policy frameworks: monetary policy independence and financial openness may mitigate the volatility caused by global commodity price swings in resource-based economies (Aizenman, Chinn, and Ito 2010).

Economic structure in EMDEs. About two-thirds of EMDEs rely heavily on commodity exports. In these countries, the commodity sector accounts for 30-80 percent of exports, 20-70 percent of government revenues, and 5-20 percent of GDP. The fall in commodity prices from their peaks in early 2011 has encouraged some economic diversification. In 2016, the share of exports accounted for by commodities in these countries had fallen to 25-70 percent.

Correlation with inflation. The oil price plunge during 2014-16 helped reduce inflation, particularly among EMDEs with a high share of energy imports in GDP. For every additional 10 percentage points of GDP in higher energy

[11] These measures are unavailable for a panel of countries from the 1970s to the 1990s. Hence, labor market variables were not included in the panel regression.

FIGURE 1.17 Labor markets and inflation

Over the past two decades, wage-setting institutions and labor markets more broadly, have become more flexible.

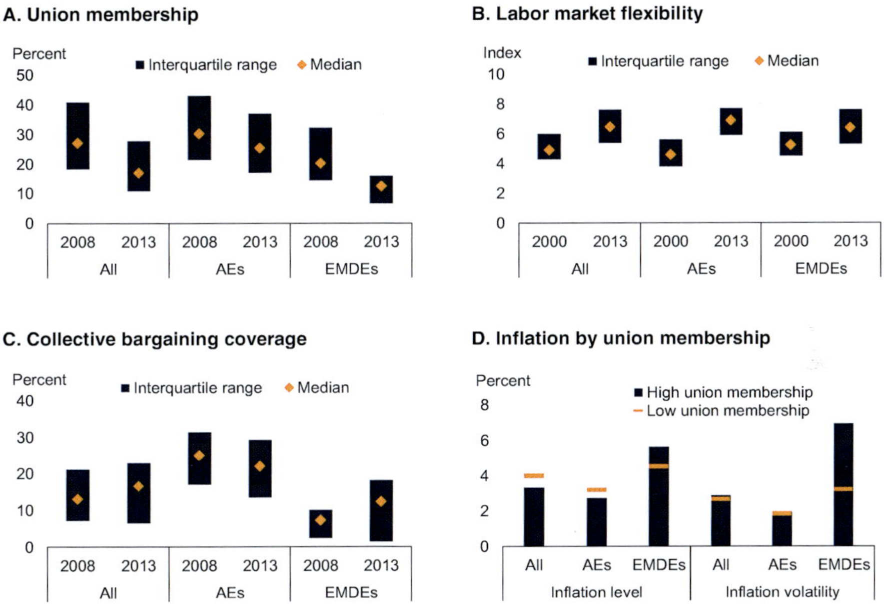

Source: Fraser Institute's Economic Freedom of the World Database; ILOStat; World Bank.

Note: AEs = advanced economies; EMDEs = emerging market and developing economies.

A. Median trade union density rate in 2000 and 2013 for all, AEs, and EMDEs, with 25th and 75th percentile error bars. Data available from 2000 to 2013.

B. Median labor market flexibility index of the Fraser Institute's Economic Freedom Index in 2000 and 2013 for all, AEs, and EMDEs, with 25th and 75th percentile error bars.

C. Median and interquartile range of share of workers covered by collective bargaining in 2008 and 2013. For 2008, data are only available for four advanced economies and five EMDEs.

D. Low union membership indicates the bottom third (below 17 percent) of the sample, high union membership indicates the top third (above 30 percent) of the sample. The sample includes 75 economies for 2000-13.

imports, disinflation over the past four decades was about 0.7 percentage point steeper. In contrast, higher net food imports were associated with slower disinflation over the past four decades.

Other factors

In some countries, disinflation has been attributed to population aging and the growing digitalization of services.

Population aging. In Japan, population aging may have contributed to chronically low inflation, as the burden of rising pension bills weighed on consumption of the working-age population; asset sales of older households depressed asset prices; and shifts toward lower-risk household assets (especially household holdings of government bonds) by older households reduced the funding envelope for fixed investment.[12] Studies based on broader groups of countries have been less conclusive.[13]

Digitalization of services. In some advanced economies, disinflation has been attributed partly to the growing digitalization of services, including e-commerce or sharing services (Goolsbee and Klenow 2018). Although electronic sales by enterprises may still be modest, they have grown rapidly (Ciccarelli and Osbat 2017). By introducing cheaper distribution channels and increasing price transparency, these services may increase competitive pressures and, by increasing efficiency, generate cost savings (Dong, Fudurich, and Suchanek 2017). However, digitalized services may foster market concentration and the emergence of "superstar firms" that reduce competitive pressures in the long run (Autor et al. 2017).[14] Empirical studies have found little evidence of significant deflationary pressures from such digitalization (Charbonneau et al. 2017). For example, using big data techniques, Cavallo and Rigobon (2016) and Cavallo (2017) find that inflation in online retail prices closely matches official U.S. price indexes. In eight other G20 countries, the evolution of online prices has also been similar to that of offline prices, although possibly with more frequent but smaller price changes.[15]

Conclusion

The chapter documents the widespread (across countries) and broad-based (across components) decline in global inflation over the past four to five decades. Global inflation fell from a peak of 16.6 percent (annual average) in 1974 to 2.6 percent in 2017 and further to 2.3 percent in the second half of 2018. In advanced economies, it has fallen steadily since the mid-1980s and in EMDEs since the mid-1990s. In EMDEs, inflation declined from a peak of 17.3 percent (annual average) in 1974 to 3.5 percent in 2017 and, in LICs, from 24.9 percent (annual average) in 1994 to 5.0 percent in 2017. By 2000, global inflation had stabilized at historically low levels before the global financial crisis set off a

---

[12] Andersen, Botman, and Hunt (2014); Imam (2013); Katagiri (2018).

[13] Although the Japan-specific studies referred to in the preceding footnote agree that population aging has been deflationary, studies based on groups of OECD countries are mixed: Yoon, Kim, and Lee (2014); Bobeica et al. (2017); and Inoue et al. (2016) find a negative relationship between the population share of elderly and inflation, and Juselius and Tákáts (2015) find the opposite.

[14] Rapid technological change has also raised concerns that inherent quality improvements are underestimated and, hence, price levels and inflation are overestimated. Empirical studies have found little evidence to support this hypothesis (Cavallo 2017).

[15] Cavallo (2017); Gorodnichenko, Sheremirov and Talavera (2016); Gorodnichenko and Talavera (2017).

period of renewed disinflation. Lower inflation has been accompanied by lower inflation volatility, especially in advanced economies.

The global disinflation has been broad-based. It has occurred in most countries, all EMDE regions, all measures of inflation, and all components of inflation. The current low and stable inflation episode resembles that during the Bretton Woods fixed exchange rate system in the post-war period until 1971 and during the gold standard of the early 1900s. When these historical exchange rate systems faltered, inflation surged. In today's context also, there are reasons to believe that structural factors that have supported disinflation over the past five decades may be fading.

Global disinflation has been supported by a confluence of structural, cyclical, and policy-related factors. A major structural change has been the unprecedented international trade and financial integration along with rapid technological progress. In the median EMDE, like in the median advanced economy, trade has increased by half since 1970, to 75 percent of GDP in 2017, and international assets and liabilities have more than tripled, to 166 percent of GDP in 2016 (although still only half the level in advanced economies).

On the policy front, the adoption of stronger monetary, exchange rate, and fiscal policy frameworks has changed policy makers' approach to price stability. Twenty-three EMDEs have followed in the footsteps of Poland, the first EMDE to introduce an inflation targeting monetary policy framework, in 1998. Reforms of labor and product markets have made EMDEs more flexible by improving competition and reducing price rigidities. Technological changes have been transforming production processes in ways that also affect the formation of prices. In addition to these long-term structural changes, severe global and country-specific shocks have depressed inflation for an extended period.

The gains of the past four to five decades in terms of inflation are by no means guaranteed. Inflation can easily make a comeback if the fundamental structural and policy changes that have compressed inflation over the past five decades lose momentum or even reverse. However, as long as strong monetary policy frameworks are supported by sound fiscal policies and institutional structures, it would be possible to keep in check the inflationary implications of fluctuations in business and financial cycles, and movements in commodity prices.

EMDEs are particularly vulnerable to rising external inflation pressures. Their inflation expectations are less well anchored than in advanced economies. In the absence of strong monetary policy frameworks, exchange rate movements can amplify inflation pressures. Hence, a temporary, externally driven inflation surge can translate into an increase in inflation that EMDE central banks would struggle to rein in. If that happens, little support for macroeconomic stabilization may be forthcoming from fiscal policy, since EMDE fiscal positions are vulnerable to rising borrowing costs when investors reassess risks.

Future research could take two directions. First, the relative contributions of long-term structural changes to global disinflation over recent decades could be more formally quantified. This could be done in a general equilibrium framework, since most regression models are poorly suited to uncovering the relationships between such slow-moving variables. Second, future work could examine more formally the degree of comovement in long-term inflation trends, as Chapters 2 and 3 do for comovement in short-term inflation. This could be set in the context of a more refined measure of trend inflation, such as trends of different lengths that could be identified in frequency domain analysis.

ANNEX 1.1 Effects of inflation on inequality and poverty

Poorer households may suffer greater welfare losses from inflation than wealthier households. In general, poorer households are less able to protect the real value of their income and assets from the impact of inflation. Although the evidence of a positive correlation between inflation and inequality or poverty is mixed at the aggregate level, the links are more established at the household level. The adoption of a credible monetary policy regime that maintains low and stable inflation may help reduce poverty and inequality. In addition, targeted pro-poor fiscal interventions and structural reforms to improve access to financial services for the poor could further mitigate any adverse effects of inflation on inequality and poverty.

Introduction

Inflation can have adverse economic effects on households and other sectors of the economy through direct and indirect channels.[1] Its effects can also differ among different groups of households. For example, poorer households tend to be less able than wealthier households to protect the real value of their income and assets from the impact of anticipated inflation, as poorer households are more reliant on wage income, have less access to interest-bearing accounts, and are unlikely to have significant holdings of other financial or real assets apart from cash. They may also face a higher or more volatile rate of inflation than wealthier households, due to differences in the composition of their consumption baskets—for instance, poorer households may be relatively more exposed to food price volatility. Less directly, there are close links between inflation, monetary policy, and growth. If high inflation results in tighter monetary policy or lower economic growth, it can thereby indirectly affect poverty and inequality.

If the negative effects of inflation fall disproportionately on the poor, it could worsen poverty rates, inequality, or both. Furthermore, because inflation has typically been higher in emerging market and developing economies (EMDEs) than in advanced economies over the past half-century, any negative effects arising from inflation on inequality and poverty may be larger in EMDEs. Although the empirical evidence at the aggregate level is somewhat mixed, the negative effects at the household level are more established. Policy measures to control inflation or mitigate its regressive effects, such as the adoption of a credible monetary policy regime, and targeted pro-poor fiscal interventions have

[1] Fischer and Modigliani (1978) document 25 direct and 25 indirect channels through which inflation can affect different sectors of the economy.

the potential to attenuate inequality and poverty. For EMDEs that are implementing structural reforms and macroeconomic stabilization policies, the potentially beneficial effects of controlling inflation may offset some of the negative effects associated with such policies.

Against this background, this annex addresses the following questions:

- What are the direct channels through which inflation affects inequality and poverty at the household level?
- What are the indirect channels through which inflation affects inequality and poverty?
- What is the impact of inflation on overall inequality and poverty?
- What are the major policy implications?

Direct channels from inflation to inequality and poverty

Inflation can have different effects on different groups of households. In a survey of almost 32,000 households in 38 countries, Easterly and Fischer (2001) found that the poor were much more likely than the rich to state that inflation was a problem. The composition of income, assets, and consumption baskets tends to be such that poorer households suffer greater losses in the real value of their income and wealth as a result of inflation than wealthier households, so that inflation leads to increases in inequality. However, the very poor—households living below the global poverty line of $1.90 per day—may be less vulnerable to inflation as they have minimal wage income or assets. Inflation is also closely linked to monetary policy and economic growth and can indirectly affect poverty and inequality.

Composition of income. In advanced economies, the poor tend to rely more heavily on wage income, transfers, and pensions, and less on income from capital than higher-income households (Erosa and Ventura 2002) (Figure A.1.1.1). As wages tend to lag price inflation, inflation can reduce the real value of nominal wages, reducing the incomes of the poorest households relative to those of the richest. This also shifts income away from labor income toward profits, which, given the distribution of income between rich and poor, will also tend to worsen inequality (Laidler and Parkin 1975; Fischer and Modigliani 1978). Poorer households may also be less likely to benefit from indexed wages (for example, through unions) or through inflation-proof benefits such as health insurance (Bulir 2001). The impact of inflation on pensions and transfers depends on their prevalence in society, as well as on the level of indexation. Welfare payments in most developed countries have some form of indexation, although adjustments

FIGURE A.1.1.1 Composition of household income, wealth, and consumption

The composition of household income, wealth, and consumption varies significantly by income bracket and country. In the United States, the poorest households rely more heavily on wages and transfers, while the richest derive more income from capital. In EMDEs, such as Brazil, nonmonetary income is more important for poorer households. In EMDEs, the poorest households spend a greater share of their income on necessities such as food than the wealthy. EMDEs also spend more on food than higher-income countries such as the United States.

A. Sources of U.S. household income, by income percentile

B. Sources of Brazilian household income, by income percentile

C. Composition of EMDE consumption expenditure, by income group

D. Composition of U.S. consumption expenditure, by income group

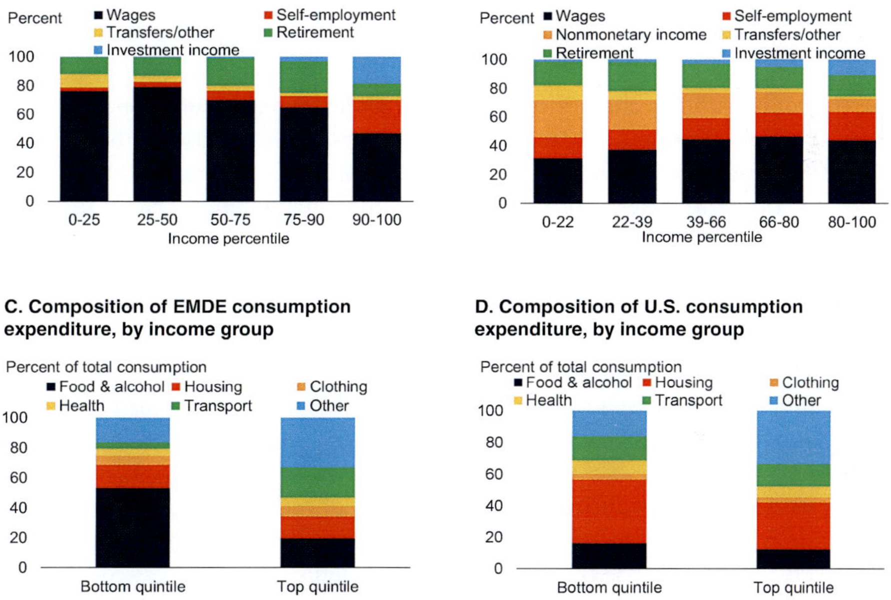

Source: Eurostat; Federal Reserve Board Survey of Consumer Finances; World Bank.

Note: EMDEs = emerging market and developing economies.

A.B Investment income includes interest income, dividends, and capital gains.

B. Income percentiles in Brazil imputed from published income levels to be broadly comparable with U.S. brackets. Data are not published in standard income quintiles. Aggregate data on EMDEs for source of income by income group were not available.

C.D. "Housing" includes utilities such as electricity and gas. "Transport" includes purchases of new vehicles as well as motor fuel. "Other" includes furnishings, personal care, and finance and insurance services.

C. Sample of 90 EMDEs, including 24 low-income countries.

tend to lag inflation, which can result in erosion of real incomes for some income groups in the short run (Minarik 1979; Burdick and Fisher 2007).

Although the channels outlined above also apply to EMDEs, households in EMDEs often rely heavily on nonmonetary income, such as subsistence farming or barter. For example, in Brazil, nonmonetary income accounts for more than a quarter of total income among the poorest fifth of households. Being nonmonetary, this source of income is less vulnerable to inflation than is wage income. For households living below the poverty line of $1.90 a day per head, nonmonetary income may form most of their income, reducing their vulnerability to inflation.

Composition of assets during sustained high inflation. The poor tend to hold most of their assets in cash and have less access to financial products that can protect them against inflation, as these products typically have some entry cost associated with their use (Kahn 1997; Mulligan and Sala-i-Martin 2000; Erosa and Ventura 2002). For example, in the United States, most households have a transaction or current account at a financial institution, with 94 percent of the poorest 20 percent of households holding one. However, many fewer households have savings products, and the distribution is very skewed: the wealthiest 20 percent of households are four times as likely as the poorest to hold certificates of deposit and six times as likely to hold savings bonds. The very richest households (top 10 percent) are 12 times as likely as the poorest 20 percent to hold equities and 23 times as likely to hold pooled investment funds. New financial technologies are beginning to broaden access to financial services for poorer households (Demirgüç-Kunt et al. 2018). The differences are even more stark when considering differences in wealth. Although an inability to protect against inflation is unlikely to affect the very poor, because their holdings of cash will be minimal, episodes of high inflation and especially hyperinflation could tip some households into poverty by eroding the value of their savings and lead to greater inequality (Cysne, Maldonado, and Monteiro 2005; Areosa and Areosa 2016).

Composition of assets during unexpected spells of inflation. A surprise increase in inflation can erode the real value of assets. Because the wealthy tend to be net creditors, such an episode of unanticipated inflation could lead to a reduction in their wealth and a corresponding increase in the wealth of net debtors, by reducing the real value of their debt (Palmer and Barth 1977). In practice, this channel is unlikely to benefit the poorest households, because they tend to have minimal holdings of assets and liabilities (Romer and Romer 1998). For example, in Brazil, 0.9 percent of the poorest decile of households have a mortgage and 6.3 percent have a credit card, compared with 6.1 percent and 44.2 percent, respectively, for the wealthiest decile. This channel seems unlikely to have much of an impact on poverty rates, particularly in EMDEs. It may have some impact on inequality by eroding the real value of assets among the top income percentiles. For example, in a study of U.S. households, Doepke and Schneider (2006) find that unanticipated inflation has tended to benefit young, middle-class households with fixed-rate mortgage debt, but it hurts older and wealthier households. However, holders of equities, who tend to be in the upper income deciles, typically fare better, because these instruments and the associated income streams are more inflation-proof.

Composition of consumption baskets. Although measures of consumer price inflation are calculated using a basket of goods that is representative of the average consumer, the actual composition of consumption baskets varies significantly by income group—because households choose different goods and services or use differently priced versions of the same goods and services. For example, the bottom quintile of households (by income) in EMDEs spend roughly half their income on food, compared with just 20 percent for the top quintile. This difference is more pronounced in EMDEs than in advanced economies, as the share of food in total consumption is much smaller in general in the latter.

In addition to differences in the composition of consumption baskets, other factors can play a role. Using data from 5 million retail scanner transactions, Kaplan and Schulhofer-Wohl (2017) find that differences in the prices paid for the same goods explain two-thirds of the heterogeneity in inflation rates among U.S. households. High-income households are more able to substitute away from higher-quality goods toward lower-quality goods during times of economic crisis, and they can also take greater advantage of discounts on bulk purchases and sales, as they do not face the same liquidity constraints as the poor (Argente and Lee 2015; Orhun and Palazzolo 2018).

In general, the evidence suggests that inflation rates vary among income groups, although there is disagreement about whether these effects are temporary or permanent. Some studies have found substantial, long-term differences in effective inflation rates between the poorest and wealthiest households, with the inflation rates faced by the poor outpacing those faced by the rich by 0.4 to 0.8 percentage point a year (Levell and Oldfield 2011; Kaplan and Schulhofer-Wohl 2017; Weichenrieder and Gurer 2018). Other studies have found significant cyclical, but not permanent, differences in inflation rates between income groups (Hobijn and Lagakos 2005; Oosthuizen 2007), with some evidence that more vulnerable groups are prone to greater variability in inflation (McGranahan and Paulson 2006). In addition, the choice of deflator used in the calculation of the poverty line or the indexation of welfare benefits can affect the incomes of the poor (Gibson, Le, and Kim 2017). Adjusting for different rates of inflation for different groups can also have a material impact on inequality measures (Weichenrieder and Gurer 2018).

Special case of food price inflation. Although the poor in EMDEs are more affected by increases in food prices than are higher-income households, a large number of the poor in EMDEs are food producers as well as consumers. A rise in food prices could therefore raise the incomes of these households. More than one-fifth of households around and below the poverty line are net food sellers in the average EMDE and would therefore benefit from higher food prices.

However, in the aggregate, the majority of the poor in EMDEs and low-income countries (LICs) are net buyers of food and, as a result, food price spikes tend to increase poverty overall. For example, the rise in food prices between 2006 and 2008 is estimated to have increased the number of poor by 105 million (Ivanic and Martin 2008). This topic is covered in Chapter 6.

Indirect channels from inflation to inequality and poverty

Economic growth. Inflation can indirectly affect poverty and inequality through its impact on economic growth. Historically, low and stable inflation, combined with well-anchored inflation expectations, has been associated with greater short-term stability of output and employment growth and higher long-term economic growth (Bruno and Easterly 1998; Eggoh and Khan 2014) (Figure A.1.1.2). These effects seem to be nonlinear, with several studies finding a negative relationship between inflation and growth if inflation is higher than a certain threshold, but they find no relationship when inflation is below that threshold (Barro 1996; Khan and Senhadji 2001). Several channels account for the beneficial effects of low and stable inflation on economic activity, including reduced uncertainty for investors and households, greater pricing transparency, and greater financial stability (Box 1.1). In turn, higher economic growth typically reduces poverty.

Stronger economic growth has generally been found to be beneficial for the poor and has been associated with steeper declines in poverty rates (Dollar and Kraay 2004; Dollar, Kleineberg, and Kraay 2016). The relationship has been highly nonlinear, with poverty responding less to growth when the initial poverty rate is high (Ravallion 2012; World Bank 2010). The relationship between economic development and inequality has been hypothesized by the so-called Kuznets curve, which proposes an inverse U-shape relationship (Kuznets 1955). At low levels of economic development, inequality is low, with little differentiation between households. As economies develop, inequality tends to rise amid increasing differentials in productivity and pay between workers. Finally, inequality starts to fall beyond a certain level of development, as societies choose to reduce inequality through taxes and transfer payments (Milanovic 1994). However, there is limited empirical evidence to support this theory, with many studies showing no evidence of such a relationship (Gallup 2012). Piketty (2014) finds that growth in the recent episode of globalization has been accompanied by greater inequality in high-income countries.

Conventional monetary policy. Inflation can also have indirect effects on inequality and poverty through its close links with unemployment, growth, and monetary policy. It is well established that monetary policy has redistributive effects, although these may be temporary. Romer and Romer (1998) distinguish between short-run and long-run effects. In the short run, expansionary monetary

FIGURE A.1.1.2 Inflation, inequality, and poverty

The relationship between inflation, growth, inequality, and poverty varies across countries. Low and stable inflation has been associated with higher rates of economic growth, although the relationships can be nonlinear. In turn, higher economic growth has been associated with declines in poverty rates.

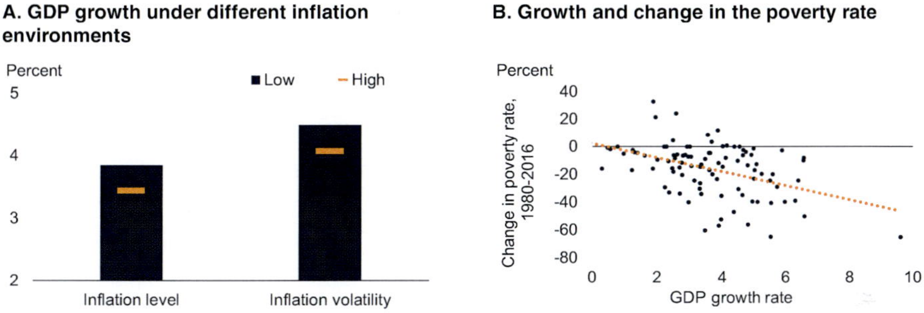

Source: World Bank.

Note: GDP = gross domestic product.

A. Average real GDP growth from 1980 to 2016 for countries with average inflation or standard deviation of inflation in the top quartile ("High") and in the bottom quartile ("Low").

B. Inflation and GDP data are averaged over 1980-2016.

policy raises output, lowers unemployment, and reduces poverty. However, the effects are only temporary, as a persistent expansion is inflationary, which requires monetary policy tightening, which in turn increases unemployment, causing poverty to rise again (a mechanism modeled in a dynamic stochastic general equilibrium framework by Areosa and Areosa 2016). The empirical results are somewhat mixed: Furceri, Loungani, and Zdzienicka (2018) find that a contractionary monetary policy shock increases inequality in the short run, while Ballabriga and Davtyan (2017) find that it can lead to a decline in inequality. In the long run, however, credible monetary policy that results in low and stable inflation can improve outcomes for the poor, by providing favorable conditions for economic growth.

Unconventional monetary policy. More recently, unconventional monetary policy tools have been utilized by central banks in advanced economies amid concerns about persistently low inflation or deflation and short-term interest rates that are close to their zero lower bound. Although the channels through which these tools operate are similar to those used by conventional tools, the strength of these channels may vary (Bank of England 2012). Empirical evidence thus far suggests that, using unconventional tools, the impact of monetary expansion on inequality is fairly neutral to negative (lowers inequality). The poor benefit from an increase in labor income via a reduction in unemployment and increase in wages and, for savers, the decrease in returns on assets is offset by increased capital gains (Casiraghi et al. 2018; Ampudia et al. 2018).

Effects of inflation on overall inequality and poverty

Although the evidence on the effects via individual links suggests that poorer households are generally more adversely affected by inflation than wealthier ones, the empirical results for the overall link between inflation and inequality are inconclusive. Much of the literature was produced in the late 1990s, and there are relatively few recent studies. Inflation trends have evolved substantially over the past 20 years, with a generalized downward trend globally. The results vary between single-country studies and cross-country studies, and between advanced economies and EMDEs. Although correlations between the variables have been found, there is less evidence of clear causation from inflation to inequality and poverty, with some studies suggesting the causality goes in the opposite direction.[2] In general, the literature suggests that slightly higher inflation is associated with mildly lower inequality in countries where inflation is already low (typically, advanced economies), but that high inflation is associated with higher inequality in countries where inflation is already high (typically, EMDEs).

Single-country studies. Parker (1998) surveys the early literature, based on 12 single-country studies, and finds that all but three show that higher inflation is associated with lower inequality (for example, Ashworth 1994; Balke and Slottje 1993). However, almost all these studies focus on advanced economies (mainly the United States), so the results may be less applicable to EMDEs. Other studies focusing on single advanced economies come to a similar conclusion (Doepke and Schneider 2006; Maestri and Roventini 2012), except for Jantti and Jenkins (2010), who find little evidence of a relationship between inflation and income inequality in the United Kingdom. Single-country studies on EMDEs, such as India (Datt and Ravallion 1998), the Philippines (Blejer and Guerrero 1990), and Brazil (Ferreira and Litchfield 2001), find that higher inflation is associated with a lower share of income held by the poor or higher inequality. Looking at seven single studies of advanced economies and EMDEs together, Bulir and Gulde (1995) find that the impact of inflation on different income groups within countries varies between countries, with a positive correlation between inflation and inequality more likely in LICs that have a less developed financial sector.

Cross-country studies. Galli and van der Hoeven (2001) review single-country and cross-country studies prior to 2000. They find that the time-series studies (the majority of which focus on the United States) almost always find higher

[2] In a study of Brazil during 1981-93, a fall in inequality, despite being associated with declining inflation, was attributed to structural and policy changes including convergence of incomes between rural and urban areas, and social transfers to the poor (Ferreira and Litchfield 2001).

inflation to be associated with lower inequality, whereas the cross-country studies find higher inflation to be associated with higher inequality and poverty (Figure A.1.1.2). Several other studies that use cross-country samples also document a positive correlation between inflation and income inequality (Romer and Romer 1998; Easterly and Fischer 2001; Agenor 2002; Albanesi 2007; Thalassinos, Ugurlu, and Muratoğlu 2012). However, even studies that find statistically significant coefficients on inflation typically find little explanatory power of their models, and the relationship between the poverty rate and inflation is less apparent than the relationship with inequality.

Nonlinear relationship between inflation and inequality. These mixed empirical results may reflect nonlinear relationships between inflation and inequality or poverty. Several studies find evidence of a nonlinear relationship, with considerable differences in the correlation between inflation and inequality depending on the initial rate of inflation (Galli and van der Hoeven 2001; Bulir 2001; Monnin 2014; Siami-Namini and Hudson 2017). Bulir (2001) reports that countries in hyperinflation had Gini coefficients that were 8 points higher, on average, than countries with high inflation but not hyperinflation. The benefit of moving from hyperinflation to high inflation was significant, but moving from high inflation to very low inflation (less than 5 percent) had a negligible effect.

Policy recommendations

Maintain a low-inflation environment. Although it is not definite, the evidence suggests that achieving stable and low inflation is associated with better poverty and inequality outcomes, with the benefits being greatest among low-income, high-inflation countries. Lowering income inequality by controlling inflation may be less costly than through other social choices (Bulir 2001). This suggests that the adoption of a credible monetary policy regime by policy makers in EMDEs can lead to improved inequality and poverty outcomes. The results are less clear-cut for advanced economies, where low inflation is already established, with some evidence that the opposite relationship holds, so that slightly higher inflation may reduce inequality.

Improve competition. Policy makers have a range of tools beyond monetary policy to improve income inequality and poverty, but they have few tools to address the effects arising specifically from inflation. Structural reforms to improve competition in the financial sector can lower costs and increase access to savings products that can help poorer households protect the real value of their assets from inflation (Beck, Demirgüç-Kunt, and Levine 2004; Claessens 2006). Such reforms have also been found to increase informal business ownership, employment, and income, with a larger benefit accruing to lower-income households (Bruhn and Love 2014).

Improve granularity in inflation measures and fiscal support. The calculation of alternative indexes of inflation for different income groups would provide greater information on the inflation rates actually experienced by the poor and could be used as an alternative benchmark for indexing welfare payments. This would reduce the erosion of their real value if inflation for poorer households was higher than the economywide inflation rate. Finally, the use of targeted subsidies could help alleviate poverty and inequality if they are focused on products, particularly food items, that are disproportionately consumed by the poor and prone to more volatile inflation.

ANNEX 1.2 Low-income countries

Low-income countries (LICs) are defined as those with gross national income (GNI) per capita, calculated using the World Bank Atlas method, of $995 or less in 2017; middle-income countries as those with GNI per capita between $996 and $12,055 in 2017; and high-income countries as those with GNI per capita of $12,056 or more in 2017. These classifications are revised in July every year.

As of 2018, LICs include Afghanistan, Benin, Burkina Faso, Burundi, Central African Republic, Chad, the Comoros, the Democratic Republic of Congo, Eritrea, Ethiopia, The Gambia, Guinea, Guinea-Bissau, Haiti, the Democratic People's Republic of Korea, Liberia, Madagascar, Malawi, Mali, Mozambique, Nepal, Niger, Rwanda, Senegal, Sierra Leone, Somalia, South Sudan, the Syrian Arab Republic, Tajikistan, Tanzania, Togo, Uganda, the Republic of Yemen, and Zimbabwe. Annual inflation data since 1970 are available for 27 LICs (excluding Eritrea, the Democratic People's Republic of Korea, Somalia, South Sudan, Syria, Tajikistan, and Yemen).

In 1987, the first year classifications were published, 49 economies (excluding most economies affiliated with the Soviet Union) were classified as LICs. Of today's LICs, Senegal, Syria, Yemen, and Zimbabwe were classified as middle-income countries in 1987. In addition to today's LICs, Bangladesh, Bhutan, Cambodia, China, Equatorial Guinea, Ghana, Guyana, India, Indonesia, Kenya, the Lao People's Democratic Republic, Lesotho, Maldives, Mauritania, Myanmar, Nigeria, Pakistan, São Tomé and Príncipe, Solomon Islands, Sri Lanka, Sudan, Vietnam, and Zambia were classified as LICs in 1987.

ANNEX 1.3 Regression analysis

A series of bivariate regressions is estimated to identify the main correlates of the decline in inflation between the 1980s and the 2010s. The sample includes 73-77 countries (depending on the availability of the correlates of inflation), of which 49-53 countries are emerging market and developing economies. Countries with populations of less than 3 million are dropped, since they tend to be outlier observations.

Specifically, the regression is estimated as $\Delta inflation_{it} = \alpha + \beta X_{it}$, with robust standard errors. All changes are between averages for 1980-89 and 2010-17. The constant α in this regression denotes the unconditional average decline in inflation over the three decades. To avoid multicollinearity, since most of the regressors are highly correlated with each other, the regression only estimates bivariate correlations.

The regressors X_{it} include the change in trade openness (identified as trade as a percentage of gross domestic product [GDP]); the change in capital account openness (defined as the Chinn-Ito index of financial openness); the switch to an inflation targeting regime; the switch to a pegged exchange rate regime (as defined by Shambaugh [2004]); the change in Dincer and Eichengreen's (2014) central bank independence and transparency index; the switch to a status of being highly integrated into global value chains (as defined in the Appendix); the initial level of government debt as a percentage of GDP; net energy imports as a percentage of GDP; and net food imports as a percentage of GDP.

TABLE A.1.3.1 Correlates of change in CPI inflation: Full sample

Panel A

Variables				
Net food imports (percent of GDP)	0.3077** [0.160]			
Net energy imports (percent of GDP)		-0.0672*** [0.024]		
Change to inflation targeting regime			-6.5383*** [2.285]	
Change to pegged exchange rate regime				-3.3842* [2.235]
Change in central bank transparency index (point increase)				
Constant	-3.5727*** [0.714]	-3.8800*** [0.802]	-2.8199*** [0.724]	-3.5029*** [0.812]
Observations	79	79	81	81
R-squared	0.068	0.036	0.129	0.048

Panel B

Variables					
Change in central bank transparency index (point increase)	-0.9784*** [0.370]				
Change in trade openness (percentage points of GDP)		-0.0182 [0.026]			
Change in capital account openness index (point increase)			-9.3815*** [2.199]		
Change in international assets and liabilities (percentage points of GDP)				-0.0003 [0.001]	
Initial government debt (percent of GDP)					-0.0005 [0.023]
Constant	-2.1583*** [0.976]	-3.4944*** [0.830]	-2.6809*** [0.656]	-3.6822*** [0.867]	-4.0227*** [1.466]
Observations	77	80	80	81	77
R-squared	0.092	0.007	0.219	0.001	0.000

Note: Standard errors are in square brackets. The dependent variable is the change between the average inflation rate during 2010-17 and the average inflation rate during 1980-89. All changes are between averages for 2010-17 and 1980-89. Inflation targeting regime and pegged exchange rate regime (as defined by Shambaugh [2016]) are dummy variables. Euro Area economies are considered floating rate regimes. The central bank transparency index (0 = least, 15 = most) is from Dincer and Eichengreen (2014). The capital account openness index (0 = closed, 1 = open) is from Chinn and Ito (2008). The dummy variable for high participation in global value chains is defined in the Appendix. CPI = consumer price index; GDP = gross domestic product.

*** indicates statistical significance at the 1 percent confidence level, ** at the 5 percent level, and * at the 10 percent level.

TABLE A.1.3.2 Correlates of change in CPI inflation: EMDEs

Panel A

Variables				
Net food imports (percent of GDP)	0.3891*** [0.164]			
Net energy imports (percent of GDP)		-0.0748** [0.039]		
Change to inflation targeting regime			-9.1011*** [3.001]	
Change to pegged exchange rate regime				-2.8823 [2.921]
Constant	-3.8778*** [1.044]	-4.0871*** [1.170]	-3.0054*** [1.105]	-4.1452*** [1.160]
Observations	46	46	47	47
R-squared	0.125	0.027	0.176	0.030

Panel B

Variables					
Change in central bank transparency index (point increase)	-1.2126** [0.589]				
Change in trade openness (percentage points of GDP)		-0.0101 [0.037]			
Change in capital account openness index (point increase)			-8.9658*** [3.332]		
Change in international assets and liabilities (percentage points of GDP)				-0.0050** [0.003]	
Initial government debt (percent of GDP)					0.0122 [0.032]
Constant	-2.5910*** [1.326]	-4.4366*** [1.238]	-3.6367*** [1.017]	-4.1563*** [1.150]	-5.2233*** [2.334]
Observations	45	46	47	47	46
R-squared	0.092	0.002	0.149	0.033	0.003

Note: Standard errors are in square brackets. The dependent variable is the change between the average inflation rate during 2010-17 and the average inflation rate during 1980-89. All changes are between averages for 2010-17 and 1980-89. Inflation targeting regime and pegged exchange rate regime (as defined by Shambaugh [2016]) are dummy variables. Euro Area economies are considered floating rate regimes. The central bank transparency index (0 = least, 15 = most) is from Dincer and Eichengreen (2014). The capital account openness index (0 = closed, 1 = open) is from Chinn and Ito (2006). The dummy variable for high participation in global value chains is defined in the Appendix. CPI = consumer price index; EMDEs = emerging market and developing economies; GDP = gross domestic product.

*** indicates statistical significance at the 1 percent confidence level, ** at the 5 percent level, and * at the 10 percent level.

ANNEX 1.4 Lessons from U.S. disinflation in 1979-82

U.S. inflation declined from double-digits in August 1979 to below 4 percent by the end of 1982. This disinflation highlighted the benefits of shifting central banks' focus to price stability, building credibility, and establishing stabilizing monetary policy rules.

The Great Inflation of 1965-82 has been described as the defining macroeconomic event of the second half of the 20th century (Bryan 2018). Siegel (1994) described it as "the greatest failure of American post-war history." Meltzer (2005) attributed to the Great Inflation the fall of the Bretton Woods system of fixed exchange rates, the bankruptcy of the thrift industry (U.S. savings banks), heavy capital taxation, and a redistribution of wealth and income. The challenges associated with the subsequent disinflation transformed the understanding of the role of central banks and monetary policy.

Against this backdrop, this annex discusses the following questions:

- How did U.S. disinflation evolve during the 1980s?
- What was the role of monetary policy in U.S. disinflation?
- What lessons have been drawn from U.S. disinflation?

Evolution of disinflation during 1979-82

By August 1979, U.S. inflation had reached 12 percent (Figure A.1.4.1). High inflation reflected multiple one-time jumps in key prices and accommodative demand policies that perpetuated high inflation. Oil prices rose seven-fold between December 1972 and January 1974 and tripled again between November 1978 and November 1979, amid supply disruptions around the Iranian Revolution. From the 1960s, monetary policy was accommodative on the understanding that permanently lower unemployment could be "bought" with higher inflation—the standard understanding of the Phillips curve at the time (Bryan 2018). The resulting accommodative monetary policy stance combined with loose fiscal policy—for example, to finance the Vietnam War, Great Society social spending, or the Kennedy tax cuts—to generate considerable domestic demand pressures.

By the end of 1982, inflation had declined to below 4 percent, in part thanks to an aggressive tightening of monetary policy, including a hike in the federal funds rate from 11 percent in August 1979 to a peak of 19 percent in July 1981.[1] In

[1] In parts of advanced-economy Europe, central banks responded more strongly and earlier than in the United States to rising inflation, but disinflation was also accompanied by output losses in the early 1980s (Beyer et al. 2009; Söderström 2005; Miles et al. 2017; Berg et al. 2015; Nguyen et al. 2017).

FIGURE A.1.4.1 Macroeconomic developments during 1979-82

The U.S. disinflation from double-digits in August 1979 to inflation below 4 percent by end-1982 was associated with two recessions (together termed the "Volcker recession").

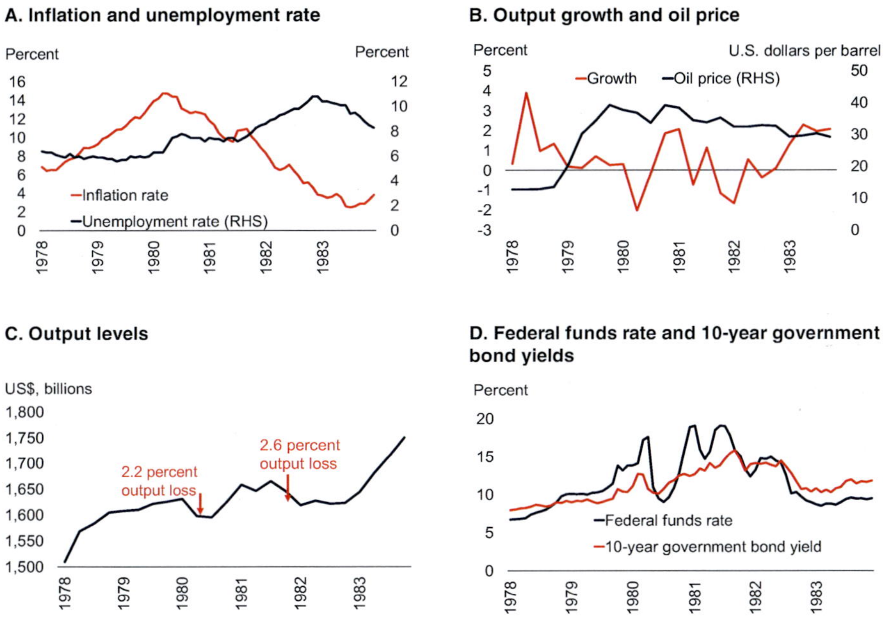

Source: Haver Analytics.

A. Inflation is in year-on-year terms.

B. Output growth is in quarter-on-quarter seasonally adjusted annualized terms. Nominal oil price is in U.S. dollars

C. Chain-weighted real gross domestic product, seasonally adjusted and annualized, in billions of U.S. dollars at 2009 prices. Vertical lines and text show cumulative output losses between the troughs of the two recessions and the preceding peaks.

October 1979, the Federal Reserve also overhauled its operations to switch from targeting the federal funds rate to targeting nonborrowed reserves. Over the same period, fiscal policy tightened by about 1 percentage point of gross domestic product (Congressional Budget Office 2017). The disinflation was associated with two recessions, together termed the "Volcker recession," after the Chairman of the Federal Reserve Board. In 6 of 12 quarters during 1980-82, output contracted. The cumulative output losses during both recessions (peak to trough) amounted to more than 2 percent. Unemployment rates doubled from 6 percent in August 1979 to almost 12 percent at the end of 1982 (Figure A.1.4.1).

Role of monetary policy in U.S. disinflation

The stagflation of the 1970s, as well as the recessions during 1979-82, have been attributed to varying degrees to changes in monetary policy. For example,

Barsky and Kilian (2002) argue that the stagflation that preceded the 1979-82 recession was mostly attributable to excessively loose monetary policy, compounded by oil price increases.

In particular, although the tripling of oil prices during 1978-79 is generally recognized as the trigger of the recession, the monetary policy response to the oil price spike deepened it. Bernanke, Gertler, and Watson (1997) showed that the nonaccommodative monetary policy response to the oil price spike accounted for its disproportionate effect on the economy. Rotemburg and Woodford (1997) also found that unexpectedly tight monetary policy in early 1982 deepened the 1982 recession.[2]

The Federal Reserve's switch in operational procedures allowed it to meet more effectively its reserve money growth targets.[3] The shift was followed by considerable volatility and a sharp rise in the federal funds rate (Goodfriend 1983). It was eventually reversed by 1987 because of the instability of the money demand function (Thornton 2004; Gilbert 1985).

Lessons from U.S. disinflation

The Great Inflation and the output losses during the subsequent disinflation have helped transform the understanding of a central bank's role. It is now widely recognized that (i) monetary policy can only have short-term effects on real output (that is, the Phillips curve changes over time); (ii) some monetary policy rules are more stabilizing than others; and (iii) central bank credibility that anchors inflation expectations is a critical precondition for effective monetary policy.

Lack of long-term real-economy effects of monetary policy. During the 1970s, monetary policy was guided by the Phillips curve, an empirical inverse relationship between (wage) inflation and unemployment. This relationship suggested that monetary policy could lower unemployment at the cost of higher inflation. However, as central banks sought to exploit this relationship, it became clear that the trade-off existed only in the short term: as inflation expectations adjusted, the Phillips curve shifted, possibly in a nonlinear way (Akerlof et al. 2000). Hence, the inflation-unemployment trade-off disappeared

[2] In contrast, Uhlig (2005) argues that the role of monetary policy has been exaggerated by previous authors' methodology, in particular by imposing timing restrictions or the restriction of a negative relationship between inflation and growth. When such restrictions are lifted, Uhlig (2005) finds that monetary policy did not have a significant effect on growth during the Volcker recession.

[3] In the previous operational procedures, money growth targets were achieved within some tolerance bands by guiding the federal funds rate. Under the new procedures, money growth targets were achieved by guiding nonborrowed reserves while maintaining the federal funds rate within a wide tolerance band (Poole 1982).

over the long run. This meant that the persistent use of monetary policy to boost employment and output beyond their long-run potential was fruitless and simply raised inflation (Clarida, Gali, and Gertler 1999).

Switch to stabilizing monetary policy rules. The increasing awareness of central banks' inability to achieve a sustained improvement in output led to an increased focus on monetary policy rules, in particular rules that emphasized the goal of stabilization. Indeed, Dennis (2006) shows that there was large uncertainty around estimated U.S. monetary policy rules before 1979 but, thereafter, U.S. monetary policy could be modeled more precisely. Other studies have also found evidence supporting a measurable change in U.S. monetary policy rules. In a dynamic stochastic general equilibrium model, Bianchi (2013) shows that the U.S. monetary policy regime switched from "dove" (favoring output growth over disinflation) to "hawk" (vice versa) in the second half of 1980. Clarida, Gali, and Gertler (2000) demonstrate that the U.S. monetary policy rule after 1979 responded more strongly to expected inflation than during the preceding period. This new rule ensured greater macroeconomic stability than earlier monetary policy rules. Owyang and Wall (2006) also document a structural change between the pre-Volcker and Volcker-Greenspan eras in the effect of monetary policy across U.S. regions.

Establishing central bank credibility. Bernanke, Gertler, and Watson (1997) note that, by guiding expectations, the choice of a credible monetary policy is key for macroeconomic stabilization. They acknowledge that econometric models typically find a modest role (about 20 percent) for monetary policy shocks—that is, *unexpected* monetary policy changes—in explaining output movements. Blanchard (1984) demonstrates that a Phillips curve relationship explained actual disinflation and output losses reasonably well until the end of 1981 but not thereafter. He interprets this as evidence that inflation expectations initially remained unchanged from the Great Inflation, and the Federal Reserve still lacked credibility.[4] Research has also shown that the wrong monetary policy rule can undermine central bank credibility. Barro and Gordon (1983a, 1983b) demonstrate that rational households and investors will anticipate the behavior of central banks that systematically attempt to reduce unemployment by surprise monetary stimulus. To reduce unemployment, the central bank needs to engineer ever-greater inflation surprises. Taking this into account, since 1979, the Fed's monetary policy has arguably been guided by an informal inflation targeting framework, even if its dual mandate was never abolished (Goodfriend 2003).

[4] With the benefit of more years of data, Alogoskoufis and Smith (1991) demonstrate the shift in the Phillips curve during the Volcker recession.

Conclusion

The experience of the Great Inflation of 1965-82, stagflation in the 1970s, and disinflation during 1979-82 transformed monetary policy in the United States and the understanding of monetary policy more broadly. The Phillips curve is no longer considered a useful policy tool, and instead it is recognized that a credible central bank can reduce inflation with less output loss. As a result, "the concept of credibility has become a central concern of the scholarly literature on monetary policy" (Blinder 2000; Bordo and Orphanides 2013), and inflation has become the "organizing focus of monetary policy" (Clarida, Gali, and Gertler 2000).

References

Abbas, S. K., P. S. Bhattacharya, and S. Pasquale. 2016. "The New Keynesian Phillips Curve: An Update on Recent Empirical Advances." *International Review of Economics and Finance* 43 (May): 378-403.

Agénor, P. 2002. "Macroeconomic Adjustment and the Poor: Analytical Issues and Cross-Country Evidence." Policy Research Working Paper 2788, World Bank, Washington, DC.

Aisen, A., and F. J. Veiga. 2006. "Does Political Instability Lead to Higher Inflation? A Panel Data Analysis." *Journal of Money, Credit and Banking* 38 (5): 1379-89.

Aizenman, J., M. D. Chinn, and H. Ito. 2008. "Assessing the Emerging Global Financial Architecture: Measuring the Trilemma's Configurations over Time." NBER Working Paper 14533, National Bureau of Economic Research, Cambridge, MA.

———. 2010. "The Emerging Global Financial Architecture: Tracing and Evaluating New Patterns of the Trilemma Configuration." *Journal of International Money and Finance* 29(4): 615-41.

———. 2011. "Assessing the Emerging Global Financial Architecture: Measuring the Trilemma's Configurations Over Time." Working Paper No. 08-14, Santa Cruz Center for International Economics, Santa Cruz, CA.

Akerlof, G. A., W. T. Dickens, G. L. Perry, T. F. Bewley, and A. S. Blinder. 2000. "Near-Rational Wage and Price Setting and the Long-Run Phillips Curve." *Brookings Papers on Economic Activity* 2000 (1): 1-60.

Aksoy, G., D. Bredin, D. Corcoran, and S. Fountas. 2017. "Relative Price Dispersion and Inflation: Evidence for the U.K. and the U.S." *Credit and Capital Markets* 50 (1): 3-24.

Al Nasser, O. M., A. Sachsida, and M. Mário. 2009. "The Openness-Inflation Puzzle: Panel Data Evidence." *International Research Journal of Finance and Economics* 28: 169-81.

Albanesi, S. 2007. "Inflation and Inequality." *Journal of Monetary Economics* 54 (4): 1088-1114.

Alogoskoufis, G. S., and R. Smith. 1991. "The Phillips Curve, the Persistence of Inflation, and the Lucas Critique: Evidence from Exchange-Rate Regimes." *American Economic Review* 81 (5): 1254-75.

Ampudia, M., D. Georgarakos, J. Slacalek, O. Tristani, P. Vermeulen, and G. Violante. 2018. "Monetary Policy and Household Inequality." Working Paper Series 2170, European Central Bank, Frankfurt am Main.

Anand, R., E. Prasad, and B. Zhang. 2015. "What Measure of Inflation Should a Developing Country Central Bank Target?" *Journal of Monetary Economics* 74 (C): 102-16.

Andersen, P., and D. Gruen. 1995. "Macroeconomic Policies and Growth." In *Productivity and Growth,* edited by P. Anderson, J. Dwyer, and D. Gruen. Sydney: Reserve Bank of Australia.

Anderson, M. D., D. P. Botman, and M. B. Hunt. 2014. "Is Japan's Population Aging Deflationary?" IMF Working Paper 14/139, International Monetary Fund, Washington, DC.

Andrade, P., G. Jordi, H. Le Bihan, and J. Matheron. 2018. "The Optimal Inflation Target and the Natural Rate of Interest." NBER Working Paper 24328, National Bureau of Economic Research, Cambridge, MA.

Areosa, W., and M. Areosa. 2016. "The Inequality Channel of Monetary Transmission." *Journal of Macroeconomics* 48 (June): 214–30.

Argente, D., and M. Lee. 2015. "Cost of Living Inequality during the Great Recession." Meeting Papers 1372, Society for Economic Dynamics.

Arteta, C., M. A. Kose, M. Stocker, and T. Taskin. 2016 "Negative Interest Rate Policies: Sources and Implications." Policy Research Working Paper 7791, World Bank, Washington, DC.

Ashworth, J. 1994. "An Empirical Estimation of Macroeconomic Activity and Income Distribution in the United States." Department of Economics Working Paper 130, Durham University, Durham, U.K.

Auer, R. A., C. E. V. Borio, and A. J. Filardo. 2017. "The Globalization of Inflation: The Growing Importance of Global Value Chains." CESifo Working Paper 6387, Munich.

Autor, D., D. Dorn, L. F. Katz, C. Patterson, and J. Van Reenen. 2017. "The Fall of the Labor Share and the Rise of Superstar Firms." Discussion Paper 1482, Centre for Economic Performance, London School of Economics.

Badinger, H. 2009. "Globalization, the Output-Inflation Tradeoff and Inflation." *European Economic Review* (53) 8: 888-907.

Baig, T., J. Decressin, T. Feyzioglu, M. S. Kumar, and C. Faulkner-MacDonagh. 2003. "Deflation; Determinants, Risks, and Policy Options." IMF Occasional Paper 221, International Monetary Fund, Washington, DC.

Baldacci, E., A. L. Hillman, and N. C. Kojo. 2004. "Growth, Governance, and Fiscal Policy Transmission Channels in Low-Income Countries." *European Journal of Political Economy* 20 (3): 517-49.

Baldini, A., and M. Poplawski-Ribeiro. 2011. "Fiscal and Monetary Determinants of Inflation in Low-Income Countries: Theory and Evidence from Sub-Saharan Africa." *Journal of African Economies* 20 (3): 419-62.

Balke, N., and D. Slottje. 1993. "Poverty and Change in the Macroeconomy: A Dynamic Macroeconometric Model." *Review of Economics and Statistics* 75 (1): 117-22.

Ball, L. M. 2014. "The Case for a Long-Run Inflation Target of Four Percent." IMF Working Paper 14/92, International Monetary Fund, Washington, DC.

Ball, L. M., and N. Sheridan. 2005. "Does Inflation Targeting Matter?" In *The Inflation-Targeting Debate*, edited by B. Bernanke and M. Woodford. Chicago: University of Chicago Press.

Ballabriga, F., and K. Davtyan. 2017. "The Distributive Impact of Monetary Policy: Evidence from the UK." ESADE Business School Research Paper No. 269, ESADE, Barcelona.

Banerjee, R. N., and A. Mehrotra. 2018. "Deflation Expectations." BIS Working Paper 699, Bank for International Settlements, Basel.

Bank of England. 2012. "The Distributional Effects of Asset Purchases." *Bank of England Quarterly Bulletin* 52 (3): 254-66.

Barrios, S., L. Bertinelli, and E. Strobl. 2010. "Trends in Rainfall and Economic Growth in Africa: A Neglected Cause of the African Growth Tragedy." *Review of Economics and Statistics* 92 (2): 350-66.

Barro, R. J. 1996. "Inflation and Growth." *Federal Reserve Bank of St. Louis Review* 78 (3): 153-69.

Barro, R. J., and D. B. Gordon. 1983a. "A Positive Theory of Monetary Policy in a Natural Rate Model." *Journal of Political Economy* 91 (4): 589-610.

———. 1983b. "Rules, Discretion and Reputation in a Model of Monetary Policy." *Journal of Monetary Economics* 12 (1): 101-21.

Barsky, R. B., and L. Kilian. 2002. "Do We Really Know That Oil Caused the Great Stagflation? A Monetary Alternative." In *NBER Macroeconomics Annual 2001,* Vol. 16, edited by B. S. Bernanke and K. Rogoff. Cambridge, MA: MIT Press.

Batini, N., B. Jackson, and S. Nickell. 2005. "An Open-Economy New Keynesian Phillips Curve for the U.K." *Journal of Monetary Economics* 52 (6): 1061-71.

Batini, N., and D. Laxton. 2007. "Under What Conditions Can Inflation Targeting Be Adopted? The Experience of Emerging Markets." In *Monetary Policy under Inflation Targeting*, edited by F. S. Mishkin and K. Schmidt-Hebbel. Santiago: Central Bank of Chile.

Bayoumi, T., and J. D. Ostry. 1997. "Macroeconomic Shocks and Trade Flows within Sub-Saharan Africa: Implications for Optimum Currency Arrangements." *Journal of African Economies* 6 (3): 412-44.

Beck, T., A. Demirgüç-Kunt, and R. Levine. 2004. "Finance, Inequality and Poverty: Cross-Country Evidence." Policy Research Working Paper 3338, World Bank, Washington, DC.

Benabou, R. 1992. "Inflation and Markups: Theories and Evidence from the Retail Trade Sector." *European Economic Review* 36 (2-3): 566-74.

Benati, L. 2008. "Investigating Inflation Persistence across Monetary Regimes." *Quarterly Journal of Economics* 123 (3): 1005-60.

Benigno, P., and E. Faia. 2016. "Globalization, Pass-Through, and Inflation Dynamics." *International Journal of Central Banking* 12 (4): 263-306.

Berg, A., S. O'Connell, C. Pattillo, R. Portillo, and F. Unsal. 2015. "Monetary Policy Issues in Sub-Saharan Africa." In *Oxford Handbook of Africa and Economics,* Vol. 2, edited by C. Monga and J. Yifu. Oxford: Oxford University Press.

Bernanke, B. S. 2004. "The Great Moderation." Speech at the meetings of the Eastern Economic Association, Washington, DC. https://www.federalreserve.gov/boarddocs/speeches/2004/20040220.

Bernanke, B. S., M. Gertler, and M. Watson. 1997. "Systematic Monetary Policy and the Effects of Oil Price Shocks." *Brookings Papers on Economic Activity* 1: 91-142.

Bernanke, B. S., and H. James. 1991. "The Gold Standard, Deflation, and Financial Crisis in the Great Depression: An International Comparison." In *Financial Markets and Financial Crises,* edited by R. G. Hubbard. Chicago: University of Chicago Press.

Bernanke, B. S., and F. S. Mishkin. 1997. "Inflation Targeting: A New Framework for Monetary Policy?" *Journal of Economic Perspectives* 11 (2): 97-116.

Bernanke, B. S., T. Laubach, F. S. Mishkin, and A. S. Posen. 2001. *Inflation Targeting: Lessons from the International Experience.* Princeton University Press.

Bernanke, B. S., V. R. Reinhart, and B. B. Sack. 2004. "Monetary Policy Alternatives at the Zero Bound: An Empirical Assessment." *Brookings Papers on Economic Activity* 2: 1-100.

Beyer, A., V. Gaspar, C. Gerberding, and O. Issing. 2009. "Opting Out of the Great Inflation: German Monetary Policy after the Break Down of Bretton Woods." Working Paper Series 1020, European Central Bank, Frankfurt am Main.

Bhattarai, K. 2016. "Unemployment-Inflation Trade-Offs in OECD Countries." *Economic Modeling* 58 (November): 93-103.

Bianchi, F. 2013. "Regime Switches, Agents' Beliefs, and Post-World War II U.S. Macroeconomic Dynamics." *Review of Economic Studies* 80 (2): 463-90.

Bianchi, F., and A. Civelli. 2015. "Globalization and Inflation: Evidence from a Time-Varying VAR." *Review of Economic Dynamics* 18 (2): 406-33.

Bick, A. 2010. "Threshold Effects of Inflation on Economic Growth in Developing Countries." *Economic Letters* 108 (2): 126-29.

Biroli, P., G. Mourre, and A. Turrini. 2010. "Adjustment in the Euro Area and Regulation of Product and Labour Markets: An Empirical Assessment." Economic Papers 428, European Commission, Brussels.

Blanchard, O. J. 1984. "The Lucas Critique and the Volcker Effect." NBER Working Paper 1326, National Bureau of Economic Research, Cambridge, MA.

Blanchard, O. J., G. Dell'Ariccia, and P. Mauro. 2010. "Rethinking Macroeconomic Policy." *Journal of Money, Credit, and Banking* 42 (s1): 199-215.

Blanchard, O. J., and J. Galí. 2007. "Real Wage Rigidities and the New Keynesian Model." *Journal of Money, Credit and Banking* 39 (s1): 35-65.

———. 2008. "Labor Markets and Monetary Policy: A New-Keynesian Model with Unemployment." NBER Working Paper 13897, National Bureau of Economic Research, Cambridge, MA.

Bleaney, M. 1999. "Trade Reform, Macroeconomic Performance and Export Growth in Ten Latin American Countries, 1979–95." *Journal of International Trade and Economic Development* 8(1): 89-105.

Bleaney, M., and D. Fielding. 2002. "Exchange Rate Regimes, Inflation and Output Volatility in Developing Countries." *Journal of Development Economics* 68 (1): 233-45.

Bleaney, M., and M. Francisco. 2018. "Is the Phillips Curve Different in Poor Countries?" *Bulletin of Economic Research* 70 (1): E17-E28.

Bleaney, M., A. Morozumi, and Z. Mumuni. 2016. "Fiscal Deficits and Inflation: Institutions Matter." University of Nottingham, U.K.

Blejer, M., and I. Guerrero. 1990. "The Impact of Macroeconomic Policies on Income Distribution: An Empirical Study of the Philippines." *Review of Economics and Statistics* 72 (3): 414-23.

Blinder, A. S. 2000. "Central-Bank Credibility: Why Do We Care? How Do We Build It?" *American Economic Review* 90 (5): 1421-31.

Bobeica, E., C. Nickel, E. Lis, and Y. Sun. 2017. "Demographics and Inflation." ECB Working Paper 2006, European Central Bank, Frankfurt am Main.

Bohl, M. T., and P. L. Siklos. 2018. "The Anatomy of Inflation: An Economic History Perspective." CAMA Working Paper 8/2018, Center for Applied Macroeconomic Analysis, Canberra, Australia.

Bordo, M. D., and A. Orphanides. 2013. *The Great Inflation: The Rebirth of Modern Central Banking.* Chicago: University of Chicago Press.

Borio, C., M. Erdem, A. Filardo, and B. Hofmann. 2015. "The Costs of Deflations: A Historical Perspective." *BIS Quarterly Review* 2015 (1): 31-54.

Borio, C. E., and A. J. Filardo. 2007. "Globalisation and Inflation: New Cross-Country Evidence on the Global Determinants of Domestic Inflation." BIS Working Paper 227, Bank for International Settlements, Basel.

Bowdler, C., and A. Malik. 2005. "Openness and Inflation Volatility: Cross-Country Evidence." Economics Papers 2005-W14, Economics Group, Nuffield College, University of Oxford.

Branch, W. A., and G. W. Evans. 2017. "Unstable Inflation Targets." *Journal of Money, Credit and Banking* 49 (4): 767-806.

Briault, C. 1995. "The Cost of Inflation." *Bank of England Quarterly Bulletin* 35 (1): 33-45.

Bruhn, M., and I. Love. 2014. "The Real Impact of Improved Access to Finance: Evidence from Mexico." *Journal of Finance* 69: 1347-76.

Bruno, M., and W. Easterly. 1998. "Inflation Crises and Long-Run Growth." *Journal of Monetary Economics* 41 (1): 3-26.

Bryan, M. F. 1997. "On the Origin and Evolution of the Word *Inflation*." Economic Commentary, Federal Reserve Bank of Cleveland, Cleveland, OH.

———. 2002. "Is It More Expensive, or Does It Just Cost More Money?" Economic Commentary, Federal Reserve Bank of Cleveland, Cleveland, OH.

———. 2018. "The Great Inflation." Federal Reserve History Series, Federal Reserve Bank of Atlanta, Atlanta, GA.

Bulíř, A. 2001. "Income Inequality: Does Inflation Matter?" *IMF Staff Papers* 48 (1): 139-59.

Bulíř, A., and A. Gulde. 1995. "Inflation and Income Distribution: Further Evidence on Empirical Links." IMF Working Paper 95/86, International Monetary Fund, Washington, DC.

Burdick, C., and T. Fisher. 2007. "Social Security Cost-of-Living Adjustments and the Consumer Price Index." *Social Security Bulletin* 67 (3): 73-88.

Burstein, A., C. Kurz, and L. Tesar. 2008. "Trade, Production Sharing and the International Transmission of Business Cycles." *Journal of Monetary Economics* 55 (4): 775-95.

Caceres, C., Y. Carrière-Swallow, and B. Gruss. 2016. "Global Financial Conditions and Monetary Policy Autonomy." IMF Working Paper 16/108, International Monetary Fund, Washington, DC.

Cachia, F. 2014. "Regional Food Price Inflation Transmission." Working Paper ESS/14-01, FAO Statistics Division, Food and Agriculture Organization of the United Nations, Rome.

Calvo, G. A. 1983. "Staggered Prices in a Utility-Maximizing Framework." *Journal of Monetary Economics* 12 (3): 383-98.

Calvo, G. A., and C. A. Végh. 1994. "Inflation Stabilization and Nominal Anchors." *Contemporary Economic Policy* XII (April): 35-45.

Camba-Méndez, G., J. A. García, and D. Rodriguez-Palenzuela. 2003. "Relevant Economic Issues Concerning the Optimal Rate of Inflation." Working Paper 278, European Central Bank, Frankfurt am Main.

———. 2017. "Inflation Targeting and Inflation Persistence: New Evidence from Fractional Integration and Cointegration." *Journal of Economics and Business* 92 (July-August): 45-62.

Canarella, G., and S. M. Miller. 2017. "Inflation Targeting and Inflation Persistence: New Evidence from Fractional Integration and Cointegration." *Journal of Economics and Business* 92 (July-August): 45-62.

Casiraghi, M., E. Gaiotti, L. Rodano, and A. Secchi. 2018. "A 'Reverse Robin Hood'? The Distributional Implications of Non-Standard Monetary Policy for Italian Households." *Journal of International Money and Finance* 85 (July): 215-35.

Catão, L., and M. Terrones. 2001. "Fiscal Deficits and Inflation—A New Look at the Emerging Market Evidence." IMF Working Paper 01/74, International Monetary Fund, Washington, DC.

———. 2005. "Fiscal Deficits and Inflation." *Journal of Monetary Economics* 52 (3): 529-54.

Cavallo, A. 2017. "Are Online and Offline Prices Similar? Evidence from Large Multi-Channel Retailers." *American Economic Review* 107 (1): 283–303.

Cavallo, A., and R. Rigobon. 2016. "The Billion Prices Project: Using Online Prices for Measurement and Research." *Journal of Economic Perspectives* 30 (2): 151-78.

Cecchetti, S. G., P. Hooper, B. C. Kasman, K. L. Schoenholtz, and M. Watson. 2007. "Understanding the Evolving Inflation Process." U.S. Monetary Policy Forum 2007, Washington, DC.

Cecchetti, S. G., and S. Krause. 2002. "Central Bank Structure, Policy Efficiency, and Macroeconomic Performance: Exploring Empirical Relationships." *Federal Reserve Bank of St. Louis Review* 84 (4): 47-60.

Charbonneau, K., A. Evans, S. Sarker, and L. Suchanek. 2017. "Digitalization and Inflation: A Review of the Literature." Staff Analytical Note 2017-20, Bank of Canada, Ottawa.

Chinn, M. D., and H. Ito. 2006. "What Matters for Financial Development? Capital Controls, Institutions, and Interactions." *Journal of Development Economics*, 81(1): 163-92.

———. 2017. "The Chinn-Ito Index—A de Jure Measure of Financial Openness." http://web.pdx.edu/~ito/Chinn-Ito_website.htm.

Chortareas, G., D. Stasavage, and G. Sterne. 2001. "Does It Pay to Be Transparent? International Evidence from Central Bank Forecasts." Bank of England Working Paper 143, London.

Ciccarelli, M., and B. Mojon. 2010. "Global Inflation." *Review of Economics and Statistics* 92 (3): 524-35.

Ciccarelli, M., and C. Osbat. 2017. "Low Inflation in the Euro Area: Causes and Consequences." Occasional Paper 181, European Central Bank, Frankfurt am Main.

Claessens, S. 2006. "Access to Financial Services: A Review of the Issues and Public Policy Objectives." *World Bank Research Observer* 21 (2): 207–40.

Clark, T. 2009. "Is the Great Moderation Over? An Empirical Analysis." *Federal Reserve Bank of Kansas City Economic Review* 94 (4): 5-42.

Clarida, R., J. Galí, and M. Gertler. 1999. "The Science of Monetary Policy: A New Keynesian Perspective." *Journal of Economic Literature* 37: 1661-1707.

———. 2000. "Monetary Policy Rules and Macroeconomic Stability: Evidence and Some Theory." *Quarterly Journal of Economics* 115 (1): 147-80.

Coibion, O., and Y. Gorodnichenko. 2012. "Why Are Target Interest Rate Changes So Persistent?" *American Economic Journal: Macroeconomics* 4 (4): 126-62.

Coibion, O., Y. Gorodnichenko, and J. F. Wieland. 2012. "The Optimal Inflation Rate in New Keynesian Models: Should Central Banks Raise Their Inflation Targets in Light of the Zero Lower Bound?" *Review of Economic Studies* 79 (4): 1371-1406.

Congressional Budget Office. 2017. Budget and Economic Data. https:// www.cbo.gov/about/products/budget-economic-data#8.

Contessi, S., L. Li, and P. De Pace. 2014. "An International Perspective on the Recent Behavior of Inflation." *Federal Reserve Bank of St. Louis Review* 96 (3): 267-94.

Cysne, R., W. Maldonado, and P. Monteiro. 2005. "Inflation and Income Inequality: A Shopping-Time Approach." *Journal of Development Economics* 78 (2): 516-28.

Datt, G., and M. Ravallion. 1998. "Why Have Some Indian States Done Better Than Others at Reducing Rural Poverty?" *Economica* 65 (257): 17-38.

Demertzis, M., and A. H. Hallett. 2007. "Central Bank Transparency in Theory and Practice." *Journal of Macroeconomics* 29 (4): 760-89.

Demirgüç-Kunt, A., L. Klapper, D. Singer, S. Ansar, and J. Hess. 2018. *The Global Findex Database 2017: Measuring Financial Inclusion and the Fintech Revolution.* Washington, DC: World Bank.

Dennis, R. 2006. "The Policy Preferences of the U.S. Federal Reserve." *Journal of Applied Econometrics* 21 (1): 55-77.

Diercks, A. 2017. "The Reader's Guide to Optimal Monetary Policy." Board of Governors of the Federal Reserve System, Washington, DC.

Dincer, N., and B. Eichengreen. 2010. "Central Bank Transparency: Causes, Consequences and Updates." *Theoretical Inquiries in Law* 11 (1): 75-123.

———. 2014. "Central Bank Transparency and Independence: Updates and New Measures." *International Journal of Central Banking* 10 (1): 189-259.

Doepke, M., and M. Schneider. 2006. "Inflation and the Redistribution of Nominal Wealth." *Journal of Political Economy* 114 (6): 1069-97.

Dollar, D., T. Kleineberg, and A. Kraay. 2016. "Growth Still Is Good for the Poor." *European Economic Review* 81(C): 68-85.

Dollar, D., and A. Kraay. 2004. "Trade, Growth, and Poverty." *Economic Journal* 114 (493): 22-49.

Domaç, I., K. Peters, and Y. Yuzefovichî. 2003. "Does the Exchange Rate Regime Matter for Inflation? Evidence from Transition Economies." Working Paper 0304, Central Bank of Turkey, Ankara.

Dong, W., J. Fudurich, and L. Suchanek. 2017. "Digital Transformation in the Service Sector: Insights from Consultations with Firms in Wholesale, Retail and Logistics." Staff Analytical Note No. 2017-19, Bank of Canada, Ottawa.

Dorich, J., N. Labelle St-Pierre, V. Lepetyuk, and R. Mendes. 2018. "Could a Higher Inflation Target Enhance Macroeconomic Stability?" BIS Working Paper 720, Bank for International Settlements, Basel.

Dornbusch, R. 1986. "Flexible Exchange Rates and Excess Capital Mobility." *Brookings Papers on Economic Activity* 1986 (1): 209-26.

Draghi, M. 2015. "Global and Domestic Inflation." Speech by Mario Draghi, President of the European Central Bank, Economic Club of New York.

Drukker, D., P. Gomis-Porqueras, and P. Hernandez-Verme. 2005. "Threshold Effects in the Relationship Between Inflation and Growth: A New Panel-Data Approach." MPRA Paper 38225, Munich Personal RePEc Archive, Munich.

Dynan, K. E., J. Skinner, and S. P. Zeldes. 2004. "Do the Rich Save More?" *Journal of Political Economy* 112 (2): 397-444.

Easterly, W., and S. Fischer. 2001. "Inflation and the Poor." *Journal of Money, Credit and Banking* 33 (2): 160–78.

Edwards, S. 1989. "Real Exchange Rates in the Developing Countries: Concepts and Measurement." NBER Working Paper 2950, National Bureau of Economic Research, Cambridge, MA.

Eggertsson, G. B., and M. Woodford. 2003. "The Zero Bound on Interest Rates and Optimal Monetary Policy." *Brookings Papers on Economic Activity* 1: 139-233.

Eggoh, J. C., and M. Khan. 2014. "On the Nonlinear Relationship Between Inflation and Economic Growth." *Research in Economics* 68 (2): 133-43.

Eickmeier, S., and M. Kühnlenz. 2013. "China's Role in Global Inflation Dynamics." Deutsche Bundesbank Discussion Paper 07/2013, Frankfurt am Main.

Eickmeier, S., and K. Pijnenburg. 2013. "The Global Dimension of Inflation—Evidence from Factor-Augmented Phillips Curves." *Oxford Bulletin of Economics and Statistics* 75 (1): 103-22.

End, M. N., M. S. J. A. Tapsoba, M. G. Terrier, and R. Duplay. 2015. "Deflation and Public Finances: Evidence from the Historical Records." IMF Working Paper 2015/176, International Monetary Fund, Washington, DC.

Erosa, A., and G. Ventura. 2002. "On Inflation as a Regressive Consumption Tax." *Journal of Monetary Economics* 49 (4): 761-95.

Espinoza, R., H. Leon, and A. Prasad. 2012. "When Should We Worry about Inflation?" *World Bank Economic Review* 26 (1): 100-27.

Fang, W. S., S. Miller, and C. S. Lee. 2012. "Short- and Long-Run Differences in the Treatment Effects of Inflation Targeting on Developed and Developing Countries." Department of Economics Working Paper 1003, University of Nevada, Las Vegas.

Federal Reserve Bank of San Francisco. 1999. *What Is Deflation and How Is It Different from Disinflation?* Federal Reserve Bank San Francisco, San Francisco, CA.

Feldstein, M. S. 1997. "The Costs and Benefits of Going from Low Inflation to Price Stability." NBER Working Paper 5469, National Bureau of Economic Research, Cambridge, MA.

———. 1999. *The Costs and Benefits of Price Stability.* Chicago: University of Chicago Press.

———. 2002. "The Role for Discretionary Fiscal Policy in a Low Interest Rate Environment." NBER Working Paper 9203, National Bureau of Economic Research, Cambridge, MA.

Fernández-Villaverde, J., P. A. Guerrón-Quintana, and J. Rubio-Ramírez. 2010. "Reading the Recent Monetary History of the U.S., 1959-2007." NBER Working Paper 15929, National Bureau of Economic Research, Cambridge, MA.

Ferreira, F., and J. Litchfield. 2001. "Education or Inflation? The Micro and Macroeconomics of the Brazilian Income Distribution during 1981-1995." *Cuadernos de Economía* 38 (114): 209-38.

Fischer, S. 1983. "Inflation and Growth." NBER Working Paper 1235, National Bureau of Economic Research, Cambridge, MA.

———. 1993. "The Role of Macroeconomic Factors in Growth." *Journal of Monetary Economics* 32 (3): 485-512.

———. 2001. "Exchange Rate Regimes: Is the Bipolar View Correct?" *Journal of Economic Perspectives* 15 (2): 3-24.

Fischer, S., and F. Modigliani. 1978. "Towards an Understanding of the Real Effects and Costs of Inflation." NBER Working Paper 303, National Bureau of Economic Research, Cambridge, MA.

Fischer, S., R. Sahay, and C. A. Végh. 1996. "Stabilization and Growth in Transition Economies: The Early Experience." *Journal of Economic Perspectives* 10 (2): 45-66.

———. 2002. "Modern Hyper- and High Inflations." NBER Working Paper 8930, National Bureau of Economic Research, Cambridge, MA.

Fisher, I. 1933. "The Debt-Deflation Theory of Great Depressions." *Econometrica* 1 (4): 337-57.

Frankel, J. A. 2007. "The Simple Geometry of Transmission and Stabilization in Closed and Open Economies: Comment." In *NBER International Seminar on Macroeconomics*. Cambridge, MA: National Bureau of Economic Research.

Friedman, M., and A. J. Schwartz. 1963. *A Monetary History of the United States, 1867-1960*. Princeton, NJ: Princeton University Press.

Fuhrer, J. C. 2009. "Inflation Persistence." FRB Boston Working Paper 09-14, Federal Reserve Bank of Boston, Boston, MA.

Furceri, D., P. Loungani, J. Simon, and S. Wachter. 2015. "Global Food Prices and Domestic Inflation: Some Cross-Country Evidence." IMF Working Paper 15/133, International Monetary Fund, Washington, DC.

Furceri, D., P. Loungani, and A. Zdzienicka. 2018. "The Effects of Monetary Policy Shocks on Inequality." *Journal of International Money and Finance* 85 (C): 168-86.

Galí, J. 2010. "The Return of the Wage Phillips Curve." NBER Working Paper 15758, National Bureau of Economic Research, Cambridge, MA.

Galli, R., and R. van der Hoeven. 2001. "Is Inflation Bad for Income Inequality: The Importance of the Initial Rate of Inflation." ILO Employment Paper 29, International Labour Organization, New York.

Gallup, J. L. 2012. "Is There a Kuznets Curve?" Portland State University Working Paper, Portland, OR.

Gamber, E. N., and J. H. Hung. 2001. "Has the Rise in Global Inflation Reduced U.S. Inflation in the 1990s?" *Economic Inquiry* 39 (1): 58-73.

Gerlach, S., and P. Tillmann. 2012. "Inflation Targeting and Inflation Persistence in Asia." *Journal of Asian Economics* 23 (4): 360-73.

Geronikolaou, G., E. Spyromitros, and P. Tsintzos. 2016. "Inflation Persistence: The Path of Labor Market Structural Reforms." *Economic Modelling* 58 (C): 317-22.

Ghosh, A. R., A.-M. Gulde, J. D. Ostry, and H. C. Wolf. 1997. "Does the Nominal Exchange Rate Regime Matter?" NBER Working Paper 5874, National Bureau of Economic Research, Cambridge, MA.

Gibson, J., T. Le, and B. Kim. 2017. "Prices, Engel Curves, and Time-Space Deflation: Impacts on Poverty and Inequality in Vietnam." *World Bank Economic Review* 31 (2): 504-30.

Gilbert, R. A. 1985. "Operating Procedures for Conducting Monetary Policy." *Federal Reserve Bank of St. Louis Review* 67 (2): 13-21.

Gonçalves, C. E. S., and J. M. Salles. 2008. "Inflation Targeting in Emerging Economies: What Do the Data Say?" *Journal of Development Economics* 85 (1-2): 312-18.

Goodfriend, M. 1983. "Discount Window Borrowing, Monetary Policy, and the Post-October 6, 1979 Federal Reserve Operating Procedure." *Journal of Monetary Economics* 12 (3): 343-56.

———. 2003. "The Phases of U.S. Monetary Policy: 1987-2001." In *Central Banking, Monetary Theory and Practice: Essays in Honour of Charles Goodhart*, edited by P. Mizen. Cheltenham, U.K.: Edward Elgar Publishing.

Goolsbee, A. D., and P. J. Klenow. 2018. "Internet Rising, Prices Falling: Measuring Inflation in a World of E-Commerce." *AEA Papers and Proceedings* 108: 488-92.

Gorodnichenko, Y., V. Sheremirov, and O. Talavera. 2016. "Price Setting in Online Markets: Does It Click?" NBER Working Paper 20819, National Bureau of Economic Research, Cambridge, MA.

Gorodnichenko, Y., and O. Talavera. 2017. "Price Setting in Online Markets: Basic Facts, International Comparisons, and Cross-Border Integration." *The American Economic Review* 107 (1): 249–82.

Granato, J., M. Lo, and M. C. Sunny Wong. 2006. "Testing Monetary Policy Intentions in Open Economies." *Southern Economic Journal* 72 (3): 730-746.

Greenwood, J., Z. Hercowitz, and P. Krusell. 1997. "Long-Run Implications of Investment-Specific Technological Change." *The American Economic Review* 87 (3): 342-362.

Greville, R. P., and M. Reddell. 1990. "The Costs of Inflation." *Reserve Bank of New Zealand Bulletin* 53 (1): 37-51.

Gruben, W. C., and D. McLeod. 2002. "Capital Account Liberalization and Inflation." *Economics Letters* 77 (2): 221-225.

Guerrieri, L., G. Gust, and D. López-Salido, 2010. "International Competition and Inflation: A New Keynesian Perspective." *American Economic Journal: Macroeconomics* 2 (4): 247-280.

Hakkio, C. C. 2013. "The Great Moderation—1982-2007." Federal Reserve Bank of Kansas City, Kansas City, MO.

Hobijn, B., and D. Lagakos. 2005. "Inflation Inequality in the United States." *Review of Income and Wealth* 51: 581-606.

Iakova, D. 2007. "Flattening of the Phillips Curve: Implications for Monetary Policy." IMF Working Paper 07/76, International Monetary Fund, Washington, DC.

Ibarra, R., and D. Trupkin. 2011. "The Relationship between Inflation and Growth: A Panel Smooth Transition Regression Approach for Developed and Developing Countries." Banco Central del Uruguay Working Paper 6, Central Bank of Chile, Santiago.

———. 2016. ""Reexamining the Relationship Between Inflation and Growth: Do Institutions Matter in Developing Countries?"" *Economic Modelling* 52 (PB): 332-51.

Ihrig, J., S. B. Kamin, D. Lindner, and J. Marquez. 2010. "Some Simple Tests of the Globalization and Inflation Hypothesis." *International Finance* 13 (3): 343-75.

Imam, P., 2013. "Demographic Shift and the Financial Sector Stability: The Case of Japan." *Journal of Population Ageing* 6 (4): 269-303.

IMF (International Monetary Fund). 2001. "The Decline of Inflation in Emerging Markets: Can It Be Maintained?" Chapter in *World Economic Outlook*. Washington, DC: International Monetary Fund.

———. 2006. "How Has Globalization Affected Inflation?" In *World Economic Outlook*. Washington, DC: International Monetary Fund.

———. 2011a. *New Growth Drivers for Low-Income Countries: The Role of BRICs*." Washington, DC: International Monetary Fund.

———. 2011b. *World Economic Outlook: Slowing Growth, Rising Risks*. October. Washington, DC: International Monetary Fund.

———. 2015. *Evolving Monetary Policy Frameworks in Low-Income and Other Developing Countries*. Washington, DC: International Monetary Fund.

———. 2016. "Global Disinflation in an Era of Constrained Monetary Policy." In *World Economic Outlook: Subdued Demand: Symptoms and Remedies*. Washington, DC: International Monetary Fund.

Inoue, T., C. Shimizu, K. G. Nishimura, and Y. Deng. 2016. "Aging, Inflation and Property Prices." Working Paper, University of Tokyo.

Ivanic, M., and W. Martin. 2008. "Implications of Higher Global Food Prices for Poverty in Low-Income Countries." Policy Research Working Paper 4594, World Bank, Washington, DC.

Jantti, M., and S. Jenkins. 2010. "The Impact of Macroeconomic Conditions on Income Inequality." *Journal of Economic Inequality* 8 (2): 221-40.

Jaumotte, F., and H. Morsy. 2012. "Determinants of Inflation in the Euro Area: The Role of Labor and Product Market Institutions." IMF Working Paper 12/37, International Monetary Fund, Washington, DC.

Judson, R., and A. Orphanides. 1999. "Inflation, Volatility and Growth." *International Finance* 2 (1): 117-38.

Juselius, M., and E. Takáts. 2015. "Can Demography Affect Inflation and Monetary Policy?" BIS Working Paper No. 485, Bank for International Settlements, Basel.

Khan, L. M. 1980. "Bargaining Power, Search Theory and the Phillips Curve." *Cambridge Journal of Economics* 4 (3): 233-44.

Khan, M., and A. Senhadji. 2001. "Threshold Effects in the Relationship between Inflation and Growth." *IMF Staff Papers* 48 (1): 1-21.

Kahn, S. 1997. "Evidence of Nominal Wage Stickiness from Microdata." *American Economic Review* 87 (5): 993-1008.

Kaplan, G., and S. Schulhofer-Wohl. 2017. "Inflation at the Household Level." *Journal of Monetary Economics* 91 (C): 19-38.

Katagiri, M. 2018. "Economic Consequences of Population Aging in Japan: Effects through Changes in Demand Structure." *Singapore Economic Review:* 1-23.

Khan, M., and A. Senhadji. 2001. "Threshold Effects in the Relationship between Inflation and Growth." IMF Staff Papers 48 (1): 1-21.

Kiley, M., and J. Roberts. 2017. "Monetary Policy in a Low Interest Rate World." *Brookings Papers on Economic Activity* 48 (1): 317-96.

Kohn, D. L. 2006. "The Effects of Globalization on Inflation and Their Implications for Monetary Policy." Remarks at Federal Reserve Bank of Boston's 51st Economic Conference, Chatham, MA.

Kremer, S., A. Bick, and D. Nautz. 2013. "Inflation and Growth: New Evidence from a Dynamic Panel Threshold Analysis." *Empirical Economics* 44 (2): 861-78.

Krugman, P. 2014. "Inflation Targets Reconsidered." In *ECB Forum on Central Banking, Conference Proceedings,* 110–122. Frankfurt am Main: European Central Bank.

Kuznets, S. 1955. "Economic Growth and Income Inequality." *American Economic Review* 45 (1): 1-28.

Kwon, G., L. McFarlane, and W. Robinson. 2009. "Public Debt, Money Supply, and Inflation: A Cross-Country Study." *IMF Staff Papers* 56 (3): 476-515.

Laidler, D., and M. Parkin. 1975. "Inflation: A Survey." *Economic Journal* 85 (345): 741-809.

Lane, P. R. 1997. "Inflation in Open Economies." *Journal of International Economics* 42 (3-4): 327-47.

Levell, P., and Z. Oldfield. 2011. *The Spending Patterns and Inflation Experience of Low-Income Households over the Past Decade.* London: Institute for Fiscal Studies.

Levin, A. T., F. M. Natalucci, and J. M. Piger. 2004. "The Macroeconomic Effects of Inflation Targeting." *Federal Reserve Bank of St. Louis Review* 86 (4): 51-80.

Levin, A. T., and J. M. Piger. 2006. "Is Inflation Persistence Intrinsic in Industrial Economies?" http://pages.uoregon.edu/jpiger/research/working-papers/levin-and-piger_is-inflatio.pdf.

Lin, H.-Y., and H.-P. Chu. 2013. "Are Fiscal Deficits Inflationary?" *Journal of International Money and Finance* 32 (C): 214-33.

Lin, S., and H. Ye. 2007. "Does Inflation Targeting Really Make a Difference? Evaluating the Treatment Effect of Inflation Targeting in Seven Industrial Countries." *Journal of Monetary Economics* 54 (8): 2521-33.

———. 2009. "Does Inflation Targeting Make a Difference in Developing Countries?" *Journal of Development Economics* 89 (1): 118-23.

Logue, D. E., and T. D. Willett. 1976. "A Note on the Relation between the Rate and Variability of Inflation." *Economica* 43 (17): 151-58.

Lombardo, G., and F. Ravenna. 2014. "Openness and Optimal Monetary Policy." *Journal of International Economics* 93 (1): 153-72.

Lopez-Villavicencio, A., and V. Mignon. 2011. "On the Impact of Inflation on Output Growth: Does the Level of Inflation Matter?" *Journal of Macroeconomics* 33 (3): 455-64.

Lucas, R. E. 1972. "Expectations and the Neutrality of Money." *Journal of Economic Theory* 4 (2): 103-24.

Lünnemann, P., and T. Mathä. 2005. "Regulated and Services' Prices and Inflation Kohn, D. L. 2006. "The Effects of Globalization on Inflation and Their Implications for Monetary Policy." Remarks at Federal Reserve Bank of Boston's 51st Economic Conference, Chatham, MA.

Kremer, S., A. Bick, and D. Nautz. 2013. "Inflation and Growth: New Evidence from a Dynamic Panel Threshold Analysis." *Empirical Economics* 44 (2): 861-78.

Krugman, P. 2014. "Inflation Targets Reconsidered." In *ECB Forum on Central Banking, Conference Proceedings*, 110–122. Frankfurt am Main: European Central Bank.

Kuznets, S. 1955. "Economic Growth and Income Inequality." *American Economic Review* 45 (1): 1-28.

Kwon, G., L. McFarlane, and W. Robinson. 2009. "Public Debt, Money Supply, and Inflation: A Cross-Country Study." *IMF Staff Papers* 56 (3): 476-515.

Laidler, D., and M. Parkin. 1975. "Inflation: A Survey." *Economic Journal* 85 (345): 741–809.

Lane, P. R. 1997. "Inflation in Open Economies." *Journal of International Economics* 42 (3-4): 327-47.

Levell, P., and Z. Oldfield. 2011. *The Spending Patterns and Inflation Experience of Low-Income Households over the Past Decade.* London: Institute for Fiscal Studies.

Levin, A. T., F. M. Natalucci, and J. M. Piger. 2004. "The Macroeconomic Effects of Inflation Targeting." *Federal Reserve Bank of St. Louis Review* 86 (4): 51-80.

Levin, A. T., and J. M. Piger. 2006. "Is Inflation Persistence Intrinsic in Industrial Economies?" http://pages.uoregon.edu/jpiger/research/working-papers/levin-and-piger_is-inflatio.pdf.

Lin, H.-Y., and H.-P. Chu. 2013. "Are Fiscal Deficits Inflationary?" *Journal of International Money and Finance* 32 (C): 214-33.

Lin, S., and H. Ye. 2007. "Does Inflation Targeting Really Make a Difference? Evaluating the Treatment Effect of Inflation Targeting in Seven Industrial Countries." *Journal of Monetary Economics* 54 (8): 2521-33.

———. 2009. "Does Inflation Targeting Make a Difference in Developing Countries?" *Journal of Development Economics* 89 (1): 118-23.

Logue, D. E., and T. D. Willett. 1976. "A Note on the Relation between the Rate and Variability of Inflation." *Economica* 43 (17): 151-58.

Lombardo, G., and F. Ravenna. 2014. "Openness and Optimal Monetary Policy." *Journal of International Economics* 93 (1): 153-72.

Lopez-Villavicencio, A., and V. Mignon. 2011. “On the Impact of Inflation on Output Growth: Does the Level of Inflation Matter?” *Journal of Macroeconomics* 33 (3): 455-64.

Lucas, R. E. 1972. “Expectations and the Neutrality of Money.” *Journal of Economic Theory* 4 (2): 103-24.

Lünnemann, P., and T. Mathä. 2005. "Regulated and Services' Prices and Inflation Persistence." Working Paper 466, European Central Bank, Frankfurt am Main.

Maestri, V., and A. Roventini. 2012. “Inequality and Macroeconomic Factors: A Timeseries Analysis for a Set of OECD Countries.” University of Verona Working Paper 34, Verona, Italy.

Mankiw, N. G., and R. Reis. 2002. “Sticky Information versus Sticky Prices: A Proposal to Replace the New Keynesian Phillips Curve.” *Quarterly Journal of Economics* 117 (4): 1295-1328.

McGranahan, L., and A. Paulson. 2006. “Constructing the Chicago Fed Income Based Economic Index–Consumer Price Index: Inflation Experiences by Demographic Group: 1983-2005.” Working Paper 2005-20, Federal Reserve Bank of Chicago, Chicago, IL.

Meltzer, A. H. 2005. “Origins of the Great Inflation.” *Federal Reserve Bank of St. Louis Review* (March/April): 145-76.

Milani, F. 2012. “Has Globalization Transformed U.S. Macroeconomic Dynamics?” *Macroeconomic Dynamics* 16 (2): 204-29.

Milanovic, B. 1994. “Determinants of Cross-Country Income Inequality: An Augmented Kuznets Hypothesis.” Policy Research Working Paper 1246, World Bank, Washington, DC.

Miles, D., U. Panizza, R. Reis, and Á. Ubide. 2017. *And Yet It Moves: Inflation and the Great Recession*. Geneva: International Center for Monetary and Banking Studies.

Minarik, J. 1979. “The Size Distribution of Income during Inflation.” *Review of Income and Wealth* 25 (4): 377-92.

Mishkin, F. S. 2000. “Inflation Targeting in Emerging-Market Countries.” *American Economic Review* 90 (2): 105-09.

———. 2007. “Inflation Dynamics.” *International Finance* 10 (3): 317-34.

———. 2008a. “Can Inflation Targeting Work in Emerging Market Countries?” In *Money, Crises, and Transition: Essays in Honor of Guillermo A. Calvo*, edited by C. M. Reinhart, C. A. Vegh, and A. Velasco. MIT Press: Cambridge, MA.

———. 2008b. “Does Stabilizing Inflation Contribute to Stabilizing Economic Activity?” NBER Working Paper 13970, National Bureau of Economic Research, Cambridge, MA.

———. 2018. “Rethinking the Inflation Target.” Presentation at Brookings Conference, “Should the Fed Stick with the 2 Percent Inflation Target or Rethink It?” Brookings Institution, Washington, DC.

Mishkin, F., and K. Schmidt-Hebbel. 2007. “Does Inflation Targeting Make a Difference?” NBER Working Paper 12876, National Bureau of Economic Research, Cambridge, MA.

Mishra, P., and P. Montiel. 2013. “How Effective Is Monetary Transmission in Low-Income Countries? A Survey of the Empirical Evidence.” *Economic Systems* 37 (2): 187-216.

Mishra, P., P. J. Montiel, and A. Spilimbergo. 2012. "Monetary Transmission in Low-Income Countries: Effectiveness and Policy Implications." *IMF Economic Review* 60 (2): 270-302.

Moghadam, R., R. Teja, and P. Berkmen. 2014. "Euro Area—'Deflation' Versus 'Lowflation.'" https://blogs.imf.org/2014/03/04/euro-area-deflation-versus- lowflation/.

Monnin, P. 2014. "Inflation and Income Inequality in Developed Economies." Working Paper 1, Centre for Economic Performance, London School of Economics.

Moreno, R. 2001. "Pegging and Stabilization Policy in Developing Countries." *Economic Review of the Federal Reserve Bank of San Francisco* 12 (99): 17-29.

Mulligan, C., and X. Sala-i-Martin. 2000. "Measuring Aggregate Human Capital." *Journal of Economic Growth* 5 (3): 215-52.

Mussa, M., P. Masson, A. Swoboda, E. Jadresic, P. Mauro, and A. Berg. 2000. "Exchange Rate Regimes in an Increasingly Integrated World Economy." IMF Occasional Paper 193, International Monetary Fund, Washington, DC.

Ndoricimpa, A. 2017. "Threshold Effects of Inflation on Economic Growth in Africa: Evidence from a Dynamic Panel Threshold Regression." Working Paper 249, African Development Bank, Abidjan, Côte d'Ivoire.

Nguyen, A. D. M., J. Dridi, F. Unsal, and O. H. Williams. 2017. "On the Drivers of Inflation in Sub-Saharan Africa." *International Economics* 151 (October): 71-84.

Omay, T., and E. Öznur Kan. 2010. "Re-examining the Threshold Effects in the Inflation-Growth Nexus with Cross-Sectionally Dependent Non-Linear Panel: Evidence from Six Industrialized Economies." *Economic Modelling* 27 (5): 996-1005.

Oosthuizen, M. 2007. "Consumer Price Inflation across the Income Distribution in South Africa." DPRU Working Paper 07-129, Development Policy Research Unit, University of Cape Town, South Africa.

Orhun, Y., and M. Palazzolo. 2018. "Frugality Is Hard to Afford." Ross School of Business Paper 1309, Kilts Center for Marketing at Chicago Booth–Nielsen Dataset Paper Series 2-031.

Osorio, C., and D. F. Unsal. 2013. "Inflation Dynamics in Asia: Causes, Changes, and Spillovers from China." *Journal of Asian Economics* 24 (1): 26-40.

Owyang, M.T., J. Piger and H. J. Wall. 2005. "Business Cycle Phases in US States." *Review of Economics and Statistics* 87(4): 604-616.

Owyang, M. T., and H. J. Wall. 2006. "Regional VARs and the Channels of Monetary Policy." Federal Reserve Bank of St. Louis Working Paper 2006-002A, Federal Reserve Bank of St. Louis, St. Louis, MO.

Palmer, J., and M. Barth. 1977. "The Distributional Effects of Inflation and Higher Unemployment." In *Improving Measures of Economic Well-Being,* edited by M. Moon and E. Smolensky. New York: Academic Press.

Parker, S. 1998. "Income Inequality and the Business Cycle: A Survey of Evidence and Some New Results." *Journal of Post Keynesian Economics* 21 (2): 201-25.

Phillips, A. W. 1958. "The Relationship between Unemployment and the Rate of Change of Money Wages in the United Kingdom, 1861-1957." *Economica* 25 (100): 283-99.

Piketty, T. 2014. *Capital in the Twenty-First Century*. Cambridge, MA: Harvard University Press.

Poole, W. 1982. "Federal Reserve Operating Procedures: A Survey and Evaluation of the Historical Record Since October 1979." *Journal of Money, Credit and Banking* 14 (4): 575-96.

Ravallion, M. 2012. "Why Don't We See Poverty Convergence?" *American Economic Review* 102 (1): 504-23.

Razîn, A., and A. Binyamini. 2007. "Flattening of the Short-Run Trade-Off between Inflation and Domestic Activity: The Analytics of the Effects of Globalization." Kiel Working Paper 1363, Kiel Institute for the World Economy, Kiel, Germany.

Reifschneider, D., and J. C. Williams. 2000. "Three Lessons for Monetary Policy in a Low-Inflation Era." *Journal of Money, Credit and Banking* 32 (4-2): 936-66.

Roberts, J. M. 2006. "Monetary Policy and Inflation Dynamics." *International Journal of Central Banking* 2 (3): 193-23.

Rodrik, D. 1990. "Premature Liberalization, Incomplete Stabilization: The Ozal Decade in Turkey." NBER Working Paper 3300, National Bureau of Economic Research, Cambridge, MA.

Rogoff, K. 2003. "Globalization and Global Disinflation." *Federal Reserve Bank of Kansas City Economic Review* 88 (4): 45-78.

———. 2015. "Costs and Benefits of Phasing Out Paper Currency." In *NBER Macroeconomics Annual 2014*, edited by J. A. Parker and M. Woodford. Chicago: University of Chicago Press.

Romer, C. D., and D. H. Romer. 1997. "Institutions for Monetary Stability." In *Reducing Inflation: Motivation and Strategy*, edited by C. D. Romer and D. H. Romer. Chicago: University of Chicago Press.

———. 1998. "Monetary Policy and the Well-Being of the Poor." NBER Working Paper 6793, National Bureau of Economic Research, Cambridge, MA.

Romer, D. 1993. "Openness and Inflation: Theory and Evidence." *Quarterly Journal of Economics* 108 (4): 869-903.

Roncaglia de Carvalho, A. 2014. "Structural Change, De-Industrialization and Inflation Inertia in Brazil." https://ssrn.com/abstract=2509254.

Rose, A. K. 2007. "A Stable International Monetary System Emerges: Inflation Targeting Is Bretton Woods, Reversed." *Journal of International Money and Finance* 26 (5): 663-81.

———. 2011. "Exchange Rate Regimes in the Modern Era: Fixed, Floating, and Flaky." *Journal of Economic Literature* 49 (3): 652-72.

Rotemberg, J. J. 1982. "Sticky Prices in the United States." *Journal of Political Economy* 90 (6): 1187-1211.

Rotemberg, J. J., and M. Woodford. 1997. "An Optimization-Based Econometric Framework for the Evaluation of Monetary Policy." In *NBER Macroeconomics Annual 1997,* Vol. 12, edited by B. S. Bernanke and J. Rotemberg. Cambridge, MA: MIT Press.

Rumler, F. 2007. "Estimates of the Open Economy New Keynesian Phillips Curve for Euro Area Countries." *Open Economies Review* 18 (4): 427-51.

Sargent, T., and N. Wallace. 1981. "Some Unpleasant Monetarist Arithmetic." *Federal Reserve Bank of Minneapolis Quarterly Review* 5 (3): 1-17.

Sbordone, A. M. 2007. "Globalization and Inflation Dynamics: The Impact of Increased Competition." NBER Working Paper 13556, National Bureau of Economic Research, Cambridge, MA.

Schembri, L. 2017. "Getting to the Core of Inflation." Remarks at the Department of Economics, Western University, London, Ontario, February 9.

Schmitt-Grohé, S., and M. Uribe. 2010. "The Optimal Rate of Inflation." In *Handbook of Monetary Economics* 1 (3): 653-722.

Schwartz, A. J. 1995. "Why Financial Stability Depends on Price Stability." *Economic Affairs* 15 (4): 21-25.

Shambaugh, J. C. 2004. "The Effect of Fixed Exchange Rates on Monetary Policy." *Quarterly Journal of Economics* 119 (1): 301-52.

———. 2016. *China's Future.* Malden, MA: Polity Press.

Siami-Namini, S., and D. Hudson. 2017. "Inflation and Income Inequality in Developed and Developing Countries." Unpublished, Texas Tech University, Lubbock, Texas.

Siegel, J. J. 1994. *Stocks for the Long Run: A Guide to Selecting Markets for Long-term Growth.* Burr Ridge, IL: Irwin Professional Publishing.

Siklos, P. L. 2003. "Assessing the Impact of Changes in Transparency and Accountability at the Bank of Canada." *Canadian Public Policy / Analyse de Politiques* 29 (3): 279-99.

Sims, C. A., and T. Zha. 1998. "Does Monetary Policy Generate Recessions?" Federal Reserve Bank of Atlanta Working Paper 98-12, Federal Reserve Bank of Atlanta, Atlanta, GA.

Söderström, U. 2005. "Targeting Inflation with a Role for Money." *Economica* 72 (288): 577-96.

Stock, J. H., and M. W. Watson. 2003. "Has the Business Cycle Changed and Why?" In *NBER Macroeconomics Annual 2002,* Vol. 17, edited by M. Gertler and K. Rogoff. Cambridge, MA: MIT Press.

———. 2007. "Why Has U.S. Inflation Become Harder to Forecast?" *Journal of Money, Credit and Banking* 39 (1): 3-33.

———. 2010. "Modeling Inflation after the Crisis." NBER Working Paper 16488, National Bureau of Economic Research, Cambridge, MA.

———. 2016. "Core Inflation and Trend Inflation." *Review of Economics and Statistics* 98 (4): 770-84.

Svensson, L. E. O. 2003. "Escaping from a Liquidity Trap and Deflation: The Foolproof Way and Others." *Journal of Economic Perspectives* 17 (4): 145-66.

Szafranek, K. 2017. "Flattening of the New Keynesian Phillips Curve: Evidence for an Emerging, Small Open Economy." *Economic Modelling* 63 (C): 334-48.

Taylor, J. B. 1979. "Staggered Wage Setting in the Macro Model." *American Economic Review* 69 (2): 108-13.

———. 1980. "Aggregate Dynamics and Staggered Contracts." *Journal of Political Economy* 88 (1): 1-23.

———. 2000. "Low Inflation, Pass-Through, and the Pricing Power of Firms." *European Economic Review* 44 (7): 1389-1408.

———. 2014. "Inflation Targeting in Emerging Markets: The Global Experience." Speech at the Conference on Fourteen Years of Inflation Targeting in South Africa and the Challenge of a Changing Mandate, South African Reserve Bank, Pretoria.

Temple, J. 2002. "Inflation and Growth: Stories Short and Tall." *Journal of Economic Surveys* 14 (4): 395-426.

Terra, C. T. 1998. "Openness and Inflation: A New Assessment." *Quarterly Journal of Economics* 113 (2): 641-48.

Thalassinos, E., E. Ugurlu, and Y. Muratoğlu. 2012. "Income Inequality and Inflation in the EU." *European Research Studies* XV (1): 127-40.

Thanh, S. D. 2015. "Threshold Effects of Inflation on Growth in the ASEAN-5 Countries: A Panel Smooth Transition Regression Approach." *Journal of Economics, Finance and Administrative Science* 20 (38): 41-48.

Thornton, D. L. 2004. "When Did the FOMC Begin Targeting the Federal Funds Rate? What the Verbatim Transcripts Tell Us." Working Paper 2004-015B, Federal Reserve Bank of St. Louis, St. Louis, MO.

Uhlig, H. 2005. "What Are the Effects of Monetary Policy on Output? Results from an Agnostic Identification Procedure." *Journal of Monetary Economics* 52 (2): 381-419.

van der Cruijsen, C., and M. Demertzis. 2007. "The Impact of Central Bank Transparency on Inflation Expectations." *European Journal of Political Economy* 23 (1): 51-66.

Vaona, A., and S. Schiavo. 2007. "Nonparametric and Semiparametric Evidence on the Long-Run Effects of Inflation on Growth." *Economics Letters* 94 (3): 452-58.

Vinayagathasan, T. 2013. "Inflation and Economic Growth: A Dynamic Panel Threshold Analysis for Asian Economies." *Journal of Asian Economics* 26 (June): 31-41.

Vuletin, G., and L. Zhu. 2011. "Replacing a 'Disobedient' Central Bank Governor with a 'Docile' One: A Novel Measure of Central Bank Independence and Its Effect on Inflation." *Journal of Money, Credit and Banking* 43 (6): 1185-1215.

Weber, C. S. 2016. "Central Bank Transparency and Inflation (Volatility)—New Evidence." *International Economics and Economic Policy* 15: 21-67.

Weichenrieder, A., and E. Gürer. 2018. "Pro-Rich Inflation in Europe: Implications for the Measurement of Inequality." SAFE Working Paper 209, Sustainable Architecture for Finance in Europe, Frankfurt.

Weidmann, J. 2013. "Who Calls the Shots? The Problem of Fiscal Dominance." Speech at the BdF-BBk Macroeconomics and Finance Conference. Deutsche Bundesbank Eurosystem, Paris.

White, W. R. 2006. "Is Price Stability Enough?" BIS Working Paper 205, Bank for International Settlements, Basel.

Woodford, M. 2003. *Interest and Prices: Foundations of a Theory of Monetary Policy.* Princeton, NJ: Princeton University Press.

World Bank. 2010. *Global Monitoring Report 2010: The MDGs after the Crisis.* Washington, DC: World Bank.

———. 2015. *Global Economic Prospects: Having Fiscal Space and Using It.* January. Washington, DC: World Bank.

———. 2016. *Global Economic Prospects: Spillovers Amid Weak Growth.* January. Washington, DC: World Bank.

———. 2017a. *World Development Indicators 2017.* Washington, DC: World Bank.

———. 2017b. "World Integrated Trade Solution." https://wits.worldbank.org/.

Wright, J. 2011. "Term Premia and Inflation Uncertainty: Empirical Evidence from an International Panel Dataset." *American Economic Review* 101 (4): 1514-34.

Yellen, J. 2006. "Monetary Policy in a Global Environment." FRBSF Economic Letter. June. Speech at the Euro and the Dollar in a Globalized Economy Conference, U.C. Santa Cruz, Santa Cruz, CA.

Yoon, J. W., J. Kim, and J. Lee. 2014. "Impact of Demographic Changes on Inflation and the Macroeconomy." IMF Working Paper 14/210, International Monetary Fund, Washington, DC.

Zhang, C. 2015. "The Effect of Globalization on Inflation in New Emerging Markets." *Emerging Markets Finance and Trade* 51 (5): 1021-33.

CHAPTER 2

Understanding Global Inflation Synchronization

Inflation movements have become increasingly synchronized internationally over time: a common global factor accounts for about 22 percent of changes in national annual inflation rates in the period since 2001. Inflation synchronization has also become more broad-based: while it was previously much more pronounced among advanced economies than among emerging market and developing economies, it has become substantial in both groups over the past two decades. In addition, inflation synchronization has become significant across all inflation measures since 2001, whereas it was previously prominent only for inflation measures that included mostly tradable goods. Greater inflation synchronization over time has coincided with improvements in economic policy institutions in many countries, stronger global trade linkages, and greater similarity of monetary policy frameworks that trigger similar policy responses.

Introduction

Inflation has recently appeared to move in tandem among countries around the globe. As documented in the previous chapter, inflation and inflation volatility have trended downward in advanced economies since the mid-1980s and in emerging market and developing economies (EMDEs) since the mid-1990s, regardless of the price index examined. A wide range of structural factors have contributed to declining inflation in recent decades. These factors appear to have depressed inflation and changed the responsiveness of inflation to global and domestic shocks.

This chapter expands on this analysis by exploring the extent to which global and group-specific factors have driven movements in national inflation rates. A growing number of studies provide evidence on highly synchronized national inflation rates (Hakkio 2009; Cicarelli and Mojon 2010; Auer, Levchenko, and Sauré 2017). Some of these also examine the extent of synchronization in other real and nominal variables, in addition to inflation (Mumtaz, Simonelli, and Surico 2011).

In theory, a wide range of factors could be responsible for the global synchronization of inflation, such as common shocks, similar policy responses, and structural features of economies, including openness to international trade and financial flows. Early studies often highlighted the contribution of

---

Note: This chapter was prepared by Jongrim Ha, M. Ayhan Kose, Franziska Ohnsorge, and Filiz Unsal.

synchronized or coordinated monetary policies as a major source of inflation comovement, especially among advanced economies (Clarida, Gali, and Gertler 2002; Rogoff 2003). More recent work has emphasized the roles of international spillovers of technology and increased trade integration through global value chains (Henriksen, Kydland, and Šustek 2013; Auer, Borio, and Filardo 2017).

This chapter expands empirical research on the topic by addressing the following questions:

- How has inflation synchronization among countries evolved over the past four to five decades?
- Which goods and price indexes have been associated with greater inflation synchronization?
- What country characteristics have been associated with greater inflation synchronization?

To answer these questions, the chapter examines synchronization in inflation using a dynamic factor model that allows the estimation of latent global and group-specific factors. In a unified framework, these factors capture commonalities in multiple measures of inflation in a large, balanced sample of countries (25 advanced economies and 74 EMDEs) over a long period (1970-2017). The chapter makes four unique contributions to the literature.

First, it systematically explores the evolution of inflation synchronization among many countries and over time. It identifies a truly global inflation factor that captures common movements in inflation in a large sample of countries, including many EMDEs. This contrasts with earlier studies that typically included only advanced economies (Box 2.1). In this global sample, the evidence of increased global inflation synchronization since 2001 is unambiguous, whereas some earlier studies based on advanced economy samples have found no such increase.

Second, in recognition of differences in economic structures and policy frameworks between EMDEs and advanced economies, the model explicitly allows for the role of an EMDE inflation factor that is distinct from an advanced economy factor; the focus in the literature thus far has been on global factors.

Third, the chapter examines commonalities and differences in inflation synchronization among a wide range of inflation measures. By choosing price indexes that differ in their tradables content, this allows for a more precise interpretation of the global factor and broadens the evidence for increased inflation synchronization since 2001.

BOX 2.1 Global inflation synchronization: A review

This box summarizes the evidence in the literature that inflation has become highly synchronized internationally over time. Global inflation synchronization depends on the frequency of common shocks; the strength of cross-border inflation spillovers, especially from major economies; the openness of economies to international trade and financial flows; and the extent to which there are similar policy frameworks among countries, generating similar policy responses. It is therefore not surprising that there is evidence of an increase in inflation synchronization in recent decades, since this has been a period of strengthening global economic linkages, increasingly developed and internationally integrated financial markets, and a growing prevalence of monetary policy frameworks focused on the objective of low and stable inflation.

Using a wide range of methodologies, a large literature has studied various aspects of inflation synchronization across countries and its evolution over time. This box provides a brief summary of what this literature says on the following questions:

- How has global inflation synchronization evolved over time?
- Which factors have contributed to global inflation synchronization?

How has global inflation synchronization evolved?

Many studies have documented the high degree of inflation synchronization in recent decades, mostly, but not exclusively, in advanced economies.[1] Some of these studies also report that the degree of synchronization has increased over the past three decades.

Existence of a global inflation factor. Several studies have documented that a global factor has accounted for a substantial proportion—ranging from 20 to 51 percent—of inflation variation among various groups of advanced economies, with the estimated contribution differing somewhat by inflation measure, time period, methodology, and sample composition (Table A.2.1.1 in Annex 2.1). In a well-known study, Ciccarelli and Mojon (2010) extract a common global factor from the consumer price index (CPI) inflation of 22 Organisation for Economic Co-operation and Development (OECD) countries over 1960-2008. They find that the global factor accounts for almost 37 percent of the variance of national

[1] The majority of studies on inflation synchronization employ variants of dynamic factor models developed by Stock and Watson (1999); Forni et al. (2005); and Kose, Otrok, and Whiteman (2003).

BOX 2.1 Global inflation synchronization: A review *(continued)*

FIGURE 2.1.1 Contribution of the global factor to inflation: Literature

The estimates of the contribution of the global factor presented in this chapter are in the range of those reported elsewhere in the literature, although at the lower end of the range.

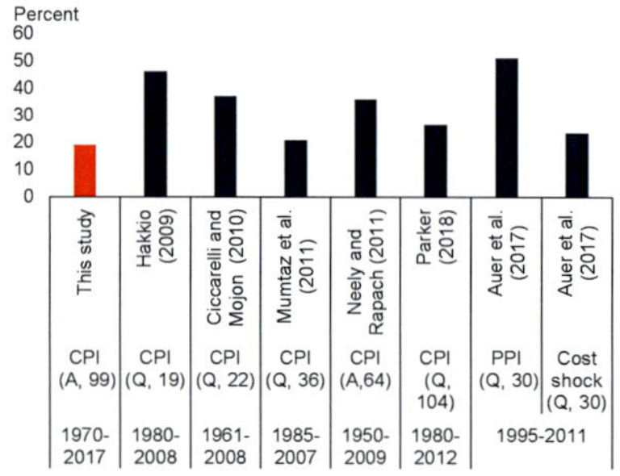

Source: Hakkio 2009; Ciccarelli and Mojon 2010; Mumtaz, Simonelli, and Surico 2011; Neely and Rapach 2011; Auer, Levchenko, and Sauré 2017; Parker 2018.

Note: Numbers in parentheses indicate the number of countries included. The figures for "This study," for consistency with other studies, shows the average contribution of the global factor to inflation variation. A = annual data set; CPI = consumer price index; PPI = producer price index; Q = quarterly data set.

inflation rates.[2] Ferroni and Mojon (2014) update this analysis through 2013, confirming a strong role for global factors among advanced economies.

Hakkio (2009) extracts a global factor from 19 OECD countries' inflation rates for 1960-2008 but adds a regional factor
and expands the set of inflation measures to include overall CPI inflation, cyclical CPI inflation, core CPI inflation, and cyclical core CPI inflation. He finds that the global factor explains, on average, 41 percent of cyclical inflation variation. Auer, Levchenko, and Sauré (2017) estimate a global inflation factor using a sample of 30 countries and find that the global factor accounts for 51 percent of inflation variation, half of which reflects common cost shocks propagated through input-output linkages (see also Auer and Mehrotra 2014).

These studies use considerably smaller and more homogeneous country samples than the sample used in this chapter. This helps to explain why, in their studies, the global factors account for larger shares of inflation variation (Figure 2.1.1). Nevertheless, the shares presented in this chapter are within the range—although toward the low end—of those reported in the literature.

[2] Although they do not explicitly quantify the contribution of global factors to inflation variation, Cecchetti et al. (2007) document coincident inflation developments around the world, such as the widespread start of the Great Inflation in the late 1960s and synchronized inflation stabilization in the mid-1980s.

BOX 2.1 Global inflation synchronization: A review *(continued)*

Other studies estimate, typically in a Phillips curve framework, the impact of specific global variables on domestic inflation—with mixed success. For example, Eickmeier and Pijnenburg (2013), using data for 24 OECD countries during 1980-2007, estimate a Phillips curve model of domestic inflation using the global and idiosyncratic factors of output gaps and changes in unit labor costs. They find that the global factor of changes in unit labor costs has a notable impact on domestic inflation. Lodge and Mikolajun (2016) also find that global commodity prices were important determinants of inflation in 19 advanced economies, although other global variables were not.

In related work, Borio and Filardo (2007) and Auer, Borio, and Filardo (2017) show that global inflation and the foreign output gap add explanatory power to conventional Phillips curve models of domestic inflation for several OECD countries. However, Gerlach et al. (2008) find that this result is not robust to the measurement of the global output gap, controlling for additional variables, or the estimation period. Ihrig et al. (2010) find that in estimates of the Phillips curve for 11 countries, the globalization hypothesis has little support. Kabukçuoğlu and Martínez-García (2018) model inflation expectations for 14 advanced economies in a Phillips curve framework augmented by the global output gap and global inflation. Their results for global output gaps are mixed—which they attribute to measurement error—but the results still indicate a strong role for global inflation in domestic inflation.

Evolution of global inflation synchronization over time. Neely and Rapach (2011) extract a global factor and seven regional factors from CPI inflation in 64 mostly advanced economies during 1950-2009. They find that the global factor, on average, accounted for 35 percent of inflation variance, and the regional factors accounted for 16 percent—and these shares have risen substantially since the 1980s. Neely and Rapach (2011) document that the regional (world) factor has increased in importance for several North American and European (Latin American and Asian) countries since 1980. Mumtaz and Surico (2012) estimate global and regional factors from 164 inflation indicators for 13 OECD economies during 1961-2004. They find that, in most countries, the degree of inflation synchronization has strengthened since the 1980s. Mumtaz, Simonelli, and Surico (2011) focus on an unbalanced panel of 36 countries

BOX 2.1 Global inflation synchronization: A review *(continued)*

between 1860 and 2007. They show that the share of inflation variation due to the global factor has grown since 1985.[3]

Which factors have contributed to global inflation synchronization?

Several studies document strong economic policy institutions, trade openness, and financial development as factors associated with a higher degree of cross-country inflation synchronization. Two types of approaches have been employed. First, the country characteristics associated with a greater share of inflation explained by the global factor are analyzed. Second, sectoral, goods, or subnational factor decompositions are used to identify more granular patterns in inflation synchronization.

Country characteristics. Neely and Rapach (2011), in their sample of 64 mostly advanced economies during 1950-2009, correlate the share of CPI inflation variance accounted for by the global factor with country characteristics. They find that the share is higher in advanced economies with stronger economic policy institutions, more developed financial markets, lower inflation, and more independent central banks. Parker (2018) shows that energy prices appear to be less synchronized with global inflation factors in less developed economies. Ciccarelli and Mojon (2010) document that the impact of a global inflation factor on domestic inflation is stronger in countries with lower inflation. In a Phillips curve framework, Auer, Levchenko, and Sauré (2017) present evidence that cross-border trade in intermediate goods and services is the main channel through which global economic slack influences domestic CPI inflation; cost shocks propagated through input-output linkages account for about one-quarter of inflation variability.

Sectoral decompositions. Monacelli and Sala (2009) estimate the contributions of a global factor to inflation variance in a large cross-section of sectoral price data (948 CPI products) for four OECD countries during 1991-2004. They find that, on average, the global factor explains 15-30 percent of the variation in disaggregated consumer price inflation, the share being higher in sectors with greater trade openness. Förster and Tillmann (2014) extract global, sectoral, and regional factors from CPI inflation in

---

[3] Using wavelet analysis, Bhanja et al. (2013) and Bhanja, Dar, and Tiwari (2016) document that inflation synchronization among Group of Seven and Euro Area countries has increased over time.

BOX 2.1 Global inflation synchronization: A review *(continued)*

40 mostly OECD countries for 1996-2011.[4] They find that about two-thirds of overall inflation volatility is due to country-specific determinants. For CPI inflation net of food and energy, the global factor and the CPI basket-specific factor account for less than 20 percent of inflation variation. Only energy price inflation in advanced economies is dominated by common factors.

Parker (2018) extends Förster and Tillmann's (2014) analysis to 223 countries and territories over 1980-2012. He finds that the global factor explains around two-thirds of the variance of advanced economies' inflation but only about one-fifth for middle-income countries and one-tenth for low-income countries. Regardless of the country group, common factors account for a larger share of variability in energy and food price inflation than housing price inflation or, more broadly, headline CPI inflation.

Subnational decompositions. Beck, Hubrich, and Marcellino (2009) extract Euro Area, national, and subnational factors from subnational inflation rates in six Euro Area countries. They find that the Euro Area factor accounted for about half the inflation variation, and national and regional components accounted for 32 and 18 percent, respectively.

Goods decompositions. Auer, Levchenko, and Sauré (2017) show, for disaggregated producer price index (PPI) inflation for 30 mostly OECD countries and 17 sectors during 1995 to 2011, that the global factor explains nearly half the fluctuations in PPI inflation in the average economy. They argue that this PPI synchronization across countries is driven primarily by common sectoral shocks and amplified by input-output linkages.

Conclusion

The literature has documented that inflation is highly synchronized internationally, but that the degree of inflation synchronization varies with country characteristics and other factors, including the measure of inflation used. Findings have typically been restricted to headline CPI inflation, largely disregarding sectoral differences in inflation synchronization.

[4] Their novel dynamic hierarchical factor model allows a decomposition into a global factor, a factor specific to a given subcomponent of the CPI (energy price inflation, food price inflation, and CPI inflation net of food and energy items), a country-group factor driving the particular CPI basket in industrial or emerging economies, and a country-specific component.

Fourth, the chapter studies a wide range of country characteristics that are conducive to high inflation synchronization; the literature often confines itself to only a few characteristics.

The chapter's principal conclusions are as follows:

- In the median country, the global inflation factor accounted for one-eighth (12 percent) of total variation in national inflation rates over 1970-2017. Its contribution was much more pronounced in the median advanced economy (24 percent) than in the median EMDE (10 percent) and negligible in the median low-income country (LIC).

- The global factor's contribution to inflation variation was greater between 1970 and 1985—a period of two global oil price spikes and two global recessions—than between 1986 and 2000. Partly as a result of the 2008-09 global financial crisis and the 2014-16 oil price plunge, global inflation synchronization strengthened significantly in 2001-17. During this last period, the global factor explained 22 percent of national inflation in the full sample. It accounted for 18 percent of inflation variation in the median EMDE and 27 percent in the median advanced economy, compared with 7 and 22 percent, respectively, during 1986-2000. In LICs as well, the global factor's contribution increased to 17 percent in 2001-17 from a 3-4 percent previously.

- In addition to global synchronization, group-specific inflation synchronization has emerged among advanced economies and EMDEs. Like global inflation synchronization, group-specific inflation synchronization increased after 2000. Since 2001, the group-specific inflation factors have accounted for 8 percent of inflation variation in the median EMDE, one-third more than during 1986-2000, and for 21 percent in the median advanced economy, one-sixth more than during 1986-2000.

- Global inflation synchronization has broadened across different measures of inflation. In 1970-85, the extent of inflation synchronization was pronounced only for inflation measures with a large portion of tradable goods and services (import prices and producer prices); it has more recently become sizable across all inflation measures. During 1970-2017, it was most pronounced for the inflation measures with the largest share of tradables: it was highest for import prices (54 percent), followed by the producer price index (PPI), headline consumer price index (CPI), gross domestic product (GDP) deflator, and core CPI (5 percent). Since 2001, it has grown to one-third even for core CPI inflation and growth of the GDP deflator.

- Inflation synchronization has tended to be greater among countries with higher trade openness, greater commodity-import intensity, and lower trade concentration. Among EMDEs, the share of the global factor was particularly high in East Asia and Pacific, Latin America and the Caribbean, and South Asia. Since 2001, however, systematic differences in the role of the global factor among countries with different characteristics have faded.

The next section documents the evolution of global and group-specific factors that have driven the increased synchronization of inflation rates. The subsequent section explores the synchronization across different measures of inflation, including headline and core consumer price inflation, and measures based on producer prices and import prices. The penultimate section examines the main factors that explain the global synchronization of inflation. The final section concludes with a brief summary, discussion of policy implications, and future research directions.

Evolution of inflation synchronization

Using results from estimates of a dynamic factor model, this section documents that global inflation synchronization has increased, in degree and breadth.

Data and methodology

The analysis is based on annual inflation data for 25 advanced economies and 74 EMDEs (including 16 LICs) for 1970-2017. In the benchmark estimation, inflation is measured as annual headline CPI inflation. To analyze the extent of synchronization in multiple measures of inflation, the database is augmented with core CPI inflation, PPI inflation, import price inflation, and GDP deflator growth for a subset of 38 countries (of which 13 are EMDEs) (Table A.2.1.2, Annex 2.1).

A dynamic factor model is employed to decompose inflation in each country into *a global inflation fact*or that is shared across all countries, an advanced economy or EMDE factor that is shared within the respective groups (that is, two *group-specific inflation factors*), and an *idiosyncratic inflation factor* that is unique to each individual country (see Annex 2.1 for details about the model and estimation).[1] Dynamic factor models are designed to extract a few unobservable common elements from a large number of (observable) variables. Thus, the model allows a parsimonious representation of the data in terms of the unobservable common elements, which are typically referred to as factors. The degree of global inflation synchronization is simply measured by the share of the variance of national inflation attributable to the global factor. In a similar

[1] These types of models are used extensively to analyze global business and financial cycles (Kose, Otrok, and Whiteman 2008; Kose, Otrok, and Prasad 2012; Ha et al. 2017; Neely and Rapach 2011; Mumtaz and Surico 2012).

fashion, the extent of inflation synchronization within each country group is measured by the fraction of variance that is explained by the group-specific factor.[2]

Inflation synchronization: Global and group factors

Behavior of the global and group-specific factors. The model identifies a global inflation factor that, as expected, registers sharp movements around oil price spikes and global recessions (Figure 2.1). Within a year of an average global recession (such recessions having occurred in 1975, 1982, 1991, and 2009) and during the average oil price plunge (these having occurred in 1986, 1990-91, 1997-98, 2001, 2008, and 2014-16), annual global inflation fell by 0.5 and 0.2 percentage point, respectively, below its long-term trend. Conversely, in the average year preceding a global recession, global inflation was almost 2 percentage points above trend. The global factor moved in tandem with median inflation across countries.[3] The advanced economy and EMDE factors also exhibited common (although more muted) movements with their respective group-specific median inflation rates.

Importance of the global inflation factor. During 1970-2017, the global inflation factor accounted for a sizable share of within-country inflation variance in advanced economies and EMDEs (Figure 2.2; Table 2.1). In the median country, the global factor accounted for 12 percent of inflation variation, but its role varied widely across and within country groups (from near zero to 70 percent). For example, for the full sample period, the contribution of the global inflation factor was much greater in the median advanced economy (24 percent) than in the median EMDE (10 percent).

Importance of group-specific inflation factors. The group-specific factors have also played an important role in driving inflation. For example, in the median advanced economy, the group-specific factor accounted for 8 percent of inflation variation during 1970-2017.

The contributions of the global inflation factor to inflation variation reported in this chapter are consistent with, but at the low end of, the range of estimates

[2] The results are qualitatively robust to different detrending methods (for example, the Hodrick-Prescott or Butterworth filter), the use of a three-factor model (including country-specific factors), and the use of quarterly data.

[3] For 90 percent of the countries in the sample, the factor loadings on the global factor (coefficients associated with the global factor in the model) are positive (and statistically significant within 90 percent confidence intervals), indicating that national inflation rates generally move in tandem with the global factor. The remaining 10 percent of the countries are mostly, although not exclusively, in Sub-Saharan Africa (Algeria, Cameroon, Central African Republic, Democratic Republic of Congo, Gabon, Gambia, Mali, Niger, Saudi Arabia, and Senegal). In these countries, the factor loadings on the global factor are not statistically significantly different from zero.

FIGURE 2.1 Global and group inflation factors

The global factor troughs around global recessions and oil price plunges. The global factor and, especially, the advanced-economy factor move in tandem with median inflation across countries.

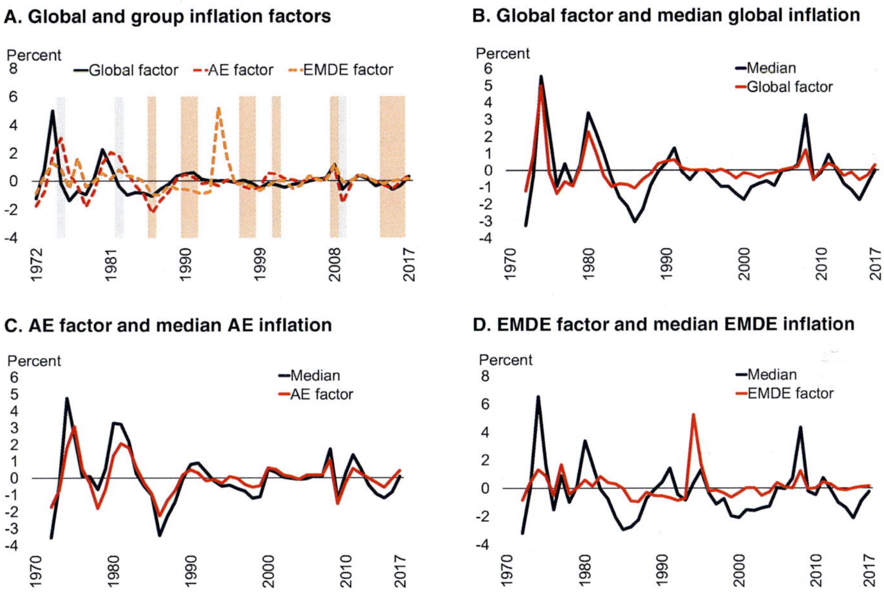

Source: World Bank.

Note: The global and group inflation factors are estimated with the baseline dynamic factor model (two-factor model with a global and a group-specific factor) for 1970-2017 (Annex 2.1). The sample includes 99 countries (25 AEs and 74 EMDEs, including 16 low-income countries). "Median" denotes cross-country median headline inflation. AE = advanced economy; EMDE = emerging market and developing economies.

A. Grey shades indicate periods of global recessions (1975, 1982, 1991, and 2009) and slowdowns (1998 and 2001); red shades indicate periods of oil price plunges (1986, 1990-91, 1997-98, 2001, 2008, and 2014-16) (Kose and Terrones 2015; Baffes et al. 2015). Identification of these global events is explained in more detail in Chapter 3.

reported in other studies (see Box 2.1). Earlier studies have reported that the global inflation factor has contributed 20-50 percent to the variation in national inflation rates, with estimates differing depending on the methodology, sample periods, country groups, and data transformations. The differences in the estimates presented here may reflect the more extensive inclusion of EMDEs in the country sample in this study than in earlier work.

Evolution of inflation synchronization

Increasing synchronization over time. Global inflation synchronization has risen over the past four to five decades (Figure 2.2; Table 2.2). This is illustrated by estimates of the model for three approximately equal subperiods: 1970-85, 1986-2000, and 2001-17. The first period, 1970-85, overlaps with the Great Inflation of 1965-84 (Annex 1.4 in Chapter 1); the second, 1986-2000, was a

FIGURE 2.2 Contributions of global and group factors to inflation

In the full sample period, 1970-2017, the global and group-specific inflation factors together explain around 16 percent of the variation in inflation rates, but more in the median advanced economy (32 percent) than in the median EMDE (13 percent). The share of inflation variance explained by the global factor declined after 1985 but rose again after 2000. Since 2001, the global inflation factor has accounted for a larger share of inflation variation in a greater number of countries than in the 1970s and 1980s.

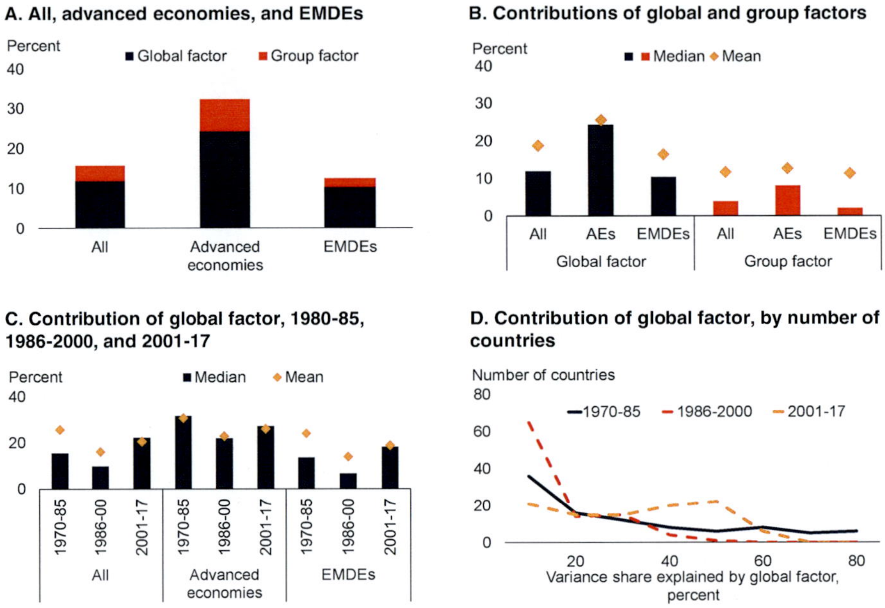

Source: World Bank.

Note: The contribution of global and group factors to inflation variance is estimated with the dynamic factor model over 1970-2017 and three subsample periods (Annex 2.1). The sample includes 99 countries (25 AEs and 74 EMDEs, including 16 low-income countries). AEs = advanced economies; EMDEs = emerging market and developing economies.

B.C. Unweighted means or medians.

TABLE 2.1 Variance decompositions: Headline CPI , 1970-2017 (percent)

Factor	All countries	Advanced economies	EMDEs
Global	11.9	24.3	10.4
	(18.8, 2.9 - 29.4)	(25.6, 10.4 - 35.2)	(16.4, 2.2 - 21.8)
Group	3.9	8.1	2.1
	(11.6, 0.7 - 16.6)	(12.7, 4.2 - 18.4)	(11.3, 0.5 - 12.7)
Global + Group	27.2	37.2	21.4
	(30.4, 14.0 - 44.2)	(38.3, 30.6 - 49.6)	(27.8, 11.5 - 41.8)

Note: All numbers indicate percent contributions of global and group-specific factors to the variance of headline CPI inflation during 1970-2017. The contributions of global and group-specific inflation factors are estimated using the dynamic factor model described in Annex 2.1. The data set includes 99 countries (25 advanced economies and 74 EMDEs). In each pair of rows, the numbers in the first row indicate medians across countries. The first number in the second row (in parentheses) is the unweighted mean across countries. The second and third numbers in the second row (in parentheses) indicate the interquartile range (25th and 75th percentiles). CPI = consumer price index; EMDEs = emerging market and developing economies.

period of widespread disinflation; and the third, 2001-17, was a period of low but typically stable inflation (Chapter 1).

The *global* factor's contribution to inflation variation was sizable—16 percent for the median country in the full sample—in 1970-85, when economies were considerably more energy-intensive than more recently and oil price spikes lifted inflation globally (Baffes et al. 2015). Then, the global factor's contribution dipped to 10 percent during 1986-2000, as many countries implemented policies to rein in inflation. But in 2001-17, it rose beyond its level in 1970-85, to 22 percent for the median economy in the full sample and 18 percent for the median EMDE; for the median advanced economy it rose to 27 percent but remained below its level in 1970-85. Similarly, the contribution of the *group* factor to inflation variation has grown since the 1970s and 1980s, to 21 percent in the median advanced economy in 2001-17 (from 18 percent in 1970-85) and 8 percent in the median EMDE (from 6 percent).

Increasingly broad-based inflation synchronization. Global inflation synchronization has become more broad-based over time. During 1986-2000, for example, the global factor contributed more than 10 percent to inflation variation in around one-third of the countries in the sample (compared with half the countries in 1970-85), and during 2001-17, this was the case in two-thirds of the countries. The distribution of the contribution of the *global* factor has clearly shifted to the right between 1970-85 and 2001-17 for all country groups (Figure 2.2). The distribution of the contribution of the *group* factor to inflation variation only shifted to the right for advanced economies: for EMDEs, the distribution in 2001-17 resembled that in 1970-85.[4]

Inflation synchronization in LICs. Until 2000, the contribution of the global factor to inflation variation in LICs was negligible (3-4 percent in the median LIC). Since 2001, however, the global factor's contribution has quintupled to 17 percent in the median LIC, a level broadly in line with the median EMDE. The share of LICs with a contribution of the global factor to inflation variation in excess of 10 percent has risen from one-quarter before 2000 to two-thirds since 2001. In addition to the growing contribution of the common global factor to short-term inflation movements, global factors have also contributed considerably to long-term inflation movements. Chapter 6 documents that a benign external environment was the main reason for the decline in trend inflation in LICs over the past two

[4] These trends are robust to estimating the dynamic factor model by subsample periods of 15-year rolling windows. The combined importance of global and group-specific factors declined until 2006, but it has since increased again. The share of variance due to the global factor was often higher for rolling samples that overlapped with the post-2007 period, reflecting the highly synchronized movements in inflation across countries following the global financial crisis.

TABLE 2.2 Variance decompositions, over time: Headline CPI (percent)

	1970-2017	1970-85	1986-2000	2001-17
Factor	**All countries**			
Global	11.9 (18.8, 2.9 - 29.4)	15.5 (25.8, 4.1 - 40.1)	9.9 (16.2, 1.5 - 29.0)	22.1 (20.7, 8.6 - 30.9)
Group	3.9 (11.6, 0.7 - 16.6)	7.9 (12.2, 2.3 - 18.2)	6.7 (19.4, 2.8 - 22.0)	9.0 (13.7, 3.8 -19.5)
Global + Group	27.2 (30.4, 14.0 - 44.2)	31.0 (38.0, 18.3 - 59.5)	34.8 (35.6, 16.1 - 48.7)	33.6 (34.4, 19.0 - 49.3)
Factor	**Advanced economies**			
Global	24.3 (25.6, 10.4 - 35.2)	31.6 (30.8, 10.8 - 39.7)	22.0 (22.9, 9.9 - 35.5)	27.3 (26.1, 21.6 - 32.9)
Group	8.1 (12.7, 4.2 - 18.4)	18.0 (18.1, 7.3 - 24.0)	15.7 (21.0, 4.9 - 33.6)	20.5 (22.7, 9.4 - 34.8)
Global + Group	37.2 (38.3, 30.6 - 49.6)	47.2 (48.8, 36.3 - 64.6)	45.0 (43.9, 26.9 - 55.4)	50.7 (48.8, 39.1 - 62.8)
Factor	**EMDEs**			
Global	10.4 (16.4, 2.2 - 21.8)	13.6 (24.1, 2.9 - 38.9)	6.6 (14.0, 0.7 - 26.7)	18.1 (18.9, 5.8 - 30.3)
Group	2.1 (11.3, 0.5 - 12.7)	6.3 (10.3, 1.9 - 15.1)	6.4 (18.9, 2.7 - 19.0)	7.8 (10.7, 3.2 - 16.9)
Global + Group	21.4 (27.8, 11.5 - 41.7)	25.8 (34.4, 13.8 - 52.3)	27.4 (32.9, 13.0 - 43.8)	28.9 (29.6, 17.2 - 39.4)

Note: All numbers indicate percentage contributions of the global and group-specific factors to the variance of headline CPI inflation. The contributions of global and group-specific inflation factors are estimated using the dynamic factor model described in Annex 2.1. The data set includes 99 countries (25 advanced economies and 74 EMDEs). In each pair of rows, the numbers in the first row indicate medians across countries. The first number in the second row (in parentheses) is the unweighted mean across countries. The second and third numbers in the second row (in parentheses) indicate the interquartile range (25th and 75th percentiles). CPI = consumer price index; EMDEs = emerging market and developing economies.

decades. Growing synchronization coincided with LICs' rapid integration into global trade networks as well as a shift toward greater exchange rate flexibility (Box 1.2, Chapter 1).

Extent of synchronization: Inflation and output

How high is the degree of global inflation synchronization reported here relative to the synchronization of other, comparable economic variables? To answer this question, it is useful to compare the extent of inflation synchronization with that of business cycles. A large literature reports that there is a global business cycle, evidenced by a high degree of synchronization of various measures of national economic activity, including output growth.

Inflation tends to exhibit stronger global synchronization than output growth (Box 2.2). For the full sample of countries over 1970-2017, the median contributions of the global factor to variations in inflation and output growth were 12 and 5 percent, respectively. The difference was somewhat more pronounced for EMDEs than for advanced economies. The global factor accounted for 10 percent of inflation variation in the median EMDE but only 3 percent of output growth variation. In the median advanced economy, the contribution of the global factor was also more sizable for variations in inflation (24 percent) than in output growth (19 percent). Since 2001, the median contributions of the global factor to variation in inflation and output growth have increased significantly, to 22 and 12 percent, respectively, for the full sample of countries.

Synchronization across different measures of inflation

The inflation synchronization discussed thus far refers to headline CPI inflation. However, the degree of inflation synchronization differs across various measures of inflation. To analyze these differences, a dynamic factor model is estimated using five measures of inflation with varying tradables content (headline CPI, core CPI, PPI, GDP deflator, and import prices).[5] Separately, a common factor to represent nontradables inflation is extracted from the three measures with below-average tradables content (core CPI, headline CPI, and GDP deflator), and a common factor to represent tradables inflation is extracted from the three measures with above-average tradables content (import prices, headline CPI, and PPI). Global and group-specific factors for each inflation measure are estimated separately for annual data for 38 countries (25 advanced economies and 13 EMDEs) over 1970-2016.

Inflation synchronization: Different measures

Behavior of global inflation measures. Global factors were typically more volatile for inflation measures with greater tradables content.

- Global factors for *PPI* and *import price* inflation tended to move together over the past four to five decades, but with considerably greater variability in the global factor for import price inflation—as may be expected for goods prices that are heavily exposed to, if not determined in, global markets (Figure 2.3). During global recessions and episodes of large oil price swings,

[5] In price indexes for the United States, for example, the share of tradable goods and services is greatest for the PPI (54 percent), followed by headline CPI (53 percent), GDP deflator (26 percent), and core CPI (15 percent), according to the U.S. Bureau of Labor Statistics. The classification of sectors into tradables and nontradables here follows the earlier literature: agriculture, hunting, forestry and fishing, mining and quarrying, and manufacturing are classified as tradable sectors and the rest as nontradable (Knight and Johnson 1997).

BOX 2.2 Global synchronization of inflation and output growth

International synchronization of inflation has tended to be higher than that of output growth over the past four to five decades. This result is mainly driven by the much higher degree of inflation synchronization during 1970-85, which witnessed multiple common shocks. Over the past three decades, the degree of synchronization of output growth has increased to become comparable to that of inflation. The differences in the degree of synchronization in inflation and output growth over time may reflect changes in the nature and frequency of global shocks and structural factors, including the evolution of policy frameworks.

Relative to what is the degree of international inflation synchronization reported in this chapter "high"? A comparison with the extent of business cycle synchronization offers a possible standard of reference for this question. A large literature reports the degree of international synchronization of various measures of business cycles, including output growth. This box examines the evidence on the relative degrees of synchronization of inflation and output growth to address the following questions:

- How does the degree of synchronization of inflation compare with that of output growth?
- What are the major factors that could explain the difference between the extent of synchronization of inflation and output growth?

Inflation versus output synchronization

Full sample comparison. To examine the relative degrees of synchronization in output growth and inflation, global factors for the two variables were separately estimated using the baseline two-factor model for 99 countries over 1970-2017. Inflation movements tended to exhibit a stronger degree of synchronization than output growth (Figure 2.2.1).[1] Specifically, the median contributions of the global factors to variation in inflation and output growth for the full country sample in this period are

[1] This is consistent with the findings in earlier theoretical and empirical studies (Henriksen, Kydland, and Šustek 2013; Mumtaz, Simonelli, and Surico 2011; Wang and Wen 2007). For instance, Wang and Wen (2007) offer sticky-price and sticky-information New Keynesian models to explain inflation synchronization that is high and well in excess of output synchronization; neither model can account for the phenomenon. They conclude that neither nominal rigidities nor monetary shocks are likely sources of inflation synchronization.

BOX 2.2 Global synchronization of inflation and output growth *(continued)*

12 and 5 percent, respectively. The difference reflects weak output growth synchronization in advanced economies and emerging market and developing economies (EMDEs): the global factor accounted for 10 percent of inflation variation in the median EMDE but only 3 percent of output growth variation. In contrast, in the median advanced economy, the contribution of the global factor was sizable for variations in inflation (24 percent) and output growth (19 percent). These results are consistent with findings in earlier studies.[2]

Inflation and output synchronization over time. Over the past three decades, the degree of synchronization of output growth has grown to become comparable to that for inflation (Figure 2.2.1). During 1970-85, inflation synchronization (with a median variance contribution of the global factor of 16 percent) was stronger than output growth synchronization (5 percent). During 1986-2000, however, the median share of the global factor in the variance of inflation declined to 10 percent, and the share of the global output growth factor remained low (6 percent), with wide differences across countries. Since 2001, the median contribution of the global factor to variation in output growth and inflation have increased significantly, to 12 and 22 percent, respectively. For the median advanced economy, the share is now greater for output growth (34 percent) than for inflation (27 percent). For the median EMDE, the global factor still contributed more to inflation variation (18 percent) than to output growth variation (7 percent).

The trends in the relative importance of global and group-specific factors over time were similar for output growth and inflation. Output growth and inflation were explained more by global factors than group-specific factors during 1970-85, but the relative importance of the group-specific factors increased during 1986-2000.[3] However, since 2001, the global factors have again become more important than the group-specific factors for output growth and inflation. Although these trends were similar in direction, they were more pronounced for inflation than for output growth.

---

[2] For example, among 60 mostly advanced economies, the global factor accounts for 25-50 percent of the variance of output growth (Kose, Otrok, and Whiteman 2003).

[3] This is consistent with the findings on the "decoupling of macroeconomic variables between advanced economies and EMDEs" reported by Kose, Otrok, and Prasad (2012).

BOX 2.2 Global synchronization of inflation and output growth *(continued)*

FIGURE 2.2.1 Synchronization in output growth and inflation

Global inflation synchronization has been stronger than global synchronization of output growth, especially in EMDEs. In advanced economies, inflation synchronization has been comparable to, or lower than, output growth synchronization since the mid-1980s.

A. Contribution of the global factor to output growth and inflation variation, 1970-2017

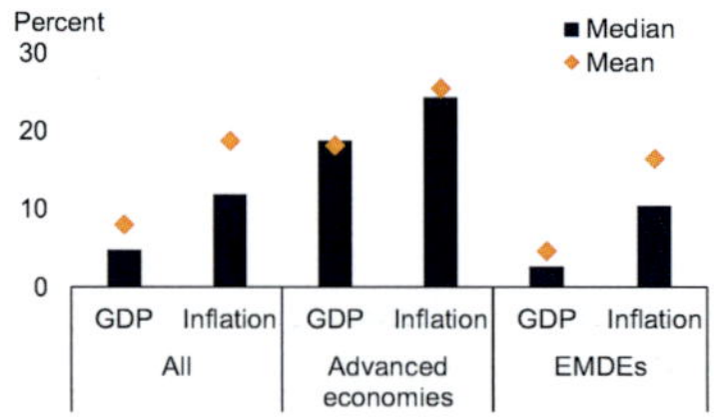

B. Contribution of the global factor to output growth and inflation variation, over time

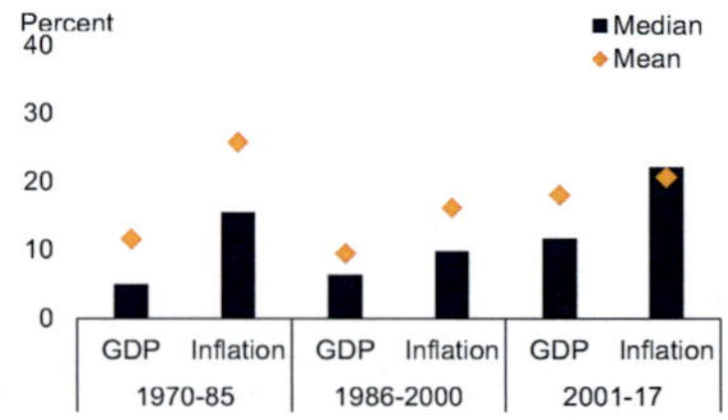

C. Contribution of the global factor to output growth and inflation variation: Advanced economies

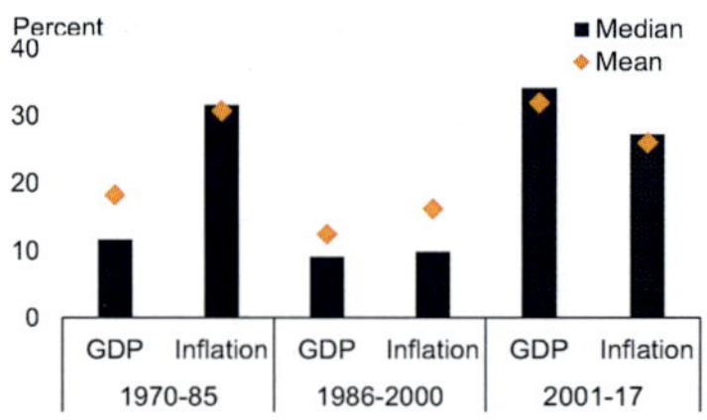

D. Contribution of the global factor to output growth and inflation variation: EMDEs

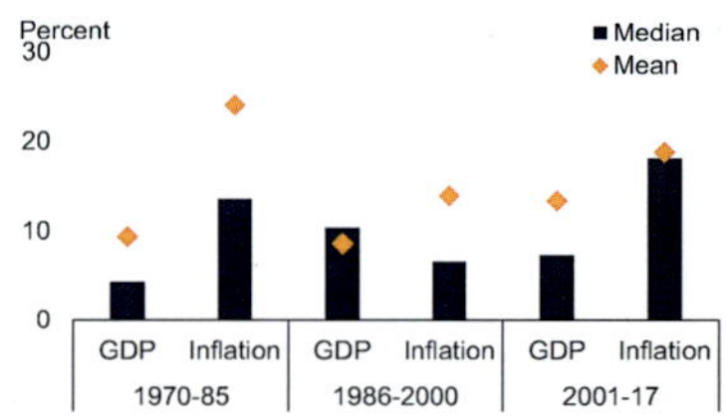

E. Contribution of global and group factors to output and inflation variation, over time

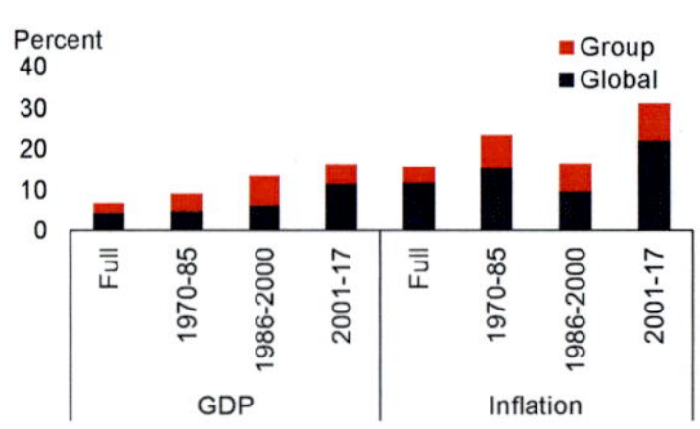

F. Contribution of global and group factors to output and inflation variation, by country group

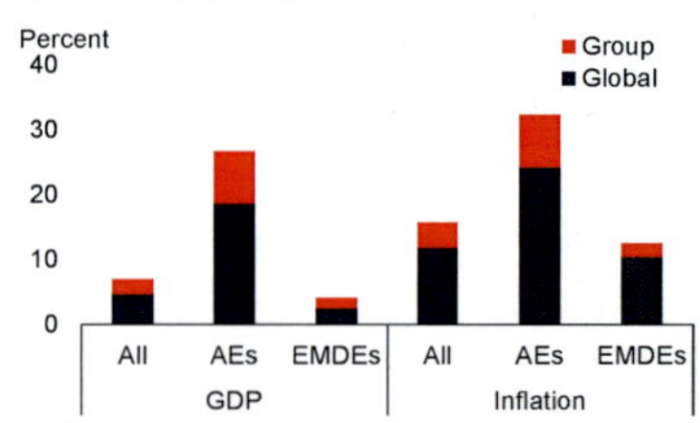

Source: World Bank.

Note: Contribution of global and group factors to the variance of real output growth and inflation in 99 economies (25 AEs and 74 EMDEs, including 16 low-income countries), based on a two-factor dynamic factor model (Annex 2.1). AEs = advanced economies; EMDEs = emerging market and developing economies; GDP = gross domestic product.

BOX 2.2 Global synchronization of inflation and output growth *(continued)*

Evolution of global factors for output growth and inflation. Around the global oil price spikes in the 1970s and the oil price plunge in the mid-2010s, global (and group-specific) factors for output growth and inflation moved in opposite directions, possibly indicating a major role of global supply shocks as the main drivers of global business and inflation cycles during these episodes. However, around global recessions and slowdowns, especially around the global financial crisis in 2008-09, the two global factors moved in tandem, probably due to demand shocks. This time-varying correlation between the two global factors is clearly observed for EMDE-specific factors (Figure 2.2.2).

Reasons for differences in inflation and output growth synchronization

Henriksen, Kydland, and Šustek (2013) examine this question in an international business cycle model with common technology shocks as well as cross-border technology spillovers. In their model, central banks' policy rules are combined with a no-arbitrage condition between domestic and foreign interest rates to render *current* prices (and interest rates) a function of expected *future* output. This results in a stronger cross-country correlation in prices than in output.

Alternatively, the difference in the degrees of synchronization may reflect the nature of global shocks or differential impacts of cross-border spillovers of shocks on inflation and output. If movements in the prices of internationally traded goods, such as swings in commodity prices, play an important role as global shocks, their impact on inflation could be greater and more immediate than their impact on output. Indeed, the degree of inflation synchronization is much higher than that of output growth during 1970-85, a period that witnessed multiple global shocks associated with sharp movements in oil prices.

Considering that cross-border spillovers of shocks can drive global synchronization in inflation and output, structural changes can also influence real and nominal linkages across countries. For instance, the strong degree of output synchronization among advanced economies during 2001-17, which was slightly more pronounced than inflation synchronization during the same period, might partly reflect widespread and major economic disruptions during the global financial crisis.

BOX 2.2 Global synchronization of inflation and output growth *(continued)*

FIGURE 2.2.2 Global inflation and output growth factors

Around global recessions and slowdowns, especially around the global financial crisis in 2008-09, global inflation and output growth factors moved in tandem, probably due to demand shocks.

A. Global factors for output growth and inflation

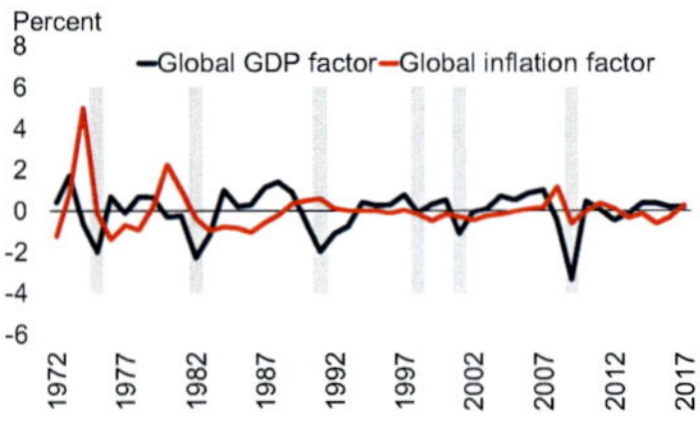

B. EMDE factors for output growth and inflation

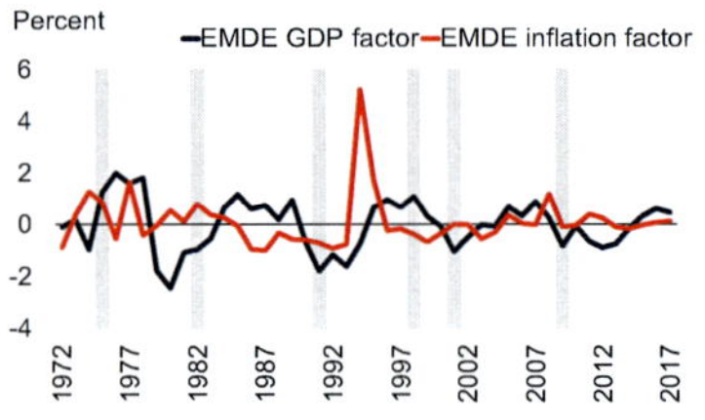

Source: World Bank.

Note: The global and group inflation and output growth factors are estimated with the baseline dynamic factor model (two-factor model with a global and a group-specific factor) for 1970-2017 (Annex 2.1). The sample includes 99 countries (25 advanced economies and 74 EMDEs, including 16 lowincome countries). Grey shades indicate the periods of global recessions and slowdowns (Kose and Terrones 2015). EMDEs = emerging market and developing economies; GDP = gross domestic product.

Conclusion

Is the degree of inflation synchronization reported in this chapter "high"? A comparison with output growth synchronization suggests that the answer is a qualified yes. Since 1970, global inflation synchronization has been more than twice as large as global output synchronization. The difference may reflect a multitude of shocks to internationally traded prices, which affected domestic inflation more directly than output, or technology spillovers that affected prices more than output because central banks responded proactively to the shocks. Over time, inflation and output synchronization have risen.

the global PPI and import price factors exhibited sharper movements than the global headline CPI factor. With a larger share of nontradable goods and services prices in the *GDP deflator*, the global factor for this measure has been considerably less volatile than those for headline CPI, PPI, and import price inflation.

- Since the mid-1980s, the global factor for *core CPI* inflation—which contains the largest share of nontradable goods and services among the

FIGURE 2.3 Global inflation factors: Various inflation measures

Global factors for PPI and import price inflation have tended to move together over the past four to five decades, and they have been considerably more volatile than the global factor for headline CPI inflation. With a larger share of nontradable goods and services prices in the GDP deflator, the contribution of the global factor to variations in GDP deflator growth has been smaller and considerably less volatile than those for PPI and import price inflation. The contribution of the global factor to core CPI inflation variation—which contains the largest share of nontradable goods and services among the inflation measures used here—has been the smallest among various inflation measures.

A. Global factors: Headline CPI, PPI, and import price

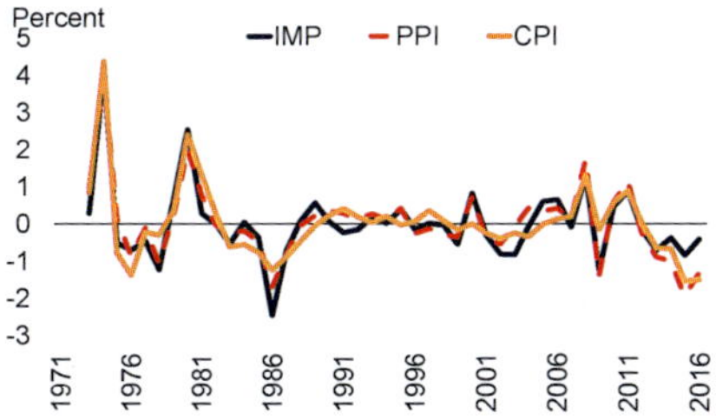

B. Global factors: Headline CPI, core CPI, and GDP deflator

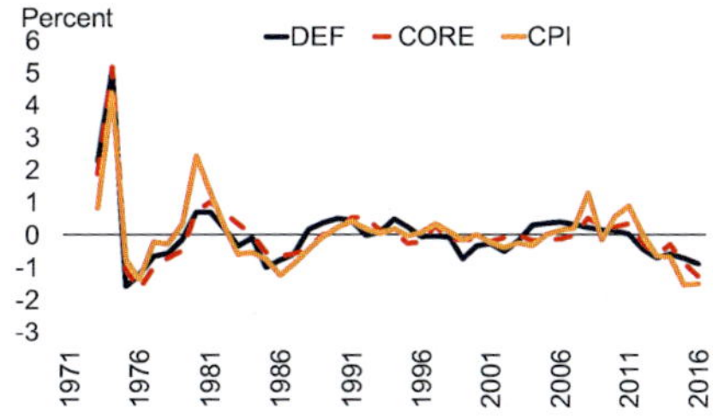

C. Contribution of global and group-specific factors to inflation variation: Various measures

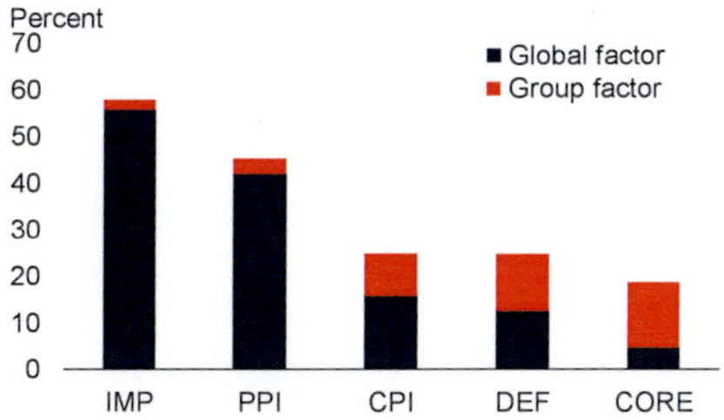

D. Correlations of headline and core CPI inflation factors with other global factors

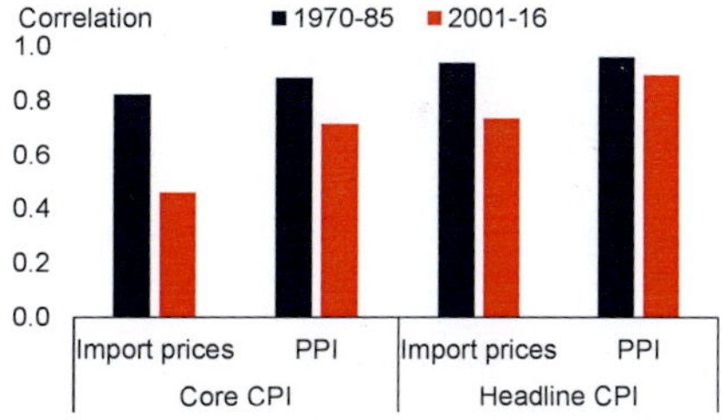

Source: World Bank.

Note: The global and group inflation factors are estimated with a baseline dynamic factor model (two-factor model) using detrended inflation rates in 38 countries (25 advanced economies and 13 EMDEs) for 1970-2016. CORE = core CPI; CPI = headline consumer price index; DEF = GDP deflator; GDP = gross domestic product; IMP = import prices; PPI = producer price index.

inflation measures examined here—has been less volatile than those for the other inflation measures. This may reflect the exclusion of energy prices (which tend to comove globally), as well as strengthened monetary policy frameworks and better-anchored inflation expectations, as a growing number of central banks succeeded in lowering inflation from high levels and began to employ inflation-targeting frameworks (as discussed in Chapters 1 and 4). The decoupling of core inflation from other inflation measures was also reflected in declining correlations between the global factors for core CPI and other measures of inflation. Thus, the correlation of the global factor for core CPI inflation with that for import price inflation halved between 1970-85 (0.8) and 2001-16 (0.4), while the correlation of PPI or headline CPI inflation with import price inflation remained high, at around 0.7-0.9.

Contribution of global factors to inflation variation. The estimated global factor's contribution to inflation variation was higher in inflation measures with greater tradable goods and services content (Figure 2.3; Table 2.3). For example, the global factor's contribution to inflation variation was largest for import prices (54 percent in the median country) and smallest for core CPI inflation (5 percent). Between these two extremes, the global factor's contribution to variation in PPI inflation was 42 percent and that to GDP deflator growth was on the order of 13 percent, which was comparable to that for headline CPI inflation.

Contribution of the group-specific factor to inflation variation. In contrast to the results for the global factor, the group-specific inflation factor contributed more to variation in inflation measures with less tradables content: it was largest for the core CPI, followed by the GDP deflator, headline CPI, PPI, and import prices. The median contribution of the group-specific factor to the variation in core CPI inflation was 14 percent—considerably more than that of the global factor (5 percent). For GDP deflator growth, the median contributions of the global and group-specific factors were similar, at 13 and 12 percent, respectively. For import prices and PPI, the contributions of the group-specific factors were negligible (less than 5 percent).

Evolution of inflation synchronization: Different measures

Trends in inflation synchronization over time were similar across the five inflation measures (Figure 2.4; Table A.2.1.3). During 1970-85, the role of the global inflation factor was sizable for all five inflation measures except core CPI inflation; global inflation synchronization weakened during 1986-2000, but returned in the 2000s to levels similar to those of 1970-85. During 1970-85, the median contribution of the global inflation factor was 68 percent for inflation variation in import prices, followed by PPI (52 percent) and core CPI (8 percent).

During 1970-85, the contribution of the global factor to inflation variation was much greater than that of the group-specific factor for all inflation measures except core CPI inflation. During 1986-2000, however, the global factor's contribution fell below 10 percent for all five measures, and the contribution of the group-specific factor rose to match or even exceed that of the global factor for virtually all inflation measures. Since 2001, the contribution of the global

TABLE 2.3 Variance decompositions: Various inflation measures (percent)

	Import prices	PPI	Headline CPI	GDP deflator	Core CPI
Factor			**All countries**		
Global	54.4 (51.8, 45.6-66.1)	42.1 (41.1, 15.3-61.7)	15.7 (22.9, 6.2-36.5)	12.6 (18.7, 3.2-30.5)	4.7 (12.5, 1.7-15.4)
Group	2.1 (8.5, 1.1-15.1)	3.2 (6.6, 0.9-8.8)	9.1 (12.8, 3.4-21.4)	12.1 (16.0, 4.6-25.5)	14.1 (18.8, 2.9-26.6)
Global + Group	63.2 (60.4, 51.5-70.4)	49.9 (45.2, 19.7-67.3)	34.1 (35.7, 25.4-44.6)	35.3 (33.8, 19.1-45.0)	26.3 (27.2, 10.9-40.4)
Factor			**Advanced economies**		
Global	54.4 (52.7, 45.6-66.1)	56.1 (48.4, 33.9-63.7)	21.4 (23.7, 11.0-36.6)	13.4 (19.1, 6.5-31.5)	7.9 (15.5, 3.1-21.4)
Group	2.5 (7.5, 1.4-15.1)	4.5 (7.7, 1.1-9.6)	11.5 (14.0, 4.1- 24.1)	12.6 (15.9, 3.5- 25.0)	17.7 (21.9, 8.7-34.8)
Global + Group	63.2 (60.2, 49.5-72.5)	60.6 (51.6, 31.2-68.1)	35.9 (37.7, 31.1-44.8)	37.3 (33.6, 18.1- 45.8)	34.3 (33.5, 18.9-46.4)
Factor			**EMDEs**		
Global	56.9 (48.2, 40.2-64.9)	16.2 (28.3, 11.1-40.4)	11.6 (21.4, 3.4-36.3)	9.3 (18.0, 2.2-26.1)	1.7 (8.0, 1.3-9.1)
Group	1.0 (12.8, 0.7-13.1)	1.4 (4.7, 0.8-4.0)	7.7 (10.4, 0.9- 11.8)	9.5 (16.2, 6.2- 25.5)	2.9 (11.5, 1.5-13.5)
Global + Group	61.4 (61.1, 57.0-65.5)	22.6 (33.0, 13.5-41.0)	25.6 (31.9, 16.7-43.9)	33.7 (34.2, 22.2-37.4)	11.8 (15.0, 3.0-16.5)

Note: The contributions of global and group inflation factors to inflation variance are estimated with a two-factor dynamic factor model for each of the five different inflation measures: Import prices, PPI, headline CPI, GDP deflator, and core CPI (Annex 2.1). The sample includes 38 countries (25 advanced economies and 13 EMDEs), except for import prices, which are only available for 21 countries (17 advanced economies and 4 EMDEs). In each pair of rows, the first number in the first row indicates medians across countries. The first number in the second row (in parentheses) is the unweighted mean variance share across countries. The second and third numbers in the second row (in parentheses) indicate the interquartile range (25th and 75th percentiles). The results for headline inflation may differ from Tables 2.1 and 2.2 because of a smaller sample size, to match the sample with available data for other measures of inflation. CPI = consumer price index; EMDEs = emerging market and developing economies; GDP = gross domestic product; PPI = producer price index.

FIGURE 2.4 Contribution of global and group factors to inflation over time: Various inflation measures

Across all measures of inflation, global inflation synchronization decreased in the mid-1980s and 1990s before rising again in the 2000s.

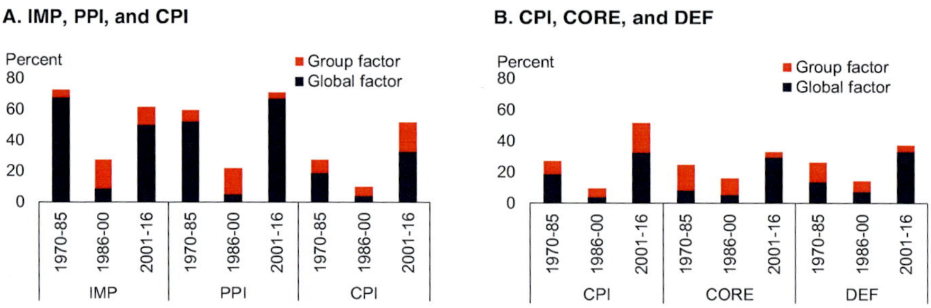

Source: Haver Analytics; OECD; World Bank.

Note: The global and group inflation factors are estimated with a dynamic factor model using annual inflation in 38 countries (25 advanced economies and 13 EMDEs) for 1970-2016 (Annex 2.1). CORE = core consumer price index; CPI = headline consumer price index; DEF = GDP deflator; IMP = import prices; PPI = producer price index.

inflation factor has risen to around two-thirds for PPI inflation variation and around one-third for core CPI inflation and GDP deflator growth variation.

Inflation synchronization: Tradable versus nontradable goods and services

Similar results are obtained from an exercise that extracts separate global and group-specific factors for mainly tradables (headline CPI, PPI, and import prices) and mainly nontradables (headline CPI, GDP deflator, and core CPI) inflation measures.[6] The global factor accounted for a much larger share of tradables inflation (40 percent) than nontradables inflation variation (13 percent) (Figure 2.5; Table 2.4). The median contribution of the group-specific factor to inflation variation was similarly low for the nontradables sector as for the tradables sector (6 percent). The differences between the contributions of global and group-specific factors to tradables and nontradables inflation were larger for advanced economies than for EMDEs.

Sources of inflation synchronization

A wide range of factors could be responsible for the global synchronization of inflation. This section starts with a brief conceptual discussion of three broad factors that could explain inflation synchronization: shocks, policy responses, and structural changes. This discussion is followed by an analysis of country-

[6] The results are robust to the exclusion of headline CPI from the estimation of the global factor for the nontradables sector.

FIGURE 2.5 Global and group inflation factors: Tradables and nontradables

Global inflation factors for tradable and nontradable goods moved broadly together until the late 1990s when the nontradables factor stabilized while the tradables factor did not. The share of inflation variance explained by the global inflation factor is greater for tradable goods than nontradable goods and larger for advanced economies than for EMDEs. Group -specific inflation synchronization is stronger for nontradable goods and services than for tradables.

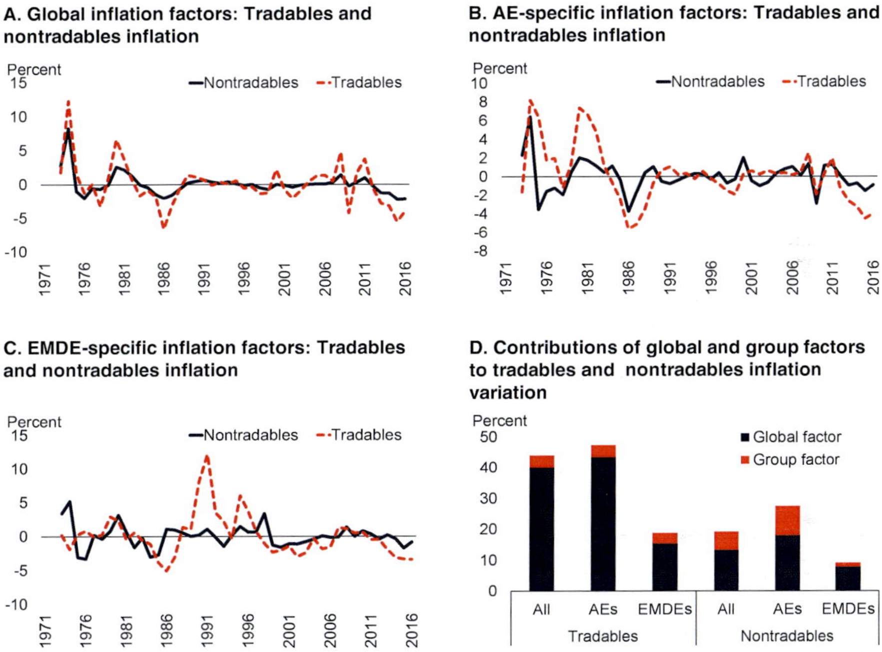

Source: World Bank.

Note: The global and group inflation factors for tradable and nontradable goods are estimated with a two-factor dynamic factor model for 1970-2016 (Annex 2.1). The common factor from three measures for domestic inflation (import prices, PPI, and headline CPI) is used as a proxy variable for the common component for tradable goods. Similarly, common factors for headline CPI, core CPI, and the GDP deflator are extracted as a proxy for global inflation factor for nontradable goods. The data are detrended annual inflation for 25 AEs and 13 EMDEs for 1970-2016. AEs = advanced economies; CPI = consumer price index; EMDEs = emerging market and developing economies; GDP = gross domestic product; PPI = producer price index.

specific structural and policy-related features that correlate with inflation synchronization.

Conceptual considerations

Shocks. Inflation synchronization across countries could be driven by common shocks that spread evenly (or at least simultaneously) across countries, and/or by country-specific shocks that spill over from one country or a subset of countries to others. Commodity price shocks, internationally correlated productivity

TABLE 2.4 Variance decompositions: Tradables and nontradables (percent)

	Nontradable sector	Tradable sector
Factor	All countries	
Global	13.2 (19.3, 4.3 - 31.6)	40.1 (36.7, 14.5 - 53.6)
Group	5.9 (10.9, 0.7 - 15.4)	3.8 (7.2, 1.7 - 9.8)
Global + Group	30.2 (30.2, 13.3 - 41.8)	45.7 (43.9, 24.1 - 62.8)
Factor	Advanced economies	
Global	17.9 (21.5, 9.3 - 32.1)	43.4 (41.7, 29.7 - 55.2)
Group	9.4 (11.3, 2.8 - 16.6)	3.9 (7.4, 1.3 - 10.1)
Global + Group	33.7 (32.8, 20.0 - 43.3)	52.4 (49.0, 34.4 - 63.7)
Factor	EMDEs	
Global	7.8 (15.2, 2.5 - 21.0)	15.3 (25.6, 8.6 - 40.4)
Group	1.2 (10.0, 0.2 - 8.5)	3.4 (6.7, 1.9 - 7.1)
Global + Group	13.3 (25.2, 8.7 - 39.8)	24.1 (32.3, 12.7 - 52.4)

Note: The global and group inflation factors for tradable and nontradable goods and services are estimated with the baseline two-factor dynamic factor model for 1970-2016 (Annex 2.1). The common factor from three measures of domestic inflation (import prices, PPI, and headline CPI) is used as a proxy variable for the common component for tradable goods. Similarly, common factors for headline CPI, core CPI, and the GDP deflator are extracted as a proxy for the global inflation factor for nontradable goods. The sample includes annual inflation in 38 countries (25 advanced economies and 13 EMDEs) for 1970-2016. The long-term trend (15-year moving average) is eliminated from annual inflation rates. For each pair of rows, the number in the first row indicates medians across countries. The first number in the second row (in parentheses) is the unweighted mean across countries. The second and third numbers in the second row (in parentheses) indicate the interquantile range (25th and 75th percentiles). CPI = consumer price index; EMDEs = emerging market and developing economies; GDP = gross domestic product; PPI = producer price index.

shocks, other cost-push shocks, and real demand shocks that trigger global recessions or expansions could all affect national inflation rates widely and often in the same direction, which would represent inflation synchronization. For example, the 2009 global recession was followed by a prolonged period of globally depressed inflation. Other shocks could affect countries asymmetrically. For example, oil price shocks would affect oil importers and oil exporters differently (Baffes et al. 2015).

Similarly, a recession in a relatively large economy could have greater spillover effects on activity and inflation in its close trading partners than elsewhere (Huidrom, Kose, and Ohnsorge 2017). Exchange rate changes, especially ones that go beyond movements warranted by real-economy developments, such as domestic currency crises or confidence shocks, will also tend to pass through into national inflation rates asymmetrically (Shambaugh 2008). On average, traded goods account for over 60 percent of consumer baskets in EMDEs and 47 percent of consumer baskets in advanced economies. Hence, exchange rate movements would tend to affect consumer prices directly and significantly. The extent of such exchange rate pass-through is discussed in detail in Chapter 5.

Similar policy responses. Earlier studies have often highlighted the contribution of correlated or coordinated monetary policies as a main source of inflation comovement, especially among advanced economies (Clarida, Gali, and Gertler 2002; Rogoff 2003). Even if there is no deliberate coordination of policies, similar monetary policy frameworks can trigger similar policy responses to global shocks. This policy synchronicity would then translate into inflation synchronicity.

For example, a growing number of countries have introduced inflation targeting monetary policy frameworks. In many of these countries, inflation targets have been lowered over the past three decades, and in advanced economies the targets are now virtually universally at or around 2 percent (Chapter 1). In EMDEs, inflation targeting has been associated with lower inflation, and the switch to inflation targeting has been associated with larger declines in inflation (Fang, Miller, and Lee 2012; Gonçalves and Salles 2008). Henriksen, Kydland, and Šustek (2013) develop an international business cycle model with technological spillovers in which central banks' Taylor rules trigger monetary policy responses to productivity shocks that are similar across countries. As a result, their model generates movements in inflation that are synchronized across countries.

Structural changes. Over the past four to five decades, the degree of global integration in trade and financial markets has grown rapidly (Chapter 1). These structural changes have often strengthened cross-country spillovers of real and nominal shocks, which have in turn led to more synchronized movements in inflation.

- *Stronger trade linkages* increase an economy's exposure to external shocks. With growing trade linkages, import prices have accounted for rising shares of global production costs and domestic prices of final goods and services. As a result, domestic inflation has become more sensitive to global shocks that raise or lower import prices (Bianchi and Civelli 2015).[7] The results in the previous section indicate that inflation synchronization has been greater

[7] This study is broadly in line with the literature that investigates the role of international input-output linkages in driving the synchronization of global business cycles (Kose and Yi 2006; di Giovanni and Levchenko 2010; Johnson 2014). Martínez-García (2015) develops a new open-economy macro model for the United States and 38 of its trading partners. The model can account for inflation synchronization even in the absence of common shocks, simply through the presence of strong spillovers associated with trade linkages.

for measures with larger tradables content and, since 2001, has increased across inflation measures. These findings likely reflect that prices are more likely to be internationally determined in sectors with strong trade linkages to global markets where they are subject to common demand and supply shocks (Karagedikli, Mumtaz, and Tanaka 2010; Parker 2018). Over time, the impact of global shocks in traded goods prices tend to be passed through to other prices, with the degree and speed of the pass-through depending on country characteristics, including trade and financial openness and the credibility of the central bank's inflation objective (Chapter 5).

- *Rapidly expanding global supply chains* allow global supply and demand shocks as well as commodity price swings to ripple through global input-output linkages and global labor markets and cause comovement in national inflation rates (Rogoff 2003; Auer, Borio, and Filardo 2017).

- Greater international competition has made *domestic inflation less sensitive to domestic output gaps*, flattening Phillips curves (Eickmeier and Pijnenburg 2013; Carney 2017; Kabukçuoğlu and Martínez-García 2018).

- *Financial linkages.* Increased international integration of financial markets has been accompanied by greater synchronization of financial conditions—including financial stress—across countries (Neely and Rapach 2011; Carney 2017). As financial stress spreads (or recedes) across global financial markets, it tightens (or loosens) credit and financial conditions in a wide range of countries. As a result, movements in domestic demand and disinflationary or inflationary pressures are also synchronized across countries.

- *Technological changes*, in addition to deepening supply chains, can also help globalize markets for nontradable service sectors. This may extend and deepen the impact of global forces on domestic inflation (Henriksen, Kydland, and Šustek 2013; Carney 2017).

Country-specific features

The results in the previous sections indicate that, since 2001, the global factor has accounted for 27 percent of domestic inflation variation in advanced economies and 18 percent in EMDEs. Similarly, the group factor has grown in importance such that, since 2001, it has accounted for 21 percent in the median advanced economy and 8 percent in the median EMDE. However, there has been wide heterogeneity in these shares across countries, especially among EMDEs, pointing to the importance of country characteristics (Monacelli and Sala 2009; Neely and Rapach 2011). This section briefly examines the country-specific correlates of the contribution of the global and group-specific factors to EMDE inflation variation.

Correlates of the contribution of the global factor. The global factor has generally contributed more to inflation variation in advanced economies than in EMDEs and, among EMDE regions, has contributed most in East Asia and Pacific, Latin America and the Caribbean, and South Asia. The global inflation factor also explains a larger share of inflation variation in commodity-importing and more trade-open EMDEs (Figure 2.6). Lower trade openness and the heavy reliance on commodity exports in three-quarters of LICs may, in part, explain the weak inflation synchronization in LICs.

A panel regression of the contribution of global or group factors to inflation variation on indicators of integration into the global economy and policy frameworks helps identify those features that are most significantly correlated with greater inflation synchronization. The data set includes annual data for 25 advanced economies and 58 EMDEs (of which 16 are LICs) for 1970-2017. The results suggest that the global factor was significantly more important for inflation in countries with higher trade openness, greater commodity-import intensity, and lower trade concentration (Table A.2.1.4, Annex 2.1). This is consistent with studies that have attributed inflation synchronization to trade or supply chain integration in advanced economies (Box 2.1).[8]

Evolution of the contribution of the global factor over time. The cross-country heterogeneity in the contribution of the global factor to inflation variation seems to have been a phenomenon of the 1970s-1990s that largely disappeared in the 2000s. During 1970-85, as in the full sample period, higher trade openness, commodity importer status, and a more flexible exchange rate regime were each associated with greater contributions of the global factor to inflation. Since 2001, these differences have become less pronounced: the range of contributions of the global factor narrowed from 0-87 percent in 1970-85 to 0-58 percent in 2001-17, without any evidence of systematic differences by country characteristics (Figure 2.6; Table A.2.1.4, Annex 2.1).[9]

Correlates of the contribution of the EMDE factor. Overall, the contributions of the EMDE-specific factor to inflation variation were more homogeneous than those for the global factor and have, if anything, also become more homogeneous over time. That said, there are some systematic differences by country characteristics. In particular, the group factor contributed more to

[8] See Monacelli and Sala (2009); Karagedikli, Mumtaz, and Tanaka (2010); Martínez-García (2015); and Auer, Borio, and Filardo (2017). For instance, in a Phillips curve framework, Auer, Borio, and Filardo (2017) present evidence that cross-border trade in intermediate goods and services is the main channel through which global economic slack influences domestic CPI inflation.

[9] In the regression analysis, this loss of systematic differences is apparent in the lack of statistically significant coefficients in the subsample for 2001-17 in Table A.2.1.4, Annex 2.1.

FIGURE 2.6 Contribution of the global factor to inflation: EMDEs

Among EMDEs, the share of the global factor in domestic inflation variance has been particularly high in East Asia and Pacific, Latin America and the Caribbean, and South Asia. In trade-open EMDEs and commodity-importing EMDEs, the global factor also explains a larger share of domestic inflation variance than elsewhere. Since 2001, the differences across EMDE country groups have narrowed, and the contribution of the global factor has become more broad-based.

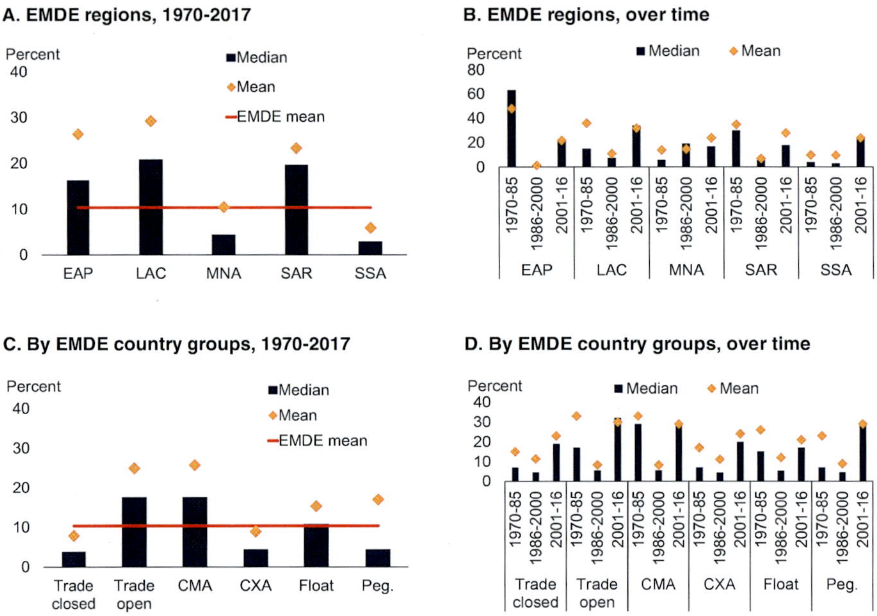

Source: World Bank

Note: Contribution of global and group inflation factors to inflation variance. The global and group inflation factors are estimated with the baseline two-factor dynamic factor model for 1970-2017 (Annex 2.1). The sample includes 25 advanced economies and 74 EMDEs, including 16 low-income countries. CMA = commodity importing EMDEs; CXA = commodity exporting EMDEs; EAP = East Asia and Pacific; EMDEs = emerging market and developing economies; Float = EMDEs with floating exchange rate regimes; LAC = Latin America and the Caribbean; MNA = Middle East and North Africa; Peg. = EMDEs with pegged exchange rate regimes; SAR = South Asia; SSA = Sub-Saharan Africa; Trade closed = EMDEs with lower trade openness, measured by the trade-to-GDP ratio (below the median across countries); Trade open = EMDEs with higher trade openness measured by the trade-to-GDP ratio (above the median across countries).

inflation variation in commodity exporters as well as in countries with pegged exchange rates (Figure 2.6; Table A.2.1.5, Annex 2.1). However, these correlates have shifted over time such that, since 2001, the exchange rate regime has no longer been systematically correlated with the contribution of the group factor. Instead, since 2001, as a growing number of EMDEs shifted toward inflation targeting monetary policy regimes, a systematic negative correlation has emerged between the contribution of the group factor to inflation variation and inflation targeting.

Conclusion

This chapter examines three questions about the extent of global inflation synchronization.

How has inflation synchronization evolved over time? Inflation has become increasingly synchronized globally: 18 percent (in the median EMDE) to 27 percent (in the median advanced economy) of inflation variation since 2001 has been accounted for by the global factor. Over the past four decades, an EMDE-specific factor has emerged that has explained about 8 percent of EMDE inflation variation since 2001, one-quarter higher than in the 1970s although still below the contribution of an advanced economy factor (21 percent). Inflation synchronization varies widely across countries but has become more broad-based over time. During 1986-2000, the global factor contributed more than 10 percent to inflation variation in around one-third of the countries in the sample; by 2001-17, this share had risen to two-thirds.

Which goods and price indexes have been associated with greater inflation synchronization? Inflation synchronization has become more pronounced across inflation measures over time. Although the global factor continues to contribute much more to inflation measures with a higher tradables content (import prices and the PPI) than to measures with a lower tradables content (core and headline CPI and the GDP deflator), this contribution has risen for all inflation measures: to two-thirds for PPI inflation and around one-third for core CPI inflation and GDP deflator growth.

Which country characteristics have been associated with greater inflation synchronization? Countries differ widely in the degree to which global factors and, to a lesser extent, group factors account for domestic inflation variation. The global factor has accounted for a larger share of domestic inflation variation in countries that have been more open to global trade, relied on commodity imports, had more concentrated trade, were more economically developed, or were EMDEs in the East Asia and Pacific, Latin America and the Caribbean, and South Asia regions. That said, over the past four to five decades, this heterogeneity has narrowed such that, since 2001, no country characteristic appears to account systematically for the greater contributions of global factors. Since 2001, the EMDE group factor has explained a greater share of inflation variability in EMDEs that did not have inflation targeting monetary policy frameworks.

The increased synchronicity of global inflation could pose challenges for policy makers. Inflation synchronization in and of itself need not warrant policy intervention (IMF 2018). However, it increases the risk of policy errors when the appropriate response to excessively low or high inflation differs depending on the origin (domestic or foreign) of the underlying inflation shock (Hartmann and McAdam 2018). In the context of exchange rate pass-through, this issue is explored in detail in Chapter 5.

Inflation synchronization raises concerns that central banks' control over domestic inflation may have weakened (Carney 2017). Heads of major advanced economy central banks have acknowledged the need to consider the global environment in setting monetary policy (Bernanke 2007; Draghi 2015; Carney 2015). Weaker monetary policy transmission would increase the burden on fiscal policy to respond to excessive or deficient domestic demand. It would also increase the need for product and labor market flexibility to be able to adjust before relative price changes driven by foreign shocks turn into general inflation. Global inflation synchronization could also strengthen the case for coordinated policy action (IMF 2018). A coordinated response to uncomfortably low or high global inflation could amplify the impact of policies advanced by an individual country.

Future research could take two directions. First, it could delve further into the sources of the inflation synchronization that has been documented here. Synchronization could be generated by common shocks that affect all countries, or by country-specific shocks that spill over between countries. This chapter—as well as the next one—is agnostic about these two sources. Second, this chapter estimates synchronization in short-term inflation movements, not in long-term inflation trends. Yet, as documented in Chapter 1, inflation has trended downward steeply around the world over the past four decades. Future research could aim to quantify the extent of synchronization in these long-term inflation trends.

ANNEX 2.1 Methodology and database

Dynamic factor model

Following Kose, Otrok, and Prasad (2012), this chapter decomposes fluctuations in inflation into one or more latent factors in the context of a dynamic factor model. Dynamic factor models are designed to extract a small number of unobservable common elements from the covariance or comovement between (observable) macroeconomic time series across countries. Thus, the model allows for a parsimonious representation of the data in terms of the unobservable common elements—typically referred to as factors. From a theoretical standpoint, dynamic factor models are appealing because they can be framed as reduced-form solutions to a standard dynamic stochastic general equilibrium (DSGE) model.

This chapter estimates two types of common driving forces in fluctuations in global inflation.

- **Global inflation factor.** This is the broad common elements in inflation fluctuations across countries.

- **Group-specific inflation factors.** These are common elements in the cyclical inflation fluctuations in the countries in a particular group. Here, it is assumed that national inflation rates are explained by a "country group" factor and advanced economy and EMDE factors.

- **Residual ("idiosyncratic") factors.** These capture elements in the fluctuations of an individual variable in a country that cannot be attributed to the other factors.

Thus, the inflation equation for each country takes the following form:

$$\pi_{i,t} = \beta^i{}_{Global} f_t^{Global} + \beta^i{}_{Group} f_t^{Group} + \varepsilon_{i,t}$$

where π_i denotes inflation in country i; the global and group factors are represented by f_t^{Global} and f_t^{Group}, respectively; and the coefficients before them (β), typically referred to as factor loadings, capture the sensitivities of the macroeconomic series to these factors. The error terms ($\varepsilon_{i,t}$) are assumed to be uncorrelated across countries at all leads and lags. The error terms and factors follow an autoregressive process. The model is estimated using Bayesian techniques as described in Kose, Otrok, and Whiteman (2003).

The importance of each factor in explaining inflation is measured by the fraction of total variance of inflation due to the respective factor. This is computed by applying the variance operator to each equation in the system. Specifically, for inflation in country *i*:

$$Var\ (\pi_i) = (\beta^i{}_{Global})^2\ Var\ (f^{Global}) + (\beta^i{}_{Group})^2\ Var\ (f^{Group}) + Var\ (\varepsilon_i{}^{\pi})$$

Since there are no cross-product terms between the factors, the variance in inflation attributable to the global factor is:

$$\frac{(\beta^i{}_{Global})^2\ Var\ (f^{Global})}{Var\ (\pi_i)}$$

The variance shares due to the group factors and idiosyncratic terms are calculated using a similar approach.

Regression analysis between the variance contributions of the inflation factors and country characteristics

To explore the relations between the impact of global and group-specific inflation factors on domestic inflation, the contributions of the global and group factors in individual countries are regressed on a variety of indicators for country characteristics. They include variables on the structure of an economy as well as policy frameworks. The variables include dummy variables for above-average commodity import intensity, income groups, and regions; dummy variables for exchange rate and monetary policy regimes; measures of trade and financial openness (trade-to-GDP ratio, capital account openness index by Chinn and Ito [2017], and index of trade concentration) and degree of participation in global value chains (share of foreign value added in exports); and measures of central bank independence and transparency and the turnover ratio of central bank heads. A more detailed description of the country characteristics is provided in the Appendix.

The regression analysis starts with a set of bivariate regressions that include a variable of interest and the constant as explanatory variables for the global or group factor's variance share of inflation. Based on the results from bivariate regressions, a multivariate regression is estimated using Bayesian model averaging (baseline) or multivariate least squares (for robustness). Considering that regional dummy variables are highly correlated with other structural and policy variables, each set of multivariate regressions is executed with and without the regional dummy variables. The estimations are conducted for the full sample (1970-2017) as well as three subsamples (1970-85, 1986-2000, and 2001-17). The list of countries is provided in Table A.2.1.2, Annex 2.1.

TABLE A.2.1.1 Factor models for inflation synchronization in the literature

Related work	Inflation measures	Data coverage	Empirical framework (economic factors)	Results
Ciccarelli and Mojon (2010)	Headline CPI	22 OECD countries (1960-2008, quarterly)	Static factor model (one global factor)	A simple average of 22 OECD countries' inflation, which the authors call global inflation, accounts for almost 70 percent of the variance of inflation in these countries between 1960Q1 and 2008Q2. First, at business cycle frequencies, the variance explained by global inflation is about 37 percent on average and much larger in many countries. Second, domestic inflation reverts to the global component. Third, in countries that have experienced stronger commitment to price stability (such as Germany) global inflation has a lesser impact on domestic inflation than in those with weaker inflation discipline (such as Italy).
Hakkio (2009)	Headline and core CPI	30 OECD and 6 non-OECD countries (1960-2008, quarterly)	Principal component analysis (global and regional factors)	The first common factor is an important determinant of national inflation rates in industrial countries and non-industrial and regional inflation rates (with R squareds of regressions of national inflation on the first common factor averaging 0.71). The commonality of industrial inflation rates appears to reflect the commonality of macro variables that are determinants of inflation.
Auer, Levchenko, and Sauré (2017)	Sectoral PPI	30 countries (1995-2011, monthly)	Dynamic factor model (global, sectoral, and country factors)	For the median country, the global component accounts for 51percent of the variance of the PPI. Input-output linkages account for half of this global component of PPI inflation. On average, a shock that raises inflation by 1 percent in the other countries in the world other than the country under observation raises domestic PPI by 0.19 percent. PPI synchronization across countries is driven primarily by common sectoral shocks and input-output linkages amplify comovement primarily by propagating sectoral shocks.
Parker (2018)	Sub-components of headline CPI	223 countries (unbalanced panel) (1980-2010, quarterly)	Dynamic hierarchical model (global, index-specific, and group factors)	Global inflation accounts for a large share of the variance of national inflation rates in OECD countries. For middle-income countries the share of national inflation variance explained by global factors is on the order of 15 to 20 percent, falling to around 10 percent for low-income countries. Higher income, greater financial sector development, and more transparent central banks are associated with a larger influence of global inflation. Relatively rich countries with deep domestic capital markets and good monetary policy are likely to be better able to mitigate idiosyncratic, domestic shocks. Global inflation factors also have greater influence on the national inflation rates of countries with fixed exchange rates. There is a more marked influence of global energy and food prices on the respective national inflation rates. Housing prices appear for the most part idiosyncratic and unrelated to global factors.

TABLE A.2.1.1 Factor models for inflation synchronization in the literature (*continued*)

Related work	Inflation measures	Data coverage	Empirical framework (economic factors)	Results
Mumtaz and Surico (2012)	Headline CPI other inflation indicators	10 advanced economies (1961-2004, quarterly)	Dynamic factor model (global and country factors)	The historical decline in the level and persistence of inflation is shared by most countries. An international factor tracks the level and persistence of national inflation rates reasonably well. The rise and fall of national contributions to inflation fluctuations are not synchronized across economies and their timing confirms conventional wisdom on the conduct of national policies: income policies and accommodative monetary policies are associated with periods of volatile inflation in the United Kingdom, the United States, Italy, and Japan. The fall in inflation predictability is a common feature of the industrialized world since the late 1980s. Differences in the pace of productivity growth appear important to explain differences in the national factors. International comovements in money growth are significantly related to international comovements in inflation.
Neely and Rapach (2011)	Headline CPI	64 countries (1950-2009, annual)	Dynamic factor model(global and regional factors)	The global factor explains 35 percent of annual inflation variability on average across the 64 countries; the regional factor explains 16 percent of inflation variability on average; and the country-specific component explains 49 percent. Although the world factor explains about a third of inflation variability on average across countries, its importance within that group varies substantially (83 percent of inflation variability in Canada; less than 10 percent in some other countries). The global inflation factor more strongly influences advanced economies with strong institutions, developed financial markets, low average inflation, and independent central banks. The relative importance of the factors is fairly stable over subsamples 1951-79 and 1980-2009, although the regional (global) factor clearly increases in importance for several North American and European (Latin American and Asian) countries during the second subsample.
Forster and Tillmann (2014)	Headline, food and energy CPI	101 economies (1996:1-2011:4)	Hierarchical factor model	About two-thirds of overall inflation volatility is due to country-specific determinants. For CPI inflation net of food and energy, the global factor and CPI basket–specific factor account for less than 20 percent of inflation variation. Only energy price inflation is dominated by common factors.
Karagedikli, Mumtaz and Tanaka (2010)	CPI of 28 product categories	14 advanced economies (1998:1 -2008:2)	Dynamic factor model	Category-specific (for 28 product categories) factors account for a large part of the comovement in the prices of goods in advanced economies which are intensive in internationally traded primary commodities; but this is less evident for other traded goods. The world factor and the category-specific factors become more significant in explaining the movement in the relative prices in the second half of the sample (2003-08).

TABLE A.2.1.1 Factor models for inflation synchronization in the literature (*continued*)

Related work	Inflation measures	Data coverage	Empirical framework (economic factors)	Results
Ferroni and Mojon (2018)	Headline CPI	22 OECD countries (1991:1-2013:3)	Forecasting model suite	The share of volatility explained by global inflation remains dominant. In a (pseudo) out-of-sample exercise, global inflation remains the only variable that can help to improve the one-year-ahead inflation forecast relative to univariate models. Commodity prices do not seem to be better predictors of domestic inflation dynamics than measures of global inflation.
Henriksen, Kydland and Šustek (2013)	Headline CPI	6 advanced economies (1974:1-2006:4)	Bilateral correlations	Fluctuations in nominal variables—aggregate price levels and nominal interest rates—are documented to be substantially more synchronized across countries at business cycle frequencies than bilateral correlations fluctuations in real output. Specifically, for 1960:1-2006:4 the average bilateral correlation of price levels is 0.52, that of short-term nominal interest rates 0.57, while that of real GDP is only 0.25.
Wang and Wen (2006)	Headline CPI	18 advanced economies	Correlations	The average cross-country correlation of inflation is significantly and systematically stronger than that of output, and the cross-country correlation of money growth is essentially zero. Yet, movements in the money stock are not significantly and systematically correlated across countries. Neither the new Keynesian sticky-price model nor the sticky-information model can fully explain the data.

Note: CPI = consumer price index; OECD = Organisation for Economic Co-operation and Development; PPI = producer price index.

TABLE A.2.1.2 List of countries

A. Full-sample country group (headline CPI inflation)	
Advanced economies (25)	Australia; Austria; Belgium; Canada; Cyprus; Denmark; Finland; France; Germany; Greece; Iceland; Ireland; Italy; Japan; Korea, Rep.; Luxembourg; New Zealand; Norway; Portugal; Singapore; Spain; Sweden; Switzerland; United Kingdom; and United States
EMDEs (58)	Algeria; Antigua and Barbuda; The Bahamas; Bahrain; Bangladesh; Barbados; Belize; Bhutan; Botswana; Cabo Verde; Cameroon; China; Colombia; Congo, Rep.; Côte d'Ivoire; Dominica; Dominican Republic; Ecuador; Egypt, Arab Rep.; El Salvador; Equatorial Guinea; Fiji; Gabon; Grenada; Guatemala; Honduras; Hungary; India; Indonesia; Iran, Islamic Rep.; Jordan; Kenya; Kuwait; Lesotho; Libya; Malaysia; Maldives; Mauritius; Morocco; Oman; Pakistan; Panama; Papua New Guinea; Paraguay; Philippines; Samoa; Saudi Arabia; Seychelles; South Africa; Sri Lanka; St. Kitts and Nevis; St. Lucia; St. Vincent and the Grenadines; Eswatini; Thailand; Trinidad and Tobago; Tunisia ;and Vanuatu
LICs (16)	Benin; Burkina Faso; Burundi; Central African Republic; Comoros; Ethiopia; The Gambia; Guinea; Madagascar; Mali; Nepal; Niger; Rwanda; Senegal; Tanzania; and Togo

B. Subsample country group (five inflation measures)	
Advanced economies (25)	Australia; Austria; Belgium; Canada; Cyprus; Denmark; Finland; France; Germany; Greece; Ireland; Italy; Japan; Korea, Rep.; Luxembourg; Netherlands; New Zealand; Norway; Portugal; Singapore; Spain; Sweden; Switzerland; United Kingdom; and United States
EMDEs (13)	Egypt, Arab Rep.; El Salvador; Hungary; India; Indonesia; Iran, Islamic Rep.; Kuwait; Pakistan; Panama; Philippines; South Africa; Thailand; and Tunisia

Note: Numbers in the parentheses indicate the number of countries in each group. EMDEs exclude LICs. CPI = consumer price index; EMDEs = emerging market and developing economies; LICs = low-income countries.

TABLE A.2.1.3 Variance decompositions over time: Various inflation measures—Panel A. Import Prices (Percent)

Factor	1970-85	1986-2000	2001-16
		All countries	
Global	67.7 (62.6, 54.9 - 74.9)	8.7 (15.5, 3.1 - 24.5)	50.1 (49.2, 42.6 - 63.3)
Group	5.1 (10.7, 0.7 - 13.9)	18.5 (25.7, 2.8 - 44.5)	11.4 (13.7, 6.1 - 19.2)
Global + Group	77.5 (73.2, 64.3 - 85.5)	37.6 (41.2, 18.5 - 58.8)	67.7 (62.9, 48.6 - 77.6)
Factor		Advanced economies	
Global	66.3 (62.3, 54.9 - 74.9)	8.7 (14.9, 3.4 - 24.5)	59.2 (50.9, 44.3 - 63.3)
Group	5.1 (8.7, 0.7 - 10.5)	18.5 (28.6, 3.9 - 52.3)	11.4 (13.6, 6.1 - 18.4)
Global + Group	71.7 (71.1, 61.8 - 85.5)	39.1 (43.5, 18.5 - 69.2)	68.0 (64.4, 52.0 - 77.6)
Factor		EMDEs	
Global	70.1 (63.5, 56.8 - 76.8)	9.9 (18.2, 2.9 - 25.1)	42.2 (42.4, 36.9 - 47.8)
Group	8.2 (18.9, 1.8 - 25.2)	11.8 (13.2, 2.5 - 22.5)	12.9 (13.9, 5.0 - 21.8)
Global + Group	82.5 (82.4, 79.9 - 85.0)	33.9 (31.4, 23.8 - 41.4)	49.4 (56.4, 47.0 - 58.7)

Note: The contribution of global and group inflation factors to inflation variance is estimated over the three subsample periods with a two-factor dynamic factor model for each of the five different inflation measures: import prices, PPI, headline, GDP deflator, and core CPI. The data set includes 38 countries (25 advanced economies and 13 EMDEs) except import prices for 21 countries (17 advanced economies and 4 EMDEs). The first argument in the first row indicates the unweighted median across countries. The first argument in the second row (in parentheses) is the mean variance share across countries. The second and third arguments in the second row (in parentheses) indicates the interquartile range (25th and 75th percentiles) of variance shares. CPI = consumer price index; EMDEs = emerging market and developing economies; GDP = gross domestic product; PPI = producer price index.

TABLE A.2.1.3 Variance decompositions over time: Various inflation measures—Panel B. PPI (Percent)

	1970-2016	1970-85	1986-2000	2001-16
Factor		**All countries**		
Global	42.1 (41.1, 15.3 - 61.7)	52.3 (45.2, 22.1 - 67.5)	5.2 (9.2, 2.3 - 11.2)	67.2 (61.4, 55.1 - 76.4)
Group	6.6 (3.2, 0.9 - 8.8)	7.3 (12.6 , 2.2 - 18.3)	16.7 (22.5, 7.1 - 29.9)	3.9 (6.1, 1.3 - 8.1)
Global + Group	49.9 (45.2, 19.7 - 67.3)	65.0 (54.8, 32.9 - 81.0)	24.9 (30.0, 16.1 - 42.7)	71.3 (63.9, 54.9 - 82.1)
Factor		**Advanced economies**		
Global	56.1 (48.4, 33.9 - 63.7)	62.1 (50.0, 27.5 - 70.7)	4.0 (9.0, 2.3 - 8.3)	71.7 (68.3, 65.8 - 77.0)
Group	4.5 (7.7, 1.1 - 9.6)	7.1 (13.2, 3.2 - 23.1)	20.7 (28.6, 11.9 - 45.8)	5.9 (6.8, 1.1 - 8.4)
Global + Group	60.6 (51.6, 31.2 - 68.1)	71.7 (58.1, 38.9 - 85.1)	35.8 (34.5, 19.1 - 52.1)	77.3 (69.1, 66.8 - 87.8)
Factor		**EMDEs**		
Global	16.2 (28.3, 11.1 - 40.4)	33.7 (36.9, 12.9 - 57.8)	6.9 (9.8, 3.1 - 11.6)	49.4 (49.0, 27.6 - 63.4)
Group	1.4 (4.7, 0.8 - 4.0)	11.4 (11.6, 2.2 - 16.6)	13.2 (11.7, 5.2 - 15.9)	3.5 (4.8, 2.4 - 7.4)
Global + Group	22.6 (33.0, 13.5 - 41.0)	50.3 (48.4, 31.5 - 70.0)	20.0 (21.4, 14.9 - 26.6)	57.6 (53.9, 41.2 - 66.6)

Note: The contribution of global and group inflation factors is estimated over the three subsample periods with the dynamic factor model (two-factor model) for each of the five different inflation measures: import prices, PPI, headline, GDP deflator, and core CPI. The data set includes 38 countries (25 advanced economies and 13 EMDEs) except import prices for 21 countries (17 advanced economies and 4 EMDEs). The first argument in the first row indicates the unweighted median across countries. The first argument in the second row (in parentheses) is the mean variance share across countries. The second and third arguments in the second row (in parentheses) indicate the interquartile range (25th and 75th percentiles) of variance shares. CPI = consumer price index; EMDEs = emerging market and developing economies; GDP = gross domestic product; PPI = producer price index.

TABLE A.2.1.3 Variance decompositions over time: Various inflation measures—Panel C. Headline CPI (Percent)

	1970-2016	1970-85	1986-2000	2001-16
Factor		All countries		
Global	15.7 (22.9, 6.2 - 36.5)	18.7 (28.2, 10.3 - 42.4)	4.0 (5.8, 1.9 - 7.5)	32.8 (30.8, 19.5 - 44.7)
Group	9.1 (12.8, 3.4 - 21.4)	8.6 (14.5, 3.8- 22.9)	5.7 (9.5, 4.8 - 10.3)	19.1 (20.2, 10.3 - 24.7)
Global + Group	34.1 (35.7, 25.4 - 44.6)	42.9 (42.7, 25.0 - 56.7)	12.1 (15.3, 8.1 - 19.0)	55.2 (51.2, 47.7 - 60.8)
Factor		Advanced economies		
Global	21.4 (23.7, 11.0 - 36.6)	20.0 (27.3, 8.7 - 42.6)	4.3 (6.2, 1.9 - 7.6)	37.0 (35.0, 28.8 - 44.9)
Group	11.5 (14.0, 4.1 - 24.1)	19.8 (18.9, 4.3 - 29.7)	5.5 (6.4, 4.7 - 7.0)	17.3 (16.6, 9.1 - 19.9)
Global + Group	35.9 (37.7, 31.1 - 44.8)	45.1 (46.1, 28.3 - 59.1)	12.0 (12.6, 7.8 - 14.6)	54.4 (52.8, 48.5 - 58.3)
Factor		EMDEs		
Global	11.6 (21.4, 3.4 - 36.3)	17.4 (30.0, 13.8 - 41.9)	3.2 (5.1, 1.0 - 5.2)	18.1 (21.0, 3.4 - 24.7)
Group	7.7 (10.4, 0.9 - 11.8)	6.8 (6.2, 3.2 - 8.6)	10.2 (15.5, 5.7 - 19.2)	25.6 (30.4, 12.4 - 42.6)
Global + Group	25.6 (31.9, 16.7 -43.9)	26.2 (36.2, 23.0 - 45.1)	12.6 (20.6, 10.1 - 27.8)	59.2 (48.3, 28.8 - 64.7)

Note: The contribution of global and group inflation factors is estimated over the three subsample periods with the dynamic factor model (two-factor model) for each of the five different inflation measures: import prices, PPI, headline, GDP deflator, and core CPI. The data set includes 38 countries (25 advanced economies and 13 EMDEs) except import prices for 21 countries (17 advanced economies and 4 EMDEs). The first argument in the first row indicates the unweighted median across countries. The first argument in the second row (in parentheses) is the mean variance share across countries. The second and third arguments in the second row (in parentheses) indicate the interquartile range (25th and 75th percentiles) of variance shares. The results differ from Tables 2.1 and 2.2 because of the smaller sample size to match the sample with available data for other measures of inflation. CPI = consumer price index; EMDEs = emerging market and developing economies; GDP = gross domestic product; PPI = producer price index.

TABLE A.2.1.3 Variance decompositions over time: Various inflation measures —Panel D. GDP deflator (Percent)

	1970-2016	1970-85	1986-2000	2001-16
Factor	All countries			
Global	12.6 (18.7, 3.2 - 30.5)	13.7 (25.9, 5.5 - 43.0)	7.4 (16.7, 3.1 - 28.8)	33.4 (32.4, 16.2 - 50.0)
Group	12.1 (16.0, 4.6 - 25.5)	12.7 (18.6, 5.8 - 28.3)	7.1 (11.7, 3.4 - 18.8)	4.1 (11.3, 0.8 - 10.9)
Global + Group	35.3 (33.8, 19.1 - 45.0)	45.3 (43.3, 19.9 - 63.2)	25.0 (27.6, 11.8 - 37.8)	44.8 (42.6, 30.7 - 58.0)
Factor	Advanced economies			
Global	13.4 (19.1, 6.5 - 31.5)	14.8 (27.1, 9.4 - 42.1)	12.8 (18.1, 3.4 - 28.9)	35.7 (34.4, 19.5 - 48.0)
Group	12.6 (15.9, 3.5 - 25.0)	9.3 (13.8, 5.0 - 23.0)	7.2 (11.5, 3.4 - 15.9)	2.3 (3.2, 0.6 - 5.2)
Global + Group	33.6 (37.3, 18.1 - 45.8)	37.8 (39.3, 19.9 - 59.3)	29.7 (28.4, 15.9 - 42.8)	39.2 (36.1, 22.1 - 47.6)
Factor	EMDEs			
Global	9.3 (18.0, 2.2 - 26.1)	9.8 (23.7, 1.9 - 44.5)	3.5 (14.2, 3.1 - 15.5)	19.7 (28.7, 10.3 - 50.0)
Group	9.5 (16.2, 6.2 - 25.5)	19.6 (27.5, 9.1 - 44.5)	7.1 (12.0, 3.4 - 18.8)	25.5 (26.3, 10.4 - 44.4)
Global + Group	33.7 (34.2, 22.2 - 37.4)	54.9 (51.2, 32.5 - 70.1)	22.8 (26.2, 10.5 - 35.9)	56.7 (55.0, 53.0 - 65.5)

Note: The contribution of global and group inflation factors is estimated over the three subsample periods with the dynamic factor model (two-factor model) for each of the five different inflation measures: import prices, PPI, headline, GDP deflator, and core CPI. The data set includes 38 countries (25 advanced economies and 13 EMDEs) except import prices for 21 countries (17 advanced economies and 4 EMDEs). The first argument in the first row indicates the unweighted median across countries. The first argument in the second row (in parentheses) is the mean variance share across countries. The second and third arguments in the second row (in parentheses) indicate the interquartile range (25th and 75th percentiles) of variance shares. CPI = consumer price index; EMDEs = emerging market and developing economies; GDP = gross domestic product; PPI = producer price index.

TABLE A.2.1.3 Variance decompositions over time: Various inflation measures —Panel E. Core CPI (Percent)

	1970-2016	1970-85	1986-2000	2001-16
Factor		All countries		
Global	4.7 (12.5, 1.7 - 15.4)	8.4 (14.2, 6.9 - 14.5)	5.4 (17.5,1.3 - 29.1)	29.8 (27.8, 9.7 - 42.1)
Group	14.1 (18.8, 2.9 - 26.6)	16.5 (18.9, 5.2 - 31.8)	10.6 (15.3, 3.1 - 25.6)	3.5 (5.8, 2.1 - 7.7)
Global + Group	26.5 (27.9, 10.9 - 40.4)	28.6 (29.6, 11.6 - 44.3)	31.3 (29.2, 11.9 - 44.9)	33.0 (30.0, 13.8 - 46.9)
Factor		Advanced economies		
Global	7.9 (14.5, 3.1 - 21.4)	8.5 (16.0, 7.7 - 22.6)	5.3 (16.1, 2.3 - 26.3)	31.9 (29.5, 25.0 - 44.1)
Group	17.7 (21.9, 8.7 - 34.8)	16.9 (21.0, 5.2 - 35.7)	17.9 (17.1, 2.3 - 29.2)	3.1 (5.8, 2.0 - 5.4)
Global + Group	34.6 (34.9, 18.9 - 46.4)	40.1 (35.5, 13.2 - 53.7)	31.8 (30.9, 20.6 - 46.6)	35.1 (33.0, 20.6 - 47.7)
Factor		EMDEs		
Global	1.7 (8.0, 1.3 - 9.1)	10.1 (8.9, 2.5 - 12.9)	26.3 (26.2, 0.7 - 29.1)	22.2 (23.3, 0.6 - 29.0)
Group	2.9 (11.5, 1.5 - 13.5)	9.4 (11.5, 5.3 - 19.2)	7.0 (6.9, 4.6 - 10.9)	6.4 (7.6, 4.2 - 13.2)
Global + Group	11.8 (15.0, 3.0 - 16.5)	17.2 (18.7, 5.6 - 27.5)	22.4 (24.9, 5.9 - 33.6)	11.8 (22.9, 1.1 - 31.1)

Note: The contribution of global and group inflation factors is estimated over the three subsample periods with the dynamic factor model (two-factor model) for each of the five different inflation measures: import prices, PPI, headline, GDP deflator, and core CPI. The data set includes 38 countries (25 advanced economies and 13 EMDEs) except import prices for 21 countries (17 advanced economies and 4 EMDEs). The first argument in the first row indicates the unweighted median across countries. The first argument in the second row (in parentheses) is the mean variance share across countries. The second and third arguments in the second row (in parentheses) indicate the interquartile range (25th and 75th percentiles) of variance shares. CPI = consumer price index; EMDEs = emerging market and developing economies; GDP = gross domestic product; PPI = producer price index.

TABLE A.2.1.4 Correlates of the variance share of the global inflation factor

	All	1970-85	1986-2000	2001-17
EMDE	0.03	0.033	0.01	-0.02
	(0.07)	(0.09)	(0.04)	(0.06)
GDP per capita	0.00	0.00	0.00	0.00
	(0.00)	(0.00)	(0.00)	(0.00)
Commodity exporter	-0.11**	-0.059	0.04	-0.02
	(0.04)	(0.06)	(0.04)	(0.04)
Inflation target	-0.06	-0.09	0.07	-0.03
	(0.05)	(0.07)	(0.04)	(0.05)
Exchange rate peg (R)	0.004	0.003	0.002	0.001
	(0.02)	(0.03)	(0.02)	(0.02)
Exchange rate peg (S)	-0.05	-0.11**	-0.02	0.03
	(0.04)	(0.05)	(0.03)	(0.03)
Trade openness	0.001**	0.001	0.00	0.00
	(0.00)	(0.00)	(0.00)	(0.00)
Trade concentration	-0.33**	-0.58***	-0.004	-0.047
	(0.12)	(0.17)	(0.1)	(0.10)
Financial openness	0.06	0.13	0.02	0.088
	(0.07)	(0.09)	(0.06)	(0.06)
Global value chain	-0.003	-0.004	-0.001	-0.001
	(0.00)	(0.00)	(0.00)	(0.00)
Debt-to-GDP ratio	-0.001	-0.001	0.002**	0.00
	(0.00)	(0.00)	(0.00)	(0.00)
Central bank independence and transparency	-0.004	-0.027*	-0.01	-0.003
	(0.01)	(0.01)	(0.01)	(0.01)

Note: Results of an ordinary least squares regression of the variance share of the global factor in inflation variation on a number of country characteristics as explanatory variables. The global factor is estimated with the dynamic factor model described in this Annex for the period of a full sample (1970-2017) and three subsamples (1970-85, 1986-2000, and 2001-17). The global factor is estimated in a sample of 99 countries (25 advanced economies and 74 EMDEs, including 16 low-income countries). Of these, 25 advanced economies and 58 EMDEs are included in this regression. The numbers in parentheses refer to standard errors (*** $p < 0.01$, ** $p < 0.05$, *$p < 0.1$). Inflation targeting regimes are defined as in IMF (2016). A value of 1 indicates the existence of an inflation targeting regime, a value of 0 its absence. Exchange rate regime (R) is based on Ilzetzki, Reinhart, and Rogoff (2017), and exchange rate regime (S) is based on Shambaugh (2004). A higher value indicates greater exchange rate flexibility. The measures of trade and capital account openness are, respectively, trade (exports plus imports)-to-GDP ratios (in percent) and the index compiled by Chinn and Ito (2006). Trade concentration is based on product concentration and diversification indexes of exports and imports by UNCTAD. Central bank independence and transparency is based on Dincer and Eichengreen (2014). A higher value indicates greater central bank independence and transparency. The EMDE dummy equals 1 for any EMDE and 0 for any other country. Dependent variables are based on median values over the country-specific sample periods except that the variables on exchange rate regime and inflation targeting are based on the mode. For details on the data definitions, refer to the Appendix.
EMDEs = emerging market and developing economies; GDP = gross domestic product.

TABLE A.2.1.5 Correlates of the variance share of the group inflation factor

	All	1970-85	1986-2000	2001-17
EMDE	-0.13*	0.00	-0.17	-0.20**
	(0.07)	(0.02)	(0.11)	(0.10)
LIC	0.00	-0.02	0.04	-0.25**
	(0.06)	(0.04)	(0.1)	(0.13)
GDP per capita	0.00	0.00	0.00	0.00
	(0.00)	(0.00)	(0.00)	(0.00)
Commodity exporter	0.09**	-0.02	0.08	0.04
	(0.04)	(0.03)	(0.06)	(0.03)
Inflation target	-0.07	0.005	-0.12	-0.07*
	(0.05)	(0.05)	(0.08)	(0.04)
Exchange rate regime (S)	0.13***	0.06**	0.20***	0.02
	(0.04)	(0.03)	(0.05)	(0.03)
Trade openness	0.00	0.00	0.00	0.00
	(0.00)	(0.00)	(0.00)	(0.00)
Trade concentration	0.10	0.11	0.20	-0.17*
	(0.11)	(0.10)	(0.16)	(0.09)
Financial openness	-0.10	0.04	-0.19**	0.03
	(0.06)	(0.05)	(0.09)	(0.05)
Global value chain	0.00	0.00	0.00	0.00
	(0.00)	(0.00)	(0.00)	(0.00)
Debt-to-GDP ratio	0.00	0.00	0.00	0.00
	(0.00)	(0.00)	(0.00)	(0.00)
Central bank independence and transparency	0.01	0.02**	0.03**	-0.01
	(0.01)	(0.01)	(0.01)	(0.01)

Note: Results of an ordinary least squares regression of the variance share of the EMDE factor in inflation variation on a number of country characteristics as explanatory variables. The global factor is estimated with the dynamic factor model described in this Annex for the period of a full sample (1970-2017) and three subsamples (1970-85, 1986-2000, and 2001-17). The global factor is estimated in a sample of 99 countries (25 advanced economies and 74 EMDEs, including 16 LICs). Of these, 25 advanced economies and 58 EMDEs are included in this regression. The numbers in parentheses refer to standard errors (*** $p < 0.01$, ** $p < 0.05$, *$p < 0.1$). Inflation targeting regimes are defined as in IMF (2016). A value of 1 indicates the existence of an inflation targeting regime, a value of 0 its absence. Exchange rate regime (S) is based on Shambaugh (2004). A higher value indicates greater exchange rate flexibility. The measures of trade and capital account openness are, respectively, trade (exports plus imports)-to-GDP ratios (in percent) and the index compiled by Chinn and Ito (2006). Trade concentration is based on product concentration and diversification indexes of exports and imports by UNCTAD. Central bank independence and transparency is based on Dincer and Eichengreen (2014). A higher value indicates greater central bank independence and transparency. The LIC dummy equals 1 for any LIC and 0 for any other country. The EMDE dummy equals 1 for any EMDE and 0 for any other country. Dependent variables are based on median values over the country-specific sample periods except that the variables on exchange rate regime and inflation targeting are based on the mode. For details on the data definitions, refer to the Appendix. EMDEs = emerging market and developing economies; GDP = gross domestic product; LIC = low-income country.

References

Auer, R. A., C. Borio, and A. Filardo. 2017. "The Globalisation of Inflation: The Growing Importance of Global Value Chains." BIS Working Paper 602, Bank for International Settlements, Basel.

Auer, R. A., A. Levchenko, and P. Sauré. 2017. "International Inflation Spillovers through Input Linkages." NBER Working Paper 23246, National Bureau of Economic Research, Cambridge, MA.

Auer, R. A., and A. Mehrotra. 2014. "Trade Linkages and the Globalisation of Inflation in Asia and the Pacific." *Journal of International Money and Finance* 49 (December): 129-51.

Baffes, J., M. A. Kose, F. Ohnsorge, and M. Stocker. 2015. "The Great Plunge in Oil Prices: Causes, Consequences, and Policy Responses." Policy Research Note 15/01, World Bank, Washington, DC.

Beck, G. W., K. Hubrich, and M. M. Marcellino. 2009. "Regional Inflation Dynamics within and across Euro Area Countries and a Comparison with the United States." *Economic Policy* 24 (57): 141-84.

Bernanke, B. S. 2007. "Globalization and Monetary Policy." Speech at the Fourth Economic Summit, Stanford Institute for Economic Policy Research, Stanford, CA.

Bhanja, N., A. B. Dar, O. Olayeni, and A. K. Tiwari. 2013. "Analyzing Time-Frequency Based Comovement in Inflation: Evidence from G-7 Countries." *Computational Economics* 45 (1): 91-109.

Bhanja, N., A. B. Dar, and A. K. Tiwari. 2016. "Frequency Based Co-movement of Inflation in Selected Euro Area Countries." *OECD Journal of Business Cycle Measurement and Analysis* 2015 (2): 1-13.

Bianchi, F., and A. Civelli. 2015. "Globalization and Inflation: Evidence from a Time Varying VAR." *Review of Economic Dynamics* 18 (2): 406-33.

Borio, C. E. V., and A. Filardo. 2007. "Globalisation and Inflation: New Cross-Country Evidence on the Global Determinants of Domestic Inflation." BIS Working Paper 227, Bank for International Settlements, Basel.

Carney, M. 2015. "How Is Inflation Affected by Globalisation?" Remarks by the Governor of the Bank of England, World Economic Forum, Jackson Hole, WY, August 29.

———. 2017. "[De]Globalization and Inflation." 2017. IMF Camdessus Central Banking Lecture, International Monetary Fund, Washington, DC.

Cecchetti, S. G., P. Hooper, B. C. Kasman, K. L. Schoenholtz, and M. W. Watson. 2007. "Understanding the Evolving Inflation Process." U.S. Monetary Policy Forum 2007, University of Chicago Booth School of Business, Chicago, IL.

Chinn, M. D., and H. Ito. 2006. "What Matters for Financial Development? Capital Controls, Institutions, and Interactions." *Journal of Development Economics* 81 (1): 163-92.

———. 2017. "The Chinn-Ito Index—A de Jure Measure of Financial Openness." http://web.pdx.edu/~ito/Chinn-Ito_website.htm.

Ciccarelli, M., and B. Mojon. 2010. "Global Inflation." *Review of Economics and Statistics* 92 (3): 524-35.

Clarida, R., J. Gali, and M. Gertler. 2002. "A Simple Framework for International Monetary Policy Analysis." *Journal of Monetary Economics* 49 (5): 879-904.

di Giovanni, J., and A. A. Levchenko. 2010. "Putting the Parts Together: Trade, Vertical Linkages, and Business Cycle Comovement." *American Economic Journal: Macroeconomics* 2 (2): 95-124.

Dincer, N., and B. Eichengreen. 2014. "Central Bank Transparency and Independence: Updates and New Measures." *International Journal of Central Banking* 10 (1): 189-259.

Draghi, M. 2015. "Global and Domestic Inflation." Speech presented to Economic Club of New York, December 4.

Eickmeier, S., and K. Pijnenburg. 2013. "The Global Dimension of Inflation: Evidence from Factor-Augmented Phillips Curves." *Oxford Bulletin of Economics and Statistics* 75 (1): 103-22.

Fang, W. S., S. Miller, and C. S. Lee. 2012. "Short- and Long-Run Differences in the Treatment Effects of Inflation Targeting on Developed and Developing Countries." Department of Economics Working Paper 1003, University of Nevada, Las Vegas, NV.

Ferroni, F., and B. Mojon. 2014. "Domestic and Global Inflation," Federal Reserve Bank of Cleveland, OH.

Forni, M., M. Hallin, M. Lippi, and L. Reichlin. 2005. "The Generalized Dynamic Factor Model: One-Sided Estimation and Forecasting." *Journal of the American Statistical Association* 100 (471): 830-840.

Förster, M., and P. Tillmann. 2014. "Reconsidering the International Comovement of Inflation." *Open Economies Review* 25 (5): 841-63.

Gerlach, S., A. Giovannini, C. Tille, and J. Vinals. 2008. "Low Inflation: Testing Times for Central Banks." ICMB Geneva Report on the World Economy 10, International Center for Monetary and Banking Studies, Geneva.

Gonçalves, C. E. S., and J. M. Salles. 2008. "Inflation Targeting in Emerging Economies: What Do the Data Say?" *Journal of Development Economics* 85 (1-2): 312-18.

Ha, J., M. A. Kose, C. Otrok, and E. S. Prasad. 2017. "Global Macro-Financial Cycles and Spillovers." Paper presented at the 18th Jacques Polak Annual Research Conference, International Monetary Fund, November 2-3, Washington, DC, November 2-3.

Hakkio, C. S. 2009. "Global Inflation Dynamics." Research Working Papers 09-01, Federal Reserve Bank of Kansas City, Kansas City, MO.

Hartmann, P., and P. McAdam. 2018. "Price and Wage-Setting in Advanced Economies: Take-Aways from the ECB's 2018 Sintra Forum." European Central Bank, Frankfurt am Main.

Henriksen, E. R., F. E. Kydland, and R. Šustek. 2013. "Globally Correlated Nominal Fluctuations." *Journal of Monetary Economics* 60 (6): 613-31.

Huidrom, R., M. A. Kose, and F. Ohnsorge. 2017. "How Important Are Spillovers from Major Emerging Markets?" Policy Research Working Paper 8093, World Bank, Washington, DC.

Ihrig, J., S. B. Kamin, D. Lindner, and J. Marquez. 2010. "Some Simple Tests of the Globalization and Inflation Hypothesis." *International Finance* 13 (3): 343-75.

Ilzetzki, E., C. M. Reinhart, and K. S. Rogoff. 2017. "Exchange Arrangements Entering the 21st Century: Which Anchor Will Hold?" NBER Working Paper 23134, National Bureau of Economic Research, Cambridge, MA.

IMF (International Monetary Fund). 2016. "Global Disinflation in an Era of Constrained Monetary Policy?" In *World Economic Outlook*, October. Washington, DC: IMF.

———. 2018. "House Price Synchronization: What Role for Financial Factors?" In *Global Financial Stability Report.* April 2018. Washington, DC: IMF.

Johnson, R. C. 2014. "Trade in Intermediate Inputs and Business Cycle Comovement. "*American Economic Journal: Macroeconomics* 6 (4): 39-83.

Kabukçuoğlu, A., and E. Martínez-García. 2018. "Inflation as a Global Phenomenon—Some Implications for Inflation Modeling and Forecasting." *Journal of Economic Dynamics and Control* 87 (C): 46-73.

Karagedikli, Ö., H. Mumtaz, and M. Tanaka. 2010. "All Together Now: Do International Factors Explain Relative Price Comovements?" Working Paper 381, Bank of England, London.

Knight, G., and L. Johnson. 1997. *Tradables: Developing Output and Price Measures for Australia's Tradable and Non-Tradable Sectors.* Canberra, Australia: Australian Bureau of Statistics.

Kose, M. A., C. Otrok, and E. Prasad. 2012. "Global Business Cycles: Convergence or Decoupling?" *International Economic Review* 53 (2): 511-38.

Kose, M. A., C. Otrok, and C. H. Whiteman. 2003. "International Business Cycles: World, Region, and Country-Specific Factors." *American Economic Review* 93 (4): 1216-39.

———. 2008. "Understanding the Evolution of World Business Cycles." *Journal of International Economics* 75 (1): 110-30.

Kose, A., and M. Terrones. 2015. *Collapse and Revival: Understanding Global Recessions and Recoveries.* Washington, DC: International Monetary Fund.

Kose, M. A., and K.-M. Yi. 2006. "Can the Standard International Business Cycle Model Explain the Relation between Trade and Comovement?" *Journal of International Economics* 68 (2): 267-95.

Lodge, D., and I. Mikolajun. 2016. "Advanced Economy Inflation: The Role of Global Factors." ECB Working Paper 1948, European Central Bank, Frankfurt am Main.

Martínez-García, E. 2015. "The Global Component of Local Inflation: Revisiting the Empirical Content of the Global Slack Hypothesis with Bayesian Methods." In *Monetary Policy in the Context of the Financial Crisis: New Challenges and Lessons,* edited by W. A. Barnett and Fredj Jawadi, 51-112. Bingley, United Kingdom: Emerald Group Publishing Limited.

Monacelli, T., and L. Sala. 2009. "The International Dimension of Inflation: Evidence from Disaggregated Consumer Price Data." *Journal of Money, Credit, and Banking* 41(s1): 101-20.

Mumtaz, H., S. Simonelli, and P. Surico. 2011. "International Comovements, Business Cycle and Inflation: A Historical Perspective." *Review of Economic Dynamics* 14 (1): 176-98.

Mumtaz, H., and P. Surico. 2012. "Evolving International Inflation Dynamics: World and Country-Specific Factors." *Journal of the European Economic Association* 10 (4): 716-34.

Neely, C. J., and D. E. Rapach. 2011. "International Comovements in Inflation Rates and Country Characteristics." *Journal of International Money and Finance* 30 (7): 1471-90.

Parker, M. 2018. "How Global Is 'Global Inflation'?" *Journal of Macroeconomics* 58 (December): 174-97.

Rogoff, K. 2003. "Globalization and Global Disinflation." *Federal Reserve Bank of Kansas City Economic Review* 88 (4): 45.

Shambaugh, J. C. 2004. "The Effect of Fixed Exchange Rates on Monetary Policy." *Quarterly Journal of Economics* 119 (1): 301-52.

———. 2008. "A New Look at Pass-Through." *Journal of International Money and Finance* 27 (4): 560-91.

Stock, J. H., and M. W. Watson. 1999. "Forecasting Inflation." *Journal of Monetary Economics* 44 (Oct.): 293-335.

Wang, P., and Y. Wen. 2007. "Inflation Dynamics: A Cross-Country Investigation." *Journal of Monetary Economics* 54 (7): 2004-31.

CHAPTER 3

Sources of Inflation: Global and Domestic Drivers

This chapter examines the key drivers of fluctuations in global and domestic inflation. It finds, first, that global demand shocks and oil price shocks have been the main drivers of variations in global inflation. Global demand shocks have become increasingly more important in explaining global inflation movements since 2001. Second, domestic shocks have explained the lion's share of domestic inflation variation. Domestic supply shocks have accounted for a larger share of inflation variance than other domestic shocks, but their importance has declined since the 1970s and 1980s. Global shocks have been responsible for around one-quarter of the variation in domestic inflation. Third, global shocks have contributed more to domestic inflation variation in advanced economies than in emerging market and developing economies. They have been a more important source of domestic inflation movements in countries with stronger global trade and financial linkages, greater dependence on commodity imports, and fixed exchange rate regimes.

Introduction

Since 1970, global inflation—defined here as the median of national inflation rates—has undergone considerable swings around a pronounced downward trend. These swings in inflation have often been associated with cyclical fluctuations in the global economy or sharp movements in oil prices (Figure 3.1). Between the early 1970s and the mid-1990s, inflation rose in many emerging market and developing economies (EMDEs) amid jumps in oil prices, currency crises, and price liberalization programs that followed economic collapse (especially in the countries of the former Soviet Union) (Chapter 1). Conversely, short-lived oil price plunges in the mid-1980s and early 1990s were accompanied by declines in inflation in advanced economies and EMDEs.

The period since the global financial crisis has been marked by an unusually pronounced and broad-based disinflation around the world. About 80 percent of countries worldwide experienced disinflation in 2008-09 and 75 percent of EMDEs experienced another bout of disinflation in the 2010s—the highest proportions since the 1980s. Roughly 80 percent of advanced economies and 40 percent of EMDEs experienced outright deflation—also exceptionally high proportions (Figure 3.2).

Note: This chapter was prepared by Jongrim Ha, M. Ayhan Kose, Franziska Ohnsorge, and Hakan Yilmazkuday. Annex 3.1 was prepared by Wee Chian Koh. Background materials for the literature review were provided by Atsushi Kawamoto.

FIGURE 3.1 Global and domestic inflation

Since 1970, global inflation has undergone considerable swings around a pronounced downward trend. These swings often coincided with global recessions or slowdowns and recoveries or large oil price fluctuations.

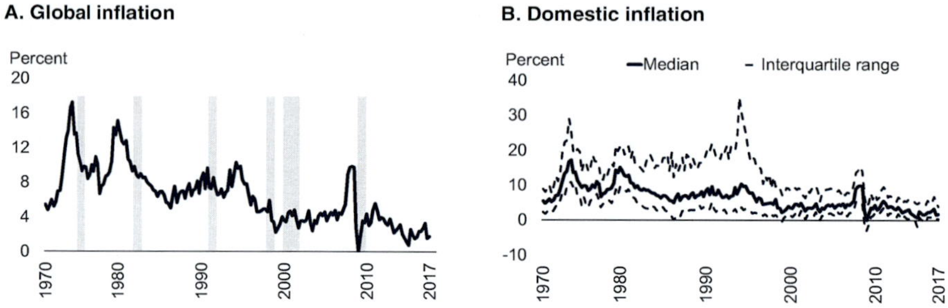

Source: OECD; Haver Analytics; World Bank.

A. Global inflation is defined as median quarter-on-quarter annualized inflation among 168 economies. Shaded areas indicate global recessions and slowdowns (Annex 3.2)

B. Median and interquartile range of quarter-on-quarter annualized inflation among 168 economies.

A growing body of research has examined the roles played by a wide range of global and domestic shocks in driving fluctuations in domestic inflation. The theoretical literature has extended the closed-economy macroeconomic models to open-economy settings that establish links between global shocks and movements in domestic inflation.[1] Empirical studies have estimated the roles played by different types of global and domestic disturbances in explaining domestic inflation variation. The results from studies using Phillips curve models have been mixed, whereas studies using vector autoregression (VAR)–based methodologies have generally identified sizable contributions of global shocks to domestic inflation. Studies for the Euro Area have found a particularly important role for the commodity price plunge of 2014-16 (Annex 3.1). This research program has typically focused on one shock or transmission channel without quantifying its importance relative to other shocks. Moreover, although the literature has established the importance of a global factor in driving domestic inflation, it has not provided a detailed analysis of the underlying drivers of global and domestic inflation. Although global demand, supply, and oil price shocks have all been mentioned as important drivers of global inflation, their quantitative importance has not been examined in a unified setup.

Against this background, this chapter studies the main drivers of movements in global and domestic inflation. The chapter addresses the following questions:

[1] For theoretical studies, see Kabukçuoğlu and Martínez-García (2018), Gali and Monacelli (2008), and Martínez-García and Wynne (2010). For empirical work, see Rogoff (2003), Borio and Filardo (2007), Bianchi and Civelli (2015), Altansukh et al. (2017), and Eickmeier and Kühnlenz (2016).

FIGURE 3.2 Countries with disinflation and deflation

Inflation has been on a pronounced and broad-based downward trend since the mid-1970s. The share of countries with slowing inflation has closely tracked global economic downturns and oil price plunges. Advanced economies are more likely than EMDEs to face disinflation during downturns. Exceptionally high proportions of advanced economies (more than three-quarters) and EMDEs (more than half) were in outright deflation at some point during 2010-17.

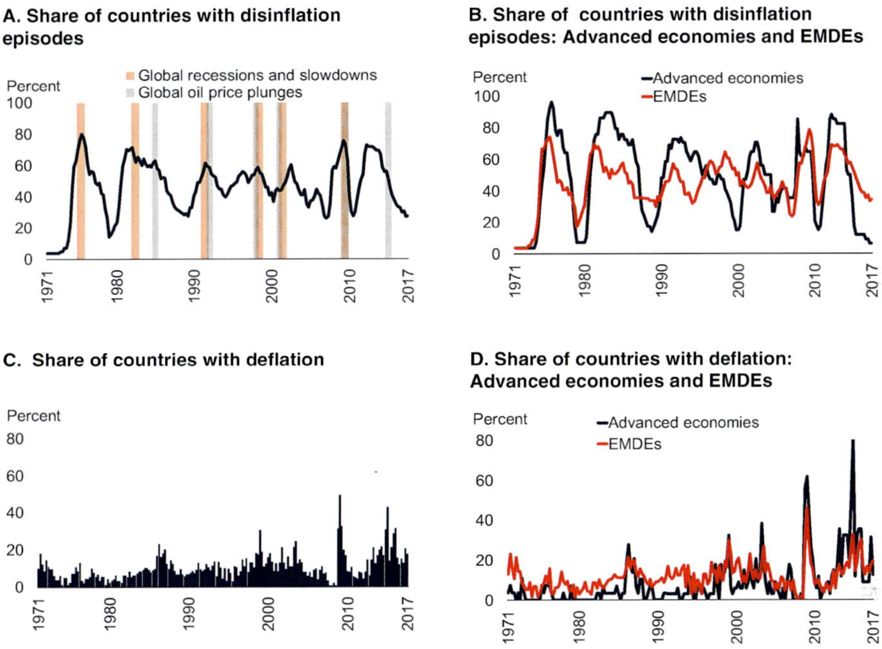

Source: World Bank.

Note: Deflation is defined as negative inflation; disinflation is defined as declining (but still positive) inflation.

A.B. Figures are based on 841 disinflation episodes, defined as in Annex 3.2, in 168 countries (of which 134 are EMDEs) between 1970:1 and 2017:3.

C.D. Deflation is defined as negative quarter-on-quarter inflation rates. Figures are based on data for 168 countries.

- What have been the main drivers of *global* inflation?
- What have been the main drivers of *domestic* inflation?
- How have the main drivers of domestic inflation differed by country characteristics?

This is the first study in the literature to present a comprehensive examination of the roles of the main drivers of global and domestic inflation for a large panel of countries over several decades. The chapter makes the following contributions to the literature:

Rich model, rich set of shocks. The chapter is the first study to examine, in a single, consistent framework, global and domestic inflation and global and domestic sources of variation in domestic inflation. It estimates a series of factor-augmented vector autoregression (FAVAR) models to quantify the roles of global demand, global supply, oil prices, and a wide range of domestic shocks in driving global and domestic inflation. Domestic shocks include domestic demand, domestic supply, monetary policy, and exchange rate shocks.

Global sample and long series. The chapter is the first to employ data for a large and globally diverse sample of countries (55 countries, including 26 EMDEs) that allows an analysis of inflation dynamics in advanced economies and EMDEs over a long period (1970-2017).

- **Historical context.** The chapter employs event studies to analyze the movements in global and domestic inflation during major economic events since 1970. By putting the post-crisis disinflation into historical context, the chapter highlights its exceptional severity.

- **Country characteristics.** In addition, the chapter considers a wide range of country characteristics that are associated with the differing contributions of global and domestic shocks to domestic inflation variability.

The chapter's principal conclusions are as follows:

- The past decade witnessed a pronounced and broad-based disinflation that depressed global inflation well below its (downward) trend. Exceptionally large fractions of advanced economies (more than three-quarters) and EMDEs (more than one-half) were in outright deflation at some point during 2010-17. Rapid decelerations or accelerations in global inflation have tended to coincide with turning points in the global business cycle or sharp movements in global oil prices.

- Global demand and oil price shocks have each accounted for 40 percent of the variation in *global* inflation since 1970. The relative importance of global demand shocks has increased since the Great Moderation (1986-2000), to account for 60 percent of global inflation variation during 2001-17. The 2014-16 oil price plunge, however, was a major source of post-crisis global disinflation.

- On average during the past four to five decades, *domestic* shocks accounted for about three-quarters of domestic inflation variation. The most important domestic shocks were supply shocks. They accounted for more of domestic inflation variation than any other domestic shocks and about as much as all global shocks combined. Since 2001, however, the role of domestic supply shocks has declined. Global demand and oil price shocks were the main source of *global* shocks' contributions to *domestic* inflation variation. During 1970-2017, they accounted for about 14 and 8 percent, respectively, of domestic inflation variation whereas global supply shocks played a minor role. Since 2001, however, in part as a result of the global financial crisis and the 2014-16 oil price plunge, the contributions of global demand and oil price shocks have increased to 22 and 17 percent, respectively, of domestic inflation variation.

- The contribution of global shocks to domestic inflation variation was larger in advanced economies and countries with higher trade and financial openness, fixed exchange rate regimes, and greater reliance on commodity imports. In EMDEs, the median contribution of global shocks to domestic inflation variance in countries with fixed exchange rate regimes and greater trade and financial openness was more than twice that in other EMDEs.

The next section examines the behavior of inflation during major events of the past four to five decades and puts the current episode of broad-based disinflation in historical context. The following section examines the main drivers of global inflation, in particular, global demand, global supply, and oil price shocks. The subsequent two sections estimate the roles of global and domestic shocks in driving movements in domestic inflation. The final section concludes with a discussion of policy implications and directions for future research.

Evolution of global and domestic inflation

It is important to distinguish at the outset between disinflation and deflation. *Disinflation* refers to a period of slowing, but still positive, inflation.[2] *Deflation* refers to a decrease in the overall price level, or a negative inflation rate.

Over the past half-century, global inflation has experienced significant movements. Some of these were disinflation episodes that were generally associated with global recessions, economic slowdowns, or large declines in global oil prices. For the purposes of this historical exploration, global inflation is defined as the median of the national trend inflation rates of 25 advanced economies and 40 EMDEs during 1970-2017.[3]

---

[2] Federal Reserve Bank of San Francisco (1999); Rogoff (2003); Goodfriend and King (2005); Coibion and Gorodnichenko (2015); Cogley, Matthes, and Sbordone (2015).

[3] In the event study, global inflation is defined as median inflation among 65 countries. The trend is defined as the nine-quarter centered moving average, as in Ball (1994). For the econometric model below, global inflation is estimated using a dynamic factor model. The estimation of a global factor model requires a balanced sample, which restricts the sample size.

Identification of global events. Turning points of global business cycles are identified using global per capita gross domestic product (GDP) and the algorithm in Harding and Pagan (2002). The method identifies four troughs of global business cycles or global recessions in 1975, 1982, 1991, and 2009 (Annex 3.2). These recessions were associated with a wide range of adverse developments, including financial crises in advanced economies or EMDEs (Kose and Terrones 2015). Global slowdowns, not involving declines in per capita GDP, took place during the Asian financial crisis in 1998 and the U.S. contraction in 2001. In contrast, peaks of global business cycles or global expansions are observed in 1973, 1981, 1990, and 2008.

Since the 1970s, there have been six oil price plunges. In 1986, 1990-91, 1997-98, 2001, 2008, and 2014-16, oil prices dropped by more than 30 percent over a seven-month period (Baffes et al. 2015). Conversely, there have been 14 oil price spikes (of which nine were reversed within two quarters), periods in which oil prices jumped by more than 30 percent over a seven-month period. Many of these episodes were associated with conflict (for example, the first Gulf War in the early 1990s or the Libyan conflict in the mid-2000s) or geopolitical tensions (for example, the Iranian Revolution in the 1970s).

Global disinflation during global recessions. Global inflation has fallen following sharp declines in global output, with a lag of one to three years. During global recessions, median global trend inflation declined 3 percentage points, on average, between the year before the trough of the global recession and the year after. The most recent global recession, in 2009, was followed by a pronounced drop in inflation (2.3 percentage points on a median basis, from 4.7 percent initial inflation). The disinflation was more than twice as steep among EMDEs as among advanced economies, but from a higher starting rate. Despite a quick rebound in both groups after 2009, inflation remained low throughout the 2010s—around 5 percent in EMDEs and 2 percent in advanced economies (Figure 3.3).

Global inflation around global expansions. With few exceptions, global trend inflation increased in the run-up to peaks of global expansions, with a slowdown after the business cycle turned (Figure 3.4). In the two years preceding the business cycle peak, median trend inflation rose by about 2.2 percentage points, on average, over all cyclical peaks since 1970. In the run-up to the most recent global business cycle peak in 2008:2, EMDE inflation rose considerably faster (by about 2 percentage points) than advanced economy inflation (0.2 percentage point) in the two years before the peak. These inflation accelerations were followed by steep subsequent declines during global recessions or slowdowns.

Global disinflation during oil price plunges. Two of the six oil price plunges since 1970—1985-86 and 2014-16—largely reflected supply decisions by the

FIGURE 3.3 Global inflation around global recessions and oil price plunges

Global recessions and oil price plunges were typically associated with slowing global inflation.

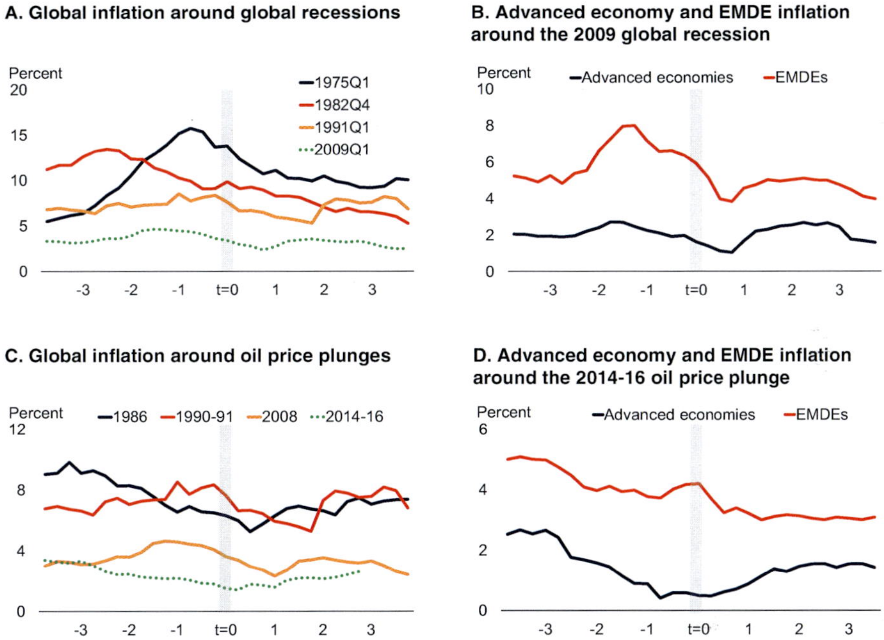

Source: World Bank; Baffes et al. 2015.

Note: Horizontal axes indicate years before and after the troughs of global recessions or local troughs of the short-term oil price cycle, as defined in Annex 3.2 (shaded area, t = 0). Global inflation is defined as median trend inflation (nine-quarter moving average) across 65 countries (balanced samples), consisting of 25 advanced economies and 40 EMDEs. EMDEs = emerging market and developing economies; GDP = gross domestic product.

A.B. Troughs of global recessions are identified using global per capita GDP and the algorithm in Harding and Pagan (2002) and are consistent with the results in Kose and Terrones (2015).

C.D. There were six oil price plunges of more than 30 percent (1986, 1990-91, 1997-98, 2001, 2008, and 2014-16) (Baffes et al. 2015). Panel C shows the four episodes with the largest oil price plunges.

Organization of the Petroleum Exporting Countries (OPEC). The organization raised output limits when faced with growing oil supply from non-OPEC producers in Mexico and the North Sea in the 1980s and the U.S. shale oil industry in the 2000s. The other four episodes predominantly reflected weak demand amid global recessions or slowdowns (World Bank 2015). On average during all six episodes, median global inflation slowed by around 1 percentage point between the year before the trough of oil prices and the year after. The 2014-16 oil price plunge was followed by a modest fall in global trend inflation, which was already low. In the two years to the trough of the most recent oil price plunge of 2014-16, the decline in EMDE inflation was broadly on par with that in advanced economy inflation.

FIGURE 3.4 Global inflation around global business cycle peaks and oil price spikes

Peaks of global expansions and oil price spikes were typically associated with rising global inflation.

A. Global inflation around global expansions **B. Global inflation around oil price spikes**

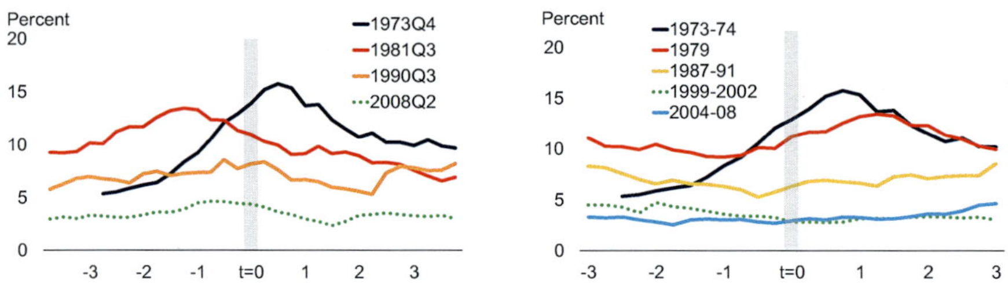

Source: World Bank; Baffes et al. 2015.

Note: Horizontal axes indicate years before and after peaks of global expansions or peaks of the short-term oil price cycle, as defined in Annex 3.2 (shaded area, t = 0). Global inflation is defined as median trend inflation across 65 countries, including 25 advanced economies and 40 EMDEs. EMDEs = emerging market and developing economies; GDP = gross domestic product.

A. Peaks of global expansions are identified using global per capita GDP and the algorithm in Harding and Pagan (2002).

B. There were five oil price spikes of more than 30 percent over a seven-month period that were not reversed within two quarters (1973-74, 1979, 1987-91, 1999-2002, 2004-08).

Global inflation around oil price spikes. Following oil price spikes, global trend inflation rose, on average across the spikes, by 2.4 percentage points within a year. The impact of the supply-driven oil price spikes in the 1970s and 1980s was much more pronounced (3.5 percentage points, on average, within a year) than the impact of the largely demand-driven oil price increases of the 1990s and 2000s (1.1 percentage points, on average, within a year). The steady rise in oil prices during 2004:3-2008:2 (when oil prices tripled) was associated with only a modest increase in trend inflation (about 1.4 percentage points), which mostly reflected sharply rising inflation in EMDEs.

Drivers of global inflation

The event study discussion above suggests that global inflation has exhibited significant movements over the global business cycle and oil price swings. Global business cycles are driven by shocks related to global supply and demand, and oil price shocks. This section quantifies the contributions of these shocks to global inflation variation.

Methodology

Model and data. A FAVAR model is estimated with three global variables—global inflation, global output growth, and global oil price growth—all expressed in quarter-on-quarter growth rates over 1970-2017, in seasonally adjusted annualized terms, with two lags (Annex 3.3).

Global inflation is defined as the common factor for detrended headline consumer price index (CPI) inflation estimated using a dynamic factor model. In parallel, the global output factor is defined as the common factor for real GDP growth estimated in a separate dynamic factor model (Figure 3.5). The database for quarterly inflation and output includes the largest country sample possible over the period 1970- 2017.[4] Global oil price growth is proxied by quarter-on-quarter growth rates of the nominal price of oil in U.S. dollar terms (average of Dubai, West Texas Intermediate, and Brent prices), as in Baffes et al. (2015).

Evolution of the global inflation and output factors. The global inflation factor was highly volatile until the 1990s (Figure 3.5). It stabilized at low levels in the 1990s and early 2000s before declining further during the global financial crisis and remaining low throughout the post-crisis period. In line with the event study above, the global inflation factor typically declined during global recessions and slowdowns. It fell sharply during the global financial crisis and after the 1975 and 1991 global recessions. Similarly, the global output factor registered significant declines during global recessions and slowed during global slowdowns. Oil price spikes during the 1970s and early 1980s, as well as before the global financial crisis, coincided with rising global inflation.

Identification of shocks. Global demand shocks, global supply shocks, and oil-price shocks are identified using a set of sign restrictions on interactions between these three variables during the first four quarters of impulse responses.[5] The restrictions to identify the structural shocks are consistent with theoretical predictions (Fry and Pagan 2011) and follow other empirical studies in the literature, although earlier studies differ in the types of variables and structural shocks on which they focus.

- A positive *global demand shock* is assumed to increase global output growth, global inflation, and oil price growth. This is consistent with similar assumptions in earlier work. Melolinna (2015) assumes that a demand shock raises output, inflation, and domestic interest rates. Charnavoki and Dolado (2014) assume that a demand shock raises output, inflation, and commodity prices. Gambetti, Pappa, and Canova (2005) assume that a

[4] The selection of countries included in the estimation of the global inflation and output growth factors reflects data availability. A balanced set of inflation series is available for 47 countries between 1970 and 2017 (accounting for 67 percent of global GDP in 2017), and that of output series is available for 29 countries (accounting for 66 percent of global GDP in 2017). The results are robust to using a smaller set of countries (25 countries, accounting for 63 percent of global GDP in 2017) with available data for inflation and output growth. The global inflation factor behaves in line with (detrended) median or average inflation, and the results are robust to defining global inflation as cross-country median or average inflation. The results are also robust to using real oil prices or nominal energy prices (Annex 3.3).

[5] The results are robust to imposing these sign restrictions for two quarters.

FIGURE 3.5 Global inflation and global output growth

Inflation comovement (captured by the contribution of a global factor to inflation variance) has been stronger than output growth comovement. For inflation and output growth, this comovement declined between 1970-85 and 1986-2000 but subsequently rebounded.

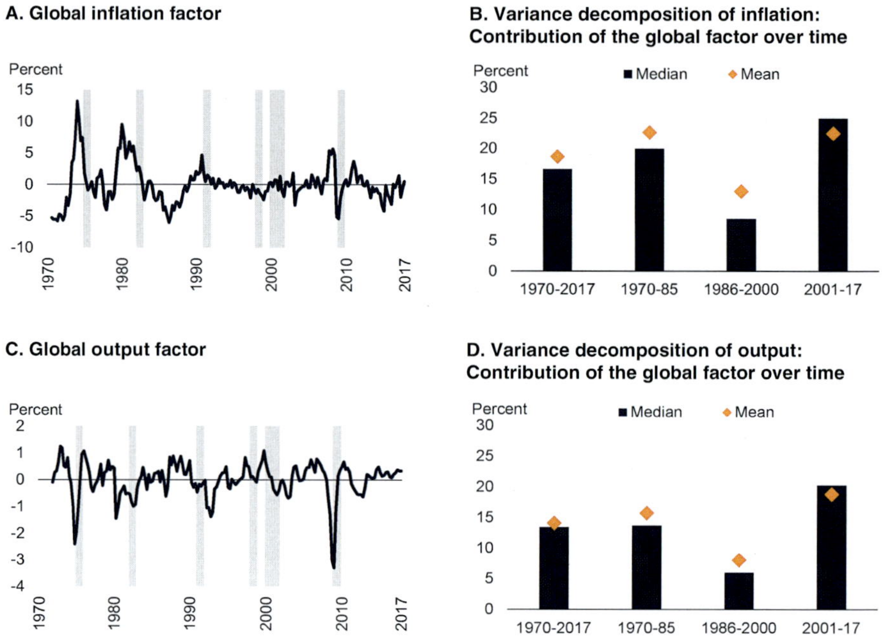

Source: World Bank.

Note: Global inflation and output factors are de-meaned. Shaded areas indicate global recessions and slowdowns (1975, 1982, 1991, 1998, 2000-01, and 2009).

A.B. The global inflation factor is extracted from 47 detrended national inflation rates using a dynamic factor model.

B.D. Variance shares of inflation (B) and output growth (D) accounted for by the global inflation factor (B) or global output factor (D) are unweighted cross-country averages or medians.

C.D. Global output growth factor is extracted from 29 detrended national output growth rates using a dynamic factor model.

demand shock raises output, inflation and commodity prices. Gambetti, Pappa, and Canova (2005) assume that a (government) demand shock raises output, inflation, domestic interest rates, and money demand. Ferroni and Mojon (2014) assume that a positive global demand shock raises output, global inflation, and commodity prices and appreciates the exchange rates of five Group of Seven (G7) economies and the Euro Area. The results presented here are robust to imposing an additional (positive) sign restriction on domestic interest rates.

- A positive *global non-oil supply shock* (hereafter "*global supply shock*") is assumed to raise global output and oil price growth but reduce global inflation. This is consistent with assumptions used by other studies.

Charnavoki and Dolado (2014) assume that a negative non-commodity supply shock raises input cost, reduces output and commodity prices, and raises inflation. Gambetti, Pappa, and Canova (2005) assume that a positive supply (technology) shock raises output but reduces inflation, domestic interest rates, and money demand. Ferroni and Mojon (2014) assume that a positive supply shock raises output, reduces inflation, and appreciates the exchange rates of five G7 economies and the Euro Area.

- A positive *oil price shock* is defined as raising oil prices and global inflation but depressing global output growth. This assumption also closely follows other studies. Melolinna (2015), Charnavoki and Dolado (2014), and Ferroni and Mojon (2014) assume that a positive cost (commodity price) shock reduces output and raises commodity prices and inflation. Baumeister and Peersman (2013) assume that a negative oil supply shock that raises the price of oil reduces output and oil consumption.

Correlates of global shocks

The model identifies a series of global demand, global supply, and oil price shocks from 1972 onward (Figure 3.6). These shocks have often been associated with turning points in the global business cycle and sharp movements in oil prices.

Global demand shocks. Negative global demand shocks were associated with global recessions (1982, 1991, and 2009) and slowdowns (1998 and 2000-01). Large positive global demand shocks often coincided with the year before the global economy began to slide into a global recession or slowdown.

Oil price shocks. Positive oil price shocks were associated with oil supply disruptions during the mid-1970s (1973-74), the Iranian Revolution (1979), the Iran-Iraq War (1979-80), the First Persian Gulf War (1990), Venezuelan unrest (2002-03), as well as militant attacks on pipelines in Iraq and Nigeria and legal disputes over oil production in República Bolivariana de Venezuela (2007-08) (Hamilton 2011; Baffes et al. 2015). Negative oil price shocks were associated with the major OPEC decision to end production restraint amid the development of new sources of oil supply (1986), the normalization of oil prices after the First Persian Gulf War (1991), the global slowdown around the Asian financial crisis (1997-98), and U.S. recessions (1990-91 and 2001). In 2014-16, OPEC's decision to abandon production restraint amid rising output from unconventional sources also constituted a negative oil price shock (Baffes et al. 2015).[6]

[6] Changes in global demand can also trigger oil price movements, such as the collapse in oil prices during the global recession of 2009. In the framework used here, these would be captured as global demand shocks.

FIGURE 3.6 Global demand, supply, and oil price shocks

Negative global demand shocks have been associated with global recessions and slowdowns. Negative oil price and global supply shocks have been associated with major supply disruptions and changes in OPEC policy. Negative global supply shocks have been associated with the disruptions following the oil price spikes of 1973 and 1979 and the global recessions or slowdowns in 1998, 2001, and 2009.

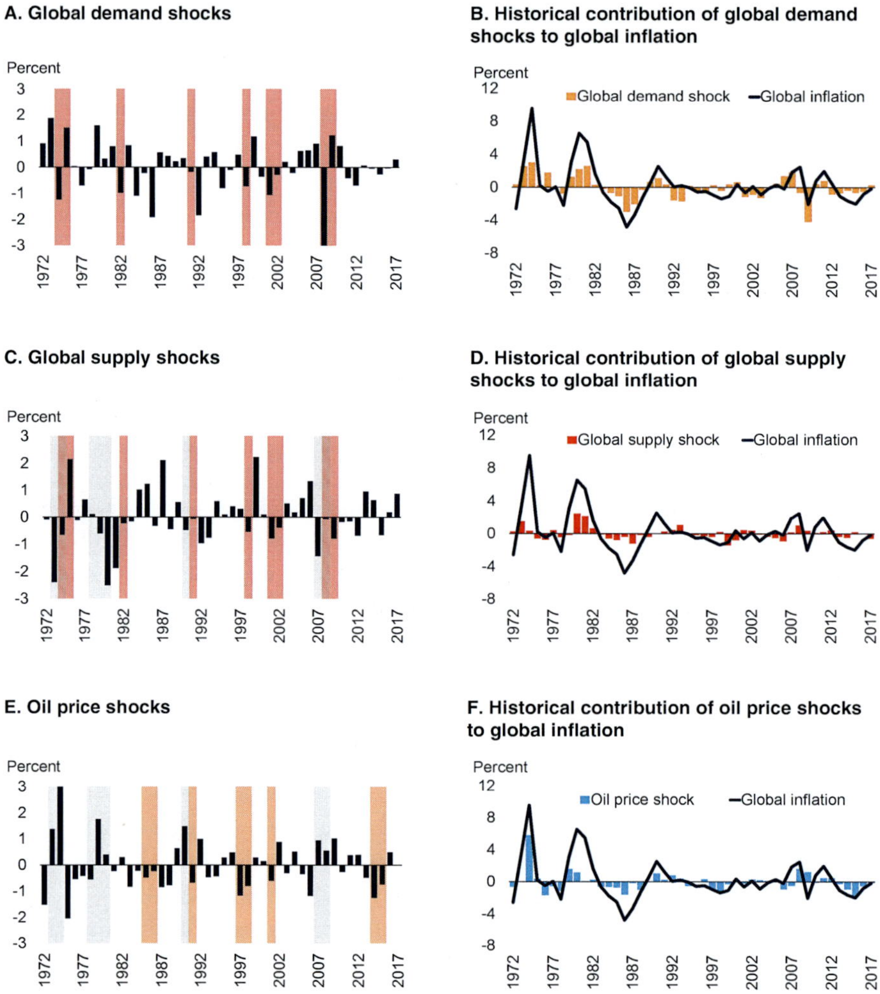

Source: World Bank.

Note: The structural shocks and their historical contributions are estimated with the global factor-augmented vector autoregression model discussed in Annex 3.3. OPEC = Organization of the Petroleum Exporting Countries.

A.C. Red-shaded areas indicate periods around global recessions and slowdowns (1975, 1982, 1991, 1998, 2000-01, and 2009).

C.E. Grey-shaded areas indicate periods around oil price spikes (1973-74, 1979, 1987-91, 1999-2002, and 2004-08).

E. Orange-shaded areas indicate periods around oil price plunges (1986, 1990-91, 1997-98, 2001, 2008, and 2014-16).

Global supply shocks. The widespread rise in inflation during the 1970s and early 1980s has been partly attributed to negative global supply shocks that compounded the impact of oil price shocks (Charnavoki and Dolado 2014). In the 1990s, global supply shocks were modest. The global economic recovery starting in the late 1990s into the mid-2000s, however, has been attributed to positive global supply shocks associated with rising productivity linked to advances in information technology and widespread trade liberalization programs in EMDEs (Charnavoki and Dolado 2014).

Role of global shocks in global CPI inflation

Impact of global shocks on global inflation. A positive one-standard-deviation global demand shock (corresponding to a 1.2 percentage point increase in annual global output growth) raised annual global inflation by 0.9 percentage point after one quarter and, cumulatively, by 5 percentage points after two years (Figure 3.7).[7] Similarly, a positive one-standard-deviation oil price shock (corresponding to an increase in annual oil price growth of around 70 percentage points) raised annual global inflation by 4.4 percentage points after two years. Although global supply shocks were modest over the sample period, a positive one-standard-deviation global supply shock reduced annual global inflation by 2.6 percentage points within two years.

Contributions of global shocks to global inflation variation. Global demand shocks and oil price shocks, in almost equal measure, have been the main drivers of global inflation variation since the 1970s (Figure 3.8). These two types of shocks together have accounted for about 80 percent of the variation in global inflation since the 1970s, each contributing about 40 percent. In contrast to global inflation, the variance of global output growth has been driven mostly by global demand shocks (accounting for 60 percent of growth variance during the full sample period), with a more modest role for oil price shocks (accounting for 22 percent of growth variation). As would be expected, fluctuations in oil prices mostly reflect shocks specific to oil prices (accounting for 76 percent of oil price variation) over the sample period.[8]

Evolution of contributions of global shocks to global inflation variation. Global shocks differed in their variability over the three subperiods. This, as well

[7] The direction of the impact of global shocks on inflation is determined by the sign restrictions for the first four quarters, but their magnitude and persistence remain of interest.

[8] These numbers refer to the variance decompositions for one-year-ahead forecast errors of global inflation. Over a medium- to long-term (5-10 years) forecasting horizon, the variance contribution of the global demand shocks (44 percent) is slightly greater than that of oil price shocks (38 percent), since global demand shocks are somewhat more persistent than oil price shocks. This is consistent with the results of Melolinna (2015) for the Euro Area, the United Kingdom, and the United States. Melolinna (2015) finds similar responses of inflation to global shocks over the past four decades.

FIGURE 3.7 Impact of global shocks on global inflation

A positive one-standard-deviation global demand shock raised global inflation by 0.9 percentage point within one quarter and, cumulatively, by 5 percentage points within two years. A positive one-standard-deviation oil price shock raised global inflation by 4.4 percentage points within two years. A positive one-standard-deviation global supply shock reduced global inflation by 2.6 percentage points within two years.

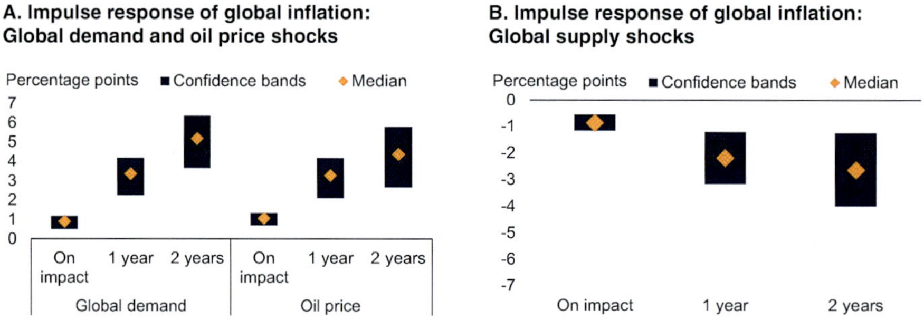

Source: World Bank.

Note: The results are estimated with the global factor-augmented vector autoregression model discussed in Annex 3.3. The cumulative impulse response of global inflation to a one-standard-deviation increase in global oil prices (corresponding to 70 percentage points higher oil price growth), global supply, or global demand (corresponding to 1.2 percentage points higher output growth) on impact, after one year, and after two years. Orange diamonds indicate the median responses and blue or red bars indicate the 16th-84th percentile confidence intervals.

as the changing responses of global inflation to these shocks, was reflected in shifts in the contribution of global shocks to global inflation variability over time. In particular, the contribution of supply shocks to global inflation variability has receded over time, while that of global demand shocks has strengthened (Figure 3.8). Global supply shocks were the main source (42 percent) of, in this case modest, global inflation variability during 1986-2000. Since 2001, however, the variance share of global supply shocks has fallen to 7 percent.

Conversely, the contribution of global demand shocks to global inflation variability has grown to 60 percent since 2001, partly reflecting the global recession of 2009 and the global slowdown of 2001. During the past decade, 2008-17, global demand shocks accounted for three-quarters of global inflation variation. However, the 2014-16 oil price plunge had a significant impact on global inflation: oil price shocks have accounted for 57 percent of global inflation variability since 2010, whereas global demand shocks have accounted for only 30 percent.[9]

[9] This is in line with ECB (2015); Sussman and Zohar (2015); and Berganza, Borallo, and del Río (2016). For instance, ECB (2015) estimates that the decline in Euro Area headline CPI inflation to zero in 2015, from 1.4 percent in 2013, was mostly driven by energy price developments.

FIGURE 3.8 Impact of global shocks on global inflation over time

Oil price shocks and global demand shocks, in approximately equal measure, have been the main sources of short-term variations in global inflation since the 1970s. The role of supply shocks receded in the two most recent decades, while that of global demand shocks strengthened. Since 2010, oil price shocks have been the main driver of global headline inflation.

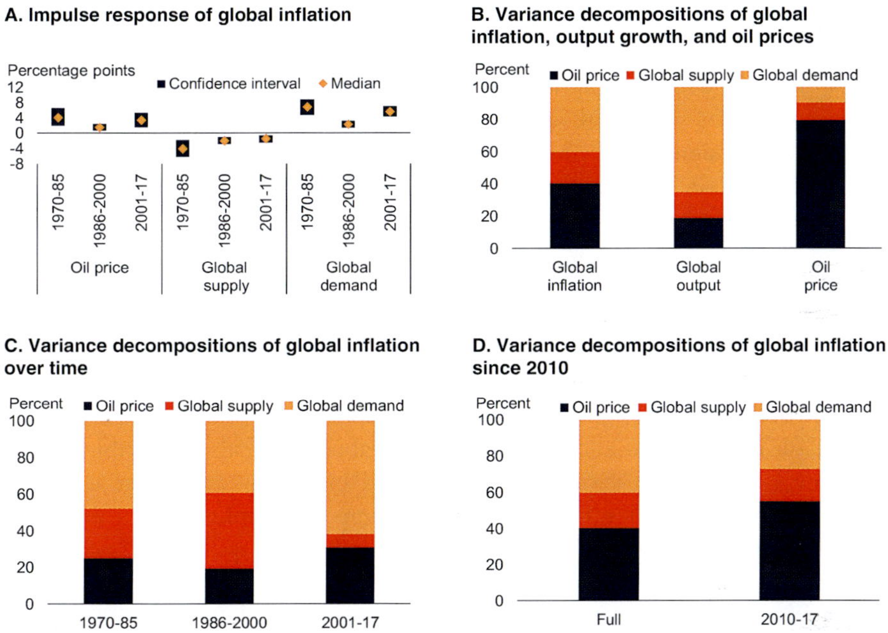

Source: World Bank.

Note: Cumulative impulse responses to one-standard-deviation shocks after two years (A) and variance decompositions (B-D) estimated by the global factor-augmented vector autoregression model discussed in Annex 3.3.

A. Cumulative response of global inflation after two years to a one-standard-deviation increase in global oil prices (corresponding to 70 percentage points higher oil price growth), global supply, or global demand (corresponding to 1.2 percentage points higher output growth). Confidence interval indicates 16th-84th percentiles.

D. Full sample period indicates 1970-2017.

Role of global shocks in different measures of global inflation

The importance of oil prices for inflation partly reflects the sizable share of energy in consumer baskets and, therefore, headline CPI inflation (Altansukh et al. 2017). On average, energy accounts for around 20 percent of headline CPI weights.[10] To explore the role of energy and other tradables in the contribution of global shocks to inflation, the same FAVAR exercise is conducted for global core CPI inflation and global producer price inflation. Producer price indexes

[10] This estimate is based on the average share of housing, water, electricity, gas, and other fuels in CPI baskets for 71 advanced economies and EMDEs (source: OECD).

(PPIs) tend to have a larger tradables content than headline CPI indexes, whereas core CPI indexes tend to have a smaller tradables content than headline CPI indexes (Chapter 2).[11]

Impact of global shocks on global core and PPI inflation. Global PPI inflation is more sensitive to global demand shocks than global headline and CPI inflation. A positive one-standard-deviation global demand shock would raise global PPI inflation by almost twice as much as it raises global CPI—headline or core—inflation over the following two years (Figure 3.9). Global PPI inflation appears to be also somewhat (one-and-a-half to two times) more sensitive, albeit not statistically significantly more, to oil price shocks than global CPI—headline or core—inflation. All three measures respond broadly similarly to a global supply shock.

Relative contributions of global shocks to inflation variability. The contribution of global demand shocks to global inflation variation was similar across all three measures (45-50 percent), but the relative contributions of oil prices and global supply shocks differed (Figure 3.9). The smaller energy content may account for the modest contribution of oil price shocks to global core CPI inflation variation (20 percent)—about half the contribution to headline CPI inflation variation. Less affected by energy and other tradables price shocks, core CPI inflation reflects an important role for global supply shocks: global productivity shocks or their cross-country spillovers, as captured by global supply shocks, appear to have been the main source of variation in core CPI inflation (38 percent), more than twice as much as for PPI inflation (14 percent) and headline CPI inflation. Over the past four to five decades, the impact of global demand, supply, and oil price shocks on global core inflation has become steadily more muted, with global demand shocks being the predominant source of global shocks. This may reflect better anchoring of inflation expectations associated with the shift toward more resilient monetary policy frameworks (Chapter 4).

Drivers of domestic inflation

The previous section establishes that global demand shocks and oil price shocks have been the main drivers of the variation in *global* inflation. This section examines the roles of global shocks along with domestic shocks in explaining the variation in *domestic* inflation.

[11] For example, the share of tradable goods and services in the United States is the greatest for the PPI (54 percent), followed by headline CPI (53 percent) and core CPI (15 percent, U.S. Bureau of Labor Statistics).

FIGURE 3.9 Impact of global shocks on global inflation: Various inflation measures

Global PPI inflation responds more strongly than other inflation measures to global demand and oil price shocks. Oil price shocks contributed about 20 percent—half as much as for headline inflation—to global core inflation variance. Meanwhile, the variance share of supply shocks in total variation in core CPI is larger than in other measures of inflation.

A. Impulse responses of headline CPI, core CPI and PPI inflation

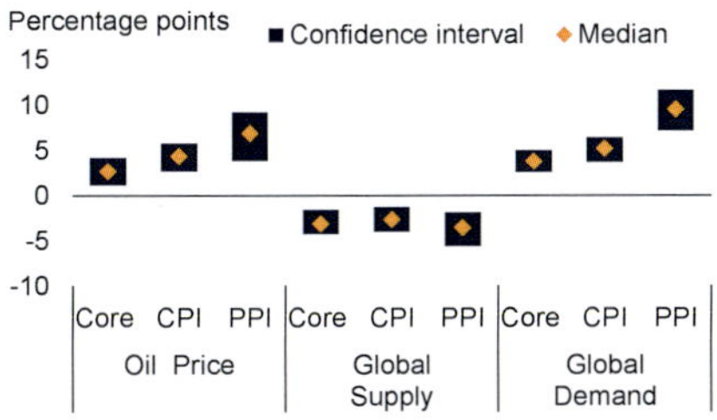

B. Variance decompositions of headline CPI, core CPI and PPI inflation

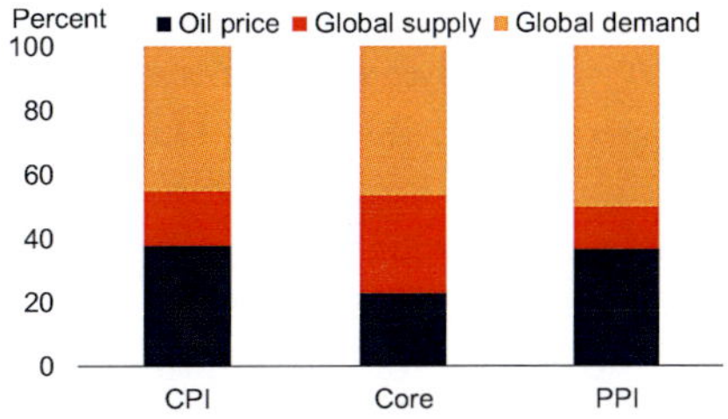

Source: World Bank.

Note: Cumulative impulse responses to positive one-standard-deviation shocks after two years (A) and variance decompositions (B) are estimated by the global factor-augmented vector autoregression model discussed in Annex 3.3, for the full sample period 1970-2017. CPI = consumer price index; PPI = producer price index.

A. Blue bars indicate 16th-84th percentile confidence intervals.

Methodology

Model and data. The FAVAR model above is expanded to include four country-specific variables, along with three global variables (global inflation, global real output growth, and oil prices): headline CPI inflation, output growth, nominal interest rates (three-month Treasury bill rates or monetary policy rates), and nominal effective exchange rates. The extension of the model here follows earlier work by Forbes, Hjortsoe, and Nenova (2017, 2018) and Conti, Neri, and Nobili (2015). All the variables are seasonally adjusted quarterly growth rates (except interest rates) between 1970 and 2017. The model is estimated on a country-by-country basis for 29 advanced economies and 26 EMDEs. For details of the model and data set, see Annex 3.3.

Identification of shocks. On top of the three global shocks (global demand, global supply, and oil price shocks) identified in the global block of the FAVAR model, four types of domestic shocks are specified: domestic supply, domestic demand, monetary policy, and exchange rate shocks.[12] The shocks are identified under the following assumptions:

[12] Gambetti, Pappa, and Canova (2005), for instance, show that a combination of technology, demand, and monetary shocks explains variations in the persistence and volatility of inflation in G7 countries.

- For global inflation, global output growth, and oil price growth, the same sign restrictions described in the previous section are imposed.
- Global variables are assumed to affect country-specific variables contemporaneously (without any sign restrictions), but the feedback from country-specific variables to global variables is assumed to be delayed by at least one quarter (block zero restriction).

To identify domestic shocks, a set of sign restrictions is imposed on the contemporaneous impulse responses of country-specific variables (Annex 3.3):[13]

- A positive *domestic demand shock* is assumed to raise domestic output growth and inflation. This is consistent with, but less restrictive than, the sign restrictions of Gambetti, Pappa, and Canova (2005), who also impose the assumption that a positive demand shock raises money demand; Forbes, Hjortsoe, and Nenova (2018) and Conti, Neri, and Nobili (2015), who also impose the assumptions that a demand shock raises interest rates and appreciates the domestic currency; and Ferroni and Mojon (2014), who also assume that a positive demand shock depreciates the domestic currency. The results presented here are robust to an additional positive sign restriction on the response within one quarter of short-term interest rates to an increase in the positive domestic demand shock.
- A positive domestic supply shock raises domestic output growth but reduces inflation. This is consistent with the sign restrictions of Forbes, Hjoertsoe, and Nenova (2018) and Gambetti, Pappa, and Canova (2005), who also impose a restriction that a positive supply shock reduces interest rates and money demand, and of Ferroni and Mojon (2014), who also assume that a positive supply shock appreciates the exchange rate.
- A contractionary (positive) *monetary policy* (or *short-term rate*) *shock* triggers nominal effective appreciation, lower output growth, and lower inflation. This is consistent with the sign restrictions of Forbes, Hjoertsoe, and Nenova (2018) and Conti, Neri and Nobili (2015). Gambetti, Pappa, and Canova (2005) impose a restriction that a monetary policy shock that raises interest rates lowers output, inflation, and money demand.
- The impact of a positive *exchange rate shock* (corresponding to an appreciation of the domestic currency) is unrestricted. Forbes, Hjoertsoe, and Nenova (2018) impose the restriction that a positive exchange rate

[13] Conti, Neri, and Nobili (2015) and Canova and Paustian (2011) argue that sign restrictions imposed on the contemporaneous relationships among variables are robust to several types of model misspecification. The results here are also robust to imposing sign restrictions for two quarters, as in Forbes, Hjortsoe, and Nenova (2017).

shock reduces inflation and interest rates. Other authors do not impose sign restrictions on responses to exchange rate shocks (Ferroni and Mojon 2014; Conti, Neri, and Nobili 2015; Gambetti, Pappa, and Canova 2008; Melolinna 2015).

The sign restrictions imposed in this chapter are therefore standard except in the identification of domestic demand shocks and exchange rate shocks. Some studies put sign restrictions on the impact of domestic demand shocks on domestic interest rates (or monetary policy rates), and others do not. For lack of a clear economic motivation for imposing this restriction on all the countries, this chapter refrains from imposing sign restrictions. That said, the results are robust to the imposition of additional sign restrictions, as done in several other studies (Annex 3.3). Separately, the sign restrictions used here could lead to ambiguity between domestic monetary shocks and domestic demand shocks (Fry and Pagan 2011). In practice, however, the number of Bayesian draws that are subject to such ambiguity (that is, where all variables have exactly the same directional response to the two shocks) is less than 1 percent for virtually all countries. Finally, also for lack of economic motivation, no sign restrictions are imposed on exchange rate responses. This could also potentially create ambiguity between exchange rates and other shocks. However, the results are robust to eliminating any potentially ambiguous draws.

Role of global shocks in domestic inflation

Overall impact of global shocks on domestic inflation. Global shocks had a significant impact on domestic inflation, although the impact was somewhat more muted than for global inflation (Figure 3.10). A negative one-standard-deviation global demand shock (about one-third the size of the average negative demand shock of 2008-09) or oil price shock (about the size of the average negative oil price shock of 2014-15) was associated with lower inflation in the median country by 0.5 percentage point after a quarter and around 1.5 percentage points after two years on a cumulative basis. A negative one-standard-deviation global supply shock raised domestic inflation by around 0.4 percentage point after a quarter, and 1.1 percentage points after two years.

Broad-based impact of global shocks on domestic inflation. The impact of global shocks on domestic inflation was statistically significant for most countries. In 90 percent of the countries, domestic inflation responded significantly within a quarter to global demand, global supply, and oil price shocks. In three-quarters of the countries, the cumulative responses of domestic inflation after two years to global demand shocks were statistically significant. In more than 60 percent of the countries, the cumulative responses to global supply or oil price shocks after two years were statistically significant (Figure 3.10).

FIGURE 3.10 Impact of global shocks on domestic inflation

Domestic inflation responded strongly—and in the majority of countries statistically significantly—to global shocks.

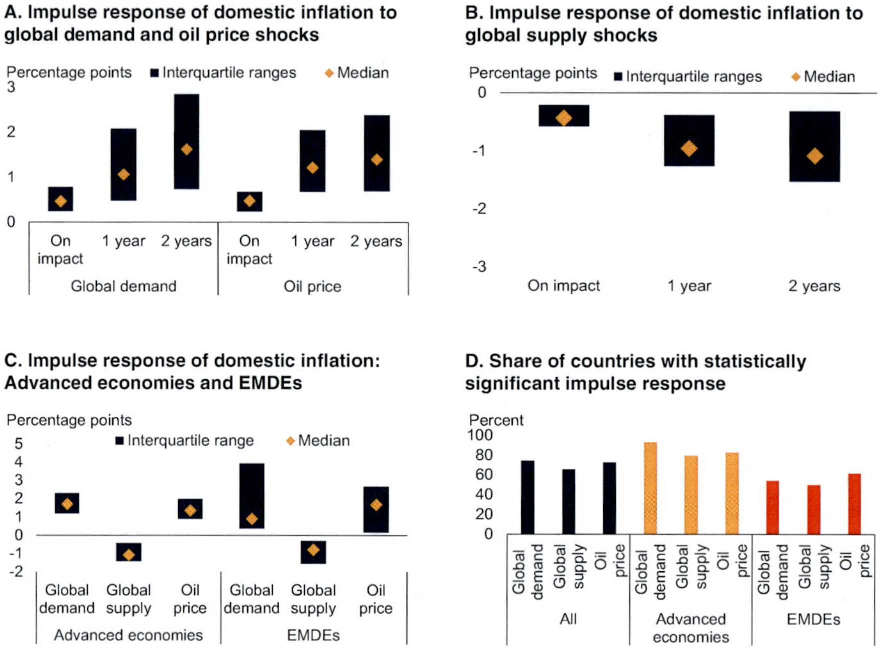

Source: World Bank.

Note: The results are based on the country-specific factor-augmented vector autoregression models discussed in Annex 3.3, estimated for 29 advanced economies and 26 EMDEs for 1970-2017. EMDEs = emerging market and developing economies.

A.-C. The figures present cumulative impulse responses after two years of domestic inflation to positive one-standard-deviation global shocks. Orange diamonds indicate medians and blue or red bars indicate the 25th-75th percentiles of country-specific impulse responses.

D. Share of countries in each group with statistically significant (within 16-84 percent confidence band) cumulative response after two years to a one-standard-deviation shock to global demand, supply, and oil prices.

Impact of global shocks on domestic inflation in advanced economies and EMDEs. The impulse responses of domestic inflation to global shocks were comparable across the two groups of countries, although they ranged much more widely among EMDEs than advanced economies (Figure 3.10). Inflation in the median country in both groups increased by around 1.5 percentage points two years after a positive one-standard-deviation oil price shock and decreased by around 1 percentage point two years after a positive one-standard-deviation global supply shock.[14] The response of domestic inflation after two years in the

[14] Using a panel of 72 countries, Choi et al. (2018) also find similar point estimates for advanced economies and EMDEs, although the effect of oil price shocks is more precisely estimated for advanced economies than for EMDEs.

median EMDE to a positive one-standard-deviation global demand shock was somewhat smaller (1 percentage point) than in the median advanced economy (1.8 percentage points). However, the range of impact among EMDEs was much wider (from 0.5 to 4 percentage points), such that the difference between advanced economies and EMDEs was not statistically significant.

Relative contribution of global shocks to domestic inflation variation. In the full sample period, global shocks accounted for over a quarter of domestic inflation variance (27 percent) in the median country, but with wide heterogeneity (contributions ranging from 0 to 70 percent).[15] As found by other studies (Conti, Neri, and Nobili 2015; Parker 2018), the main global shocks transmitted to domestic inflation were global demand shocks and oil price shocks. In the median country, they accounted for 14 and 8 percent, respectively, of domestic inflation variation (Figure 3.11).

Consistent with the results presented in Chapter 2, the contribution of global shocks to domestic inflation variation was considerably larger (33 percent median) in advanced economies—with global demand shocks and oil price shocks important—than in EMDEs (14 percent). The greater contribution of global shocks to advanced economy inflation may reflect their stronger global trade and financial linkages, more deeply integrated supply chains, more diversified export bases, and more similar monetary policy regimes. EMDEs are a more heterogeneous group of countries that may be expected to respond in a widely heterogeneous manner to external shocks (Cárdenas and Levy-Yeyati 2011).

Evolution of the role of global shocks in domestic inflation

Country-specific FAVAR models are estimated over the three subperiods of 1970-85, 1986-2000, and 2001-17. The results suggest that the role of global shocks in domestic inflation has strengthened considerably since 2001 in an era of rapidly deepening global trade and financial integration (Chapter 1).

Evolution of the impact of global shocks on domestic inflation. The response of domestic inflation to global shocks has risen since 2001, after falling slightly during 1986-2000 (Figure 3.11). The impulse responses of domestic inflation to oil price shocks during 2001-17 were similar to those in the 1970s and early 1980s, after falling to virtually nil during 1986-2000. The impulse responses to global demand shocks were larger during 2001-17 than during 1986-2000 but somewhat more moderate than those during 1970-85, although not statistically

[15] In Chapter 2, the global inflation factor accounts for 12 percent of domestic inflation variation during 1970-2017. This share cannot be easily compared with the results reported here because of the differences in samples and methodologies. The estimation in Chapter 2 reflects a much larger sample than here where the estimation requires quarterly data.

significantly so. Finally, since the mid-1980s, the impulse responses to global supply shocks have been modest, and significantly smaller than during the 1970s and early 1980s.

Evolution of the relative contribution of global shocks to domestic inflation variation. The contribution of global shocks to domestic inflation variation depends on the responsiveness of domestic inflation to global shocks and the magnitude and frequency of global shocks.[16] Since 2001, the contribution of global shocks to domestic inflation variation has grown significantly (to 43 percent, from 20-23 percent previously), and in all country groupings (to more than one-half in advanced economies and one-quarter in EMDEs), as a result of considerably larger global demand and oil price shocks. To a large extent, this may reflect the impacts of the global financial crisis, propagated through global supply chains and trade networks, and the 2014-16 oil price plunge (Baffes et al. 2015; Nguyen et al. 2017). Nevertheless, the contribution of global supply shocks has decreased over time, from 10 percent during 1970-85 to less than 5 percent since 1986.

Domestic drivers of domestic inflation

Notwithstanding the increase since 2001 in the contribution of global shocks to domestic inflation variation, domestic shocks remained the main source of domestic inflation variation. Over the full sample period, domestic shocks accounted for about three-quarters of domestic inflation variation in the median country (about six-sevenths in the median EMDE and two-thirds in the median advanced economy). Domestic supply shocks were the largest domestic source of inflation variation. In EMDEs, for example, domestic supply shocks alone contributed more than half as much to domestic inflation variation as all global shocks combined.

An abundant literature has explored the role of various domestic drivers of inflation in a wide range of country samples and methodologies (Annex 3.1). The methodology used in this chapter quantifies the four most commonly discussed domestic shocks (domestic demand and supply, monetary policy, and exchange rates) in a consistent framework after controlling for global shocks.

[16] The evolution of the volatility of structural shocks can be indirectly measured by the standard deviation of the structural shocks for the subperiods of interest. The standard deviation of oil price shocks halved from 1970-85 (1.45 percent) to 1986-2000 (0.78 percent) and remained low during 2001-17 (0.72 percent). The standard deviation of global demand shocks also decreased from 1970-85 to 1986-2000 (from 1.06 to 0.79 percent) but increased again to 1.1 percent during 2001-17. The standard deviation of global supply shocks evolved in a similar pattern to that of oil price shocks.

FIGURE 3.11 Contributions of global shocks to domestic inflation

Global shocks accounted for around a quarter of domestic inflation variation, but considerably more in advanced economies (one-third) than in EMDEs (one-seventh). Since 2001, however, this contribution has grown in all country groups—to more than one-half in advanced economies and one-quarter in EMDEs—as a result of considerably larger global demand shocks.

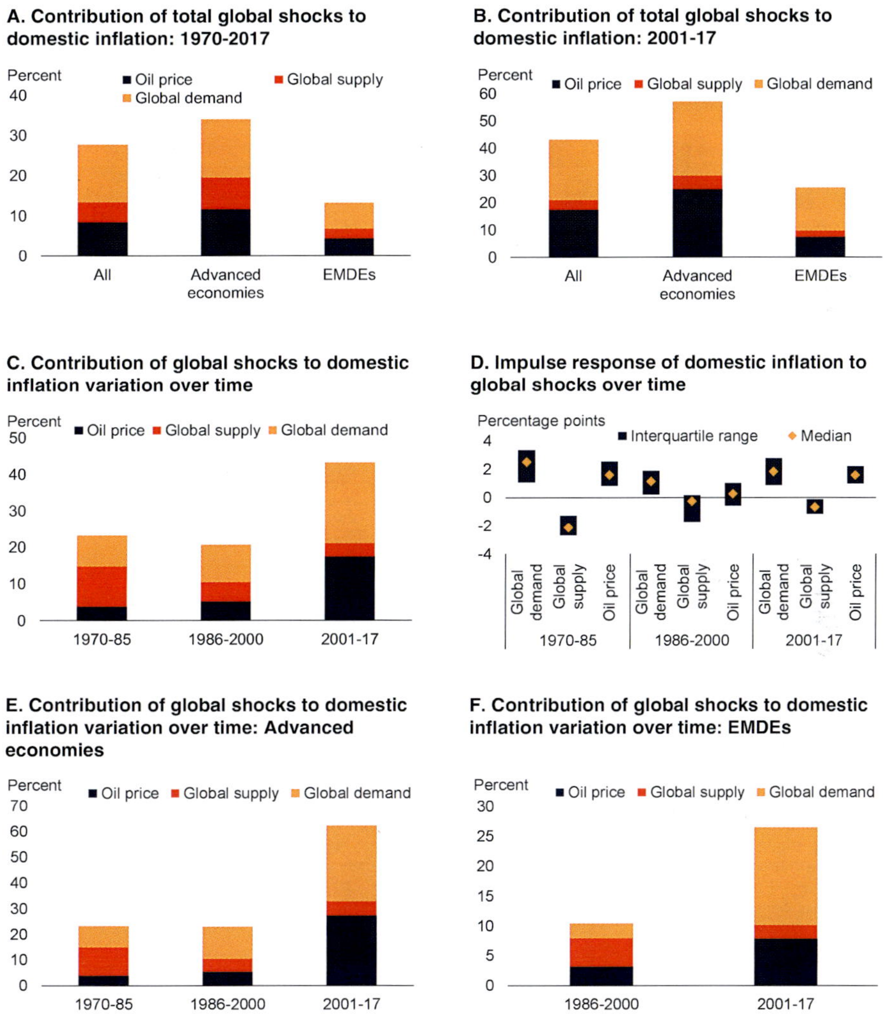

Source: World Bank.

Note: EMDEs = emerging market and developing economies.

A.-C., E., F. Median shares of country-specific inflation variance accounted for by global shocks (global demand, global supply, and oil prices) based on the country-specific factor-augmented vector autoregression models discussed in Annex 3.3, estimated for 29 advanced economies and 26 EMDEs for 1970-2017, unless otherwise noted.

D. Cumulative impulse responses of domestic inflation after two years, following one-standard-deviation shocks. Orange diamonds indicate medians and blue bars indicate the 25th-75th percentile of country-specific impulse responses.

FIGURE 3.12 Correlates of domestic shocks

Negative domestic demand shocks were associated with domestic recessions, especially when they coincided with global recessions. Negative supply shocks were associated with low (or negative) productivity growth and were most pronounced around financial crises. Positive (contractionary) monetary policy shocks were associated with interest rate hikes, especially during economic downturns, and accommodative monetary policy shocks were associated with interest rate cuts. Exchange rate shocks were most pronounced during currency crises but were also sizable during debt and banking crises.

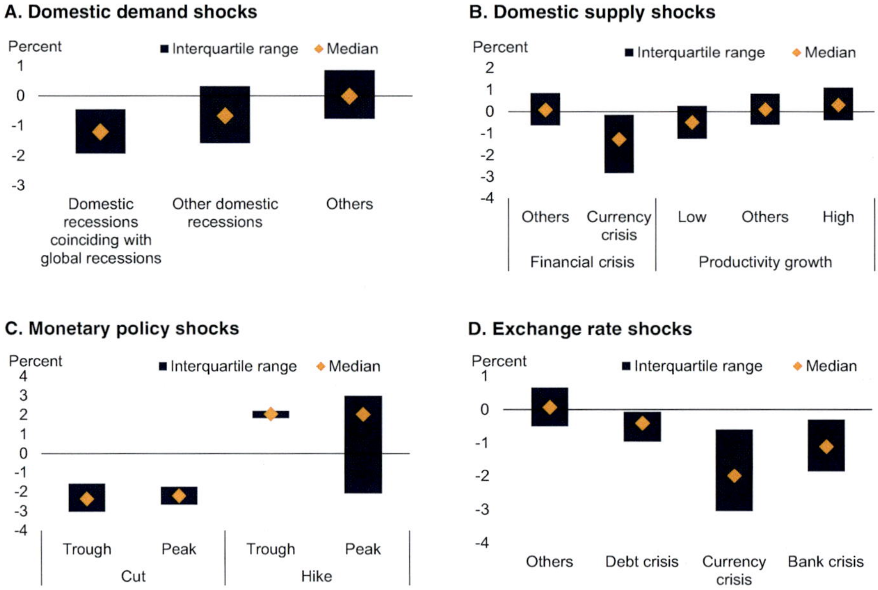

Source: Economic Cycle Research Institute; World Bank.

Note: Orange diamonds indicate median and blue bars indicate the 25th-75th percentile of identified shocks in the full sample period 1970-2017. The results are based on the country-specific factor-augmented vector autoregression estimation discussed in Annex 3.3, estimated for 29 advanced economies and 26 emerging market and developing economies.

A.C. For 21 countries, business cycle turning points are used. For the other countries, the turning points are identified as in Harding and Pagan (2002).

B. Productivity growth defined as total factor productivity (TFP) growth the from Penn World Tables. "High" ("low") indicates the year in which TFP growth is in the highest (lowest) quartile for 1970-2017.

C. Positive (interest rate "hikes") and negative (interest rate "cuts)" monetary policy shocks exceeding one standard deviation.

D. Currency, banking, and debt crises as defined in Laeven and Valencia (2013).

Correlates of domestic shocks

The model identifies a series of domestic supply, domestic demand, monetary policy, and exchange rate shocks from 1972 onward. These estimated shocks have tended to be associated with the turning points of domestic business cycles, dynamics of productivity growth, monetary policy decisions, and developments during financial crises.

Domestic demand shocks. Negative domestic demand shocks have been closely associated with domestic recessions (Figure 3.12). The demand shocks were more pronounced when domestic recessions overlapped with global recessions. Global recessions may have amplified domestic recessions by generating spillovers through trade and financial links. Ferroni and Mojon (2014) also find that Euro Area disinflation during 2008-09 was largely a reflection of negative demand shocks caused by the global financial crisis.

Domestic supply shocks. Negative supply shocks appear to be associated with low (or negative) productivity growth. They were also particularly pronounced around financial crises. Indeed, Forbes, Hjortsoe, and Nenova (2018) identify strong negative supply shocks in the United Kingdom during the global financial crisis. Currency, debt, and banking crises may have caused severe disruptions to economic activity that were reflected in these negative supply shocks.

Monetary policy shocks. Accommodative monetary policy shocks were associated with policy interest rate cuts. Similarly, contractionary monetary policy shocks were associated with policy rate hikes, especially when they were implemented around business cycle troughs. Many monetary policy rate hikes around business cycle peaks were not identified as contractionary, suggesting that they were largely an endogenous response to inflationary pressures. The model correctly identifies the aggressive U.S. monetary policy tightening in 1979-82 (Annex 1.4 in Chapter 1) as well as the monetary policy loosening in major Euro Area countries in the early to mid-2010s in response to the Euro Area sovereign debt crisis (Conti, Neri, and Nobili 2015).

Exchange rate shocks. As expected, exchange rate shocks were most pronounced during currency crises. They were also significant during debt and banking crises, but they were about one-fifth and one-half, respectively, of the size of exchange rate shocks during currency crises.

Role of domestic shocks in explaining domestic inflation

Overall impact of domestic shocks on domestic inflation. The estimated response of domestic inflation to domestic *demand* shocks is slightly stronger than its response to global demand shocks: a one-standard-deviation positive domestic demand shock raised annual domestic inflation by 1.6 percentage points within two years (Figure 3.13).[17] In the median country, domestic *supply*

[17] Many studies document a growing role for domestic demand shocks in explaining domestic inflation variation (Leeper, Sims, and Zha 1996; Domaç and Yücel 2005; Ahmad and Pentecost 2012; Nguyen et al. 2017).

FIGURE 3.13 Impact of domestic shocks on domestic inflation

Domestic inflation responded somewhat more strongly to domestic demand shocks than to global demand shocks. In the median country, domestic supply shocks had about twice the impact of global supply shocks on domestic inflation. The impact of monetary policy shocks was comparable to that of domestic demand shocks.

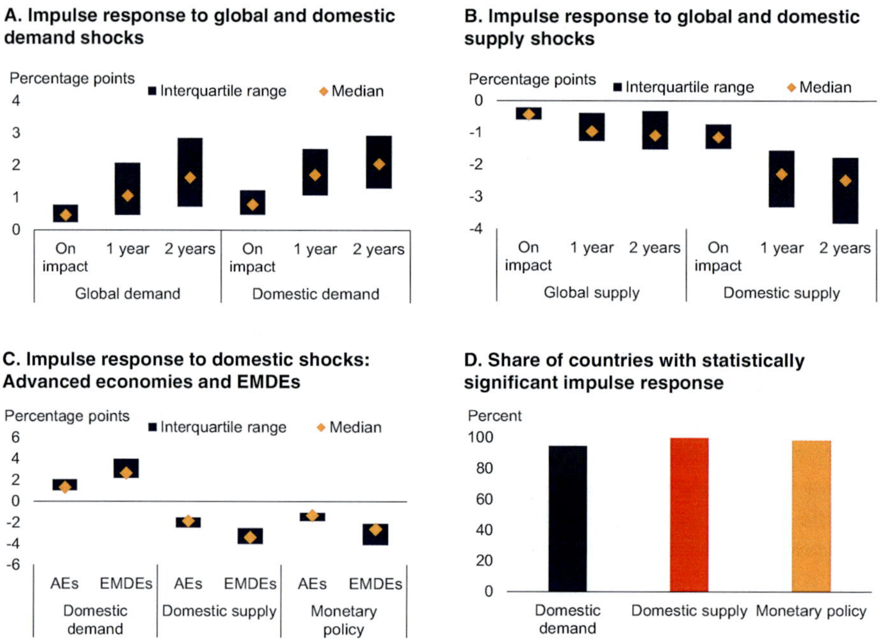

Source: World Bank.

Note: AEs = advanced economies; EMDEs = emerging market and developing economies.

A.-C. Cumulative impulse responses of domestic inflation on impact, after one (A, B) or two (A, B, C) years to one-standard-deviation shocks based on the country-specific factor-augmented vector autoregresson models discussed in Annex 3.3, estimated for 29 AEs and 26 EMDEs for 1970-2017. Diamonds show median and blue or red bars indicate 25th-75th percentiles of country-specific results. In the median country, a positive one-standard-deviation domestic demand shock increases domestic output growth by 1.6 percentage points, a positive supply shock decreases domestic inflation by 1.1 percentage points, a positive (contractionary) monetary policy shock increases short-term interest rates (or policy rates) by 0.27 percentage point, and a positive exchange rate shock drives a 15 percentage point increase (appreciation) in nominal effective exchange rates.

D. Share of countries with a statistically significant (at the 16th-84th percentile range) cumulative response of domestic inflation after two years.

shocks had about twice the impact of global supply shocks on domestic inflation. A one-standard-deviation positive domestic supply shock reduced domestic inflation by about 2.5 percentage points after two years.[18] The impact of monetary policy shocks was comparable to that of domestic demand shocks: a one-standard-deviation increase in short-term interest rates reduced domestic

[18] A role for supply shocks has been found by Globan, Arčabić, and Sorić (2015); Ahmad and Pentecost (2012); and Nguyen et al. (2017).

inflation by 2 percentage points after two years.[19] The impact of exchange rate shocks was smaller (less than 1 percentage point after two years) than that of other domestic shocks.

Broad-based impact of domestic shocks on domestic inflation. The effects of domestic demand, supply, and monetary policy shocks were broad-based: the cumulative impacts after two years were statistically significant in 92 percent of the countries. As explored in Chapter 5, monetary shocks are an important source of exchange rate fluctuations and are often associated with a larger exchange rate pass-through to domestic prices than are other types of shocks. In contrast, few countries display a statistically significant response of domestic inflation to pure exchange rate shocks, in part due to the wide range of sources of exchange rate shocks and the wide range of country characteristics that determine the effects of such shocks on inflation.[20] Possibly reflecting the higher level and volatility of inflation in EMDEs, the response of domestic inflation to domestic shocks was stronger in the median EMDE than in the median advanced economy, although the difference was not statistically significant.

Relative contribution of domestic shocks to domestic inflation. In the median country in the full sample period, domestic shocks contributed more than three times as much as global shocks to domestic inflation variation. Domestic shocks accounted for 67 percent of the variation in domestic inflation in advanced economies, and 85 percent in EMDEs (Figure 3.14). In contrast to *global* supply shocks, which played a limited role in global and domestic inflation variation, *domestic* supply shocks accounted for a greater variance share of domestic inflation (26 percent) than every other type of domestic shock and, in EMDEs, a greater share than all global shocks combined. The predominant role of domestic supply shocks is consistent with previous studies.[21]

Domestic demand shocks and monetary policy shocks each accounted for around 15 percent and exchange rate shocks for about 17 percent of domestic

[19] The transmission of monetary policy has been extensively documented, especially for advanced economies. The recent literature includes Disyatat and Vongsinsirikul (2003); Maćkowiak (2007); Osorio and Unsal (2013); Elbourne and Haan (2009); Globan, Arčabić, and Sorić (2015); Tena and Salazar (2008); Mallick and Sousa (2012); Mishra, Montiel, and Sengupta (2016); Ngalawa and Viegi (2011); and Nguyen et al. (2017).

[20] In part, the wide range of impulse responses for exchange rate shocks reflects that, being largely unrestricted, they capture a large variety of shocks.

[21] Supply shocks, which tend to be associated with changes in relative prices, have tended to be more important than shifts in demand. Nguyen et al. (2017) find that the main drivers of inflation dynamics in Sub-Saharan African countries in the previous 25 years were shocks to domestic supply, the exchange rate, and monetary variables. In 33 mostly EMDE countries between 1986 and 2010, Osorio and Unsal (2013) estimate that domestic shocks explain the majority (around 70 percent) of inflation variation. For European Union countries, the evidence is mixed. Vašíček (2011) estimates that global shocks were the main drivers of inflation in the Czech Republic, Hungary, Poland, and the Slovak Republic during 1998-2007.

FIGURE 3.14 Evolution of the impact of domestic shocks on inflation

During 1970-2017, domestic supply shocks explained about one-quarter of domestic inflation variation in advanced economies and EMDEs. Other domestic shocks contributed less and in almost equal measure to domestic inflation variation. The contribution of domestic shocks, especially exchange rate and domestic supply shocks, to domestic inflation variation has decreased over time.

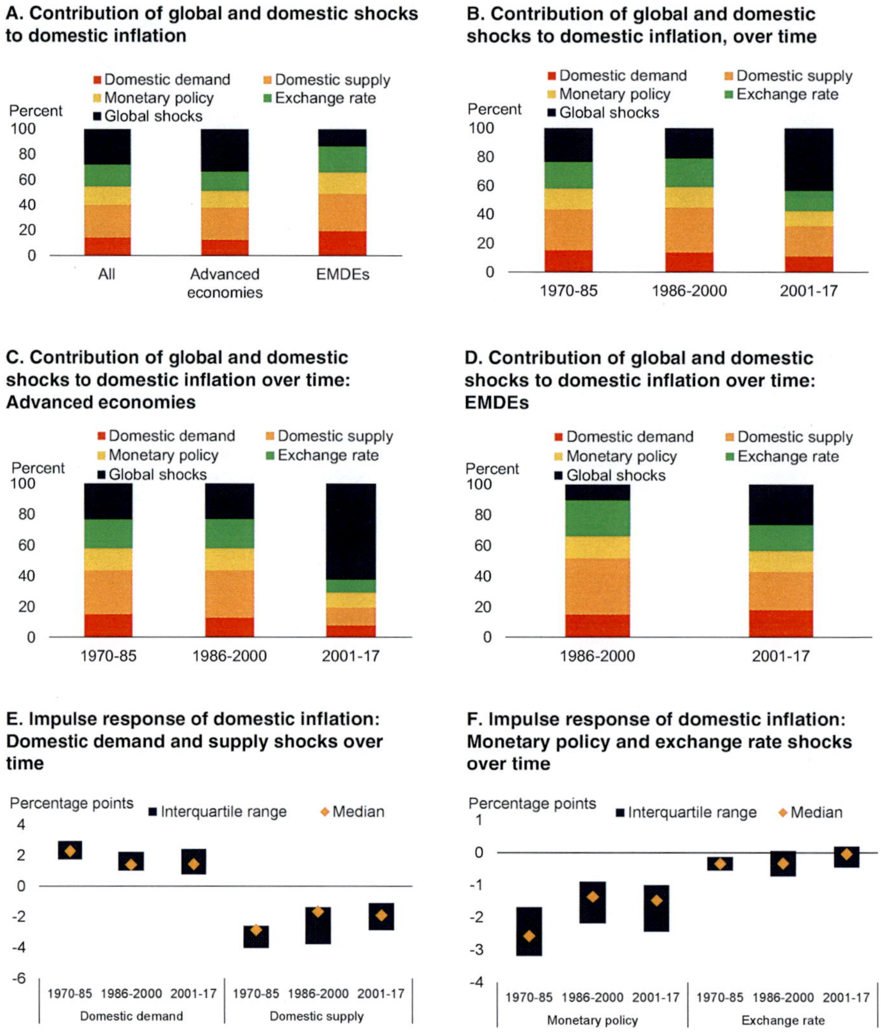

Source: World Bank.

Note: Median share of country-specific inflation variance accounted for by domestic shocks (domestic demand, supply, exchange rates, and interest rates) based on the country-specific factor-augmented vector autoregression models discussed in Annex 3.3, estimated for 29 advanced economies and 26 EMDEs for 1970-2017. EMDEs = emerging market and developing economies.

E.F. Orange diamonds indicate the median and blue bars indicate the 25th-75th percentile of country-specific impulse responses. Cumulative impulse responses after two years for 1970-85, 1986-2000, and 2001-17.

inflation variation. The variance share of domestic supply shocks was somewhat more pronounced in EMDEs (30 percent) than in advanced economies (25 percent). In advanced economies and EMDEs, the other three types of domestic shocks contributed in broadly equal measure (but always more in EMDEs than in advanced economies) to domestic inflation variation.

Evolution of the role of domestic shocks in domestic inflation

Evolution of the impact of domestic shocks on domestic inflation. Since the mid-1980s, the sensitivity of domestic inflation to domestic shocks has declined (Figure 3.14). During 2001-17, the responses of domestic inflation to all four types of domestic shocks were half or less of those during 1970-85. These declines largely occurred during the Great Moderation and, in contrast to the response to global shocks, there has not been a rebound in the response to domestic shocks since 2001. The impact of exchange rate shocks, which was modestly negative during 1970-85, all but disappeared during 2001-17. It is possible that a gradual improvement in the anchoring of inflation expectations has contributed to this lower responsiveness of inflation to domestic shocks. The role of inflation expectations is explored in detail in Chapter 4.

Evolution of the relative contribution of domestic shocks to domestic inflation variation. Since 2001, the contribution of domestic shocks to domestic inflation variation has declined to 53 percent, from 77-80 percent during the preceding decades. This decline has affected all types of domestic shocks broadly similarly. As a result, domestic supply shocks have remained the main source of domestic inflation variation since 2001, accounting for 16 percent of total domestic inflation variation. This broad-based decline in the contribution of all domestic shocks since 2001 is particularly evident in EMDEs. In contrast, in advanced economies, the contribution of supply shocks has shrunk considerably more than that of other shocks, such that, since 2001, domestic supply shocks have contributed less to advanced economy domestic inflation than monetary policy shocks.

Cross-country variation in the role of global and domestic shocks in domestic inflation

Role of global shocks. The role of global factors in explaining domestic inflation has varied widely across countries. The median contribution of global shocks was considerably larger in countries that were open to global trade and finance and were commodity importers (Figure 3.15). Monetary policy and exchange rate regimes also mattered: global shocks were more important inflation drivers

FIGURE 3.15 Contribution to domestic inflation, by country groups

Global shocks have been a more important source of domestic inflation movements in countries with stronger global trade and financial linkages, greater dependence on commodity imports, and fixed exchange rate regimes.

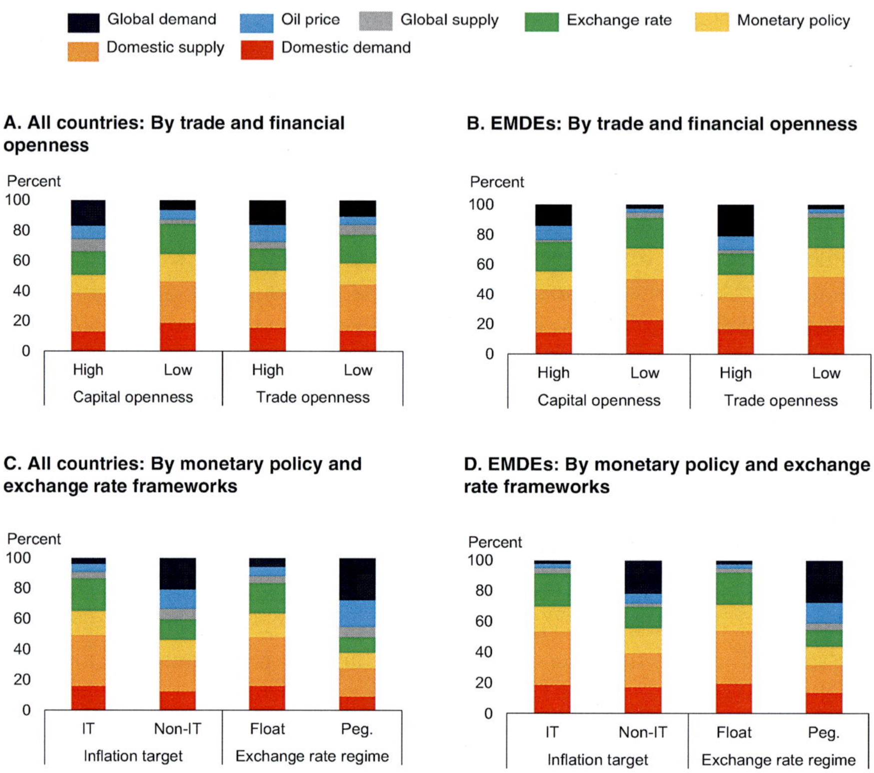

Source: Ilzetzki, Reinhart, and Rogoff 2017; World Bank.

Note: Median share of country-specific inflation variance accounted for by domestic shocks (domestic demand, supply, exchange rates, and interest rates) and global shocks based on country-specific factor-augmented vector autoregression models discussed in Annex 3.3, estimated for 29 advanced economies and 26 EMDEs for 1970-2017. EMDEs = emerging market and developing economies; GDP = gross domestic product; IT = inflation targeting.

A.B. Countries with "high" capital openness are defined as those above the median, as in Chinn and Ito (2017); all others are considered to have "low" capital openness. Countries with "high" trade openness are defined as those with trade-to-GDP ratios above the median; all others are considered to have "low" trade openness.

C.D. IT regimes are defined as in IMF (2016). Flexible exchange rate regimes (Float) are defined as freely floating and managed floating exchange rate regimes, as defined in Ilzetzki, Reinhart, and Rogoff (2017). All other regimes are defined as pegged exchange rate regimes (Peg). See the Appendix for more details on country characteristics.

in countries without inflation targeting and fixed exchange rate regimes.[22] In EMDEs, the median contribution of global shocks to domestic inflation variances in countries without inflation targeting and fixed exchange rate

[22] These results do not qualitatively change when the results are based on averages across countries. They are mostly consistent with earlier studies.

regimes, and with greater trade and financial openness was more than twice that in other EMDEs. The variance share of global demand shocks was particularly sizable (20 percent or more) for EMDEs with above-median trade and financial openness, with fixed exchange rate regimes, and without inflation targeting regimes.[23] The variance share of global oil price shocks was particularly sizable in countries, especially EMDEs, that were commodity importers, open to trade and international finance, with fixed exchange rates, and without inflation targeting regimes.[24] The variance share of global supply shocks was particularly large in EMDEs with less independent central banks.

Conclusion

Over the past decade—since the global financial crisis of 2008-09 and the oil price plunge of 2014-16—global inflation has been exceptionally low. The results in this chapter suggest that the recent decline in *global* inflation stemmed in part from the severe global recession and that was prolonged by the oil price plunge. Global demand shocks have accounted for most of the variation in global inflation variation since 2008, and oil price swings have accounted for 60 percent since 2010.

More broadly than the post-crisis period, this chapter has explored systematically, in a unified framework, the roles of domestic and global demand, supply, and commodity price shocks, as well as monetary policy and exchange rate shocks, in explaining movements in global and domestic inflation. The following are the key findings.

First, this chapter highlights the role of global demand shocks and oil price shocks in explaining variations in global inflation since 1970. Oil price shocks and global demand shocks together contributed 80 percent (about 40 percent each) to the variation in global inflation in this period. The roles of global demand shocks and oil price shocks have strengthened considerably over time, while that of global supply shocks has receded.

Second, global shocks have accounted for about one-quarter of domestic inflation variation since the 1970s, but with wide heterogeneity across countries.

---

[23] Bianchi and Civelli (2015) find that the impulse responses of inflation to global slack are higher in countries that are more open to trade and with higher business cycle integration. Theoretical considerations developed by Martínez-Garcia and Wynne (2010) suggest that inflation is less responsive to domestic slack in countries that are more open to trade. Andrews, Gal, and Witheridge (2018) also find that a high level of global value chain integration can strengthen the transmission of global shocks by accentuating the impact of global economic slack on domestic inflation.

[24] Berganza, Borallo, and del Río (2016) find that the direct effects of falling oil prices have been greater in countries with a larger share of oil in the CPI and higher energy taxation (usually in the form of unit tax rates), as well as currency depreciations after the oil price drop.

The role of global shocks was considerably larger (33 percent) in the median advanced economy—with global demand shocks and oil price shocks about equally important—than in the median EMDE (14 percent) where only global demand shocks played a major role.

Third, it follows that domestic shocks have accounted for about three-quarters of domestic inflation variation and more in EMDEs. In contrast to *global* supply shocks, which played a limited role in global and domestic inflation variation, *domestic* supply shocks accounted for 26 percent of inflation variation and, in EMDEs, for more than any other type of domestic shock. Domestic demand and monetary policy shocks explained about 15 percent, each, of domestic inflation variation.

Fourth, the contribution of global shocks to domestic inflation variation tended to be higher in EMDEs without inflation targeting regimes, with more open capital accounts, with greater trade openness, and with global value chain participation.

Policy makers need to build resilience to global shocks, since their importance as a source of domestic inflation variation has grown over time. This is particularly relevant for policy makers in small, open economies with deep or rapidly growing integration into global trade and financial networks and supply chains. A menu of policy options is available to offset the impact of global shocks in EMDEs. These include active use of countercyclical policies as well as strengthening institutions, including through greater central bank independence. In addition, ample fiscal space and a sound long-term framework for fiscal sustainability can ensure that fiscal policy can support macroeconomic stabilization.

Future research could examine more formally the role of country characteristics. This could be done in a regression framework or by conditioning impulse responses on country characteristics. In addition, changes in the role of global and domestic shocks in domestic and global inflation could be examined in greater detail, for example, by allowing for time-varying coefficients or dynamic factor loadings.

ANNEX 3.1 Literature review: Drivers of domestic inflation

The evidence for a major contribution of global shocks to domestic consumer price inflation is mixed but strongest for global commodity price shocks, particularly in the case of the oil price collapse of 2014-16. The role of global factors, whether global demand and supply shocks or global commodity price shocks, appears to be stronger in countries that are more open to trade, more integrated into global supply chains, and with a greater share of traded goods in the consumer price index basket. The literature on the impact of domestic shocks in emerging market and developing economies (EMDEs) suggests that they explain a substantial portion of the variance of inflation. Domestic supply shocks are at least as important as shocks to demand, but the role of demand shocks has been growing. In EMDEs, the transmission of monetary shocks to inflation is hampered by underdeveloped financial markets as well as by institutional weaknesses.

A large literature has documented the growing role of global factors in domestic inflation. Although strong comovement of inflation among countries is a well-established finding, explanations vary: spillovers from global demand, common supply or commodity price shocks, and trade and financial linkages (Chapter 2). Meanwhile, empirical studies have also typically found an important, albeit diminishing, role of domestic shocks in domestic inflation. Domestic monetary policy is, over the long run, the determining factor for domestic inflation, a principle recognized in the numerical inflation targets set for central banks in many countries. That said, nonmonetary factors, on the demand and supply sides of the economy, and movements in foreign exchange rates can drive short- and medium-term movements in inflation. With increasing globalization, external factors may play a more prominent role (Table A.3.1.1). Against this background, this annex presents a brief survey of the literature to address the following questions:

- How much do global shocks contribute to domestic inflation, and how does the contribution differ by country characteristics?
- How much have oil price shocks contributed to post-crisis inflation?
- What is the relative importance of global and domestic shocks in inflation dynamics?

Role of global shocks in domestic inflation

Empirical studies have documented the role of global shocks in the dynamics of domestic inflation in individual countries using two approaches: a Phillips curve framework and structural vector autoregression (SVAR) or factor-augmented vector autoregression (FAVAR) models. Phillips curve-based evidence on the role of global factors has been mixed, possibly reflecting measurement error in global output gap estimates. In contrast, vector autoregression (VAR)–based studies have typically found an important contribution of global shocks, especially commodity price shocks, to inflation.[1]

Phillips curve framework. A group of studies has tested the hypothesis that inflation is driven by global slack, in addition to, or instead of, domestic slack. The results have been mixed.

- **Global output gap matters.** Borio and Filardo (2007), in a sample of 15 Organisation for Economic Co-operation and Development (OECD) economies during 1985-2005, find that global inflation and the global output gap add explanatory power to conventional Phillips curve models of domestic inflation.[2] Filardo and Lombardi (2014) also find an important role for global demand shocks, in part transmitted through global commodity price shocks, in inflation in Asian countries. Altansukh et al. (2017) test for structural breaks in the correlation between the components (energy, food, and core) of domestic and trade-weighted foreign inflation in 13 OECD countries during 1970-2013. They find that the short-run sensitivity of headline inflation to foreign energy inflation has increased significantly, but that the synchronization of movements in core inflation has not.
- **Global output gap does not matter.** In contrast, Ihrig et al. (2010) find that in estimates of the Phillips curve for a subset of 11 OECD countries during 1977-2005, the sensitivity of inflation to the global output gap was generally insignificant and often of the wrong sign, and that the sensitivity of inflation to domestic output gaps remained unchanged over time. Similarly, in a broader sample of 24 OECD economies during 1980-2007, Eickmeier and Pijnenburg (2013) find a statistically significant impact on domestic inflation, only for global unit labor cost growth—not global output gaps. Mikolajun and Lodge (2016) estimate Phillips curves augmented by global output gaps, global inflation, and global commodity prices for 19 OECD countries and find little support for a significant role of global economic slack in domestic inflation.[3] Kabukçuoğlu and Martínez-

[1] In a rare study using micro data, Andrade and Zachariadis (2016) find that individual prices adjust to global shocks more slowly than to domestic shocks.

[2] Some studies have examined the role of other external shocks, such as U.S. monetary policy shocks. Using an SVAR framework, Maćkowiak (2007) analyzes the importance of external shocks in the determination of output and inflation in eight Asian countries between 1986 and 2000 and finds that external shocks explained nearly half the variation in inflation.

[3] Moreover, the results suggest that the importance of global inflation in forecasting domestic inflation has its roots solely in its ability to capture slow-moving trends in inflation rates. In the Phillips curve context, the same role is performed by domestic forward-looking inflation expectations.

García (2018) model inflation expectations for 14 OECD countries in a Phillips curve framework that is augmented by the global output gap and global inflation. Again, they find no robustly statistically significant role for global output gaps—which they attribute to measurement error—although they find a significant role for global inflation.

Vector autoregression models. VAR models have more successfully demonstrated a significant role for global developments in driving domestic inflation. Ciccarelli and Mojon (2010) attribute a third of inflation variation to global factors in 22 OECD countries during 1960-2008. Neely and Rapach (2011) attribute more than half of the inflation variation in 64 countries during 1951-2009 to international (global and regional) factors. Mumtaz, Simonelli, and Surico (2011) find a growing share of inflation variation contributed by global factors in 36 mostly advanced economies since 1960. Commodity price shocks are also an important driver of inflation. Using a structural dynamic factor model for Canada, Charnavoki and Dolado (2014) find that global demand, supply, and commodity price shocks played an important role in Canadian inflation during 1975-2010. Furceri, Loungani, and Zdzienicka (2018), in a sample of 34 advanced economies during the 2000s, find that a hypothetical 10 percent increase in global food inflation would have raised domestic inflation by about 0.5 percentage point after a year, but the estimated impact declined over time and became less persistent.

Role of global oil price shocks in post-crisis domestic inflation

Euro Area evidence. Using a Bayesian VAR model, ECB (2017) documents a particularly pronounced contribution of global demand and oil supply shocks to Euro Area inflation in 2008-09 and 2014-16. The authors argue that commodity price movements were the main driver of the global common factor in inflation. However, also in a Bayesian VAR model for the Euro Area, Conti, Neri, and Nobili (2015) find that inflation during 2013-14 was depressed as much by monetary and demand shocks as by oil price movements.

Evidence from the 2014-16 oil price plunge. A recent group of studies focuses on the 70 percent drop in the price of oil from the peak in July 2014 to the trough in January 2016. World Bank (2015, 2018) and Sussman and Zohar (2015) attribute the oil price decline largely to a positive oil supply shock, as the Organization of the Petroleum Exporting Countries decided to protect its global oil market share amid growing U.S. shale oil production. Weak demand played a more prominent role in the subsequent decline in late 2015-16. Berganza, Boralla, and del Río (2016) document that extremely low inflation since the Great Recession has in part reflected the sharp decline in oil prices during 2014-16.

Role of country characteristics

Carney (2015) voices broader concerns among central banks that increased competition from overseas and global financial market integration may have changed the relationship between inflation and domestic economic conditions. Several studies, discussed here, have established empirically that global factors play a greater role in driving domestic inflation in countries with greater trade and global value chain integration, and with a greater share of goods in the consumer price index (CPI) whose prices are highly correlated with global shocks.

Trade integration. Auer, Borio, and Filardo (2017) estimate a Phillips curve model for producer price inflation, augmented by global slack, for 18 OECD countries for 1982-2006. The significantly positive coefficient estimate of the interaction between global slack and global value chain participation indicates that global value chains form an important transmission channel from global slack to domestic inflation. In time-varying-coefficient VAR models, Bianchi and Civelli (2015) find that the impulse responses of inflation to global slack are larger in more trade-open economies and in those with higher business cycle integration. Theoretical considerations developed by Martínez-Garcia and Wynne (2010) suggest that inflation will generally be less responsive to domestic slack the more open the economy is to international trade.

Exposure to food and energy price shocks. Furceri, Loungani, and Zdzienicka (2018) provide evidence that the global food price shocks of the 2000s had a larger impact on domestic inflation in emerging market and developing economies (EMDEs) than in advanced economies. They attribute this to the greater share of food in the consumption baskets of EMDEs and the weaker anchoring of inflation expectations in EMDEs than in advanced economies. Berganza, Boralla, and del Río (2016) find that the post-crisis oil price drop depressed global inflation between 2014 and 2016. The direct effects of falling oil prices were greater in countries with larger shares of oil in the CPI and higher energy taxation (usually in the form of per unit tax rates), as well as in countries where currency depreciations were associated with the oil price drop.

Role of domestic shocks in domestic inflation

In the past two decades, empirical studies have typically found an important, albeit diminishing, role of domestic shocks in domestic inflation. A summary of selected empirical studies on the importance of domestic shocks in inflation dynamics is provided in Table A.3.1.1.

Evidence on advanced economies. Several studies have offered evidence that domestic shocks play a key role in domestic inflation dynamics. Globan, Arčabić, and Sorić (2015) find, for non-Euro Area new European Union member states, that short-run inflation dynamics could be explained mainly by domestic factors, even if foreign shocks became the major driver of inflation in the medium term. Bobeica and Jarociński (2017), using a medium-scale, reduced-form VAR, document that domestic shocks can explain the "missing disinflation" and "missing inflation" episodes in the United States and the Euro Area in the 2010s. However, Pain, Koske, and Sollie (2006) find, for OECD countries since the mid-1990s, that the sensitivity of inflation to domestic economic conditions has declined.

Evidence on EMDEs. Studies on EMDEs have similarly found that domestic shocks play a predominant role in domestic inflation dynamics, even if the role of global shocks may have grown. For European Union countries, the evidence is mixed, with Vašíček (2011) arguing that global shocks were the main drivers of inflation in the Czech Republic, Hungary, Poland, and the Slovak Republic during 1998-2007 but Halka and Kotlowski (2017) finding that domestic shocks played an important role in inflation dynamics in the Czech Republic, Poland, and Sweden, including by transmitting global demand shocks through the domestic output gap. For Asia, Osorio and Unsal (2013) estimate that domestic shocks explain around 70 percent of total variation in domestic inflation in 33 countries.

Role of monetary policy in domestic inflation

There is an extensive literature on the transmission of monetary policy to the domestic economy. One of the challenges this research has had to address is the simultaneity between monetary policy and economic development: monetary policy responds to the economy, as well as vice versa (Leeper, Sims, and Zha 1996; Gertler and Karadi 2015). Most studies of the transmission of monetary policy to the economy have focused on advanced economies. Using structural model frameworks, many of these studies have shown that monetary policy explains a substantial part of the variation in domestic inflation, with statistical significance.[4] The literature has evolved by developing more advanced empirical frameworks that purport to address the problem of simultaneity. Surveys of this work are provided by Boivin, Kiley, and Mishkin (2010); Benati and Goodhart (2010); and Bhattarai and Neely (2016). Ramey (2016) and Stock and Watson (2017) discuss the evolution of estimation strategies.

[4] For instance, Canova and De Nicolo (2002) show that monetary disturbances explain large portions of output and inflation fluctuations in the G7 economies. The explanatory power of monetary disturbances for output variability in Canada, Germany, Italy, and the United Kingdom is found to exceed 22 percent; for inflation variability in Italy, Japan, the United Kingdom, and the United States, it is found to exceed 54 percent.

Evidence on EMDEs. The evidence on the transmission of monetary policy to macroeconomic conditions is less clear for EMDEs than for advanced economies. A group of earlier studies focused on challenges that EMDEs face in the implementation of monetary policy and specific channels of monetary policy transmission.[5] These challenges include higher default risk, underdeveloped financial markets, and weaker institutions.[6] Although the interest rate and asset price channels of monetary policy transmission are limited, and sometimes insignificant (Mohanty and Turner 2008; Vonnák 2008), some studies have found that the exchange rate channel plays a significant role in EMDEs (Neaime 2008; Bhattacharya, Patnaik, and Shah 2011). In low-income countries, because of undeveloped financial markets, monetary policy transmission relies heavily on the bank lending channel. The evidence on its effectiveness is mixed .[7]

Role of domestic demand and supply shocks in domestic inflation

Several studies have examined nonmonetary macroeconomic shocks as drivers of domestic inflation. Domestic demand shocks include, for example, unanticipated changes in government spending, while domestic supply shocks include unanticipated changes in the availability of goods or services resulting from such factors as severe weather events, labor strikes, and changes in productivity. The effects of such shocks on prices may be transitory or permanent, depending partly on the nature of the shock and partly on the monetary policy regime and anchoring of inflation expectations.

Evidence on advanced economies. Melolinna (2015) uses a FAVAR framework to study inflation dynamics in the Euro Area, the United Kingdom, and the United States. The results suggest that headline inflation in the three economies reacted in a similar fashion to macroeconomic shocks over the previous four decades, with demand shocks having the most persistent effects. Gambetti, Pappa, and Canova (2005) examine the dynamics of U.S. output and inflation using a structural time-varying coefficient VAR. They find that a combination of technology, demand, and monetary shocks explained variations in the persistence and volatility of inflation. These and other studies have found that, along with monetary policy shocks, real macroeconomic shocks, both demand and supply, help to explain inflation dynamics in advanced economies.

Evidence on EMDEs. Several empirical studies have analyzed the effects of supply and demand shocks on inflation in EMDEs. A broad finding is that

[5] Hammond, Kanbur, and Prasad (2009); Mishra, Montiel, and Spilimbergo (2012).

[6] Frankel (2011); Agenor and Aynaoui (2010); Wu, Luca, and Jeon (2011).

[7] Mishra, Montiel, and Sengupta (2016); Mishra and Montiel (2012); Disyatat and Vongsinsirikul (2003); Golenelli and Rovelli (2005); Catao and Pagan (2010); Singh and Kalirajan (2007); Aleem (2010).

supply shocks, which tend to be associated with changes in relative prices, have to be more important than shifts in demand, but that the role of demand shifts has grown. Mohanty and Klau (2001), in a study of 14 EMDEs during the 1980s and 1990s, find significant effects from supply shocks, especially from those affecting food prices. Several studies focus on regional groups of EMDEs:

- *Asia.* Osorio and Unsal (2013), using a set of global VAR and SVAR models, study the drivers of inflation in 33 Asian countries during 1986-2010. They find that supply shocks explained around 45 percent of total variation in cyclical inflation, and monetary shocks around 35 percent, but that the role of demand factors had increased since 2000.[8] Dua and Gaur (2009) investigate the determinants of inflation in the framework of an open-economy Phillips curve model for eight Asian countries during 1990-2005. They find that agriculture-related supply shocks were a significant determinant of inflation for EMDEs but not for advanced economies.

- *Sub-Saharan Africa.* Nguyen et al. (2017) analyze inflation dynamics in Sub-Saharan African countries, using a global VAR model. They find that in the previous 25 years, the main drivers of inflation were shocks to domestic supply, the exchange rate, and monetary variables, but, in the most recent decade, domestic demand pressures and global shocks played larger roles than previously. Similarly, using the SVAR framework of Blanchard and Quah (1989), Ahmad and Pentecost (2012) study inflation dynamics in 22 African countries. They find that the most important source of inflation was demand shocks, which accounted for between 50 and 90 percent of inflation variation in all countries.

- *Middle East.* Hasan and Alogeel (2008) find, for Saudi Arabia and Kuwait between 1964 and 2007, that, in the long run, inflation in trading partners was the main factor affecting inflation, with a smaller contribution from exchange rate pass-through. The estimated impacts of domestic demand and monetary shocks were confined to the short run. Kandil and Morsy (2010) study the determinants of inflation in Gulf Cooperation Council countries during 2003-08, using a model that includes domestic and external factors. They find that binding capacity constraints (supply side) and government spending (demand side) helped to explain short-term movements in inflation.

[8] However, the supply and demand shocks include external factors, for example, commodity price shocks and inflation spillovers from other Asian countries. The contribution to inflation of domestic supply shocks varied from one country to another, between zero and 40 percent.

TABLE A.3.1.1 Literature review: Drivers of inflation—Panel A. Studies on advanced economies

Paper	Sample countries	Sample period	Methodology	Shocks				Main results
				DD	DS	MP	ER	
Amisano and Tristani (2007)	Euro Area	1970:1-2004:4	DSGE		√	√		Inflation targeting and monetary policy shocks explain 76 and 9 percent of inflation variation, respectively. Tax and technology shocks are less important.
Bobeica and Jarociński (2017)	Euro Area and U.S.	1990:1-2014:4	BVAR	√	√	√	√	Domestic shocks are more important in the missing inflation episode, whereas global shocks are more important in the missing disinflation episode.
Canova and De Nicolò (2002)	G7	1973-95	VAR			√		Monetary shocks are the dominant source of output and inflation fluctuations in three of the seven countries.
Conti, Neri, and Nobili (2017)	Euro Area	1995:1-2015:3	BVAR	√		√		Foreign shocks (oil supply and global demand) and aggregate demand are the main drivers of inflation; monetary policy is less important.
Gambetti, Pappa, and Canova (2005)	US	1970-2002	SVAR	√	√	√		Technology, demand, and monetary shocks explain the variation in inflation, with technology contributing 25 percent, demand 17 percent, and monetary policy 14 percent, on average.
Globan, Arčabić, and Sorić (2015)	Bulgaria, Croatia, Czech Republic, Hungary, Latvia, Lithuania, Poland, and Romania	2001-13	SVAR		√	√		Foreign shocks are the major factor in explaining inflation dynamics in the medium run; short-run inflation dynamics are mainly influenced by domestic shocks.
Melolinna (2015)	Euro Area, UK, U.S.	1975M1-2012M12	FAVAR	√	√	√		Demand shocks are more persistent drivers of inflation.
Mumtaz, Zabczyk, and Ellis (2011)	UK	1964:1-2005:1	FAVAR	√	√	√		Supply shocks are the key drivers of inflation, with monetary policy shocks having a small initial impact that slowly increases over time.
Pain, Koske, and Sollie (2006)	OECD countries	1985-2005	VAR		√			The sensitivity of inflation to domestic economic conditions has declined, whereas the sensitivity to foreign economic conditions has risen, working through import prices.

Note: BVAR = Bayesian vector autoregression; DD = domestic demand; DS = domestic supply; DSGE = dynamic stochastic general equilibrium; ER = exchange rate; FAVAR = factor-augmented vector autoregression; G7 = Group of Seven; MP = monetary policy; OECD = Organisation for Economic Co-operation and Development; SVAR = structural vector autoregression; VAR = vector autoregression.

TABLE A.3.1.1 Literature review: Drivers of inflation—Panel B. Studies on EMDEs

Paper	Sample countries	Sample period	Methodology	Shocks				Main results
				DD	DS	MP	ER	
Ahmad and Pentecost (2012)	22 African countries	1980-2015	SVAR	√	√			Demand shocks account for between 50 and 90 percent of inflation variation; domestic supply shocks account for about 10 to 40 percent.
Bhattacharya, Patnaik, and Shah (2009)	India	1997-2009	VAR			√	√	Monetary policy impacts inflation through the exchange rate.
Dua and Gaur (2010)	Japan; Hong Kong SAR, China; Korea, Rep.; Singapore; Philippines; Thailand;	1990s-2005	Open economy Phillips curve	√	√		√	The output gap is important in explaining inflation in almost all the countries. In developing countries, agricultural supply shocks are important but not so in advanced economies.
Halka and Kotlowski (2017)	Czech Republic, Poland, and Sweden	2000:1-2014:2	SVAR	√	√		√	Domestic shocks are important in inflation dynamics with transmission via the domestic output gap and exchange rate channel.
Hasan and Alogeel (2008)	Saudi Arabia and Kuwait	1966-2007	ECM	√	√			In the long run, inflation in trading partners is the main driving factor of inflation, with significant but lower contribution from exchange rate pass-through. Demand shocks and money supply shocks are important in the short run, but tend to dissipate quickly.
Jongwanich and Park (2008)	China; India; Indonesia; Korea, Rep.; Malaysia; Philippines; Singapore; Thailand; and Vietnam	1996:1-2008:1	SVAR	√			√	Inflation is largely due to excess aggregate demand and inflation expectations rather than external price shocks.
Jongwanich, Wongcharoen, and Park (2016)	China; Hong Kong SAR, China; India; Indonesia; Korea, Rep; Malaysia; Philippines; Singapore; Thailand; and Vietnam	2000:1-2015:2	SVAR			√	√	Cost-push factors such as oil and food prices are more important in explaining PPI than CPI. For CPI, demand-pull factors still explain much of the inflation.

Note: CPI = consumer price index; DD = domestic demand; DS = domestic supply; ECM = error correction model; ER = exchange rate; MP = monetary policy; PPI = producer price index; SVAR = structural vector autoregression; VAR = vector autoregression.

TABLE A.3.1.1 Literature review: Drivers of inflation—Panel B. Studies on EMDEs (*continued*)

Paper	Sample countries	Sample Period	Methodology	Shocks DD	DS	MP	ER	Main results
Kandil and Morsy (2010)	Bahrain, Kuwait, Oman, Qatar, Saudi Arabia, and United Arab Emirates	1970-2007	VECM			√	√	Inflation in major trading partners is an important foreign factor. In addition, oil revenues have reinforced inflationary pressures through growth of credit and aggregate spending.
Khan and Hanif (2012)	Pakistan	1992-2011	SVAR	√	√	√		Supply shocks explain 48 percent of variation in inflation, while the share of real demand shocks was around 10 percent and the remaining 42 percent attributed to nominal shocks.
Mohanty and Klau (2001)	14 EMDEs	1981:1-1999:4	Open economy Phillips curve	√	√	√	√	The output gap is a significant determinant of inflation. Supply side factors and import prices (especially food prices, via the exchange rate channel) are also important, but money supply is less relevant.
Neaime (2008)	Egypt, Arab Rep.; Jordan; Turkey; Lebanon; Morocco; and Tunisia	1990s-2000s	VAR			√	√	In Egypt and Turkey, the exchange rate played a dominant role in the transmission mechanism of monetary policy; for Jordan, Lebanon, Morocco, and Tunisia, it was the interest rate.
Nguyen et al. (2017)	33 Sub-Saharan African countries	1988-2013	VAR	√	√	√	√	Main drivers of inflation have been domestic supply shocks and shocks to exchange rate and monetary variables. However, in recent years, domestic demand and global shocks have played a larger role in driving inflation.
Osorio and Unsal (2013)	33 Asian countries	1986-2010	GVAR, SVAR	√	√	√	√	Monetary and supply shocks are the main drivers of inflation, but more recently demand shocks are increasing in importance.
Porter (2010)	China	1996:1-2010:1	BVAR	√		√	√	Global shocks are more important than domestic demand and monetary conditions.
Vašíček (2011)	Czech Republic, Hungary, Poland, and Slovak Republic	1998:1-2007:3	New Keynesian Phillips curve	√	√		√	Inflation seems to be driven by external factors.

Note: BVAR = Bayesian vector autoregression; DD = domestic demand; DS = domestic supply; EMDEs = emerging market and developing economies; ER = exchange rate; GVAR = global vector autoregression; MP = monetary policy; SVAR = structural vector autoregression; VAR = vector autoregression; VECM = vector error correction model.

ANNEX 3.2 Event studies

Global business cycles and oil price swings. The chapter conducts an event study of inflation around peaks of global expansionary periods and troughs of global recessions, and oil price plunges and spikes. It uses quarterly per capita gross domestic product and the algorithm in Harding and Pagan (2002) to identify turning points of global business cycles. The exercise finds four peaks of global expansions (1973:4, 1981:3, 1990:3, and 2008:2) and four troughs of global recessions (1975:1, 1982:4, 1991:1, and 2009:1). In addition to these four global recessions, Kose and Terrones (2015) identify two global slowdowns (1998 and 2000-01) since 1960. World Bank (2015) identifies oil price plunges as episodes of 30 percent or more declines in oil prices over a six-month period, of which there have been six since 1970 (1985-86, 1990-91, 2001, 1997-98, 2007-09, and 2014-16). Oil price spikes are similarly identified and occurred in 1973-74, 1979, 1987-91,1999-2002, and 2004-08.

Disinflation episodes. Country-specific disinflation episodes are defined, using a variation of Ball (1994), as quarters in which the nine-quarter centered moving average of headline consumer price index inflation (quarter-on-quarter, seasonally adjusted) declines by at least 1 percentage point from the peak to the trough. A trough is the quarter in which trend inflation is lower than in the previous four quarters and following four quarters. A peak is defined as the quarter in which trend inflation is above the previous four quarters and following four quarters. This yields 190 disinflation episodes and 179 inflation episodes in 34 advanced economies, and 719 disinflation episodes and 729 inflation episodes in 134 EMDEs during 1970-2017:3.

ANNEX 3.3 Methodology and database

Global block

This chapter employs a factor-augmented vector autoregression (FAVAR) model. In the first step, a global block is estimated in isolation to examine the roles of different types of global shocks in driving global inflation. In the second step, the global block is combined with a country-specific block to compare the roles of global and domestic shocks in driving domestic inflation.

The global block includes three variables: global inflation, global output growth, and oil price growth (for precise variable definitions, see below). All variables are detrended using a 60-quarter centered moving average. Global output growth and global inflation correspond to the global output growth and global inflation factors estimated separately using the following dynamic factor models:[1]

$$Y_t^i = \beta_{global}^{Y,i} f_t^{Y,\,global} + e_t^{Y,i}$$

$$\pi_t^i = \beta_{global}^{\pi,\,i} f_t^{\pi,\,global} + e_t^{\pi,i}$$

where π_t^i and y_t are inflation and output growth in country i in quarter t, respectively, while $f_t^{\pi,global}$ and $f_t^{Y,global}$ are the global common factors for inflation and output growth in quarter t, respectively.[2]

In its structural form, the FAVAR model is represented by:

$$B_o Z_t = \alpha + \sum_{i=1}^{L} B_i Z_{t-1} + \varepsilon_t$$

where ε_t is a vector of orthogonal structural innovations, and Z_t consists of global inflation ($f_t^{\pi,\,global}$), global output growth ($f_t^{y,\,global}$), and oil price growth (Δop). The vector ε_t consists of a shock to the global supply of goods and services ("*global supply shock*"), a shock to the global demand for goods and services ("*global demand shock*"), and a shock to oil prices ("*oil price shock*").

The chapter follows the methodology in Charnavoki and Dolado (2014) in using sign restrictions to identify global demand, global supply, and oil price

[1] The main assumptions in the estimation of the global factors follow those in Kose, Otrok, and Whiteman (2008) and Kose, Otrok, and Prasad (2012).

[2] The model is specified in terms of growth, not levels, since the variable of interest (inflation) is itself a growth rate.

shocks. Postulating that B_0^{-1} in our model has a recursive structure such that the reduced form errors (u_t) can be decomposed according to $u_t = B_0^{-1}\varepsilon_t$, the sign restrictions that are imposed over the first four quarters can be written as follows:

$$\begin{bmatrix} u_t^{Y,global} \\ u_t^{OilPrice} \\ u_t^{\pi,global} \end{bmatrix} = \begin{bmatrix} + & - & + \\ + & + & + \\ + & + & - \end{bmatrix} \begin{bmatrix} \varepsilon_t^{GlobalDemand} \\ \varepsilon_t^{OilPrice} \\ \varepsilon_t^{GlobalSupply} \end{bmatrix}$$

where a positive *global demand shock* increases global output, global inflation, and oil prices; a positive *oil price shock* increases oil prices and global inflation but reduces global output growth; and a positive *global supply shock* increases global output growth and oil price growth but reduces global inflation.

Structural shocks are assumed to have unit variance, and the magnitude of each shock is defined as a one-standard-deviation increase in the identified structural shocks. Based on the full sample results, it is estimated that a one-standard-deviation shock to global demand represents a 1.2 percentage point increase in global output growth; a one-standard-deviation global supply shock represents a 0.9 percentage point increase in global inflation; and a one-standard-deviation oil price shock a 70 percentage point increase in oil price growth.

The model is estimated by using quarterly data with two lags, as in Charnavoki and Dolado (2014). The lag length is supported by statistical tests (Akaike information criterion [AIC] and Schwartz information criterion [SIC]). Alternative specifications with three or four lags were tested, and the robustness of the VAR estimation results were confirmed. In the Bayesian estimation, the estimation first searches for 1,000 successful draws from at least 2,000 iterations with 1,000 burn-ins; the results reported here are based on the median of these 1,000 successful draws, along with 16-84 percent confidence intervals.

Domestic block

To compare the impact of global and domestic shocks, the model is, in a second step, expanded by a country-specific block. The country-specific block includes four domestic variables: inflation, output growth, nominal effective exchange rates, and nominal short-term interest rates (or policy rates). The model is estimated with two lags (identified as optimal lag length according to the SIC and AIC criteria) on a country-by-country basis, and median results and interquartile ranges are presented. The results are robust to using averages instead of medians.

Similar to Forbes, Hjortsoe, and Nenova (2018, 2017), the global block and the country-specific block are combined as follows:[3]

$$\begin{bmatrix} u_t^{Y,global} \\ u_t^{OilPrice} \\ u_t^{\pi,global} \\ u_t^{Y,domestic} \\ u_t^{\pi,domestic} \\ u_t^{InterestRate} \\ u_t^{ExchangeRate} \end{bmatrix} = \begin{bmatrix} + & - & + & 0 & 0 & 0 & 0 \\ + & + & + & 0 & 0 & 0 & 0 \\ + & + & - & 0 & 0 & 0 & 0 \\ * & * & * & + & + & - & * \\ * & * & * & + & - & - & * \\ * & * & * & * & * & + & * \\ * & * & * & * & * & + & + \end{bmatrix} \begin{bmatrix} \varepsilon_t^{GlobalDemand} \\ \varepsilon_t^{OilPrice} \\ \varepsilon_t^{GlobalSupply} \\ \varepsilon_t^{DomesticDemand} \\ \varepsilon_t^{DomesticSupply} \\ \varepsilon_t^{MonetaryPolicy} \\ \varepsilon_t^{ExchangeRate} \end{bmatrix}$$

where * stands for an unrestricted initial response. While country-specific shocks do not affect global variables contemporaneously, global shocks can affect country-specific variables (without any sign or zero restrictions).

A positive country-specific *supply* or a positive country-specific *demand* shock increases country-specific output growth. Country-specific inflation falls by a positive country-specific supply shock. A positive *interest rate* shock (corresponding to a contractionary monetary policy) initially increases both the domestic interest rate and the exchange rate, and decreases output growth and inflation. Finally, a positive *exchange rate* shock (corresponding to the appreciation of the domestic currency) is assumed to increase the exchange rate, but other effects on domestic variables are left unrestricted.

In the median country, a positive one-standard-deviation domestic demand shock increases domestic output growth by 1.6 percentage points. A one-standard-deviation positive supply shock decreases domestic inflation by 1.1 percentage points. A one-standard-deviation positive (contractionary) monetary

[3] Using a country-specific structural vector autoregression (SVAR) framework with sign restrictions into global and domestic variables in 26 advanced economies for the period of 1992-2015, Forbes, Hjortsoe, and Nenova (2018) identify domestic demand, supply, and monetary policy, and exchange rate shocks along with global permanent and temporary shocks as drivers of domestic inflation and exchange rates. Conti, Neri, and Nobili. (2015) similarly identify global and domestic structural shocks using cross-country data in the Euro Area between 1995 and 2005. In line with those studies, this chapter identifies global and domestic macroeconomic shocks as drivers of inflation. However, this chapter differs from these earlier studies in estimating latent global factors and augmenting country-specific VAR models with these global factors. Instead of estimating the standard single-equation, country-specific Phillips curve, which includes unemployment or output gap as core explanatory variables for inflation, the FAVAR model in this chapter includes domestic and foreign drivers of inflation and allows feedback loops over time among variables. The model is thus expected to enhance the explanatory power for domestic inflation and reduce concerns about omitted variables in single-equation, country-specific Phillips curves.

policy shock increases short-term interest rates (or policy rates) by 0.27 percentage point. A positive one-standard-deviation exchange rate shock represents a 15 percentage point increase (appreciation) in nominal effective exchange rate appreciation.

The results for the roles of global and domestic shocks in explaining the variation in domestic inflation are presented as median point estimates across countries.[4] Interquartile ranges indicate the range from the 25th to the 75th quartile of country-specific estimates (for example, Forbes, Hjortsoe, and Nenova 2017).

Bayesian estimation

The system is estimated on a country-by-country basis. The Bayesian estimation searches for 1,000 successful draws of at least 2,000 iterations with 1,000 burn-ins. The results shown in the chapter are based on the median of these 1,000 successful draws and 68 percent confidence intervals at the country level, although alternative presentation methodologies (for example, the median target, as in Fry and Pagan [2011]) are considered as a robustness check. In the Bayesian estimation, the Minnesota priors proposed by Litterman (1986) are used; since the Minnesota prior assumes that the variance-covariance matrix of residuals is known, the entire variance-covariance matrix of the variance autoregression is estimated by ordinary least squares. For the estimation, the identification strategy through the algorithm introduced by Arias, Rubio-Ramirez, and Waggoner (2014) is used, where the standard Cholesky decomposition is employed with an additional orthogonalization step that is necessary to produce a posterior draw from the correct distribution for structural vector autoregression coefficients.

Database

The sample includes 29 advanced economies and 26 emerging market and developing economies (EMDEs) with at least 10 years (40 quarters) of continuous data for the variables in the domestic block, but the sample period differs across countries (Table A.3.3.1). Long-term components of quarterly growth rates are proxied by 15-year moving averages, benchmarking Stock and Watson (2012).[5] The following variables are used as inputs in the FAVAR estimation:

---

[4] Focusing on cross-country medians mitigates concerns that, for the United States and China, the domestic block might affect the global block contemporaneously.

[5] Unit-root tests of 55 quarterly inflation rates indicate that most of the country-specific inflation rates are stationary or trend-stationary at the 5 percent significance level. Based on these results, long-term trends in inflation rates are eliminated. As in Chapter 2, the results are qualitatively robust to different detrending methods (for example, the Hodrick-Prescott or Butterworth filters).

- Global output growth is the global common factor of quarter-on-quarter, seasonally adjusted real gross domestic product (GDP) growth in a sample of 29 advanced economies and EMDEs for 1970:1-2017:4.
- Global inflation is defined as the global common factor of quarter-on-quarter headline consumer price index (CPI) inflation (seasonally adjusted) in a sample of 47 advanced economies and EMDEs. For robustness, the estimation is repeated using core inflation and producer price index inflation, similarly defined.
- Oil price growth is the quarter-on-quarter growth rate of nominal oil prices (average of Dubai, West Texas Intermediate, and Brent).
- Domestic inflation is quarter-on-quarter, seasonally adjusted headline CPI inflation.
- Domestic output growth is quarter-on-quarter, seasonally adjusted real GDP growth.
- Domestic interest rates are quarter-on-quarter differences in three-month Treasury bill rates or monetary policy rates.
- Nominal effective appreciation is quarter-on-quarter appreciation in trade-weighted nominal exchange rates against 52 currencies, as provided by the Bank for International Settlements.

Robustness exercises

Since the FAVAR estimation in this chapter rests on various assumptions about the relationships among endogenous variables, several robustness checks on the assumptions are performed. The results presented in this chapter are robust to the following changes:

- Alternative measures of global inflation and global output in the estimation of the global block: (i) global inflation and output factors estimated with an identical group of 25 countries and (ii) median GDP growth and inflation rates among countries.
- Alternative measures of oil prices in the global block: real oil prices and nominal energy prices.
- Use of averages, instead of medians, in reporting all country-specific results on the contribution of global and domestic shocks to domestic inflation (Table A.3.3.2).
- An alternative number of periods (that is, two-quarters periods) in imposing sign restrictions in identifying country-specific structural shocks.

- Alternative sign restrictions: positive domestic demand shocks lead to contemporaneous increases in country-specific, short-term interest rates (or policy rates).
- Alternative presentations of 1,000 successful draws following Fry and Pagan (2011): instead of presenting the median across 1,000 successful draws, use of the draw that is closest to the median across 1,000 successful draws (that is, the median target). The same strategy has been applied to calculate the corresponding 68 percent confidence sets, again by following Fry and Pagan (2011).
- Country-specific FAVAR estimation results for 2001-17 instead of full-sample results.

TABLE A.3.3.1 List of countries and sample periods

Country sample periods			
Country	**Sample period**	**Country**	**Sample period**
Australia	1970:2 - 2017:4	India	1993:3 - 2017:4
Austria	1990:1 - 2017:4	Israel	1985:3 - 2017:4
Azerbaijan	2005:3 - 2017:4	Italy	1979:2 - 2017:4
Belgium	1970:2 - 2017:4	Jordan	1999:3 - 2017:4
Bulgaria	1994:4 - 2017:4	Japan	1989:3 - 2017:4
Brazil	1998:3 - 2017:4	Korea, Rep.	1991:3 - 2017:4
Botswana	1994:4 - 2017:4	Luxembourg	1999:3 - 2017:4
Canada	1970:2 - 2017:4	Mexico	1989:1 - 2017:4
Switzerland	1970:3 - 2017:4	Macedonia, FYR	2008:1 - 2017:4
Chile	1986:3 - 2017:4	Malta	1999:3 - 2017:4
China	1984:4 - 2017:4	Malaysia	2004:4 - 2017:4
Colombia	1994:4 - 2017:4	Morocco	1995:4 - 2017:4
Costa Rica	1997:3 - 2017:4	Netherlands	1982:3 - 2017:4
Czech Republic	1992:4 - 2017:4	Norway	1979:2 - 2017:4
Germany	1970:2 - 2017:4	New Zealand	1974:3 - 2017:4
Denmark	1970:2 - 2017:4	Philippines	1987:3 - 2007:3
Dominican Republic	2004:3 - 2017:3	Poland	1992:1 - 2017:4
Egypt, Arab Rep.	2002:4 - 2017:2	Portugal	1986:2 - 2017:4
Spain	1977:3 - 2017:4	Russian Federation	2000:1 - 2017:4
Finland	1987:3 - 2017:4	Slovak Republic	1996:1 - 2017:4
France	1970:2 - 2017:4	Slovenia	2002:3 - 2017:4
United Kingdom	1970:2 - 2017:4	South Africa	1981:3 - 2017:4
Greece	1994:4 - 2017:4	Sweden	1983:3 - 2017:4
Honduras	2005:4 - 2017:4	Thailand	2000:4 - 2017:4
Hungary	1995:4 - 2017:4	Tunisia	2000:4 - 2017:4
Indonesia	1990:3 - 2017:4	Turkey	2007:1 - 2017:4
Ireland	1984:3 - 2017:4	United States	1970:2 - 2017:4
Iceland	1988:3 - 2017:4		

Note: Countries with at least 40 quarters of data have been included.

TABLE A.3.3.2 Contribution of domestic shocks to domestic inflation

Panel A. Income groups

	All countries		AEs		EMDEs	
	Median	Mean	Median	Mean	Median	Mean
Total global shocks	27.7	32.5	33.3	37.0	13.6	19.7
Total domestic shocks	72.3	67.5	66.7	63.0	86.4	80.3
Domestic demand shock	14.5	13.8	12.9	12.2	19.5	19.5
Domestic supply shock	26.0	24.4	25.2	23.8	29.7	25.3
Monetary policy shock	14.4	14.2	13.2	12.5	16.9	16.6
Exchange rate shock	17.3	15.1	15.4	14.5	20.3	18.8

Panel B. Subperiods

	1970-85		1986-2000		2001-17	
	Median	Mean	Median	Mean	Median	Mean
Total global shocks	23.2	30.3	20.6	26.1	43.2	44.3
Total domestic shocks	76.8	69.7	79.4	73.9	56.8	55.8
Domestic demand shock	15.5	13.5	13.9	13.7	11.3	12.0
Domestic supply shock	28.3	26.2	31.1	27.9	20.8	19.3
Monetary policy shock	14.4	14.0	14.4	14.3	10.6	11.8
Exchange rate shock	18.7	16.1	19.9	18.1	14.2	12.6

Note: The table shows median across countries' shares of country-specific inflation variance accounted for by domestic shocks (domestic demand, supply, exchange rates, and interest rates) and global shocks based on country-specific factor-augmented vector autoregression models estimated for 29 advanced economies and 26 EMDEs for 1970-2017 (panel A) and three subsamples (panel B). AEs = advanced economies; EMDEs = emerging market and developing economies.

References

Agénor, P., and K. E. Aynaoui. 2010. "Excess Liquidity, Bank Pricing Rule, and Monetary Policy." *Journal of Banking and Finance* 34 (5): 923-33.

Ahmad, A. H., and E. Pentecost. 2012. "Identifying Aggregate Supply and Demand Shocks in Small Open Economies: Empirical Evidence from African Countries." *International Review of Economics and Finance* 21 (1): 272-91.

Aleem, A. 2010. "Transmission Mechanism of Monetary Policy in India." *Journal of Asian Economics* 21 (2): 186-97.

Altansukh, G., R. Becker, G. J. Bratsiotis, and D. R. Osborn. 2017. "What Is the Globalisation of Inflation?" *Journal of Economic Dynamics and Control* 74 (January): 1-27.

Amisano, G., and O. Tristani. 2007. "Euro Area Inflation Persistence in an Estimated Nonlinear DSGE Model." ECB Working Paper 754, European Central Bank, Frankfurt am Main.

Andrade, P., and M. Zachariadis. 2016. "Global versus Local Shocks in Micro Price Dynamics." *Journal of International Economics* 98 (C): 78-92.

Andrews, D., P. Gal, and W. Witheridge. 2018. "A Genie in a Bottle? Globalisation, Competition and Inflation." OECD Working Paper 1462, Organisation for Economic Co-operation and Development, Paris.

Arias, J. E., J .F. Rubio-Ramirez, and D. F. Waggoner. 2014. "Inference Based on SVARs Identified with Sign and Zero Restrictions: Theory and Applications." International Finance Discussion Papers 1100, Board of Governors of the Federal Reserve System, Washington, DC.

Auer, R., C. Borio, and A. Filardo. 2017. "The Globalisation of Inflation: The Growing Importance of Global Value Chains." BIS Working Paper 602, Bank for International Settlements, Basel.

Baffes, J., M. A. Kose, F. Ohnsorge, and M. Stocker. 2015. "The Great Plunge in Oil Prices—Causes, Consequences, and Policy Responses." Policy Research Note 1, World Bank, Washington, DC.

Ball, L. 1994. "What Determines the Sacrifice Ratio?" In *Monetary Policy,* edited by G. Mankiw. Chicago: Chicago University Press.

Baumeister, C., and G. Peersman. 2013. "Time-Varying Effects of Oil Supply Shocks on the US Economy." *American Economic Journal: Macroeconomics* 5 (4): 1-28.

Benati, L., and C. Goodhart. 2010. "Monetary Policy Regimes and Economic Performance: The Historical Record, 1979-2008." In *Handbook of Monetary Economics,* Vol. 3, edited by B. M. Friedman and M. Woodford, 1159-1236. New York: Elsevier.

Berganza, J. C., F. Borrallo, and P. del Río. 2016. "Determinants and Implications of Low Global Inflation Rates." Working Paper 1608, Banco de España, Madrid.

Bhattacharya, R., I. Patnaik, and A. Shah. 2011. "Monetary Policy Transmission in an Emerging Market Setting." IMF Working Paper 11/5, International Monetary Fund, Washington, DC.

Bhattarai, S., and C. J. Neely. 2016. "A Survey of the Empirical Literature on U.S. Unconventional Monetary Policy." Working Paper 2016(21), Federal Reserve Bank of St. Louis, St. Louis, MO.

Bianchi, F., and A. Civelli. 2015. "Globalization and Inflation: Evidence from a Time Varying VAR." *Review of Economic Dynamics* 18 (2): 406-33.

Blanchard, O., and D. Quah. 1989. "The Dynamic Effect of Aggregate Demand and Supply Disturbances." *American Economic Review* 79 (4): 655-73.

Bobeica, E., and M. Jarociński. 2017. "Missing Disinflation and Missing Inflation: The Puzzles That Aren't." ECB Working Paper Series 2000, European Central Bank, Frankfurt am Main.

Boivin, J., M. T. Kiley, and F. S. Mishkin. 2010. "How Has the Monetary Transmission Mechanism Evolved over Time?" In *Handbook of Monetary Economics,* Vol. 3, edited by B. M. Friedman and M. Woodford, 369-422. New York: Elsevier.

Borio, C., and A. Filardo. 2007. "Globalisation and Inflation: New Cross-Country Evidence on the Global Determinants of Domestic Inflation." BIS Working Paper 227, Bank for International Settlements, Basel.

Canova, F., and G. De Nicolo. 2002. "Monetary Disturbances Matter for Business Fluctuations in the G-7." *Journal of Monetary Economics* 49 (6): 1131-59.

Canova, F., and M. Paustian. 2011. "Business Cycle Measurement with Some Theory." *Journal of Monetary Economics* 58 (4): 345-61.

Cárdenas, M., and E. Levy-Yeyati. 2011. "Graduation Season: Moving towards Advanced-Economy Status." Op-ed, June 1, Brookings Institution, Washington, DC.

Carney, M. 2015. "How Is Inflation Affected by Globalisation?" Remarks by the Governor of the Bank of England, World Economic Forum, Jackson Hole, WY, August 29.

Catão, L., and A. Pagan. 2010. "The Credit Channel and Monetary Transmission in Brazil and Chile: A Structural VAR Approach." Working Paper 579, Central Bank of Chile, Santiago.

Charnavoki, V., and J. J. Dolado. 2014. "The Effects of Global Shocks on Small Commodity-Exporting Economies: Lessons from Canada." *American Economic Journal: Macroeconomics* 6 (2): 207-37.

Chinn, M. D., and H. Ito. 2017. "The Chinn-Ito Index—A de Jure Measure of Financial Openness." http://web.pdx.edu/~ito/Chinn-Ito_website.htm.

Choi, S., D. Furceri, P. Loungani, S. Mishra, and M. Poplawski-Ribeiro. 2018. "Oil Prices and Inflation Dynamics: Evidence from Advanced and Developing Economies." *Journal of International Money and Finance* 82: 71-96.

Ciccarelli, M., and B. Mojon. 2010. "Global Inflation." *Review of Economics and Statistics* 92 (3): 524-35.

Cogley, T., C. Matthes, and A. M. Sbordone. 2015. "Optimized Taylor Rules for Disinflation When Agents Are Learning." *Journal of Monetary Economics* 72 (May): 131-47.

Coibion, O., and Y. Gorodnichenko. 2015. "Is the Phillips Curve Alive and Well after All? Inflation Expectations and the Missing Disinflation." *American Economic Journal: Macroeconomics* 7 (1): 197-232.

Conti, A. M., S. Neri, and A. Nobili. 2015. "Why Is Inflation So Low in the Euro Area?" Economic Working Papers 1019, Bank of Italy, Rome.

———. 2017. "Low Inflation and Monetary Policy in the Euro Area." ECB Working Paper 2005, European Central Bank, Frankfurt am Main.

Disyatat, P., and P. Vongsinsirikul. 2003. "Monetary Policy and the Transmission Mechanism in Thailand." *Journal of Asian Economics* 14 (3): 389-418.

Domaç, I., and E. M. Yücel. 2005. "What Triggers Inflation in Emerging Market Economies?" *Review of World Economics* 144 (1): 141-64.

Dua, P., and U. Gaur. 2009. "Determination of Inflation in an Open Economy Phillips Curve Framework—The Case of Developed and Developing Asian Countries." Working Paper 178, Centre for Development Economics, Delhi School of Economics, New Delhi, India.

ECB (European Central Bank). 2015. *Annual Report.* https://www.ecb.europa.eu/ pub/pdf/annrep/ar2015en.pdf.

———. 2017. "Exchange Rate Pass-Through into Euro Area Inflation." Occasional Paper, European Central Bank, Frankfurt am Main.

Eickmeier, S., and M. Kühnlenz. 2016. "China's Role in Global Inflation Dynamics." *Macroeconomic Dynamics* 22 (2): 225-54.

Eickmeier, S., and K. Pijnenburg. 2013. "The Global Dimension of Inflation: Evidence from Factor-Augmented Phillips Curves." *Oxford Bulletin of Economics and Statistics* 75 (1): 103-22.

Elbourne, A., and J. Haan. 2009. "Financial Structure and Monetary Policy Transmission in Transition Countries." *Journal of Comparative Economics* 34 (1): 1-23.

Federal Reserve Bank of San Francisco. 1999. "What Is Deflation and How Is It Different from Disinflation?" https://www.frbsf.org/education/publications/doctor-econ/1999/september/deflation-disinflation-causes.

Ferroni, F., and B. Mojon. 2014. "Domestic and Global Inflation." Federal Reserve Bank of Cleveland, OH.

Filardo, A. J., and M. J. Lombardi. 2014. "Has Asian Emerging Market Monetary Policy Been Too Procyclical When Responding to Swings in Commodity Prices?" Working Paper 77, Bank for International Settlements, Basel.

Forbes, K. J., I. Hjortsoe, and T. Nenova. 2017. "Shocks versus Structure: Explaining Differences in Exchange Rate Pass-Through across Countries and Time." Discussion Paper 50, Bank of England, London.

———. 2018. "The Shocks Matter: Improving Our Estimates of Exchange Rate Pass-Through." *Journal of International Economics* 114 (September): 255-75.

Frankel, J. 2011. "Monetary Policy in Emerging Markets: A Survey." Working Paper 11-003, John F. Kennedy School of Government, Harvard University, Cambridge, MA.

Fry, R., and A. Pagan. 2011. "Sign Restrictions in Structural Vector Autoregressions: A Critical Review." Journal of Economic Literature 49 (4): 938-60.

Furceri, D., P. Loungani, and A. Zdzienicka. 2018. "The Effects of Monetary Policy Shocks on Inequality." *Journal of International Money and Finance* 85 (July): 168-86.

Gali, J., and T. Monacelli. 2008. "Monetary Policy and Exchange Rate Volatility in a Small Open Economy." *Review of Economic Studies* 72 (3): 707-34.

Gambetti, L., E. Pappa, and F. Canova. 2005. "The Structural Dynamics of U.S. Output and Inflation: What Explains the Changes?" Economics Working Papers 921, Department of Economics and Business, Universitat Pompeu Fabra, Barcelona.

———. 2008. "The Structural Dynamics of U.S. Output and Inflation: What Explains the Changes?" *Journal of Money, Credit and Banking* 40 (2-3): 369-88.

Gertler, M., and P. Karadi. 2015. "Monetary Policy Surprises, Credit Costs, and Economic Activity." *American Economic Journal: Macroeconomics* 7 (1): 44-76.

Globan, T., V. Arčabić, and P. Sorić. 2015. "Inflation in New EU Member States: A Domestically or Externally Driven Phenomenon?" *Emerging Markets Finance and Trade* 51 (6): 1-15.

Golinelli, R., and R. Rovelli. 2005. "Monetary Policy Transmission, Interest Rate Rules and Inflation Targeting in Three Transition Countries." *Journal of Banking and Fina*nce 29 (1): 183-201.

Goodfriend, M., and R. G. King. 2005. "The Incredible Volcker Disinflation." *Journal of Monetary Economics* 52 (5): 981-1015.

Hałka, A., and J. Kotłowski. 2017. "Global or Domestic? Which Shocks Drive Inflation in European Small Open Economies?" NBP Working Paper 232, Narodowy Bank Polski, Warsaw, Poland.

Hamilton, J. D. 2011. "Historical Oil Shocks." NBER Working Paper 16790, National Bureau of Economic Research, Cambridge, MA.

Hammond, G., R. Kanbur, and E. S. Prasad. 2009. "Monetary Policy Challenges for Emerging Market Economies." Working Paper 36, Global Economy and Development Series, Brookings Institution, Washington, DC.

Harding, D., and A. Pagan. 2002. "Dissecting the Cycle: A Methodological Investigation." *Journal of Monetary Economics* 49 (2): 365-81.

Hasan, M., and H. Alogeel. 2008. "Understanding the Inflationary Process in the GCC Region: The Case of Saudi Arabia and Kuwait." IMF Working Paper 08/193, International Monetary Fund, Washington, DC.

Ihrig, J., S. B. Kamin, D. Lindner, and J. Marquez. 2010. "Some Simple Tests of the Globalization and Inflation Hypothesis." *International Finance* 13 (3): 343-75.

Ilzetzki, E., C. M. Reinhart, and K. S. Rogoff. 2017. "Exchange Arrangements Entering the 21st Century: Which Anchor Will Hold?" NBER Working Paper 23134, National Bureau of Economic Research, Cambridge, MA.

IMF (International Monetary Fund). 2016. *World Economic Outlook October 2016: Subdued Demand: Symptoms and Remedies.* Washington, DC: IMF.

Jongwanich, J., and D. Park. 2008. "Inflation in Developing Asia: Demand-Pull or Cost-Push?" ERD Working Paper Series 121, Asian Development Bank, Manila.

Jongwanich, J., P. Wongcharoen, and D. Park. 2016. "Determinants of Consumer Price Inflation versus Producer Price Inflation in Asia." ADB Economics Working Paper Series 491, Asian Development Bank, Manila.

Kabukçuoğlu, A., and E. Martínez-García. 2018. "Inflation as a Global Phenomenon—Some Implications for Inflation Modeling and Forecasting." *Journal of Economic Dynamics and Control* 87 (C): 46-73.

Kandil, M., and H. Morsy. 2010. "Fiscal Stimulus and Credibility in Emerging Countries." IMF Working Paper 10/123, International Monetary Fund, Washington, DC.

Khan, M. H., and M. N. Hanif. 2012. "Role of Demand and Supply Shocks in Driving Inflation: A Case Study of Pakistan. *Journal of Independent Studies and Research* 10 (20): 113-22.

Kose, M. A., C. Otrok, and E. Prasad. 2012. "Global Business Cycles: Convergence or Decoupling?" *International Economic Review* 53 (2): 511-38.

Kose, M. A., C. Otrok, and C. Whiteman. 2008. "Understanding the Evolution of World Business Cycles." *Journal of International Economics* 75 (1): 110-30.

Kose, M. A., and M. Terrones. 2015. *Collapse and Revival: Understanding Global Recessions and Recoveries*. Washington, DC: International Monetary Fund.

Laeven, L., and F. Valencia. 2013. "Systemic Banking Crisis Database." *IMF Economic Review* 61 (2): 225-70.

Leeper, E. M., C. A. Sims, and T. Zha. 1996. "What Does Monetary Policy Do?" *Brookings Papers on Economic Activity* 1996 (2): 1-63.

Litterman, R. B. 1986. "Forecasting with Bayesian Vector Autoregressions—Five Years of Experience." *Journal of Business and Economic Statistics* 4 (1): 25-38.

Mackowiak, B. 2007. "External Shocks, U.S. Monetary Policy and Macroeconomic Fluctuations in Emerging Markets." *Journal of Monetary Economics* 54 (8): 2512-20.

Mallick, S. K., and R. M. Sousa. 2012. "Real Effects of Monetary Policy in Large Emerging Markets." *Macroeconomic Dynamics* 16 (S2): 190-212.

Martínez-García, E., and M. Wynne. 2010. "The Global Slack Hypothesis." Staff Papers 10, Federal Reserve Bank of Dallas, Dallas, TX.

Melolinna, M. 2015. "What Has Driven Inflation Dynamics in the Euro Area, the United Kingdom and the United States?" ECB Working Paper 1802, European Central Bank, Frankfurt am Main.

Mikolajun, I., and D. Lodge. 2016. "Advanced Economy Inflation: The Role of Global Factors." ECB Working Paper 1948, European Central Bank, Frankfurt am Main.

Mishra, P., and P. Montiel. 2012. "How Effective Is Monetary Transmission in Low-Income Countries? A Survey of the Empirical Evidence." IMF Working Paper 12/143, International Monetary Fund, Washington, DC.

Mishra, P., P. Montiel, and R. Sengupta. 2016. "Monetary Transmission in Developing Countries: Evidence from India." IMF Working Paper 16/167, International Monetary Fund, Washington, DC.

Mishra, P., P. J. Montiel, and A. Spilimbergo. 2012. "Monetary Transmission in Low-Income Countries: Effectiveness and Policy Implications." *IMF Economic Review* 60 (2): 270-302.

Mohanty, M. S., and M. Klau. 2001. "What Determines Inflation in Emerging Market Economies?" In *Modelling Aspects of the Inflation Process and the Monetary Transmission Mechanism in Emerging Market Countries*, 1-38. Basel: Bank for International Settlements.

Mohanty, M. S., and P. Turner. 2008. "Monetary Policy Transmission in Emerging Market Economies: What Is New?" In *Transmission Mechanisms for Monetary Policy in Emerging Market Economies*, 1-59. Basel: Bank for International Settlements.

Mumtaz, H., S. Simonelli, and P. Surico. 2011. "International Comovements, Business Cycle and Inflation: A Historical Perspective." *Review of Economic Dynamics* 14 (1): 176-98.

Neaime, S. 2008. "Monetary Policy Transmission and Targeting Mechanisms in the MENA Region." ERF Working Paper 395, Economic Research Forum, Giza, Arab Republic of Egypt.

Neely, C. J., and D. E. Rapach. 2011. "International Comovements in Inflation Rates and Country Characteristics." *Journal of International Money and Finance* 30 (7): 1471-90.

Ngalawa, H., and N. Viegi. 2011. "Dynamic Effects of Monetary Policy Shocks in Malawi." *South African Journal of Economics* 79 (3): 224-50.

Nguyen, A. D. M., J. Dridi, F. D. Unsal, and O. H. Williams. 2017. "On the Drivers of Inflation in Sub-Saharan Africa." *International Economics* 151 (C): 71-84.

Osorio, C., and D. F. Unsal. 2013. "Inflation Dynamics in Asia: Causes, Changes, and Spillovers from China." *Journal of Asian Economics* 24 (February): 26-40.

Pain, N., I. Koske, and M. Sollie. 2006. "Globalisation and Inflation in the OECD Economies." Working Paper 524, Organisation for Economic Co-operation and Development, Paris.

Parker, M. 2018. "How Global Is 'Global Inflation'?" *Journal of Macroeconomics* 58 (December): 174-97.

Porter, N. 2010. "Price Dynamics in China." IMF Working Paper 10/221, International Monetary Fund, Washington, DC.

Ramey, V. A. 2016. "Macroeconomic Shocks and Their Propagation." NBER Working Paper 21978, National Bureau of Economic Research, Cambridge, MA.

Rogoff, K. S. 2003. "Globalization and Global Disinflation." *Federal Reserve Bank of Kansas City Economic Review* Q (IV): 45-78.

Singh, K., and K. Kalirajan. 2007. "Monetary Transmission in Post-Reform India: An Evaluation." *Journal of the Asia Pacific Economy* 12 (2): 158-87.

Stock, J. H., and M. W. Watson. 2012. "Disentangling the Channels of the 2007-2009 Recession." NBER Working Paper 18094, National Bureau of Economic Research, Cambridge, MA.

———. 2017. "Identification and Estimation of Dynamic Causal Effects in Macroeconomics." Working Paper, Harvard University, Cambridge, MA.

Sussman, N., and O. Zohar. 2015. "Oil Prices, Inflation Expectations and Monetary Policy." Discussion Paper, Central Bank of Israel, Jerusalem.

Tena, J. D., and C. Salazar. 2008. "Explaining Inflation and Output Volatility in Chile: An Empirical Analysis of Forty Years." *Cuadernos de Economía* 27 (49): 259-79.

Vašíček, B. 2011. "Inflation Dynamics and the New Keynesian Phillips Curve in Four Central European Countries." *Emerging Markets Finance and Trade* 47 (5): 71-100.

Vonnák, B. 2008. "The Hungarian Monetary Transmission Mechanism: An Assessment." In *Transmission Mechanisms for Monetary Policy in Emerging Market Economies*, 235-57. Basel: Bank for International Settlements.

World Bank. 2015. *Global Economic Prospects: The Global Economy in Transition.* Washington, DC: World Bank.

———. 2018. *Global Economic Prospects: Broad-Based Upturn, but for How Long?* Washington, DC: World Bank.

Wu, J., A. C. Luca, B. N. Jeon. 2011. "Transmission of Monetary Policy via Domestic and Foreign Banks in Emerging Economies: Evidence from Bank-Level Data." *Journal of International Money and Finance* 30 (6): 1128-56.

In an interconnected world, fulfilling the Federal Reserve's objectives under its dual mandate requires that we pay close attention to how our own actions affect other countries and how developments abroad, in turn, spill back into U.S. economic conditions.

Stanley Fischer (2015)

PART B

INFLATION

Expectations and Pass-Through

CHAPTER 4

Inflation Expectations: Review and Evidence

Inflation expectations play a critical role in enabling the proper formulation of monetary policy. As such, it is essential for policy makers to have a good understanding of how inflation expectations are determined. This chapter provides a comprehensive examination of the determination and evolution of inflation expectations, with a focus on emerging market and developing economies (EMDEs). It finds that long-term inflation expectations in EMDEs are not as well anchored as those in advanced economies, despite notable improvements over the past two decades. Indeed, in EMDEs, long-term inflation expectations are more sensitive to both domestic and global inflation shocks. However, EMDEs tend to be more successful in anchoring inflation expectations in the presence of an inflation targeting regime, high central bank transparency, strong trade integration, and a low level of public debt.

Introduction

Inflation expectations play a critical role in the effective implementation of monetary policy. A central bank is more likely to be successful in achieving low and stable inflation if it can anchor economic agents' long-term inflation expectations close to its inflation objective. This is because inflation expectations are key in the transmission of monetary policy, as they affect current inflation through their impact on the setting of wages and prices (Bernanke et al. 2001). Measures of inflation expectations are therefore important yardsticks in assessing the credibility of a central bank in meeting its inflation objective.

Given the importance of inflation expectations for monetary policy, it is essential for central banks to have a good understanding of how they are affected by domestic and global shocks. This is especially critical for central banks in emerging market and developing economies (EMDEs), since these economies tend to experience more pronounced business and financial cycles than advanced economies, and therefore may face greater challenges in anchoring expectations.

There is a rich theoretical and empirical literature on inflation expectations. Theoretical studies have examined how public and private information is used by economic agents in formulating inflation expectations. A large body of empirical work has tested the predictions of theoretical models and assessed how firmly inflation expectations are anchored, by measuring the sensitivity of

---

Notes: This chapter was prepared by M. Ayhan Kose, Hideaki Matsuoka, Ugo Panizza, and Dana Vorisek. Yohei Okawa provided background material for a country case study in Annex 4.5.

expectations to various shocks, such as macroeconomic news shocks or oil or other price shocks. The literature, however, has mainly focused on advanced economies.

This chapter presents the first comprehensive analysis of the evolution and determinants of inflation expectations in EMDEs, with emphasis on three main questions:

- How does the degree of anchoring of inflation expectations differ between advanced economies and EMDEs?
- How sensitive are inflation expectations to global and domestic shocks?
- What are the main determinants of the degree of anchoring of inflation expectations?

The chapter makes several contributions to the literature on inflation expectations. First, it employs a large and diverse sample of countries (24 advanced economies and 23 EMDEs) for a period of close to three decades. Second, it analyzes the sensitivity of long-term inflation expectations to global and domestic inflation shocks using a time-varying parameter regression model. Third, it examines the determinants of the degree of anchoring of expectations, using a dynamic panel regression framework. Fourth, it complements the empirical analysis with case studies that examine the role of inflation targeting in stabilizing inflation expectations in three EMDEs. In addition, it provides a summary of the literature with a special focus on empirical studies on the anchoring of inflation expectations in EMDEs.

The chapter begins by discussing the measurement of inflation expectations, comparing survey-based and market-based measures. Survey-based measures have the advantage of being able to incorporate the views of large groups of economic agents and to canvass different types of agents. Market-based measures (that is, measures based on comparisons of certain yields in financial markets) have the advantage of being available at a higher frequency and more extensive range of horizons than survey-based measures.[1]

The following section reviews the theoretical and empirical literature on the formation and anchoring of inflation expectations. Despite a lack of consensus on the theoretical framework that best captures the behavior of inflation expectations, the empirical literature has concluded that an inflation targeting regime helps improve the anchoring of expectations in both advanced economies and EMDEs.

[1] For background on market- and survey-based measures of inflation expectations, see Coibion et al. (2018) and Grothe and Meyler (2018) for the United States and the Euro Area, and Sousa and Yetman (2016) for EMDEs.

The next section examines trends in long-term (five-year-ahead) inflation expectations in advanced economies and EMDEs, from the 1990s to the present. It then assesses the anchoring of inflation expectations. It finds that although expectations have become more firmly anchored during the past decade in both advanced economies and EMDEs, this has been less evident in EMDEs than in advanced economies. The section also reports that inflation expectations in EMDEs are more sensitive to both global and domestic shocks than are inflation expectations in advanced economies, although sensitivity to global shocks has fallen in both groups of economies and sensitivity to domestic shocks has fallen in EMDEs.

The subsequent section identifies the main factors that determine the anchoring of inflation expectations. It presents evidence that inflation expectations are better anchored in both advanced economies and EMDEs when the central bank employs an inflation targeting regime and is highly transparent. For EMDEs, low public debt and a high degree of trade openness are also associated with better anchoring of expectations, while the use of a fixed exchange rate regime is associated with weaker anchoring of expectations. These results suggest that the institutions and framework of monetary policy, the macroeconomic environment (including fiscal policy), and structural characteristics all matter for the anchoring of long-term inflation expectations in EMDEs.

The penultimate section presents case studies on the experience of inflation targeting in Brazil, Chile, and Poland. The conclusions of the case studies are in line with the empirical findings. In Brazil, less than ideal fiscal conditions and worsening central bank transparency during part of the inflation targeting period may have impeded the anchoring of expectations. By contrast, the combination of high central bank credibility and an effective fiscal framework may have helped anchor expectations in Chile. In Poland, the transition to a flexible exchange rate regime concurrent with the adoption of inflation targeting may have helped to anchor expectations.

The final section concludes with a summary of major findings and a discussion of future research directions.

Measuring inflation expectations

Robust measurement is key to evaluating inflation expectations, and typically two sources exist. Survey-based measures are derived from surveys of households, firms, or professional forecasters, in which respondents are asked about their expectations for inflation at various horizons. Market-based measures are calculated from the prices of assets linked to prospective inflation. Each measure has advantages and drawbacks.

Survey-based measures

Surveys of households and firms. Among advanced economies, commonly referenced surveys of households' inflation expectations include the University of Michigan's Surveys of Consumers (monthly frequency for the United States), the European Commission's consumer survey for the countries of the European Union (monthly), and the Bank of England's consumer survey (quarterly) for the United Kingdom.[2] High-frequency surveys of households' or firms' inflation expectations are also conducted by Australia, Canada, the Czech Republic, Italy, Japan, the Republic of Korea, New Zealand, and Sweden. Among EMDEs, survey-based measures of households' or firms' expectations are produced by central banks in East Asia (for example, Indonesia, the Philippines, and Thailand), Europe and Central Asia (for example, Kazakhstan and Turkey), and India and South Africa.[3]

Surveys of professional forecasters. The most commonly used survey of professional forecasters is produced by Consensus Economics, which incorporates the views of more than 700 professional forecasters in 85 advanced economies and EMDEs. Consensus Economics publishes short-term expectations at a monthly frequency and long-term expectations at a semi-annual or quarterly frequency.[4] Other surveys of professional forecasters include the Survey of Professional Forecasters by the Federal Reserve Bank of Philadelphia, which provides data on expectations up to 10 years ahead, and the European Central Bank's Survey of Professional Forecasters. Central banks in several other economies (for example, Argentina, Brazil, Iceland, Indonesia, Israel, Mexico, South Africa, and Turkey) also produce professional survey-based measures of inflation expectations. Surveys of inflation expectations in EMDEs typically have smaller samples than those in advanced economies, but the number of EMDEs included in Consensus Economics' surveys has increased over time, from seven in 1990 to 52 in 2018.[5]

Differences between surveys of households or firms and surveys of professional forecasters. On average, households' and firms' inflation expectations are higher

[2] Most survey results are presented as median responses. Discrepancies among respondents can be informative as a proxy of inflation uncertainty (Mankiw, Reis, and Wolfers 2003; Miles et al. 2017).

[3] For the European Union, a data set on inflation expectations has been collected by the European Commission since 2003. Although it has been used for research purposes, it has not yet been published (Arioli et al. 2017). Some central banks (for example, those of China, Poland, and Romania) release survey results showing the percentage of respondents who expect inflation to change.

[4] In addition, Germany's Ifo Institute has provided data on five-year-ahead inflation expectations for more than 70 countries since the end of 2014.

[5] The International Monetary Fund's *World Economic Outlook* has the broadest country coverage of long-term inflation projections (39 advanced economies and 154 EMDEs).

than professional forecasters' expectations in advanced economies and EMDEs (Figure 4.1). The volatility of households' inflation expectations is also larger than that of professional forecasters' expectations. Households' beliefs about past inflation are found to be a strong predictor of their inflation expectations (Jonung 1981; Malmendier and Nagel 2016). Households' inflation expectations are thus more backward looking than professional forecasters' expectations.[6]

Several reasons for these differences have been suggested. First, households' and firms' expectations are subject to "sticky information" and are updated more slowly than those of professional forecasts (Carroll 2003). Second, household surveys give the same weight to "informed" and "uninformed" consumers. Because uninformed consumers likely give excess weight to goods that are purchased frequently (for example, food) or have highly visible price changes (for example, gasoline), their assessment of inflation expectations can be biased upward when the prices of these products increase (Coibion and Gorodnichenko 2015; Coibion, Gorodnichenko, and Kamdar, forthcoming; Sousa and Yetman 2016). Yet, surveys of households and firms also have important advantages relative to surveys of professional forecasters—for instance, they can be designed to include a large number of respondents and have the flexibility to canvass different types of economic agents. For surveys of professional forecasters, bias may arise from respondents' reluctance to reveal their expectations about inflation because they consider the information private (Cunningham, Desroches, and Santor 2010).

Market-based measures

The most commonly used market-based measure of inflation expectations is the break-even inflation rate—that is, the difference between yields on comparable nominal and inflation-indexed bonds. In general, however, this difference consists of four components: expected inflation, an inflation risk premium, a liquidity premium, and other factors (Hördahl 2009; Christiansen, Dion, and Reid 2004). Hence, extracting expected inflation requires the use of strong assumptions, and any estimate of expected inflation is necessarily imprecise (Galati, Heemeijer, and Moessner 2011).

Another common market-based measure is the inflation swap rate based on derivative instruments, which again includes not only inflation expectations, but

[6] Kumar et al. (2015) and Kabundi, Schaling, and Some (2015) document that in New Zealand and South Africa, some firms do not understand the central bank's objective function. Hence, even if professional forecasters' expectations are well anchored by inflation targeting in these countries, the same is not necessarily true of firms' inflation expectations. The latter may be more important for actual inflation, because firms may incorporate expected marginal costs into their product prices.

FIGURE 4.1 Survey-based measures of inflation expectations: Country evidence

Inflation expectations derived from surveys of households tend to be higher, and their volatility larger, than inflation expectations derived from surveys of professional forecasters. This finding holds for both advanced economies and EMDEs where both types of surveys are conducted.

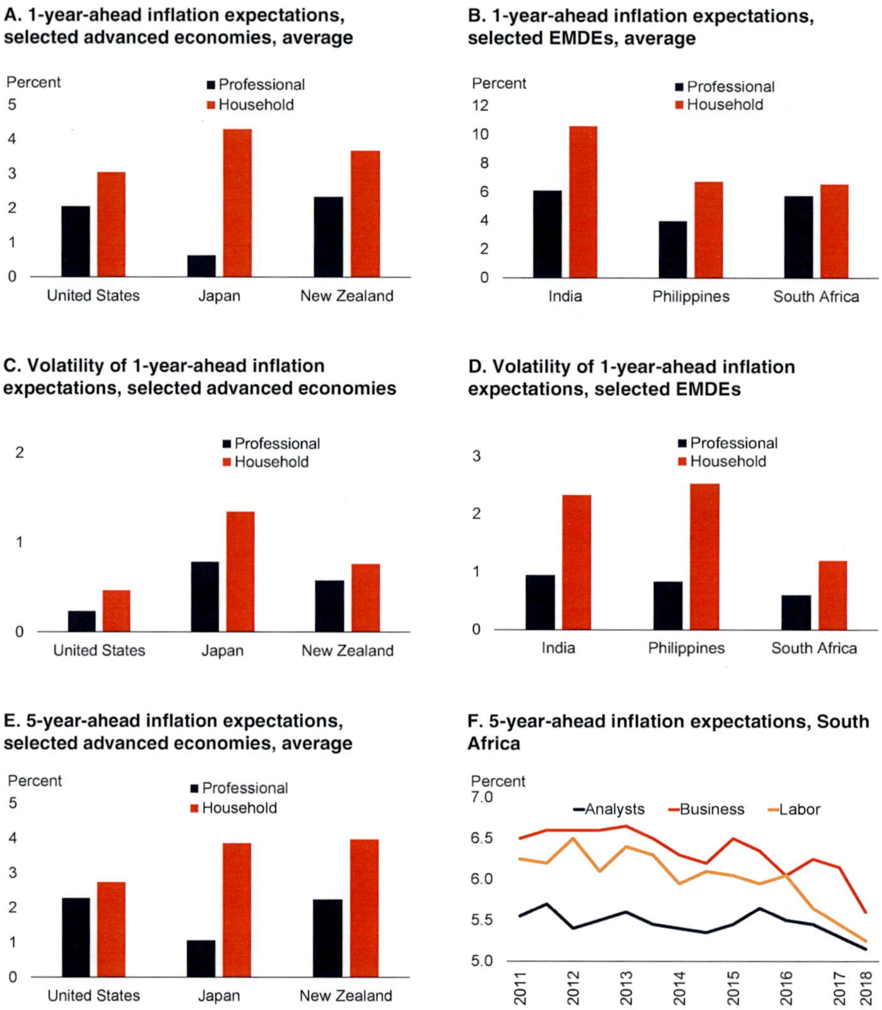

Source: Bank of Japan; Bloomberg; Bureau of Economic Research, South Africa; Central Bank of the Philippines; Consensus Economics; Haver Analytics; International Monetary Fund; Reserve Bank of India; Reserve Bank of New Zealand; University of Michigan; World Bank.

Note: EMDEs = emerging market and developing economies.

A.C. The sample period is 2006H1-2018H1.

B.D. The sample period is 2007H2-2018H1.

C.D. Volatility is measured by standard deviation.

E. The sample period is 2009H1-2018H1.

also the inflation risk premium and liquidity premium. A key advantage of the swap rate is that, unlike for break-even inflation rates, liquidity has a limited impact on its movements (Grothe and Meyler 2018). Both types of market-based measures have the advantage of being available at very high frequencies, which may help policy makers develop an understanding of how inflation expectations are formed and may be calculated at a wider range of forecast horizons than is possible using surveys. However, swap markets in EMDEs are typically insufficiently developed to allow such a measure to be reliably extracted. Therefore, central banks in several large EMDEs (for example, Brazil, Chile, Colombia, Mexico, Peru, Poland, the Russian Federation, South Africa, Thailand, and Turkey) typically derive their market-based measures of inflation expectations from inflation-indexed government bonds (Sousa and Yetman 2016; De Pooter et al. 2014).

Differences between survey-based and market-based measures. In terms of the level of inflation expectations, those derived from surveys of professional forecasters are not systematically higher or lower than market-based measures (Figure 4.2). However, professional forecasters' inflation expectations tend to be close to central bank inflation forecasts, as has been shown for New Zealand and the United States (Coibion and Gorodnichenko 2015). In addition, the volatility of professional forecaster-based expectations tends to be lower than that of market-based expectations. During periods of market stress, break-even inflation rates can be particularly volatile because "flight-to-liquidity" flows raise demand for government bonds sharply.[7] This could push nominal yields to extremely low levels and put strong downward pressure on measured break-even inflation rates (Hördahl 2009). Relative to survey-based measures of inflation expectations, an advantage of market-based measures is that they cannot be influenced by poorly crafted surveys.

Expectations measure used in this chapter

Due to the breadth of its country coverage and length of its time coverage, the main long-term inflation expectations series used in this chapter are the survey-based, five-year-ahead expectations produced on a semi-annual basis by Consensus Economics. In the empirical work, the change in long-term inflation expectations is measured as the difference between five-year-ahead inflation expectations in the current period and five-year-ahead inflation expectations in the previous period (that is, six months prior).

[7] During periods of market stress, investors may have a strong preference for holding very liquid securities, such as government bonds. This preference can lead to sharp movements in bond markets (that is, flight to liquidity), similar to market movements driven by flight to quality.

FIGURE 4.2 Survey-based and market-based measures of inflation expectations: Country evidence

Across countries, inflation expectations derived from surveys of professional forecasters are not systematically higher or lower than market-based measures of expectations. However, the volatility of market-based inflation expectations tends to be higher than that of survey-based expectations in both advanced economies and EMDEs.

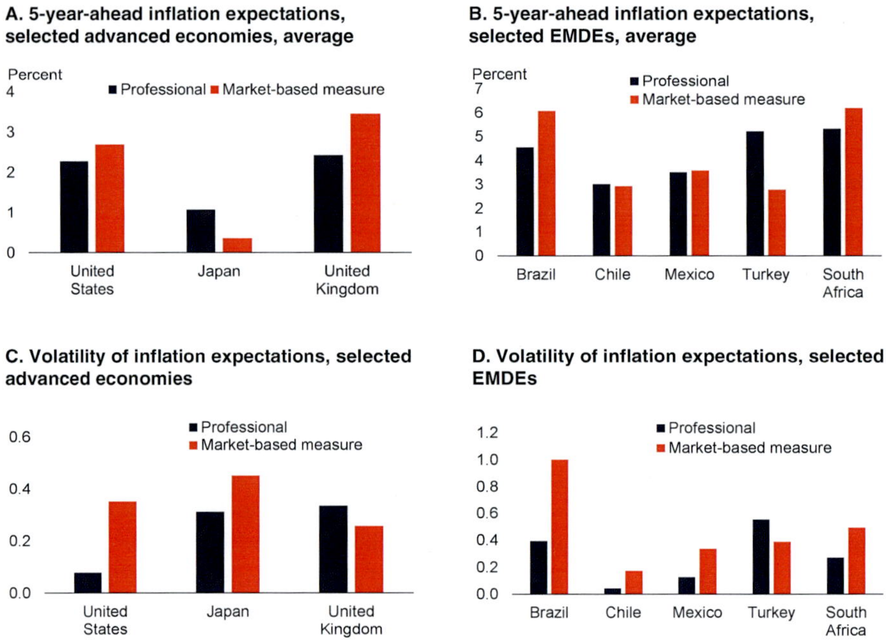

Source: Bloomberg; Consensus Economics; International Monetary Fund; World Bank.

Note: EMDEs = emerging market and developing economies.

A.-D. Market-based inflation expectations are inflation swap rates (five-year, five-year forward) for advanced economies and break-even inflation rates (five-year-ahead) for EMDEs.

A.C. The sample period is 2007H1-2018H1.

B.D. The sample period is 2012H2-2018H1.

C.D. Volatility is measured by standard deviation.

Literature on inflation expectations

Theories of inflation expectations have mainly focused on how expectations reflect public and private information. There remain different views on which conceptual framework is best.[8] Empirical studies, most of which have focused on

[8] Coibion, Gorodnichenko, and Kamdar (forthcoming) and Mankiw and Reis (2018) survey the literature on the formation of expectations. Annex 4.1 presents a brief overview of how views on the linkages between inflation expectations and monetary policy have evolved over time.

advanced economies, concentrate on testing the implications of the theoretical literature and evaluating the degree of anchoring of expectations.[9]

Conceptual considerations

The theoretical literature on the determinants of inflation expectations ranges from models that assume agents have "full-information rational expectations" (FIRE) to models that allow for constraints on agents' ability to process information.[10] There is still no consensus on an ideal framework to describe how inflation expectations are determined (Mankiw and Reis 2018).

With its simple formulation of the relationship between inflation and economic activity, the New Keynesian model has been used extensively in policy and academic circles. However, it has also been subject to criticism—in particular, that it does not take into account the constraints that economic agents typically face in forming their expectations about inflation. For example, Friedman (1979) argues that FIRE does not explain how "economic agents derive the knowledge which they then use to formulate expectations."

FIRE models have also been criticized for their inability to explain the persistence of inflation that is usually found in the data. These criticisms have led to two alternate approaches in modeling the role of information in the formation of inflation expectations: the sticky-information model and the noisy-information model. In the sticky-information model, forecasts are updated slowly because acquiring information is costly (Mankiw and Reis 2002). The assumption of sticky-information flow can be rationalized in terms of an "epidemic" model of news diffusion (Carroll 2003).[11]

Models of noisy information and rational inattention instead assume that economic agents continuously update their information but receive imperfect, "noisy" signals or do not pay attention to all news (Woodford 2002; Sims 2003; Maćkowiak and Wiederholt 2009; Coibion, Gorodnichenko, and Kamdar 2018). Departures from the full-information assumption can also be rationalized in the context of "learning" models, which assume that agents need to use statistical methods to learn about the central bank's objective function and the overall structure of the economy (Evans and Honkapohja 2009).[12]

---

[9] Annex 4.2 lists a number of empirical studies on the evolution, determinants, and anchoring of inflation expectations in advanced economies and EMDEs.

[10] Agents with FIRE are assumed to understand perfectly the structure and functioning of the economy and the policy makers' objective function (Bernanke 2007).

[11] In the "epidemic" model, households' inflation forecasts are affected by media and professional inflation forecasts.

[12] Coibion, Gorodnichenko, and Kamdar (forthcoming) discuss models featuring other departures from FIRE, including bounded rationality and adaptive learning models. Models with bounded rationality assume that agents build a simplified model of the world, paying attention to only some of the relevant variables. Adaptive learning models assume that agents behave like econometricians, using the available information at the time of the forecast and following a specific updating mechanism.

On the operational side, the assumption that a fraction of firms is not fully rational and instead sets prices using a rule of thumb that depends on past inflation led to the development of the hybrid New Keynesian Phillips curve. In this specification, current inflation depends on both expected and lagged inflation (Fuhrer and Moore 1995; Galí and Gertler 1999). In particular, the model takes into account backward- and forward-looking inflation expectations (that is, inflation expectations are determined by past inflation and expectations about those variables viewed as determining actual inflation). Some specifications of the model also control for foreign inflation (for example, IMF 2016).

In addition to fitting the data better, the hybrid New Keynesian Phillips curve is well suited to the reality of constantly evolving economic structures. The standard New Keynesian Phillips curve implies that long-run inflation expectations do not respond to news because the public knows the long-run equilibrium. The hybrid curve is consistent with an environment in which the structure of the economy is not perfectly understood by policy makers or the public. The hybrid curve can also fit environments in which the central bank's objective function is not completely known by economic agents or it is not optimal for all agents to update their information constantly (Bernanke 2007; Kumar et al. 2015).[13]

Learning models and models of noisy information also allow for a more sophisticated formalization of the drivers of expectation anchoring. For example, these types of models imply that long-run expectations will be well anchored—and thus will not respond to news—if private agents are confident about their estimates of future inflation. In an inflation targeting framework, the anchoring of expectations is therefore related to the public's confidence that the central bank is willing and able to reach the target.[14]

Empirical evidence

Formation of expectations. One strand of studies examines the empirical relevance of the sticky-information and noisy-information models. Mean inflation forecasts from professional forecasters, consumers, firms, and central bankers have all been found to respond to macroeconomic shocks with a delay (Coibion and Gorodnichenko 2012). Because mean forecasts adjust gradually, it

[13] The presence of lagged inflation in the hybrid New Keynesian Phillips curve signifies that the central bank is not fully credible; this lack of credibility impairs the effectiveness of monetary policy (Ball 1995; Woodford 2005).

[14] Demertzis and Viegi (2008) present a model in which a monetary policy regime with well-defined objectives (such as an inflation target) could help improve the anchoring of inflation expectations.

is possible to predict ex post forecast errors using ex ante changes in mean expectations (Coibion and Gorodnichenko 2015). Carroll (2003) shows that households' inflation expectations are updated slowly and in part based on media coverage of professional forecasters' inflation projections.

Another strand of studies examines the relevance of forward- and backward-looking expectations in the hybrid New Keynesian Phillips curve. Backward-looking inflation expectations have been shown not to matter (that is, the associated coefficient is not statistically significant) if the trend inflation is determined by the long-run inflation target (Cogley and Sbordone 2008).[15] Similarly, if the New Keynesian model accounts for positive trend inflation, price-setting firms become more forward looking and the inflation rate becomes less sensitive to current economic conditions as trend inflation increases (Ascari and Sbordone 2014).

Anchoring of inflation expectations in advanced economies. A transparent central bank communicates to the public its intent, strategy, assessments, procedures, and policies in an open, clear, and timely manner. An inflation targeting regime provides a disciplined framework that helps improve monetary policy transparency. Broadly, the empirical work on advanced economies suggests that monetary regimes that increase central bank transparency, including through inflation targeting, are associated with a decrease in the persistence of movements of inflation away from trend.

For example, in Canada, New Zealand, Sweden, and the United Kingdom, inflation persistence disappeared after the adoption of an inflation targeting regime (Benati 2008). In the United States, by contrast, where inflation targeting had not yet been adopted, the persistence parameter remained low but positive and statistically significant. These results are corroborated by Gürkaynak, Levin, and Swanson (2010), who show that the response of market-based inflation expectations to macroeconomic news was larger in the United States than in Sweden and the United Kingdom. They also show that in the United Kingdom, expectations became better anchored after the Bank of England's monetary policy was made operationally independent in May 1997. Moreover, increased trust in the European Central Bank has been associated

[15] Bernanke (2007) argues that the decline in the volatility of the trend component of inflation, as estimated by the approach of Stock and Watson (2007, 2016), is consistent with the view that inflation expectations have become better anchored. Employing the New Keynesian model, Ascari and Sbordone (2014) show that the inflation rate becomes less sensitive to current economic conditions when trend inflation makes price-setting firms more forward looking. Trend inflation could instead be measured with long-term inflation expectations (Clark and Nakata 2008; Garnier, Mertens, and Nelson 2015; Mertens 2016).

with a decline in uncertainty about future inflation in the Euro Area, thus contributing to the anchoring of inflation expectations (Christelis et al. 2016).[16]

Other research studies the conditions under which inflation may not be well anchored under an inflation targeting regime. For example, even with an inflation targeting framework, expectations were not well anchored in New Zealand when forecasters did not understand the central bank's objective function (Kumar et al. 2015). Inflation expectations in 10 advanced economies were not as well anchored during periods of persistently below-target inflation as during periods when inflation was close to target (Ehrmann 2015).

Several studies have examined whether inflation expectations became unanchored during and after the global financial crisis, which was followed by a wave of unconventional monetary policy actions. During the period immediately following the crisis, market-based inflation expectations in the United States and the United Kingdom became more sensitive to macroeconomic news, but neither survey-based nor market-based long-term inflation expectations in the Euro Area became unanchored (Galati, Heemeijer, and Moessner 2011; Galati, Poelhekke, and Zhou 2011).

During a longer post-crisis period in the Euro Area, when inflation fell and was persistently below target, there is evidence that the anchoring of inflation expectations weakened (Grishchenko, Mouabbi, and Renne 2017; Garcia and Werner 2018). The findings, which are based on different methodologies and different measures of inflation expectations, are less consistent for the United States, where anchoring is alternately found to have improved and deteriorated significantly in the post-crisis period (Ciccarelli, Garcia, and Montes-Galdón 2017; Grishchenko, Mouabbi, and Renne 2017). Overall, given the size of the shocks during the crisis, expectations in advanced economies remained fairly well anchored (Miles et al. 2017).[17]

Anchoring of inflation expectations in EMDEs. Evidence on the anchoring of inflation expectations in EMDEs is more limited, but some studies suggest that inflation targeting plays a role (Annex 4.2). Using monthly survey data from

[16] An alternative way to assess the anchoring of inflation expectations is to employ Stock and Watson's (2007, 2016) approach, which decomposes the inflation process into trend and volatility components. Data for Japan, the United Kingdom, and the United States show that shocks to trend inflation are persistent (and can be modeled as a unit root process), but that the volatility of trend inflation declined markedly during the 1980s (Miles et al. 2017). These findings are consistent with the finding that inflation expectations have become more firmly anchored than in the past, although not perfectly so.

[17] Strohsal and Winkelmann (2015) examine the anchoring of inflation expectations, as well as the sensitivity to news shocks, using a sample of four advanced economies. They find that the degree of anchoring did not change during the crisis.

Consensus Economics for a sample of 22 EMDEs and 14 advanced economies in a structural vector autoregressive model, Davis (2014) finds evidence that the introduction of inflation targeting is associated with a statistically significant reduction in the response of 12-month-ahead inflation expectations to shocks in both oil prices and observed inflation. Using market-based measures of inflation expectations for Brazil, Chile, and Mexico, De Pooter et al. (2014) document that long-term inflation expectations became better anchored in these countries over the preceding decade, especially in Chile and Mexico. Although they do not specifically test for the role of inflation targeting, they ascribe this result to recent improvements in the credibility of these countries' central banks.

IMF (2016) estimates a hybrid New Keynesian Phillips curve using data from a large sample of countries (24 advanced economies and 20 EMDEs). It reports that although the coefficient on lagged inflation (backward-looking expectations) started declining in the early 2000s, there was a reversal in this trend in the aftermath of the Great Recession, with the coefficient returning close to its value in the early 1990s. This study also finds that the sensitivity of inflation expectations to macroeconomic news (proxied by the difference between expected and realized inflation) is negatively correlated with standard measures of central bank independence and transparency, and that expectations become better anchored when countries adopt an inflation targeting regime.[18] IMF (2018) reports that multiple measures of the degree of anchoring of inflation expectations point to an improvement in the anchoring of expectations over the past two decades. However, there has been considerable heterogeneity in the extent of anchoring across emerging market economies.[19]

In the context of Brazil, the literature examines a wide range of factors that might diminish the beneficial effects of inflation targeting on anchoring, broadly concluding that central bank transparency, central bank credibility, and the

[18] Estimations that allow for time-varying coefficients indicate that, although inflation expectations are better anchored in advanced economies than in EMDEs, anchoring has improved in both groups over time (IMF 2016). Other studies offer similar findings. Capistrán and Ramos-Francia (2010) and Mehrotra and Yetman (forthcoming) conclude from data for a large sample of EMDEs that inflation targeting has affected inflation expectations. Studies of Mexico, Brazil, and South Africa find that the adoption of inflation targeting has helped anchor expectations in each case (Carrasco and Ferreiro 2013; Cerisola and Gelos 2009; and Reid 2009, respectively). However, Kabundi, Schaling, and Some (2015) show that, in South Africa, even with inflation targeting, expectations of price and wage setters (businesses and trade unions) were higher than the upper bound of the official target band, while expectations of analysts were within the target band. This study also finds that expectations of price and wage setters were substantially influenced by lagged inflation, but that those of analysts were not.

[19] IMF (2018) focuses on four measures: absolute deviation of three-year-ahead inflation forecast from target, variability of inflation forecasts, dispersion of inflation forecasts, and sensitivity to inflation shocks. In the context of a small macroeconomic model, IMF (2018) also shows that better-anchored inflation expectations reduce inflation persistence and limit the pass-through of currency movements to domestic prices.

country's fiscal position are all important in shaping inflation expectations. De Mendonça and Galveas (2013) show that, when controlling for central bank transparency, the forward-looking and hybrid specifications of the Phillips curve are more suitable for explaining current inflation than the purely backward-looking specifications. Yet, inflation expectations react more strongly to actual inflation, exchange rate movements, and output shocks when there is a problem of central bank credibility (Cortes and Paiva 2017). A deterioration in the fiscal position could also impede the anchoring of inflation expectations because of fears that monetary policy will be constrained, especially in cases where high interest rates imply unstable public debt dynamics (Cerisola and Gelos 2009; de Mendonça and Veiga 2014).[20]

Inflation expectations: Trends and anchors

Inflation expectations can provide valuable evidence about the credibility of a central bank. As documented by many studies, there is a close link between inflation expectations and monetary policy effectiveness. The more credible households and firms consider the central bank, the more likely inflation expectations are well anchored. In turn, well-anchored inflation expectations are found to support the effectiveness of monetary policy. Assessing and improving the degree of anchoring of inflation expectations are thus critical tasks for monetary policy makers.

Evolution of inflation expectations

In both advanced economies and EMDEs, long-term (five-year-ahead) inflation expectations have fallen during the past two to three decades. After declining rapidly during the 1990s, inflation expectations in advanced economies have remained stable at around 2 percent per year since the mid-2000s, with very little cross-country variation (Figure 4.3). In EMDEs, inflation expectations decreased markedly in the second half of the 1990s. Although they have not regained their mid-1990s peak, expectations trended upward from 2005 to 2014, before retreating somewhat in recent years. Throughout the entire sample period, inflation expectations in EMDEs displayed wider cross-country dispersion than in advanced economies, as did measures of central bank transparency. However, the rise in inflation expectations during 2005-14 coincided with an improvement in central bank transparency in EMDEs as a group.

---

[20] Using a dynamic stochastic general equilibrium model calibrated to the United States, Eusepi and Preston (2018a, 2018b) conclude that government liabilities can reduce the effectiveness of monetary policy in controlling inflation in economies with high government debt under imperfect knowledge.

Differences in anchoring between advanced economies and EMDEs. If inflation expectations are well anchored, they should be relatively insensitive to news, because economic agents assume that transitory shocks do not affect inflation over the long run. The degree of anchoring can be assessed empirically by regressing changes in five-year-ahead inflation expectations on macroeconomic news.[21] Relevant news can be proxied by inflation shocks—the difference between realized inflation and short-term inflation expectations in the previous period (that is, six months prior). Following earlier studies, this chapter employs two simple empirical strategies to study the extent of anchoring inflation expectations: a panel regression model with country and time fixed effects, and a time-varying model that provides a flexible framework to track time variation in the degree of anchoring (Annex 4.3). The first approach provides an overview of how well expectations are anchored in different country groups (for example, advanced economies versus EMDEs) and time periods. The second approach shows how country-specific and time-varying measures of the degree of anchoring have evolved.

The empirical exercises produce three major results. First, the sensitivity of long-term (five-year-ahead) inflation expectations to inflation shocks in both advanced economies and EMDEs is greater than zero for 1990-2018, indicating imperfect anchoring of inflation expectations (Figure 4.4; Annex 4.4). Second, the sensitivity is lower in advanced economies than in EMDEs, and the difference in sensitivity between these two groups is statistically significant. This finding, which indicates that expectations are better anchored in the advanced economies, is consistent with the view that monetary policy is less credible in EMDEs than in advanced economies.

Third, in both country groups, inflation expectations have become better anchored over time (that is, coefficients for both country groups are statistically significantly smaller in the latter time periods). Especially during 2005-18, expectations in advanced economies are found to have been very well anchored (the coefficient is not statistically significantly different from zero). In EMDEs, anchoring improved markedly during 2005-18, despite the slight increase in inflation expectations in these economies since 2005.

[21] The sensitivity of long-term inflation expectations to inflation shocks is used in this chapter to measure the degree of anchoring of inflation expectations. This measure is employed in several previous studies (Beechey, Johannsen, and Levin 2011; Galati, Poelhekke, and Zhou 2011; Gürkaynak, Levin, and Swanson 2010; IMF 2016; Garcia and Werner 2018; De Pooter et al. 2014). Other previous studies employ different measures of anchoring of inflation expectations: the deviation of long-term inflation expectations from an inflation target (Buono and Formai 2018; Bordo and Siklos 2017), variance of inflation expectations (Grishchenko, Mouabbi, and Renne, 2017), and dispersion of inflation forecasts (Capistrán and Ramos-Francia 2010). These measures are highly correlated (IMF 2018). The measure employed here is useful for at least three reasons: it is available for a large sample of countries; it can be used in a time-varying model; and the findings using it can be compared to others in the literature.

FIGURE 4.3 Long-term inflation expectations

Long-term (five-year-ahead) inflation expectations in advanced economies declined during the 1990s. Since the mid-2000s, they have remained stable at around 2 percent, with limited cross-country variation. Inflation expectations in EMDEs also fell in the second half of the 1990s, but have risen somewhat since 2005, and remain higher than in advanced economies. Inflation expectations in EMDEs also display wider cross-country dispersion. Among EMDEs, those with highly transparent central banks have relatively lower inflation expectations.

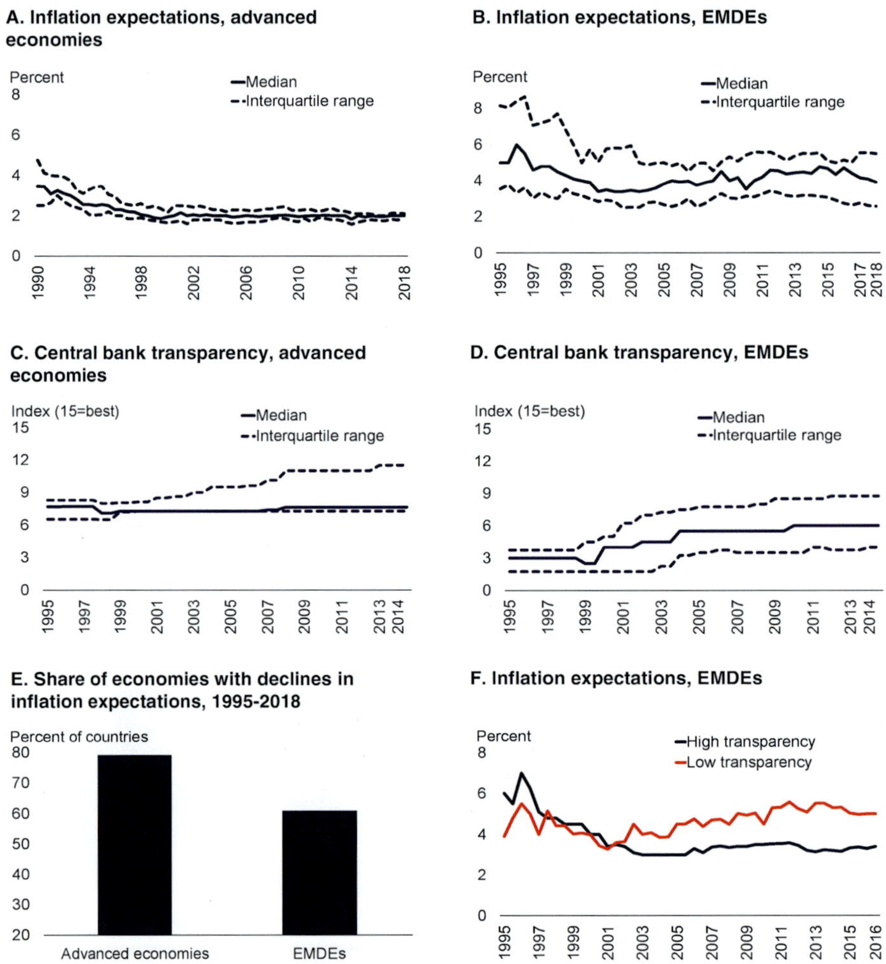

Source: Consensus Economics; Dincer and Eichengreen 2014; International Monetary Fund; World Bank.

Note: EMDEs = emerging market and developing economies.

A.B.E.F. Inflation expectations are five-year-ahead expectations of annual inflation.

A. Based on a sample of 24 advanced economies during 1990H1-2018H1.

B. Based on a sample of 23 EMDEs during 1995H1-2018H1.

C. Based on a sample of 24 advanced economies.

D.F. Based on a sample of 23 EMDEs.

F. High (low) transparency countries are defined as those with central bank transparency above the 75th (below the 25th) percentile of EMDEs.

Roles of global and domestic shocks in anchoring inflation expectations

The time-varying model described above is extended to estimate the response of inflation expectations to shocks from two sources, global and domestic. Examples of domestic shocks include unexpected electoral outcomes, wage disputes, and currency movements. Global shocks (surprises) could stem from sudden movements in food prices, oil prices, global economic activity, and financial conditions in major advanced economies.[22] In the model, a global inflation shock is defined as the first principal component of national inflation shocks for the full sample of countries (Annex 4.3). A domestic inflation shock is defined as the residual from a regression of the national inflation shock on the global inflation shock.

The regressions produce four major results (Figure 4.5). First, for the median economy in each country group, the sensitivity of inflation expectations to both types of shocks is positive, indicating imperfect anchoring. Second, in the case of advanced economies, there was a gradual decline in the sensitivity of inflation expectations to global shocks from the 1990s to the late 2000s, followed by a large one-time drop during the global financial crisis. There was a much less pronounced downward trend in the sensitivity of inflation expectations to domestic shocks than to global shocks. These results imply that, in advanced economies, the improved anchoring of expectations has been partly driven by the reduction in the sensitivity of inflation expectations to global shocks.

Third, for EMDEs, the sensitivity of inflation expectations to domestic shocks gradually fell during 2005-12, and since 2012 has been stable. There has also been a slight decline in the sensitivity of expectations to global shocks since 2000. Finally, inflation expectations appear to be more sensitive to both global and domestic shocks in EMDEs than in advanced economies, implying weaker anchoring of expectations in the former group. The robustness of the results is tested by replacing the global shock, as described above, with an oil price shock, food price shock, global liquidity shock, and global output gap shock. These exercises lead to broadly consistent findings with the headline results.

Determinants of anchoring expectations

The improved anchoring of five-year-ahead inflation expectations over time in advanced economies and EMDEs, as suggested by the time-varying model in the

[22] De Pooter et al. (2014) examine how foreign and domestic news surprises affect (market-based) inflation expectations in Brazil, Chile, and Mexico, using daily data. In their framework, foreign news surprises stem from macroeconomic developments in the United States and China and fluctuations in oil and food prices. They report that U.S. nonfarm payroll data releases have a significant impact on long-term inflation expectations in Chile and Mexico, while there is no corresponding impact in Brazil. The impact of news related to oil and food prices is not statistically significant.

FIGURE 4.4 Sensitivity of inflation expectations to inflation shocks

The sensitivity of long-term inflation expectations to inflation shocks has fallen in the past decade in both advanced economies and EMDEs but remains comparatively higher in EMDEs. A similar pattern is observed when measuring the sensitivity of expectations using a time-varying model.

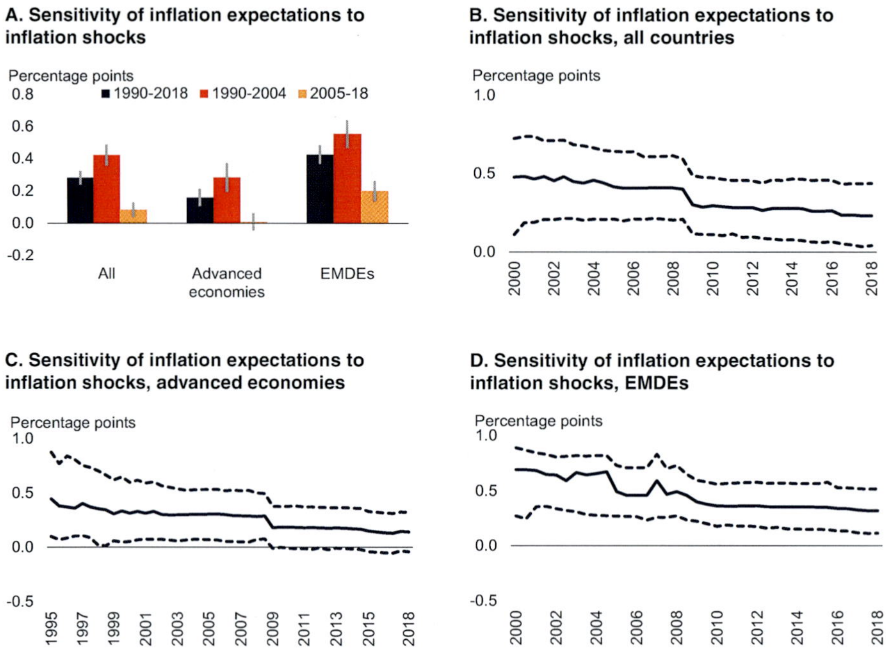

Note: EMDEs = emerging market and developing economies.

A.-D. Inflation expectations are five-year-ahead expectations of annual inflation. Inflation shocks are defined as the difference between realized inflation and short-term inflation expectations in the previous period.

Sensitivity is estimated using a panel regression of the change in five-year-ahead inflation expectations on inflation shocks, as described in Annex 4.3. Bars denote medians and vertical lines denote 90 percent confidence intervals. Based on a sample of 24 advanced economies and 23 EMDEs during 1990H2-2018H1.

B.-D. Time-varying sensitivity is estimated by regressing the change in five-year-ahead inflation expectations on inflation shocks, as described in Annex 4.3. Solid lines denote the median of estimates and the dotted lines indicate the median of 68 percent confidence intervals.

B. Based on a sample of 24 advanced economies and 23 EMDEs during 2000H1-2018H1.

C. Based on a sample of 24 advanced economies during 1995H1-2018H1.

D. Based on a sample of 23 EMDEs during 2000H1-2018H1.

previous section, may be associated with policy reforms aimed at increasing central bank credibility since the early 1990s (Mishkin 2007). Using the estimated sensitivity of inflation expectations as a dependent variable, panel regression models are used to assess which factors determine the degree of anchoring of expectations (Annex 4.3). The explanatory variables in the models include the presence of an inflation targeting regime, central bank transparency, the presence of a fixed exchange rate regime, financial openness, trade openness, and fiscal sustainability.

FIGURE 4.5 Sensitivity of inflation expectations to global and domestic inflation shocks

Inflation shocks can be associated with global and domestic factors. Long-term inflation expectations in EMDEs are more sensitive to both global and domestic shocks than are inflation expectations in advanced economies.

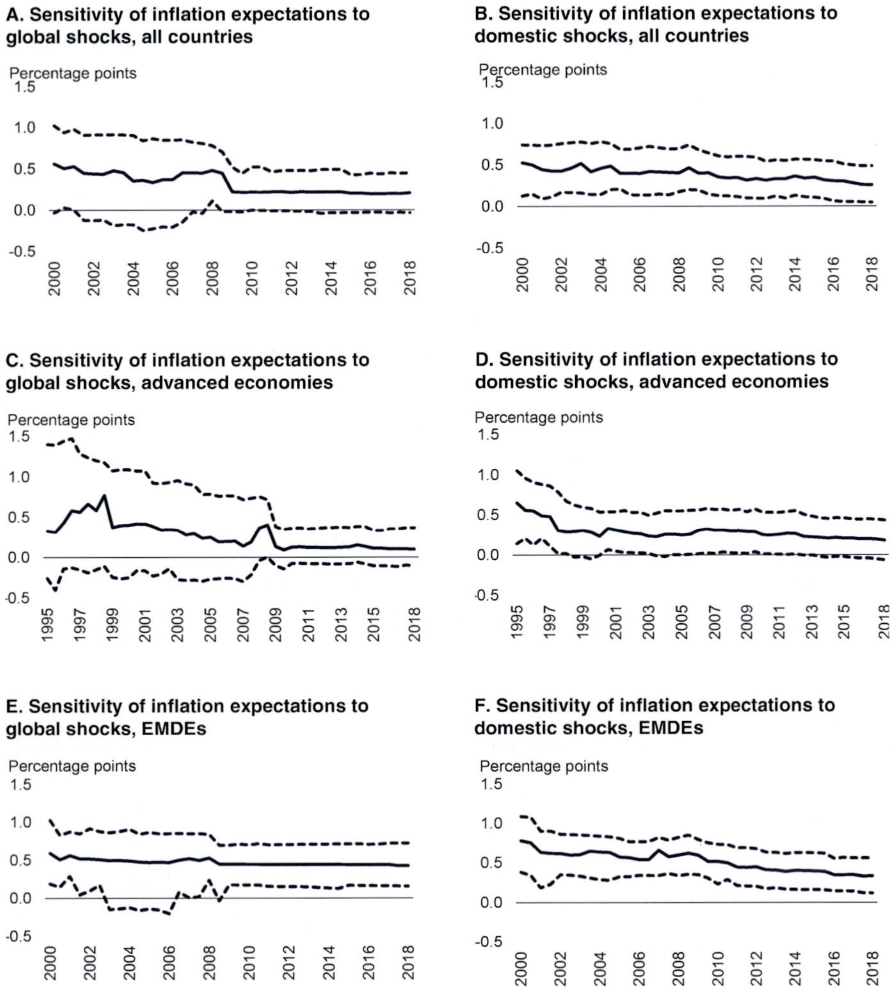

Source: World Bank.

Note: EMDEs = emerging market and developing economies.

A.-F. Inflation expectations are five-year-ahead expectations of annual inflation.

A.-F. Time-varying sensitivity is estimated by regressing the change in five-year-ahead inflation expectations on global and domestic shocks, as described in Annex 4.3. Solid lines denote the median of estimates and dotted lines indicate the median of 68 percent confidence intervals.

A.B. Based on a sample of 24 advanced economies and 23 EMDEs during 2000H1-2018H1.

C.D. Based on a sample of 24 advanced economies during 1995H1-2018H1.

E.F. Based on a sample of 23 EMDEs during 2000H1-2018H1.

Inflation targeting and central bank transparency. If central banks in advanced economies are perceived as credible, they can successfully anchor inflation expectations without explicit inflation targets or formal transparency rules. However, in EMDEs, where central banks still need to build credibility, explicit targets and transparency rules are more likely to be necessary to anchor expectations. The regression results show that the coefficient on inflation targeting is statistically significant and negative, meaning it is associated with lower sensitivity of inflation expectations to shocks (Figure 4.6).[23] For central bank transparency, the coefficient is only statistically significant and negative for the full sample of countries and the EMDE subsample. Central bank transparency has improved in EMDEs over the past two decades. In advanced economies, although the degree of central bank transparency is higher than in EMDEs, it has not changed much during this period.

Financial integration and exchange rate regime. Financial integration appears to exert a disciplining effect on macroeconomic policy (Tytell and Wei 2004; Gupta 2008; Kose et al. 2010). For example, integration could raise the cost of loose monetary policy in the form of larger capital outflows. However, more financially open economies are more vulnerable to external shocks, which may make it more difficult for policy makers to anchor inflation expectations. The results indicate that the correlation between financial openness and the anchoring of inflation expectations is not statistically significant for the full sample of countries or the EMDE subsample. However, as documented above, long-term inflation expectations in EMDEs are more sensitive to global shocks. Hence, large external shocks could offset the benefits of financial integration to anchoring expectations in EMDEs.

The use of pegged exchange rates might be a signal for a credibility crutch in countries with limited monetary policy credibility (Levy Yeyati, Sturzenegger, and Reggio 2010). As is well-known from the impossible trinity argument, employing a fixed exchange rate regime when capital movements are free could hamper the independence of monetary policy.[24] Although the exchange rate regime by itself does not appear to be relevant for anchoring inflation expectations, the results show that when financial openness is interacted with the fixed exchange rate regime dummy, the interaction term becomes significant.

[23] Capistrán and Ramos-Francia (2010) also find that inflation targeting affects inflation expectations only in EMDEs, with no effect on the dispersion of inflation expectations in advanced economies. They argue that given the recent relative stability of inflation in advanced economies, professional forecasters may have homogeneous views about future inflation, so that the dispersion remains unchanged even after the introduction of an explicit inflation target.

[24] The impossible trinity is the argument that a country cannot have more than two of the following: fixed exchange rate, free capital movement, and independent monetary policy. As a result, countries with inflation targeting regimes typically also operate with flexible exchange rates (De Gregorio 2009a).

FIGURE 4.6 Determinants of the sensitivity of inflation expectations to shocks

Long-term inflation expectations in EMDEs are found to be better anchored in the presence of an inflation targeting regime, a high degree of central bank transparency, low public debt, and a high degree of trade openness.

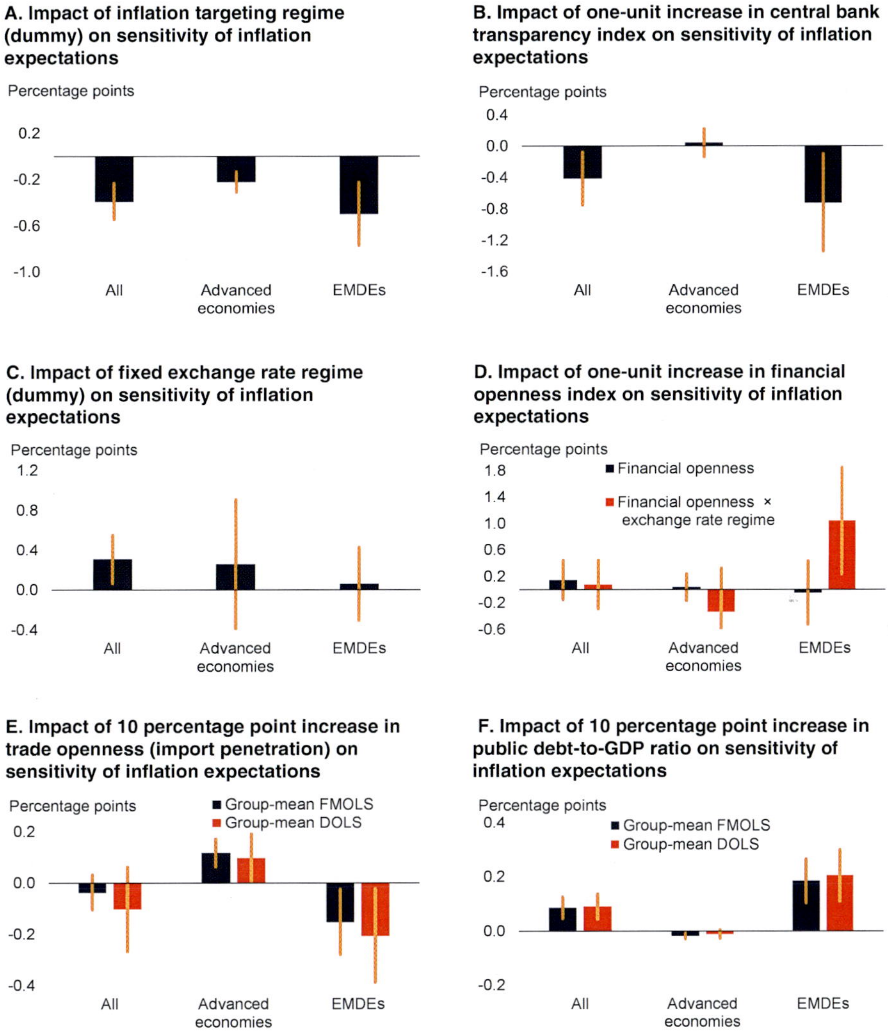

Sources: Chinn and Ito 2017; Dincer and Eichengreen 2014; International Monetary Fund; Shambaugh 2004; World Bank.

Note: DOLS = dynamic ordinary least squares; EMDEs = emerging market and developing economies; FMOLS = fully modified ordinary least squares; GDP = gross domestic product.

A.-D. Inflation expectations are five-year-ahead expectations of annual inflation. Bars denote coefficients of panel regressions of 24 advanced economies and 23 EMDEs using annual data for 1995-2016, as described in Annex 4.3. Vertical lines denote 90 percent confidence intervals.

D. Financial openness x exchange rate regime is the interaction of these two explanatory variables.

E.F. Bars denote coefficients of group mean panel FMOLS and group mean DOLS regressions of 24 advanced economies and 23 EMDEs using annual data for 1995-2016, as described in Annex 4.3. Vertical lines denote 90 percent confidence intervals.

This result suggests that the exchange rate regime does matter for anchoring inflation expectations in more financially open economies.[25]

Trade integration. Trade integration could affect inflation expectations through competition in product markets that could increase the responsiveness of domestic prices to shocks. For example, one line of research finds that higher price flexibility steepens the Phillips curve, reducing the short-run output gain from a monetary expansion, and lowering the incentive for central banks to adopt inflationary policies (Romer 1993; Rogoff 2006). Alternatively, outsourcing of labor through global value chains may reduce the responsiveness of wages to domestic labor market conditions and hence flatten the Phillips curve (Blanchard, Cerutti, and Summers 2015; Blanchard 2016; Miles et al. 2017). However, at least for the United States, lower marginal costs, rather than globalization, are the key driver of the flattening of the Phillips curve.[26]

The regression results show that the correlation between import penetration and sensitivity of inflation expectations to shocks is negative and statistically significant for the subsample of EMDEs. Thus, for EMDEs only, the anchoring of inflation expectations improves as import penetration rises, consistent with theories suggesting that globalization is associated with improved anchoring.[27]

Fiscal sustainability. Inflation expectations are unlikely to be well anchored if there are questions about fiscal sustainability because of fears that monetary policy will be constrained, especially in cases where high interest rates imply unstable public debt dynamics. The regression results for the full sample of countries, and for the EMDE subsample, are consistent with this prediction, showing a positive and statistically significant correlation between the ratio of

[25] The baseline regressions use Chinn and Ito's (2017) de jure measure of financial openness and Shambaugh's (2004) classification of exchange rate regimes. The baseline results do not change when a de facto measure of capital account liberalization (sum of foreign assets and liabilities as percentage of GDP) and an alternative measure of exchange rate regime classification (from Ilzetzki, Reinhart, and Rogoff 2017) are used as explanatory variables.

[26] The empirical literature examining whether globalization affects domestic inflation produces mixed results. For example, Calza (2009) and Ihrig et al. (2010) find no robust evidence that global slack affects the parameters of the inflation process. Gaiotti (2010) finds that the flattening of the Phillips curve is due to globalization. In contrast, Borio and Filardo (2007) argue that global slack may become a key driver of domestic inflation, while Auer, Borio, and Filardo (2017) show that the rise of global value chains has amplified the importance of global slack in driving domestic inflation. Forbes (2018) suggests that inflation models should allow key global factors, including global slack, to adjust over time. As a robustness check, government effectiveness (measured by the World Bank's Worldwide Governance Indicators) is also included as an explanatory variable in the regressions here. It is not statistically significant.

[27] Using a New Keynesian model, Martínez-García (2017) argues that the impact of globalization on monetary policy effectiveness is underestimated if the analysis uses the standard trade openness measures, and that what matters is the elasticity of substitution between locally produced and imported goods.

public debt to GDP and the sensitivity of long-term inflation expectations to inflation shocks.[28]

Anchoring expectations: Country experiences

The findings from the empirical exercises on the degree and determinants of inflation anchoring in advanced economy and EMDE country groups are broadly consistent with the behavior of inflation expectations at the country level. Yet, there are still lessons to be learned from individual countries' experiences.

Among advanced economies, the sensitivity of inflation expectations to inflation shocks tends to be lower under inflation targeting. Yet, at the country level, inflation targeting does not necessarily guarantee firm anchoring of inflation expectations (Figure 4.7). In Canada, New Zealand, and the United Kingdom, for instance, the sensitivity of expectations to inflation shocks has been close to zero since 2000. In these countries, the early introduction of inflation targeting may have helped anchor expectations.[29] Japan has had difficulty anchoring expectations after introducing its inflation targeting regime in 2013, perhaps because of its recent history of persistently low inflation. Inflation expectations are not as well anchored under persistently below-target inflation as when inflation is close to target (Ehrmann 2015).

In the Euro Area, where the European Central Bank's main objective since its inception in 1999 has been to maintain price stability (defined as inflation of less than, but close to, 2 percent in the medium term), the sensitivity of inflation expectations was lower than that in the United States in 2005 (Beechey, Johannsen, and Levin 2011). This pattern reversed in 2010-15, when sensitivity in the United States was close to zero—lower than that in the Euro Area—due in part to persistent undershooting of the European Central Bank's target and perhaps also to the U.S. Federal Reserve's adoption of an official inflation target in 2012.[30]

[28] De Mendonça and Veiga (2014) argue that even under an inflation targeting regime, interest rate hikes to reach target inflation imply increases in the primary surplus required for stabilizing the public debt, and that this fiscal deterioration could constrain monetary policy. These authors also show that the public-debt-to-GDP ratio has a statistically significant relationship with the deviation between inflation and its target.

[29] New Zealand, Canada, the United Kingdom, and Korea introduced inflation targeting in 1990, 1991, 1992, and 1998, respectively. Kumar et al. (2015) argue that expectations (based on firm-level data rather than those of professional forecasters) are not well anchored in New Zealand because forecasters do not understand the central bank's objective function. Yetman (2017) and Beaudry and Ruge-Murcia (2017) find that the implementation of inflation targeting in Canada and the United Kingdom has been more successful than that in other inflation targeting countries.

[30] Garcia and Werner (2018) find that there has been a decline in the extent of anchoring inflation expectations in the Euro Area since 2013.

The record of EMDE central banks in anchoring inflation expectations under inflation targeting regimes has been mixed. Annex 4.5 provides case studies for Brazil, Chile, and Poland. In Brazil, although long-term inflation expectations have been relatively stable under the inflation targeting regime that began in 1999, the sensitivity of expectations to shocks remains elevated relative to that in Chile and Poland. Less than ideal fiscal conditions and worsening central bank transparency during part of the inflation targeting period may have contributed to this outcome (Cerisola and Gelos 2009; de Mendonça and Galveas 2013; de Mendonça and Veiga 2014).

In contrast, Chile has had considerable success: the sensitivity of inflation expectations to shocks has for some years been close to the median for advanced economies. The gradual introduction of inflation targeting in the 1990s gave the central bank time to build its credibility. From the outset of the inflation targeting regime, the central bank pursued a robust communications effort that included the publication of a quarterly Monetary Policy Report with strong analytical content.[31] Chile's adoption of an inflation target as part of a comprehensive, credible macroeconomic policy framework may have helped generate favorable macroeconomic outcomes (De Gregorio, Tokman, and Valdés 2005; Valdés 2007).

Poland has also succeeded with inflation targeting, which it began in 1999, even though domestic financial markets were immature, and the central bank had limited knowledge of monetary policy transmission at the time of introduction. The transition to a flexible exchange rate regime concurrent with the adoption of inflation targeting may have helped to anchor expectations. Over time, inflation expectations fell, eventually settling near the policy target rate, and the sensitivity of expectations to shocks became quite low.

In India and South Africa, the sensitivity of inflation expectations to shocks fell markedly after the introduction of inflation targeting. In South Africa, the combination of inflation targeting and consistently high central bank transparency may have been key to anchoring expectations.[32] In India, however, lagged inflation, as well as current and lagged changes in fuel and food prices, have been found to have significantly affected inflation expectations (Benes et al. 2017; Patra and Ray 2010).

[31] For instance, the Central Bank of Chile's quarterly inflation report included, from its inception, inflation forecasts with confidence intervals displayed in fan charts of the type pioneered by the Bank of England (Mishkin 2007).

[32] Kabundi, Schaling, and Some (2015) and Miyajima and Yetman (2018) show that, even in the presence of an inflation targeting framework, expectations of price setters (businesses and unions) in South Africa are higher than the upper bound of the official target band; the expectations of analysts are within the target band. In addition, expectations of price setters put a greater weight on past inflation, whereas analysts' expectations are more forward looking.

FIGURE 4.7 Time-varying sensitivity of inflation expectations to shocks: Country experiences

Inflation targeting does not guarantee the anchoring of long-term inflation expectations. However, sensitivity to inflation shocks in advanced economies with inflation targets tends to be low. The success of central banks in emerging market and developing economies in anchoring inflation expectations under inflation targeting has been mixed.

A. Sensitivity of inflation expectations to inflation shocks, advanced economies (1)

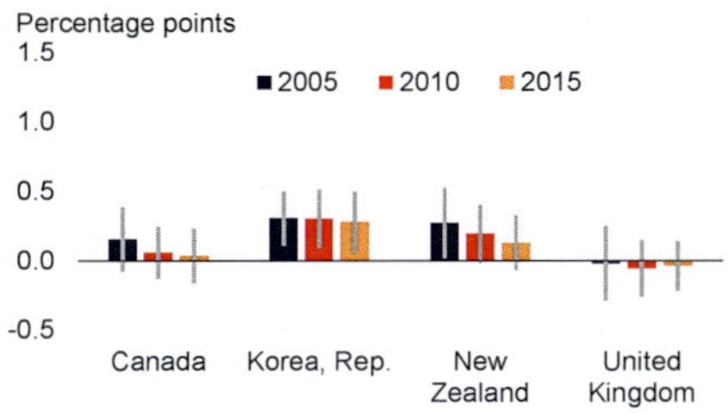

B. Sensitivity of inflation expectations to inflation shocks, advanced economies (2)

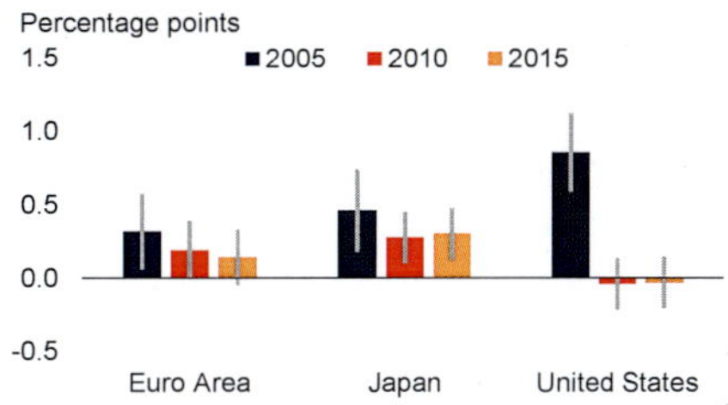

C. Sensitivity of inflation expectations to inflation shocks, Europe and Central Asia

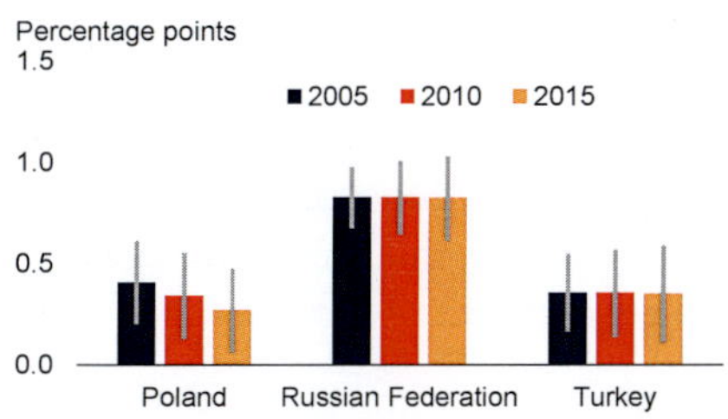

D. Sensitivity of inflation expectations to inflation shocks, Latin America

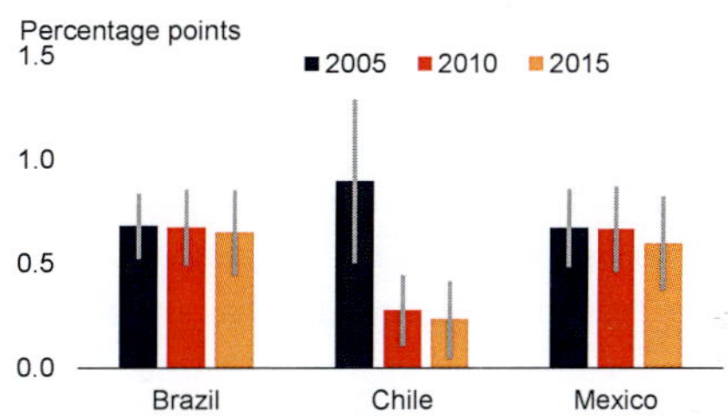

E. Sensitivity of inflation expectations to inflation shocks, India

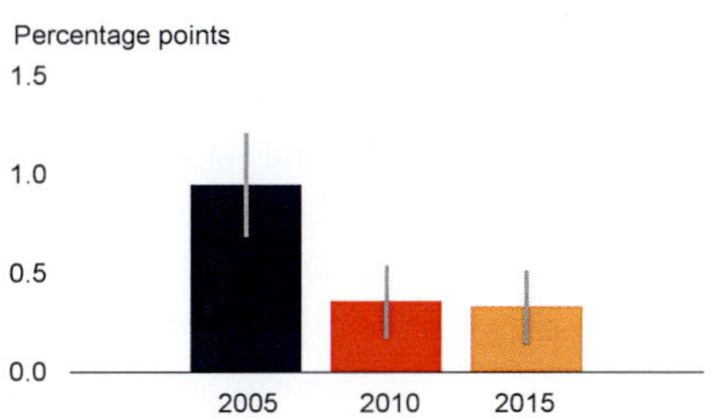

F. Sensitivity of inflation expectations to inflation shocks, South Africa

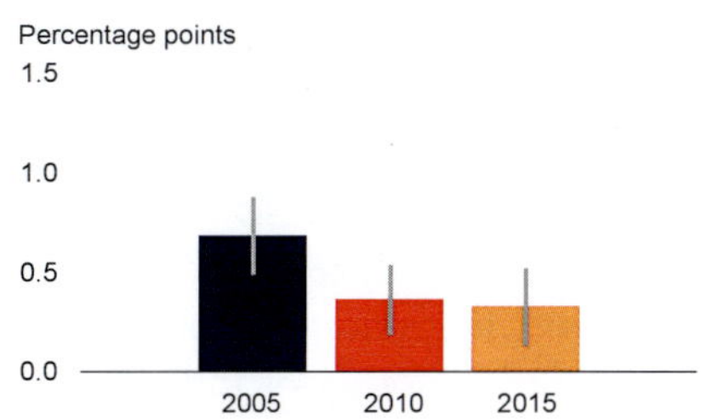

Source: World Bank.

A-F. Inflation expectations are five-year-ahead expectations of annual inflation. Time-varying sensitivity is estimated by regressing long-term inflation forecast revisions on inflation shocks. Vertical lines denote 68 percent confidence intervals. The model is described in Annex 4.3.

B. The Euro Area here comprises Austria, Belgium, Finland, France, Germany, Greece, Ireland, Italy, the Netherlands, Portugal, and Spain.

Mexico has been less successful than Chile in anchoring inflation expectations under an inflation targeting regime. The Bank of Mexico did not publish its own inflation forecasts for several years after adopting inflation targeting (Batini and Laxton 2006; De Pooter et al. 2014). Over time, however, the central bank's communication strategy has improved, and it now publishes its inflation forecasts and releases the minutes of its monetary policy meetings (Carrasco and Ferreiro 2013). Finally, in Russia, high, positive sensitivity of inflation expectations to inflation shocks may reflect low central bank transparency (Dincer and Eichengreen 2014). However, Russia is relatively new to inflation targeting, having introduced the regime in 2015.

Conclusion

This chapter contributes to the literature on inflation expectations in EMDEs by answering three questions. First, how does the degree of anchoring of long-term inflation expectations differ between advanced economies and EMDEs? Second, how sensitive are inflation expectations to global and domestic shocks? Third, what are the main determinants of the degree of anchoring of inflation expectations? The principal conclusions are the following:

- Long-term inflation expectations have declined and become more firmly anchored in the past two decades in both advanced economies and EMDEs. However, anchoring in EMDEs remains notably weaker than in advanced economies. This finding is consistent with the view that monetary policy is less credible in EMDEs than in advanced economies.

- Long-term inflation expectations in EMDEs are more sensitive to both global and domestic shocks than are inflation expectations in advanced economies. The sensitivity of EMDE inflation expectations to domestic shocks gradually fell between 2005 and 2012 and has since been mostly stable, while the sensitivity of EMDE inflation expectations to global shocks has fallen slightly since 2000. In advanced economies, a large drop in the sensitivity of inflation expectations to global shocks in the wake of the global financial crisis followed a steady decline from the late 1990s to the late 2000s; there has been a much less pronounced downward trend in sensitivity to domestic shocks. These findings suggest that the improvement in the anchoring of inflation expectations in advanced economies is partly due to the decline in sensitivity to global shocks.

- The institutional and monetary policy environment matters for the anchoring of inflation expectations, as do the general macroeconomic environment and structural characteristics of the economy. The chapter finds that the presence of an inflation targeting regime and a rise in central bank transparency are associated with better anchoring of long-term inflation expectations. For EMDEs, lower public debt and greater trade openness are also associated with better anchoring of expectations. This finding implies that the anchoring of inflation expectations in EMDEs depends not only on monetary policy, but also on structural factors and fiscal policy. Case studies for Brazil, Chile, and Poland provide examples of these multiple factors at work. In Brazil, for instance, fiscal policy, together with backtracking on central bank transparency for a period, may have held back progress on improving the anchoring of inflation expectations. In Chile, a highly transparent central bank, together with a credible macroeconomic framework, may have contributed to the central bank's success in achieving well-anchored inflation expectations. And in Poland, the simultaneous adoption of inflation targeting and a floating exchange rate regime may have helped anchor expectations.

Although inflation expectations have become significantly better anchored during the past decade, the results show that there is still room for improvement, especially in EMDEs. Although inflation targeting seems to have been useful in reducing the sensitivity of inflation expectations to shocks, inflation targeting should not be considered necessary or sufficient for improved anchoring of expectations. The overall macroeconomic policy framework, including fiscal conditions and the transparency of the central bank, is also important for success.

These findings point to several research avenues to explore. First, research could examine the determinants of a wider range of measures of inflation expectations in EMDEs. This research direction would be particularly worthwhile if data availability could be improved. Second, it would be useful to consider nonlinearities between institutional factors and the anchoring of inflation expectations. In addition, there is a need to investigate how complementarities between institutional factors and fiscal and monetary policy frameworks help improve the anchoring of inflation expectations.

ANNEX 4.1 Primer on expectations and monetary policy

The effectiveness of monetary policy depends on expectations, particularly about the future policy stance. Moreover, there is broad agreement that economic agents form their expectations by extracting signals from their experience of actual policies. Over time, there has been an evolution of views on this topic, which is reflected in the development of the models describing the links between expectations and monetary policy. This annex presents a brief history of the evolution of views on the topic.

Traditional Keynesian models

The birth of modern macroeconomics is usually associated with the publication of Keynes' (1936) *General Theory of Employment, Interest and Money*. However, the backdrop for Keynes's analysis was the Great Depression, a period of low or negative inflation and stagnant nominal wages (Samuelson and Solow 1960). The General Theory had little to say directly about the issue of inflation and, for simplicity, assumed that money wages were fixed. As the economy recovered, and with World War II posing a new set of challenges due to higher government expenditure, Keynes later discussed the trade-off between excess demand and wage and price inflation (Keynes 1940).

By the 1950s, inflation was becoming more of a problem for policy makers, and Phillips (1958) provided a breakthrough, with statistical evidence on a negative relationship between the unemployment rate and wage inflation in the United Kingdom. The Phillips curve became a standard feature of subsequent Keynesian macroeconomic models. Samuelson and Solow (1960) famously developed the notion of a policy trade-off between reduced unemployment (or increased output) and lower inflation. However, they also pointed out that this trade-off might not be stable.

Friedman (1968) established that adaptive inflation expectations would disrupt this trade-off. A change in the expected rate of inflation would shift the short-run Phillips curve, and over time output and unemployment would return to their long-run equilibrium values, regardless of the rate of inflation. Keynesian modelers incorporated the concepts of endogenous expectations and the natural rate of unemployment (or, equivalently, potential output) into their estimated Phillips curves. Policy makers would no longer be able to run the economy "hot" without facing accelerating inflationary pressure.

Views advanced by Friedman and Phelps

Friedman (1968) forcefully argued that estimates of a stable relationship between inflation and unemployment would exist only when inflation expectations were well anchored. He warned that any attempt to exploit the short-run relationship as if it were permanent would cause expectations to become unanchored, leading to a shift in the Phillips curve. Thus, starting at the natural rate of unemployment, a stimulative monetary policy would lead to higher inflation without any benefit in terms of lower unemployment in the long run.

Friedman's point—made independently by Phelps (1967)—was that rational workers care only about real wages, and that real wages need to adjust so that labor supply equals labor demand at a uniquely determined natural rate of unemployment. An expansionary monetary (or fiscal) policy aimed at pushing unemployment below the natural rate would lead to an increase in aggregate demand, which would then feed into both higher prices and wages. If the increase in wages is smaller than the increase in prices, firms are willing to hire more workers because the real wage has decreased. However, workers will soon realize that their real wage has decreased and request wage increases that match price inflation. The outcome is a rightward shift of the Phillips curve with an equilibrium characterized by higher inflation and unemployment back at the natural rate. In this framework, the short-run Phillips curve is negatively sloped, but it shifts up the vertical long-run Phillips curve.

In the expectations-augmented Phillips curve, inflation depends on expected inflation as well as the deviation between actual unemployment and the natural rate of unemployment. In the long run, expected inflation is always equal to actual inflation and unemployment is always at the natural rate. However, the short-run Phillips curve will move up as expectations adjust, eventually to a point where a new short-run Phillips curve crosses the vertical long-term curve. The new equilibrium will be characterized by higher inflation and no gains in terms of lower unemployment. Any attempt to keep the unemployment rate below its natural level would require a continuous acceleration of inflation. A corollary of the expectations-augmented Phillips curve is that, in the long run, the natural rate of unemployment is compatible with any rate of inflation and the rate of inflation is completely driven by economic agents' expectations of future inflation.

In the Friedman-Phelps formulation of the Phillips curve, there is a short-run trade-off between inflation and economic activity. Lucas (1972) introduced rational expectations about monetary policy itself into macroeconomic models. This led Sargent and Wallace (1975, 1976) to conclude that systematic monetary policy is irrelevant even in the short run. In this new classical approach, forward-looking agents incorporate policy makers' reaction function into their expectations and thus make policy actions ineffective by fully anticipating them. In this view, only random (that is, surprise) changes in monetary policy can affect the real economy.

New Keynesian model

It soon became clear that the policy irrelevance proposition required the assumption of fully flexible prices and wages. Pioneering work by Fischer (1977), Taylor (1980), Rotemberg (1982), and Calvo (1983) showed that in the presence of staggered contracts monetary policy can be effective even under the assumption of rational expectations. Calvo's pricing model is one of the key building blocks of modern New Keynesian models. This workhorse model combines forward-looking optimizing agents with monopolistic competition and sticky prices. Although agents are assumed to have full-information rational expectations (FIRE), in the presence of distortions associated with market power and sticky prices, monetary policy can be welfare enhancing and achieve an efficient allocation of resources.

In effect, the New Keynesian approach reverts to ideas first clearly expressed in the writings of Keynes's contemporary, Hawtrey (for example, *Monetary Reconstruction*, 1923). Hawtrey argued that the effectiveness of monetary policy depends on expectations about the future policy stance and that agents form their expectations by extracting signals from the current policy actions. This view underlies the endogenous expectations in modern monetary economics (for example, Woodford 2003).

The standard New Keynesian Phillips curve describes inflation as a function of expected inflation and the output gap (Galí and Gertler 1999). This curve is the basis of Bernanke's (2007) statement that expectations "greatly influence actual inflation and thus the central bank's ability to achieve price stability." In addition, expectations affect the transmission of monetary policy through the term structure of interest rates and changes in asset prices. Although the central bank can control the short-term nominal interest rate, investment and consumption decisions depend on the long-term real interest rate, which, in turn, depends on expectations about long-term inflation and future movements of the short-term nominal rate.[1] Economic decisions are also affected by movements in asset prices (wealth effects), which again depend on expected real returns. A problem with the standard New Keynesian Phillips curve is that it does not fit the data well. Fuhrer (1997) documents that inflation expectations are not significant in explaining inflation using a purely forward-looking model. Several studies employ the hybrid New Keynesian Phillips curve, in which current inflation depends on both expected and lagged inflation (Galí and Gertler 1999).

[1] Although the New Keynesian Phillips curve allows for a short-term trade-off between inflation and unemployment, it maintains the neoclassical view that there is no long-run trade-off. However, at low levels of inflation, the long-run Phillips curve may become negatively sloped and allow for such a trade-off (Akerlof, Dickens, and Perry 2000; Benigno and Ricci 2011). Blanchard (2016) argues that the Great Recession led to a substantial anchoring of inflation expectations and that now the U.S. Phillips curve looks more like the Phillips curve of the 1960s than the accelerationist Phillips curve of standard New Keynesian models.

ANNEX 4.2 Studies on the anchoring of inflation expectations

TABLE A.4.2.1 Studies on advanced economies

Authors	Questions	Economies (sample period and frequency)	Methodology	Results
Beaudry and Ruge-Murcia (2017)	Has inflation targeting been successful in Canada?	Australia, Canada, New Zealand, Sweden, United Kingdom, and United States (1991-2016, monthly and quarterly)	Descriptive statistics	The implementation of inflation targeting in Canada has been particularly successful compared with the experiences of other inflation targeting countries and the United States.
Beechey, Johannsen, and Levin (2011)	Are inflation expectations anchored more firmly in the Euro Area than in the United States?	Euro Area and the United States (2003-07, daily)	Regression of changes in inflation expectations on macroeconomic news	Inflation expectations are better anchored in the Euro Area than in the United States.
Carroll (2003)	How are households' inflation expectations formed?	United States (1981-2000, quarterly)	Regression of household expectations on professional forecasts or news	Household forecasts are affected by media and professional forecasts.
Ciccarelli, Garcia, and Montes-Galdón (2017)	Did the financial crisis and the Great Recession affect the anchoring of long-term inflation expectations?	United States (2005-15, monthly)	Estimating the time-varying coefficient measuring the pass-through from short- to long-term inflation expectations	The anchoring of inflation expectations has deteriorated significantly since late 2008.
Coibion and Gorodnichenko (2015)	Was the absence of disinflation during the Great Recession linked to a change in inflation expectations?	United States (1981-2013, monthly)	Regression of difference between household and professional inflation expectations on the change in oil price	The absence of disinflation during 2009-11 can be attributed to rising inflation expectations, which were in turn affected by rising oil prices.
Ehrmann (2015)	How do inflation expectations behave under inflation targeting?	10 advanced economies (1990s-2014, monthly)	Regression of inflation expectations on lagged inflation and dummy variable for times of (persistently) low inflation	Inflation expectations are not as well anchored when inflation is persistently low as when inflation is around the target: inflation expectations are more dependent on lagged inflation.

TABLE A.4.2.1 Studies on advanced economies *(continued)*

Authors	Questions	Economies (sample period and frequency)	Methodology	Results
Galati, Poelhekke, and Zhou (2011)	Did the global financial crisis affect inflation expectations?	Euro Area, United Kingdom, and United States (2004-09, daily)	Test for anchoring by regression of changes in inflation expectations on macroeconomic news	There is some evidence that market-based inflation expectations in the United Kingdom and the United States became more sensitive to macroeconomic news during the global financial crisis.
Garcia and Werner (2018)	Are Euro Area inflation expectations well anchored?	Euro Area, Germany, Italy, and Spain (2005-17, daily)	Test for anchoring by regression of changes in inflation expectations on macroeconomic news	The anchoring of inflation expectations has weakened in the Euro Area since 2013.
Grishchenko, Mouabbi, and Renne (2017)	Are long-term inflation expectations well anchored?	Euro Area and United States (1999:1-2016:2)	Estimation of inflation expectations and inflation uncertainty by dynamic latent factor model with stochastic volatility	Inflation anchoring improved in the United States, while mild de-anchoring occurred in the Euro Area.
Gürkaynak, Levin, and Swanson (2010)	Does inflation targeting anchor long-term inflation expectations?	Sweden, United Kingdom, and United States (1990s to early 2000s, daily)	Test for anchoring by regression of changes in inflation expectations on macroeconomic news	The response of market-based inflation expectations to macroeconomic news is larger in the United States than in Sweden and the United Kingdom. Inflation targeting affects long-term inflation expectations.
IMF (2016)	1. Have inflation expectations become increasingly sensitive to inflation outturns in recent years? 2. How do monetary policy frameworks affect the degree of anchoring of inflation expectations?	24 advanced economies and 20 EMDEs (1990s-2016)	1. Estimation of a hybrid New Keynesian Phillips curve (regression of actual inflation on inflation expectations, past inflation, and other control variables) 2. Test for anchoring by regression of changes in inflation expectations on macroeconomic news, using a time-varying parameter model	1. The coefficient on lagged inflation started declining in the mid-1990s, but this trend reversed in the aftermath of the Great Recession, and the coefficient is now similar to that in the early 1990s. 2. The sensitivity of inflation expectations to macroeconomic news is inversely correlated with standard measures of central bank independence and transparency; expectations become better anchored when countries adopt an inflation targeting regime. Estimations that allow for time-varying coefficients indicate that, while expectations are better anchored in advanced economies, anchoring has improved in both advanced economies and EMDEs.

TABLE A.4.2.1 Studies on advanced economies *(continued)*

Authors	Questions	Economies (sample period and frequency)	Methodology	Results
Kumar et al. (2015)	Are firms' inflation expectations well anchored?	New Zealand (2014Q3-2014Q4)	Quantitative survey of cross-section of firms	Firm managers display little anchoring of inflation expectations, despite 25 years of inflation targeting by the Reserve Bank of New Zealand. Managers are generally poorly informed about recent inflation dynamics. Their forecasts of future inflation reflect high levels of uncertainty and are volatile at both short- and long-run horizons.
Johnson (2003)	Does inflation targeting affect long-term inflation expectations?	Australia, Canada, New Zealand, Sweden, and the United Kingdom (1990s, monthly)	Comparison of forecasts of actual inflation with predicted forecasts, which are derived by multiplying the estimated coefficients of Phillips curves using the same independent variables before and after the target announcement	Inflation targeting stabilizes long-term inflation expectations.
Strohsal, Melnick, and Nautz (2016)	Did the global financial crisis affect inflation expectations?	United States (2004-14, monthly)	Regression of deviations of long-term inflation expectations from the inflation target on observed inflation or news-driven short-term inflation expectations using a model with time-varying parameters	Inflation expectations in the United States became partially de-anchored during the global financial crisis, but this de-anchoring was temporary.
Strohsal and Winkelmann (2015)	Are long-term inflation expectations well anchored?	Euro Area, Sweden, United Kingdom, and United States (2004-11, daily)	Estimation of a market-perceived inflation target using an exponential smooth transition autoregressive (ESTAR) model	Expectations appear to be best anchored in the Euro Area, followed by the United States, Sweden, and the United Kingdom. In most of these countries, the degree of anchoring did not change during the global financial crisis.

Note: EMDEs = emerging market and developing economies.

TABLE A.4.2.2 Studies on EMDEs (some including advanced economies)

Authors	Questions	Economies (sample period and frequency)	Methodology	Results
Baskaya, Gulsen, and Kara (2012)	Are inflation expectations well anchored in Turkey?	Turkey (2006-12, monthly)	Regression of inflation expectations on the lagged inflation rate	Inflation expectations are more sensitive to inflation realization at higher levels, but this sensitivity has decreased over time.
Capistrán and Ramos-Francia (2010)	Does inflation targeting affect inflation expectations?	12 advanced economies and 13 EMDEs (1989-2006, monthly)	Regression of dispersion of inflation expectations on a dummy for inflation targeting, the actual inflation rate, and world average inflation	Inflation targeting affects inflation expectations only in EMDEs. There is no effect of inflation targeting on the dispersion of inflation expectations in advanced economies.
Carrasco and Ferreiro (2013)	Does inflation targeting anchor inflation expectations?	Mexico (2004-11, monthly)	Tests whether inflation expectations follow a normal distribution under inflation targeting using the Shapiro-Wilk test, Jarque-Bera test, and Doornik-Hansen test. If the inflation expectations are anchored, they are assumed to follow a normal distribution where the mean is the inflation target and the variance is constant.	Inflation expectations are anchored to the inflation target.
Cerisola and Gelos (2009)	Does inflation targeting anchor inflation expectations? Is the inflation targeting framework supported by the perceived sustainability of public finances?	Brazil (2000-04, monthly)	Recursive OLS regression of inflation expectations on inflation target, lagged inflation rate, primary balance as a percent of GDP, and other control variables	The adoption of inflation targeting helped anchor expectations; the stance of fiscal policy was important in shaping inflation expectations.
Cortes and Paiva (2017)	How does the loss of credibility affect inflation expectations?	Brazil (2004-16, monthly)	Using VARs, estimation of impulse responses of inflation expectation to actual inflation, exchange rate movements, and output gap with two subsamples: 2004-10 and 2011-16	During 2011-16, inflation expectations reacted more strongly to actual inflation, exchange rate movements, and output shocks than during 2004-10.

TABLE A.4.2.2 Studies on EMDEs (some including advanced economies) (*continued*)

Authors	Questions	Economies (sample period and frequency)	Methodology	Results
Davis (2014)	Does inflation targeting anchor long-term inflation expectations?	14 advanced economies and 22 EMDEs (1990-2011, monthly)	SVAR to test whether 12-month-ahead inflation expectations respond to shocks to inflation and oil prices	The introduction of inflation targeting is associated with a statistically significant reduction in the response of short-term inflation expectations to shocks in oil prices and observed inflation.
de Mendonça and Galveas (2013)	How does central bank transparency affect the central bank's commitment to inflation targeting?	Brazil (2001-10, monthly)	Estimation of backward-looking, forward-looking, and hybrid New Keynesian Phillips curves (regression of actual inflation on inflation expectations, past inflation, and other control variables)	Given the degree of central bank transparency, the forward -looking and hybrid specifications of the Phillips curve are more suitable for explaining current inflation.
de Mendonça and Veiga (2014)	Are fiscal imbalances a constraint to monetary policy?	Brazil (1999-2010, monthly)	Regression of the deviation between inflation and its target on the net public debt-to-GDP ratio and other control variables	The deviation of realized inflation from target inflation tends to be higher when the public debt-to-GDP ratio is larger.
De Pooter et al. (2014)	Are long-term inflation expectations in EMDEs well anchored?	Brazil, Chile, and Mexico (2000s-2013, daily)	Test for anchoring by regression of changes in inflation expectations on news	Long-term inflation expectations have become better anchored during the decade to 2013, especially in Chile and Mexico.
IMF (2018)	How has the extent of anchoring of inflation expectations evolved in recent decades?	19 EMDEs (2004-17, biannual)	Facts about four measures of inflation anchoring: absolute deviation of the three-year-ahead inflation forecast from target, variability of inflation forecasts,dispersion of inflation forecasts, and sensitivity to inflation surprises	The degree of anchoring of inflation expectations has improved significantly over the past two decades. However, there is heterogeneity in the extent of anchoring across emerging markets.
Kabundi, Schaling, and Some (2015)	Are long-term inflation expectations of individual agents well anchored?	South Africa (2000-13, quarterly)	Estimation of a market-perceived inflation target of individual agents using panel regression with dummy variables	The inflation expectations of price setters (businesses and unions) are higher than the upper bound of the official target band, while the expectations of professional forecasters are within the target band. In addition, price setters' expectations are associated with lagged inflation but analysts' expectations are not.

TABLE 4.2.2 Studies on EMDEs (some including advanced economies) (*continued*)

Authors	Questions	Economies (sample period and frequency)	Methodology	Results
Lei, Lu, and Zhang (2015)	Do consumers and professional forecasters update their inflation forecasts with information from the news media?	China (2001-12, quarterly)	Regression of inflation expectations on news about prices	The news media can have a strong influence on inflation expectations.
Mehrotra and Yetman (forthcoming)	Are long-term inflation expectations well anchored?	23 advanced economies and 21 EMDEs (2005-12, monthly)	Estimation of the decay function such that inflation forecasts monotonically diverge from a long-run anchor toward actual inflation as the forecast horizon shortens	Inflation expectations have become more tightly anchored over time in both inflation targeting economies and in those following other monetary policy regimes.
Minella et al. (2003)	Does inflation targeting anchor inflation expectations?	Brazil (2000-03, monthly)	Regression of inflation expectations on inflation target, lagged inflation rate, exchange rate, and other control variables	In Brazil, actual inflation was above the upper limit of the tolerance interval in 2001 and 2002 after the introduction of inflation targeting in 1999. Inflation expectations react significantly to the inflation target and past inflation. The inflation targeting regime has been successful in helping to anchor expectations.
Miyajima and Yetman (2018)	Are long-term inflation expectations of individual agents well anchored?	South Africa (2001-17, quarterly; 1993-2017, monthly)	Estimation of the decay function such that inflation forecasts monotonically diverge from a long-run anchor toward actual inflation as the forecast horizon shortens	Inflation expectations of businesses and trade unions are anchored to levels above the official target range although overall, inflation expectations have become more strongly anchored in South Africa in recent years.
Patra and Ray (2010)	What are the determinants of inflation expectations?	India (1997-2008, monthly)	Regression of inflation expectations on lagged inflation, changes in prices of fuel and primary articles, the output gap, and real interest rate	Lagged inflation and movements in fuel and food prices affect inflation expectations.
Reid (2009)	Are long-term inflation expectations well anchored?	South Africa (2001-07, quarterly)	Test for anchoring by regression of changes in inflation expectations on macroeconomic news	Inflation expectations are well anchored in South Africa due to the inflation targeting framework.

Note: EMDEs = emerging market and developing economies.

ANNEX 4.3 Methodology and database

Methodology

Panel regressions

If long-term expectations are well-anchored, they will not be highly responsive to macroeconomic news. Figure 4.4, panel A, presents the results of a panel regression model that estimates the sensitivity of changes in long-term inflation expectations to macroeconomic news shocks. The change in long-term inflation expectations (dependent variable) is measured by the difference between five-year-ahead inflation expectations in the current period and five-year-ahead inflation expectations in the previous period. The macroeconomic news shock corresponds to an inflation shock (a regressor) that is measured by the difference between realized inflation and short-term inflation expectations in the previous period.[1]

The model includes an interaction dummy variable to allow for different elasticities of inflation expectations in advanced economies and EMDEs:

$$E_t \pi_{i,t+5} - E_{t-1} \pi_{i,t+5} = \beta_1(\pi_{i,t} - E_{t-1} \pi_{i,t}) + \beta_2 D_i (\pi_{i,t} - E_{t-1} \pi_{i,t}) + \mu_i + \tau_t + \varepsilon_{i,t} \quad (1)$$

where i denotes country and t refers to time. $E_t \pi_{i,t+5}$ and $E_{t-1} \pi_{i,t+5}$ are five-year-ahead inflation expectations in the current and previous periods, respectively. $\pi_{i,t}$ refers to realized inflation and $E_{t-1} \pi_{i,t}$ is short-term inflation expectations in the previous period. D_i is a dummy variable that is equal to 0 for advanced economies and 1 for EMDEs, implying that β_1 and $(\beta_1 + \beta_2)$ are the estimated sensitivities for advanced economies and EMDEs, respectively. When the estimated sensitivity is small (that is, β_1 is not statistically significantly different from zero), inflation expectations are well anchored. The model includes country fixed effects (μ_i) and time fixed effects (τ_t) that are estimated for three periods: 1990H2-2004H2, 2005H1-18H1, and 1990H2-2018H1.[2]

Regressions with time-varying parameters: Country-specific models

Figure 4.4, panels B, C, and D, presents the results of a time-varying model, estimated using a Kalman filter, that captures the time variation in the sensitivity of changes in long-term inflation expectations to inflation shocks. The model is a version of model (1), but it includes time-varying coefficients:

[1] The model follows Beechey, Johannsen, and Levin (2011); Gürkaynak, Levin, and Swanson (2010); and De Pooter et al. (2014).

[2] Because there are no available data for most EMDEs in the early 1990s, the panel data set is unbalanced. The sample was split at 2004 to produce two samples of roughly equal length.

$$E_t\pi_{t+5} - E_{t-1}\pi_{t+5} = \alpha_t + \beta_t(\pi_t - E_{t-1}\pi_t) + \varepsilon_t, \varepsilon_t \sim iid\ N(0,\sigma_\varepsilon)^2 \quad (2)$$

where the measures of expected and realized inflation are the same as those in model (1). The model is estimated for each of the 24 advanced economies and 23 EMDEs in the sample, using semiannual data for 1990H1-2018H1 and 1995H1-2018H1, respectively. The time-varying parameters are assumed to follow a random walk:[3]

$$\alpha_t = \alpha_{t-1} + \xi_t, \xi_t \sim iid\ N(0,\sigma_\xi)^2$$

$$\beta_t = \beta_{t-1} + \eta_t, \eta_t \sim iid\ N(0,\sigma_\eta)^2$$

where α_t captures changes in long-term inflation expectations that are independent of inflation shocks, and β_t measures the sensitivity of inflation expectations to inflation shocks.[4] In other words, α_t and β_t are assumed to be the sensitivity to the permanent and temporary shocks, respectively. If forecasters believe that the central bank's monetary policy is credible, they do not react to inflation shocks. This implies that if β_t is not statistically significantly different from zero, inflation expectations are well anchored.

Regressions with time-varying parameters: Global and domestic shocks

A simple regression model with time-varying parameters is estimated to analyze the sensitivity of inflation expectations to global and domestic inflation shocks. The results are presented in Figure 4.5. The global inflation shock is defined as the first principal component of inflation shocks for the full sample of 24 advanced economies for 1990H2-2018H1 and 23 EMDEs for 1995H1-2018H1. The domestic inflation shock is defined as the residual from a regression of the inflation shock on the first principal component of inflation shocks, as in the following model:

$$\pi_t - E_t\pi_{t-1} = \delta_t f_t + \epsilon_t \quad (3)$$

where f_t is the first principal component of inflation shocks and δ_t is the time-varying parameter. $\delta_t f_t$ represents the global inflation shock and the remaining term ϵ_t is defined as the domestic inflation shock. The sensitivity of five-year-ahead inflation expectations to global and domestic inflation shocks is then modeled as:

---

[3] IMF (2016) and Buono and Formai (2018) also estimate models with the time-varying parameters. IMF (2016) also uses a Kalman filter model but does not include other factors (α_t). Buono and Formai (2018) estimate their model over a rolling window in which the sample periods change over time.

[4] The results remain robust when α_t is not included in the model.

$$E_t \pi_{t+5} - E_{t-1} \pi_{t+5} = \alpha_t + \beta_{1t} G_t + \beta_{2t} D_t + \varepsilon_t \quad (4)$$

where $G_t (= \delta_t f_t)$ is the global shock and $D_t (= \epsilon_t)$ is the domestic shock. Models (3) and (4) are estimated using a Kalman filter and with the assumption that the time-varying parameters follow a random walk.

Panel cointegration regressions

The determinants of the degree of anchoring of inflation expectations are studied using a set of panel regression models. The results of these exercises, using annual data for 24 advanced economies and 23 EMDEs for 1995-2016, are presented in Figure 4.6. The degree of anchoring is measured as the sensitivity (β_t) of changes in long-term inflation expectations to inflation shocks (as estimated in model (2) above). Six determinants are considered: the presence of an inflation targeting regime, the degree of central bank transparency, the exchange rate regime, financial openness, trade openness, and the degree of fiscal sustainability. Inflation targeting regime and fixed exchange rate regime are dummy variables for which the presence of the indicated regime equals one. Exchange rate regime is determined using Shambaugh (2004). Central bank transparency and financial openness (capital account openness) are measured using indexes produced by Dincer and Eichengreen (2014) and Chinn and Ito (2017), respectively. Trade openness is measured as imports divided by domestic demand (domestic demand is defined as gross domestic product (GDP) + imports - exports). Fiscal sustainability is measured as the ratio of gross public debt to GDP.

The empirical exercise is undertaken in four steps. First, all variables are tested in a panel setting for unit roots.[5] Some tests do not reject the null hypothesis of nonstationarity of trade openness and gross public debt-to-GDP ratio (Table A.4.4.2). Second, since some variables (including the inflation targeting dummy, fixed exchange rate regime dummy, and financial openness index) are stationary, residual series are obtained from a panel regression of sensitivity of inflation expectations on these stationary variables. Specifically, the following model is estimated:

$$\beta_{i,t} = \theta_i + \varphi_t + \gamma MP_{i,t} + \delta X_{i,t} + \epsilon_{i,t} \quad (5)$$

where $\beta_{i,t}$ is the time-varying estimate of the country-specific estimate of the elasticity of inflation expectations to inflation shocks, as explained in the

[5] This test follows Im, Pesaran, and Shin (2003); Maddala and Wu (1999); and Choi (2001). Although the time-varying parameters are constructed under the assumption of a random walk, most results of panel unit root tests reject the null hypothesis of nonstationarity.

discussion of regressions with time-varying parameters. $MP_{i,t}$ is (i) a dummy variable that takes a value of one in countries with an inflation targeting framework or (ii) a measure of central bank transparency. $X_{i,t}$ includes a dummy variable that takes a value of one for countries with a fixed exchange rate regime and financial openness index. θ_i captures country-fixed effects and φ_t refers to time fixed effects.

Third, the existence of cointegration between the residuals from the panel regression in model (5) and the gross public debt-to-GDP ratio and trade openness is tested by employing Pedroni's (1999) cointegration test (Table A.4.4.3). The results indicate that the residuals are cointegrated with the two variables. Fourth, following Pedroni (2000, 2001), a grouped mean fully modified ordinary least squares (FMOLS) regression model and a grouped mean dynamic OLS (DOLS) regression model are estimated to correct for endogeneity bias and serial correlation. The dependent variable is the estimated residual from the panel regression in model (5). The independent variables are trade openness (measured by the import penetration ratio) and the gross public debt-to-GDP ratio.

Database

TABLE A.4.3.1 List of countries

Country group	Countries
Advanced economies (24)	Australia, Austria, Belgium, Canada, Denmark, Finland, France, Germany, Greece, Ireland, Israel, Italy, Japan, Korea, the Netherlands, New Zealand, Norway, Portugal, Singapore, Spain, Sweden, Switzerland, the United Kingdom, the United States
EMDEs (23)	Argentina, Bangladesh, Brazil, Chile, China, Colombia, the Arab Republic of Egypt, India, Indonesia, the Islamic Republic of Iran, Kuwait, Malaysia, Mexico, Pakistan, Peru, Poland, the Russian Federation, Saudi Arabia, South Africa, Thailand, Tunisia, Turkey, Zambia

Note: The numbers in parentheses are the number of countries in the sample. EMDEs = emerging market and developing economies.

TABLE A.4.3.2 Description of the variables

Variable	Description	Sources
Inflation expectations (advanced economies: 1990H1-2018H1 EMDEs: 1995H1-2018H1)	Current year, one-year-ahead, five-year-ahead inflation forecasts based on surveys conducted biannually for 30 countries by Consensus Economics, complemented by current year, one-year-ahead, and five-year-ahead annual average headline CPI inflation forecasts produced biannually for 17 countries in the IMF's World Economic Outlook database.	Consensus Economics, Consensus Forecast; IMF, World Economic Outlook database
Inflation targeting regime (1995-2016)	A dummy variable equal to 1 for inflation targeting regime and 0 for no inflation targeting regime.	IMF, Annual Report on Exchange Arrangements and Exchange Restrictions database
Central bank transparency (1995-2014)	Index calculated from responses to 15 questions. To expand the sample, the index was extrapolated to 2015-16 using 2014 data.	Dincer and Eichengreen (2014)
Exchange rate regime (1995-2014)	The exchange rate regime classification developed in Shambaugh (2004) is used to determine whether a country has a pegged or flexible exchange rate. To expand the sample, the index was extrapolated to 2015-16 using 2014 data.	Shambaugh (2004)
Financial openness (1995-2015)	Index of de jure capital account openness. To expand the sample, the index was extrapolated to 2016 using 2015 data.	Chinn and Ito (2017)
Trade openness (1995-2016)	Imports divided by domestic demand (domestic demand = GDP + imports - exports).	IMF, International Financial Statistics database
Gross public debt (1995-2016)	Gross public debt divided by nominal GDP.	IMF, World Economic Outlook database
Oil prices (1990H1-2017H2)	Index is in nominal U.S. dollars.	World Bank, Commodity Price Data (the Pink Sheet)
Food prices (1990H1-2017H2)	Index is in nominal U.S. dollars.	World Bank, Commodity Price Data (the Pink Sheet)
Global liquidity (1990H1-2017H2)	International claims on all sectors (annual change).	Bank for International Settlements, Global Liquidity Indicators database
Global output gap (1990H1-2017H2)	Real GDP-weighted average of country specific output gaps estimated using a multivariate filter.	World Bank (2018)

Note: CPI = consumer price index; EMDEs = emerging market and developing economies; IMF = International Monetary Fund.

ANNEX 4.4 Estimation results

TABLE A.4.4.1 Sensitivity of long-term inflation expectations to inflation shocks

A. 1990H2-2018H1

	Dependent variable: Change in long-term inflation expectations			
	All countries	All countries	Advanced economies	EMDEs
All countries	0.282*** (0.021)			
Advanced economies		0.159*** (0.028)	0.154*** (0.032)	
EMDEs		0.425*** (0.030)		0.425*** (0.030)
Observations	2,408	2,408	1,344	1,064
R-squared	0.069	0.086	0.019	0.169

B. 1995H1-2004H2

	Dependent variable: Change in long-term inflation expectations			
	All countries	All countries	Advanced economies	EMDEs
All countries	0.423*** (0.035)			
Advanced economies		0.284*** (0.049)	0.278*** (0.052)	
EMDEs		0.554*** (0.048)		0.558*** (0.046)
Observations	1,139	1,139	696	443
R-squared	0.119	0.131	0.044	0.261

C. 2005H1-2018H1

	Dependent variable: Change in long-term inflation expectations			
	All countries	All countries	Advanced economies	EMDEs
All countries	0.083***			
Advanced economies		0.008 (0.028)	-0.001 (0.031)	
EMDEs		0.201*** (0.034)		0.206*** (0.037)
Observations	1,269	1,269	648	621
R-squared	0.011	0.028	0.000	0.049

Note: Standard errors are in parentheses. EMDEs = emerging market and developing economies.

A.-C. Results for the full sample of 47 countries, 24 advanced economies, and 23 EMDEs, with country and time fixed effects.

*** p < 0.01, ** p < 0.05, * p <0.1 significance level.

TABLE A.4.4.2 Panel unit root tests

A. All countries

	Intercept and trend			Intercept		
	Im-Pesaran-Shin	ADF Fisher	PP Fisher	Im-Pesaran-Shin	ADF Fisher	PP Fisher
Total sensitivity	-23.1 (0.00)***	1167.2 (0.00)***	560.8 (0.00)***	-15.2 (0.00)***	853.4 (0.00)***	444.3 (0.00)***
Gross public debt	0.0 (0.52)	102.0 (0.27)	42.9 (1.00)	-4.9 (0.00)***	405.2 (0.00)***	78.2 (0.88)
Penetration	-2.2 (0.01)***	145.3 (0.00)***	112.2 (0.10)*	-0.9 (0.19)	96.1 (0.42)	89.2 (0.62)

B. Advanced economies

	Intercept and trend			Intercept		
	Im-Pesaran-Shin	ADF Fisher	PP Fisher	Im-Pesaran-Shin	ADF Fisher	PP Fisher
Total sensitivity	-3.7 (0.00)***	96.7 (0.00)***	95.2 (0.00)***	-0.4 (0.34)	71.8 (0.01)***	98.4 (0.00)***
Gross public debt	1.1 (0.86)	38.2 (0.84)	14.2 (1.00)	-0.6 (0.26)	55.8 (0.21)	27.9 (0.99)
Penetration	-3.4 (0.00)***	86.3 (0.00)***	53.3 (0.28)	-0.9 (0.18)	49.3 (0.42)	47.2 (0.50)

C. EMDEs

	Intercept and trend			Intercept		
	Im-Pesaran-Shin	ADF Fisher	PP Fisher	Im-Pesaran-Shin	ADF Fisher	PP Fisher
Total sensitivity	-29.1 (0.00)***	1070.5 (0.00)***	465.6 (0.00)***	-21.3 (0.00)***	781.6 (0.00)***	345.9 (0.00)***
Gross public debt	-1.0 (0.16)	63.8 (0.04)**	28.6 (0.98)	-6.4 (0.00)***	349.5 (0.00)***	50.3 (0.31)
Penetration	1.0 (0.85)	48.2 (0.38)	60.5 (0.07)*	0.1 (0.53)	43.9 (0.56)	43.8 (0.56)

Note: P-values are in parentheses. ADF = augmented Dickey-Fuller unit-root test; EMDEs = emerging market and developing economies; PP = Phillips-Perron unit-root test.

A. Results for the full sample of 47 countries, using data for 1995-2016.

B. Results for 24 advanced economies, using data for 1995-2016.

C. Results for 23 EMDEs, using data for 1995-2016.

The null hypothesis of a unit root is rejected at significance levels of *** $p < 0.01$, ** $p < 0.05$, * $p < 0.1$.

TABLE A.4.4.3 Panel cointegration tests

	Intercept and trend					
	All countries		Advanced economies		EMDEs	
	Statistic	p-value	Statistic	p-value	Statistic	p-value
Panel v-statistic	-1.7	0.96	2.0	0.03**	-1.2	0.88
Panel rho-statistic	-9.7	0.00***	1.0	0.84	-7.0	0.00***
Panel PP-statistic	-27.8	0.00***	-3.0	0.00***	-19.5	0.00***
Panel ADF-statistic	-22.4	0.00***	-3.8	0.00***	-15.7	0.00***
Group rho-statistic	0.3	0.60	3.1	1.00	-0.5	0.30
Group PP-statistic	-13.9	0.00***	-0.9	0.18	-10.8	0.00***
Group ADF-statistic	-11.7	0.00***	-2.7	0.00***	-10.7	0.00***

	Intercept					
	All countries		Advanced economies		EMDEs	
	Statistic	p-value	Statistic	p-value	Statistic	p-value
Panel v-statistic	2.4	0.01***	-0.5	0.69	1.9	0.03**
Panel rho-statistic	-11.5	0.00***	-0.2	0.42	-8.3	0.00***
Panel PP-statistic	-19.4	0.00***	-2.8	0.00***	-13.8	0.00***
Panel ADF-statistic	-15.2	0.00***	-2.7	0.00***	-11.0	0.00***
Group rho-statistic	-1.3	0.09*	1.9	0.97	-1.1	0.14
Group PP-statistic	-10.0	0.00***	-1.6	0.06*	-7.0	0.00***
Group ADF-statistic	-9.5	0.00***	-2.9	0.00***	-8.7	0.00***

Note: Results for the full sample of 47 economies, 24 advanced economies, and 23 EMDEs, all using data for 1995-2016. ADF = augmented Dickey-Fuller unit-root test; EMDEs = emerging market and developing economies; PP = Phillips-Perron unit-root test.

The null hypothesis of no cointegration is rejected at significance levels of *** $p<0.01$, ** $p<0.05$, * $p<0.1$.

TABLE A.4.4.4 Determinants of sensitivity of inflation expectations

A. Panel regressions

	Dependent variable: Estimated sensitivity					
	All countries	All countries	Advanced economies	Advanced economies	EMDEs	EMDEs
Model	FE	FE	FE	FE	FE	FE
Inflation targeting	-0.390***		-0.222***		-0.498***	
	(0.094)		(0.053)		(0.165)	
Central bank transparency		-0.414**		0.040		-0.724*
		(0.204)		(0.108)		(0.377)
Exchange rate regime	0.306**	0.307**	0.255	0.012	0.060	0.079
	(0.147)	(0.149)	(0.395)	(0.405)	(0.222)	(0.224)
Financial openness	0.141	0.046	0.032	-0.094	-0.059	-0.186
	(0.178)	(0.177)	(0.121)	(0.125)	(0.289)	(0.286)
Exchange rate regime x financial openness	0.070	-0.046	-0.343	-0.069	1.037**	1.001**
	(0.222)	(0.225)	(0.400)	(0.410)	(0.490)	(0.493)
Observations	1,034	1,034	528	528	506	506
R-squared	0.067	0.055	0.203	0.178	0.078	0.067

Note: Results of panel regressions for the full sample of 47 countries, 24 advanced economies, and 23 EMDEs, with country and time fixed effects, using data for 1995-2016. Standard errors are in parentheses. EMDEs = emerging market and developing economies; FE = fixed effects.

*** p < 0.01, ** p < 0.05, * p < 0.1 significance level.

B. Panel cointegration regressions (fully modified OLS and dynamic OLS)

	Dependent variable: Residual from the first regression					
	All countries	All countries	Advanced economies	Advanced economies	EMDEs	EMDEs
Model	FMOLS	DOLS	FMOLS	DOLS	FMOLS	DOLS
Penetration	-0.004	-0.010	0.012	0.010	-0.015	-0.021
	(0.004)	(0.010)	(0.003)***	(0.006)*	(0.008)**	(0.011)*
Gross public debt	0.008	0.009	-0.002	-0.001	0.018	0.020
	(0.002)***	(0.003)***	(0.001)***	(0.001)	(0.005)***	(0.006)***

Note: Results of group mean panel fully modified ordinary least squares regressions (FMOLS) and group mean dynamic ordinary least squares regressions (DOLS) the full sample of 47 countries, 24 advanced economies, and 23 EMDEs. Standard errors in parentheses. DOLS = dynamic ordinary least squares; EMDEs = emerging market and developing economies; FMOLS = fully modified ordinary least squares; OLS = ordinary least squares.

*** p < 0.01, ** p < 0.05, * p < 0.1 significance level.

ANNEX 4.5 Inflation targeting: Country experiences

Inflation targeting in Brazil

Rationale. Brazil adopted inflation targeting in July 1999 after it became clear that five years of exchange rate targeting had failed. Despite the success of the Central Bank of Brazil (BCB) in reducing historically high inflation through exchange rate stabilization measures, which began in 1994, a lack of fiscal discipline resulted in a gradual buildup of government debt, which in turn made the Brazilian *real* vulnerable to speculative attacks (Mishkin and Savastano 2002). Amid a severe currency crisis that began in early 1999, Brazil shifted to an inflation targeting regime to "coordinate market expectations and control inflation" (Barbosa-Filho 2008).

Process. The inflation targeting framework, adopted by presidential decree, established that the National Monetary Council would set inflation targets no later than two years in advance, following a transition period concluding in 2002. The BCB was granted instrument independence to this end (Bognanski, Tombini, and Werlang 2000). If end-year annual inflation is out of the established tolerance range, which has been changed over time, the governor of the BCB is required to provide an open (public) letter to the minister of finance explaining why the target was not met and what actions will be taken to return inflation to the target range. The framework also required the BCB to issue a quarterly inflation report detailing the results of its recent monetary policy actions and its projections for inflation.

Several aspects of Brazil's inflation targeting framework are distinctive. For one, the BCB is not solely responsible for setting the inflation target range. The entity that establishes the targets, the National Monetary Council, is composed of the governor of the BCB, the minister of finance, and the minister of planning, development, and management. In addition, Brazil's target band was for a long time quite wide compared to that in other inflation targeting countries (IMF 2015).[1] Official assessment of whether the annual target has been met is based only on the December/December change in the consumer price index (CPI). Furthermore, although Brazil has maintained a de jure flexible exchange rate under its inflation targeting regime, the BCB has at times intervened in foreign exchange markets to manage excess volatility of the currency.

[1] However, after the target was held at 4.5 percent and the tolerance band at 2.5-6.5 percent since 2006, the band was narrowed to 3-6 percent in 2018. Over 2019-21 the target and tolerance band will be incrementally lowered on an annual basis, to a target of 3.75 percent within a band of 2.25-5.25 percent in 2021.

When inflation targeting was adopted in 1999, Brazil had a sound banking system and was in the process of strengthening its fiscal profile. The banking system had been restructured after a crisis in the early 1990s. Although government debt was still rising in 1999, fiscal adjustment was underway. A series of debt restructuring agreements between individual states and the federal government had been negotiated a few years prior. Fiscal discipline improved with the passing of the Fiscal Responsibility Law in 2000 (López Vicente and Serena Garralda 2014).

Results. Brazil's inflation targeting regime was successful in the first years after its inception. Inflation was within the target range in 1999 and 2000, and BCB transparency improved markedly (Figure A.4.5.1). A major challenge developed in 2001, however, when a combination of shocks—a severe drought and energy crisis, slowing global growth, and contagion from a financial crisis in Argentina—led to another bout of currency depreciation (Minella et al. 2003). The currency pressure was exacerbated in 2002 by a sharp rise in bond spreads, a weak external position (Brazil had insufficient capital inflows to finance its current account deficit and foreign exchange reserves were low), and uncertainty about macroeconomic policy during the presidential election cycle. As the *real* depreciated, inflation spiked to more than 17 percent in May 2003, and concerns about debt sustainability rose (at the time, half of Brazil's public debt was denominated in or indexed to the U.S. dollar). Inflation far exceeded the upper bound of the target band for three consecutive years to 2003, and three-year-ahead inflation expectations were around the upper limit of the target inflation band in 2002 and 2003. Five-year-ahead expectations, however, remained better anchored and within the band, reaching a maximum of 5.2 percent in the first half of 2003, below the 6.5 percent upper limit at the time.

The deviations from the target in 2001-03 were followed by a long period of better performance. Although headline inflation remained above the upper limit of the target band through mid-2005, five-year-ahead inflation expectations for Brazil declined toward the middle of the band. However, disinflation during these years occurred in large part due to exchange rate appreciation, which resulted from a combination of relatively high domestic policy interest rates and a supportive global trade and financing environment (Barbosa-Filho 2008; Arestis, Ferrari-Filho, and de Paula 2011).

Brazil managed to keep inflation within the target band during the global financial crisis. Headline inflation rose in the leadup to the global financial crisis in response to rising oil prices, strong capital inflows, and growing domestic demand, but was still within the target band as Lehman Brothers collapsed. Inflation expectations increased in 2007 and 2008, but not sharply, providing evidence that expectations had become better anchored under the inflation

FIGURE A.4.5.1 Inflation targeting in Brazil

Inflation in Brazil has overshot the target range significantly at times since the Central Bank of Brazil's adoption of inflation targeting. Although long-term inflation expectations are not as well anchored as in some other inflation targeting EMDEs, the sensitivity of inflation to shocks has been permanently lower and remarkably constant following a large initial drop after the introduction of inflation targeting.

A. Actual inflation and inflation expectations

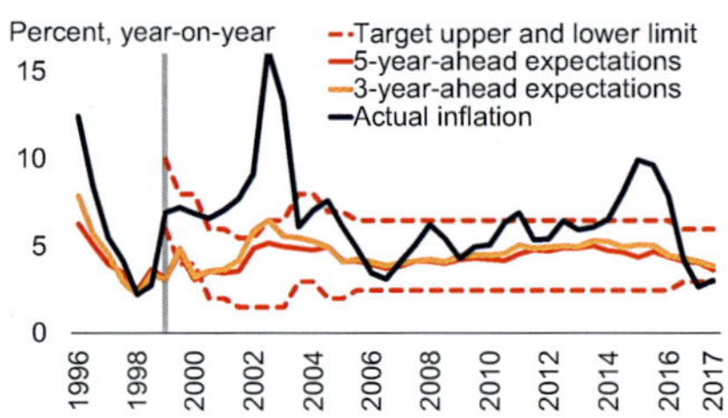

B. Central bank transparency

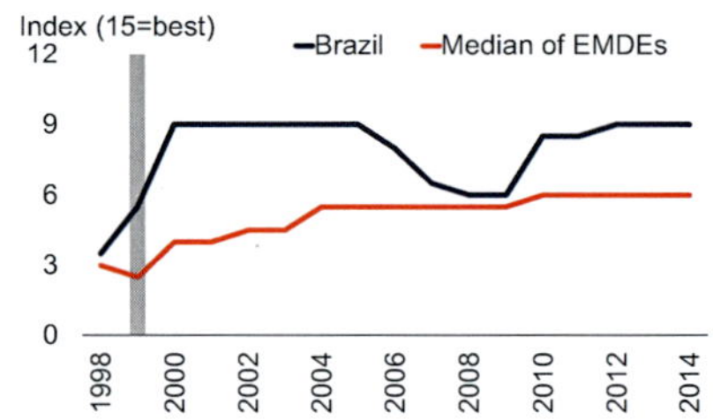

C. General government primary balance and gross debt

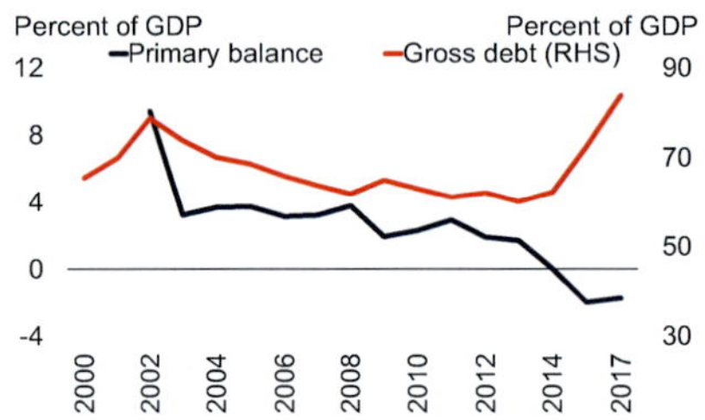

D. Sensitivity of inflation expectations to shocks

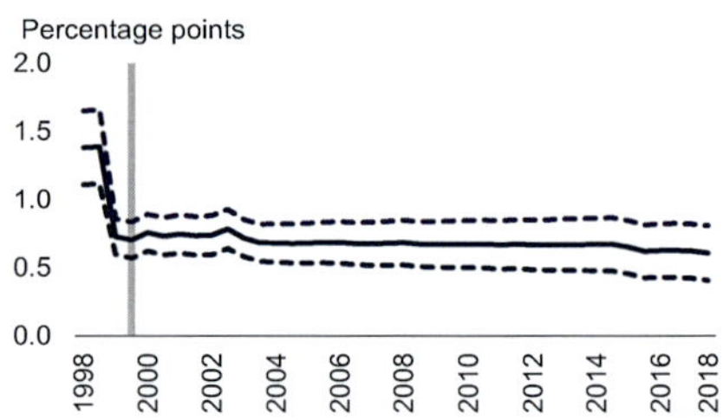

Source: Consensus Economics; Dincer and Eichengreen 2014; Haver Analytics; International Monetary Fund; World Bank.
Note: EMDEs = emerging market and developing economies; GDP = gross domestic product.
A.B.D. The start of the inflation targeting regime is shaded in gray.
B. Transparency is based on information from the Central Bank of Brazil's website, statutes, annual reports, and other published documents, as calculated by Dincer and Eichengreen (2014).
C. The primary balance is net government lending and borrowing, excluding net interest payments.
D. Time-varying sensitivity is estimated by regressing long-term inflation forecast revisions on inflation shocks. Dotted lines denote the 68 percent confidence interval. Annex 4.3. provides details on the methodology.

targeting regime. As the crisis deepened and capital inflows dropped sharply, BCB prioritized stabilizing the exchange rate and maintaining adequate liquidity, in part through foreign exchange market interventions and reducing reserve requirements (Céspedes, Chang, and Velasco 2014).

From 2011 to mid-2014, headline inflation in Brazil was near or slightly above the upper limit of the target band, reflecting currency depreciation, rising wage costs, continued price indexation, and, in the latter part of this period, drought conditions in parts of the country that were aggravated by the onset of the El

Niño weather phenomenon (IMF 2015). In response, BCB began raising interest rates in mid-2013. Yet, inflationary pressures intensified after increases in regulated gasoline and diesel prices in late 2014 and electricity tariffs in early 2015. From mid-2014 through late 2016, headline inflation was persistently above the upper bound of the target range, and more than 4 percentage points above the upper bound of 6.5 percent over the 12 months ending December 2015. Moreover, the government's primary balance deteriorated sharply, raising the public debt-to-GDP ratio. However, despite rapidly rising inflation, five-year -ahead inflation expectations remained firmly in the middle of the band, suggesting that the inflation targeting regime retained credibility.

After peaking in early 2016 following the realignment of administered prices, inflation gradually moderated, and the BCB began an extended period of interest rate easing late in the year. By the end of 2017, inflation was slightly below the 3 percent lower bound of the target band, largely due to food price deflation that in turn reflected very strong agricultural production. Five-year-ahead inflation expectations continued to moderate during this period.

The behavior of inflation expectations in Brazil has been broadly consistent with the estimated sensitivity of long-term inflation expectations to shocks. Following a large initial drop in the sensitivity of expectations to shocks after the introduction of the inflation targeting regime in 1999, sensitivity has been more or less constant, suggesting that the inflation targeting regime has been successful in anchoring expectations. Yet the sensitivity to shocks is still higher than in some other inflation targeting emerging market and developing economies (EMDEs). A deterioration of fiscal balances could have impeded the anchoring of inflation expectations (Cerisola and Gelos 2009; de Mendonça and Veiga 2014). An additional factor may have been that central bank independence was less well established in Brazil than in other countries (Cortes and Paiva 2017; Minella et al. 2003).

Lessons learned. Brazil's experience with inflation targeting offers two key lessons. First, long-term inflation expectations can remain stable during sharp fluctuations in actual inflation even in the absence of typical elements of inflation targeting regimes elsewhere (for example, the central bank having sole power to set inflation targets, fixed-term appointment of central bank governors, and use of a narrow inflation target band). Further, inflation expectations in Brazil have been stable despite periodic questions about the credibility of the inflation targeting regime arising from its unique institutional arrangements (IMF 2015). However, some of the specifics of the regime (that is, a wide target band and use of only December data for measuring results) have arguably made formal compliance with targets easier than in most other inflation targeting countries.

Second, fiscal policy can be a key factor in determining the outcome of inflation targeting and controlling inflation expectations (Cerisola and Gelos 2009; de Mendonça and Veiga 2014). For instance, during the 2001-03 currency crisis, Brazil avoided a prolonged growth contraction thanks to the fiscal adjustments put in place in the late 1990s. These measures lent support to the inflation targets and the BCB's well-articulated strategy for reverting inflation to target levels (Giavazzi, Goldfajn, and Herrera 2005). At the same time, the structure of public debt in Brazil at the time—a large share of debt was short term or denominated in foreign currency—was a constraint on the central bank's ability to target inflation freely, since interest rate hikes abroad had a significant adverse impact on debt service obligations. Similarly, the high level of foreign currency–denominated debt may have also dissuaded the central bank from allowing the exchange rate to float freely, despite the stated commitment to floating (López Vicente and Serena Garralda 2014). Over time, the structure of public debt has changed, and the vast majority of domestic debt is now issued domestically. However, the stock of debt has risen rapidly in recent years.

Inflation targeting in Chile

Rationale. Expansionary macroeconomic policies in Chile in the late 1980s, together with the oil price spike that accompanied the Gulf War in the early 1990s, resulted in a sharp increase in inflation, to a peak of 30 percent in October 1990. These factors triggered the decision to adopt inflation targeting (Morandé 2002). Policy makers recognized that the fundamental historical driver of the inflation trends was excessive credit expansion by the Central Bank of Chile (BCC) (Corbo 2005). To better discipline monetary policy, the BCC first announced a numerical target for inflation in 1990. Since the target was set for just one year ahead, it did not amount to the complete adoption of inflation targeting. But it was the first step in the transition toward such a regime.

Process. Gradual implementation, a hallmark of Chile's inflation targeting experience, allowed the BCC to build credibility. Legislation passed in 1989 made the BCC fully independent and declared price stability to be the primary monetary policy objective. The BCC was given authority to define this objective (that is, goal independence) and control the instruments of monetary policy (that is, instrument independence). Its new framework of banking sector regulation and supervision was among the strongest of all emerging markets (Mishkin 2004).

Starting in 1991, the BCC adopted a partial inflation targeting regime. Under this arrangement, it announced a headline target for annual inflation in December each year, gradually reducing the level of the target, but continued to target an exchange rate band and retained the right to use short-term capital controls if needed.[2] Chile used unremunerated (non-interest bearing) reserve requirements on selective capital inflows through most of the 1990s to discourage buildups of short-term liabilities, favored a weaker exchange rate, and provided more operating space for monetary policy (De Gregorio, Tokman, and Valdés 2005). The exchange rate band was widened during the decade, allowing more flexible adjustment to external shocks (Bordo and Siklos 2014).

In September 1999, Chile shifted to a floating exchange rate regime and formally adopted a flexible inflation targeting framework that recognized the lag effect in monetary policy and the short-run trade-off with output. Key components of the framework included bolstering the statistical and analytical capacity of the BCC, publication of a monetary policy report (initially three issues per year, and four per year since 2009), and the release of minutes of monetary policy meetings with a short lag. In addition, the BCC announced its intent to deepen the foreign exchange derivatives market and intervene in the foreign exchange market only in extraordinary circumstances (Valdés 2007).

Over time, Chile's inflation target has been fine-tuned. In 1999, the BCC set the target band for annual inflation at 2-4 percent (to be achieved in 2001) and later extended this target indefinitely. In 2001, the target was redefined as 3 percent with at ± 1 percentage point tolerance range, and the horizon for achieving the 3 percent target, from any current deviation, was lengthened from 12-24 months to 24 months to account more realistically for the lag in the monetary transmission mechanism.

In 2001, the government adopted a balanced budget rule that constrained public expenditures, to ensure that the structural balance, measured as a share of GDP, met a specific target or range (De Gregorio 2009b; Llédo et al. 2017). The fiscal targets are were then regularly adjusted in line with changes in potential growth and forecasts of long-term copper prices.[3] Two independent committees, one focused on potential output and the other on copper prices, advise on the practical calculation of the structural balance.

Results. Despite some large fluctuations of inflation around the target range, long-term inflation expectations in Chile have been remarkably well anchored since the adoption of inflation targeting, and the sensitivity of inflation expectations to shocks is among the lowest in EMDEs. During the early years of the inflation targeting regime, inflation fell and became less volatile. Even under the partial inflation targeting regime, there was a sustained decline in headline

[2] The new framework also included current account deficit targets (Céspedes and Soto 2005).

[3] Prior to 2015, long-term molybdenum prices were also considered in setting structural balance targets. Llédo et al. (2017) provide additional details.

FIGURE A.4.5.2 Inflation targeting in Chile

Inflation has shown wide fluctuations around the target range under Chile's inflation targeting regime. Yet inflation expectations have been stable, perhaps reflecting the presence of a comprehensive, credible macroeconomic policy framework that includes the use of a fiscal rule. The sensitivity of long-term inflation expectations in Chile to shocks has diminished to a remarkably low level.

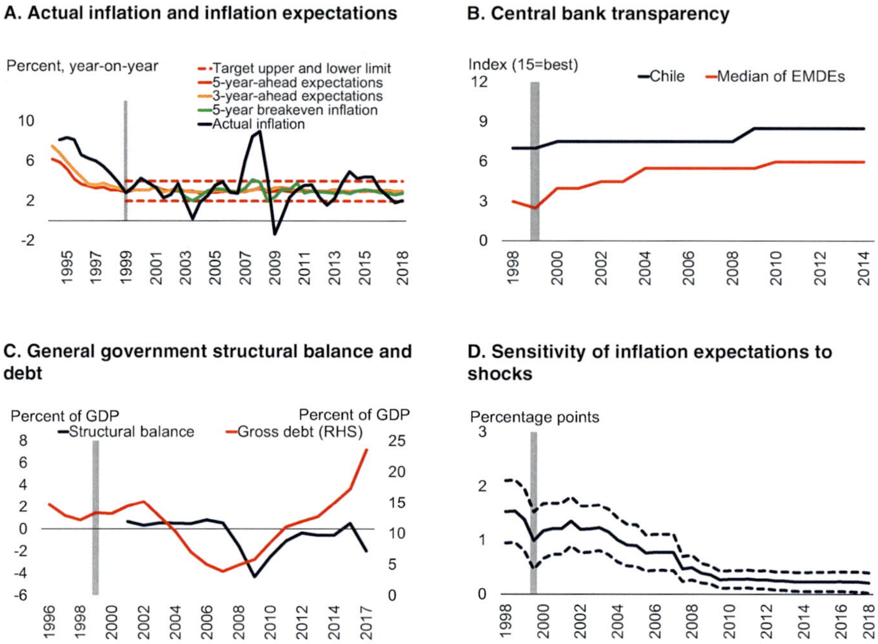

Source: Bloomberg, Consensus Economics, Dincer and Eichengreen (2014), Haver Analytics, International Monetary Fund, World Bank.

A.-D. The start of the inflation targeting regime is shaded in gray.

B. Transparency is based on information from the Central Bank of Chile's website, statutes, annual reports, and other published documents, as calculated by Dincer and Eichengreen (2014).

C. Structural balance is the difference between government revenues and expenditures, adjusted for effects due to economic cycles.

D. Time-varying sensitivity is estimated by regressing long-term inflation forecast revisions on inflation shocks. Dotted lines denote 68 percent confidence interval. Annex 4.3 provides details on the methodology.

inflation and inflation expectations (Figure A.4.5.2). Average inflation fell from 15.5 percent in 1991-94 to 5.7 percent in 1995-98. Moreover, the exchange rate pass-through to inflation dropped significantly starting in the mid-1990s and continued falling after the adoption of formal inflation targeting in 1999 (Schmidt-Hebbel and Tapia 2002).

A period of low inflation in 2003 and 2004 challenged the credibility of Chile's inflation target. In the second half of 2003, Chile experienced a significant and unexpected deceleration in inflation, as the peso appreciated and competition in the retail sector intensified (Central Bank of Chile 2004). Although survey-based inflation expectations remained close to the target of 3 percent (that is, well anchored), five-year-ahead, market-based inflation expectations declined significantly.

Long-term inflation expectations varied only slightly during the global financial crisis, despite large gyrations in actual inflation. From mid-2007 to late 2008, headline inflation in Chile experienced upward pressure from international factors—namely, rising food and energy prices. Headline inflation peaked at 9.9 percent (year-on-year) in October 2008. Although short-term expectations increased significantly as inflation rose, the reaction of five-year-ahead expectations was much more muted, reaching a high of 3.2 percent in the second half of 2008. Thereafter, as the global financial crisis deepened and global activity slowed, inflation in Chile rapidly became negative, prompting a 775 basis point reduction in the policy interest rate in the seven months to July 2009 and the introduction of several liquidity support measures. Yet five-year-ahead inflation expectations dropped only slightly, to 2.9 percent in the second half of 2009, suggesting that expectations were by that point very well anchored.

Inflation rose well above the target band in 2014-16, due to peso depreciation following the slump in copper prices. However, excess capacity in the economy and a cautious monetary policy stance helped reduce inflationary pressure, and by mid-2017, inflation began to slightly undershoot the target band. Food price deceleration and, initially, peso appreciation, contributed to the undershooting. Through these fluctuations, long-term inflation expectations were impressively stable.

Indeed, inflation expectations at the three-year-ahead and five-year-ahead horizons have been stable at around 3 percent since 1999. At the same time, the sensitivity of long-term inflation expectations to revisions in the short-term inflation forecast and other factors steadily declined during the decade after the adoption of full-fledged inflation targeting. Since 2009, the sensitivity of long-term expectations to shocks has been close to zero, consistent with findings by De Pooter et al. (2014) that inflation expectations have become better anchored in Chile over time.

Lessons learned. Chile's experience with inflation targeting offers three key lessons. First, gradual and successful implementation of the regime can have a lasting impact on inflation expectations. Second, deviations of actual inflation from the target, although substantial at times in Chile's case, need not weaken the credibility of the central bank. A clear strategy for returning inflation to target during the medium term, taking into account the lagged effect of monetary policy and the short-run trade-off between output and inflation, is more important than precise targeting from one year to the next. Third, a comprehensive, credible macroeconomic policy framework has yielded positive returns in Chile. A credible fiscal rule, strong financial sector regulation and supervision, and well-functioning capital markets—as well as the monetary policy regime of inflation targeting with a flexible exchange rate—have all helped generate favorable macroeconomic outcomes (De Gregorio, Tokman, and Valdés 2005; Valdés 2007).

Inflation targeting in Poland

Rationale. During the 1990s, monetary policy in Poland embodied two intermediate strategies: maintaining a stable exchange rate and controlling money supply growth (NBP 1998). Amid the challenges related to the transition to a market economy, inflation was reduced from an extremely high level in 1990 to around 10 percent by the end of the decade. But the two strategies also generated tension in the conduct of monetary policy. Inflation stabilization stalled, while episodes of excessive capital inflows, as Poland integrated more deeply into global markets, stoked fears of inflation persistence. Growing current account deficits highlighted a primary disadvantage of exchange rate targeting, since a flexible rate offers a key adjustment mechanism for balance of payments disequilibria. Coupled with the need to meet certain price stability and exchange rate criteria as Poland began accession discussions with the European Union (EU), this triggered the announcement by the National Bank of Poland (NBP) in 1998 that it would adopt an inflation target beginning in 1999 (Gottschalk and Moore 2001; Jonas and Mishkin 2003).

Process. Major legislative changes in the late 1990s paved the way for the adoption of inflation targeting. A new constitution in early 1997, together with the Act on the National Bank of Poland passed later the same year, established goal and instrument independence for the NBP (Polański 2004). Monetary policy would henceforth be conducted by a Monetary Policy Council composed of 10 members serving fixed-duration terms. The new constitution also enshrined two Maastricht Treaty fiscal requirements into law: it barred direct NBP financing of government deficits and imposed a public debt ceiling of 60 percent of GDP.[4] These legislative changes followed the development of indirect instruments of monetary policy in the early 1990s, including Treasury bills and bonds, which allowed the NBP to begin to conduct open market operations.

[4] However, the risk of fiscal dominance over monetary policy was perceived to be already low at the time (Gottschalk and Moore 2001).

Introducing the medium-term strategy for inflation targeting, the Monetary Policy Council committed to achieving inflation-reduction targets and publishing a semi-annual inflation report (NBP 1998). The medium-term target for CPI inflation was defined as below 4 percent by 2003. By the end of 2002, inflation was less than 2 percent, well below the target ceiling. Poland took a cautious approach to liberalizing its exchange rate, indicating that the date of floating would depend on foreign exchange market developments and the pace of capital account liberalization. The eventual flotation of the zloty in April 2000 was smooth, however, with no speculative attack despite a large current account deficit.

Over time, Poland's inflation targeting regime has been fine-tuned. In 2003, the NBP redefined the target to be 2.5 percent, within a band of ± 1 percentage point (NBP 2003).

Results. When inflation targeting was announced in 1998, inflation was falling. Yet, the short-term inflation target was still overshot in 1999-2001, even after the target band was raised and widened in 2001 (Figure A.4.5.3). This was followed by four years of below-target inflation. Several factors may explain the undershooting of inflation relative to the target. First, the immature domestic bond market limited the ability of the NBP to estimate the transmission of monetary policy to inflation (Christoffersen, Slok, and Wescott 2001; Polański 2004). Second, deficiencies in data availability and quality prevented timely identification of inflation pressures, and excess liquidity produced by foreign exchange intervention and institutional issues in the banking sector distorted monetary policy transmission (Schaechter, Stone, and Zelmer 2000). Despite the misses, the NBP communicated the deviations sufficiently far in advance that the public was not surprised by them (Bulíř et al. 2008). The avoidance of surprises helped build the credibility of inflation targeting.

Inflation overshot the target band during and after the global financial crisis but persistently undershot it in 2013-16. In 2013, the slowdown of the Euro Area led to region-wide disinflation, including in Poland, where inflation fell below target. The plunge in oil prices that began in mid-2014 accelerated the deflationary trend, contributing to negative inflation during 2014-16. However, the impact of low inflation in the Euro Area on the Polish economy was smaller than in economies with more rigid exchange rate regimes (Iossifov and Podpiera 2014). During the period of undershooting, the NBP kept its policy rate at 1.5 percent amid concerns about macroeconomic stability (NBP 2016). Inflation recovered to the target range in 2017, as oil prices rose and the Euro Area economy strengthened.

Measures of long-term inflation expectations in Poland have stabilized under the inflation targeting regime, mostly fluctuating within the target band. Five-year-

FIGURE A.4.5.3 Inflation targeting in Poland

After the introduction of inflation targeting in Poland, inflation converged toward the target range, long-term inflation expectations became better anchored, and a measure of central bank transparency improved markedly. Over time, the sensitivity of inflation expectations to shocks has declined.

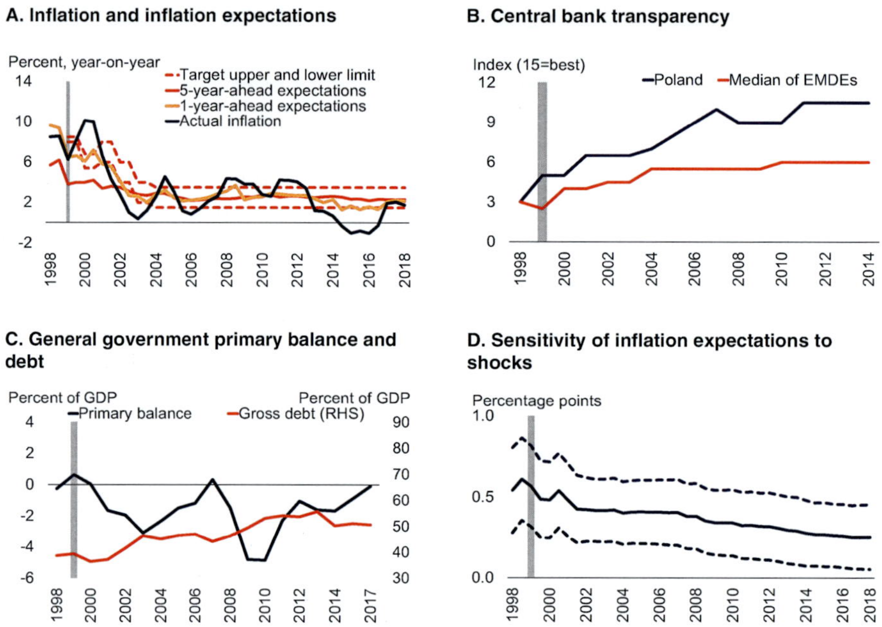

Source: Consensus Economics; Dincer and Eichengreen 2014; Haver Analytics; International Monetary Fund; World Bank.
Note: EMDEs = emerging market and developing economies; GDP = gross domestic product.
A.-D. The start of the inflation targeting regime is shaded in gray.
B. Transparency is based on information from the National Bank of Poland's website, statutes, annual reports, and other published documents, as calculated by Dincer and Eichengreen (2014).
C. The primary balance is net government lending and borrowing, excluding net interest payments.
D. Time-varying sensitivity is estimated by regressing long-term inflation forecast revisions on inflation shocks. Dotted lines denote the 68 percent confidence interval. Annex 4.3 provides details on the methodology.

ahead inflation expectations stabilized immediately after the shift to inflation targeting—initially, to a level well below the target band. Since 2003, the year the short- and medium-term targets were merged, five-year-ahead expectations have been firmly anchored at about 3 percent. This is consistent with the low and steadily moderating sensitivity of inflation expectations to shocks and an improvement in monetary policy credibility (NBP 2003).

Lessons learned. Poland's experience with inflation targeting offers two key lessons. First, it is possible to control inflation, despite limitations on the relevant data and the presence of much uncertainty about monetary policy transmission. When inflation targeting was adopted in 1999, domestic financial markets in Poland were still developing, and the transmission of monetary policy in the emerging market economy was untested. Although these conditions limited the NBP's ability to respond to shocks in a timely manner, the NBP succeeded in bringing down the inflation rate, broadly in line with the medium-term targets. Inflation volatility as well fell significantly after the introduction of inflation targeting.

Second, the combination of inflation targeting and a flexible exchange rate seems to have reduced spillovers from external shocks, in line with results in the literature on macroeconomic adjustment (for example, Georgiadis 2016). Real exchange rate depreciation supported Poland's growth during the global financial crisis, even as other European economies experienced a sharp slowdown in activity (Andrle, Garcia-Saltos, and Ho 2014). Moreover, spillovers to Poland from the recent period of ultra-low inflation in the Euro Area were lower than in other EU countries with lower exchange rate flexibility (for example, Bulgaria and Croatia) (Iossifov and Podpiera 2014).

References

Akerlof, G., W. Dickens, and G. Perry. 2000. "Near-Rational Wage and Price Setting and the Long-Run Phillips Curve." *Brookings Papers on Economic Activity* 31: 1-60.

Andrle, M., R. Garcia-Saltos, and G. Ho. 2014. "A Model-Based Analysis of Spillovers: The Case of Poland and the Euro Area." IMF Working Paper 14/186, International Monetary Fund, Washington, DC.

Arestis, P., F. Ferrari-Filho, and L. F. de Paula. 2011. "Inflation Targeting in Brazil." *International Review of Applied Economics* 25 (2): 127-48.

Arioli, R., C. Bates, H. Dieden, I. Duca, R. Friz, C. Gayer, G. Kenny, A. Meyler, and I. Pavlova. 2017. "EU Consumers' Quantitative Inflation Perceptions and Expectations: An Evaluation." Occasional Paper Series 186, European Central Bank, Frankfurt am Main.

Ascari, G., and A. M. Sbordone. 2014. "The Macroeconomics of Trend Inflation." *Journal of Economic Literature* 52 (3): 679-739.

Auer, R., C. Borio, and A. Filardo. 2017. "The Globalisation of Inflation: The Growing Importance of Global Value Chains." BIS Working Paper 602, Bank for International Settlements, Basel.

Ball, L. 1995. "Disinflation with Imperfect Credibility." *Journal of Monetary Economics* 35 (1): 5-23.

Barbosa-Filho, N. 2008. "Inflation Targeting in Brazil: 1999-2006." *International Review of Applied Economics* 22 (2): 187-200.

Baskaya, Y. S., E. Gulsen, and H. Kara. 2012. "Inflation Expectations and Central Bank Communication in Turkey." *Central Bank Review* 12 (2): 1-10.

Batini, N., and D. Laxton. 2006. "Under What Conditions Can Inflation Targeting Be Adopted? The Experience of Emerging Markets." Central Bank of Chile Working Paper 406, Central Bank of Chile, Santiago.

Beaudry, P., and F. Ruge-Murcia. 2017. "Canadian Inflation Targeting." *Canadian Journal of Economics* 50 (5): 155-72.

Beechey, M. J., B. K. Johannsen, and A. T. Levin. 2011. "Are Long-Run Inflation Expectations Anchored More Firmly in the Euro Area Than in the United States?" *American Economic Journal: Macroeconomics* 3 (2): 104-29.

Benati, L. 2008. "Investigating Inflation Persistence across Monetary Regimes." *Quarterly Journal of Economics* 123 (3): 1005-60.

Benes, J., K. Clinton, A. George, J. John, O. Kamenik, D. Laxton, P. Mitra, G. V. Nadhanael, H. Wang, and F. Zhang. 2017. "Inflation-Forecast Targeting for India: An Outline of the Analytical Framework." IMF Working Paper 17/32, International Monetary Fund, Washington, DC.

Benigno, P., and L. Ricci. 2011. "The Inflation-Output Trade-Off with Downward Wage Rigidities." *American Economic Review* 101 (4): 1436-66.

Bernanke, B. S. 2007. "Inflation Expectations and Inflation Forecasting." Speech at the Monetary Economics Workshop of the National Bureau of Economic Research Summer Institute, Cambridge, MA, July 10.

———, T. Laubach, F. S. Mishkin, and A. S. Posen. 2001. *Inflation Targeting: Lessons from the International Experience.* Princeton, NJ: Princeton University Press.

Blanchard, O. 2016. "The Phillips Curve: Back to the '60s." *American Economic Review: Papers & Proceedings* 106 (5): 31-34.

———, E. Cerutti, and L. Summers. 2015. "Inflation and Activity - Two Explorations and Their Monetary Policy Implications." NBER Working Paper 21726, National Bureau of Economic Research, Cambridge, MA.

Bognanski, J., A. A. Tombini, and S. R. C. Werlang. 2000. "Implementing Inflation Targeting in Brazil." Working Paper 1, Central Bank of Brazil, Brasilia.

Bordo, M., and P. Siklos. 2014. "Central Bank Credibility, Reputation and Inflation Targeting in Historical Perspective." Working Paper 20693, National Bureau of Economic Research, Cambridge, MA.

———. 2017. "Central Bank Credibility before and after the Crisis." *Open Economies Review* 28 (1): 19-45.

Borio, C., and A. Filardo. 2007. "Globalisation and Inflation: New Cross-Country Evidence on the Global Determinants of Domestic Inflation." BIS Working Paper 227, Bank for International Settlements, Basel.

Bulíř, A., K. Šmídková, V. Kotlán, and D. Navrátil. 2008. "Inflation Targeting and Communication: It Pays Off to Read Inflation Reports." Working Paper 08/234, International Monetary Fund, Washington, DC.

Buono, I., and S. Formai. 2018. "New Evidence on the Evolution of the Anchoring of Inflation Expectations." *Journal of Macroeconomics* 57 (C): 39-54.

Calvo, G. 1983. "Staggered Prices in a Utility-Maximizing Framework." *Journal of Monetary Economics* 12 (3): 383-98.

Calza, A. 2009. "Globalization, Domestic Inflation and Global Output Gaps: Evidence from the Euro Area." *International Finance* 12 (3): 301-20.

Capistrán, C., and M. Ramos-Francia. 2010. "Does Inflation Targeting Affect the Dispersion of Inflation Expectations?" *Journal of Money, Credit and Banking* 42 (1): 113-34.

Carrasco, A., and J. Ferreiro. 2013. "Inflation Targeting and Inflation Expectations in Mexico." *Applied Economics* 45 (10): 3295-3304.

Carroll, C. D. 2003. "Macroeconomic Expectations of Households and Professional Forecasters." *Quarterly Journal of Economics* 118 (1): 269-98.

Central Bank of Chile. 2004. "Monetary Policy Report: January 2004." Central Bank of Chile, Santiago.

Cerisola, M., and G. Gelos. 2009. "What Drives Inflation Expectations in Brazil? An Empirical Analysis." *Applied Economics* 41 (10): 1215-27.

Céspedes, L. F., R. Chang, and A. Velasco. 2014. "Is Inflation Targeting Still on Target?" *International Finance* 17 (2): 185-207.

Céspedes, L. F., and C. Soto. 2005. "Credibility and Inflation Targeting in an Emerging Market: Lessons from the Chilean Experience." *International Finance* 8 (3): 545-75.

Chinn, M., and H. Ito. 2017. "The Chinn-Ito Index: A De Jure Measure of Financial Openness." http://web.pdx.edu/~ito/Chinn-Ito_website.htm.

Choi, I. 2001. "Unit Root Tests for Panel Data." *Journal of International Money and Finance* 20 (2): 249-72.

Christelis, D., G. D. Georgarakos, T. Jappelli, and M. van Rooij. 2016. "Trust in the Central Bank and Inflation Expectations." DNB Working Papers 537, Netherlands Central Bank, Amsterdam.

Christiansen, I., F. Dion, and C. Reid. 2004. "Real Return Bonds, Inflation Expectations, and the Break-Even Inflation Rate." Working Paper 2004-43, Bank of Canada, Ottawa.

Christoffersen, P., T. Slok, and R. Wescott. 2001. "Is Inflation Targeting Feasible in Poland? *Economics of Transition* 9 (1): 153-74.

Ciccarelli, M., J. A. Garcia, and C. Montes-Galdón. 2017. "Unconventional Monetary Policy and the Anchoring of Inflation Expectations." Working Paper 1995, European Central Bank, Frankfurt am Main.

Clark, T., and T. Nakata. 2008. "Has the Behavior of Inflation and Long-Term Inflation Expectations Changed?" *Federal Reserve Bank of Kansas City Economic Review* 93 (1): 17-50.

Cogley, T., and A. Sbordone. 2008. "Trend Inflation, Indexation, and Inflation Persistence in the New Keynesian Phillips Curve." *American Economic Review* 98 (5): 2101-26.

Coibion, O., and Y. Gorodnichenko. 2012. "What Can Survey Forecasts Tell Us about Information Rigidities?" *Journal of Political Economy* 120 (1): 116-59.

———. 2015 "Is the Phillips Curve Alive and Well after All? Inflation Expectations and the Missing Disinflation." *American Economic Journal: Macroeconomics* 7 (1): 197-232.

Coibion, O., Y. Gorodnichenko, and R. Kamdar. 2018. "The Formation of Expectations, Inflation, and the Phillips Curve." *Journal of Economic Literature.*

———. Forthcoming. "How Do Firms Form Their Expectations? New Survey Evidence." *American Economic Review* 108 (9): 2671-2713.

———, and M. Pedemonte. 2018. "Inflation Expectations as a Policy Tool?" NBER Working Paper 24788, National Bureau of Economic Research, Cambridge, MA.

Corbo, V. 2005. "Monetary Policy under Inflation Targeting in Chile and around the World." Speech at the 9th Annual Conference of the Central Bank of Chile, Santiago, October 20.

Cortes, G., and C. A. C. Paiva. 2017. "Deconstructing Credibility: The Breaking of Monetary Policy Rules in Brazil." *Journal of International Money and Finance* 74 (June): 31-52.

Cunningham, R., B. Desroches, and E. Santor. 2010. "Inflation Expectations and the Conduct of Monetary Policy: A Review of Recent Evidence and Experience." *Bank of Canada Review* (Spring): 13-25.

Davis, J. S. 2014. "Inflation Targeting and the Anchoring of Inflation Expectations: Cross-Country Evidence from Consensus Forecasts." Globalization and Monetary Policy Institute Working Paper 174, Federal Reserve Bank of Dallas, Dallas, TX.

De Gregorio, J. 2009a. "Inflation Targeting and Financial Crises." Speech at the at the Seminar on Financial Crises, Banco de la República de Colombia and the Fondo de Garantías de Instituciones Financieras de Colombia, Bogota.

———. 2009b. "Chile: Foreign Shocks and Policy Responses." *World Economics* 10 (4): 5-24.

———, A. Tokman, and R. Valdés. 2005. "Flexible Exchange Rate with Inflation Targeting in Chile: Experience and Issues." Working Paper 540, Inter-American Development Bank, Washington, DC.

de Mendonça, H. F., and K. A. Galveas. 2013. "Transparency and Inflation: What Is the Effect on the Brazilian Economy?" *Economic Systems* 37 (1): 69-80.

de Mendonça, H. F., and I. S. Veiga. 2014. "A Note on Openness and Inflation Targeting: Implications for the Unpleasant Fiscal Arithmetic." *Macroeconomic Dynamics* 18 (5): 1187-1207.

De Pooter, M., P. Robitaille, I. Walker, and M. Zdinak. 2014. "Are Inflation Expectations Well Anchored in Brazil, Chile, and Mexico?" *International Journal of Central Banking* 10 (2): 337-400.

Demertzis, M., and M. Viegi. 2008. "Inflation Targets as Focal Points." *International Journal of Central Banking* 4: 55-86.

Dincer, N. N., and B. Eichengreen. 2014. "Central Bank Transparency and Independence: Updates and New Measures." *International Journal of Central Banking* 10 (1): 189-253.

Ehrmann, M. 2015. "Targeting Inflation from Below: How Do Inflation Expectations Behave?" *International Journal of Central Banking* 11 (S1): 213-49.

Eusepi, S., and B. Preston. 2018a. "Central Bank Communication and Expectations Stabilization." *Journal of Economic Literature* 56: 3-59.

———. 2018b. "Fiscal Foundations of Inflation: Imperfect Knowledge." *American Economic Review* 108 (9): 2551-89.

Evans, G., and S. Honkapohja. 2009. "Learning and Macroeconomics." *Annual Review of Economics* 1: 421-49.

Fischer, S. 1977. "Long-Term Contracts, Rational Expectations, and the Optimal Money Supply Rule." *Journal of Political Economy* 85 (1): 191-205.

Forbes, K. 2018. "Has Globalization Changed the Inflation Process?" Paper presented at the 17th Bank for International Settlements Annual Research Conference, Zurich, June 22.

Friedman, B. 1979. "Optimal Expectations and the Extreme Information Assumptions of 'Rational Expectations' Macromodels." *Journal of Monetary Economics* 5 (1): 23-41.

Friedman, M. 1968. "The Role of Monetary Policy." *American Economic Review* 58 (1): 1-17.

Fuhrer, J. C. 1997. "The (Un)Importance of Forward-Looking Behavior in Price Specifications." *Journal of Money, Credit, and Banking* 29 (3): 338-50.

———, and G. Moore. 1995. "Inflation Persistence." *Quarterly Journal of Economics* 110 (1): 127-59.

Gaiotti, E. 2010. "Has Globalization Changed the Phillips Curve? Firm-Level Evidence on the Effect of Activity on Prices." *International Journal of Central Banking* 6 (4): 51-84.

Galati, G., P. Heemeijer, and R. Moessner. 2011. "How Do Inflation Expectations Form? New Insights from a High-Frequency Survey." BIS Working Paper 349, Bank for International Settlements, Basel.

Galati, G., S. Poelhekke, and C. Zhou. 2011. "Did the Crisis Affect Inflation Expectations?" *International Journal of Central Banking* 7 (1): 167-207.

Galí, J., and M. Gertler. 1999. "Inflation Dynamics: A Structural Economic Analysis." *Journal of Monetary Economics* 44 (2): 195-222.

Garcia, J. A., and S. Werner. 2018. "Inflation News and Euro Area Inflation Expectations." IMF Working Paper 18/167, International Monetary Fund, Washington, DC.

Garnier, C., E. Mertens, and E. Nelson. 2015. "Trend Inflation in Advanced Economies." *International Journal of Central Banking* 11 (4): 65-136.

Georgiadis, G. 2016. "Determinants of Global Spillovers from U.S. Monetary Policy." *Journal of International Money and Finance* 67 (C): 41-61.

Giavazzi, F., I. Goldfajn, and S. Herrera. 2005. *Inflation Targeting, Debt, and the Brazilian Experience, 1999 to 2003.* Cambridge, MA: MIT Press.

Gottschalk, J., and D. Moore. 2001. "Implementing Inflation Targeting Regimes: The Case of Poland." *Journal of Comparative Economics* 29 (1): 24-39.

Grishchenko, O., S. Mouabbi, and J.-P. Renne. 2017. "Measuring Inflation Anchoring and Uncertainty: A US and Euro Area Comparison." Finance and Economics Discussion Series 2017-002, Board of Governors of the Federal Reserve System, Washington, DC.

Grothe, M., and A. Meyler. 2018. "Inflation Forecasts: Are Market-Based and Survey-Based Measures Informative?" *International Journal of Financial Research* 9 (1): 171-88.

Gupta, A. S. 2008. "Does Capital Account Openness Lower Inflation?" *International Economic Journal* 22: 471-87.

Gürkaynak, R. S., A. Levin, and E. Swanson. 2010. "Does Inflation Targeting Anchor Long-Run Inflation Expectations? Evidence from the U.S., UK, and Sweden." *Journal of the European Economic Association* 8 (6): 1208-42.

Hawtrey, R. G. 1923. *Monetary Reconstruction.* London: Longmans, Green and Co.

Hördahl, P. 2009. "Disentangling the Drivers of Recent Shifts in Break-Even Inflation Rates." *BIS Quarterly Review* (March): 10-11.

Ihrig, J., S. B. Kamin, D. Lindner, and J. Marquez. 2010. "Some Simple Tests of the Globalization and Inflation Hypothesis." *International Finance* 13 (3): 343-75.

Ilzetzki, E., C. Reinhart, and K. Rogoff. 2017. "Exchange Arrangements Entering the 21st Century: Which Anchor Will Hold?" NBER Working Paper 23134, National Bureau of Economic Research, Cambridge, MA.

Im, K. S., M. H. Pesaran, and Y. Shin. 2003. "Testing for Unit Roots in Heterogeneous Panels." *Journal of Econometrics* 115 (1): 53-74.

IMF (International Monetary Fund). 2015. "Brazil: 2014 Article IV Consultation." IMF, Washington, DC.

———. 2016. "Global Disinflation in an Era of Constrained Monetary Policy." In *World Economic Outlook,* 121-70. Washington, DC: IMF.

———. 2018. "Challenges for Monetary Policy in Emerging Markets as Global Financial Conditions Normalize." *World Economic Outlook*. Washington, DC: IMF.

Iossifov, P., and J. Podpiera. 2014. "Are Non-Euro Area EU Countries Importing Low Inflation from the Euro Area?" Working Paper 14/191, International Monetary Fund, Washington, DC.

Johnson, D. R. 2003. "The Effect of Inflation Targets on the Level of Expected Inflation in Five Countries." *Review of Economics and Statistics* 85: 1076-81.

Jonas, J., and F. Mishkin. 2003. "Inflation Targeting in Transition Countries: Experience and Prospects." Working Paper 9667, National Bureau of Economic Research, Cambridge, MA.

Jonung, L. 1981. "Perceived and Expected Rates of Inflation in Sweden." *American Economic Review* 71 (5): 961-68.

Kabundi, A., E. Schaling, and M. Some. 2015. "Monetary Policy and Heterogeneous Inflation Expectations in South Africa." *Economic Modelling* 45 (February): 109-17.

Keynes, J. M. 1936. *The General Theory of Employment, Interest and Money*. London: Macmillan.

———. 1940. *How to Pay for the War: A Radical Plan for the Chancellor of the Exchequer*. London: Macmillan and Co.

Kose, M. A., E. Prasad, K. Rogoff, and S.-J. Wei. 2010. "Financial Globalization and Economic Policies." In *Handbook of Development Economics*, Volume 5, edited by D. Rodrik and M. Rosenzweig, 4283-362. Oxford, U.K.: North-Holland.

Kumar, S., H. Afrouzi, O. Coibion, and Y. Gorodnichenko. 2015 "Inflation Targeting Does Not Anchor Inflation Expectations: Evidence from Firms in New Zealand." *Brookings Papers on Economic Activity* 2: 151-225.

Lei, C., Z. Lu, and C. Zhang. 2015. "News on Inflation and the Epidemiology of Inflation Expectations in China." *Economic Systems* 39 (4): 644-53.

Levy Yeyati, E., F. Sturzenegger, and I. Reggio. 2010. "On the Endogeneity of Exchange Rate Regimes." *European Economic Review* 54 (5): 659-77.

Lledó, V., S. Yoon, X. Fang, S. Mbaye, and Y. Kim. 2017. "Fiscal Rules at a Glance." Background paper, International Monetary Fund, Washington, DC.

López Vicente, F., and J. M. Serena Garralda. 2014. "Macroeconomic Policy in Brazil: Inflation Targeting, Public Debt Structure and Credit Policies." Occasional Paper 1405, Banco de España, Madrid.

Lucas, R. E. 1972. "Expectations and the Neutrality of Money." *Journal of Economic Theory* 4 (2): 103-24.

Maćkowiak, B., and M. Wiederholt. 2009. "Optimal Sticky Prices under Rational Inattention." *American Economic Review* 99 (3): 769-803.

Maddala, G. S., and S. Wu. 1999. "A Comparative Study of Unit Root Tests with Panel Data and a New Simple Test." *Oxford Bulletin of Economics and Statistics* 61 (S1): 631-52.

Malmendier, U., and S. Nagel. 2016. "Learning from Inflation Experiences." *The Quarterly Journal of Economics* 131 (1): 53-87.

Mankiw, N. G., and R. Reis. 2002. “Sticky Information versus Sticky Prices: A Proposal to Replace the New Keynesian Phillips Curve.” *Quarterly Journal of Economics* 117 (4): 1295-1328.

———. 2018. “Friedman’s Presidential Address in the Evolution of Macroeconomic Thought.” *Journal of Economic Perspectives* 32 (1): 81-96.

———, and J. Wolfers. 2003. “Disagreement about Inflation Expectations.” In *NBER Macroeconomics Annual,* Volume 18, edited by M. Gertler and K. Rogoff, 209-48. Cambridge, MA: MIT Press.

Martínez-Garcia, E. 2017. “Good Policies or Good Luck? New Insights on Globalization and the International Monetary Policy Transmission Mechanism.” *Computational Economics* 1-36.

Mehrotra, A., and J. Yetman. Forthcoming. “Decaying Expectations: What Inflation Forecasts Tell Us about the Anchoring of Inflation Expectations.” *International Journal of Central Banking.*

Mertens, E. 2016. “Measuring the Level and Uncertainty of Trend Inflation.” *The Review of Economics and Statistics* 98 (5): 950-67.

Miles, D., U. Panizza, R. Reis, and Á. Ubide. 2017. “And Yet It Moves: Inflation and the Great Recession.” Geneva Reports on the World Economy 19, Centre for Economic Policy Research, London.

Minella, A., P. Springer de Freitas, I. Goldfajn, and M. Kfoury Muinhos. 2003. “Inflation Targeting in Brazil: Constructing Credibility under Exchange Rate Volatility.” *Journal of International Money and Finance* 22 (7): 1015-40.

Mishkin, F. 2004. “Can Inflation Targeting Work in Emerging Market Countries?” Working Paper 10646, National Bureau of Economic Research, Cambridge, MA.

———. 2007. *Monetary Policy Strategy.* Cambridge, MA: MIT Press.

Mishkin, F., and M. Savastano. 2002. “Monetary Policy Strategy for Emerging Market Countries: Lessons from Latin America.” *Comparative Economic Studies* 24 (2): 45-82.

Miyajima, K., and J. Yetman. 2018. “Inflation Expectations Anchoring across Different Types of Agents: The Case of South Africa.” IMF Working Paper 18/177, International Monetary Fund, Washington, DC.

Morandé, F. 2002. “A Decade of Inflation Targeting in Chile: Developments, Lessons, and Challenges.” In *Inflation Targeting: Design, Performance, Challenges*, 583-626. Santiago: Central Bank of Chile.

National Bank of Poland. 1998. “Medium-Term Strategy of Monetary Policy, 1999–2003.” Monetary Policy Council, National Bank of Poland, Warsaw.

———. 2003. “Monetary Policy Strategy beyond 2003.” Monetary Policy Council, National Bank of Poland, Warsaw.

———. 2016. “Report on Monetary Policy Implementation in 2015.” National Bank of Poland, Warsaw.

Patra, M. D., and P. Ray. 2010. “Inflation Expectations and Monetary Policy in India: An Empirical Exploration.” IMF Working Paper 10/84, International Monetary Fund, Washington, DC.

Pedroni, P. 1999. "Critical Values for Cointegration Tests in Heterogeneous Panels with Multiple Regressors." *Oxford Bulletin of Economics and Statistics* 61 (S1): 653-70.

———. 2000. "Fully-Modified OLS for Heterogeneous Cointegrated Panels." *Advances in Econometrics* 15: 93-130.

———. 2001. "Purchasing Power Parity Tests in Cointegrated Panels." *The Review of Economics and Statistics* 83 (4): 727–31.

Phelps, E. S. 1967. "Phillips Curves, Expectations of Inflation and Optimal Unemployment Over Time." *Economica* 34 (135): 254–281.

Phillips, A.W. 1958. "The Relationship between Unemployment and the Rate of Change of Money Wage Rates in the United Kingdom, 1861–1957." *Economica* 25 (100): 283-99.

Polański, Z. 2004. "Poland and the European Union: The Monetary Policy Dimension: Monetary Policy before Poland's Accession to the European Union." *Bank i Kredyt* 5: 4-18.

Reid, M. 2009. "The Sensitivity of South African Inflation Expectations to Surprises." *South African Journal of Economics* 77: 414–429.

Rogoff, K. 2006. "Impact of Globalization on Monetary Policy." Paper prepared for the Federal Reserve of Kansas City Jackson Hole Conference, "The New Economic Geography: Effects and Policy Implications," Jackson Hole, WY, August 24-26.

Romer, D. 1993. "Openness and Inflation: Theory and Evidence." *The Quarterly Journal of Economics* 108 (4): 869-903.

Rotemberg, J. 1982. "Sticky Prices in the United States." *Journal of Political Economy* 90 (6): 1187-211.

Samuelson, P., and R. Solow. 1960. "Analytical Aspects of Anti-Inflation Policy." *American Economic Review Papers and Proceedings* 50 (2): 177-94.

Sargent, T., and N. Wallace. 1975. "'Rational' Expectations, the Optimal Monetary Instrument, and the Optimal Money Supply Rule." *Journal of Political Economy* 83 (2): 241-54.

———. 1976. "Rational Expectations and the Theory of Economic Policy." *Journal of Monetary Economics* 2 (2): 169-83.

Schaechter, A., M. R. Stone, and M. Zelmer. 2000. "Adopting Inflation Targeting: Practical Issues for Emerging Market Countries." Occasional Paper 202, International Monetary Fund, Washington, DC.

Schmidt-Hebbel, K., and M. Tapia. 2002. "Inflation Targeting in Chile." *North American Journal of Economics and Finance* 13 (2): 125-46.

Shambaugh. J. 2004. "The Effect of Fixed Exchange Rates on Monetary Policy." *Quarterly Journal of Economics* 119 (1): 301-52.

Sims, C. A. 2003. "Implications of Rational Inattention." *Journal of Monetary Economics* 50 (3): 665-90.

Sousa, R., and J. Yetman. 2016. "Inflation Expectations and Monetary Policy." BIS Paper 89d, Bank for International Settlements, Basel.

Stock, J., and M. Watson. 2007. "Why Has U.S. Inflation Become Harder to Forecast?" *Journal of Money, Credit and Banking* 39 (1): 3-33.

———. 2016. "Core Inflation and Trend Inflation." *Review of Economics and Statistics* 98 (4): 770-84.

Strohsal, T., R. Melnick, and D. Nautz. 2016. "The Time-Varying Degree of Inflation Expectations Anchoring." *Journal of Macroeconomics* 48 (June): 62-71.

Strohsal, T., and L. Winkelmann. 2015. "Assessing the Anchoring of Inflation Expectations." *Journal of International Money and Finance* 50 (C): 33-48.

Taylor, J. 1980. "Aggregate Dynamics and Staggered Contracts." *Journal of Political Economy* 88 (1): 1-23.

Tytell, I., and S.-J. Wei. 2004. "Does Financial Globalization Induce Better Macroeconomic Policies?" IMF Working Paper 04/84, International Monetary Fund, Washington, DC.

Valdés, R. 2007. "Inflation Targeting in Chile: Experience and Selected Issues." Economic Policy Paper 22, Central Bank of Chile, Santiago.

Woodford, M. 2002. "Imperfect Common Knowledge and the Effects of Monetary Policy." In *Knowledge, Information, and Expectations in Modern Macroeconomics: In Honor of Edmund S. Phelps*, edited by P. Aghion, R. Frydman, J. Stiglitz, and M. Woodford. Princeton, NJ: Princeton University Press.

———. 2003. *Interest and Prices: Foundations of a Theory of Monetary Policy*. Princeton, NJ: Princeton University Press.

———. 2005. "Central-Bank Communication and Policy Effectiveness." NBER Working Paper 24788, National Bureau of Economic Research, Cambridge, MA.

World Bank. 2018. *Global Economic Prospects: Broad-Based Upturn, but for How Long?* Washington, DC: World Bank.

Yetman, J. 2017. "The Evolution of Inflation Expectations in Canada and the US." *Canadian Journal of Economics* 50 (5): 711-37.

CHAPTER 5
Inflation and Exchange Rate Pass-Through

The degree to which domestic prices adjust to exchange rate movements is key to understanding inflation dynamics, and hence to guiding monetary policy decisions. However, the exchange rate pass-through to inflation varies considerably across countries and over time. This chapter brings to light two fundamental factors accounting for these variations: the nature of the shock triggering currency movements and country-specific characteristics. First, an empirical investigation demonstrates that different domestic and global shocks can be associated with widely different pass-through ratios. This underscores the need to consider the underlying causes of currency movements before evaluating their impact on inflation. Second, country characteristics matter, including policy frameworks that govern monetary policy responses, as well as other structural features that affect an economy's sensitivity to currency fluctuations. Pass-through ratios tend to be lower in countries that combine flexible exchange rate regimes and credible inflation targets. The empirical results also suggest that central bank independence can greatly facilitate the task of stabilizing inflation following large currency movements and allows fuller use of the exchange rate as a buffer against external shocks.

Introduction

Exchange rate fluctuations are an important driver of inflation and could therefore have significant implications for the formulation of monetary policy (Fischer 2015; Forbes 2015; Mishkin 2008). The expected impact of currency movements on consumer prices will determine how the central bank should react to them. In particular, monetary authorities might look beyond the price-level effect of an exchange rate movement but may choose to respond if the impact on inflation is persistent. The risk of policy missteps if the pass-through is not properly evaluated is particularly elevated in emerging market and developing economies (EMDEs), where large currency movements are more frequent and central banks have a greater propensity to respond to them (Calvo and Reinhart 2002; Ball and Reyes 2008). This highlights the importance of correctly assessing the exchange rate pass-through ratio (ERPTR) to inflation—defined in this chapter as the percentage increase in consumer prices associated with a 1 percent depreciation of the effective exchange rate after one year.

A rich literature has demonstrated that currency movements are only partially transmitted to domestic prices, with effects dissipating through the production

Note: This chapter was prepared by Jongrim Ha, Marc Stocker, and Hakan Yilmazkuday. Background materials were provided by Sergiy Kasyanenko.

chain. The pass-through to consumer prices goes through various channels, from direct effects through energy and other commodity prices, to indirect effects through import prices, wage formation, and profit markups (Bacchetta and van Wincoop 2003; Burstein and Gopinath 2014; Ito and Sato 2008; McCarthy 2007). Even in the case of internationally traded goods, different forms of market segmentation and/or nominal rigidities may explain incomplete pass-through (see Box 5.1 for a literature review).

Many structural factors have been associated with a lower sensitivity of domestic prices to exchange rate movements, including the degree of competition among importing and exporting firms (Amiti, Itskhoki, and Konings 2016), the frequency of price adjustments (Devereux and Yetman 2003; Corsetti, Dedola, and Leduc 2008; Gopinath and Itskhoki 2010), the composition of trade (Campa and Goldberg 2010), the level of participation in global value chains (GVCs; Georgiadis, Gräb, and Khalil 2017), the share of trade invoiced in foreign currencies (Casas et al. 2017; Gopinath 2015), and the use of currency hedging instruments (Amiti, Itskhoki, and Konings 2014). A credible monetary policy framework that supports well-anchored inflation expectations has also been viewed as an effective way to reduce the pass-through to consumer prices (Carriere-Swallow et al. 2016; Gagnon and Ihrig 2004; Reyes 2004; Schmidt-Hebbel and Tapia 2002; Taylor 2000).

Beyond structural factors and country characteristics, the nature of the macroeconomic shock that triggers an exchange rate movement plays a key role in determining the size of the associated pass-through (Comunale and Kunovac 2017; Forbes, Hjortsoe, and Nenova 2017; Shambaugh 2008). This reflects the fact that shocks impacting the exchange rate concurrently affect activity, markups, productivity, and several other factors that influence price formation and inflation expectations. It is thus likely that the extent of estimated ERPTRs will vary widely depending on the shock that triggers them—a possibility that most empirical studies have not taken into account.

This chapter contributes to a recent strand of the literature that emphasizes the importance of identifying underlying shocks to assess the transmission of exchange rate movements to inflation and, therefore, to formulate the correct monetary policy response. For instance, if the ERPTR associated with monetary policy changes is higher than the one associated with other types of shocks, there is a risk that a central bank might underestimate the exchange rate channel of its actions and maintain an excessively tight (or loose) monetary policy stance relative to what is needed to stabilize inflation and output. This may lead to unnecessary fluctuations in activity and make the anchoring of inflation expectations more difficult to achieve over time.

BOX 5.1 Exchange rate pass-through: A review

Many studies have estimated the exchange rate pass-through to inflation, producing a wide range of estimates depending on country characteristics as well as the type of shocks that trigger the exchange rate changes.

Properly measuring the exchange rate pass-through is important for forecasting inflation and setting monetary policy. Earlier studies generally estimated the exchange rate pass-through ratio (ERPTR) in a reduced-form framework, treating exchange rate movements as exogenous rather than considering the underlying shocks behind such movements.

A group of recent studies emphasizes that different shocks can be associated with widely different ERPTRs. These studies usually identify underlying shocks in structural vector autoregression (SVAR) models, highlighting heterogeneity in the direction and magnitude of ERPTRs, depending on the nature of the shocks and country characteristics (Shambaugh 2008; Forbes, Hjortsoe, and Nenova 2017).

Explanatory factors include the monetary policy regime, level of central bank credibility, trade and financial market openness, degree of participation in global value chains, and structural features of product and labor markets.

Against this background, this box addresses the following questions:

- What are the theoretical underpinnings of partial exchange rate pass-throughs to inflation?
- How do pass-throughs vary depending on the source of shocks?
- What are the key country characteristics affecting pass-throughs?

What are the theoretical underpinnings of partial exchange rate pass-throughs to inflation?

An incomplete adjustment of prices to exchange rate movements can arise in the presence of international market segmentation for traded goods, because of various trade frictions or firms' ability to practice price discrimination across international locations. Nominal rigidities may also help explain the persistence of such deviations over time and lead to a declining ERPTR across the production chain.

Price discrimination by firms. Producers' ability to have different pricing strategies across different segments of international markets is a key feature

BOX 5.1 Exchange rate pass-through: A review (*continued*)

of most theoretical models of partial ERPTRs. In particular, the pricing-to-market literature (originally developed by Krugman 1987 and Dornbusch 1987) places monopolistic firms at the center of international price discrimination. Exporters can adjust their markups over marginal cost across different destinations to take into account the demand conditions and price elasticities encountered in each market (Froot and Klemperer 1989; Auer and Chaney 2009). In general, models with heterogeneous consumers give rise to more flexible demand systems that allow for "optimal" international price discrimination with incomplete ERPTRs (Goldberg and Hellerstein 2008; Hellerstein 2008; Goldberg and Verboven 2001; Nakamura and Zerom 2010).

Endogenous firm selection. International trade models of cross-border production networks have provided further rationale for partial ERPTRs. In these models, macroeconomic shocks produce a new, endogenously determined distribution of firms, impacting pricing strategies and aggregate ERPTRs (Bernard et al. 2003; Chaney 2008; Eaton, Kortum, and Kramarz 2011; Mayer, Melitz, and Ottaviano 2014; Melitz and Ottaviano 2008; Rodriguez-Lopez 2011). More competitive and productive firms, which also tend to source more of their inputs internationally, have a larger market share, which lowers average pass-throughs and deepens global value chain integration (Amiti, Itskhoki, and Konings 2014; de Soyres et al. 2018; Gopinath and Neiman 2014).

Nominal rigidities. Nominal rigidities in local-currency pricing can account for a less than full pass-through, even when markups are constant. When prices are sticky, the currency of invoices will determine the rate of pass-through (Choudhri and Hakura 2015; Devereux, Engel, and Storgaard 2004; Bacchetta and van Wincoop 2005; Gopinath and Itskhoki 2010; Flodén and Wilander 2006). In models with nominal price rigidities, producers opt to invoice in the currency of the origin or destination, depending on the desired ERPTRs. Exporters facing stronger competition in the destination markets may choose to invoice in local currencies to keep prices stable relative to competitors, thus reducing the overall exchange rate pass-through.

Nontradable input costs. Local nontradable inputs are relatively immune to exchange rate movements, which tend to lower the exchange rate pass-through to consumer prices. In particular, distribution costs drive a significant wedge between producer and retail prices (Burstein, Neves, and

BOX 5.1 Exchange rate pass-through: A review (*continued*)

Rebelo 2003; Corsetti and Dedola 2005; Berger et al. 2012). Models with consumer search (Alessandria 2009; Alessandria and Kaboski 2011) and inventories (Alessandria, Kaboski, and Midrigan 2010) work in a broadly similar fashion by creating a disconnect between the border and consumer prices of imported goods.

How do pass-throughs vary depending on the source of shocks?

Although structural features play an important role in determining ERPTRs, the nature of the macroeconomic shocks behind exchange rate movements has been increasingly emphasized as a determining factor (Forbes, Hjortsoe, and Nenova 2017). Shocks can act concurrently on inflation and exchange rates, with varying implications for ERPTRs. In a literature review, Goldberg and Knetter (1997) document that estimated exchange rate pass-throughs depend critically on how well identified the sources of the exchange rate movements are.

Shambaugh (2008) takes this argument a step further by systematically categorizing exchange rate pass-throughs by type of shock. He estimates a vector autoregression model with long-run identifying restrictions on industrial production, the real exchange rate, consumer prices, the nominal exchange rate, and import prices for 11 mostly advanced economies. ERPTRs after one year are estimated for shocks to domestic supply, domestic demand, domestic prices, foreign prices, and import prices. A *foreign price* shock has a smaller pass-through rate, close to 0.5, as does a *domestic demand* shock, at around 0.4.

Forbes, Hjortsoe, and Nenova (2017, 2018) apply a five-variable SVAR with short- and long-term identifying restrictions to the United Kingdom and 26 small, open economies with de facto floating exchange rates during 1990-2015. They estimate sizable ERPTRs in responses to domestic monetary policy shocks but modest ones in response to domestic demand shocks. Their estimates of ERPTRs following global shocks (permanent and transitory) are quite heterogeneous across countries (Figure 5.1.1). Borensztein and Queijo (2016) follow a broadly similar approach for a group of South American countries; Comunale and Kunovac (2017) for Euro Area countries; Cunningham et al. (2017) for a sample of advanced economies; and Ca'Zorzi, Hahn, and Sanchez (2007) for 12 emerging market and developing economies (EMDEs).

BOX 5.1 Exchange rate pass-through: A review (*continued*)

Although ERPTRs were historically larger in EMDEs, with currency depreciations often associated with inflation crises and subsequent sharp recessions (Frankel and Rose 1996; Reinhart and Rogoff 2008), they have recently declined in many countries, reflecting the shifting nature of shocks and institutional change (Carriere-Swallow et al. 2016; Forbes, Hjortsoe, and Nenova 2017; Tunç 2017).

FIGURE 5.1.1 Pass-through following different types of shocks

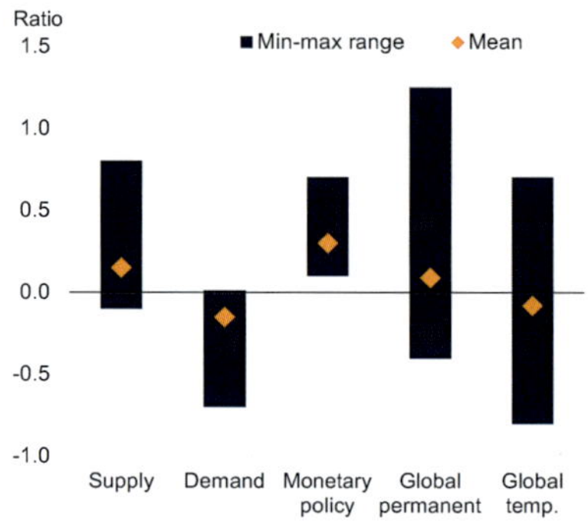

Source: Forbes, Hjortsoe, and Nenova (2017).

Notes: Blue bars depict the range of median shock-dependent pass-through estimates across 26 countries, conditional on the shock causing the exchange rate to move. The first bar shows the estimates after a domestic supply shock, the second after a domestic demand shock, the third after a domestic monetary policy shock, and the fourth and fifth after permanent and temporary global shocks, respectively. The exchange rate pass-through ratios are measured eight quarters after the shock.

What are the key country characteristics affecting pass-throughs?

Many empirical studies focus on the relationship between estimated ERPTRs and country characteristics. In general, greater openness to trade and financial transactions, less credible central banks, more volatile inflation and exchange rates, and lower levels of market competition are associated with higher ERPTRs.

Various studies emphasize trade openness and the composition of imported goods (Campa and Goldberg 2005, 2010), central bank credibility (Taylor 2000; Gagnon and Ihrig 2004; Choudri and Hakura 2006; Mishkin and Schmidt-Hebbel 2007; Coulibaly and Kempf 2010; Caselli and Roitman 2016; Carriere-Swallow et al. 2016), the degree of competition in product markets (Devereux, Tomlin, and Dong 2015; Amiti, Itskhoki, and Konings 2016), inflation volatility (Ca'Zorzi, Hahn, and Sanchez 2007; Forbes, Hjortsoe, and Nenova 2017), and exchange rate volatility (Campa and Goldberg 2005). Other studies focus on microeconomic aspects of price-setting: nominal rigidities (Devereux and Yetman 2003; Corsetti, Dedola, and Leduc 2008); the role of foreign-currency pricing, especially in invoicing (Gopinath, Itskhoki, and Rigobon 2010; Gopinath 2015; Devereux, Tomlin, and Dong 2015); the

BOX 5.1 Exchange rate pass-through: A review (*continued*)

dispersion of price changes (Berger and Vavra 2015); and the frequency of price adjustments (Gopinath and Itskhoki 2010). Korhonen and Wachtel (2006) find that high degrees of dollarization and import penetration accelerated the speed of pass-through in Commonwealth of Independent States countries relative to other emerging markets.

Other research indicates that exchange rate pass-through varies over time and may be subject to regime switching and structural breaks (Ozkan and Erden 2015; Campa and Goldberg 2005; Cunningham et al. 2017; Donayre and Panovska 2016; Khalaf and Kichian 2005). Some studies link this time-varying exchange rate pass-through to the role of domestic factors, such as the changing composition of imports and shifts in monetary policy frameworks, or to external factors, such as the increasing role of China in the global economy (Marazzi et al. 2005; Gust, Leduc, and Vigfusson 2010).

Against this background, this chapter examines the following questions:

- How have exchange rate movements impacted inflation over time?
- How does the pass-through to inflation depend on the underlying shock triggering the exchange rate movement?
- What country characteristics are associated with lower pass-throughs?

To answer these questions, the chapter first examines the extent of the comovement between inflation and exchange rates across 34 advanced economies and 138 EMDEs, including event studies of significant depreciation and appreciation episodes. Second, from a series of factor-augmented vector autoregression (FAVAR) models, the chapter estimates the impact of various global and domestic shocks on exchange rates and inflation, deriving shock-specific pass-through ratios.[1] The models are estimated from a subsample of 55 countries, including 26 EMDEs. Third, it investigates how country characteristics affect pass-through ratios, paying a particular attention to

[1] Defined as the ratio between the one-year cumulative impulse response of consumer price inflation and the one-year cumulative impulse response of the exchange rate change to three domestic shocks (monetary policy, domestic demand, and domestic supply), three global shocks (global demand, global supply, and oil prices), and one residual shock (risk premium).

monetary policy frameworks, participation in GVCs, and foreign-currency invoicing.

The main conclusions are as follows:

- Large depreciation episodes continue to be associated, on average, with more significant increases in consumer price inflation in EMDEs than in advanced economies. Unconditional pass-throughs tend to increase with the size of the depreciation in both country groups.
- The relationship between inflation and currency movements depends on the nature of the underlying shock. Monetary policy shocks are associated with a higher exchange rate pass-through compared to other domestic shocks, and global shocks have widely different effects.
- Pass-throughs are generally lower in countries with more flexible exchange rate regimes and a credible commitment to an inflation target. This, in turn, facilitates the central bank's task of stabilizing inflation and makes exchange rate movements a more effective buffer against external shocks.

The contribution of this chapter to the literature is threefold. First, it utilizes a rich set of results to shed new light on the heterogeneity of pass-through estimates across countries and over time.

Second, it supplements a burgeoning empirical literature linking exchange rate pass-through to underlying shocks in a structural vector autoregression (SVAR) model framework. This contrasts with traditional reduced-form approaches that estimate "average" pass-throughs based on conditioning variables. The estimation of shock-specific pass-throughs refines the analysis of factors affecting the link between exchange rate movements and inflation.

Third, compared to the few preceding studies that have derived state-dependent estimates of ERPTRs (Forbes, Hjortsoe, and Nenova 2017, 2018; Shambaugh 2008), this chapter investigates additional shocks and uses a larger sample of countries. It looks at the impact of three domestic shocks (monetary policy, demand, and supply), three global shocks (demand, supply, and oil price), and a residual shock capturing, among other factors, changing risk premiums. A unique FAVAR framework combining global and domestic developments allows identification of these different shocks in a unified setup. Moreover, the identification strategy uses an efficient algorithm to combine sign and zero restrictions, preserving a certain level of agnosticism (Arias, Rubio-Ramirez, and Waggoner 2014). Finally, compared to previous studies, this chapter is more focused on EMDE-specific characteristics, including monetary policy frameworks, participation in GVCs, and foreign currency invoicing.

The next sections offer key stylized facts about the link between inflation and exchange rate movements, present estimates of shock-specific ERPTRs, and demonstrate the importance of structural factors and country-specific characteristics. The conclusion discusses policy implications and suggests avenues for future research.

Exchange rate movements and inflation

This section examines the historical relationship between changes in the nominal effective (trade-weighted) exchange rate and consumer price inflation. A depreciation (decline in the effective exchange rate) is expected to cause the domestic price of imports to rise and, depending on a host of factors, higher consumer prices (a positive pass-through). The first step in this descriptive analysis examines the impact of large currency movements on consumer price inflation in cross-country event studies. The second step examines the stability of the relationship between inflation and currency movements over time.

Inflation and exchange rate movements: Event study

The event study presented in this section explores episodes of large exchange rate fluctuations, defined as quarterly movements in excess of 5 percent across 34 advanced economies and 138 EMDEs. The rationale for focusing on large currency fluctuations is twofold. First, such episodes are more likely to induce detectable changes in prices throughout the entire production chain. This helps trace factors influencing the exchange rate pass-through across countries. Second, such an event study allows the estimation of the pass-through conditional on the size and direction of the exchange rate movement. A common assumption in the literature is that the relationship between exchange rate movements and inflation is linear and symmetric. However, prices may respond differently to large changes in the exchange rate, and depreciations may generate an asymmetric reaction relative to appreciations. Computing unconditional pass-throughs associated with different types of exchange rate movements can help disentangle these effects.

Overall, depreciations of between 5 and 10 percent per quarter have been associated with a low unconditional pass-through over the past two decades (Figure 5.1). Median estimates of the same quarter pass-through are close to zero in advanced economies and around +0.1 for EMDEs (a 10 percent depreciation in the median EMDE triggers a 1 percent increase in consumer prices after one quarter). Depreciations of between 10 and 20 percent in a given quarter were generally accompanied by a higher pass-through, with median values of +0.1 for advanced economies and +0.2 for EMDEs. Depreciations in excess of 20 percent were associated with pass-throughs of around +0.4 in both groups of countries, but these events have been far less common recently, which reduces the reliability of the estimated pass-throughs.

The event study also confirms a broad-based decline in the pass-through among EMDEs over the past two decades. For depreciations of between 5 and 10 percent, the median pass-through in EMDEs fell by a factor of three from 1980-98 to 1998-2017. This decline came with a reduction in the frequency and severity of currency depreciations. Prior to 1998, large depreciation episodes in EMDEs clustered around periods of U.S. dollar appreciation, often associated with a tightening of U.S. monetary policy. In some cases, these led to full-blown currency or debt crises, particularly in Latin America during the 1980s and the early to mid-1990s, and in Asia during the second half of the 1990s. The reduced frequency of large depreciations and lower unconditional pass-throughs over the past two decades may have common causes: enhanced monetary and fiscal policy frameworks, more flexible exchange rate regimes, accumulations of foreign exchange reserves, lower current account deficits, and better external debt management (Frankel, Parsley, and Wei 2005). Unconditional pass-throughs remained higher among EMDEs with less flexible exchange rate regimes (those devaluing from currency pegs or other forms of currency arrangements) and those without inflation targeting central banks.

Appreciation episodes are generally associated with positive, but lower, pass-throughs compared to depreciations of the same magnitude, with median values of +0.02 for advanced economies and EMDEs for appreciations of between 5 and 10 percent, and only slightly higher for appreciations of between 10 and 20 percent (Figure 5.2). These results may indicate that currency appreciations induce a weaker response from import and consumer prices compared to similar-size depreciations (Brun-Aguerre, Fuertes, and Greenwood-Nimmo 2017). However, large currency appreciations are also rare events, making rigorous conclusions about asymmetric effects difficult to establish in this context. Overall, the results appear to point to the presence of nonlinearities in the relationship between exchange rate movements and inflation, including in EMDEs (Caselli and Roitman 2016).

Inflation and exchange rate correlation: Evolution over time

Although the declining sensitivity of inflation to exchange rate movements has been extensively documented, this relationship is generally assumed to be stable in the short term. However, there is growing evidence that pass-throughs can vary considerably even over short periods of time, making inference from average values unreliable and potentially misleading for policy evaluation and forecasting purposes.

FIGURE 5.1 Pass-through during significant currency depreciations

The median pass-through associated with large currency depreciations declined in EMDEs over the past two decades but remains higher among countries with less flexible exchange rate regimes and without inflation targeting central banks. The frequency and severity of depreciation episodes dropped as well.

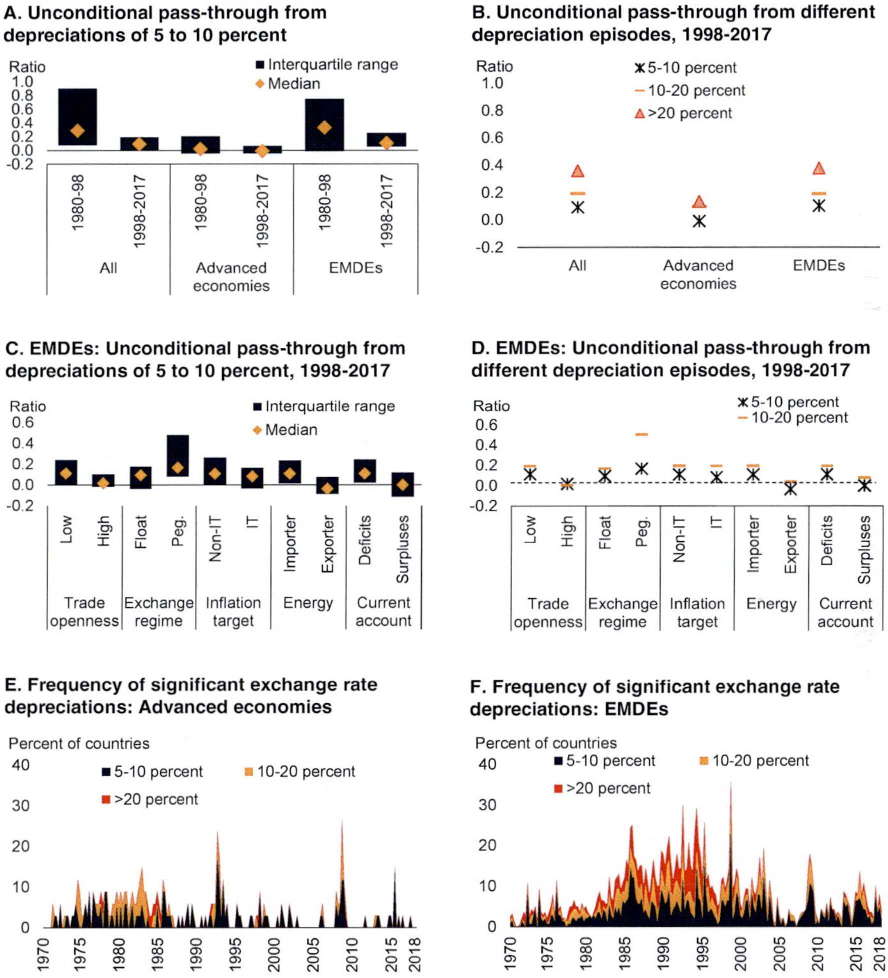

Source: World Bank.

Note: Depreciations are defined as negative quarterly changes in the nominal effective exchange rate. The sample comprises 34 advanced economies and 138 EMDEs. EMDEs = emerging market and developing economies; IMF = International Monetary Fund; IT = inflation targeting.

A.-D. Pass-throughs are defined as the change in consumer prices after one quarter divided by the depreciation of the nominal effective exchange rate. The markers refer to the median pass-through.

A.C. The bars show the interquartile range of pass-throughs.

C.D. Countries with "high" trade openness are defined as those with above median trade-to-GDP ratios; all others are considered to have "low" trade openness. Exchange rate and IT regimes are based on IMF classifications (see the Appendix for details). Energy exporters are defined as in World Bank (2018); all other countries are considered energy importers. Countries with current account deficits are those with a negative average current account balance over 1998-2017.

FIGURE 5.2 Pass-through during significant currency appreciations

The median pass-through associated with significant currency appreciations is low, but such episodes are relatively rare.

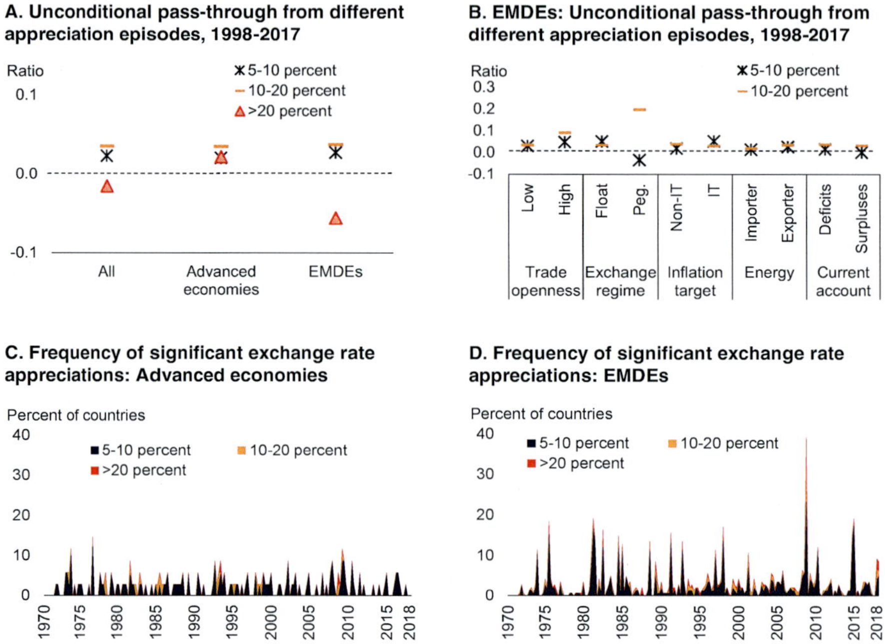

Source: World Bank.

Note: Appreciations are defined as positive quarterly changes in the nominal effective exchange rate. The sample comprises 34 advanced economies and 138 EMDEs. EMDEs = emerging market and developing economies; GDP = gross domestic product; IMF = International Monetary Fund; IT = inflation targeting.

A.B. Pass-throughs are defined as the change in consumer prices after one quarter divided by the cumulative depreciation of the nominal effective exchange rate following significant depreciation episodes. The markers refer to the median pass-through associated with different appreciation episodes.

B. Countries with "high" trade openness are defined as those with above median trade-to-GDP ratios; all others are considered to have "low" trade openness. Exchange rate and IT regimes are based on IMF classifications (see the Appendix for details). Energy exporters are defined as in World Bank (2018); all other countries are considered energy importers. Countries with current account deficits are those with a negative average current account balance over 1998-2017.

This instability in pass-through rates can be illustrated by plotting rolling correlation rates between exchange rate movements and consumer price inflation over time (Figure 5.3).[2] For advanced economies, the median correlation rate became increasingly positive during the late 1990s (+0.4 in

[2] Using a three-year window of the bivariate correlation between the nominal effective exchange rate depreciation rate in one quarter and the inflation rate in the next quarter. For advanced economies and EMDEs, correlation rates tend to peak after one quarter, indicating that exchange rate movements have the strongest impact on inflation with a one-quarter lag.

FIGURE 5.3 Correlations between inflation and nominal effective exchange rate changes

Correlations between inflation and exchange rate movements vary considerably over time.

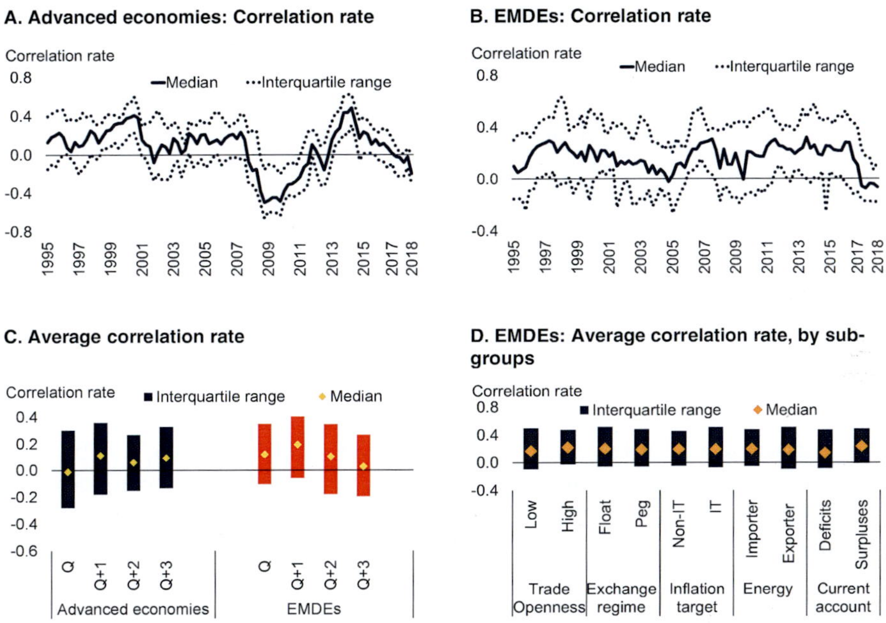

Source: World Bank.

Note: EMDEs = emerging market and developing economies; GDP = gross domestic product; IMF = International Monetary Fund; IT = inflation targeting.

A.B.D. Correlation over a three-year rolling window between inflation and nominal effective exchange rate depreciations after one quarter. The sample includes 51 economies. The median and interquartile range are for three-year window correlation during 1995-2018.

C. Q, Q+1, Q+2, and Q+3 represent the correlation between inflation and nominal effective exchange rate depreciations over the same quarter and after one, two, and three quarters, respectively.

D. Countries with "high" trade openness are defined as those with above median trade-to-GDP ratios; all others are considered to have "low" trade openness. Exchange rate and IT regimes are based on IMF classifications (see the Appendix for details). Energy exporters are defined as in World Bank (2018); all other countries are considered energy importers. Countries with current account deficits are those with a negative average current account balance over 1998-2017.

2000), during the mid-2000s (+0.2 in 2007), and again during the mid-2010s (+0.5 in 2014). These were periods marked by unusually large monetary policy shocks or heightened uncertainty over policy actions, providing some evidence of stronger exchange rate pass-through to inflation during such episodes. In contrast, correlation rates were close to zero during the recovery in the early 2000s and turned significantly negative during the global financial crisis (-0.5 in 2008-09). They were also close to zero during the latest synchronized upturn in 2017-18. These were periods dominated by shifts in domestic or global demand conditions, which appear to be associated with a lower sensitivity of inflation to exchange rate movements.[3] These trends were largely shared across countries, as reflected in similar swings in the upper and lower bands of the interquartile range of country estimates.[4]

Among EMDEs, the median correlation also moved close to zero during the economic recovery in the early 2000s and during the global financial crisis, but it became increasingly positive after 2010 amid deteriorating supply-side conditions in many countries, including commodity exporters facing the end of the commodity supercycle (Baffes et al. 2015).

A wide range of cross-country and time variation in the correlation between exchange rates and inflation is consistent with the notion that different shocks as well as country-specific characteristics can shape the response of inflation to currency movements. These two factors—the source of shocks and country characteristics—are discussed in the next two sections.

Pass-through to inflation and underlying shocks

A recent strand of the literature on the exchange rate pass-through emphasizes the importance of identifying the underlying cause of currency movements (Comunale and Kunovac 2017; Forbes, Hjortsoe, and Nenova 2017, 2018; Shambaugh 2008). For example, a depreciation driven by monetary policy easing could be accompanied by larger increases in inflation, as it raises import prices in the short term and is associated with stronger aggregate demand (and, consequently, an increase in overall pricing pressures) over the medium term. In this case, the pass-through should be expected to be positive and large, as domestic and external forces contribute to higher inflation. In contrast, a depreciation associated with weaker domestic demand could be accompanied by lower inflation over time, as the impact of rising economic slack on domestic prices could outweigh that of higher import prices. In this case, the shock-specific pass-through could be negative. Therefore, the sensitivity of inflation to exchange rate movements can vary considerably depending on the macroeconomic environment and the source of the shocks. This section quantifies differences in pass-through ratios associated with various global and domestic shocks.

Methodology. For this empirical investigation, country-specific FAVAR models were estimated for 29 advanced economies and 26 EMDEs, using quarterly data between 1971 and 2017. The model provides a multivariate, open-economy framework that maps domestic and foreign drivers of inflation and the nominal

---

[3] Sharp movements in oil prices around the global financial crisis also affected the correlation between exchange rate movement and domestic inflation trends around that period.

[4] Range between the 25th and 75th percentile of country estimates.

effective exchange rate. The identification strategy is based on the following assumptions, combining sign and short-term restrictions:[5]

- A positive *domestic demand shock* is assumed to raise domestic output growth and inflation.[6]
- A positive (contractionary) *monetary policy shock* is assumed to cause an exchange rate appreciation, decrease domestic output growth, and reduce inflation.
- A positive *supply shock* is assumed to raise output growth but to lower inflation.
- A positive *global demand shock* triggers a simultaneous upswing in global output growth, global inflation, and oil prices.[7]
- A positive *global supply shock* leads to higher global output growth and oil prices but lower global inflation.
- A positive *oil price shock* induces an increase in oil prices and global inflation but a drop in global output growth.
- *Global shocks* can have contemporaneous effects on domestic variables, but domestic shocks can only influence global variables with a lag.

A two-step procedure is applied to measure shock-specific exchange rate pass-throughs. First, the exchange rate and inflation responses to these shocks are mapped separately from impulse response functions. Second—as in Shambaugh (2008) and Forbes, Hjortsoe, and Nenova (2017, 2018)—the pass-through is defined as the cumulative impulse response of consumer price inflation relative to the impulse response of the effective exchange rate over the same period. The pass-through is measured one year after the initial shock, as in Shambaugh (2008).

A positive pass-through indicates that a shock triggering a currency depreciation is followed by an increase in consumer prices, as is generally expected. A negative value means that a shock triggering a currency depreciation is followed by a decline in consumer prices.

---

[5] Details of the modeling approach are provided in Annex 5.1.

[6] An alternative specification also assumes that positive domestic demand shocks lead to a contemporaneous increase in domestic interest rates. See Annex 5.1 for robustness results.

[7] Global shocks are derived from a separate tri-dimensional vector autoregression model that incorporates global output growth, global inflation, and oil price changes, following the approach of Charnavoki and Dolado (2014) and Uhlig (2005). See Chapter 3 for details.

Exchange rate responses

Since pass-through ratios are defined in this framework as the relative response of consumer prices and the exchange rate to different global and domestic shocks, it is important first to investigate the estimated impact of these shocks on the exchange rate. Empirical studies have shown that fundamentals have some, albeit limited, predictive power over exchange rate movements. These fundamentals include changes in relative business cycle positions, monetary policy stances, risk premiums, and terms of trade (Ca'Zorzi and Rubaszek 2018; Cheung et al. 2017). In particular, periods of domestic output or investment contraction are often associated with currency depreciations (Cordella and Gupta 2015; Landon and Smith 2009; Campa and Goldberg 1999). Monetary policy easing can also lead to currency depreciations, as a declining interest rate differential with the rest of the world tends to put downward pressure on the domestic currency (Chinn and Meredith 2005; Engel 2016). Rising risk premiums and heightened sovereign default risks can also trigger such downward pressures (Foroni, Ravazzolo, and Sadaba 2018). Finally, nominal exchange rates can respond to terms of trade shocks, particularly in commodity exporters with flexible currency regimes (Aizenman, Edwards, Riera-Crichton 2012; Schmitt-Grohé and Uribe 2018).

Impulse responses from the FAVAR model provide a basis for disentangling the impacts of different types of domestic and global shocks on the exchange rate. The results described below are based on a one-year response of the nominal effective exchange rate to one-standard-deviation shocks. Medians and interquartile ranges of country-specific estimates are reported for different groups.[8]

Domestic shocks. Monetary policy tightening leads to currency appreciations in all advanced economies and EMDEs (Figure 5.4). Interest rate driven appreciations are estimated to be larger in EMDEs, particularly among countries with inflation targeting central banks and in some commodity exporters (Brazil, Colombia, and South Africa). Stronger domestic demand causes currency appreciations as well, but the impact is statistically insignificant after one year in most cases.[9] Meanwhile, changes in domestic supply conditions have mixed effects. This is consistent with the literature arguing that productivity shocks have uncertain implications for currency movements (Alfaro et al. 2018; Corsetti, Dedola, and Leduc 2008).

[8] An interquartile range is a range between the 25th to the 75th percentile of country estimates within each country group.

[9] In this chapter, statistical inferences are based on 68 percent confidence intervals.

Global shocks. The median impact of global shocks on the exchange rate is close to zero across countries (Figure 5.5). Obviously, this result is not surprising, because one country's currency depreciation is, by definition, another's appreciation. Still, domestic currency appreciations are more likely to happen in the wake of a positive global demand shock, particularly among EMDEs. This could reflect the fact that the U.S. dollar, which remains the global currency of exchange, generally depreciates during global upturns. A weaker U.S. dollar, in turn, typically supports capital inflows and amplifies appreciations in EMDEs, particularly among countries with current account deficits (Avdjiev et al. 2018). A positive global supply-side shock has mixed effects, with currency depreciations observed among some EMDEs that run current account surpluses (for example, China) and appreciations among some commodity exporters (for example, Brazil, Colombia, Malaysia, and South Africa). Rising oil prices also tend to be associated with currency appreciations in oil-exporting economies and with depreciations in some oil importers.

Relative contributions of global and domestic shocks. On balance, domestic factors are the dominant drivers of exchange rate fluctuations, accounting for about two-thirds of currency movements in advanced economies and more than one-half in EMDEs (Figure 5.6). Although the direction and magnitude of the impact of global shocks varies substantially across countries, these shocks still explain around 7 percent of the variance of currency movements in the median advanced economy and up to 16 percent in the median EMDE. Forbes, Hjortsoe, and Nenova (2017) present similar results, but they attribute a larger share of currency movements to global shocks.[10] About 25 percent of currency movements are accounted for by other shocks, which encompass changes in sovereign and private sector risk premiums. Indeed, shifting expectations about sovereign default risks can have a significant impact on exchange rate dynamics (Alvarez, Atkeson, and Kehoe 2009; Foroni, Ravazzolo, and Sadaba 2018).

Estimated pass-through

Shock-specific ERPTRs are calculated from country-specific FAVAR models as the ratio between the impulse response of inflation and the impulse response of the exchange rate to different shocks after one year. These conditional pass-through ratios can help establish a link between cross-country and time variations in the average ERPTRs and various factors, such as different sensitivities to shocks, changes in the prevalence of some shocks, improved policy frameworks, or other structural factors.

Median estimates of pass-through ratios are reported across different country groups, as well as interquartile ranges across these country groups.

[10] At around 30 percent, on average.

FIGURE 5.4 Exchange rate responses to domestic shocks

Monetary policy tightening and, to a lesser degree, positive domestic demand shocks are accompanied by currency appreciations, particularly among EMDEs that are more open to trade, have more flexible exchange rate regimes, and have inflation targeting central banks.

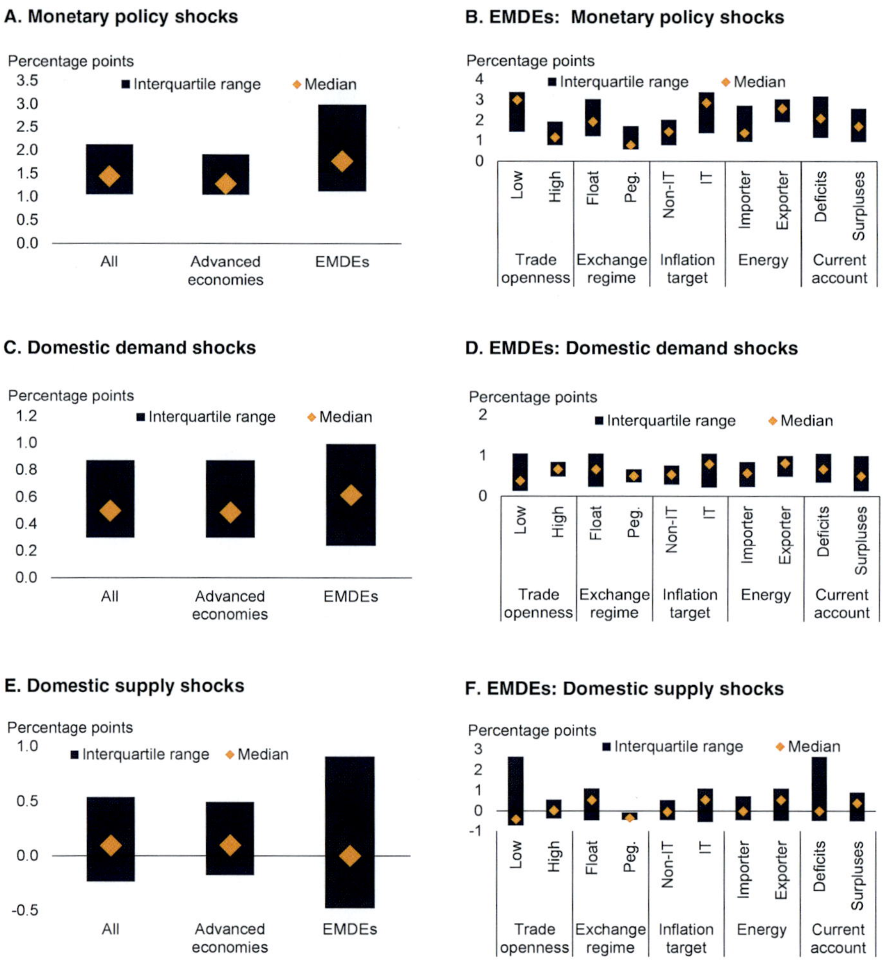

Source: World Bank.

Note: One-year impulse responses of the exchange rate to domestic shocks (monetary policy, domestic demand, and domestic supply) from country-specific factor-augmented vector autoregression models estimated for 29 advanced economies and 26 EMDEs over 1998-2017. Bars show the interquartile range and markers represent the median across countries. A positive number indicates an appreciation. EMDEs = emerging market and developing economies; IMF = International Monetary Fund; IT = inflation targeting.

B.D.F. Countries with "high" trade openness are defined as those with above median trade-to-GDP ratios; all others are considered to have "low" trade openness. Exchange rate and IT regimes are based on IMF classifications (see the Appendix for details). Energy exporters are defined as in World Bank (2018); all other countries are considered energy importers. Countries with current account deficits are those with a negative average current account balance over 1998-2017.

FIGURE 5.5 Exchange rate responses to global shocks

The effect of global shocks on exchange rates has varied considerably across countries. However, strengthening global demand is more often followed by domestic currency appreciations, particularly among EMDEs with floating exchange rate regimes and inflation targeting central banks. Oil price shocks have opposite effects on the exchange rates of energy exporters and energy importers.

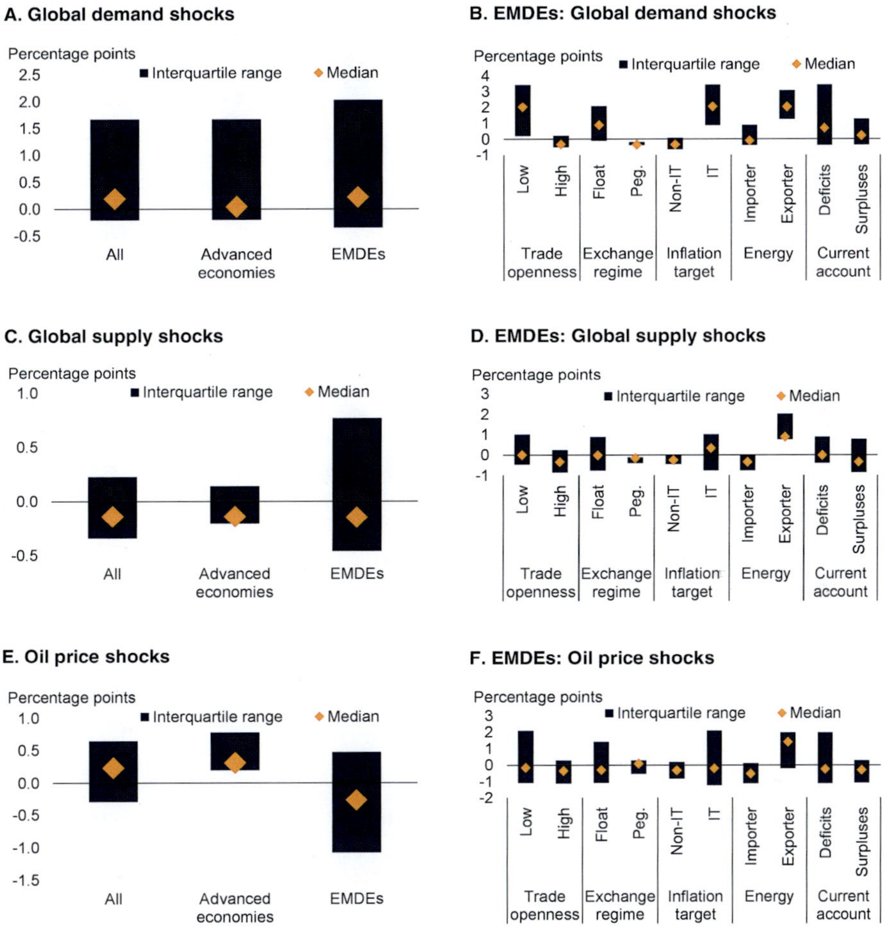

Source: World Bank.

Note: One-year impulse response of the exchange rate to global shocks (demand, supply, and oil prices) from country-specific factor-augmented vector autoregression models estimated for 29 advanced economies and 26 EMDEs over 1998-2017. Bars show the interquartile range and markers represent the median across countries. A positive number indicates an appreciation. EMDEs = emerging market and developing economies; IMF = International Monetary Fund; IT = inflation targeting.

B.D.F. Countries with "high" trade openness are defined as those with above median trade-to-GDP ratios; all others are considered to have "low" trade openness. Exchange rate and IT regimes are based on IMF classifications (see the Appendix for details). Energy exporters are defined as in World Bank (2018); all other countries are considered energy importers. Countries with current account deficits are those with a negative average current account balance over 1998-2017.

FIGURE 5.6 Variance decompositions of exchange rate movements

Domestic shocks account for about two-thirds of the variation in exchange rates in the median advanced economy and more than half in the median EMDE after one year. Monetary policy shocks contributed most to exchange rate variations.

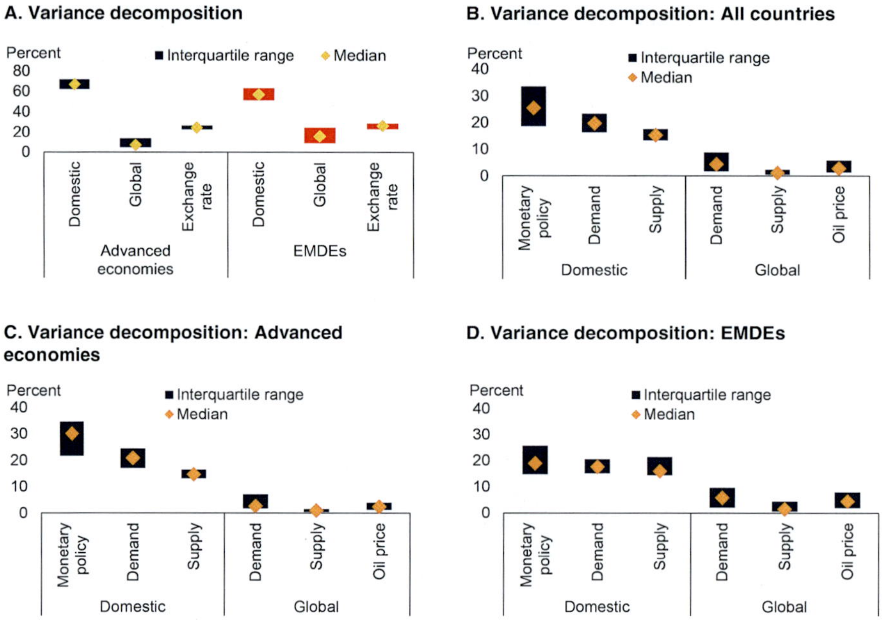

Source: World Bank.

Note: Median share of country-specific exchange rate variance accounted for by global, domestic, and exchange rate shocks based on country-specific factor-augmented vector autoregression models estimated for 29 advanced economies and 26 EMDEs over 1998-2017. Bars show the interquartile range and markers represent the median across economies. EMDEs = emerging market and developing economies.

Domestic shocks. Domestic shocks account for over half the variance of inflation and exchange rates in most countries but are associated with different ERPTRs depending on their source.

Domestic monetary policy shocks are generally associated with large, positive ERPTRs (for example, currency depreciations combined with monetary policy easing are accompanied by significant increases in inflation). Median values since 1998 are estimated to be +0.2 in advanced economies and +0.3 in EMDEs (Figure 5.7). Pass-through ratios are generally higher in small, open EMDEs that have less flexible exchange rate regimes or do not have inflation targeting central banks (for example, Azerbaijan, Botswana, Honduras, Jordan, the former Yugoslav Republic of Macedonia, and Morocco). The finding that EMDEs with inflation targeting central banks tend to have lower than average ERPTRs provides preliminary evidence that a credible commitment to price stability helps weaken the responsiveness of inflation to exchange rate movements.

In sharp contrast with *monetary policy* shocks, *domestic demand* shocks are associated with small, negative ERPTRs for most countries (for example, a negative domestic demand shock tends to be associated with currency depreciation and declining inflation). Median values at around -0.07 are similar for advanced economies and EMDEs. Among EMDEs, the ERPTR is generally more negative in countries with less flexible exchange rate regimes and without inflation targeting central banks.

Domestic supply-side shocks are associated with positive ERPTRs but with lower median values compared to monetary policy shocks (less than +0.1 in advanced economies and EMDEs). However, most of these estimates are insignificant, with wide variations across country groups.

Global shocks. Global shocks account for a smaller proportion of the variance of exchange rate movements and are associated with more variations in estimated ERPTRs.

ERPTRs associated with *global demand* shocks tend to be positive among EMDEs (for example, currency depreciation coupled with higher inflation), particularly in economies with less flexible exchange rate regimes and without inflation targeting central banks (Figure 5.8). However, in several EMDEs, ERPTRs are estimated to be negative (currency depreciation coupled with lower inflation), including among some energy exporters (for example, Azerbaijan and Colombia). Estimated ERPTRs are statistically insignificant in over one-fifth of advanced economies and one-third of EMDEs.

Oil price shocks tend to be associated with widely different ERPTRs. The median ERPTR is positive for many energy exporters (for example, Azerbaijan, Colombia, and Malaysia) but negative in advanced economies, except the United States (partly due to the negative correlation between the U.S. dollar and oil prices). The estimates are insignificant in over one-half of advanced economies and almost two-thirds of EMDEs.

Global supply shocks tend to generate large variations in ERPTRs as well, with a negative median estimate for advanced economies and a positive one for EMDEs. However, the estimates are insignificant for nearly three-quarters of advanced economies and about two-thirds of EMDEs.

Other shocks. The FAVAR models attribute nearly a quarter of currency movements to *residual* shocks that may be linked to shifting risk premiums and other unmeasured factors. The median ERPTR associated with such shocks is

FIGURE 5.7 Pass-through associated with domestic shocks

The exchange rate pass-through is large and positive when currency movements are associated with monetary policy changes. It is smaller when currency movements are associated with changes in domestic supply conditions and negative when they are associated with changes in domestic demand conditions. Among EMDEs, the pass-through is generally lower among countries with more flexible exchange rate regimes and inflation targeting central banks.

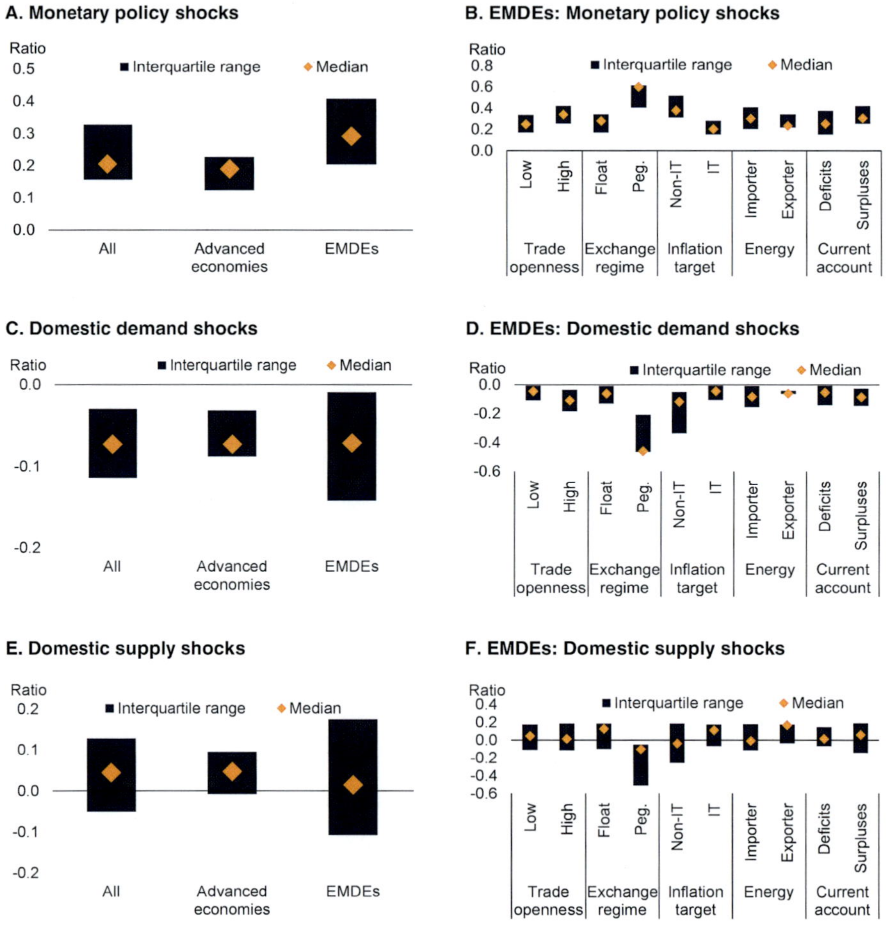

Source: World Bank.

Note: Pass-throughs are defined as the ratio between the one-year cumulative impulse response of consumer price inflation and the one-year cumulative impulse response of the exchange rate change estimated from factor-augmented vector autoregression models for 29 advanced economies and 26 EMDEs over 1998-2017. A positive pass-through means that a currency depreciation is associated with higher inflation. Bars show the interquartile range and markers represent the median across countries. EMDEs = emerging market and developing economies; IMF = International Monetary Fund; IT = inflation targeting.

B.D.F. Countries with "high" trade openness are defined as those with above median trade-to-GDP ratios; all others are considered to have "low" trade openness. Exchange rate and IT regimes are based on IMF classifications (see the Appendix for details). Energy exporters are defined as in World Bank (2018); all other countries are considered energy importers. Countries with current account deficits are those with a negative average current account balance over 1998-2017.

FIGURE 5.8 Pass-through associated with global shocks

Exchange rate pass-throughs vary widely, depending on the source of the global shock and country characteristics. For EMDEs, the pass-through is generally the lowest among countries that are less open to trade, have more flexible exchange rate regimes, and have inflation targeting central banks.

A. Global demand shocks

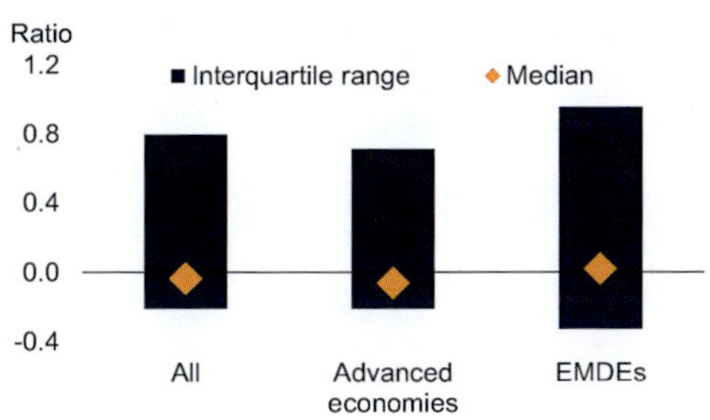

B. EMDEs: Global demand shocks

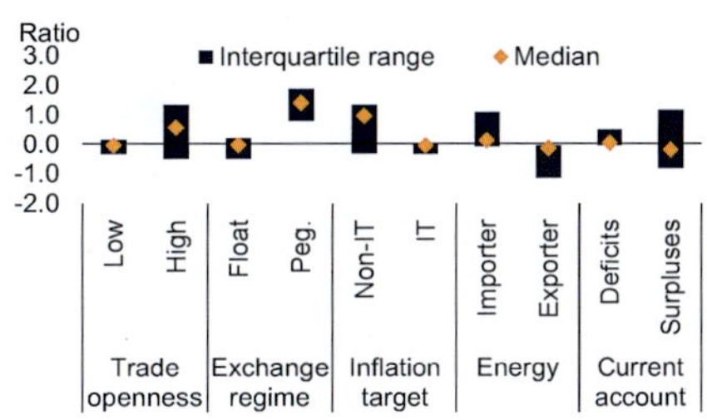

C. Global supply shocks

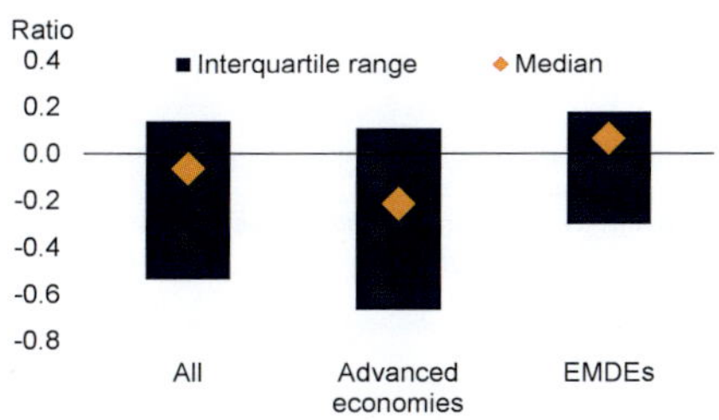

D. EMDEs: Global supply shocks

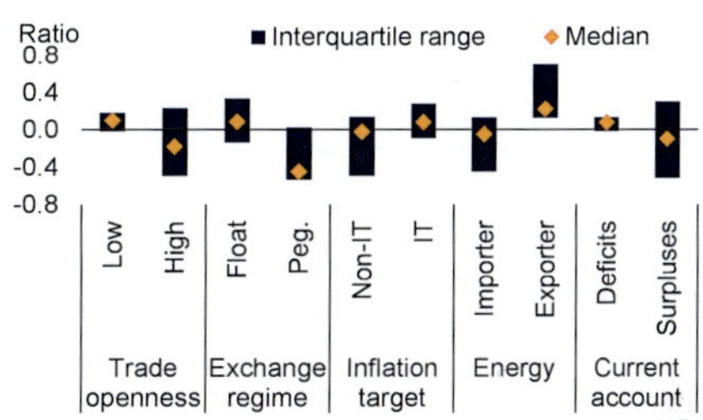

E. Oil price shocks

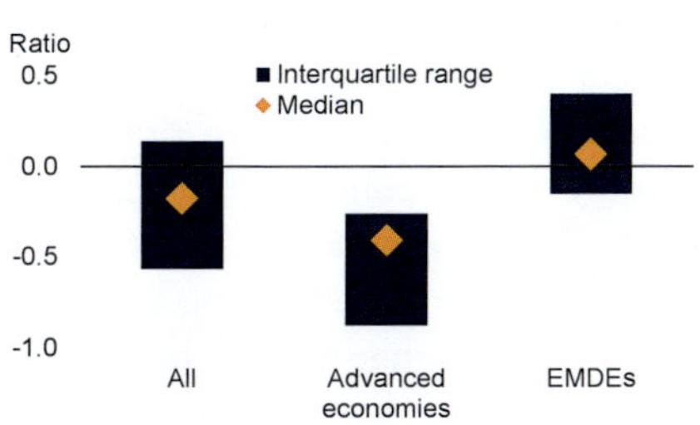

F. EMDEs: Oil price shocks

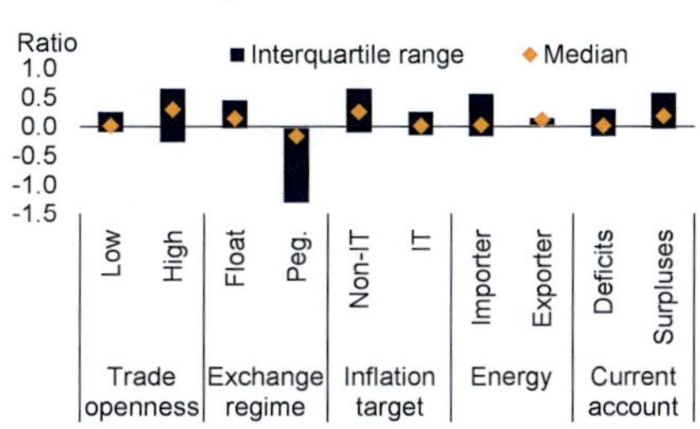

Source: World Bank.

Note: Pass-throughs are defined as the ratio between the one-year cumulative impulse response of consumer price inflation and the one-year cumulative impulse response of the exchange rate change estimated from factor-augmented vector autoregression models for 29 advanced economies and 26 EMDEs over 1998-2017. A positive pass-through means that a currency depreciation is associated with higher inflation. Bars show the interquartile range and markers represent the median across countries. EMDEs = emerging market and developing economies; IMF = International Monetary Fund; GDP = gross domestic product; IT = inflation targeting.

B.D.F. Countries with "high" trade openness are defined as those with above median trade-to-GDP ratios; all others are considered to have "low" trade openness. Exchange rate and IT regimes are based on IMF classifications (see the Appendix for details). Energy exporters are defined as in World Bank (2018); all other countries are considered energy importers. Countries with current account deficits are those with a negative average current account balance over 1998-2017.

FIGURE 5.9 Pass-through associated with exchange rate shocks

The exchange rate pass-through is close to zero when currency movements are associated with residual exchange rate shocks (not defined as domestic or global shocks).

A. Exchange rate shocks

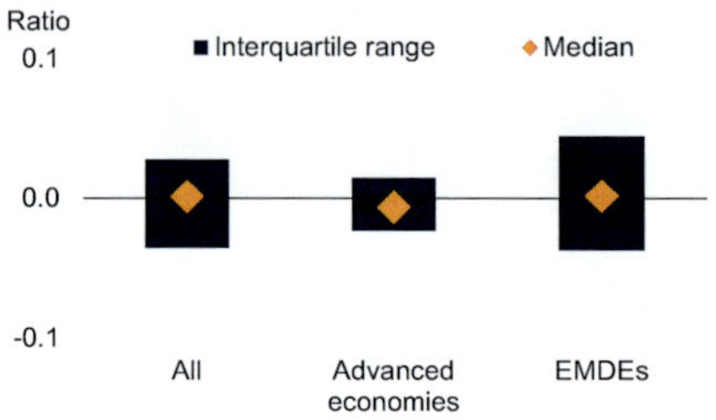

B. EMDEs: Exchange rate shocks

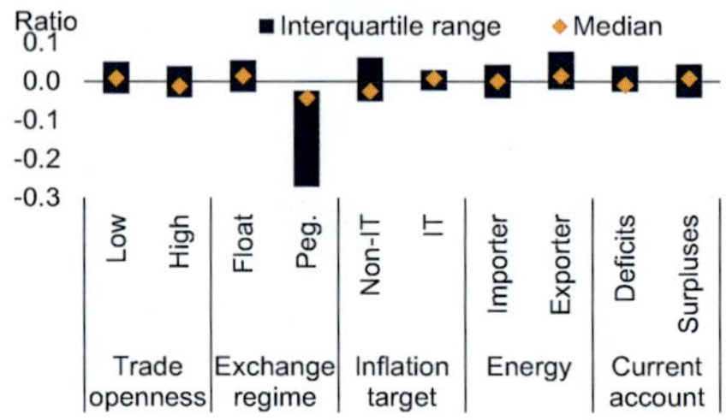

Source: World Bank.

Note: Pass-throughs are defined as the ratio between the one-year cumulative impulse response of consumer price inflation and the one-year cumulative impulse response of the exchange rate change estimated from factor-augmented vector autoregression models for 29 advanced economies and 26 EMDEs over 1998-2017. A positive pass-through means that a currency depreciation is associated with higher inflation. Bars show the interquartile range and markers represent the median across countries. EMDEs = emerging market and developing economies; IMF = International Monetary Fund; IT = inflation targeting.

B. Countries with "high" trade openness are defined as those with above median trade-to-GDP ratios; all others are considered to have "low" trade openness. Exchange rate and IT regimes are based on IMF classifications (see the Appendix for details). Energy exporters are defined as in World Bank (2018); all other countries are considered energy importers. Countries with current account deficits are those with a negative average current account balance over 1998-2017.

close to zero for advanced economies and EMDEs (Figure 5.9). However, it tends to be negative in EMDEs with less flexible exchange rate regimes, indicating that the direct effect of exchange rate changes on import prices is more than offset by other factors in those countries.

Past empirical studies disentangling the impacts of different types of shocks on exchange rates and inflation have reached broadly similar conclusions (Box 5.1). For instance, Forbes, Hjortsoe, and Nenova (2017) estimate a five-variable SVAR model with short- and long-term identifying restrictions using a sample of 26 small, open economies with de facto floating exchange rates. They report relatively large, positive ERPTRs in response to *domestic monetary policy* shocks but modest ones for responses to *domestic supply* shocks and negative ERPTRs for *domestic demand* shocks. They also find that pass-throughs associated with *global* shocks vary considerably in magnitude and direction. Shambaugh (2008) tests for cross-country differences in shock-specific ERPTRs and concludes that *domestic demand* shocks have a smaller pass-through relative to other types of shocks.

Average pass-through. To facilitate a comparison with other empirical studies, a weighted average of shock-specific pass-through ratios is computed, using shares

FIGURE 5.10 Average pass-through

Over the past two decades, the average pass-through dropped close to zero in advanced economies and somewhat below +0.1 in EMDEs, albeit with considerable differences across countries.

A. Average pass-through

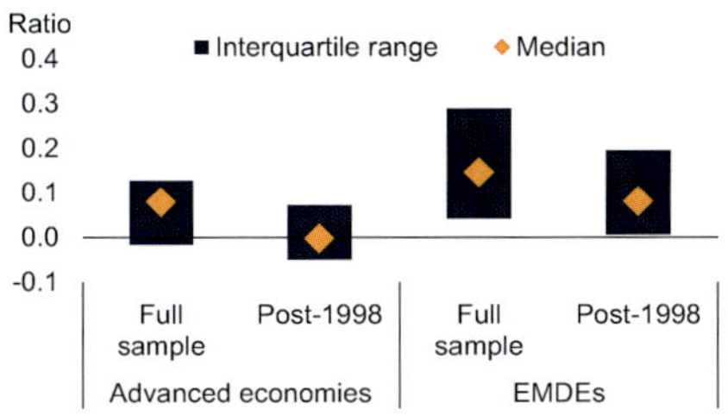

B. EMDEs: Average pass-through, 1998-2017

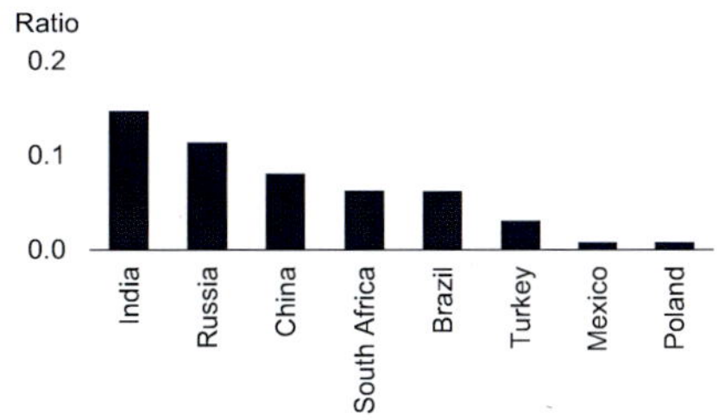

Source: World Bank.

Note: Pass-throughs are defined as the ratio between the one-year cumulative impulse response of consumer price inflation and the one-year cumulative impulse response of the exchange rate change estimated from factor-augmented vector autoregression models for 29 advanced economies and 26 EMDEs over 1998-2017. A positive pass-through means that a currency depreciation is associated with higher inflation. Bars show the interquartile range and markers represent the median across countries. Shock-specific pass-throughs are aggregated using shares of currency movements accounted for by each type of shock as weights. EMDEs = emerging market and developing economies.

A. Full sample estimations are over 1971 to 2017 but can vary at the country level depending on data availability (see the Appendix for details).

of currency movements accounted for by each type of shock as weights. This summary measure reflects the average sensitivity of inflation to exchange rate movements over the entire estimation period.

Overall, average ERPTRs are estimated to have declined in advanced economies and EMDEs in recent decades. The median estimate for advanced economies averaged +0.08 since 1970 but was close to zero over 1998-2017 (Figure 5.10). For EMDEs, the median value averaged +0.15 since 1970, but declined to +0.08 over 1998-2017.

Among larger EMDEs, the average ERPTR in China is estimated at +0.08 since 1998, somewhat below previously reported estimates (Jiang and Kim 2013; Shu and Su 2009; Wang and Li 2010). For India, the average ERPTR is estimated at +0.14, broadly in line with previous studies (Bhattacharya, Patnaik, and Shah 2008; Forbes, Hjortsoe, and Nenova 2017; Kapur and Behera 2012). For the Russian Federation, it is measured at +0.11, consistent with findings of the Central Bank of the Russian Federation (2014). For Brazil, the average ERPTR is estimated at +0.06 since 1998, toward the lower end of other studies (Forbes, Hjortsoe, and Nenova 2017; Ghosh 2013; Nogueira and Leon-Ledesmab 2009). For South Africa, the ERPTR is estimated at +0.07, broadly in line with the evidence presented in Kabundi and Mbelu (2018).

Pass-through to inflation and structural factors

The findings of this chapter confirm that the nature of the shocks behind exchange rate movements plays a critical role in determining the direction and magnitude of the exchange rate pass-through to inflation. Country characteristics matter as well. Monetary policy frameworks and structural factors, such as the degree of international trade integration and foreign-currency invoicing, can make domestic prices more or less sensitive to exchange rate fluctuations. In EMDEs, improvements in monetary policy frameworks are credited for being a major force in pushing average ERPTRs down over the past two decades.

Monetary policy framework and credibility. The empirical literature has generally found ERPTRs to be smaller among advanced economies and in EMDEs with inflation targeting or more credible central banks (Carriere-Swallow et al. 2016; Gagnon and Ihrig 2004; Reyes 2004; Schmidt-Hebbel and Tapia 2002). Over the past two decades, an increasing number of central banks have adopted inflation targets and enhanced their credibility, which has helped reduce ERPTRs (Mishkin and Schmidt-Hebbel 2007; Coulibaly and Kempf 2010). This tendency has been observed across EMDEs, including in many economies in Asia (Prasertnukul, Kim, and Kakinaka 2010), Latin America (Ghosh 2013), and Eastern Europe and Central Asia (Maria-Dolores 2010; Yüncüler 2011). More generally, countries with lower inflation and less volatile exchange rates have been found to have lower average pass-throughs as well (Forbes, Hjortsoe, and Nenova 2017).

The consequences of inflation targeting frameworks and greater central bank credibility and independence are discernible in estimated ERPTRs for domestic and global shocks. In particular, the ERPTR associated with *domestic monetary policy* shocks is significantly smaller in EMDEs with more independent centrals banks (Figure 5.11). An improvement of the central bank independence index from one standard deviation below the sample mean to one standard deviation above it can reduce the pass-through ratio associated with monetary policy shock by half. In countries with more independent central banks, inflation responds less to exchange rate movements triggered by *global demand* and *oil price* shocks as well. This implies that countries with flexible exchange rates can better absorb external shocks through currency adjustments without threatening price stability.

Trade openness and participation in global value chains. The feedback between trade openness and exchange rate pass-through is multifaceted. A larger share of foreign products in domestic markets implies a potentially larger role for exchange rate movements in driving aggregate inflation (Benigno and Faia 2016; Soto and Selaive 2003). This would be consistent with a higher average ERPTR in more open economies. However, increased foreign competition in domestic markets will tend to reduce the pricing power of domestic firms, which will tend to reduce the ERPTR (Auer 2015; Berman, Martin, and Mayer 2012; Gust, Leduc, and Vigfusson 2010). More competitive or productive firms also tend to have larger market shares and source more of their inputs internationally (Gopinath and Neiman 2014), further contributing to a decrease in the ERPTR (Amiti, Itskhoki, and Konings 2014).

The degree of GVC integration could play an important role as well. By fragmenting production and increasing the share of intermediate goods in total trade, higher GVC integration could weaken the response of import and export prices to exchange rate movements. Such an effect has been identified in advanced economies and EMDEs (Amiti, Itskhoki, and Konings 2014; de Soyres et al. 2018; Georgiadis, Gräb, and Khalil 2017).[11]

Several economies in East Asia and Pacific and Eastern Europe and Central Asia have high GVC integration and low average pass-throughs; however, a clear link between GVC integration and pass-throughs could not be established, partly reflecting the correlation between GVC participation and other variables associated with trade openness (Figure 5.12; Chinn 2014).

Foreign-currency invoicing. Having a large share of imports invoiced in a foreign currency could amplify the sensitivity of import and export prices to exchange rate movements (Devereux, Tomlin, and Dong 2015; Gopinath 2015). The ERPTR to import and export prices has been found to be particularly elevated for countries with a high share of imports priced in U.S. dollars (Casas et al. 2017; Korhonen and Wachtel 2006). More generally, domestic prices in highly dollarized economies tend to react more to currency movements relative to other countries, since tradable and nontradable goods are priced in a foreign currency (Carranza, Galdon-Sanchez, and Gomez-Biscarri 2009; Reinhart, Rogoff, and Savastano 2014; Sadeghi et al. 2015). However, the selection of the pricing currency could itself depend on the desired level of the

[11] For instance, using a structural two-country model, Georgiadis, Gräb, and Khalil (2017) show that the sensitivity of an economy's local-currency production costs to exchange rate changes rises as the country participates more in GVCs by importing a larger share of its intermediate inputs. The increased sensitivity of the economy's local-currency production costs to exchange rate changes translates into a lower sensitivity of its foreign-currency export prices to exchange rate changes. As the economy's foreign-currency export price equals its trading partner's local-currency import price, an increase in the economy's GVC participation implies a fall in its trading partner's exchange rate pass-through to local-currency import prices.

FIGURE 5.11 Central bank credibility and pass-through

A growing number of countries have adopted explicit inflation targets, and central bank independence has increased since 2000. Greater central bank independence has tended to dampen the pass-through to inflation of exchange rate movements stemming from monetary policy shocks and is also associated with lower average ERPTRs.

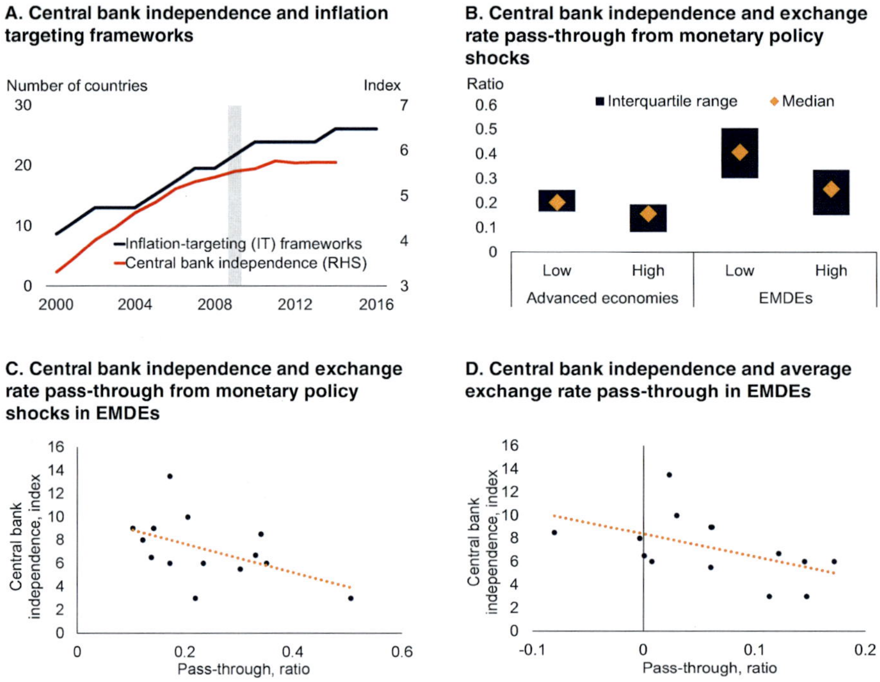

Source: World Bank.

Note: The central bank independence index is computed by Dincer and Eichengreen (2014). An increase in the index means greater central bank independence. Pass-throughs are defined as the ratio between the one-year cumulative impulse response of consumer price inflation and the one-year cumulative impulse response of the exchange rate change estimated from factor-augmented vector autoregression models for 29 advanced economies and 26 EMDEs over 1998-2017. A positive pass-through means that a currency depreciation is associated with higher inflation. Bars show the interquartile range and markers represent the median across countries. EMDEs = emerging market and developing economies; ERPTR = exchange rate pass-through ratio; IMF = International Monetary Fund; IT = inflation targeting.

B. Low and high central bank independence are defined as below or above the sample average.

C.D. The sample only includes EMDEs with floating exchange rate regimes according to the IMF classification (see the Appendix for details).

D. Shock-specific pass-throughs are aggregated using shares of currency movements accounted for by each type of shock as weights.

exchange rate pass-through, preserving the causal relationship (Gopinath, Itskhoki, and Rigobon 2010).

A significantly larger share of foreign-currency (and U.S. dollar) invoicing in most EMDEs relative to advanced economies could partly help explain a difference in average ERPTRs across these two groups. However, the

FIGURE 5.12 Global value chain participation and pass-through

Higher global value chain participation is associated with lower pass-throughs in some EMDEs, but the relationship is tenuous across the full sample.

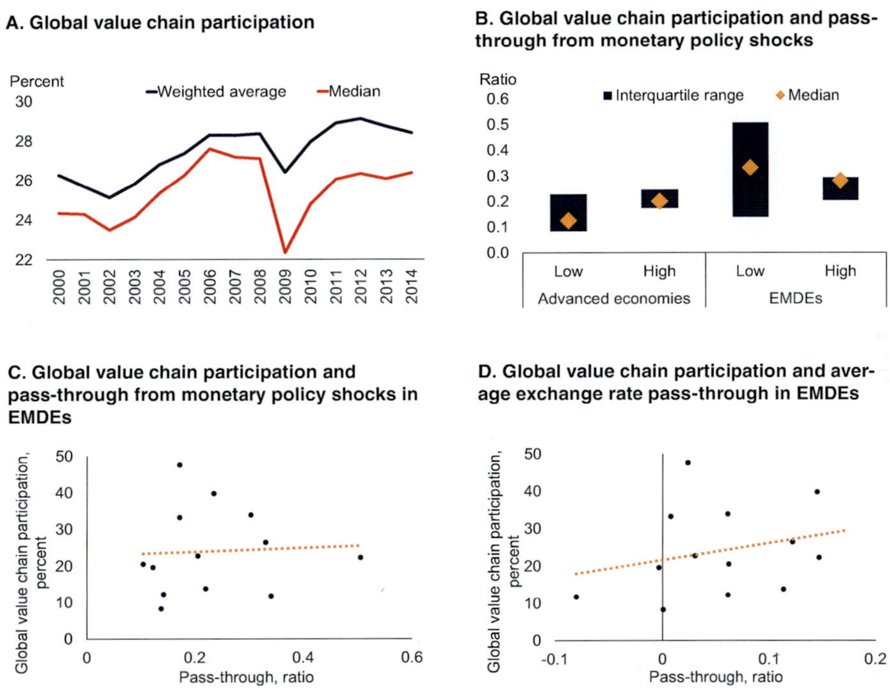

Source: OECD; World Bank.

Note: Global value chain data are from the OECD-WTO TiVA database. The selected indicator is foreign value added as a percent of gross exports. Pass-throughs are defined as the ratio between the one-year cumulative impulse response of consumer price inflation and the one-year cumulative impulse response of the exchange rate change estimated from factor-augmented vector autoregression models for 29 advanced economies and 26 EMDEs over 1998-2017. A positive pass-through means that a currency depreciation is associated with higher inflation. Bars show the interquartile range and markers represent the median across countries. EMDEs = emerging market and developing economies; IMF = International Monetary Fund; OECD = Organisation for Economic Co-operation and Development; TiVA = Trade in Value Added; WTO = World Trade Organization.

B. Low and high value chain participation are defined as below or above the sample average.

C.D. The sample only includes EMDEs with floating exchange rate regimes according to the IMF classification (see the Appendix for details).

D. Shock-specific pass-throughs are aggregated using shares of currency movements accounted for by each type of shock as weights.

relationship between the size of the pass-through and the share of imports invoiced in foreign currencies appears to be tenuous (Figure 5.13). For instance, EMDEs with a higher share of foreign-currency invoicing and more elevated ERPTRs are also characterized by less flexible currency regimes, and the absence of an inflation targeting central bank. Overall, the share of foreign-currency invoicing is merely a secondary factor explaining cross-country differences in estimated ERPTRs.

FIGURE 5.13 Foreign-currency import invoicing and pass-through

The share of foreign-currency invoicing does not seem to account for cross-country variations in ERPTRs in EMDEs.

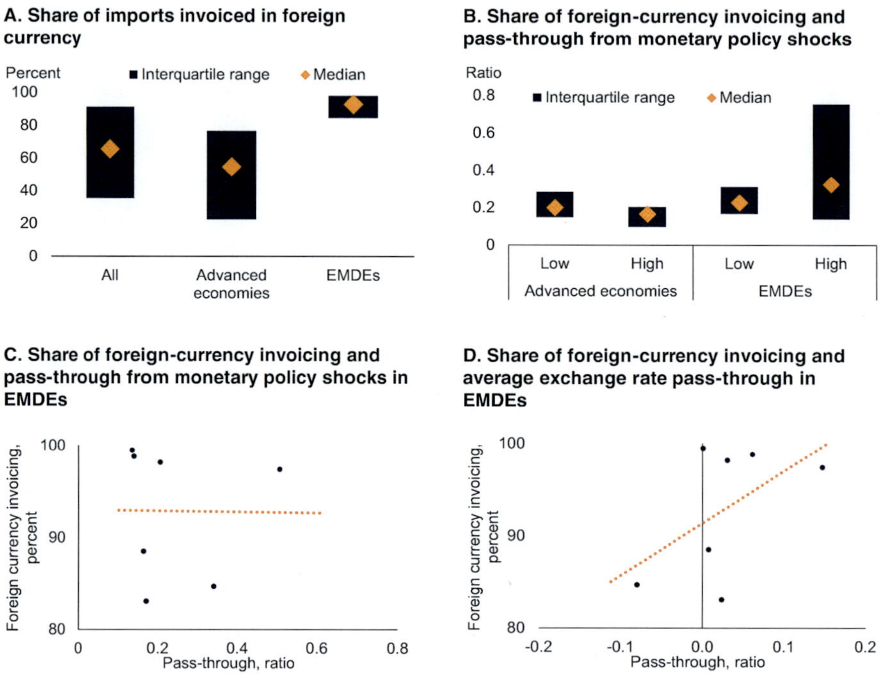

Source: Gopinath 2015; World Bank.

Note: Share of imports invoiced in foreign currency based on data for 50 countries calculated by Gopinath (2015). Pass-throughs are defined as the ratio between the one-year cumulative impulse response of consumer price inflation and the one-year cumulative impulse response of the exchange rate change estimated from factor-augmented vector autoregression models for 29 advanced economies and 26 EMDEs over 1998-2017. A positive pass-through means that a currency depreciation is associated with higher inflation. Bars show the interquartile range and markers represent the median across countries. EMDEs = emerging market and developing economies; ERPTR = exchange rate pass-through ratio; IMF = International Monetary Fund.

B. Low and high share of foreign-currency invoicing are defined as below or above the sample average.

C.D. The sample only includes EMDEs with floating exchange rate regimes according to the IMF classification (see the Appendix for details).

D. Shock-specific pass-throughs are aggregated using shares of currency movements accounted for by each type of shock as weights.

Conclusion

Monetary authorities in EMDEs have long been worried that significant exchange rate fluctuations could jeopardize price stability and force disruptive monetary policy responses. To alleviate these concerns, some countries adopted managed currency arrangements or leaned against undesirable currency movements with aggressive policy changes—a practice that has been dubbed "fear of floating" (Calvo and Reinhart 2002; Ball and Reyes 2008). However, a lack of exchange rate flexibility can amplify global shocks, encourage speculative attacks, and make it more difficult to anchor inflation expectations credibly. This in turn tends to increase the sensitivity of inflation to exchange rate movements, constraining the effectiveness of monetary policy and, as a result, limiting the adjustment of relative prices and the efficacy of expenditure-switching mechanisms as a buffer against global shocks.

This underscores the importance of properly evaluating the exchange rate pass-through to inflation under various circumstances and identifying the factors affecting it. Such an evaluation is of fundamental importance to formulating the appropriate and proportionate monetary policy response to currency movements.

This chapter investigates the relationship between inflation and exchange rate movements, contingent on the nature of the underlying shocks. The chapter uses FAVAR models to compute seven shock-specific pass-through ratios for each country. These ratios are then grouped and aggregated to identify common patterns.

Overall, *domestic* shocks are found to be a dominant driver of exchange rate fluctuations across most countries but are associated with significantly different pass-throughs to inflation, depending on their characteristics. In particular, *domestic monetary* shocks are generally accompanied by higher than average pass-throughs, particularly in countries with less flexible exchange rate regimes and without inflation targeting central banks. In contrast, *domestic demand* shocks are typically associated with negative and mostly insignificant pass-through ratios, due to the offsetting effects of growth and exchange rate channels (for example, weakening domestic demand giving rise to currency depreciation and declining inflation). *Global* shocks accounted for a smaller proportion of exchange rate movements and are associated with considerable heterogeneity of the estimated ERPTRs, depending on country characteristics and the source of the shock.

Differences in shock-specific ERPTRs could have important implications for monetary policy. For example, the exchange rate pass-through during an initial economic recovery phase could be low, reflecting the predominance of *domestic demand* shocks. However, appreciation caused by unexpected monetary policy tightening could be associated with a significantly larger degree of pass-through. Failing to take these factors into account may lead central banks to tighten policy more than needed to stabilize inflation, creating unnecessary fluctuations in activity.

Monetary policy frameworks and other country-specific characteristics affecting the sensitivity of domestic prices to currency fluctuations matter as well. In particular, a credible commitment to maintaining low and stable inflation has been one of the key factors behind the weak pass-through of even sizable depreciations to inflation in advanced economies and EMDEs over the past two decades. Looking at the cross-section of ERPTR estimates for EMDEs, an improvement of the central bank independence index from one standard deviation below the sample mean to one standard deviation above the sample mean could potentially reduce the pass-through ratio associated with *domestic monetary policy* shocks by half. This highlights a self-reinforcing feedback between central bank credibility and price stability. Similarly, currency movements triggered by *global demand* and *oil price* shocks also have more limited effects on inflation when central banks are credibly committed to an inflation target. This speeds up relative price adjustments and reinforces the benefit of flexible currency regimes.

Overall, the downward trend in exchange rate pass-through presented in this chapter can be connected to improvement in central bank policies and more solid anchoring of inflation expectations. Other structural factors, including growing integration in GVCs, may have played a role as well, but the analysis is not able to account for the cross-country differences in pass-through ratios.

Future research could investigate more formally the relationship between estimated ERPTRs and structural factors, such as the degree of value chain participation and foreign-currency invoicing practices in EMDEs. This could take the form of event studies around significant policy or other structural changes. The analysis of shock-specific pass-through could also be extended to different inflation measures, for example, import price, producer price, gross domestic product deflator, and core consumer price inflation. This could shed more light on the source of incomplete pass-through to consumer price inflation and help guide monetary policy decisions. Finally, nonlinearities in the exchange rate pass-through could be further investigated, looking at the direction and size of the various shocks under consideration.

ANNEX 5.1 Methodology and database

Estimation methodology

The analysis rests on country-specific factor-augmented vector autoregression (FAVAR) models, consisting of global and domestic variables. The global block includes three variables: global inflation, global output growth, and oil price growth. The domestic block includes four country-specific variables: inflation, output growth, changes in nominal effective exchange rates, and monetary policy (or equivalent short-term) nominal interest rates (for precise variable definitions, please see the last section in this annex).

In its structural form, the FAVAR model is represented by

$$B_o y_t = \alpha + \sum_{i=1}^{L} B_i y_{t-i} + \varepsilon_t$$

where ε_t is a vector of orthogonal structural innovations, and y_t consists of global inflation ($f_t^{\pi, global}$), global output growth ($f_t^{Y, global}$), oil price growth (Δop), country-specific inflation (π^i_t), country-specific output growth (Y^i_t), country-specific changes in nominal effective exchange rates (XR^i_t), and country-specific monetary policy (or equivalent short-term) nominal interest rates (I^i_t). The vector ε_t consists of seven global and domestic structural shocks (to be defined below). Postulating that B_0^{-1} in the econometric model has a recursive structure such that the reduced-form errors (u_t) can be decomposed according to $u_t = B_0^{-1} \varepsilon_t$, similar to Charnavoki and Dolado (2014) and Forbes, Hjortsoe, and Nenova (2017, 2018), the imposed sign and short-term restrictions can be written as follows:

$$\begin{bmatrix} u_t^{Y,global} \\ u_t^{OP} \\ u_t^{\pi,global} \\ u_t^{Y,domestic} \\ u_t^{\pi,domestic} \\ u_t^{I,domestic} \\ u_t^{ER} \end{bmatrix} = \begin{bmatrix} + & - & + & 0 & 0 & 0 & 0 \\ + & + & + & 0 & 0 & 0 & 0 \\ + & + & - & 0 & 0 & 0 & 0 \\ * & * & * & + & + & - & * \\ * & * & * & + & - & - & * \\ * & * & * & * & * & + & * \\ * & * & * & * & * & + & + \end{bmatrix} \begin{bmatrix} \varepsilon_t^{GlobalDemand} \\ \varepsilon_t^{OilPrice} \\ \varepsilon_t^{GlobalSupply} \\ \varepsilon_t^{DomesticDemand} \\ \varepsilon_t^{DomesticSupply} \\ \varepsilon_t^{MonetaryPolicy} \\ \varepsilon_t^{ExchangeRate} \end{bmatrix}$$

where * stands for an unrestricted initial response. Although country-specific shocks do not affect global variables in the first four quarters, global shocks can affect country-specific variables (without any sign or zero restrictions). A positive country-specific supply or demand shock increases country-specific output growth. Furthermore, a country-specific supply shock reduces domestic inflation, whereas a country-specific demand shock increases domestic inflation. A positive exchange rate shock (corresponding to an appreciation of the domestic currency) is assumed to increase the exchange rate, but its impact on other domestic variables is left unrestricted. Finally, a positive interest rate shock (corresponding to a contractionary monetary policy) initially increases the domestic interest rate and results in an appreciation of the domestic currency, while it decreases domestic output growth and inflation. All country-specific shocks are assumed to affect country-specific variables on impact through the corresponding sign restrictions, although the robustness checks (below) also consider such restrictions lasting for an alternative number of periods.

The system is estimated on a country-by-country basis using quarterly data with two lags, as in Charnavoki and Dolado (2014). The Bayesian estimation used searches for 1,000 successful draws of at least 2,000 iterations with 1,000 burn-ins. The results shown in the chapter are based on the median of these 1,000 successful draws and 68 percent confidence sets at the country level, although alternative presentation methodologies (for example, the median target, as in Fry and Pagan [2011]) are considered as a robustness check below. In the Bayesian estimation, Minnesota priors proposed by Litterman (1986) are used; since the Minnesota prior assumes that the variance-covariance matrix of residuals is known, we use the entire variance-covariance matrix of the vector autoregression estimated by ordinary least squares. For the actual estimation, the identification strategy through the algorithm introduced by Arias, Rubio-Ramirez, and Waggoner (2014) is used, where the standard Cholesky decomposition is employed together with an additional orthogonalization step that is necessary to produce a posterior draw from the correct distribution for structural vector autoregression coefficients.

The results for the role of global and domestic shocks in domestic inflation are presented as median point estimates across countries. Interquartile ranges indicate the range from the 25th to the 75th quartile of country-specific estimates (for example, Forbes, Hjortsoe, and Nenova [2017]). For presentational clarity, and consistent with other studies in the literature, the country-specific confidence sets are calculated but not presented.

Exchange rate pass-through

Following Shambaugh (2008) and Forbes, Hjortsoe, and Nenova (2017), for each country, the exchange rate pass-through ratio (ERPTR) is defined as the ratio of the response of country-specific inflation to the response of the nominal exchange rate changes following a given shock. The sign of the ratio is inverted, so that a positive ERPTR denotes a situation in which a currency depreciation is accompanied by rising inflation:

$$\text{ERPTR} = -\frac{\text{Response of country-specific inflation}}{\text{Response of country-specific nominal exchange rate change}}$$

As in Forbes, Hjortsoe, and Nenova (2017) and others, the ERPTR is calculated based on one-year cumulative impulse response functions of the endogenous variables. Since the Bayesian estimation results are based on 1,000 successful draws satisfying the sign restrictions, the country-specific ERPTRs are represented as the median (and 68 percent confidence sets) of successful draw-specific ERPTRs (ERPTRs are calculated for each successful draw individually before being used for a country-specific statistic).

Robustness checks

Several robustness checks were performed:

- An alternative number of periods (two-quarter periods) were considered in imposing sign restrictions in identifying country-specific structural shocks. The resulting pass-through ratios are largely comparable to the benchmark estimates (Figure A.5.1.1).
- An alternative specification of sign restrictions was considered where positive domestic demand shocks led to a contemporaneous increase in country-specific interest rates. The pass-through ratios associated with domestic demand and monetary policy shocks in this specification are very similar to the benchmark estimates (Figure A.5.1.2).
- Alternative presentations of 1,000 successful draws were considered, following Fry and Pagan (2011), such that rather than presenting the median across 1,000 successful draws, the draw that was closest to the median across 1,000 successful draws (the median target) was used. The same strategy was applied to calculate the corresponding 68 percent confidence sets, again following Fry and Pagan (2011).

Data

The sample includes 29 advanced economies and 26 EMDEs with at least 10 years (40 quarters) of continuous data for the variables in the domestic block, but the sample period differs across countries (see Table A.5.1.1 for details). Long-term trends of the variables are eliminated using the local mean method, as in Stock and Watson (2012). The following variable definitions are used as inputs into the FAVAR estimation.

FIGURE A.5.1.1 Pass-through: One versus two-quarter sign restrictions

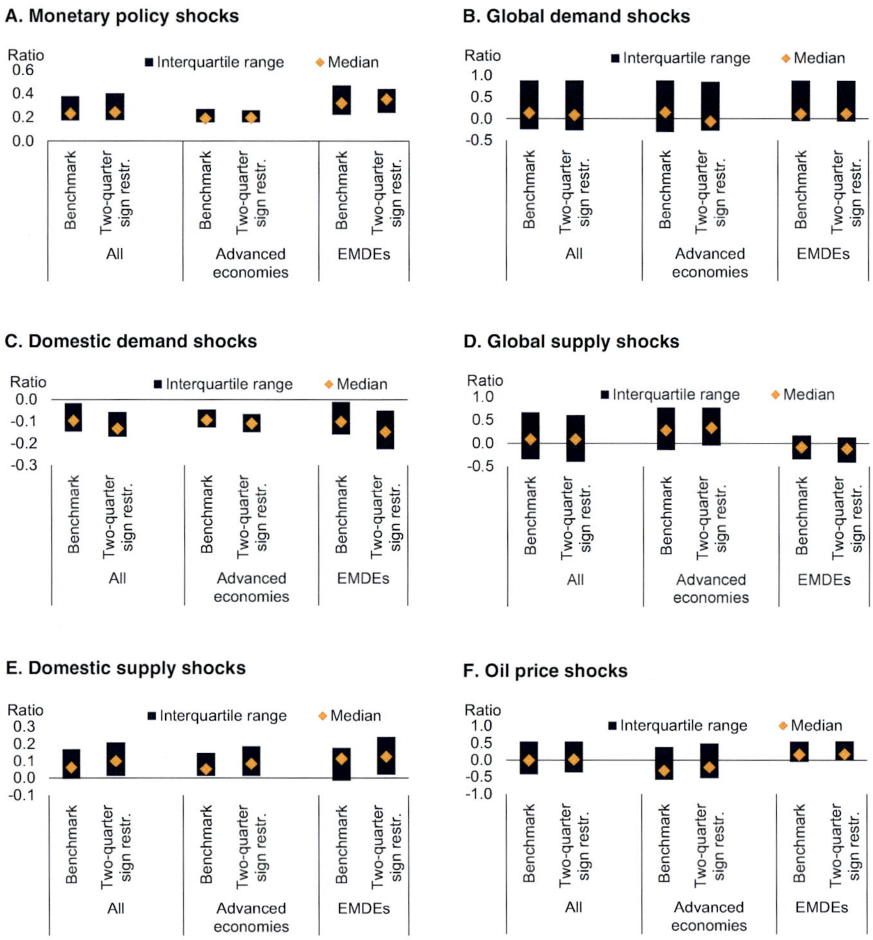

Source: World Bank.

Note: Pass-throughs are defined as the ratio between the one-year cumulative impulse response of consumer price inflation and the one-year cumulative impulse response of the exchange rate change to shocks from country-specific factor-augmented vector autoregression models estimated for 51 economies (29 advanced economies and 22 EMDEs) over 1998-2017. A positive pass-through means that a currency depreciation is associated with higher inflation. Bars show the interquartile range and markers represent the median across countries. In the alternative specification, sign restrictions are applied to the current quarter and next quarter. EMDEs = emerging market and developing economies.

FIGURE A.5.1.2 Pass-through: Additional sign restriction to identify domestic demand shocks

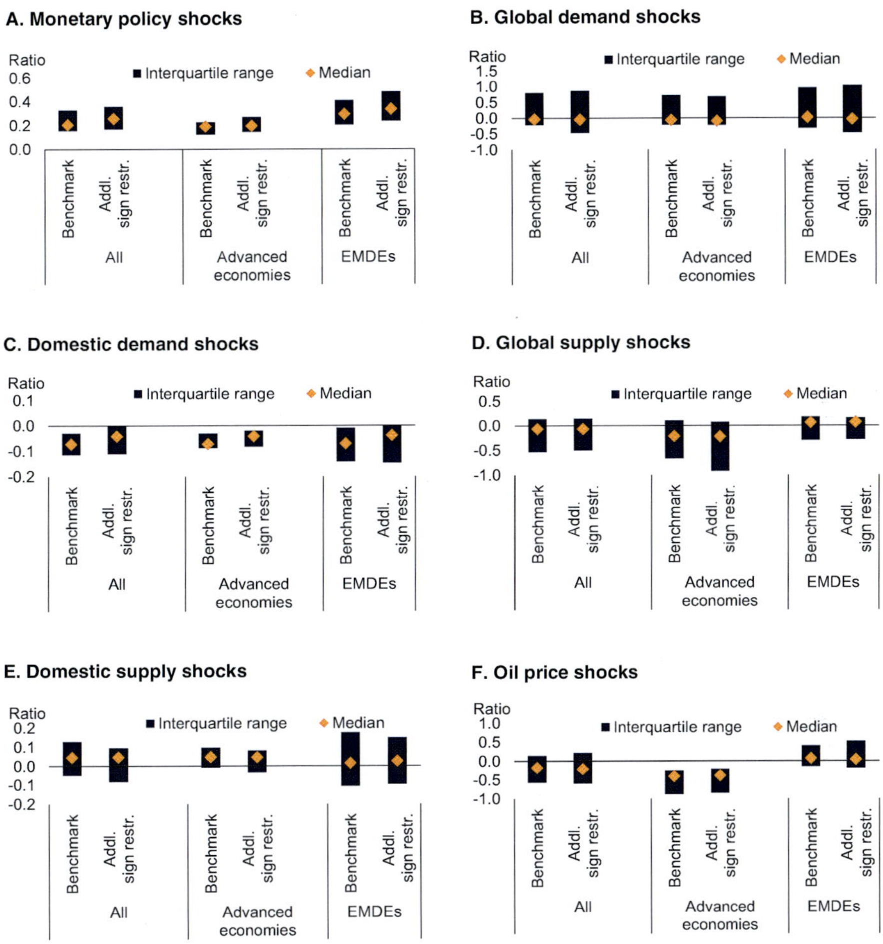

Source: World Bank.

Note: Pass-throughs are defined as the ratio between the one-year cumulative impulse response of consumer price inflation and the one-year cumulative impulse response of the exchange rate change to shocks from country-specific factor-augmented vector autoregression models estimated for 51 economies (29 advanced economies and 22 EMDEs) over 1998-2017. A positive pass-through means that a currency depreciation is associated with higher inflation. Bars show the interquartile range and markers represent the median across countries. In the alternative specification, an additional sign restriction was imposed, assuming that a positive domestic demand shock leads to a contemporaneous increase in domestic interest rates. EMDEs = emerging market and developing economies.

- Global output growth is the global common factor of quarter-on-quarter, seasonally adjusted real GDP growth in a sample of 29 countries for 1971:1-2017:4.[1]
- Global inflation is the global common factor of quarter-on-quarter headline CPI inflation (seasonally adjusted) in a sample of 47 advanced economies and EMDEs.[2]
- Oil price growth is the quarter-on-quarter growth rate of nominal oil prices (average of Dubai, West Texas Intermediate, and Brent).
- Country-specific inflation is quarter-on-quarter, seasonally adjusted headline CPI inflation.
- Country-specific output growth is quarter-on-quarter, seasonally adjusted real GDP growth.
- Domestic interest rates are annualized three-month Treasury bill rates or monetary policy rates.
- Nominal effective exchange rate changes are the quarter-on-quarter changes in the trade-weighted nominal exchange rates against 52 currencies, as provided by the Bank for International Settlements.

Global output growth and global inflation are estimated using the following two single-factor dynamic factor models:

$$Y_t^i = \beta_{global}^{Y,i} f_t^{Y,global} + e_t^{Y,i}$$

$$\pi_t^i = \beta_{global}^{\pi,i} f_t^{\pi,global} + e_t^{\pi,i}$$

where π_t^i and Y_t^i are inflation and output growth in country *i* in quarter *t*, respectively, while $(f_t^{\pi,global})$ and $(f_t^{Y,global})$ are the global common factors for inflation and output growth in quarter *t*, respectively. Details on the estimation of the global factors, including the evolution of factor estimates and variance decompositions, are presented in Chapter 3.

[1]The dynamic factor estimation of the global GDP factor requires a balanced panel throughout the full sample period. Thus, only a subset of countries is employed for this estimation.

[2]The number of countries in the estimation of the global output and inflation factors is based on data availability. As explained in Chapter 3, the estimates of global inflation and output factors do not change much when the same group of countries is employed.

TABLE A.5.1.1 List of countries and sample periods

Country	Sample period	Country	Sample period
Australia	1970:2 - 2017:4	India	1993:3 - 2017:4
Austria	1990:1 - 2017:4	Israel	1985:3 - 2017:4
Azerbaijan	2005:3 - 2017:4	Italy	1979:2 - 2017:4
Belgium	1970:2 - 2017:4	Jordan	1999:3 - 2017:4
Bulgaria	1994:4 - 2017:4	Japan	1989:3 - 2017:4
Brazil	1998:3 - 2017:4	Korea, Republic of	1991:3 - 2017:4
Botswana	1994:4 - 2017:4	Luxembourg	1999:3 - 2017:4
Canada	1970:2 - 2017:4	Mexico	1989:1 - 2017:4
Switzerland	1970:3 - 2017:4	Macedonia, FYR	2008:1 - 2017:4
Chile	1986:3 - 2017:4	Malta	1999:3 - 2017:4
China	1984:4 - 2017:4	Malaysia	2004:4 - 2017:4
Colombia	1994:4 - 2017:4	Morocco	1995:4 - 2017:4
Costa Rica	1997:3 - 2017:4	Netherlands	1982:3 - 2017:4
Czech Republic	1992:4 - 2017:4	Norway	1979:2 - 2017:4
Germany	1970:2 - 2017:4	New Zealand	1974:3 - 2017:4
Denmark	1970:2 - 2017:4	Philippines	1987:3 - 2007:3
Dominican Republic	2004:3 - 2017:3	Poland	1992:1 - 2017:4
Egypt, Arab Rep.	2002:4 - 2017:2	Portugal	1986:2 - 2017:4
Spain	1977:3 - 2017:4	Russian Federation	2000:1 - 2017:4
Finland	1987:3 - 2017:4	Slovak Republic	1996:1 - 2017:4
France	1970:2 - 2017:4	Slovenia	2002:3 - 2017:4
United Kingdom	1970:2 - 2017:4	South Africa	1981:3 - 2017:4
Greece	1994:4 - 2017:4	Sweden	1983:3 - 2017:4
Honduras	2005:4 - 2017:4	Thailand	2000:4 - 2017:4
Hungary	1995:4 - 2017:4	Tunisia	2000:4 - 2017:4
Indonesia	1990:3 - 2017:4	Turkey	2007:1 - 2017:4
Ireland	1984:3 - 2017:4	United States	1970:2 - 2017:4
Iceland	1988:3 - 2017:4		

Note: Countries with at least 40 quarters of data have been included.

References

Aizenman, J., S. Edwards, and D. Riera-Crichton. 2012. "Adjustment Patterns to Commodity Terms of Trade Shocks: The Role of Exchange Rate and International Reserves Policies." *Journal of International Money and Finance* 31 (8): 1990-2016.

Alessandria, G. 2009. "Consumer Search, Price Dispersion and International Relative Price Volatility." *International Economic Review* 50 (3): 803-29.

Alessandria, G., and J. P. Kaboski. 2011. "Pricing-to-Market and the Failure of Absolute PPP." *American Economic Journal: Macroeconomics* 3 (1): 91-127.

Alessandria, G., J. P. Kaboski, and V. Midrigan. 2010. "Inventories, Lumpy Trade, and Large Devaluations." *American Economic Review* 100 (5): 2304-39.

Alfaro, L., A. Cuñat, H. Fadinger, and L. Yanping. 2018. "The Real Exchange Rate, Innovation and Productivity: Regional Heterogeneity, Asymmetries and Hysteresis." NBER Working Paper 24633, National Bureau of Economic Research, Cambridge, MA.

Alvarez, F., A. Atkeson, and P. Kehoe. 2009. "Time-Varying Risk, Interest Rates, and Exchange Rates in General Equilibrium." *Review of Economic Studies* 76 (3): 851-78.

Amiti, M., O. Itskhoki, and J. Konings. 2014. "Importers, Exporters, and Exchange Rate Disconnect." *American Economic Review* 104 (7): 1942-78.

———. 2016. "International Shocks and Domestic Prices: How Large Are Strategic Complementarities?" NBER Working Paper 22119, National Bureau of Economic Research, Cambridge, MA.

Arias, J., J. Rubio-Ramirez, and D. Waggoner. 2014. "Inference Based on SVARs Identified with Sign and Zero Restrictions: Theory and Applications." Dynare Working Paper 30, Centre pour la recherche économique et ses applications, Paris.

Auer, R. 2015. "Exchange Rate Pass-Through, Domestic Competition, and Inflation: Evidence from the 2005-08 Revaluation of the Renminbi." *Journal of Money, Credit and Banking* 47 (8): 1617-50.

Auer, R., and T. Chaney. 2009. "Exchange Rate Pass-Through in a Competitive Model of Pricing-to-Market." *Journal of Money, Credit and Banking* 41 (s1): 151-75.

Avdjiev, S., V. Bruno, C. Koch, and H. Shin. 2018. "The Dollar Exchange Rate as a Global Risk Factor: Evidence from Investment." Paper prepared for the 18th Jacques Polak Annual Research Conference, International Monetary Fund, Washington, DC.

Bacchetta, P., and E. van Wincoop. 2003. "Why Do Consumer Prices React Less Than Import Prices to Exchange Rates?" *Journal of the European Economic Association* 1 (2-3): 662-70.

———. 2005. "A Theory of the Currency Denomination of International Trade." *Journal of International Economics* 67 (2): 295-319.

Baffes, J., M. A. Kose, F. L. Ohnsorge, and M. Stocker. 2015. "The Great Plunge in Oil Prices: Causes, Consequences, and Policy Responses." Policy Research Note 1, World Bank, Washington, DC.

Ball, C. P., and J. Reyes. 2008. "Inflation Targeting or Fear of Floating in Disguise? A Broader Perspective." *Journal of Macroeconomics* 30 (1): 308-26.

Benigno, P., and E. Faia. 2016. "Globalization, Pass-Through, and Inflation Dynamics." *International Journal of Central Banking* 12 (4): 263-306.

Berger, D., J. Faust, J. H. Rogers, and K. Steverson. 2012. "Border Prices and Retail Prices." *Journal of International Economics* 88 (1): 62-73.

Berger, D., and J. Vavra. 2015. "Consumption Dynamics during Recessions." *Econometrica* 83 (1): 101-54.

Berman, N., P. Martin, and T. Mayer. 2012. "How Do Different Exporters React to Exchange Rate Changes?" *Quarterly Journal of Economics* 127 (1): 437-92.

Bernard, A. B., J. Eaton, J. B. Jensen, and S. Kortum. 2003. "Plants and Productivity in International Trade." *American Economic Review* 93 (4): 1268-90.

Bhattacharya, R., I. Patnaik, and A. Shah. 2008. "Exchange Rate Pass-Through in India." National Institute of Public Finance and Policy, New Delhi, India.

Borensztein, E., and V. Queijo. 2016. "Exchange Rate Pass-Through in South America: An Overview." IDB Working Paper Series IDB-WP-710, Inter-American Development Bank, Washington, DC.

Brun-Aguerre, R., A. Fuertes, and M. Greenwood-Nimmo. 2017. "Heads I Win; Tails You Lose: Asymmetry in Exchange Rate Pass-Through into Import Prices." *Journal of the Royal Statistical Society* 180 (2): 587-612.

Burstein, A., and G. Gopinath. 2014. "International Prices and Exchange Rates." In *Handbook of International Economics*, edited by G. Gopinath, E. Helpman, and K. Rogoff, 391-451. Amsterdam: Elsevier.

Burstein, A., J. Neves, and S. Rebelo. 2003. "Distribution Costs and Real Exchange Dynamics during Exchange Rate-Based Stabilizations." *Journal of Monetary Economics* 50 (6): 1189-1214.

Calvo, G., and C. Reinhart. 2002. "Fear of Floating." *Quarterly Journal of Economics* 107 (2): 379-408.

Campa, J., and L. Goldberg. 1999. "Investment, Pass-Through, and Exchange Rates: A Cross-Country Comparison." *International Economic Review* 40 (2): 287-331.

———. 2005. "Exchange Rate Pass-Through into Import Prices." *Review of Economics and Statistics* 87 (4): 679-90.

———. 2010. "The Sensitivity of the CPI to Exchange Rates: Distribution Margins, Imported Inputs, and Trade Exposure." *Review of Economics and Statistics* 92 (2): 392-407.

Carranza, L., J. Galdon-Sanchez, and J. Gomez-Biscarri. 2009. "Exchange Rate and Inflation Dynamics in Dollarized Economies." *Journal of Development Economics* 89 (1): 98-108.

Carriere-Swallow, Y., G. Bertrand, E. Magud, and F. Valencia. 2016. "Monetary Policy Credibility and Exchange Rate Pass-Through." IMF Working Paper 16/240, International Monetary Fund, Washington, DC.

Casas, C., F. Diez, G. Gopinath, and P. O. Gourinchas. 2017. "Dominant Currency Paradigm." NBER Working Paper 22943, National Bureau of Economic Research, Cambridge, MA.

Caselli, F., and A. Roitman. 2016. "Non-Linear Exchange Rate Pass-Through in Emerging Markets." IMF Working Paper 16/1, International Monetary Fund, Washington, DC.

Ca'Zorzi, M., E. Hahn, and M. Sánchez. 2007. "Exchange Rate Pass-Through in Emerging Markets." ECB Working Paper Series 739, European Central Bank, Frankfurt am Main.

Ca'Zorzi, M., and M. Rubaszek. 2018. "Exchange Rate Forecasting on a Napkin." ECB Working Paper Series 2151, European Central Bank, Frankfurt am Main.

Central Bank of the Russian Federation. 2014. "Monetary Policy Report 3-2014." Central Bank of the Russian Federation, Moscow, Russia.

Chaney, T. 2008. "Distorted Gravity: The Intensive and Extensive Margins of International Trade." *American Economic Review* 98 (4): 1707-21.

Charnavoki, V., and J. Dolado. 2014. "The Effects of Global Shocks on Small Commodity-Exporting Economies: Lessons from Canada." *American Economic Journal: Macroeconomics* 6 (2): 207-37.

Cheung, Y., M. Chinn, A. Garcia Pascual, and Y. Zhang. 2017. "Exchange Rate Prediction Redux: New Models, New Data, New Currencies." NBER Working Paper 23267, National Bureau of Economic Research, Cambridge, MA.

Chinn, M. 2014. "Global Supply Chains and Macroeconomic Relationships in Asia." In *Asia and Global Production Networks: Implications for Trade, Incomes and Economic Vulnerabilities*, edited by B. Ferrarini and D. Hummels. Cheltenham, U.K.: Asian Development Bank and Edward Elgar Publishing.

Chinn, M., and G. Meredith. 2005. "Testing Uncovered Interest Parity at Short and Long Horizons during the Post-Bretton Woods Era." NBER Working Paper 11077, National Bureau of Economic Research, Cambridge, MA.

Choudhri, E., and D. Hakura. 2006. "Exchange Rate Pass-Through to Domestic Prices: Does the Inflationary Environment Matter?" *Journal of International Money and Finance* 25 (4): 614-39.

———. 2015. "The Exchange Rate Pass-Through to Import and Export Prices: The Role of Nominal Rigidities and Currency Choice." *Journal of International Money and Finance* 51 (March): 1-25.

Comunale, M., and D. Kunovac. 2017. "Exchange Rate Pass-Through in the Euro Area." ECB Working Paper Series 2003, European Central Bank, Frankfurt am Main.

Cordella, T., and P. Gupta. 2015. "What Makes a Currency Procyclical? An Empirical Investigation." *Journal of International Money and Finance* 55 (July): 240-59.

Corsetti, G., and L. Dedola. 2005. "A Macroeconomic Model of International Price Discrimination." *Journal of International Economics* 67 (1): 129-55.

Corsetti, G., L. Dedola, and S. Leduc. 2008. "High Exchange-Rate Volatility and Low Pass-Through." *Journal of Monetary Economics* 55 (6): 1113-28.

Coulibaly, D., and H. Kempf. 2010. "Does Inflation Targeting Decrease Exchange Rate Pass-Through in Emerging Countries?" Working Paper 303, Banque de France, Paris.

Cunningham, R., C. Friedrich, K. Hess, and M. J. Kim. 2017. "Understanding the Time Variation in Exchange Rate Pass-Through to Import Prices." Staff Discussion Paper, Bank of Canada, Ottawa.

de Soyres, F., E. Frohm, V. Gunnella, and E. Pavlova. 2018. "Bought, Sold and Bought Again." Policy Research Working Paper 8535, World Bank, Washington, DC.

Devereux, M. B., C. Engel, and P. E. Storgaard. 2004. "Endogenous Exchange Rate Pass-Through When Nominal Prices Are Set in Advance." *Journal of International Economics* 63 (2): 263-91.

Devereux, M. B., B. Tomlin, and W. Dong. 2015. "Exchange Rate Pass-Through, Currency of Invoicing and Market Share." NBER Working Paper 21413, National Bureau of Economic Research, Cambridge, MA.

Devereux, M. B., and J. Yetman. 2003. "Price Setting and Exchange Rate Pass-Through: Theory and Evidence." In *Price Adjustment and Monetary Policy: Proceedings of a Conference Held by the Bank of Canada*. November 2003, 347-71. Ottawa: Bank of Canada.

Dincer, N. N., and B. Eichengreen. 2014. "Central Bank Transparency and Independence: Updates and New Measures." *International Journal of Central Banking* 10 (1): 189-253.

Donayre, L., and, I. Panovska. 2016. "State-Dependent Exchange Rate Pass-Through Behavior." *Journal of International Money and Finance* 64 (June): 170-95.

Dornbusch, R. 1987. "Exchange Rates and Prices." *American Economic Review* 77 (1): 93-106.

Eaton, J., S. Kortum, and F. Kramarz. 2011. "An Anatomy of International Trade: Evidence from French Firms." *Econometrica* 79 (5): 1453-98.

Engel, C. 2016. "Exchange Rates, Interest Rates, and the Risk Premium." *American Economic Review* 106 (2): 436-74.

Fischer, S. 2015. "The Transmission of Exchange Rate Changes to Output and Inflation." Speech at Monetary Policy Implementation and Transmission in the Post-Crisis Period, a Research Conference Sponsored by the Board of Governors of the Federal Reserve System, Washington, DC, November 12.

Flodén, M., and F. Wilander. 2006. "State Dependent Pricing, Invoicing Currency, and Exchange Rate Pass-Through." *Journal of International Economics* 70 (1): 178-96.

Forbes, K. 2015. "Much Ado about Something Important: How Do Exchange Rate Movements Affect Inflation?" Speech at the Money, Macro and Finance Research Group Annual Conference, Cardiff, U.K., September 11.

Forbes, K., I. Hjortsoe, and T. Nenova. 2017. "Shocks versus Structure: Explaining Differences in Exchange Rate Pass-Through across Countries and Time." External Monetary Policy Committee Unit Discussion Paper 50, Bank of England, London.

———. 2018. "The Shocks Matter: Improving Our Estimates of Exchange Rate Pass-Through." *Journal of International Economics* 114 (September): 255-75.

Foroni, C., F. Ravazzolo, and B. Sadaba. 2018. "Assessing the Predictive Ability of Sovereign Default Risk on Exchange Rate Returns." *Journal of International Money and Finance* 81 (March): 242-64.

Frankel, J. A., D. C. Parsley, and S.-J. Wei. 2005. "Slow Pass-Through around the World: A New Import for Developing Countries." NBER Working Paper 11199, National Bureau of Economic Research, Cambridge, MA.

Frankel, J., and A. Rose. 1996. "Currency Crashes in Emerging Markets: An Empirical Treatment." *Journal of International Economics* 41 (3/4): 351-66.

Froot, K. A., and P. D. Klemperer. 1989. "Exchange Rate Pass-Through When Market Share Matters." *American Economic Review* 79 (4): 637-54.

Fry, R., and A. Pagan. 2011. "Sign Restrictions in Structural Vector Autoregressions: A Critical Review." *Journal of Economic Literature* 49 (4): 938-60.

Gagnon, J. E., and J. Ihrig. 2004. "Monetary Policy and Exchange Rate Pass-Through." *International Journal of Finance and Economics* 9 (4): 315-38.

Georgiadis, G., J. Gräb, and M. Khalil. 2017. "Global Value Chain Participation and Exchange Rate Pass-Through." Unpublished, European Central Bank, Frankfurt.

Ghosh, A. 2013. "Exchange Rate Pass-Through, Macro Fundamentals and Regime Choice in Latin America." *Journal of Macroeconomics* 35: 163-71.

Goldberg, P. K., and R. Hellerstein. 2008. "A Structural Approach to Explaining Incomplete Exchange Rate Pass-Through and Pricing-to-Market." *American Economic Review* 98 (2): 423-29.

Goldberg, P. K., and M. M. Knetter. 1997. "Goods Prices and Exchange Rates: What Have We Learned?" *Journal of Economic Literature* 35 (3): 1243-72.

Goldberg, P. K., and F. Verboven. 2001. "The Evolution of Price Dispersion in the European Car Market." *Review of Economic Studies* 68 (4): 811-48.

Gopinath, G. 2015. "The International Price System." NBER Working Paper 21646, National Bureau of Economic Research, Cambridge, MA.

Gopinath, G., and O. Itskhoki. 2010. "Frequency of Price Adjustment and Pass-Through." *Quarterly Journal of Economics* 125 (2): 675-727.

Gopinath, G., O. Itskhoki, and R. Rigobon. 2010. "Currency Choice and Exchange Rate Pass-Through." *American Economic Review* 100 (1): 304-36.

Gopinath, G., and B. Neiman. 2014. "Trade Adjustment and Productivity in Large Crises." *American Economic Review* 104 (3): 793-831.

Gust, C., S. Leduc, and R. Vigfusson. 2010. "Trade Integration, Competition, and the Decline in Exchange-Rate Pass-Through." *Journal of Monetary Economics* 57 (3): 309-324.

Hellerstein, R. 2008. "Who Bears the Cost of a Change in the Exchange Rate?" *Journal of International Economics* 76 (1): 14-32.

Ito, T., and K. Sato. 2008. "Exchange Rate Changes and Inflation in Post-Crisis Asian Economies: Vector Autoregression Analysis of the Exchange Rate Pass-Through." *Journal of Money, Credit and Banking* 40 (7): 1407-38.

Jiang, J., and D. Kim. 2013. "Exchange Rate Pass-Through to Inflation in China." *Economic Modelling* 33 (July): 900-12.

Kabundi, A., and A. Mbelu. 2018. "Has the Exchange Rate Pass-Through Changed in South Africa?" *South African Journal of Economics* 86 (3): 339-60.

Kapur, M., and H. Behera. 2012. "Monetary Transmission Mechanism in India: A Quarterly Model." Working Paper, September, Reserve Bank of India, Mumbai.

Khalaf, L., and M. Kichian. 2005. "Testing for Structural Breaks in Covariance: Exchange Rate Pass-Through in Canada." Working Paper, Bank of Canada, Ottawa.

Korhonen, I., and P. Wachtel. 2006. "A Note on Exchange Rate Pass-Through in CIS Countries." BOFIT Discussion Paper 2, Institute for Economies in Transition, Bank of Finland, Helsinki.

Krugman, P. 1987. "Pricing to Market When the Exchange Rate Changes." NBER Working Paper 1926, National Bureau of Economic Research, Cambridge, MA.

Landon, S., and C. Smith. 2009. "Investment and the Exchange Rate: Short Run and Long Run Aggregate and Sector-Level Estimates." *Journal of International Money and Finance* 28 (5): 813-35.

Litterman, R. B. 1986. "Forecasting with Bayesian Vector Autoregressions: Five Years of Experience." *Journal of Business and Economic Statistics* 4 (1): 25-38.

Marazzi, M., N. Sheets, R. Vigfusson, J. Faust, J. Gagnon, J. Marquez, R. Martin, T. Reeve, and J. Rogers. 2005. "Exchange Rate Pass-Through to U.S. Import Prices: Some New Evidence." International Finance Discussion Paper 833, Board of Governors of the Federal Reserve System, Washington, DC.

Maria-Dolores, R. 2010. "Exchange Rate Pass-Through in New Member States and Candidate Countries of the EU." *International Review of Economics and Finance* 19 (1): 23-35.

Mayer, T., M. J. Melitz, and G. Ottaviano. 2014. "Market Size, Competition, and the Product Mix of Exporters." *American Economic Review* 104 (2): 495-536.

McCarthy, J. 2007. "Pass-Through of Exchange Rates and Import Prices to Domestic Inflation in Some Industrialized Economies." *Eastern Economic Journal* 33 (4): 511-37.

Melitz, M. J., and G. Ottaviano. 2008. "Market Size, Trade, and Productivity." *Review of Economic Studies* 75 (1): 295-316.

Mishkin, F. 2008. "Exchange Rate Pass-Through and Monetary Policy." Norges Bank Conference on Monetary Policy, Oslo, Norway, March 7.

Mishkin, F., and K. Schmidt-Hebbel. 2007. "Does Inflation Targeting Make a Difference?" NBER Working Paper 12876, National Bureau of Economic Research, Cambridge, MA.

Nakamura, E., and D. Zerom. 2010. "Accounting for Incomplete Pass-Through." *Review of Economic Studies* 77 (3): 1192-1230.

Nogueira, R., and M. Leon-Ledesmab. 2009. "Fear of Floating in Brazil: Did Inflation Targeting Matter?" *North American Journal of Economics and Finance* 20 (3): 255-66.

Ozkan, I., and L. Erden. 2015. "Time-Varying Nature and Macroeconomic Determinants of Exchange Rate Pass-Through." *International Review of Economics & Finance* 38 (July): 56-66.

Prasertnukul, W., D. Kim, and M. Kakinaka. 2010. "Exchange Rates, Price Levels, and Inflation Targeting: Evidence from Asian Countries." *Japan and the World Economy* 22 (3): 173-82.

Reinhart, C., and K. Rogoff. 2008. "This Time Is Different: A Panoramic View of Eight Centuries of Financial Crises." NBER Working Paper 13882, National Bureau of Economic Research, Cambridge, MA.

Reinhart, C., K. Rogoff, and M. Savastano. 2014. "Addicted to Dollars." *Annals of Economics and Finance* 15 (1): 1-50.

Reyes, J. 2004. "Exchange Rate Pass-Through Effects and Inflation Targeting in Emerging Economies: What Is the Relationship?" *Review of International Economics* 15 (3): 538-59.

Rodriguez-Lopez, A. 2011. "Prices and Exchange Rates: A Theory of Disconnect." *Review of Economic Studies* 78 (3): 1135-77.

Sadeghi, S., M. Feshari, M. Marvasti, and Z. Ghanbari. 2015. "Exchange Rate Pass-Through and Inflation in Dollarized Economies: Evidence from the Middle Eastern and North African Countries." *Iranian Economic Review* 19 (2): 139-47.

Schmidt-Hebbel, K., and M. Tapia. 2002. "Monetary Policy Implementation and Results in Twenty Inflation-Targeting Countries." Working Paper 166, Central Bank of Chile, Santiago.

Schmitt-Grohé, S., and M. Uribe. 2018. "How Important Are Terms-of-Trade Shocks?" *International Economic Review* 59 (1): 85-111.

Shambaugh, J. 2008. "A New Look at Pass-Through." *Journal of International Money and Finance* 27 (4): 560-91.

Shu, C., and X. Su. 2009. "Exchange Rate Pass-Through in China." *China and World Economy* 17 (1): 33-46.

Soto, C., and J. Selaive. 2003. "Openness and Imperfect Pass-Through: Implications for the Monetary Policy." Working Paper 216, Central Bank of Chile, Santiago.

Stock, J. H., and M. W. Watson. 2012. "Disentangling the Channels of the 2007-2009 Recession." NBER Working Paper 18094, National Bureau of Economic Research, Cambridge, MA.

Taylor, J. 2000. "Low Inflation, Pass-Through, and the Pricing Power of Firms." *European Economic Review* 44 (7): 1389-1408.

Tunç, C. 2017. "A Survey on Exchange Rate Pass-Through in Emerging Markets." *Bulletin of Economic Theory and Analysis* 2 (3): 205-33.

Uhlig, H. 2005. "What Are the Effects of Monetary Policy on Output? Results from an Agnostic Identification Procedure." *Journal of Monetary Economics* 52 (2): 381-419.

Wang, J., and N. Li. 2010. "Exchange Rate Pass-Through: The Case of China." *Frontiers of Economics in China* 5 (3): 356-74.

World Bank. 2018. *Global Economic Prospects: The Turning of the Tide.* June. Washington, DC: World Bank.

Yüncüler, Ç. 2011. "Pass-Through of External Factors into Price Indicators in Turkey." *Central Bank Review* 11 (2): 71-84.

Global developments—perhaps technological in nature, such as the tremendous growth of online shopping—could be helping to hold down inflation in a persistent way in many countries.

Janet L. Yellen (2017)

Increased competition and changes in technology are driving down the prices of many of the things we buy.... A question we are grappling with here is how much further this process has to run.

Philip Lowe (2017)

There are reasons why low inflation is a phenomenon, and they should be set out clearly. However, there is no reason to assume that inflation will no longer rise. If the central banks aren't careful, we could very quickly end up with higher inflation rates again.... It would be totally irresponsible to declare that inflation has been conquered for once and for all.

Agustín Carstens (2018)

PART C

INFLATION

Low-Income Country Considerations

CHAPTER 6
Inflation in Low-Income Countries

Most of the variation in inflation among low-income countries (LICs) over the past decades is accounted for by external shocks. More than half of the variation in core inflation rates among LICs is due to global core price shocks, compared with one-eighth in advanced economies. Global food and energy price shocks account for another 13 percent of core inflation variation in LICs—half more than in advanced economies and one-fifth more than in non-LIC emerging market and developing economies. This points to challenges in anchoring domestic inflation expectations, which have been most evident among LICs with floating exchange rates, especially in cases where central bank independence has been weak.

Introduction

Low and stable inflation helps promote long-term economic growth, and it has become the primary objective of the monetary policies of central banks around the world (Chapter 1).[1] One of the key factors that determine the ability of central banks to achieve this objective is the degree to which inflation expectations are well anchored (Blinder et al. 2008). To steer inflation expectations, central banks typically establish a nominal policy anchor, which can either be quantity-based (for example, broad money supply or M2), price-based (for example, the exchange rate), or a target for inflation itself.[2]

Inflation expectations are shaped by many factors, including the history of inflation and the degree of credibility of the central bank (Chapter 4). If the central bank's commitment to its nominal anchor has high credibility, temporary inflation shocks—for example, due to commodity price shocks—will not set inflation expectations adrift. A central bank's credibility, in turn, depends on whether it is (i) committed to achieving its objective of low and stable inflation, (ii) has sufficient institutional capability to deliver on its commitment, and (iii) has a track record of achieving its objective.

Ensuring monetary policy credibility is particularly important for low-income countries (LICs), which have historically had to cope with frequent domestic

Note: This chapter was prepared by Jongrim Ha, Anna Ivanova, Peter Montiel, and Peter Pedroni.

[1] Central banks are responsible for maintaining not only price stability (low and stable inflation) but also (especially more recently) financial stability (the soundness of the domestic financial system). The instruments of monetary policy are generally used mainly for the former objective; a different set of instruments is generally used for the latter (Taylor 2005; Hammond, Kanbur, and Prasad 2009).

[2] The use of targets for the growth of monetary aggregates has generally fallen out of favor since the 1980s, at least in advanced economies, because of such problems as instability in relationships between monetary growth and inflation and the divergent behavior of different aggregates.

supply shocks, especially weather-related shocks to agricultural production that feed through to food prices (Frankel 2011).[3] Moreover, LIC central banks face several other impediments to their ability to anchor inflation expectations. First, they are likely to face a broader set of objectives, compared with those in advanced economies and other emerging market and developing economies (EMDEs); for example, the exchange rate is more likely to be a separate and important policy objective (Rodrik 2007; Berg and Miao 2010).[4] Second, the weak institutional capacity of central banks in LICs may complicate monetary policy management. Third, central banks in LICs generally lack a track record of low inflation. Finally, globalization has increased LICs' exposure to external price shocks.[5]

Although LICs have achieved significant progress in reducing inflation over the past two decades, they have done so in an international environment characterized by significantly lower worldwide inflation. How much of LICs' progress represents homegrown gains in central bank credibility, and how much is simply the result of a more favorable global environment? This chapter attempts to shed some light on this issue.

The chapter addresses the following questions:

- How has inflation in LICs evolved?
- How well anchored are inflation expectations in LICs?
- What country characteristics have been associated with stronger anchoring?

In this chapter, the question of the degree of anchoring of medium-term inflation expectations in LICs is tackled by estimating a novel heterogeneous panel structural vector autoregression (SVAR) model.[6] The model examines the

[3] The definition of LICs in this chapter follows the World Bank. The LICs in the sample include Afghanistan, Burundi, Benin, Burkina Faso, Comoros, Ethiopia, Guinea, Liberia, Mali, Mozambique, Malawi, Niger, Rwanda, Senegal, Sierra Leone, Togo, Tanzania, and Uganda.

[4] An important reason is that, as argued in the "fear of floating" literature (for example, Calvo and Reinhart 2002; Agénor and da Silva 2013), nominal exchange rate fluctuations may be particularly disruptive in the EMDE context, due to the prevalence of balance sheet currency mismatches arising from "original sin" and inadequate domestic financial regulation. Another reason is the thinness of the foreign exchange market in many cases, with a lack of stabilizing hedging and speculation. Under these conditions, LIC central banks may seek to pursue stability of the nominal exchange rate.

[5] This not only includes a direct channel via import prices, but also a variety of indirect channels. Annex 6.1 summarizes the literature on monetary policy challenges in LICs and the channels through which globalization may change the environment in which LIC central banks operate.

[6] The heterogeneous panel SVAR methodology, which is a variant of the Pedroni (2013) methodology, allows analyzing the consequences of various unanticipated global and domestic inflation shocks on the domestic core consumer price index. Rather than using pooled estimation, the approach incorporates group mean panel estimation methods to avoid inconsistent estimation that can occur under pooled methods when the dynamics associated with endogenous variables are heterogeneous. See Annex 6.2 for details.

extent to which core inflation in LICs has remained stable in the face of a variety of external shocks, including shocks to global core, energy, and food price inflation, and other shocks transmitted to the domestic economy through exchange rate fluctuations. The assessment is made based on the degree of sensitivity of domestic core inflation, which is determined by the degree of anchoring of inflation expectations, to external shocks. The estimation is based on a monthly panel data set that covers 104 countries (25 advanced economies and 79 EMDEs, including 18 LICs) for 1970M2-2016M12. The data set contains at least 36 months of continuous data for each country, for six variables—headline consumer price index (CPI), food CPI, energy CPI, core CPI, nominal effective exchange rate (NEER), and rainfall. Differences across income groups and subgroups in LICs in the extent to which domestic core inflation performance has been insulated from international factors are analyzed in terms of country characteristics, institutional factors, and policy regimes under a simple ordinary least squares regression framework.

The chapter's principal conclusions are as follows.

LICs, like other EMDEs, have experienced higher average levels and volatility of headline inflation than have advanced economies. However, the level and volatility of headline inflation have declined in all three country groups over the past two decades. The fall in inflation volatility in LICs is largely accounted for by declines in the volatility of core and energy price inflation. Food price inflation volatility has remained elevated.

Among LICs, core inflation has tended to be lower in countries with lower public debt ratios, fixed exchange rates, a higher degree of capital account openness, and greater central bank transparency. Although these results are largely consistent with those for advanced economies and other EMDEs, the effects of these characteristics seem to be more prominent for LICs.

Core inflation in LICs was more susceptible to external disturbances than in the other country groups. Around three-quarters of the variation in domestic core inflation rates among LICs was accounted for by external inflation shocks, and very little by shocks to domestic core inflation. This result is exactly opposite of that of advanced economies where only a quarter of the variation in domestic core inflation is explained by global inflation shocks.

Consistent with the findings in the other chapters in this report, domestic characteristics appear to matter not just for the level of domestic core inflation, but also for determining the susceptibility of core inflation to external shocks, although further research is needed to solidify this evidence.

Importantly, however, the results indicate that what sets LICs apart may not be so much that they differ from the other country groups in terms of these characteristics, but that these characteristics appear to operate differently in the LIC environment. Notably, although LICs that fix their exchange rates seem to succeed in anchoring inflation expectations about as well as other economies, those that float have had a much more difficult time in anchoring inflation expectations. This finding suggests that LICs may have in essence imported their anti-inflation credibility.

This chapter presents the results of what is the first investigation reported in the literature of the effects of various inflation shocks, domestic and global, on core inflation in a large group of countries, with a specific focus on LICs. The study takes advantage of the flexibility of a heterogeneous panel SVAR framework and a large data set that includes core inflation series for 18 LICs and 61 other EMDEs. The empirical framework makes possible the analysis of the impact of global and domestic shocks on core inflation in different groups of countries in a unified framework. Moreover, it helps identify the global component of core inflation endogenously and produces a parsimonious representation of the common and idiosyncratic components of core inflation in the countries in the sample. To help identify the exogenous component of domestic agricultural supply shocks, which are typically associated with food price inflation, the study uses rainfall data as an exogenous instrument.[7] Finally, the chapter also contributes to the literature by analyzing the country characteristics that help explain differences in core inflation responses to shocks between LICs and other country groups.

The next section documents the evolution of inflation over time and across countries, with special focus on LICs. The following section examines the impact of global and domestic inflation shocks on core inflation in LICs, using a heterogeneous panel SVAR model. The subsequent section distills the country characteristics associated with a larger role of global shocks. The final section concludes with a discussion of policy implications for LICs' control of inflation.

Evolution of inflation in LICs

Data for two periods are examined: 1980-99 and 2000-16. In both periods, LICs, like other EMDEs, generally experienced higher levels and volatility of consumer price inflation than did advanced economies (Figure 6.1). This is true of headline, core, food, and energy price inflation. The level and volatility of inflation declined between the two periods in each of the three groups, but the level and volatility of headline and core inflation in LICs remained generally higher than in advanced economies. Median headline inflation in LICs was around 6 percent in 2000-16, three times median inflation in advanced

[7] The relevance of the instrumental variable is tested using statistical methods. It is significant at the 5 percent level. Refer to Annex 6.2 for details on the test results.

economies. As Chapter 1 demonstrates, inflation performance in LICs has improved markedly over the past three decades but the decline happened later (starting in the 1990s) than in advanced economies (starting in the late 1970s).

Inflation volatility in LICs has also declined in recent decades (except food price inflation). This decline in volatility is not simply the result of the decline in median inflation among LICs: the cross-country correlation between the level of inflation and its volatility has tended to be much lower in LICs than in other country groups.[8] The higher volatility of inflation in LICs suggests that these countries may have experienced more frequent and/or larger shocks that tended to destabilize the inflation rate, or that their inflation rates have been more susceptible to shocks.

Food and energy prices, like other primary commodity prices, are known to be more volatile than the prices of services and manufactured goods. The historically high volatility and the lower correlation between inflation levels and inflation volatility in these countries, may therefore be the result of greater sensitivity of inflation in LICs to global commodity prices. Indeed, simple correlations reveal that food inflation, but not energy inflation, has been a more important driver of fluctuations in headline inflation in LICs and other EMDEs than in advanced economies (Figure 6.1). For core inflation, however, the evidence is more mixed: its correlation with food and energy inflation has not been clearly higher in LICs than in the other two country groups. The food and energy components of the CPI have historically been more volatile in LICs and other EMDEs than in advanced economies, reflecting the closer link of consumer prices with primary commodity prices in the former groups of countries, where food and energy have embed in them smaller services component than in advanced economies. Combined with the greater importance of food in LIC consumption baskets, it is expected that movements in global food price inflation have played a relatively more important role in inflation variation in LICs.

Median core inflation has tended to be lower in LICs with the following features: greater capital account openness; lower public debt ratios, fixed exchange rate regimes, higher degrees of central bank independence and transparency, higher degrees of participation in global value chains, and, to a lesser extent, higher degrees of trade openness (Figure 6.2). The findings for advanced economies and other EMDEs are similar to those for LICs, except that advanced economies with relatively high public debt have tended to have lower core inflation. Higher degrees of capital account openness, fixed exchange rate

[8] The correlation coefficient between the level and volatility of headline inflation (median across countries) is around zero in LICs for 1980-2016; the coefficients for other EMDEs and advanced economies are 0.48 and 0.50, respectively.

FIGURE 6.1 Inflation levels and volatility, by country group

Headline, food, energy, and core consumer price inflation in LICs and other EMDEs have typically been higher and more volatile than in advanced economies. Inflation and its volatility have declined across all country groups in the past two decades, with a particularly pronounced fall in inflation volatility in LICs (except for food). Nonetheless, headline and core inflation in LICs, and their volatility, have remained generally higher than in advanced economies. Food inflation has been a more important driver of fluctuations in headline inflation in LICs and other EMDEs than in advanced economies.

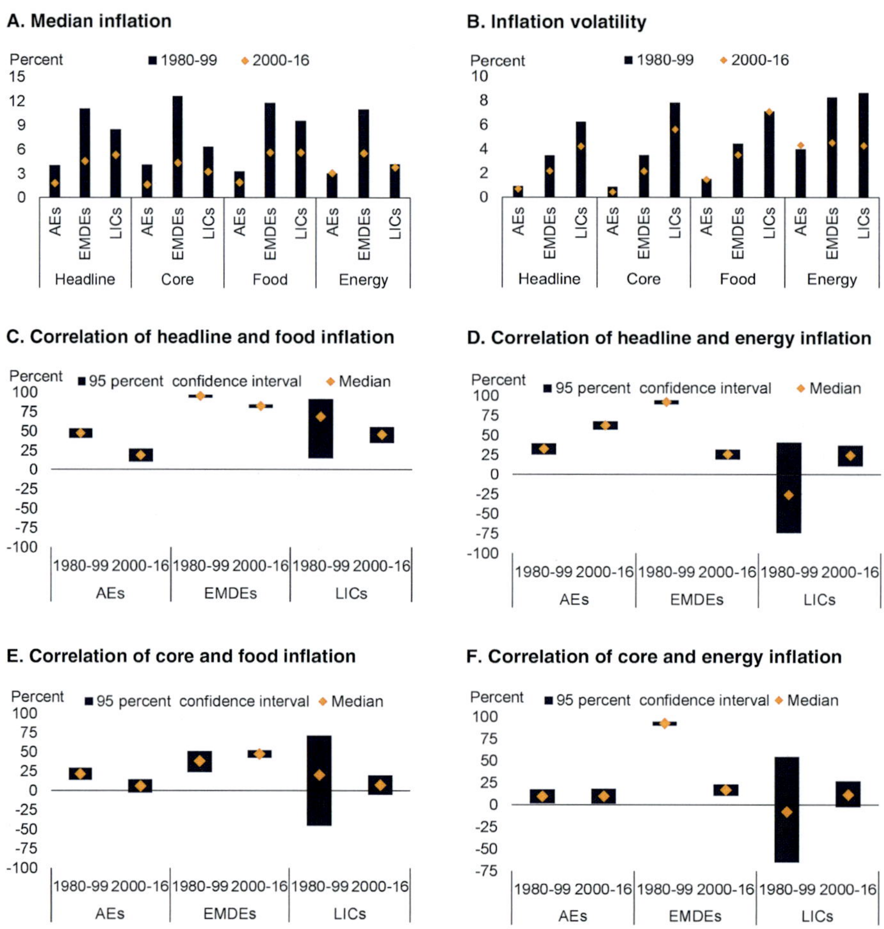

Source: Haver Analytics; International Monetary Fund *International Financial Statistics*; World Bank.

Note: All inflation rates are annual. Headline inflation uses a balanced panel for 1980-2016, including 154 countries (29 advanced economies, 98 EMDEs, and 27 LICs). Core inflation uses a balanced panel for 1980-2016, including 54 countries (27 advanced economies, 24 EMDEs, and 3 LICs). Food inflation uses a balanced panel for 1980-2016, including 104 countries (29 advanced economies, 61 EMDEs, and 14 LICs). Energy inflation uses a balanced panel for 1980-2016, including 55 countries (27 advanced economies, 25 EMDEs, and 3 LICs). EMDEs here exclude LICs. AEs = advanced economies; EMDEs = emerging market and developing economies; LICs = low-income countries.

A.B. Simple averages of median annual inflation or inflation volatility.

B. Inflation volatility is measured as the standard deviation of annual inflation rates for the past 10 years.

C.-F. The non-stationary part of each series is eliminated using the methodology by Stock and Watson (2012).

regimes, and greater central bank transparency are associated with more pronounced differences in core inflation in LICs than in advanced economies and other EMDEs.

Although greater reliance on exports of primary commodities and less financial openness than in other country groups have continued to characterize LICs in recent years, structural changes, including changes in macroeconomic institutions and policy regimes, may have helped reduce inflation and its volatility in these countries (Chapter 1). In broad terms,

- Trade openness has increased for all country groups since the early 1990s, with the degree of openness as well as its evolution over time being similar in advanced economies and EMDEs (including LICs). Although capital account openness has also increased for all groups since the early 1990s, it remains much lower in EMDEs than in advanced economies and has increased at a much slower pace.
- The proportion of EMDEs with pegged exchange rates fell sharply after the collapse of the Bretton Woods system in the early 1970s but stabilized in the mid-1990s and has been stable since then.
- An index of central bank independence and transparency is markedly lower in LICs and other EMDEs than in advanced economies, although it underwent a notable increase between 1991 and 2016.

Transmission of shocks into core price inflation

Methodology. To examine how well anchored core inflation is in LICs, a heterogeneous panel SVAR methodology is adopted to identify the effects of various global and domestic inflation shocks on domestic core CPI inflation in an orthogonalized reduced-form setting.[9] In particular, the panel SVAR structure includes a 3 x 3 block of global variables, namely, global energy, global food, and global core price inflation obtained by the cross-sectional average of individual country inflation rates, with the three variables arranged in this order.[10] It also includes a 3 x 3 block of panel variables, composed of individual

[9] The approach can be thought of as an adaptation of the Pedroni (2013) methodology, which relaxes the diagonality of the loading matrix for the common versus idiosyncratic orthogonalized shocks in a way that is particularly well suited for reduced form Cholesky analysis through the use of global versus domestic block Granger causality restrictions in the panel. See Annex 6.2 for details.

[10] One could also consider using principal component or dynamic factor estimates in place of the global variables. However, a combination of observed global variables and cross-section averages is used in this chapter for three reasons: (i) cross-sectional averages tend to be close proxies for the first principal component (Pesaran 2006); (ii) even if they differ slightly, asymptotically as the number of countries gets large, which one is used should not matter for the panel vector autoregression method in terms of orthogonalizing global core shocks from domestic shocks; and (iii) the data set is unbalanced, which makes the estimation of the dynamic factors more cumbersome.

FIGURE 6.2 Median core inflation, by country characteristics

Core inflation has tended to be relatively low in LICs, other EMDEs, and advanced economies with greater capital account openness, lower public debt ratios (except in advanced economies), fixed exchange rates, higher central bank transparency, greater participation in global value chains, and, to a lesser extent, greater trade openness.

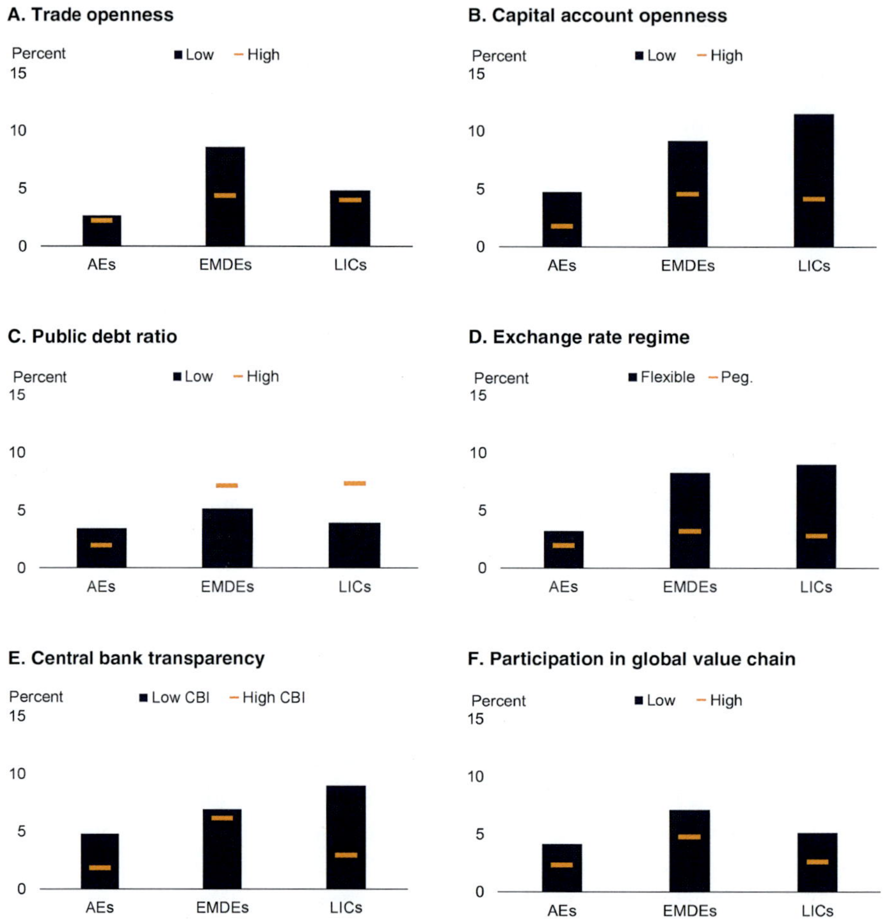

Source: Dincer and Eichengreen 2014; Haver Analytics; International Monetary Fund *International Financial Statistics*; Chinn and Ito 2018; Shambaugh 2004; World Bank; World Integrated Trade Solution.

Note: Based on median annual core inflation across 145 countries (34 advanced economies, 91 EMDEs, and 20 LICs) from 1980 to 2016. Countries with "high" are defined as those with values above the median; all others are considered "low." EMDEs here exclude LICs. AEs = advanced economies; CBI = central bank transparency index; EMDEs = emerging market and developing economies; GDP = gross domestic product; GVC = global value chain; LICs = low-income countries.

A.B. Trade and capital account openness are based on trade-to-GDP (percent) and the Chinn and Ito (2018) index, respectively.

C. Percent of GDP.

D. The exchange rate regime is based on the classification by Shambaugh (2004).

E. Based on the CBI by Dincer and Eichengreen (2014). The higher the index is, the more transparent and independent the central bank is.

F. A country is classified as well integrated into the GVC if one of the following two conditions is met: the sum of backward and forward participation in GVCs is greater than the median of the sample in a particular year, or the sum of intermediate exports and imports as a percent of GDP is greater than the median of the sample in a particular year. All other countries are defined as having "low" GVC participation.

country food inflation, core inflation, and the NEER, with the three panel variables arranged in this order. Each block is then orthogonalized via a standard Cholesky decomposition, and additional restrictions are imposed such that the domestic variables do not have an impact on the global variables, while the global variables are permitted to have an impact on the country-specific variables.[11] An important issue is that identified domestic food price shocks can be endogenous to domestic core inflation in the case that both variables are significantly influenced by common components, presumably domestic demand shocks. To avoid this, domestic food inflation is instrumented by external variables, rainfall and the square of rainfall, which reflect exogenous shocks such as weather events.[12] Finally, all dynamics are permitted to be heterogeneous across countries, so that the distribution of country-specific impulse response functions (IRFs) can be estimated (Annex 6.2).

- The cumulative response of domestic core inflation to unanticipated innovations in the three global inflation measures is computed as the response to a standardized 1 percentage point increase in the relevant global inflation rate. A muted response of domestic core inflation is interpreted as weaker transmission of the global shocks into domestic core inflation.

- Next, variance decompositions for domestic core inflation are computed, which supplement the information contained in the IRFs by providing estimates of the portion of variation in domestic core inflation that is explained by global shocks. It is expected that if inflation expectations are well anchored, then the variance of domestic core inflation is more likely to be explained primarily by its own domestic core price shocks, and that relative price shocks (global or domestic) will have more modest effects.

- The values of the IRFs and variance decompositions are then projected on institutional and policy characteristics of each country. This allows us to determine the characteristics associated with relatively high versus low response rates of domestic core inflation to various global inflation innovations, and to assess which characteristics are more closely associated with well-anchored inflation expectations in LICs.

Impact of global shocks. Medians and interquartile ranges of the cumulative IRFs of domestic core inflation (which are equivalent to responses of the level of the log CPI) in advanced economies, non-LIC EMDEs, and LICs are shown in

---

[11] In other words, this chapter takes a two-step estimation process. First, the global block is estimated and fixed. Second, the global block is used to help in the selection of parameters for the domestic block, but not vice versa (see Annex 6.2 for details).

[12] More specifically, the predicted value of domestic food inflation from a regression of food inflation rates on rainfall and rainfall squared is used as a proxy for domestic food inflation net of demand-side effects. This proxy is included as one of the endogenous variables in the vector autoregression framework.

Figure 6.3, for 6 and 18 months after the shock, to illustrate the persistence of the impact. During the sample period, 1970-2016, core inflation responded very differently in LICs, compared with advanced economies and other EMDEs, to global core price shocks. A 1 percentage point increase in global core inflation increased median core inflation in LICs by close to 0.6 percentage point after 18 months, compared with less than 0.2 percentage point in advanced economies and other EMDEs. Thus, LICs appear to import more of the fluctuations in core global inflation than do the other country groups. Next, the effects on domestic core inflation of international relative price changes is considered, in the form of separate shocks to global food and energy inflation, holding global core inflation constant. Shocks to global food inflation have more notable consequences for domestic core inflation in LICs. A 1 percentage point increase in global food inflation raised median core inflation in LICs by around 0.1 percentage point (and by up to 0.3 percentage point) within six months, larger than the effects in advanced economies and other EMDEs. With respect to shocks to global energy inflation, median core inflation in LICs responded more sharply and quickly than that in advanced economies and other EMDEs, although with more heterogeneous responses across countries.

These results likely reflect the relatively large weight of food more generally, as well as the relatively large weights of imported food and energy, in headline CPI in LICs, and the weaker response of many LIC central banks to the "second-round" effects of these shocks that allow them to be transmitted to core prices. Alternatively, it could also be the case that labor can shift wages in response to these shocks in these countries. Shocks to global core, food, and energy prices all tend to create increases in domestic core inflation in LICs. However, core inflation in LICs appears to be more sensitive to global core inflation than to changes in international relative prices of food and energy. By contrast, other EMDEs show limited sensitivity to global core price shocks, but they more closely resemble LICs in their response to international prices of food and energy. Core inflation in advanced economies displays minimal sensitivity to changes in global core inflation and international energy inflation, but some sensitivity to changes in the international price of food, although less than that of LICs.

Impact of domestic food price shocks. Next, the dynamic response of core inflation to domestic food price shocks is examined (Figure 6.4). Such shocks are likely to contain a strong endogenous component—they are likely, in part, to be responses to variables that similarly affect domestic core inflation. The estimation therefore uses rainfall measures (rainfall and rainfall squared) to isolate domestic food supply shocks. Since consumer prices in LICs contain relatively large food components, and since much of the food consumed in these

FIGURE 6.3 Response of core inflation to global price shocks

The median response of domestic core inflation to global core price shocks is relatively large for LICs, compared to other EMDEs and advanced economies, 6 and 18 months after the shocks, although with significant variation in responses among LICs. There is long-lasting impact with some delay in LICs, hinting at the possibility of spillovers from advanced economies. The median response to global energy price shocks is relatively small, with no large differences across country groups. The response to global food price shocks is larger in LICs than in advanced economies and other EMDEs, and there is also substantial variation in responses across LICs.

A. Response to global core price shocks

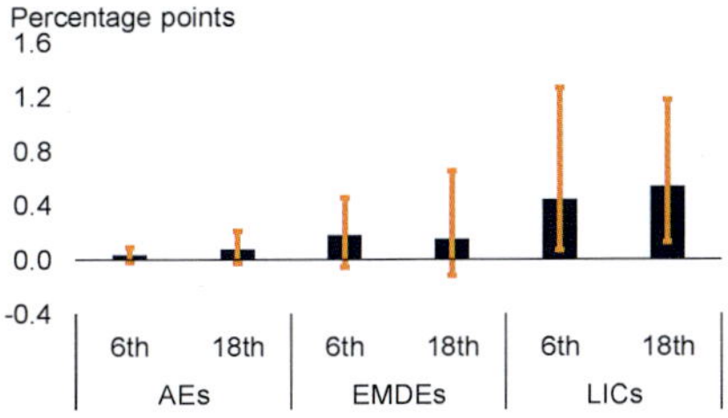

B. Response to global food and energy price shocks

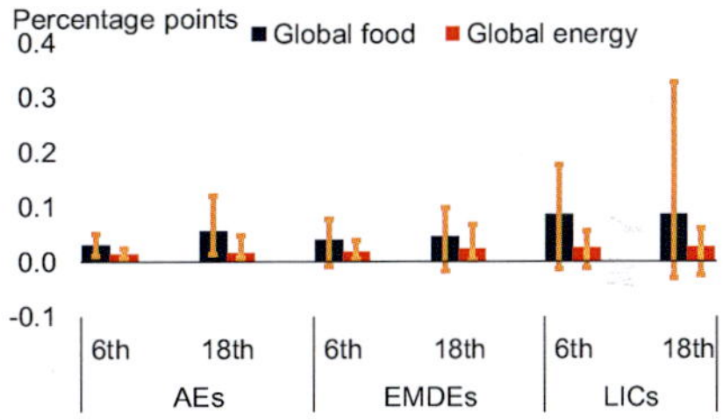

Source: World Bank.

Note: Cumulative IRFs after 6 and 18 months of domestic core inflation following a 1 percentage point increase in inflation measures. Medians and interquartile ranges (25th and 75th percentiles) of IRF distributions are shown for each country group. The results are based on a heterogeneous panel SVAR model with 104 countries (25 advanced economies, 61 EMDEs, and 18 LICs) between 1970m2 and 2016m12. EMDEs here exclude LICs. See Annex 6.2 for details.
AEs = advanced economies; EMDEs = emerging market and developing economies; IRF = impulse response function; LICs = low-income countries; SVAR = structural vector autoregression.

countries is produced in large domestic agriculture sectors, the expectation was that supply shocks to domestic food prices would tend to destabilize core inflation in LICs, with smaller effects on core inflation in other EMDEs and advanced economies. Indeed, the results find that a supply-driven domestic food price shock tended to raise median core inflation in LICs, and to have a negligible effect on core inflation in advanced economies and other EMDEs (Figure 6.4). However, the effect in LICs is short-lived, fading within six months of the shock.[13]

[13] Three possible interpretations of this finding may be mentioned. First, food price inflation seems to be more volatile and less persistent in LICs than in other countries (Figure 6.1), so that although domestic supply shocks may be more frequent and larger than in the other country groups, they may also be rapidly reversed, suggesting that, if the core price level is itself more flexible in LICs, the effects of domestic food price shocks in those countries may be short-lived. Second, food price subsidies tend to be used more commonly and more intensively in LICs than in the other country groups. To the extent that these keep the prices paid by consumers below producer prices, increases in prices received by domestic producers may have a muted effect on consumer prices. Third, assuming that domestically produced food cannot be easily substituted for imported food, the adjustment to international food price shocks through, for example, government subsidies may be costlier than the adjustment to domestic food price shocks, which can eventually be mitigated by adjustment in domestic food production.

Impact of exchange rate shocks. Finally, the NEER shock, which is the last variable in the Cholesky ordering, effectively picks up all shocks that move the NEER and are not covered by the first five shocks. Accordingly, the response of domestic core inflation to these NEER disturbances indicates the extent of the exchange rate pass-through to core inflation, irrespective of the underlying shock to the NEER. The estimated pass-through is more pronounced in LICs than in advanced economies or other EMDEs (Figure 6.4).[14] This may again reflect a weaker anchoring of inflation expectations in LICs than in the other country groups, due to weaker commitment to medium-term inflation objectives on the part of LIC central banks and greater challenges to that commitment posed by larger imported components of headline CPI.

Impacts of the shocks, by exchange rate regime. To shed more light on the differences between LICs and other country groups in the transmission of global and domestic shocks into domestic core inflation, IRFs were estimated separately for countries with fixed and flexible exchange rate regimes (Figure 6.5). For advanced economies and other EMDEs, the response of domestic core inflation to global core price shocks was larger in countries with fixed exchange rate regimes. However, the opposite was true for LICs: the response to global core inflation was found to be less pronounced for LICs with fixed exchange rate regimes. An interpretation could be that LICs with fixed exchange rates are more successful in anchoring inflation expectations than those with flexible exchange rates. This may be because weak institutions make a credible commitment to price stability difficult without a credible anchor in the form of a fixed exchange rate.

Contributions of the shocks to core inflation variation. Variance decompositions of core inflation were examined for the three country groups, using within-group medians (Figure 6.6). The key differences were found between advanced economies, on the one hand, and LICs and other EMDEs on the other. Consistent with substantially stronger anchoring of domestic inflation expectations in advanced economies, more than three-quarters of the variance of core CPI inflation rates in these economies is explained by shocks to core inflation. In LICs and other EMDEs domestic core inflation is overwhelmingly explained by shocks to global core inflation. The variance share of global core price shocks in the total variation of domestic core inflation is around 60 percent for both these income groups. The contribution of shocks to domestic core inflation, by contrast, is much smaller. The share of domestic core inflation explained by global food and energy shocks is moderately larger for

[14] This finding is overall consistent with the findings in Chapter 5 where the estimates of the pass-through ratio are on average greater in EMDEs than in advanced economies, although the country group in the chapter includes few LICs.

FIGURE 6.4 Response of core inflation to shocks to food prices and exchange rates

The median response of domestic core inflation to domestic food price shocks is notably larger in LICs than in advanced economies and other EMDEs. The response of domestic core inflation to an NEER shock (a catch-all shock) is also larger in LICs, followed by other EMDEs and advanced economies, which is consistent with the literature on exchange rate pass-through. The pass-through rate is around -0.1 (and up to -0.3) 18 months after the shock, but with substantial variation in responses across LICs; the impact is relatively long-lasting.

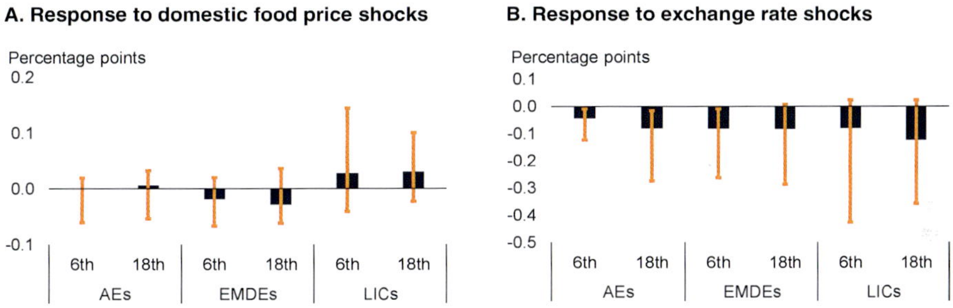

Source: World Bank.

Note: Cumulative IRFs after 6 and 18 months of domestic core inflation following a 1 percentage point increase in domestic food inflation or exchange rate change. Medians and interquartile ranges (25th and 75th percentiles) of IRF distributions are shown for each country group. The results are based on a heterogeneous panel SVAR model with 104 countries (25 advanced economies, 61 EMDEs, and 18 LICs) between 1970m2 and 2016m12. See Annex 6.2 for details.

AEs = advanced economies; EMDEs = emerging market and developing economies; IRF = impulse response function; LICs = low-income countries; NEER = nominal effective exchange rate; SVAR = structural vector autoregression.

LICs than for advanced economies and other EMDEs. In LICs, global food and energy price shocks account for 12 percent of core inflation variation—half more than in advanced economies and one-fifth more than in non-LIC EMDEs. In line with the results from the IRFs, this result may suggest that central banks in LICs have not succeeded in anchoring inflation expectations in the face of shocks to inflation rates, and that much of LIC inflation seems to have been driven by spillovers from advanced economies and other EMDEs. This is discussed in more detail in the next section.

Country characteristics and the roles of shocks

Decomposition of core inflation variation by country group

Differences in structural characteristics, institutions, and policy regimes might explain the differences in the inflation process among LICs. To shed light on the contributions of these factors, variance decompositions are compared for the estimated response of core inflation 18 months after a shock across country groups, using group medians. The country characteristics are central bank transparency and independence, the public sector debt-to-gross domestic product (GDP) ratio (an indicator of potential fiscal dominance), the exchange rate regime, and the degrees of international trade and financial integration. For each characteristic, two subgroups are distinguished in each of the three main country groups: one consisting of countries with "high" values of the relevant characteristic and the other comprising countries with "low" values. The extent to which inflation performance has been homegrown is inferred from the share of the variance of domestic core inflation that is accounted for by domestic core inflation itself, rather than by external or domestic food price shocks.[15]

- *Central bank transparency and independence.* For each country group, the differences between the two subgroups are quite pronounced: in countries with a high level of central bank transparency, external shocks play a less important role than in those with a low degree of central bank transparency (Figure 6.6). This suggests that inflation expectations are better anchored in the former than in the latter. However, although central bank transparency seems to matter for all country groups, it seems to play a greater role among LICs and other EMDEs in insulating them from external shocks than it does in advanced economies. Thus, there appear to be EMDE-specific and LIC-specific factors at play.

- *Public debt.* Even independent and transparent central banks may be unable to resist pressures to provide financing to the fiscal authorities when public sector debt is very high, such that monetary restraint might trigger a solvency crisis for the government. Empirically, across all the country groups, economies with relatively high public-sector debt-to-GDP ratios exhibit a larger role for external shocks in explaining the variance of core inflation, and this effect is particularly pronounced for LICs (Figure 6.6). Moreover, external shocks explain a larger share of the variance in core inflation in LICs with higher public sector debt ratios than in any of the other subgroups. A somewhat surprising result among advanced economies is that high debt ratios appear to be associated with low inflation (Figure 6.2). This result may reflect that once monetary policy credibility is established, as is the case in many advanced economies, countries may be able to afford to accumulate higher debt without destabilizing expectations.[16]

---

[15] The differences in IRFs between LIC subgroups are quite similar to the differences in variance decompositions. Higher public debt, lower central bank transparency, and lower capital account openness, which all may capture weaker monetary policy credibility, are associated in LICs with stronger responsiveness of domestic core inflation to global core price shocks. Trade openness does not appear to make an important difference for LICs' response to the global core.

[16] It may also capture low-inflation, high-debt outcomes in advanced economies in the wake of the global financial crisis or the role of a few advanced economies (such as Italy and Japan) where high levels of public debt have gone together with low inflation for reasons not considered here.

FIGURE 6.5 Response of core inflation to global core price shocks

LICs with fixed exchange rates are better able than floaters to insulate their domestic core inflation from global core and food price shocks. However, LIC-floaters fare better at managing global energy price shocks. In contrast, core inflation in advanced economies with floating exchange rates is generally less sensitives to global price shocks. The results for other EMDEs are mixed.

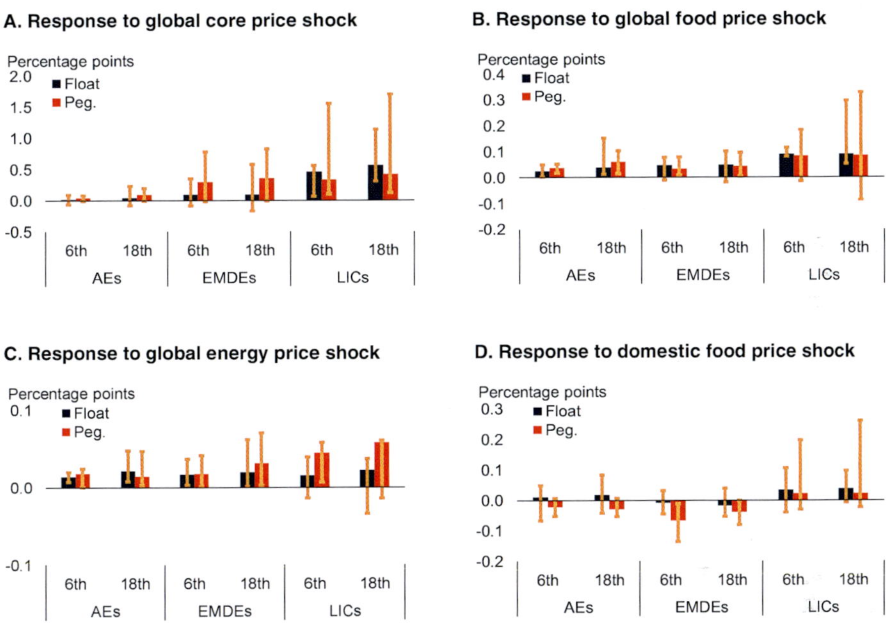

Source: Shambaugh 2004; World Bank.

Note: Cumulative IRFs after 6 and 18 months of domestic core inflation following a 1 percentage point increase in inflation measures. Medians and interquartile ranges (25th and 75th percentiles) of IRF distributions are shown for each country group. The results are based on a heterogeneous panel SVAR model with 104 countries (25 advanced economies, 61 EMDEs, and 18 LICs). Exchange rate regimes are based on the classification by Shambaugh (2004) between 1970m2 and 2016m12. EMDEs here exclude LICs. AEs = advanced economies; EMDEs = emerging market and developing economies; IRFs = impulse response functions; LICs = low-income countries; SVAR = structural vector autoregression.

- *Financial and trade openness.* Panels D and E in Figure 6.6 compare variance decompositions across countries with different degrees of international trade and financial openness. If international financial integration, which brings the possibility of an abrupt reversal in capital flows, imposes more discipline on monetary policy makers and helps anchor inflation expectations over time, this could help explain why advanced economies, which are generally more financially open, exhibit relatively low sensitivity to external inflation shocks, with the lowest sensitivity of all in their highly open subgroup. A similar relationship is exhibited by LICs: for countries with higher capital account openness, the variance share of global shocks is about 50 percent, and for countries with lower capital account openness, the

FIGURE 6.6 Contribution of inflation shocks to core inflation variation

In advanced economies, variations in core inflation are largely explained by domestic core price shocks; in LICs and other EMDEs, they are mostly explained by global core price shocks, possibly reflecting spillovers from advanced economies. The share of core inflation explained by global food and energy shocks is largest in LICs. In advanced economies and other EMDEs, the response to global core price shocks is larger in countries with fixed exchange rates, whereas the opposite is true for LICs. Higher public debt, less central bank transparency, and less capital account openness have been associated with stronger responses of core inflation in LICs to global core price shocks.

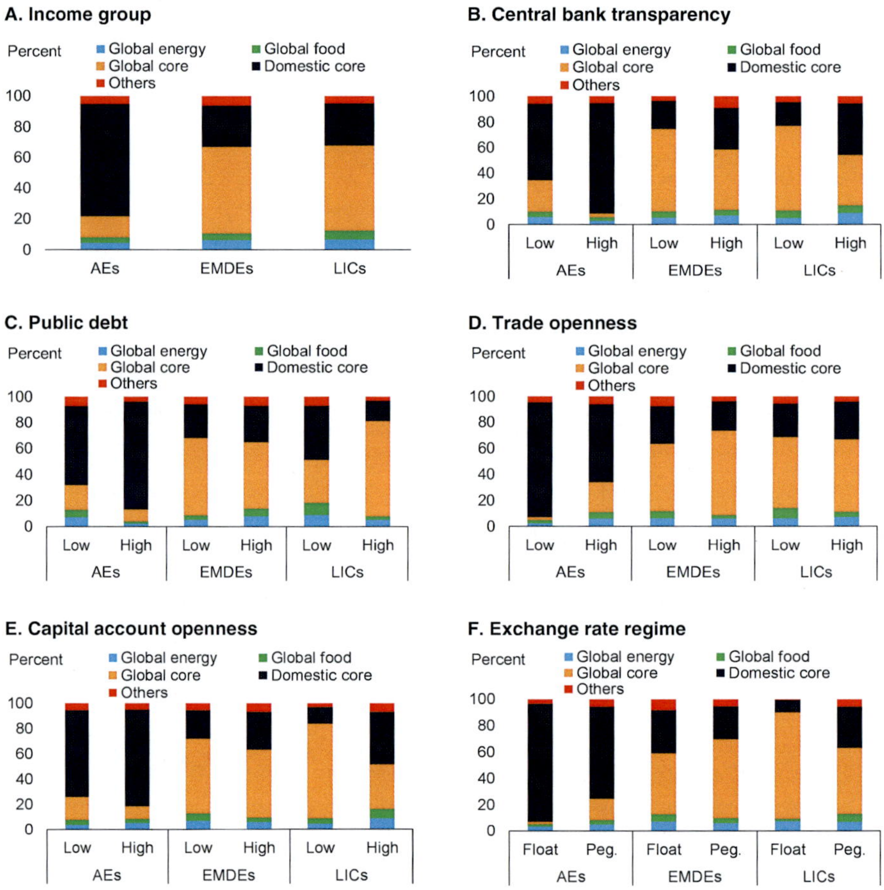

Source: Dincer and Eichengreen 2014; Haver Analytics; International Monetary Fund *International Financial Statistics*; Shambaugh 2004; World Bank.

Note: Forecast error variance decompositions (forecasting horizon: 18 months) based on medians across countries within each group. The results are based on a heterogeneous panel SVAR model with 104 countries (25 advanced economies, 61 EMDEs, and 18 LICs). EMDEs here exclude LICs. AEs = advanced economies; EMDEs = emerging market and developing economies; GDP = gross domestic product; LICs = low-income countries; SVAR = structural vector autoregression.

B.-E. Countries with "high" characteristics are defined as those with values above the median; all others are considered "low."

B. Based on the central bank transparency index by Dincer and Eichengreen (2014).

C. Classification of countries is "high" and "low" based on government debt as a percent of GDP.

D.E. Measures of trade and capital account openness are based on trade (exports plus imports)-to-GDP ratios and the Chinn and Ito (2018) index, respectively.

F. The exchange rate regime is based on Shambaugh (2004).

share is greater than 80 percent. The difference between the more and less integrated subgroups of LICs is larger than in the other country groups. Trade openness, which may also serve as a disciplining device, does not seem to play an important role in the sensitivity of domestic core inflation to global core shocks in LICs, although LICs with higher trade openness show smaller variance shares for global food and energy shocks. In the other country groups, higher trade openness has tended to be associated with higher variance shares for external factors. The latter could reflect that higher trade openness may be associated with higher exposure to global shocks.

- *Exchange rate regime.* The effects of exchange rate regimes differ between advanced economies and non-LIC EMDEs, on the one hand, and LICs on the other (Figure 6.6). Ex ante, it might be expected that fixed exchange rate regimes would be associated with stronger transmission from external inflation shocks to domestic core inflation. This is because small countries that fix will tend to import the inflation performance of their trading partners, whereas those that float can, in principle, control their domestic inflation rates independently. This indeed seems to be what is observed in the case of advanced economies, and to a lesser extent, non-LIC EMDEs: shocks to global core inflation account for a much larger fraction of the variance of domestic core inflation in fixed regimes than in floating regimes. For LICs, however, these findings are reversed: core inflation in floaters is less robust in the face of external shocks than in countries that fix. This may reflect the challenges faced by LIC central banks. Because their domestic inflation rates are determined largely by those of their trading partners, LICs with credibly fixed exchange rates may be characterized by inflation expectations that tend to be anchored to the "normal" inflation experience of their trading partners and not be disrupted by transitory external inflation shocks. By contrast, LICs with floating regimes can avail themselves of no such external anchor; their anchor for inflation expectations has to be homegrown. In the face of the challenges, LIC central banks may find it difficult to provide such an anchor. In its absence, transitory external inflation shocks may create inflation expectations, which become self-fulfilling (discussed more fully in Annex 6.1).

Correlates of the impacts of shocks on core inflation

The discussion above is suggestive and intuitive, but it does not quantify the implications of changes in the country characteristics. To investigate more comprehensively the implications of marginal variations in a wide set of country characteristics, all possible bivariate relationships between the country characteristics and estimated responses (and variance shares) 6 and 18 months after the shocks were systematically explored.

Methodology. Three conceptually distinct types of investigation were conducted.

- First, the country characteristics most likely to be important in explaining the differences in the magnitudes of the cumulative IRFs and variance decompositions between LICs and the other country groups were examined. This was done by first exploring whether an LIC dummy for the response was *significant* in a regression that also included only an EMDE (non-LIC) dummy and a constant, and then checking whether the addition of any country characteristics in the regression rendered the LIC dummy *insignificant.*

- Second, policies that would allow LICs to reduce the transmission of global food, energy, and core price shocks to domestic core inflation were explored using two approaches: studying the marginal association of country characteristics attributable to policies with the cumulative IRFs of domestic core inflation to global shocks, and studying the marginal association of similar characteristics with the variance contributions of global shocks to domestic core inflation variation.

- Third, the existence of an "LIC effect" was tested further by examining whether the responses of the dependent variables to country characteristics differed systematically between LICs and the other country groups. To this end, a series of cross-section estimations were conducted, using the entire sample of 104 countries, in an attempt to isolate the influence of individual country characteristics on the effects of external inflation shocks on the variance of domestic core inflation.

What is the LIC effect? The results of the first investigation are presented in Table 6.1 for equations in which cumulative IRFs were the dependent variable and in Table 6.2 for equations in which the variance decomposition estimates were the dependent variable. The first row of each table indicates the coefficient estimates and significance levels (shown by asterisks) of the LIC dummy when it is included in a regression with a constant and an EMDE (non-LIC) dummy only. The subsequent rows show the results of regressions in which additional variables are included individually. Each row corresponds to a different regression, which includes not only an LIC dummy, EMDE dummy, and constant, but also the variable indicated in the row title. It is important to note that the numeric values and significance levels shown in the table are not those of the additional included variable, but rather of the LIC dummy. Thus, it is for cases in which row 1 shows statistical significance and some other row in the table shows insignificance that it can be inferred that a country characteristic renders an otherwise significant LIC dummy insignificant when included in the regression.

The response of core inflation in LICs to global shocks is only statistically elevated in the case of global food price shocks (Table 6.1). However, global core price shocks explain 37-39 percentage points more of LIC core inflation variation than in other regions (Table 6.2). The latter set of results is consistent with what was noted earlier, in that global inflation shocks appear to make a larger contribution to the variation in domestic inflation in LICs than in other EMDEs or advanced economies.

For the transmission of global food-price shocks, several structural characteristics appear to be important, including dependence on commodity imports, labor market (or demographic) variables, capital account openness, and trade openness. The variable indicating the degree of central bank transparency and independence also appears to play a role. By contrast, for the transmission of global core price shocks, it was difficult to identify country characteristics that could explain the LIC dummy. To some extent, the degree of the LIC effect is influenced by central bank transparency, trade openness, and population growth, since the inclusion of these variables substantially changed the magnitude of the regression coefficients, although it did not render the coefficient on the LIC dummy insignificant. Although these results are not formal tests of causation, they suggest that the degree of central bank transparency, trade and capital account openness, as well as demographic variables are most likely associated with the higher contribution of global inflation shocks to variations in domestic core inflation in LICs. Further empirical investigation of the LIC effect is needed to identify the factors that could render the LIC dummy insignificant. Perhaps, additional structural characteristics of the economy (for example, industry structure) could help explain the LIC effect.

How can LICs reduce their vulnerability to global inflation shocks? To examine how LIC inflation rates respond to global shocks, the previous links are recomputed for LICs only, and thus without an LIC dummy. The results for IRFs of domestic core inflation as the dependent variable 1, 6, and 18 months after the original shock are shown in Table 6.3 and for variance decompositions as the dependent variable in Table 6.4. The coefficients and significance levels shown are now those of the variables indicated in the row titles.

The strength of the energy and food price shock transmissions are inversely associated with increased trade and financial openness as well as increased central bank transparency. Similarly, the results suggest that the magnitude of the transmission of the global core shock is negatively associated with increased

TABLE 6.1 Regression of the response of core inflation

Response of domestic core to	Global energy		Global food		Global core	
Time horizon (months)	6	18	6	18	6	18
LIC dummy	**0.01**	**0.02**	**0.08****	**0.07**	**0.25**	**0.22**
	[0.65]	**[0.48]**	**[2.21]**	**[0.77]**	**[0.67]**	**[0.46]**
Level of headline inflation (LIC dummy in the inclusion of each level of the headline inflation variable)	0.00	0.01	0.07*	0.05	0.62**	0.59
	[0.14]	[0.25]	[1.85]	[0.58]	[2.53]	[1.51]
Commodity importer	0.05**	0.09**	0.06	-0.05	0.55	0.35
	[2.30]	[2.34]	[1.38]	[-0.48]	[1.27]	[0.63]
GDP	0.00	0.01	0.07*	0.05	0.61**	0.62
	[-0.01]	[0.14]	[1.75]	[0.52]	[2.39]	[1.53]
Inflation target	0.00	0.00	0.07*	0.06	0.59**	0.65
	[-0.1]	[0.09]	[1.86]	[0.69]	[2.31]	[1.62]
Pegged exchange rate regime	0.00	0.00	0.066*	0.07	0.53**	0.58
	[-0.07]	[0.12]	[1.76]	[0.8]	[2.09]	[1.43]
Central bank transparency	0.01	0.02	0.05	0.01	0.48*	0.53
	[0.66]	[0.44]	[1.13]	[0.07]	[1.75]	[1.21]
Public debt	0.00	0.00	0.07*	0.07	0.61**	0.60
	[-0.12]	[0.02]	[1.91]	[0.78]	[2.42]	[1.53]
Population growth	0.02	0.02	0.04	0.02	0.39	0.30
	[0.77]	[0.58]	[0.89]	[0.15]	[1.4]	[0.67]
Labor market flexibility	0.01	0.02	0.06	0.05	0.391*	0.37
	[0.51]	[0.51]	[1.61]	[0.54]	[1.86]	[1.03]
Capital account openness	0.01	0.01	0.04	-0.06	0.90***	0.86*
	[0.36]	[0.31]	[0.91]	[-0.59]	[3.01]	[1.8]
Trade openness	0.01	0.01	0.06	0.06	0.67***	0.51
	[0.3]	[0.25]	[1.63]	[0.6]	[2.62]	[1.28]

Source: Chinn and Ito 2018; Dincer and Eichengreen 2014; International Monetary Fund; World Bank.

Note: Each row corresponds to a different regression, where the coefficients and significances (t-values) are those of the variable indicated in the row title. The dependent variables are based on a country-specific heterogeneous panel SVAR estimation for 104 countries (25 advanced economies, 61 EMDEs, and 18 LICs). EMDEs here exclude LICs. GDP is national GDP measured in U.S. dollars using purchasing power parity (not market) exchange rates. Inflation targeting regimes are defined as in IMF (2016). Central bank transparency data are based on Dincer and Eichengreen (2014). Exchange rate regimes are based on Shambaugh (2004). Labor market flexibility is based on the estimates compiled by the Fraser Institute, with a higher value representing a more flexible labor market. The measures of trade and capital account openness are, respectively, trade (exports plus imports)-to-GDP ratios (in percent) and the index compiled by Chinn and Ito (2018). Dependent variables are based on mean values over the country-specific sample periods. The numbers in brackets refer to t-statistics. EMDEs = emerging market and developing economies; GDP = gross domestic product; LIC = low-income country; SVAR = structural vector autoregression.

*** $p < 0.01$, ** $p < 0.05$, * $p < 0.1$ significance levels.

TABLE 6.2 Regression of variance decompositions of core inflation

Variance share for domestic core	Global energy		Global food		Global core	
Forecasting horizon (months)	6	18	6	18	6	18
LIC dummy	**0.01** **[0.36]**	**0.03** **[1.40]**	**0.03**** **[2.04]**	**0.02** **[1.59]**	**0.37***** **[3.83]**	**0.39**** **[4.19]**
Level of headline inflation (LIC dummy in the inclusion of each level of the headline inflation variable)	0.00 [0.2]	0.02 [1.21]	0.02* [1.88]	0.02 [1.35]	0.40*** [4.02]	0.42** [4.38]
Commodity importer	0.01 [0.56]	0.02 [1.03]	0.01 [0.81]	0.00 [0.08]	0.34*** [2.96]	0.38*** [3.39]
GDP	0.00 [0.05]	0.02 [1.01]	0.02* [1.83]	0.02 [1.23]	0.35*** [3.51]	0.38*** [3.87]
Inflation target	0.01 [0.42]	0.03 [1.33]	0.02* [1.74]	0.02 [1.28]	0.32*** [3.29]	0.34*** [3.66]
Pegged exchange rate regime	0.01 [0.29]	0.02 [1.21]	0.02* [1.65]	0.02 [1.39]	0.38*** [3.73]	0.40*** [4.08]
Central bank transparency	0.01 [0.29]	0.03 [1.3]	0.02 [1.42]	0.02 [1.04]	0.25*** [2.36]	0.29*** [2.74]
Public debt	0.01 [0.5]	0.03 [1.5]	0.02* [1.74]	0.02 [1.46]	0.40*** [3.95]	0.42*** [4.31]
Population growth	0.02 [0.87]	0.04* [1.82]	0.02 [1.53]	0.03 [1.48]	0.24*** [2.21]	0.26*** [2.53]
Labor market flexibility	0.01 [0.5]	0.03 [1.58]	0.03*** [2.23]	0.025* [1.71]	0.36*** [3.62]	0.38*** [3.99]
Capital account openness	-0.01 [-0.28]	0.02 [0.85]	0.01 [0.32]	0.00 [0.02]	0.42*** [3.44]	0.42*** [3.57]
Trade openness	0.01 [0.55]	0.03 [1.46]	0.02 [1.33]	0.01 [0.87]	0.48*** [4.88]	0.49*** [5.26]

Source: Chinn and Ito 2018; Dincer and Eichengreen 2014; International Monetary Fund; Shambaugh 2004; World Bank.

Note: Each row corresponds to a different regression, where the regression includes an LIC dummy, an EMDE dummy, a constant, and the variable indicated in the row title. The numeric values and significance levels (t-values) are not those of the additional included variable, but rather those of the LIC dummy when the variable indicated in the row title was included in the regression. Thus, it is cases where row 1 shows significance, and some other row in the table shows insignificance, that are indicative of a country characteristic that rendered an otherwise significant LIC dummy insignificant through its inclusion in the regression. The dependent variables are based on country-specific heterogeneous panel SVAR estimations for 104 countries (25 advanced economies, 61 EMDEs, and 18 LICs). EMDEs here exclude LICs. The LIC dummy equals 1 for any LIC, and 0 for any other country. GDP refers to national GDP measured in U.S. dollars using purchasing power parity (not market) exchange rates. Inflation targeting regimes are defined as in IMF (2016). Central bank transparency data are based on Dincer and Eichengreen (2014). Exchange rate regimes are based on Shambaugh (2004). Labor market flexibility is based on the estimates compiled by the Fraser Institute, with a higher value representing a more flexible labor market. The measures of trade and capital account openness are, respectively, trade (exports plus imports)-to-GDP ratios (in percent) and the index compiled by Chinn and Ito (2018). Dependent variables are based on mean values over the country-specific sample periods. The numbers in brackets refer to t-statistics. EMDEs = emerging market and developing economies; GDP = gross domestic product; LIC = low-income country; SVAR = structural vector autoregression.

*** $p < 0.01$, ** $p < 0.05$, * $p < 0.1$ significance levels.

central bank transparency.[17] Although they are less statistically significant, the results indicate that higher financial and trade openness is associated with increased strength in the transmission of global core shocks into core inflation in LICs.

Therefore, openness measures appear to play different roles for the cumulative IRFs and variance decompositions of domestic core inflation to global relative price shocks versus global core price shocks in LICs. It could be that relative price shocks (for example, shocks in energy and food prices) are mostly driven by supply shocks, and shocks to global core inflation are largely demand shocks. Thus, the differential consequences of openness for the transmission of these shocks into domestic core inflation reflect different channels through which demand and supply shocks are transmitted. Alternatively, it could also be the case that global relative price shocks are less destabilizing for domestic inflation expectations, because opening trade and the domestic financial market to global markets contributes to the anchoring of inflation expectations as a disciplining device. It is also possible that the global core price shocks could have different consequences for domestic core inflation in different groups of LICs, by interacting with other structural features, for example, exchange rate regimes.[18]

In sum, from the two types of regression analysis, it seems that the policy reactions for the LIC effect need not be the same as the causes of the LIC effect, especially for global core price shocks, which explain the largest portion of variation in LICs' core inflation. The exceptions to this might be the degree of openness and the degree of central bank independence, for the transmission of global energy and food price shocks. The above results point toward individual country characteristics that may be significant in helping to account for differences in the transmission of global shocks to domestic core inflation in LICs, or in helping to identify which policies might help reduce the magnitude and variance contribution of these transmissions. The next step is to use these results as a basis for investigating possible multivariate relationships, especially interaction effects that help identify policies that may be particularly effective in anchoring inflation expectations in LICs.

---

[17] The results do not necessarily imply a causal relation from greater central bank transparency to better anchored domestic core inflation in LICs. Central bank transparency may simply be a proxy for a whole constellation of institutional factors that may be conducive to better anchoring of core inflation expectations in LICs (see, for instance, Bordo and Siklos (2017)). The important point is that the usual policy suspects—such as central bank transparency—appear to have the type of association with the anchoring of core inflation expectations that might be expected, but of course these results are at best suggestive.

[18] This would be analogous to the observation in Figure 6.5 that shows that different types of shocks have different consequences for advanced economies and EMDEs, depending on the exchange rate regimes.

TABLE 6.3 LICs: Regression of the response of core inflation on country characteristics

Response of domestic core to	Global energy			Global food			Global core		
Time horizon (months)	1	6	18	1	6	18	1	6	18
Level of headline inflation	0.00	0.01	0.03	0.00	0.01	0.04	-0.02	-0.37	-0.22
	[0.99]	[0.32]	[1.08]	[0.02]	[0.12]	[0.4]	[-0.75]	[-0.91]	[-0.46]
Commodity importer	-0.01	-0.05	-0.06	-0.01	0.03	0.01	-0.01	2.20***	2.23**
	[-0.7]	[-1.5]	[-1]	[-0.54]	[0.32]	[0.07]	[-0.29]	[3.21]	[2.55]
GDP	0.00	0.00	0.003**	0.00	0.00	0.01	0.00	0.02	0.04*
	[1.08]	[1.56]	[2.42]	[1.02]	[1.49]	[1.58]	[-0.8]	[0.87]	[1.65]
Pegged exchange rate regime	-0.01	0.00	-0.04	0.00	-0.01	-0.06	0.04	0.87	0.63
	[-0.89]	[-0.1]	[-0.79]	[-0.07]	[-0.14]	[-0.35]	[1.05]	[1.1]	[0.65]
Central bank transparency	-0.010**	0.01	-0.01	-0.02*	-0.07	-0.15	0.03	-0.03	-0.16
	[-1.98]	[0.56]	[-0.36]	[-1.89]	[-1.14]	[-1.36]	[0.95]	[-0.05]	[-0.27]
Public debt	0.00	0.00	-0.05	-0.01	0.01	-0.06	0.03	0.84	0.26
	[-0.63]	[0.1]	[-1.14]	[-0.66]	[0.16]	[-0.38]	[0.75]	[1.34]	[0.34]
Population growth	0.01	-0.02	-0.01	0.01	0.09	0.09	0.01	0.51	0.73
	[1.07]	[-0.57]	[-0.09]	[0.75]	[0.79]	[0.44]	[0.23]	[0.56]	[0.68]
Labor market flexibility	0.01	0.01	0.08	0.01	-0.08	-0.15	-0.05	1.26*	2.39***
	[0.59]	[0.35]	[1.41]	[0.35]	[-0.66]	[-0.68]	[-1.03]	[1.72]	[3.02]
Capital account openness	0.01	0.06	-0.02	0.00	-0.31*	-0.68**	-0.01	1.42	0.48
	[0.38]	[0.94]	[-0.18]	[-0.03]	[-1.82]	[-2.2]	[-0.17]	[0.92]	[0.25]
Trade openness	-0.01	0.01	-0.09**	-0.02	-0.10	-0.25	0.06*	0.72	-0.18
	[-0.94]	[0.21]	[-2.1]	[-1.08]	[-1.14]	[-1.63]	[1.83]	[1.02]	[-0.2]

Source: Chinn and Ito 2018; Dincer and Eichengreen 2014; International Monetary Fund; Shambaugh 2004; World Bank.

Note: Each row corresponds to a different regression, where the coefficients and significances (t-values) are those of the variable indicated in the row title. The dependent variables are based on a country-specific heterogeneous panel SVAR estimation for 104 countries (25 advanced economies, 61 EMDEs, and 18 LICs). EMDEs here exclude LICs. GDP refers to national GDP measured in U.S. dollars using purchasing power parity (not market) exchange rates. Inflation targeting regimes are defined as in IMF (2016). Central bank transparency data are based on Dincer and Eichengreen (2014). Exchange rate regimes are based on Shambaugh (2004). Labor market flexibility is based on the estimates compiled by the Fraser Institute, with a higher value representing a more flexible labor market. The measures of trade and capital account openness are, respectively, trade (exports plus imports)-to-GDP ratios (in percent) and the index compiled by Chinn and Ito (2018). Dependent variables are based on mean values over the country-specific sample periods. The numbers in brackets refer to t-statistics. EMDEs = emerging market and developing economies; GDP = gross domestic product; LICs = low-income countries; SVAR = structural vector autoregression.

*** $p < 0.01$, ** $p < 0.05$, *$p < 0.1$ significance levels.

TABLE 6.4 LICs: Regression of the variance decompositions of core inflation on country characteristics

Variance share of	Global energy			Global food			Global core		
Forecasting horizon (months)	1	6	18	1	6	18	1	6	18
Level of headline inflation	0.00	0.00	0.00	0.00	0.01*	0.00	-0.02	0.06	0.02
	[0.99]	[0.35]	[-0.46]	[0.02]	[1.69]	[-0.2]	[-0.75]	[0.63]	[.1.14]
Commodity importer	0.00	0.00	0.00	-0.01	-0.01	0.00	-0.01	0.24	-0.01
	[-0.71]	[-0.06]	[0.15]	[-0.54]	[-0.75]	[-0.41]	[-0.29]	[1.32]	[-0.25]
GDP	0.00	0.00	0.00	0.00	0.001***	0.00	0.00	0.01**	0.00
	[1.08]	[0.50]	[0.72]	[1.02]	[2.61]	[0.95]	[-0.8]	[2.47]	[0.76]
Pegged exchange rate regime	-0.01	0.00	0.00	0.00	-0.02	0.00	0.04	0.01	-0.04
	[-0.89]	[-0.17]	[0.11]	[-0.07]	[-1.27]	[0.53]	[1.05]	[0.04]	[-1.27]
Central bank transparency	-0.006**	0.00	0.00	-0.02*	-0.01	0.00	0.02	-0.23**	-0.01
	[-1.98]	[-0.06]	[-0.78]	[-1.89]	[-1.38]	[-0.54]	[0.95]	[-2.41]	[-0.63]
Public debt	0.00	-0.01	0.00	-0.01	0.00	0.00	0.02	-0.12	-0.01
	[-0.63]	[-1.3]	[-1.44]	[-0.66]	[-0.21]	[0.78]	[0.74]	[-0.86]	[-0.26]
Population growth	0.01	0.00	0.00	0.01	0.01	0.01	0.01	0.28	0.02
	[1.07]	[-0.19]	[-1.09]	[0.75]	[0.71]	[1.41]	[0.24]	[1.5]	[0.42]
Labor market flexibility	0.00	-0.01	0.00	0.01	0.00	0.00	-0.05	0.46***	0.08**
	[0.58]	[-0.86]	[0.23]	[0.34]	[-0.11]	[-0.14]	[-1.03]	[2.64]	[2.38]
Capital account openness	0.00	-0.06***	-0.01**	0.00	-0.03	0.02	-0.01	0.12	0.11*
	[0.37]	[-3.59]	[-2.04]	[-0.03]	[-0.75]	[1.33]	[-0.17]	[0.34]	[1.84]
Trade openness	0.00	-0.01	-0.01**	-0.01	-0.03**	0.01	0.06*	-0.22	-0.02
	[-0.92]	[-1.31]	[-2.23]	[-1.08]	[-2.15]	[0.96]	[1.83]	[-1.44]	[-0.84]

Source: Chinn and Ito 2018; Dincer and Eichengreen 2014; International Monetary Fund; Shambaugh 2004; World Bank.

Note: Each row corresponds to a different regression, where the coefficients and significances (t-values) are those of the variable indicated in the row title. The dependent variables are based on a country -specific heterogeneous panel SVAR estimation for 104 countries (25 advanced economies, 61 EMDEs, and 18 LICs). EMDEs here exclude LICs. GDP refers to national GDP measured in U.S. dollars using purchasing power parity (not market) exchange rates. Inflation targeting regimes are defined as in IMF (2016). Central bank transparency data are based on Dincer and Eichengreen (2014). Exchange rate regimes are based on Shambaugh (2004). Labor market flexibility is based on the estimates compiled by the Fraser Institute, with a higher value representing a more flexible labor market. The measures of trade and capital account openness are, respectively, trade (exports plus imports)-to-GDP ratios (in percent) and the index compiled by Chinn and Ito (2018). Dependent variables are based on mean values over the country-specific sample periods. The numbers in brackets refer to t-statistics. EMDEs = emerging market and developing economies; GDP = gross domestic product; LICs = low-income countries; SVAR = structural vector autoregression.

*** $p < 0.01$, ** $p < 0.05$, * $p < 0.1$ significance levels.

How do the effects of country characteristics differ in LICs from other country groups? The presence of an "LIC effect" was explored further by using data for all country groups to examine whether the values of the dependent variable differ systematically for LICs. The results indicate that for LICs and other EMDEs, the share of the 18-month variance in domestic core inflation explained by global core inflation is much higher than for advanced economies, although not greatly different between these two groups (Table 6.5).

Next, the robustness of these differences to the inclusion of other variables was examined. The initial results suggested that the various cross-country differences could affect the transmission of global core inflation to domestic core inflation. Accordingly, the variables capturing trade and financial openness, exchange rate regime, and central bank transparency were included in the regressions, one at a time (columns 2 through 4 of Table 6.5). However, none of these variables made a significant difference. The coefficients on the EMDE (non-LIC) and LIC dummies were essentially unaffected, and none of the additional variables was statistically significant (to save space, these results are not reported). Instead, in column 5, all the variables were included together. Again, none was statistically significant, and the coefficients on the dummies were unaffected. These results suggest that the differences between LICs and other EMDEs, on the one hand, and advanced economies on the other, are not due to systematic differences among these sets of countries with respect to the characteristics most naturally suggested by theory.

The next question considered was whether the different inflation performance of LICs and other EMDEs, relative to advanced economies, is attributable to differences in the effects of the relevant characteristics on the transmission from global to domestic core inflation between LICs and other EMDEs, on the one hand, and advanced economies on the other. This question was explored by interacting these characteristics with the EMDE and LIC dummies, one at a time. If the interaction term is statistically significant, the implication would be that the EMDE or LIC context makes a difference in the role of the relevant characteristics. This was not the case for either of the openness variables (the results are not reported here). However, the exchange rate regime made a substantial difference, as shown in columns 6 and 7 of Table 6.5. The interaction of the pegged exchange rate regime variable, *pegged XR*, with the EMDE and LIC dummies proved highly significant in both cases, but with opposite signs. Fixed exchange rates thus had a substantial negative effect on transmission from the global to the domestic core in LICs, but a modest positive effect in other EMDEs.

The implications are that the "EMDE effect" and "LIC effect" are regime-specific. For illustrative purposes, if *Pegged XR* is set to 0 for countries with floating rates and *Pegged XR* is set to 1 for countries with fixed rates, the EMDE effect (column 6 in Table 6.5) would be 0.39 for floating regime countries and 0.59 for fixed regime countries; for LICs, the corresponding values are 0.67 and 0.04, respectively. Focusing specifically on the LIC results, the upshot is that LICs that fix their exchange rates seem to be able to anchor inflation expectations about as well as advanced economies, and those that float are not able to do so. This result is consistent with the view that LICs have found it difficult to generate homegrown anchors for the domestic core.

To investigate this issue, the possible role of central bank independence in anchoring inflation expectations among LIC floating regime countries was considered. This was done by interacting a measure of central bank independence, *central bank turnover*, with exchange rate flexibility (1 – *Pegged XR*) in LICs.[19] The results are reported in column 7 of Table 6.5. The interaction term is not significant at conventional levels, but, in view of the small number of floating regimes among the LICs in the sample, the p-value of 0.27 makes the negative coefficient at least suggestive: LICs that float may be more successful at anchoring inflation expectations in the face of shocks to global core inflation when their central banks are more independent.

Conclusion

There has been a remarkable degree of convergence of views in academic and policy circles about the principles to which monetary policy should adhere to yield the low and stable medium-term inflation that is conducive to healthy economic growth. However, central banks in LICs face significant challenges in achieving low and stable inflation and anchoring inflation expectations to such an outcome. Meanwhile, globalization has proceeded apace in LICs, as it has elsewhere, affecting, through several channels, the challenges confronted by LICs in achieving this objective.

Nevertheless, over the past two decades, inflation rates in LICs have been declining, from excessively high levels in many cases, and have converged closer to those of advanced economies and other EMDEs, despite the special challenges faced by LICs. These challenges include sizable domestic shocks, as well as large external shocks, which increasing globalization may have amplified. At the same time, inflation has stabilized at a low rate in the large advanced economies. The improvement in LIC inflation performance over the past two decades raises the question of the extent to which it reflects an improved domestic policy environment (that is, homegrown) or has effectively been

[19] The *Central bank turnover* measures central bank turnover rates, the number of changes in central bank heads before the end of the legal term of office, as in Dreher, Sturm, and de Haan (2010). This variable is used here instead of central bank transparency and independence, for wider country coverage of the data.

TABLE 6.5 Regression of the variance of core inflation explained by global core price shocks on country characteristics

Variables	1	2	3	4	5	6	7
EMDE dummy	0.49***	0.50***	0.49***	0.49***	0.49***	0.39***	0.39***
	[0.00]	[0.00]	[0.00]	[0.00]	[0.00]	[0.00]	[0.00]
LIC dummy	0.38***	0.39***	0.38***	0.38***	0.38***	0.67***	0.80***
	[0.00]	[0.00]	[0.00]	[0.00]	[0.00]	[0.00]	[0.00]
Trade openness		0.001			0.001	0.0002	0.0001
		[0.28]			[0.34]	[0.73]	[0.86]
Capital account openness			-0.004		-0.03	-0.09	-0.07
			[0.97]		[0.78]	[0.47]	[0.48]
Pegged exchange rate regime (Pegged XR)				0.04	0.03		
				[0.61]	[0.71]		
Pegged XR*EMDE						0.20**	0.20***
						[0.04]	[0.04]
Pegged XR*LIC						-0.63***	-0.76***
						[0.00]	[0.00]
CB turnover* (1-Pegged XR)*LIC							-0.81
							[0.26]
R^2	0.36	0.37	0.36	0.36	0.37	0.46	0.46

Source: Chinn and Ito 2018; Dreher, Sturm, and de Haan 2010; International Monetary Fund; Shambaugh 2004; World Bank.

Note: Each column corresponds to a different regression. The dependent variables (the variance share of global core shocks for domestic core inflation at the 18-month forecasting horizon) are based on a country-specific heterogeneous panel SVAR estimation for 104 countries (24 advanced economies, 61 EMDEs, and 18 LICs). EMDEs here exclude LICs. The LIC dummy equals 1 for any LIC and 0 for any other country. The EMDE dummy equals 1 for any EMDE and 0 for any other country. CB turnover refers to the number of changes in the head of a central bank before the end of a legal term of office, based on Dreher, Sturm, and de Haan (2010). Because of the wider availability of data for this variable, it is used instead of central bank transparency. Exchange rate regimes are based on Shambaugh (2004). The measures of trade and capital account openness are, respectively, trade (exports plus imports)-to-GDP ratios (in percent) and the index compiled by Chinn and Ito (2018). Dependent variables are based on mean values over the country-specific sample periods. The numbers in brackets refer to p-values. CB = central bank; EMDEs = emerging market and developing economies; GDP = gross domestic product; LICs = low-income countries; SVAR = structural vector autoregression; XR = exchange rate.
*** $p < 0.01$, ** $p < 0.05$, *$p < 0.1$ significance levels.

imported. It is difficult to take a firm view on this question ex ante, because globalization has affected the challenges faced by LIC central banks in complicated ways that do not unambiguously make their anti-inflation objectives easier or more difficult to achieve.

The question must therefore be approached empirically. The heterogeneous panel SVAR technique used for this chapter has allowed us to assess the relative roles of the external inflation environment and domestic factors in driving core inflation in a large group of countries, including LICs and other country groups. The inclusion of other countries provides better estimates of the influence of relevant global factors and the roles of different country characteristics in explaining the susceptibility of domestic core inflation to being dislodged by external shocks. Compared with the existing literature, the results of the analysis in this chapter lead to some new conclusions.

- LIC core inflation tends to respond more strongly to global core inflation than does core inflation in the other country groups.
- LIC core inflation responds more strongly to global food inflation than does core inflation in the other country groups.
- LIC core inflation responds more sharply, although more variably, to global energy inflation than does core inflation in the other country groups.
- Exchange rate pass-through to core inflation also appears to be much larger for LICs than for the other country groups.

Together, these results suggest that, at least in this sample, core inflation was more susceptible to external disturbances in LICs than in the other country groups. Variance decompositions support this result, indicating that most of the variation in domestic core inflation among LICs was accounted for by external inflation shocks, and very little by shocks to domestic core inflation, a result exactly opposite of that of advanced economies.

What sets LICs apart is not so much that they differ from advanced economies (and other EMDEs) in characteristics that might be expected to contribute to importing global inflation, such as trade or financial openness or the exchange rate regime. Rather, it is that these characteristics appear to operate differently in the LIC environment.

Thus, LICs with floating exchange rates have had a difficult time stabilizing inflation at a low rate, although they seem to resist external inflation shocks better when their central banks are more independent. In contrast, LICs that fix their exchange rates seem to be able to succeed in stabilizing core inflation about as well as advanced economies, suggesting that these LICs might have, in essence, imported anti-inflation credibility. This result reflects the economic principle that a fixed exchange rate against a low-inflation currency is a monetary standard in which the foreign central bank provides the nominal anchor.

A flexible exchange rate regime, in contrast, is on its own monetary standard: a domestic nominal anchor must stabilize inflation expectations. A popular, and robust, choice for the latter in this century—for many EMDEs as well as advanced economies—is to set an explicit medium- and long-term inflation target for monetary policy (Adrian, Laxton, and Obstfeld 2018). In this regime, the flexible exchange rate provides an important means of adjustment to real sector shocks, which facilitates the robustness of the regime. Fixed exchange rate regimes, in contrast, have often proven fragile, and are prone to collapse. These factors underline the need for a reform agenda to strengthen the anti-inflation credibility of domestic monetary policy.

The upshot is that LIC central banks do not yet appear to have been sufficiently successful in meeting the challenges posed for them by the environment in which they operate, and they have not yet achieved the objective of securing low and stable medium-term inflation rates on a homegrown basis. Instead, the results in this chapter suggest that their much-improved inflation performance might have largely been imported. Consequently, if global inflation were to rise, LICs would likely see their inflation rising in tandem. Hence, the reform agenda for achieving homegrown anti-inflation credibility in LICs remains unfinished.

The chapter raises some questions. The implications for inflation outcomes of differences in the characteristics of LICs and other EMDEs remain to be explored. Of immediate policy relevance are questions related to reforms of LIC central banks to achieve homegrown anti-inflation credibility. Given the challenging operating environments for LIC central banks, these may well differ from reform priorities elsewhere. Finally, it would be useful to study changes in the transmission of global shocks into LICs.

ANNEX 6.1 Monetary policy challenges in low-income countries

The level and volatility of inflation in low-income countries (LICs) have remained higher than in advanced economies and other emerging market and developing economies over the recent two decades. This divergence may partly reflect special monetary policy challenges that arise in LICs from their volatile economies, conflicts among central bank policy objectives, weaknesses in monetary policy transmission, and limited institutional capacity at central banks. There are various ways in which these challenges may be addressed.

Introduction: The role of monetary policy and its recent performance in low-income countries

Central banks around the world accept that they serve two primary objectives: price stability, meaning low and stable inflation, and financial stability, meaning maintenance of a financial system that is safe and sound (Taylor 2005; Hammond, Kanbur, and Prasad 2009). To achieve their objectives, central banks have two sets of policy instruments. One comprises the instruments of monetary policy, which are used to exert control over the general level of interest rates, particularly short-term rates, and the supply of credit. The other comprises prudential regulation and supervision, including capital requirements applying to financial institutions and constraints on their lending, which are sometimes referred to as macroprudential policies. There is today broad consensus that the instruments of monetary policy are generally best assigned to the objective of price stability, and prudential policies are generally best assigned to the objective of financial stability (Bernanke and Gertler [1999] and many others).

The primary objective of monetary policy is therefore low and stable inflation. This refers more to the medium term rather than the short term, since short-term fluctuations in inflation are unavoidable and of limited importance.

In recent decades, there has been substantial progress in many countries, and globally, toward price stability, with inflation having been lowered considerably from the relatively high levels reached in the 1970s and 1980s. Between 2000 and 2016, the inflation level more than halved in advanced economies and emerging market and developing economies (EMDEs) (excluding low-income countries [LICs]), and inflation volatility has also decreased (Figure 6.1).[1] Despite the global downward trend in the level and volatility of inflation, progress has been less pronounced in LICs. Although headline and core

[1] This trend has continued in recent years. Median consumer price inflation has fallen significantly in EMDEs, to 3.5 percent in 2017, from 5.5 percent per year, on average, in the decade before the global financial crisis. In contrast, median inflation in LICs was 5 percent in 2017, barely changed from the 6 percent average in 1999-2008.

consumer price inflation levels in LICs are still higher than those in advanced economies, the volatility has remained much higher than in advanced economies and other EMDEs (Figure 6.1). It seems that monetary policies in LICs, overall, have not been so successful in recent years for the objective of low and stable inflation, despite a global environment conducive to this aim.

This may be due partly to the particular challenges faced by monetary policy in LICs. These are the subject of this annex, which asks two questions:

- What have been the challenges facing monetary policy in LICs?
- How can the challenges be addressed?

What have been the challenges facing monetary policy in LICs?

A key factor in determining the ability of central banks to achieve low and stable inflation is their success in anchoring the inflation expectations of wage and price setters. If expectations are well anchored at a low inflation rate, temporary departures of inflation from this level will be less likely to set inflation expectations adrift and have prolonged effects on the inflation rate. Inflation expectations are shaped importantly by the credibility of the central bank, which depends partly on the clarity of its stated objectives, and partly on its demonstrated commitment to its objectives and ability to achieve them (Blinder et al. [2008], among many others). These considerations point to several challenges facing monetary policy in LICs.

One challenge is simply that the history of inflation in LICs is unfavorable for establishing confidence in future price stability. LICs therefore face more of a challenge than advanced economies in establishing a convincing track record of low and stable inflation.

More fundamentally, monetary policy in LICs faces challenges arising from conflicts among policy objectives, difficulties in specifying appropriate policy objectives, weaknesses in the instruments and transmission mechanism of monetary policy, and shortcomings in the analytical capacity of central banks. These are considered in turn.

Conflicts among policy objectives

There are several reasons why it may be more challenging in LICs than in advanced economies and many other EMDEs for central banks to focus their policies on the objective of low and stable inflation.

First, because LICs start with relatively high inflation, it is more difficult for a central bank to make a credible commitment to low and stable inflation. This commitment will require the central bank to be willing to tolerate relatively weak activity—negative output gaps—perhaps for an extended period, which will conflict with its secondary objectives (Kasa 2001; Gemayel, Jahan, and Peter 2011).

Second, in LICs there tend to be relatively more frequent supply shocks than in other country groups, arising, for example, from the effects of weather events on agricultural production (Frankel 2011). A poor harvest will tend to increase inflation in the short term while depressing economic activity. Supply shocks thus push inflation and output growth in opposite directions, tending to give rise to a conflict between monetary policy's primary objective of stabilizing prices and its secondary objectives of supporting growth and maintaining a narrow output gap. Stabilizing inflation in response to supply shocks may thus require the sacrifice of the secondary objectives of monetary policy (Nguyen et al. 2017; Adam 2011; Bashar 2011). This contrasts with demand shocks, which are relatively less prevalent in LICs than in other country groups, where stabilizing inflation should simultaneously serve the objective of containing output and employment gaps ("divine coincidence") (Blanchard and Galí 2007).

Third, central banks in LICs are more likely to face conflicts between price stability and fiscal considerations, including the demands of the authorities' fiscal policy (Mas 1995; Prasad 2010). Because they are public sector institutions with the capacity to generate seigniorage revenue through the issuance of interest-free liabilities (most notably, currency), central banks can face pressures to provide cheap financing to governments. These pressures will tend to be greater in LICs, because systems for raising revenue from taxes are relatively less well developed. In the extreme case of fiscal dominance, in which the central bank is institutionally subservient to the finance ministry, meeting the demands of fiscal policy becomes the bank's overriding objective, regardless of its adverse consequences for price stability.

Endowing central banks with legal independence has become more prevalent since the early 1990s, partly as a means to allow central banks to give primacy to price stability over fiscal objectives and enhance their anti-inflation credibility. However, such de jure independence does not necessarily translate into de facto independence. Researchers have constructed measures of the latter based on various indicators, including for EMDEs (for example, Cukierman 2008; Garriga 2016). One study found that although central bank independence increased around the world with reforms undertaken from the early 1990s, EMDEs and the subgroup of LICs remained characterized by less independent central banks than did advanced economies (Garriga 2016).[2]

[2] Garriga's index of independence, which theoretically ranges from 0 (least independence) to 1 (most independence), averaged 0.71 for 34 advanced economies, 0.57 for 110 EMDEs, and 0.62 for 26 LICs.

But even independent central banks may find their commitment to price stability undermined by fiscal constraints. To the extent that a central bank depends on the finance ministry to recapitalize it if it incurs large losses, it may be more receptive to government pressure; and to safeguard its independence in light of this possibility, it may abstain from policies that would require it to incur sustained losses (most notably the sterilization of capital inflows), even if by doing so it endangers price stability. Furthermore, a central bank may find its pursuit of price stability constrained by fiscal considerations even in the absence of concern for its own solvency. For example, when the government's solvency is itself precarious, the central bank may be reluctant to pursue anti-inflation policies that would increase the government's borrowing costs and reduce tax revenues.

Therefore, there are several ways in which fiscal considerations can constrain central banks' policies in pursuit of price stability and undermine their anti-inflation credibility in LICs.

Fourth, in LICs (as in some other EMDEs) the exchange rate may be a more important policy objective than it is in advanced economies (Taylor 2001; Mishkin and Savastano 2001; Buffie et al. 2004; IMF 2015). A declared strategy of stabilizing the nominal exchange rate against one or more currencies of trading partners that have a track record of low and stable inflation may well be compatible with the achievement of domestic price stability. Indeed, for some LICs, such a strategy may offer a particularly effective way to achieve this objective. Given the limited international financial integration of many LICs, the adoption of such an exchange rate peg may leave some scope for monetary management directed toward domestic objectives. For many LICs, therefore, monetary and exchange rate policies may remain potentially independent, as noted by Ostry, Ghosh, and Chamon (2012). This contrasts with advanced economies and many EMDEs that are highly integrated with international financial markets, where the open-economy trilemma implies that it would be impossible to maintain independent monetary and exchange rate policies.

However, conflicts between monetary and exchange rate policies may arise. Thus, an ad hoc assignment of monetary policy to an objective of exchange rate stabilization—motivated, for example, by currency mismatches in balance sheets that mean that depreciation of the domestic currency would increase debt burdens—may be attempted when important preconditions (relating, in particular, to international cost competitiveness and inflation differentials) are not met. Such an effort is likely to prove unsustainable and disruptive and a distraction from monetary stabilization. In such cases, it would be more advisable to address the causes of the balance sheet mismatches, including shortcomings in financial regulation, although constraints on official borrowing in domestic currency (associated with "original sin") may be difficult to address in the short term (Calvo and Reinhart [2002], among many others).

There may also be an inclination in LICs, as in other EMDEs, to adopt the real exchange rate as a policy objective. As argued by Rodrik (2007) and Berg and Miao (2010), the real exchange rate may have an important role to play in development policy through its impact on the traded/nontraded composition of domestic real output and, in particular, as a means to promote export-led growth. Thus, LIC central banks may be led to include a depreciated real exchange rate target among their objectives. But attempting to use monetary policy to serve this objective will not only distract from the objective of price stability, but also be destabilizing for inflation. Thus, a domestic inflation shock will call for monetary policy to be eased to generate a depreciation of the domestic currency that stabilizes the real exchange rate; but the original inflation shock will consequently be magnified.

The upshot is that central banks in LICs may be faced with a broader set of objectives than those in advanced economies.[3] Distraction from the primary objective of monetary policy—price stability—by its secondary aims (supporting employment and growth), fiscal considerations, or the aim a depreciated real exchange rate will typically call for more expansionary monetary policies than the central bank would otherwise pursue.

Difficulties in specifying appropriate policy objectives

The anchoring of inflation expectations depends on more than the central bank's commitment to the broad objective of low and stable inflation. It is also likely to require a declared, quantitatively specific inflation objective for the medium term that has public support, and against which the public can judge the central bank's performance.[4]

However, specification of an inflation objective may prove relatively challenging in LICs. It is unlikely that simply importing the inflation targets of advanced economies (about 2 percent per year) would be optimal for LICs. There are

[3] A recent survey of International Monetary Fund country desks for 44 LICs and 21 lower-middle-income countries found that, although price stability was an important objective of monetary policy in around four-fifths of the countries, more than two-thirds of the central banks were charged with two or more objectives (IMF 2015). The definition of LICs in the paper differs from the one used in this chapter.

[4] In the past, particularly in the 1970s and 1980s, "intermediate targets" for the growth of monetary aggregates were widely used, especially by advanced economies, in attempts to anchor inflation expectations. This strategy encountered several difficulties, including significant differences in the behavior of various aggregates; difficulties encountered by central banks in controlling the aggregates; and instability of relationships between the aggregates and economic developments, including inflation. Monetary aggregates are still monitored by central banks, but reliance on them is now limited and monetary targets play a small role.

grounds for believing that official inflation objectives in LICs should be somewhat higher than in advanced economies.

First, the weakness of formal tax systems in LICs, and the high collection costs frequently associated with them, point to the argument for a larger relative role of seigniorage as a source of government revenue, particularly from the relatively large informal sector, where tax collection is limited (Huang and Wei 2006; Di Bella et al. 2006). However, the argument for a larger role for seigniorage revenue, and therefore a higher optimal inflation rate than in advanced economies, depends partly on the productivity of public sector spending. Where there are grounds for believing that public sector spending yields a particularly high marginal social rate of return (for example, in areas such as health and education), the social value of marginal government revenue to finance these outlays will be high, suggesting a greater role for seigniorage revenue and therefore a higher optimal inflation rate than in countries where such marginal social returns are lower. This is one reason why appropriate inflation objectives will tend to vary from country to country.

Second, there is empirical evidence that higher inflation begins to exert negative effects on economic growth at significantly higher inflation rates in EMDEs than in advanced economies (for example, Khan and Senhadji 2001), with significant variation in the effects among individual countries.

These considerations suggest that the challenge is to identify appropriate country-specific inflation objectives. The specification of inflation objectives has indeed proven to be a challenging task for central banks in LICs. The survey of International Monetary Fund (IMF) country desk economists reported in IMF (2015) found that most low- and lower-middle-income countries that listed price stability as a central bank objective, but that had not adopted formal inflation targeting, did not have a numerical inflation target, and those that had such a target simply tended to align it with the bank's inflation forecast.[5]

To the extent that central banks in LICs have objectives in addition to low and stable inflation, such as small output or employment gaps, these will also need to be quantified. This too may pose serious challenges for LICs. Estimation of output and employment gaps, and of appropriate objectives for them, is highly problematic in advanced economies, because of instability in the relationship between unemployment and inflation and uncertainty surrounding estimates of potential output. It is likely to be even more so in LICs, for example, because of the higher incidence of supply shocks and the greater prevalence and variability of underemployment.

[5] Again, this is a different set of countries from the group of LICs used in this chapter.

Weaknesses in the instruments and transmission mechanism of monetary policy

In advanced economies and many of EMDEs, the key (conventional) monetary policy instrument is a very short-term interest rate, most often an interbank rate such as the federal funds rate in the United States. The central bank can exert close control over the interbank rate through its supply of reserves to the banking system and administration of standing facilities. In LICs, however, interbank markets are typically absent, as are liquid secondary markets in government securities, which the central bank could seek to influence through open-market operations. The government securities market in LICs tends to be a primary market in which the counterparties to the central bank are commercial banks that adopt a buy-and-hold strategy for such securities. Thus the central bank conducts monetary policy by directly lending to and borrowing from the commercial banking system (for example, through repo transactions) or by doing so indirectly through the primary market for government securities. These transactions operate by altering the cost of official funds for the banking system.

Thus, in LICs monetary policy heavily depends on the bank lending channel, and it is typically not activated through an interbank market. Other channels of transmission that are operative in advanced economies, including through interest rates on traded securities, exchange rates, and asset prices, are much weaker in LICs (Mishra, Montiel, and Spilimbergo 2012). This reflects the absence of highly liquid markets for privately issued traded securities; weak links with international financial markets, coupled with relatively inflexible exchange rates; small and illiquid markets for equities; and poorly organized real estate markets.

The strength and reliability of the bank lending channel are therefore particularly important in LICs. But they tend to be limited by several factors. First, LICs are generally characterized by limited financial inclusion and relatively small formal financial sectors that have only weak links to economic activity in the important informal sectors of the economy. Second, the institutional and legal environment in these economies—including property rights, accounting and disclosure standards, and contract enforcement—tends to be relatively weak (see, for example, Beck, Demirgüç-Kunt, and Levine [2009] on LICs in Sub-Saharan Africa). This makes financial intermediation from private savers to private borrowers costly and risky, inducing banks to limit this activity and prefer holding safer government securities. Third, productive activity in these economies is often dualistic, characterized by a few large, well-established firms and many very small, opaque, and often unstable ones. The marginal cost of bank lending to large firms tends to be relatively low despite the imperfections in the domestic institutional environment. But the marginal cost of extending credit to small firms is likely to rise steeply, so that the volume of lending to such firms may be very insensitive to fluctuations in bank funding costs induced by monetary policy. In short, Tobin's description of the effects of easing monetary policy under conditions of high liquidity preference as "pushing on a string" may be an especially apt analogy in the case of LICs, and the effects of tightening policy are also likely to be limited. A survey of studies of the strength and reliability of monetary transmission in LICs, by Mishra and Montiel (2013), and the empirical evidence based on a large panel of countries by Mishra et al. (2014) are consistent with this perspective.

The challenges created for monetary policy by weak monetary transmission could conceivably be overcome if the strength of monetary policy effects on such variables as inflation, real output, and the exchange rate could be reliably estimated, since weak effects could be offset by stronger policy measures. However, the strength of monetary transmission in LICs has proven difficult to estimate because of data limitations (Li et al. 2016). Several investigators have focused more narrowly on the extent of pass-through from policy rates to bank lending rates. Saborowski and Weber (2013), for example, find that although changes in policy rates tended to be transmitted almost one-for-one into retail bank lending rates in advanced economies, pass-through in developing countries was only in the range of 30-45 percent. Abuka et al. (2015) find similar evidence for Uganda in relation to advanced economies, and that pass-through was particularly weak in less financially developed Ugandan districts. But they find evidence that increases in policy rates were associated with a reduced supply of bank credit, suggesting that a bank lending channel was operative in Uganda, although it was weaker than in advanced economies.

Shortcomings in the analytical capacity of central banks

Because monetary policy affects the economy with lags, an important component of inflation targeting—or, for that matter, any other activist monetary policy regime—is the ability of the central bank to forecast with a modicum of accuracy its target variables on the assumption of unchanged policies as well as to assess the effects on those variables of potential changes in the settings of its instruments. In many advanced economies and non-LIC EMDEs, these tasks are performed using structural macroeconomic models of the economies in question. However, few LIC central banks have such models with proven track records (IMF 2015). Although work on such models is underway at many LIC central banks, the task is formidable, not least because of the lack of relevant historical data, insufficient knowledge about the macroeconomic structure of the economies concerned, rapid structural change in the economy, and shortages of research expertise.

The analytical capacity of LIC central banks—even their ability to monitor and assess recent and current economic developments—is generally hampered by serious data deficiencies (Gemayel, Jahan, and Peter 2011; IMF 2015). Thus, data on economic developments in informal sectors, which are often large, are typically absent or grossly inadequate. Official estimates of real gross domestic product (GDP) are typically available only with annual frequency and often with substantial lags.[6] Labor market data, including on wages and unemployment rates, are generally poor. The absence of a well-defined term structure of yields in financial markets makes it difficult to assess market expectations of future monetary policy actions. Finally, estimates of inflation expectations are generally unavailable because of the absence of survey evidence and market-based measures derived from differences between yields on comparable indexed and non-indexed securities.

Complications introduced by globalization

Finally, globalization changes the environment in which LIC central banks operate in significant ways, both aggravating and easing the challenges they face in attaining their objectives. Consider four aspects of globalization:

- Increasing size of the domestic traded goods sector.
- For many LICs, increasing volume of inflows of workers' remittances.
- Larger presence of foreign-owned banks in the domestic economy.
- Increased (although still limited) integration with the international financial market.

Understood in this way, globalization has several effects on the environment in which LIC central banks operate. First, globalization is likely to alter the stability properties of the domestic economy in complicated ways. It increases the economy's exposure to external shocks, in the form of exogenous changes in the foreign-currency prices of traded goods, remittance flows, and capital flows. Larger remittance flows, for instance, simultaneously magnify the channels of transmission from the international real economy to domestic aggregate demand.[7] Second, globalization may alter the trade-offs the central bank faces

[6] Berg et al. (2015) report that only 13 of the 45 Sub-Saharan African countries in IMF databases have any quarterly data for GDP, and only five have data on nominal and real GDP. For those with quarterly data, the median span of the data is less than nine years. As an indicator of measurement error for real GDP in LICs, Ley and Misch (2014) compare the final estimates of real GDP for a particular year, as available five years later, to the estimates made by IMF staff in the spring after the year in question. They find that differences were twice as large for LICs as for Organisation for Economic Co-operation and Development countries.

[7] By estimating a dynamic panel model over 1970-2007, Arusha and Debdulal (2013) document that international remittance inflows decrease with home country volatility.

between competing objectives. Although most LICs remain poorly integrated with international financial markets, international financial shocks will increasingly pose challenges for central banks in LIC economies as well, especially in the form of destabilizing central bank objectives such as high levels of economic activity, stable exchange rates, and financial sector robustness. This will make the potential conflicts between such objectives and the central one of achieving medium-run price stability potentially more acute. Third, globalization may affect the monetary transmission mechanism in several ways (Abuka et. al. 2015; Montiel and Pedroni 2018). Much research has found a link between individual bank characteristics and the extent to which those banks tend to pass through changes in policy interest rates to their own retail lending rates.[8] More generally, globalization may also affect the relative merits of alternative exchange rate and monetary policy regimes in LICs. For instance, a larger traded goods sector increases the effectiveness of fixed exchange rates in importing anti-inflation credibility, because a larger share of the domestic price level is directly affected by international goods arbitrage.

How can these challenges be addressed?

Many of the challenges discussed above are related to the stage of economic and financial development of LICs and should be addressed as part of the broader development process. These include the development of financial markets that may be expected to provide the central bank with more effective policy instruments, the improvement of systems for the compilation of economic statistics, and capacity development in central banks and economic ministries, including strengthening economic expertise.

The focus here, however, is on the issue of conflicts among policy objectives—a potentially serious obstacle to a central bank's success in maintaining price stability and achieving anti-inflation credibility. How can this be addressed? There are several promising options for LICs.

First, the central banks need to pay attention to the secondary objectives of its monetary policy—particularly employment and the output gap—which could be alleviated by the authorities' use of other economic policies. These could include the judicious use of budgetary policy when there is fiscal space, and structural reforms that reduce the economy's vulnerability to shocks, strengthen automatic fiscal stabilizers, increase the flexibility and effectiveness of discretionary fiscal policy, and increase the flexibility of labor markets.

[8] For example, Abuka et al. (2015) find that better-capitalized banks in Uganda were less likely to pass through changes in policy rates. Since foreign banks tend to differ from domestic banks along many of the relevant dimensions, the changing composition of the domestic banking system associated with foreign bank penetration is likely to affect aggregate pass-through.

Second, the central bank could develop or strengthen instruments separate from monetary policy to address its objective of financial stability, including capital flow management measures and macroprudential policies.

Third, entrusting a large part of the responsibility for financial stability to a supervisory and regulatory authority, separate from the central bank and associated with a well-capitalized deposit insurance agency, could relieve pressure on the central bank to concern itself with financial stability in the conduct of monetary policy.

Finally, the central bank could strengthen its efforts to convince the public of the primacy it gives to the low-inflation objective, in ways discussed by Mishkin (1997). Declaration of a specific inflation target—the strategy adopted by most advanced economies—could serve this purpose, but this strategy may not yet suit LICs, for various reasons. These include weak and uncertain monetary transmission, data deficiencies, and limited analytical capacity at central banks. For economies with weak anti-inflation records and credibility, like many LICs, a more effective option could be to peg the exchange rate to a currency or basket of currencies of one or more trading partners with well-established records of low inflation. In effect, the central bank would be piggybacking on the low-inflation credibility earned by these other countries. This would necessarily be at the cost of a loss of monetary autonomy—the central bank would be "tying its hands"—if the economy is well integrated with international financial markets. This may not be a major concern for many LICs at present, because their financial integration is limited, and some monetary autonomy may remain. However, it is important not to lost sight of the significant drawbacks of limited international financial integration, including weakening of the disciplining mechanism that financial integration may exert on a central bank and contribute to its anti-inflation credibility. The strategy of an exchange rate peg is less likely to be successful for relatively closed economies, where the exchange rate plays a small role in domestic price formation. There is also a danger that the exchange rate peg may be unsustainable—for example, if it is initially set at a level that, in real terms, makes the economy uncompetitive, or if the convergence of domestic inflation to inflation rates in the partner countries whose currencies provide the currency peg does not occur rapidly.

ANNEX 6.2 Methodology and database

Model description

This annex explains the details of the heterogeneous panel structural vector autoregression (SVAR) methodology used in this chapter. The technique is an adaptation of the heterogeneous panel SVAR methodology first developed by Pedroni (2013). The method is modified to accommodate some of the specific aspects of the analysis of this chapter.

The most important of these adaptations is to accommodate the details of the reduced form specification used in the estimation and analysis of the inflation dynamics in a way that takes advantage of the relatively abundant data sample. To provide motivation for the adaptation, it is worth noting that the original specification developed in Pedroni (2013) works under any method of orthogonalization of the white noise impulses of a vector autoregression (VAR), including the type of Cholesky orthogonalization used in this chapter. The original specification imposes a form of structural discipline on the relationship between the common and idiosyncratic components of these impulses that allows the estimation and inference to be done with very short panels, even though the dynamics are permitted to be heterogeneous among the countries of the panel. Specifically, the approach envisions that the panel vector of what are referred to as the structural impulses or "shocks" is decomposed into analogous mutually orthogonal vectors of common and idiosyncratic structural shocks such that the loadings on these vectors are diagonal.

To use a concrete example of this form of structure, taken from Pedroni (2013), if such a panel vector is thought of as composed of two composite structural shocks, "aggregate supply," ϵ_{it}^{AS}, and "aggregate demand," ϵ_{it}^{AD}, so that $\epsilon_{it} = (\epsilon_{it}^{AS}, \epsilon_{it}^{AD})'$, then the relationship between these composite shocks and the corresponding common shocks $\bar{\epsilon}_t = (\bar{\epsilon}_{it}^{AD}, \bar{\epsilon}_{it}^{AS})'$ and the corresponding idiosyncratic shocks $\tilde{\epsilon}_{it} = (\tilde{\epsilon}_{it}^{AS}, \tilde{\epsilon}_{it}^{AD})'$, becomes $\epsilon_{it} = \Lambda_i \bar{\epsilon}_t + \tilde{\epsilon}_{it}$ where Λ_i is the diagonal loading matrix. To put it simply, aggregate demand shocks load only into composite aggregate demand shocks, and not into composite aggregate supply shocks, and so forth, so that the contributions of idiosyncratic and common demand shocks sum to the contribution of the total composite demand shocks. Once the vectors ϵ_{it} and $\bar{\epsilon}_t$ have been structurally identified, the diagonality of Λ_i on the factor structure for the white noise shocks permits consistent estimation of the loadings by simple computation of the correlation between the corresponding elements of ϵ_{it} and $\bar{\epsilon}_t$, which allows for good small sample estimation properties even in relatively short panels.

By contrast, when the analysis is based on reduced form impulse shocks, as in the case of this chapter, then it may be desirable to loosen this structural aspect, since the white noise impulse shocks are themselves unknown linear combinations of any underlying structural shocks. This in turn also allows the shapes of the responses to the reduced form common and idiosyncratic components to differ more substantially from one another, again presumably because the mix of underlying structural shocks is free to differ among the common and idiosyncratic components. The econometric cost to reducing these structural aspects of the estimation is of course an increased need for data, particularly in the time series dimension. But in the application in this chapter, sufficient data were obtained to accomplish this.

Thus, to implement this adaptation, in the absence of diagonality of the loading matrix, one of the simplest and most transparent approaches is to exploit directly the remaining orthogonality between the common and idiosyncratic shocks. This can be done by thinking of the panel SVAR as a common global block and a country-specific domestic block nested within the panel, with the orthogonality between the common and idiosyncratic shocks implemented through a set of Granger noncausal restrictions. In effect, the panel SVAR is estimated recursively in multiple tiers, in this case a global tier and a domestic tier, with the global tier estimated first, and then placed within the domestic tier in a manner such that the domestic tier has no impact on the global tier. The global variables can be represented by cross-sectional averages of the national-level variables, as in Pedroni (2013), by variables reported directly at the global level, or any combination of the two.

To see the details of this adapted approach as it relates to the specific setup, let $\Delta Z_{it} = \Delta(\text{Energy}_t, \text{Food}_t, \text{Core}_t, \text{food}_{it}, \text{core}_{it}, \text{neer}_{it})'$ be the data vector, where ΔEnergy_t is global energy inflation, ΔFood_t is global food inflation, ΔCore_t is global average core inflation, Δfood_{it} is domestic food inflation instrumented by the rainfall data, Δcore_{it} is domestic core inflation, and Δneer_{it} is the nominal effective exchange rate (NEER) appreciation rate. In this case, the vector moving average form for the panel can be represented here as $\Delta Z_{it} = A_i(L)\epsilon_{it}$, $A_i(L) = \Sigma_{j=0}^{Q} A_{ij}$, with the upper left 3 x 3 block representing the global time-series block, the lower right 3 x 3 block representing the local domestic block, and the lower left 3x3 block representing the interactions running from the global block to the domestic block. In precise terms, the Cholesky orthogonalization of the error terms combined with the remaining orthogonalization into common versus idiosyncratic shocks becomes equivalent to the following set of restrictions in this notational form, namely $[A(k,\ell)_j] = 0\, \forall j, \forall k < \ell$ when $k \leq 3$, $A(k,\ell)_j = 0$ for $j = 0, \forall k < \ell$ when $k > 3$.

However, these restrictions can be implemented equivalently by implementing a recursive two-tiered estimation algorithm. The estimation algorithm for this adaptation, which implements these restrictions, can now be summarized as follows.

1. Construct the global variable block, by estimating cross-sectional averages $\Delta\bar{Z}_t = N_t^{-1}\Sigma_{i=1}^{N_t} \Delta Z_{it}$, where the notation N_t reflects that the panel need not be balanced, or use global variables directly, as desired.
2. Estimate the 3 x 3 global tier VAR $\bar{R}\ (L)\Delta\ \bar{Z}_t = \bar{\mu}\ t, \bar{R}\ (\mathrm{L}) = I - \Sigma_j^P =1\ \bar{R}_j$, E $[\bar{\mu}_t\ \bar{\mu}_t']= \bar{\Omega}\mu$ and fix this block.
3. Estimate 6 x 6 individual VARs as $R_i\ (\mathrm{L})\Delta Z_{it} = \mu_{it}$, $R_i\ (\mathrm{L}) = I - \Sigma_{j=1}^{P_i} R_{i,j}$, $\mathrm{E}[\mu_{it}\,\mu_{it}'] = \Omega_{i,\mu}\ \forall i$ with the global tier estimates imposed on the upper left 3 x 3 block and the lower right 3 x 3 block set to zero for all lags.
4. Use the Cholesky factorization $\Omega_{i,\mu} = A_i(0)A_i(0)'$ to orthogonalize the reduced form shocks such that $\epsilon_{it} = A_i(0)^{-1}\mu_{it}$, and compute the corresponding country-specific impulse responses and variance decompositions on the basis of $A_i\,(L) = R_i(\mathrm{L})^{-1}A_i(0)$.[1]
5. Use the sample distributions for individual country specific impulse responses and variance decompositions to compute the quantile responses among countries, if desired.[2]
6. Project the sample distributions for the individual impulse responses and variance decompositions onto the sample distributions of individual country characteristics x_i to study the country-specific characteristics associated with the cross-sectional heterogeneity of the dynamics, such as $\bar{A}_{i,s}(\mathrm{k}, \ell) = \alpha_s + \beta_s'x_i + \eta_{i,s}\ \forall \mathrm{k}, \ell, s, s = 0, \ldots, Q$ forecast horizons.

Data and sources

A monthly panel data set was used, covering 104 countries, including 25 advanced economies, 61 non-low-income-country (LIC) emerging market and developing economies (EMDEs), and 18 LICs for 1970M2-2016M12.[3] The

[1] In this chapter, estimation of the VAR model is done on the basis of reduced-form VAR representation and identification of the structural form, and representation of the results is based on the structural vector moving average form.

[2] Using a bootstrap method, this chapter checked the statistical significance of the impulse response functions estimated from the heterogeneous panel SVAR model. The confidence intervals indicate that the results are significant at the 5 percent level across all country groups.

[3] The 104 countries included in the data set satisfy the panel SVAR condition that for a country to be included in the sample, it must contain at least 36 months of continuous data for the intersection of the country block, for all variables, namely (i) headline CPI, (ii) food CPI, (iii) energy CPI, (iv) core CPI, (v) NEER, and (vi) rainfall.

panel data set is unbalanced, with the number of observations varying across countries. Various sources were used to construct the monthly series on headline, food, and energy inflation. The main sources for headline consumer price index (CPI) inflation include Haver Analytics, the International Monetary Fund (IMF) *International Financial Statistics*, and OECDstat. Similarly, food and energy inflation data are covered by OECDstat, the Economic and Statistical Observatory for Sub-Saharan Africa, and Haver Analytics. And, for some countries, data were obtained from national sources. The NEER data were obtained from the *International Financial Statistics*.

Core inflation. This is obtained by subtracting the contributions of volatile components of the CPI, such as food and energy inflation. First, a measure of core inflation is obtained by using official core data from OECDstat and Haver Analytics. For the countries for which official core inflation was not available, it was estimated by deducting food and energy[4] inflation multiplied by their corresponding weights from headline CPI inflation and dividing this contribution from the core by the weight of core inflation in the total CPI. The following formula for calculating core inflation was utilized:

$$\text{Core inflation} = \frac{[\pi - \omega_F \pi_F - \omega_E \pi_E]}{1 - \omega_F - \omega_E}$$

where π, π_F, and π_E are the current monthly inflation rates for headline, food, and energy, respectively, and ω_F and ω_E are the current weights for food and energy, respectively. Weights of the sub-indexes in the total index were obtained from the Consumer Price Index database published by the IMF as well from OECDstat and Haver Analytics.

Rainfall. Rainfall is used as an instrumental variable in identifying supply-driven changes in domestic food prices. Rainfall monthly data come from the World Bank's *Climate Change Knowledge Portal: Historical Data*. The data set is produced by the Climatic Research Unit of the University of East Anglia, and reformatted by the International Water Management Institute. The monthly mean historical rainfall data can be mapped to show the baseline climate and seasonality by month. Rainfall is measured as millimeters per month for all countries for 1970-2016. To test the relevancy of the instruments, panel-based Lambda-Pearson statistics (or Fischer statistics) are used.[5] Specifically, the

[4] For most LICs and other EMDEs measures of monthly energy inflation are not available. Instead, for these countries the calculation of core inflation uses the Housing, Water, Electricity, Gas and Other Fuels category of the CPI as a proxy for energy inflation.

[5] Constructing the F-statistic for joint significance of all the corresponding members of the panel would not be desirable, because F-statistics are well known to behave poorly as the number of implied restrictions grows large.

Lambda-Pearson statistic is constructed as $-2.0\text{x}\Sigma_i lnP_i$ (where, lnP_i is the natural log of the significance level associated with the F-test for significance of the rainfall instrumental variable for country *i*). Under the null hypothesis of significance of the rainfall instrumental variable for the panel, the Lambda-Pearson panel statistic will have a chi-square distribution with 2xN degrees of freedom, where N is the number of countries. The results show that the instrumental variables are significant at the 5 percent level. (In the case of LICs, they are significant at the 1 percent level.)

Country characteristics

To help explain the variation of domestic inflation, several potentially important country-specific characteristics were used that may affect a nation's inflation rate. The characteristics considered are (i) the exchange rate regime by the classification of Shambaugh (2004) (where "1" is assigned to countries that have pegged or fixed exchange rates, and "0" is assigned to those with flexible exchange rates); (ii) an indicator of whether a country has an inflation targeting framework; (iii) Dincer and Eichengreen's (2014) central bank transparency index (the higher the index is, the more transparent and independent the central bank is); (iv) gross public debt as a percentage of gross domestic product (GDP); (v) trade openness, defined as the sum of exports and imports of goods and services as a share of GDP from the World Bank's World Development Indicators and the IMF's *World Economic Outlook*; (vi) an indicator of the degree of global value chain (GVC) participation (where "1" is assigned to countries that are considered to be well-integrated into GVCs and "0" otherwise); (vii) the Chinn and Ito (2018) index of capital account openness; (viii) an indicator of whether a country is a commodity importer or exporter; and (ix) central bank turnover, using data compiled by Dreher, Sturm, and de Haan (2010). For a complete list of the country characteristics, sources, and methods used for construction of the indicators, see the Appendix.

References

Abuka, C., R. Alinda, C. Minoui, J. L. Peydro, and A. Presbitero. 2015. "The Bank Lending Channel in a Frontier Economy: Evidence from Loan-Level Data." https://www.rieti.go.jp/jp/events/15061501/pdf/7-2_presbitero.pdf.

Adam, C. 2011. "On the Macroeconomic Management of Food Price Shocks in Low-income Countries." *Journal of African Economies* 20 (1): i63-i99.

Adrian, T., D. Laxton, and M. Obstfeld, eds. 2018. *Advancing the Frontiers of Monetary Policy*. Washington, DC: International Monetary Fund.

Agénor, P. R., and L. P. da Silva, 2013. "Inflation Targeting and Financial Stability: A Perspective from the Developing World." Working Paper 324, Banco Central do Brasil, Brasília, Brazil.

Arusha, C., and M. Debdulal. 2013. "International Business Cycles and Remittance Flows." *B.E. Journal of Macroeconomics* 13 (1): 1-33.

Bashar, O. H. M. N. 2011. "The Role of Aggregate Demand and Supply Shocks in a Low-Income Country: Evidence from Bangladesh." *Journal of Developing Areas* 44 (2): 243-64.

Beck, T., A. Demirgüç-Kunt, and R. Levine. 2009. "Financial Institutions and Markets across Countries and over Time – Data and Analysis." Policy Research Working Paper 4943, World Bank, Washington, DC.

Berg, A., and Y. Miao. 2010. "The Real Exchange Rate and Growth Revisited: The Washington Consensus Strikes Back?" IMF Working Paper 10/58, International Monetary Fund, Washington, DC.

Berg, A., S. O'Connell, C. Pattillo, R. Portillo, and D. F. Unsal. 2015. "Monetary Policy Issues in Sub-Saharan Africa." In *The Oxford Handbook of Africa and Economics: Policies and Practices*, edited by C. Monga and J. Y. Lin. Oxford: Oxford University Press.

Bernanke, B., and M. Gertler 1999. "Monetary Policy and Asset Price Volatility." *Federal Reserve Bank of Kansas City Economic Review* Q (IV): 17-51.

Blanchard, O., and J. Galí. 2007. "Real Wage Rigidities and the New Keynesian Model." *Journal of Money, Credit and Banking* 39 (s1): 35-65.

Blinder, A., M. Ehrmann, M. Fratzscher, J. de Haan, and D. Jansen. 2008. "Central Bank Communication and Monetary Policy: A Survey of Theory and Evidence." *Journal of Economic Literature* 46 (4): 910-45.

Bordo, M. D., and P. L. Siklos. 2017. "Central Bank Credibility before and after the Crisis." *Open Economies Review* 28 (1): 19-45.

Buffie, E., C. Adam, S. O'Connell, and C. Pattillo. 2004. "Exchange Rate Policy and the Management of Official and Private Capital Flows in Africa." *IMF Staff Papers* 51 (s1): 126-60.

Calvo, G., and C. Reinhart. 2002. "Fear of Floating." *Quarterly Journal of Economics* CXVII (2): 379-408.

Carstens, A. 2018. "Agustín Carstens interview with Börsen-Zeitung." Available at https://www.bis.org/speeches/sp180523.htm.

Chinn, M., and H. Ito. 2018. "The Chinn-Ito Index – A de jure Measure of Financial Openness." http://web.pdx.edu/~ito/Chinn-Ito_website.htm.

Cukierman, A. 2008. "Central Bank Independence and Monetary Policymaking Institutions: Past, Present, and Future." *European Journal of Political Economy* 24 (4): 722-36.

Dincer, N. N., and B. Eichengreen. 2014. "Central Bank Transparency and Independence: Updates and New Measures." *International Journal of Central Banking* 10 (1): 189-259.

Di Bella, G., A. A. Selassie, B. Clements, J. K. Martijn, and S. Tareq. 2006. "Designing Monetary and Fiscal Policy in Low-Income Countries." IMF Occasional Papers 250, International Monetary Fund, Washington, DC.

Dreher, A., J. Sturm, and J. de Haan. 2010. "When Is a Central Bank Governor Replaced? Evidence Based on a New Data Set." *Journal of Macroeconomics* 32 (3): 766–81.

Frankel, J. A. 2011. "Monetary Policy in Emerging Markets: A Survey." In *Handbook of Monetary Economics 3B*, edited by B. M. Friedman and M. Woodford. New York: Elsevier.

Garriga, A. C. 2016. "Central Bank Independence in the World: A New Data Set." *International Interactions* 42 (5): 849-68.

Gemayel, E., S. Jahan, and A. Peter. 2011. "What Can Low-Income Countries Expect from Adopting Inflation Targeting?" IMF Working Paper 11/276, International Monetary Fund, Washington, DC.

Hammond, G., R. Kanbur, and E. Prasad. 2009. "Monetary Policy Challenges for Emerging Market Economies." In *New Monetary Policy Frameworks for Emerging Markets: Coping with the Challenges of Financial Globalization*, edited by G. Hammond, R. Kanbur, and E. Prasad. Cheltenham, UK: Edward Elgar Publishing.

Huang, H., and S.-J. Wei. 2006. "Monetary Policies for Developing Countries: The Role of Institutional Quality." *Journal of International Economics* 70 (1): 239-52.

IMF (International Monetary Fund). 2015. "Evolving Monetary Policy Frameworks in Low-Income and Other Developing Countries." Staff Report, October, International Monetary Fund, Washington, DC.

———. 2016. *World Economic Outlook: Subdued Demand: Symptoms and Remedies.* October. Washington, DC: IMF.

Kasa, K. 2001. "Will Inflation Targeting Work in Developing Countries?" *FRBSF Economic Letter* 2001 (1), Federal Reserve Bank of San Francisco, San Francisco, CA.

Khan, M. S., and A. S. Senhadji. 2001. "Threshold Effects in the Relationship between Inflation and Growth." *IMF Staff Papers* 48 (1): 1-21.

Ley, E., and F. Misch. 2014. "Output Data Revisions in Low-Income Countries." Paper presented at the conference Macroeconomic Challenges Facing Low-Income Countries: New Perspectives, International Monetary Fund, Washington, DC.

Li, B. G., S. A. O'Connell, C. Adam, A. Berg, and P. Montiel. 2016. "VAR Meets DSGE: Uncovering the Monetary Transmission Mechanism in Low-Income Countries." International Monetary Fund, Washington, DC.

Mas, I. 1995. "Central Bank Independence: A Critical View from a Developing Country Perspective." *World Development* 23 (10): 1639-52.

Mishkin, F. 1997. "Strategies for Controlling Inflation." NBER Working Paper 6122, National Bureau of Economic Research, Cambridge, MA.

Mishkin, F., and M. A. Savastano. 2001. "Monetary Policy Strategies for Latin America." Policy Research Working Paper 2685, World Bank, Washington, DC.

Mishra, P., and P. J. Montiel. 2013. "How Effective Is Monetary Transmission in Low-Income Countries? A Survey of the Empirical Evidence." *Economic Systems* 37 (2): 187-216.

Mishra, P., P. J. Montiel, and A. Spilimbergo. 2012. "Monetary Transmission in Low-Income Countries: Effectiveness and Policy Implications." *IMF Economic Review* 60 (2): 270-302.

Mishra, P., P. J. Montiel, P. Pedroni, and A. Spilimbergo. 2014. "Monetary Policy and Bank Lending Rates in Low-Income Countries: Heterogeneous Panel Estimates." *Journal of Development Economics* 111 (November): 117-31.

Montiel, P., and P. Pedroni. 2018. "Trilemma-Dilemma: Constraint or Choice? Some Empirical Evidence from a Structurally Identified Heterogeneous Panel VAR." *Open Economies Review* 29 (127): 1-18.

Nguyen, A. D. M., J. Dridi, F. Unsal, and O. H. Williams. 2017. "On the Drivers of Inflation in Sub-Saharan Africa." *International Economics* 151 (C): 71-84.

Ostry, J. D., A. R. Ghosh, and M. Chamon. 2012. "Two Targets, Two Instruments: Monetary and Exchange Rate Policies in Emerging Economies." IMF Staff Discussion Note 12/01, International Monetary Fund, Washington, DC.

Pedroni, P. 2013. "Structural Panel VARs." *Econometrics* 1(2): 180-206.

Pesaran, M. H. 2006. "Estimation and Inference in Large Heterogeneous Panels with a Multifactor Error Structure." *Econometrica* 74 (4): 967-1012.

Prasad, E. S. 2010. "Financial Sector Regulation and Reforms in Emerging Markets: An Overview." NBER Working Paper 16428, National Bureau of Economic Research, Cambridge, MA.

Rodrik, D. 2007. "The Real Exchange Rate and Economic Growth: Theory and Evidence." John F. Kennedy School of Government, Cambridge, MA.

Saborowski, C., and S. Weber. 2013. "Assessing the Determinants of Interest Rate Transmission through Conditional Impulse Response Functions." IMF Working Paper 13/23, International Monetary Fund, Washington, DC.

Shambaugh, J. 2004. "The Effect of Fixed Exchange Rates on Monetary Policy." *Quarterly Journal of Economics* 119 (1): 301-52.

Stock, J. H., and M. W. Watson. 2012. "Disentangling the Channels of the 2007-2009 Recession." NBER Working Paper 18094, National Bureau of Economic Research, Cambridge, MA.

Taylor, J. 2001. "The Roles of Exchange Rates in Monetary-Policy Rules." *American Economic Review* 91 (2): 263-67.

———. 2005. "Monetary Policy in Emerging Market Countries with Implications for Egypt." ECES (The Egypt Center for Economic Studies) Distinguished Lecture 23, Cairo, Egypt.

CHAPTER 7

Poverty Impacts of Food Price Shocks and Policies

In the event of large swings in world food prices, countries often intervene to dampen the impact of international food price spikes on domestic prices and lessen the burden of adjustment on vulnerable population groups. Although individual countries can succeed in insulating their domestic markets from short-term fluctuations in global food prices, the collective intervention of many countries exacerbates the volatility of world prices. Insulating policies introduced during the 2010-11 food price spike accounted for 40 percent of the increase in the world price of wheat and 25 percent of the increase in the world price of maize. Combined with government policy responses, the 2010-11 food price spike increased global poverty by 1 percent or 8.3 million people.

Introduction

In August 2011, international food prices hit an all-time high.[1] This followed shortly after the 2007-08 food price spike, which pushed an estimated 105 million people into extreme poverty (Ivanic and Martin 2008). This event also prompted widespread concerns about the food security of the poorest. Although food prices have declined considerably since then, in real terms, they are still significantly above their 2000 lows (Figure 7.1). New evidence points to a rise in world hunger and severe food insecurity between 2014 and 2017, reversing the declining trend observed in the previous decade. In 2017, the number of undernourished people reached 821 million, up by 5 percent since 2014 and a major step backward in achieving the second Sustainable Development Goal (SDG 2) target of hunger eradication by 2030 (FAO et al. 2018). Climate variability and the growing frequency of extreme weather events increase the risk of disruption to food production and are accompanied by food price spikes and setbacks in food availability and access to food.

Food prices are determined by the complex interaction between demand and supply forces. A dramatic increase in demand for feedstock for biofuel production in the early 2000s put considerable pressure on markets for grain and contributed to a rundown in stocks (Akiyama et al. 2001; Wright 2014).

Note: This chapter was prepared by David Laborde, Csilla Lakatos, and Will Martin. David Laborde and Will Martin acknowledge the funding support of the CGIAR Research Program on Policies, Institutions, and Markets (PIM) led by the International Food Policy Research Institute (IFPRI). The opinions expressed here belong to the authors and do not necessarily reflect those of PIM, IFPRI, or CGIAR.

[1] Unless otherwise stated, the concept of food prices as used in this chapter refers to the commodity prices of major staple foods such as rice, wheat, and maize.

Population growth and urbanization, as well as a shift in diets toward animal-based foods, created demand pressures despite an increase in agricultural productivity in emerging market and developing economies (EMDEs) (Fukase and Martin 2017). Slowing yield growth and declining availability of agricultural land also constrained food production growth. Extreme climate events (for example, El Niño, droughts, and natural disasters), particularly when stock levels have been low, have also contributed to food price volatility.

Food price increases have important macroeconomic and microeconomic impacts through several channels. At the macroeconomic level, food price increases result in higher inflation, which can significantly affect household real incomes. High food prices can also result in terms-of-trade shocks, with important implications for growth and government policy space.

The microeconomic impact of food price increases on poverty and inequality depends on the net food seller status of the poorest households. For households that are net sellers of food products (such as farmers, agricultural workers, and small landowners), rising food prices increase real incomes. By contrast, they lower the real incomes of households who are net buyers of food. In low-income countries (LICs), poor urban households spend large shares of their income on food and are likely to feel the effects of such declines in real incomes most severely. On average, sharp increases in food prices raise poverty, reduce nutrition, and curtail the consumption of essential services such as education and health care (World Bank 2011). In the longer term, once producers and consumers have adjusted to the increases and wage rates have responded, sustained increases in food prices may lower poverty (Ivanic and Martin 2014b; Gillson and Fouad 2014).

A decline in food prices can also have adverse impacts on net sellers of food, particularly in the short term, when they are highly dependent on revenues from crops. Interest groups often put pressure on governments not to allow food prices to fall too rapidly.

Countries often use policy interventions to dampen the domestic impact of international food price spikes and lessen the burden on vulnerable population groups. For example, during the 2007-08 food price spike, close to three-quarters of EMDEs took policy action to insulate their domestic prices from the sharp increase in international food prices (World Bank 2009). In the event of food price spikes, net importers usually intervene by lowering rates of protection (typically tariffs) on food, and net exporters impose export restrictions or bans. These policies are often complemented with social safety net programs, such as cash transfers or school feeding programs, that help deal with the income effects of the food price rise without distorting domestic prices.

FIGURE 7.1 Global food prices

In August 2011, shortly after the 2007-08 food price spike, international nominal food prices hit an all-time high. Although food prices have declined considerably since then, in real terms, they are still significantly above their lows in the 2000s.

A. Global food prices **B. Global food price volatility**

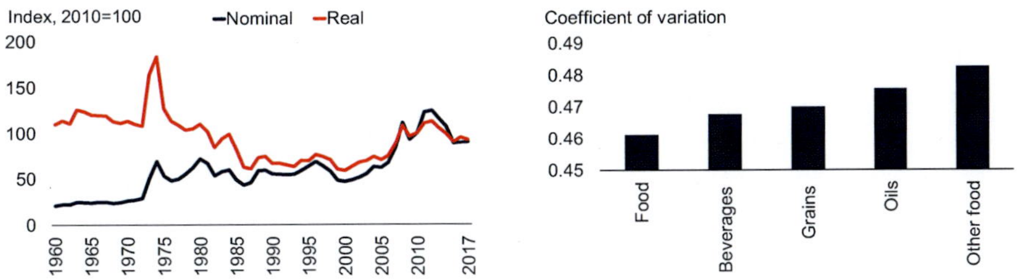

Source: World Bank.

A. Based on yearly commodity price indexes between 1960 and 2017. The World Bank manufactures unit value index is used as a deflator.

B. Based on monthly nominal commodity price indexes between January 1960 and November 2017.

To the extent that policy interventions reduce the transmission of international price spikes to domestic markets, they may appear to be successful for individual countries. However, the combined intervention of many countries raises international prices. These insulating policies tend to encourage consumption and reduce production during price spikes. This, in turn, results in higher import demand and reduced export supply that further drive up global prices. During price plunges, government interventions encourage greater exports and greater global supply, which further depresses prices. Only countries that insulate themselves to an above average degree can reduce price volatility in their domestic markets (Anderson, Martin, and Ivanic 2017).

The international community has recognized the importance of ensuring the stability and availability of food supplies as key to addressing several development objectives. The Sustainable Development Goals (SDGs) give food security a high priority: SDG 2 sets out explicitly the goal to "end hunger, achieve food security and improved nutrition, and promote sustainable agriculture." Other SDGs are strongly interconnected: food, agriculture, and nutrition play an important role in SDG 1 on ending poverty, SDG 12 on sustainable consumption and production, and SDG 13 on climate change adaptation and mitigation.

In this context, this chapter addresses the following questions:

- How do food price shocks affect EMDEs and LICs?

- How do countries intervene to reduce the impact of food price shocks?
- What was the impact of the 2010-11 food price shock on poverty?

The chapter presents the following findings:

- At the macroeconomic level, a high share of agriculture and food in total output, consumption, employment, trade, and government revenues heightens countries' vulnerability to volatility in international food prices. At the microeconomic level, food price spikes are felt most severely by the poorest segments of the population who are net food buyers.
- Governments in EMDEs tend to respond particularly strongly to sharp changes in world prices for staple foods—such as rice, wheat, and maize—to smooth volatility. Domestic food prices are considerably less volatile than world food prices in the short run, but over the longer term, there is a tendency for domestic and world prices to return to their original relationship. In the short run, a 1 percent increase in world rice, wheat, and maize prices is associated with an increase in domestic prices by 0.6, 0.7, and 0.8 percent, respectively.
- Although individual countries can succeed at insulating their domestic markets from short-term fluctuations in global food prices, their combined interventions make global food prices more volatile. Insulating policies introduced during the 2010-11 food price spike accounted for 40 percent of the increase in the world price of wheat and 25 percent of the increase in the world price of maize. In contrast, government interventions in rice markets dampened the degree to which world prices increased by about 50 percent.
- The 2010-11 food price spike increased poverty by 1 percent, or 8.3 million people, despite widespread government intervention.

The chapter contributes to two strands of the literature: the implications of government interventions to insulate domestic grain markets, and the impacts of changes in world food prices on poverty. First, the chapter discusses the features and sources of the 2010-11 food price spike. Second, it quantifies the degree to which countries intervened. Third, the chapter is the first study to quantify the poverty impact of the 2010-11 food price spike and associated trade policy interventions.

Food price shocks

At the macroeconomic level, high shares of agriculture and food in total output, consumption, employment, trade, and government revenues heighten countries' vulnerability to volatility in international food prices. At the microeconomic level, a high share of net food buyers among the poorest segments of society heightens the adverse effects of food price spikes on poverty and income distribution.

Macroeconomic channels

Reliance on food imports and production. Agriculture accounts for close to one-third of total value added and two-thirds of total employment in LICs. This is almost three times their shares in the average EMDE (Figure 7.2) (Aksoy and Beghin 2004). For example, in Burkina Faso and Burundi, agriculture accounts for more than four-fifths of total employment. In Chad and Sierra Leone, it accounts for more than half of domestic value added. In addition, more than three-quarters of LICs are net food importers compared to only half of EMDEs. In these net food-importing LICs, net food imports amount to 5.4 percent of private consumption. Benin and the Gambia are particularly vulnerable to high food prices, with net food imports at more than 10 percent of private consumption.[2]

Inflation. A surge in food prices increases consumer price index (CPI) inflation. For example, the 2007-08 and 2010-11 surges in international food prices caused substantial inflationary pressures. LIC inflation more than doubled, from 7 to 15 percent during 2007-08 and from 5 to 11 percent during 2010-11. The increase in EMDE inflation was less pronounced, from 7 to 11 percent during 2007-08 and from 5 to 6 percent during 2010-11. Food prices accounted disproportionately for these increases in inflation—for about two-thirds in LICs and more than half in EMDEs. In vulnerable LICs, such as Benin and Niger, where net food imports amount to 15 and 7 percent of household consumption, respectively, inflation surged from 1 to 8 percent and from 0.2 to 11 percent, respectively, during the 2007-08 food price spike.

Terms of trade. Sharp increases in food prices can result in significant adverse terms-of-trade shocks, especially for countries that are large net importers of food. More than three-quarters of LICs are net food importers. Accordingly, in the median LIC, the terms-of-trade index declined by 2 and 4 percent during the 2007-08 and 2010-11 food price spikes, respectively. In some, the deterioration was much steeper. For example, the terms of trade index of Sierra Leone, an LIC highly reliant on food imports, weakened by 10 percent during each of these food price spike episodes. More broadly, severe terms-of-trade shocks are considerably more common in LICs than in advanced

[2] Conversely, heavy reliance on food exports heightens vulnerability to food price declines. For example, in Malawi, net food exports amount to 12 percent of total private consumption.

FIGURE 7.2 Macroeconomic channels of transmission

At the macroeconomic level, high shares of agriculture and food in total output, consumption, employment, trade, and government revenues heighten countries' vulnerability to volatility in international food prices.

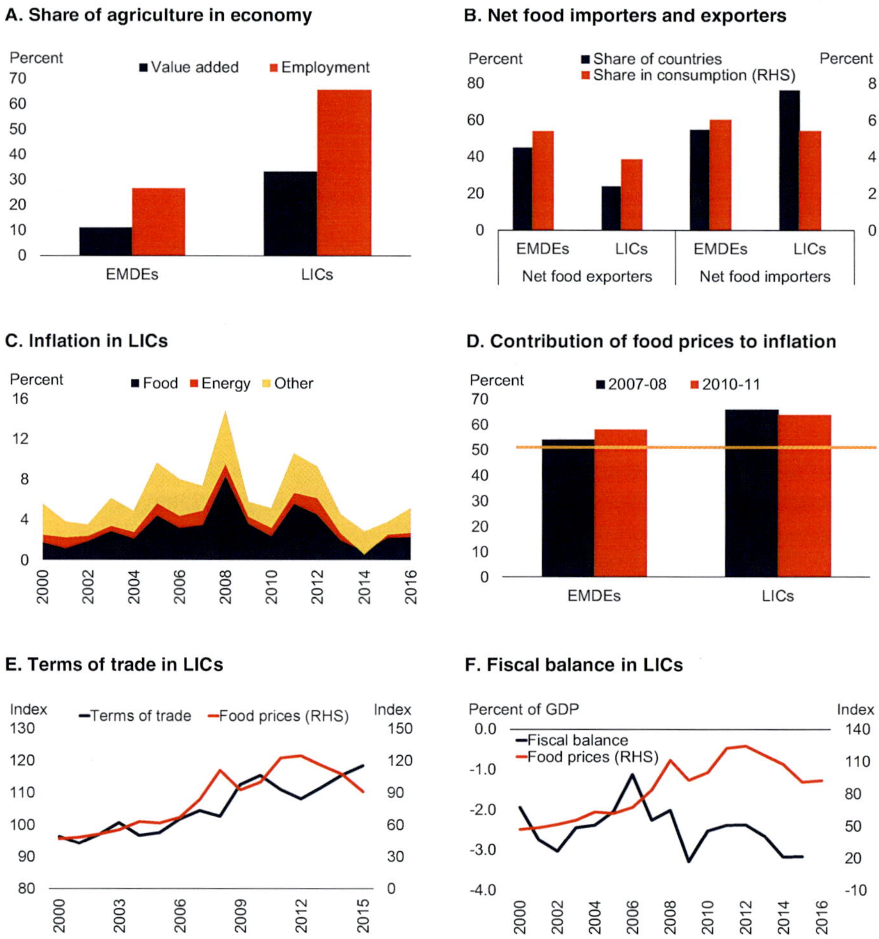

Source: World Bank; Kose et al. 2017.

Note: EMDEs = emerging market and developing economies; GDP = gross domestic product; LICs = low-income countries.

A. Based on a sample of 93 EMDEs and 21 LICs. Averages for 2010-16.

B. Blue bars show the share of EMDEs or LICs in which food imports exceed food exports ("net food importers") or food imports fall short of food exports ("net food exporters"). Red bars show net food imports relative to consumption in EMDE and LIC food exporters and importers.

C. Average inflation based on a sample of 12 LICs.

D. Share of inflation accounted for by food price inflation. The orange line indicates half.

E. Net barter terms of trade index, 2000 = 100.

F. Median based on a sample of 26 LICs.

economies (IMF 2011). In addition, of all possible external shocks, negative terms-of-trade shocks tend to have the most severe output cost in LICs (Becker and Mauro 2006).

Fiscal policy constraints. Heavy reliance on food and agricultural exports exposes many countries to the volatility of international commodity prices. Absent stabilizing fiscal arrangements, this can introduce volatility into public finances and erode fiscal sustainability: rising food prices may increase tax revenues from the agriculture sector and encourage governments to spend. Conversely, when food prices fall, revenue losses in the agriculture sector are exacerbated by political pressures to subsidize food production. Food price spikes may also cause sociopolitical instability, including political unrest and food riots (Barrett 2013). During the sharp rise in food prices in 2007-08, LICs' fiscal balances deteriorated, on average, by close to 1 percentage point of gross domestic product (GDP), partly due to higher food import bills.

Monetary policy constraints. In countries where inflation expectations are not well anchored and monetary policy frameworks are weak, the increase in inflation caused by rising food prices can compel central banks to tighten policy. In heavy food importers, this can be exacerbated by exchange rate depreciation in response to the deteriorating terms of trade. Indeed, during the 2007-08 food price spike, close to half of EMDE central banks responded to rising inflation and depreciation by tightening monetary policy.[3]

Microeconomic channels

Rising food prices impact households through price and income effects. Rising food prices reduce households' purchasing power but raise income generated from food production.

Poor households—those with per capita income less than $2.97/day—spend on average more than half of their income on food in EMDEs and close to two-thirds in LICs (Figure 7.3). In countries such as Burundi, Guinea, and Honduras, the share of food expenditures is even higher, accounting for more than three-quarters of total consumption of the poorest households. In LICs, more than one-third of the poorest households' consumption expenditure on food is spent on staple foods such as cereals and vegetables. These staple foods are considerably more exposed to international price volatility than are domestically processed food products (Figure 7.1).

[3] Based on a sample of 54 EMDEs.

FIGURE 7.3 Microeconomic channels of transmission

At the microeconomic level, a high share of net food buyers among the poorest segments of the population heightens the adverse effects of food price spikes on income distribution and poverty.

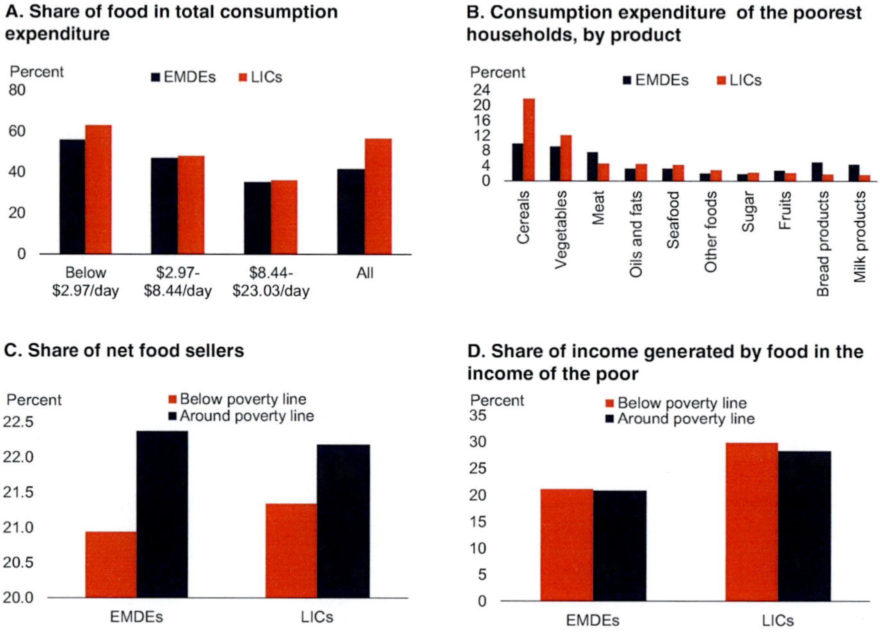

Source: World Bank; International Food Policy Research Institute.

Note: EMDEs = emerging market and developing economies; LICs = low-income countries.

A. Based on 2010 data on the share of food in the total consumption expenditure of households.

B. Based on 2010 data on the share of products in total household consumption expenditure.

C.D. Averages weighted by the number of poor for a sample of 22 EMDEs and 7 LICs. Based on a poverty line of $1.90/ day.

For households that are net sellers of agricultural and food products (for example, farmers), rising food prices raise incomes. More than one-fifth of households around and below the poverty line are net food sellers in the average EMDE and LIC. Households around and below the poverty line in these countries tend to generate about one-quarter of their incomes from food production.

The overall impact depends on the relative magnitudes of income and price effects of households in different segments of the income distribution. If the positive income effect outweighs the overall loss of purchasing power, household real incomes rise. In contrast, poor urban households, which are typically net buyers of food that spend a large share of their consumption expenditure on food, are likely to suffer real income losses (Aksoy and Hoekman 2010).

On average, many of the poor in EMDEs and LICs are net buyers of food. As a result, food price spikes tend to raise poverty, reduce nutrition, and cut consumption of essential services such as education and health care. For example, the 2007-08 rise in food prices is estimated to have raised the number of poor by 105 million (Ivanic and Martin 2008). In extreme cases, food price spikes can induce food insecurity and hunger, with severely adverse long-term impacts on human capital.

Government interventions

In the event of large swings in global food prices, governments are confronted with difficult policy choices. One option is to allow domestic prices to adjust to world food price changes, exposing domestic consumers and producers to changes in their real incomes.[4] However, this may raise inflation in the short run and, in countries where inflation expectations are poorly anchored, in the medium to long run.[5] The decline in real incomes of poor net buyers associated with higher inflation (Easterly and Fischer 2001) would entail welfare losses, especially when net consumers of food are loss- and risk-averse (Gouel and Jean 2015; Freund and Ozden 2008; Giordani, Rocha, and Ruta 2016). Meanwhile, net sellers of food may gain.

Alternatively, governments can spare consumers or producers these losses by reducing the transmission of international food price shocks to domestic markets.[6] As measured in this chapter, policy intervention is reflected in the ratio of domestic to world prices—the "protection rate." If, during a period of rising world prices, the rate of protection declines, a country is seeking to insulate its domestic markets from the increase in prices. If the protection rate rises, policy makers are compounding the increase in world prices. This may occur with the objective of correcting past "errors," because domestic prices fell below policy makers' desired long-run level, or because policy has insulated the

[4] A sizable nontradable services component in the cost of providing consumers with food (transportation, storage, retail, and so forth) dampens the pass-through of changes in world food prices into domestic markets.

[5] In principle, monetary policy tightening can also offset inflationary effects from rising global food prices to ensure that rising food prices remain a purely relative price change and do not become entrenched in higher inflation. However, this would come at the cost of reduced economic activity (Lustig 2009). Among LICs, only Uganda is formally committed to an inflation targeting regime, which aims to keep average annual core inflation at 5 percent ± 2 percent.

[6] Policy makers may also have a longer-term goal to protect (or tax) domestic agents (Grossman and Helpman 1994). In empirical work based on political economy models, protection rates vary to reduce the costs associated with adjusting prices and the costs of providing a rate of protection that differs from the long-run political equilibrium (Anderson and Nelgen 2011; Ivanic and Martin 2014a).

market from world markets and an exogenous shock, such as a harvest shortfall, has caused the domestic price to rise relative to the world price.[7]

In practice, during the 2007-08 food price spike, close to three-quarters of EMDEs took policy action to insulate their economies from the sharp increase in international food prices (World Bank 2009). The most commonly used interventions were reductions in taxes, including import duties and consumer taxes (Figure 7.4). Net importers frequently intervened by lowering import tariffs or even introducing import subsidies, and net exporters imposed export restrictions or bans to dampen the increase in domestic prices.

Domestic and world food price dynamics

Domestic food prices are considerably less volatile than global food prices in the short run, but over the longer term, there is a tendency for domestic prices to return to their original relationship with international prices (Figure 7.5). This does not necessarily imply that protection rates become zero, but that they return to their pre-spike levels.

Governments in EMDEs tend to respond particularly strongly to sharp changes in the world prices of staple foods—such as rice, wheat, and maize—to reduce the volatility of domestic prices. For staple foods, domestic price movements can diverge substantially from international price movements in the short run but converge in the longer term.

The movements of world and domestic food staple prices during the latest two food price spikes (2007-08 and 2010-11) resembled similar earlier episodes: world prices rose rapidly, and domestic prices rose only gradually. However, the 2010-11 spike was different from previous episodes in several respects. The 2007-08 increase in food prices came after a long period of stability in food prices. In 2007-08, world prices of all staple foods increased steeply, led by the strong increase in the world price of rice. Most countries reacted strongly by introducing insulating policies. In contrast, the 2010-11 episode occurred when world markets and policies were still normalizing from the 2007-08 episode. Government interventions therefore differed considerably across countries and commodities. Government interventions raised rice prices more than the modest increase in world prices.

Rice. Rice was the staple food with the largest price increase during the 2007-08 food price spike. Between January 2007 and May 2008, world rice prices almost

[7] A similar pattern was observed in the maize market in many African countries (Chapoto and Jayne 2009).

FIGURE 7.4 Food-related government policies

Countries often use policy interventions to dampen the domestic impact of international food price spikes and lessen the burden on vulnerable population groups. In the short run, domestic markets for key staple foods, such as rice, maize, and wheat, are highly insulated from global food price swings. Insulation policies undertaken during the 2010-11 episode exacerbated the volatility of world prices and accounted for about 40 percent of the increase in the world price of wheat and one-quarter of the increase in the world price of maize.

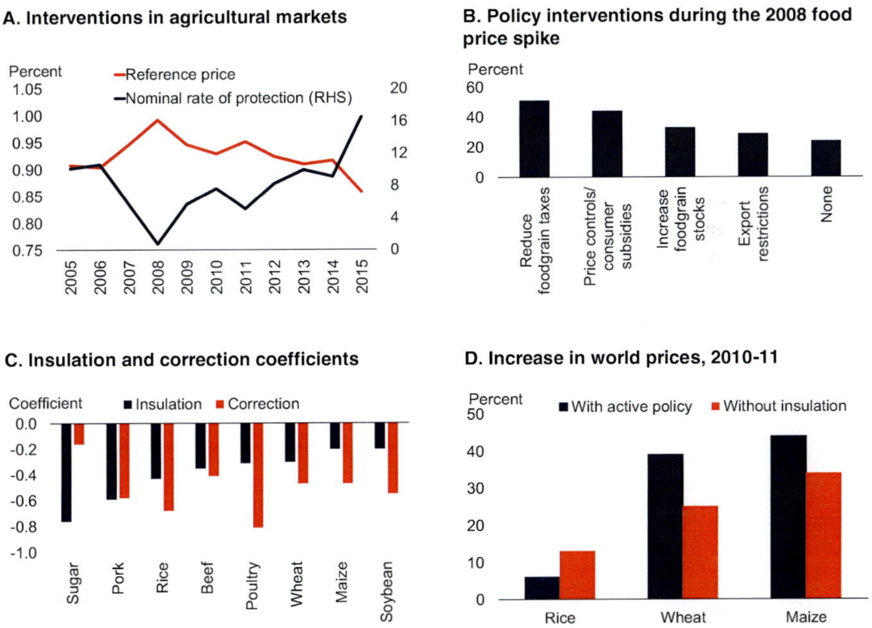

Source: Ivanic and Martin (2014a), Ag-Incentives Database, World Bank.

A. Nominal Rate of Protection (NRP) is computed as the price difference between the farm gate price received by producers and an undistorted reference price at the farm gate level. The reference price at the farm gate level is defined as the net price of the product when it leaves the farm, after marketing costs have been subtracted. The undistorted farm gate price is defined as the price prevailing in competitive world markets.

B. Percent of respondents based on a survey of 80 EMDEs.

C. Estimates based on the error correction model described in Annex 7.1. The coefficient of price insulation ranges from 0 for countries that do not insulate against the rise in world prices, to -1 for countries that adopt policies that fully insulate domestic markets. The error correction term represents the cost of being out of equilibrium or the speed with which policies achieve the target level of protection or at which policy makers move back toward this equilibrium after being forced away from it by a shock to world prices. Based on data for 82 countries, of which 26 advanced economies, 44 EMDEs, and 12 LICs for the period 1955-2011.

D. Estimates derived based on the methodology described in Annex 7.1.

tripled.[8] This sharp increase reflected export restrictions introduced by major suppliers (for example, India and Vietnam), triggered by food security concerns, panic buying by several large importers, a weak dollar, and record high prices of

[8] The world price of 5 percent broken white Thai rice increased from \$313/metric ton (mt) to \$902/mt.

FIGURE 7.5 Domestic and global food prices

Domestic food prices tend to be less volatile than global food prices. This partly reflects a sizable services component in the cost of providing domestic consumers with food, but also policy intervention.

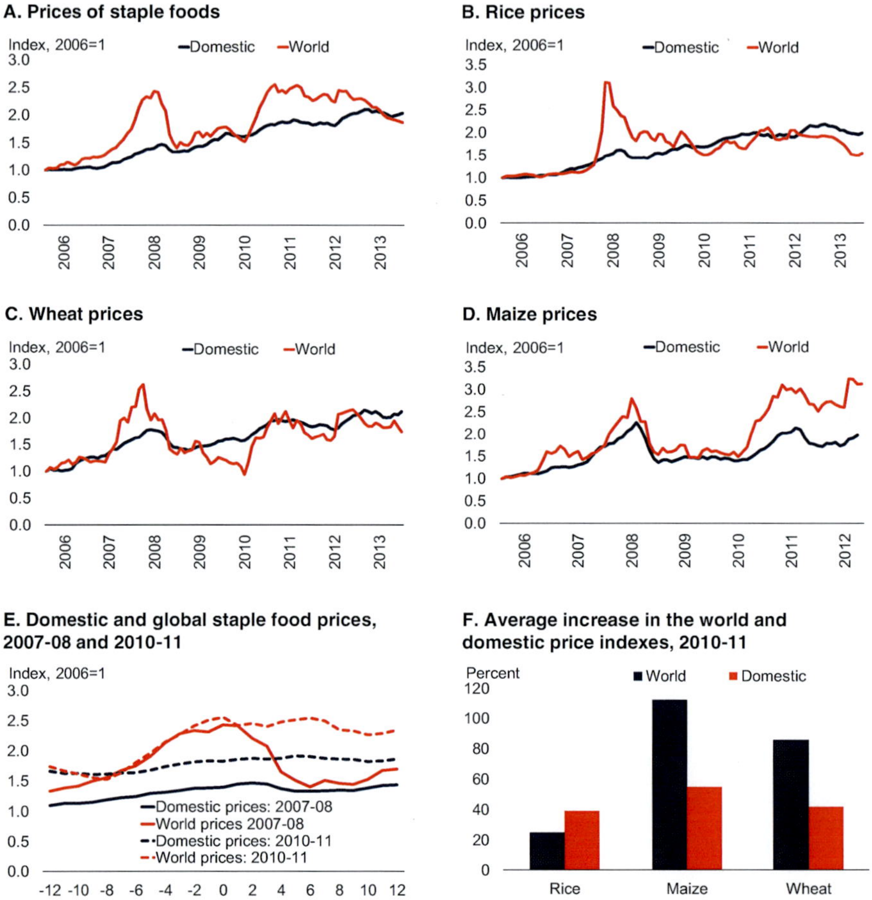

Source: Ivanic and Martin 2014a; World Bank.
Note: Trade-weighted averages.
A. Rice, wheat, maize, edible oil, and sugar prices.
E. Event study based on monthly cross-country average domestic staples prices (average of wheat, rice, and maize prices) and global staples prices (average of wheat, rice, and maize) during 2007-08 and 2010-11. Period 0 represents the month of the peak of the world food price spike.
F. Average percent increase in the price index.

oil, which is a major input into food production (Childs and Kiawu 2009). During this episode, domestic markets were largely insulated from this global rice price spike (Ivanic and Martin 2008). By contrast, during the 2010-11 price spike, rice prices increased much less, by about 30 percent between June 2010 and May 2012. In some countries, adverse supply conditions combined with the use of nontariff trade policies resulted in domestic rice prices rising above world prices.[9] Instead of insulating policies, on average, EMDEs implemented policies that raised domestic prices relative to world prices (Figure 7.5).

Wheat. Between February 2007 and March 2008, world wheat prices more than doubled, partly in response to lower than anticipated wheat production caused by drought in Australia, Ukraine, and other major exporters.[10] Strong policy intervention partially insulated domestic markets from the global wheat price spike and its subsequent collapse in the aftermath of the global financial crisis in 2009-10. Similarly, during the 2010-11 event, world wheat prices more than doubled between June 2010 and May 2011.[11] This time, the increase in world prices was partly driven by lower than expected production and exports in Kazakhstan, the Russian Federation, and Ukraine and excessive rains in Australia that damaged wheat crops (World Bank 2010). Large orders from major wheat importers in the Middle East and North Africa added to price pressures. Since 2011, global and domestic wheat prices have fluctuated, broadly synchronously.

Maize. During the 2007-08 food price spike, the world price of maize almost doubled, partly as a result of increasing U.S. demand for maize stimulated by mandatory targets for ethanol production.[12] Similarly, during the 2010-11 episode, the world price of maize increased significantly. As in the case of wheat, adverse weather-related events in major maize-exporting countries contributed to the spike in world prices. In contrast, many countries in Sub-Saharan Africa benefited from excellent maize harvests, which, in combination with unpredictable trade policies, led to sharp falls in domestic prices.

Insulation of domestic food markets

The degree of insulation of domestic markets from world food price swings can be quantified using an error correction model (ECM) (Annex 7.1). In this analytical framework, domestic food prices are represented as the outcome of a policy process in which policy makers seek to reduce the cost of adjustment as well as the cost of being out of equilibrium (Nickell 1985).

The ECM regresses the log of the protection rate on the log of world prices and the deviation from long-term "equilibrium" food prices. The sample used here includes annual data for eight food commodity prices in 82 countries, of which 44 are EMDEs and 12 are LICs, during 1955-2011.

[9] In Vietnam, for instance, domestic rice prices rose by 41 percent between July and October 2010 due to lower than expected production, prior commitments on exports, and high inflation from a depreciating currency.

[10] The world price of U.S. hard red wheat increased from \$196/mt to \$440/mt.

[11] The world price of U.S. hard red wheat increased from \$158/mt to \$355/mt.

[12] Between January 2007 and June 2008, the world price of maize increased from \$165/mt to \$287/mt.

The degree of insulation of an increase in global food prices is captured by the coefficient estimate of short-term changes in global food prices. A more negative coefficient indicates a higher degree of insulation in the short term. The degree of long-term adjustment to a 1 percent increase in global food prices is captured by the coefficient on the error correction term. A coefficient near -1 indicates that, over the long term, cumulative global and domestic price swings converge.

Estimates from the ECM point to short-term insulation in markets for key staple foods such as rice and wheat (Figure 7.4). Among these key staples, insulation is the highest for rice. In the short run, a 1 percent increase in global rice, wheat, and maize prices is associated with an increase in domestic prices of 0.6, 0.7, and 0.8 percent, respectively.

Certain types of interventions in markets for staple foods have been found to raise volatility in domestic markets. For example, during the 2008-09 food price spike, several African countries implemented pricing, marketing, and trade policy interventions to stabilize domestic maize markets. The countries that intervened most intensively experienced the highest domestic price volatility, mostly because of the ad hoc and unpredictable nature of these interventions (Chapoto and Jayne 2009).[13]

The use of an export ban during food price spikes, possibly related to a domestic drought, illustrates the trade-offs between different policy instruments:

- *Ensuring food security*. By restricting the sale of food for exports, an export ban increases domestic supply and dampens domestic food price increases. This can help net food buyers access food.

- *Alleviating poverty*. Net food-selling farmers are likely to be hardest hit by a drought. An export ban reduces their ability to mitigate their production losses with higher incomes from higher prices. If these farmers are among the poorer segments of the income distribution, the export ban will likely increase poverty, as observed in Zambia during the 2016-17 El Niño event (Al-Mamun et al. 2017).

- *Volatility*. Although export bans may alleviate pressures during a specific situation, they heighten domestic price volatility by preventing domestic shocks from being dissipated through changes in trade levels. If bans are

[13] After abstaining from the use of interventions in staple food markets for several years, policy makers in Eastern and Southern Africa extensively used pricing, marketing, and trade policy tools during the 2015-16 agricultural season to contain the impact of an El Niño-induced decline in output and food security (Al-Mamun et al. 2017; Tschirley and Jayne 2010).

backed up by stockholding measures, such as those used in India (Gouel, Gautam, and Martin 2016), they can be consistent with domestic price stabilization.

Although individual countries can succeed at insulating their domestic markets from short-term fluctuations in global food prices, their combined policies make global food prices more volatile. Government interventions tend to increase consumption and reduce production during price spikes and support production and discourage consumption during price plunges. During price spikes, this results in higher import demand and, hence, higher global demand that further drives up global prices. During price plunges, it encourages greater exports from each country and, hence, greater global supply that further depresses prices. Only countries that insulate themselves to an above average degree can reduce the transmission of international price volatility to their domestic markets (Anderson, Martin, and Ivanic 2017; Martin and Anderson 2012; Ivanic and Martin 2014a).[14]

Impact of the 2010-11 food price shock on poverty

The impact of the 2010-11 food price shock on poverty is quantified in two steps. In the first step, the degree of intervention by countries is estimated based on a framework developed by Anderson, Ivanic, and Martin (2014). In the second step, these estimates are fed into a computable general equilibrium (CGE) model to determine the impact of insulation policies on poverty. Two scenarios are modeled. In the first scenario, the impact of countries' own interventions on poverty is considered. In the second scenario, the combined effect of all policy interventions on global food markets and their feedback to domestic poverty are quantified.

Quantifying trade policy interventions

The approach to quantifying the extent of trade policy interventions builds on that used in Anderson, Ivanic, and Martin (2014). A primary shock, such as a weather shock, is assumed to generate an initial change in domestic and world prices. In attempting to insulate domestic markets from the increase in world prices, governments make offsetting changes to protection measures, such as the introduction of export bans (food exporters) or the reduction of import duties (food importers). These measures, in turn, reinforce the original shock to world prices. When a country imposes an export restriction, the availability of food to

[14] Consistent with Martin and Anderson (2012) and Anderson, Ivanic, and Martin (2014).

the rest of the world is reduced, and this tends to push up world prices. Similarly, when an importing country reduces its import tariffs, it increases the demand for imports and hence puts upward pressure on world prices (Annex 7.1).

Similarly, when an importing country reduces its import tariffs, it increases the demand for imports and, as a consequence, puts upward pressure on world prices (Annex 7.1).

The data used for quantifying the extent of trade policy interventions are taken primarily from the Ag-Incentives Consortium database.[15] The database provides estimates of changes in domestic and world prices for 57 countries and 68 agricultural and food commodities during 2005-15. Where data from the Ag-Incentives database were unavailable, alternative data were used from FAOSTAT, Global Information and Early Warning System, and Fewsnet. Overall, this analysis covers 24 major food producing and consuming countries, using data on household income sources and spending patterns from 2011. Of these, 18 are EMDEs and 6 are LICs.

During the food price spike of 2010-11, world prices of maize, wheat, and rice rose by 44, 39, and 6 percent, respectively (Figure 7.4). In contrast, domestic prices rose by considerably less, pointing to substantial insulation, with considerable heterogeneity across countries and commodities.

- *Rice.* Some countries (for example, Bangladesh, Nepal, Panama, Tanzania, and Zambia) reduced trade barriers to offset partially the rise in world rise prices. However, important net rice exporters, such as India, Pakistan, and the Republic of Yemen, implemented policy interventions that, ultimately, raised domestic rice prices more than the increase in world prices. In India, the world's second largest rice producer, quantitative restrictions initially prevented domestic price increases. However, the subsequent abolition of export quotas in September 2011 (in place since 2007) coincided with the agricultural marketing season and resulted in a surge in exports and a rise in domestic prices. In Pakistan, domestic rice prices rose relative to the world price over this same period because of heavy summer flooding that affected one-fifth of the country's land area and inflicted extensive damage to crops. A large increase in domestic prices relative to external prices occurred in the Republic of Yemen, amid persistent water shortages and a shift to less water-intensive non-staple crops. Prices also rose modestly in Ethiopia and Uganda because of drought. The combined intervention of all countries dampened the increase in the world price of rice by about 50 percent compared to a scenario without insulation policies.

[15] The data are available at www.ag-incentives.org.

- *Wheat.* Most developing countries took measures to offset the increase in global wheat prices in 2010-11. Policy actions and the degree of insulation were broadly similar to those employed during the spike in wheat prices in 2007-08. Policy makers justified efforts to dampen the impact of the global wheat price spike by noting that the world wheat price spike partly reflected a catching up with rising domestic wheat prices.[16] The combined intervention of countries accounted for close to 50 percent of the increase in the world price of wheat.

- *Maize.* Although most countries insulated their domestic maize markets against maize price increases during 2010-11, there was considerable heterogeneity in the policy responses. In Bangladesh, Ecuador, Malawi, Tanzania, and Zambia, protection rates were reduced to offset fully the rise in global maize prices. Ethiopia, Uganda, and the Republic of Yemen increased protection rates or used policies that, in combination with domestic output shocks, reinforced the effect of the increase in world prices on domestic prices.

During the 2010-11 event, the combined action of government policies raised global wheat and maize prices, accounting for about 40 percent of the increase in the world price of wheat and 25 percent of the increase in the price of maize (Figure 7.4). In the case of rice, combined policy actions reduced the rice price surge compared to a scenario of nonaction.[17]

Poverty implications

To assess the poverty implications of the 2010-11 increase in the world prices of rice, wheat, and maize, the MIRAGRODEP general equilibrium model was used in combination with household models for 285,000 households from 31 countries (Laborde, Robichaud, and Tokgoz 2013). MIRAGRODEP is a dynamic, multicountry, and multisector CGE model (Annex 7.1). The poverty impact depends on price changes, the relative reliance of households on the consumption of individual staple foods, and the net food buying status of households in different segments of the distribution (Deaton 1989).

[16] Ethiopia is an exception, where domestic wheat prices rose 28 percentage points more than world prices during 2010-11. This reflected domestic supply shocks, combined with limited access to global wheat markets to alleviate shortages. Wheat output fell by 10 percent in 2010-11 as a result of a fungus that destroyed the wheat harvest and lowered stocks in 2011. Wheat imports rose but were constrained by tight foreign exchange controls, effectively stopping private sector imports and ensuring that all grain imports were channeled through the state-owned Ethiopian Grain Trade Enterprise (Wakeyo and Lanos 2014; Negassa and Jayne 1997).

[17] This primarily reflects the elimination of export restrictions in India and increased import protection in Pakistan, Indonesia, Uganda, and the Republic of Yemen.

The results show that a hypothetical 10 percent surge in rice, wheat, and maize prices raises the number of poor by 0.22 percent, or 2.1 million people. Among staple foods, an increase in wheat prices raises the number of poor most (0.01 percentage point for a 10 percent wheat price increase). Rice price increases cause particularly large increases in the number of poor in Sub-Saharan Africa (0.13 percentage point). Finally, maize price increases tend to have a lesser impact on the number of poor.

To model the interaction between food price shocks and government interventions, the effects of a supply shock are traced in the model. The model assumes that an adverse productivity shock outside developing countries, in particular, in the Black Sea Basin and Australia, triggers the increase in world prices. In the summer of 2010, major grain producers in the Black Sea Basin, such as Russia, Ukraine, and Kazakhstan, were hit by a severe drought that significantly affected their harvest, and excessive rains in Australia caused by La Niña damaged crops, which were downgraded to feed quality (World Bank 2010). Primary shocks in these regions are assumed not to contribute directly to global changes in poverty rates, given their small share of the population living below the poverty line of $1.90/day.

The productivity shocks are calibrated to match the observed changes in protection rates and world prices given in Figure 7.6. For example, given the initial protection rates, a negative production shock of 55 percent for rice, 27 percent for wheat, and 35 percent for maize in advanced economies and Russia generates an increase of 10 percent in average world prices for these commodities. The policy experiments are implemented by eliminating individual trade policy measures for each country. In each case, world prices are recomputed endogenously in the model and therefore capture the direct and indirect effects of the policy changes.

As the model used in the simulations distinguishes between domestic and imported goods, two potential policy instruments are considered—an import duty (or subsidy) and an export subsidy (or tax).[18] The use of such policies can distort trade flows to such an extent that they switch between net-exporting and net-importing status. As a result, many countries typically put in place flanking policies. In 2007-08, for example, the Arab Republic of Egypt and Indonesia

[18] Because rice, wheat, and maize are bulk commodities that are less strongly differentiated than manufactured products, two-way trade in these goods is unusual—except when there are regional differences in varieties. Regionally differentiated varieties could create two-way trade flows such as, for example, Indian exports of basmati rice and imports of jasmine rice. Although the limited extent of two-way trade in these products might suggest treating them as homogeneous products, models of differentiated products are needed to capture adequately the bilateral trade flows in these commodities (Thursby, Johnson, and Grennes 1986).

FIGURE 7.6 Government interventions during 2010-11

Some countries reduced trade barriers to insulate themselves from increasing world prices. Others resorted to policy interventions that ultimately raised domestic prices more than the increase in world prices.

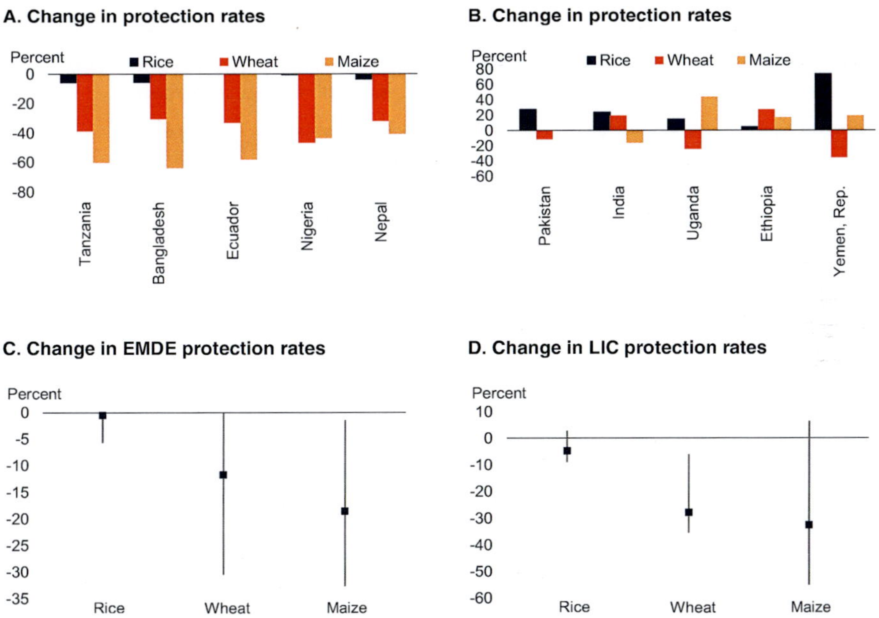

Source: Ag-Incentives Database.

Note: Estimates based on the methodology described in Annex 7.1. Changes in the rates of protection are presented in the form $T_i = \Delta t/(1+t_0)$, where t is the initial rate of protection (positive if an import tariff or export subsidy) and Δt is the change in this rate of protection. If the change in the rate of protection is negative during a period of rising world prices, countries are seeking to insulate their markets from the increase in prices. If it is positive, policy makers are compounding the increase in world prices with an increase in protection, which may be due to the correction of past "errors": if domestic prices fall below policy makers' desired long-run level of protection, or if a policy that insulated the domestic market from world markets and a subsequent exogenous shock—such as a harvest shortfall—has caused the domestic price to rise relative to the world price. EMDEs = emerging market and developing economies; LICs = low-income countries.

C.D. Median and interquartile range of the change in protection rates for rice, wheat, and maize in EMDEs (C) and LICs (D).

subsidized imports of wheat and rice, respectively, to hold down domestic consumer prices. To avoid subsidizing exports of the same goods, export restrictions were also introduced. To represent this in the model used here, it is assumed that, for every good with an import tariff that initially raises import prices by $T_0 = (1+t_0)$, there is a flanking export subsidy at rate $T_0 = (1+t_0)$. The two measures are assumed to adjust in the same proportion.

The model results suggest that the food price spikes of 2010-11 raised poverty in most countries, despite widespread government intervention (Figure 7.7; Table 7.1). On average, the share of extreme poor increased by 0.12 percentage point,

FIGURE 7.7 Poverty impact of policies implemented during 2010-11

The 2010-11 food price spike raised global poverty. The combined impact of all government interventions raised poverty worldwide, except in a few countries. Due to the dampening effect of interventions on the world price of rice, however, the impact of the combined interventions is found to have raised poverty about 14 percent less than individual action.

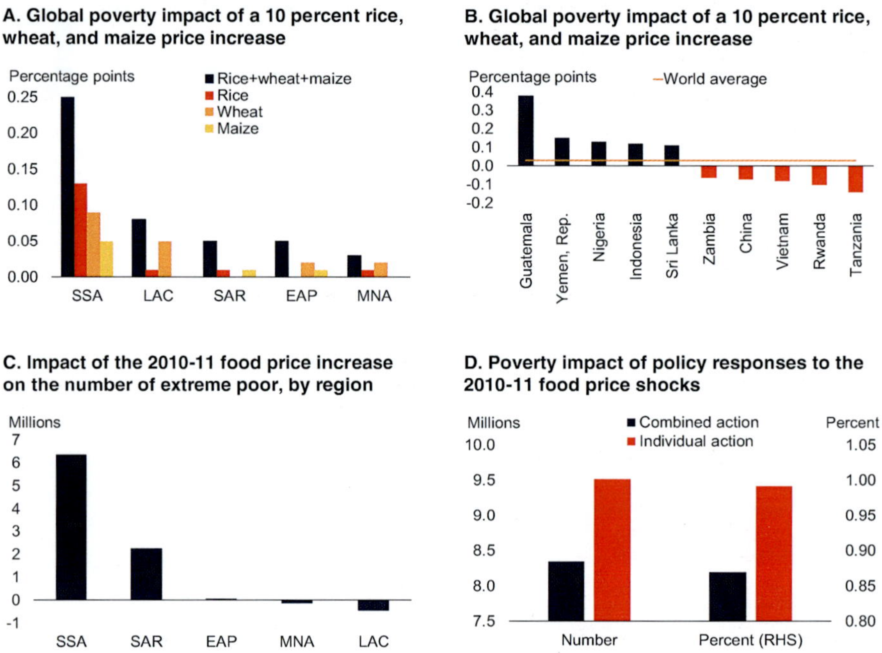

Source: World Bank staff estimates.

Note: Based on estimates using the MIRAGRODEP computable general equilibrium model described in detail in Annex 7.1. EAP = East Asia and Pacific; LAC = Latin America and the Caribbean; MNA = Middle East and North Africa; SAR = South Asia; SSA = Sub-Saharan Africa.

A.B. Change in poverty headcount.

C.D. Assuming increases in the price of maize, rice, and wheat as represented in Figure 7.4, panel D, and based on a poverty line of $1.90/day.

from 13.7 percent. This is equivalent to an additional 8.3 million people, or a 1 percent increase in the number of extreme poor. The increase in world food prices, combined with government intervention, was most strongly felt in countries such as India and Uganda, where the extreme poor tend to be net food buyers, whose real incomes declined.[19]

[19] The results reported here do not take into account the impact of safety net programs, such as India's Public Distribution System, which distributes food to poor households at fixed prices and so automatically makes larger transfers to the poor when food prices rise.

The poverty impact of the 2010-11 food price spike on some regions, such as East Asia and Pacific and Latin America and the Caribbean, is estimated to be limited: low rates of poverty combined with the benefits of the price increase for countries that are heavy exporters of rice (East Asia and Pacific) or maize (Latin America and the Caribbean) offset some of the losses incurred due to the increase in prices. Even in Sub-Saharan Africa—the region that accounts for two-thirds of the global increase in poverty—countries like Ethiopia and Nigeria implemented insulation policies that reduced poverty.

The results reported here contrast with those of Anderson, Ivanic, and Martin (2014), who find that during the 2007-08 food price spike, most countries' own policies, considered individually, reduced poverty, and the combined effect of all policy interventions was close to zero. The overall impacts are different because the 2007-08 price shocks were much larger; the transmission of price changes from world to domestic markets was assumed to be more pronounced; and there was a fall in poverty rates over time (the poverty headcount in India, for instance, fell from 33 to 21 percent).[20]

Conclusion

The unusual occurrence of two food price spikes in short succession—in 2007-08 and 2010-11—raised concerns about the stability of food markets and global poverty. During the 2007-08 event, coming after a long period of relatively stable prices, many countries used trade policies that insulated domestic food prices from the surge in world prices. Although each country's policies can dampen domestic price movements, the result of the combined use of policies increases global food price volatility. For example, widespread insulation policies accounted for 40 percent of the increase in world wheat prices and 25 percent for world maize prices.

The 2010-11 food price rise differed from the 2007-08 price surge in its economic context, policy responses, and poverty implications. Although the 2007-08 episode was led by rice prices, exacerbated by export restrictions imposed by major rice producers, the 2010-11 food price surge was led by maize and wheat prices, triggered by adverse weather events in major wheat and maize producers in Australia and the Black Sea Basin. During 2007-08, large rice consumers, such as India, imposed export restrictions to contain domestic rice price increases. These were gradually unwound over the following years. In

[20] There is uncertainty around poverty estimates due to systematic measurement errors in household surveys, which may bias the poor's dependence on food purchases (Headey and Martin 2016), and because sustained periods of higher prices result in declines in poverty (Ivanic and Martin 2014b; Jacoby 2016).

2010-11, some large wheat and maize producers, such as Russia and Ukraine, also introduced export restrictions and import bans to contain domestic price pressures.

During the 2007-08 food price spike, the policy interventions of individual countries helped to reduce poverty (Anderson, Ivanic, and Martin 2014). In contrast, during the 2010-11 food price spike, individual government policy responses raised global poverty by 1 percent, about the same amount as the increase in poverty of these interventions considered collectively.

The 2010-11 food price spike preceded a rise in world hunger and severe food insecurity between 2014 and 2017, reversing the declining trend observed in the previous decade. In 2017, the number of undernourished people reached 821 million, up by 5 percent since 2014 and a major step backward in achieving SDG 2 of eradicating hunger by 2030 (FAO et al. 2018).

The results presented in this chapter highlight that the use of trade policy interventions to insulate domestic markets from food price shocks compounds the volatility of international prices and may or may not be effective in protecting the most vulnerable population groups. Instead, storage policies and targeted safety net interventions, such as cash transfers, food and in-kind transfers, and so forth, can mitigate the negative impact of food price shocks while reducing the economywide distortionary impacts of trade policies. Additional measures, such as crop and weather insurance, warehouse receipt systems, commodity exchanges, and futures markets, could also be used as risk management instruments.

Despite the growing body of literature on food price stabilization policies, several questions remain to be explored. How can measures that seek to influence market outcomes—such as trade and storage policies—be combined with social safety net policies to optimize their development impacts? In a second-best environment, when trade policy interventions are still used, how can coordination between countries be improved to reduce their negative effects? We leave these questions open for future research.

TABLE 7.1 Impact of policy responses to the 2010-11 food price increase on the number of extreme poor (thousands)

	Combined action	Individual action
Bangladesh	644.3	628.3
China	42.4	401.7
Ecuador	42.4	45.9
Ethiopia	-51.2	41.2
Guatemala	33.8	0.0
Indonesia	-13.8	-68.1
India	1,797.2	1,819.7
Kenya	376.9	441.5
Cambodia	15.6	11.6
Sri Lanka	0.0	0.0
Malawi	77.6	172.5
Nigeria	-359.8	-150.7
Nicaragua	-4.0	-1.5
Nepal	2.1	4.1
Pakistan	-211.2	-354.3
Panama	-0.9	-1.5
Peru	-18.2	-39.7
Rwanda	45.0	47.4
Tanzania	514.4	525.7
Uganda	668.7	550.4
Vietnam	198.7	108.5
Yemen, Rep.	-123.5	-233.0
South Africa	0.0	476.0
Zambia	5.8	78.4
Sub-Saharan Africa	6,350.0	6,721.2
Central America	28.9	-3.0
Latin America	-476.4	-328.8
Middle East and North Africa	-124.2	-226.7
South Asia	2,232.3	2,097.9
Southeast Asia	36.9	14.0
Developed countries	-5.5	6.2
Developing countries	8,350.0	9,513.0
World	8,344.5	9,519.2

Source: World Bank staff estimates.

Note: Based on estimates using the computable general equilibrium model MIRAGRODEP, described in detail in Annex 7.1. Assuming increases in the price of maize, rice, and wheat as represented in Figure 7.4, panel D, and based on a poverty line of $1.90/day.

ANNEX 7.1 Methodology and database

Error correction model

The analytical framework used to represent the imperfect transmission of changes in international prices into domestic markets relies on an error correction model (ECM), as described in Ivanic and Martin (2014b). As noted by Nickell (1985), this model represents a situation in which policy makers seek to reduce the costs of change and of being out of equilibrium. A simplified version of the model used by Ivanic and Martin (2014b), expressed in logs, is as follow:

$$\Delta\tau = \alpha\ (p^{w} - p^{w}_{t\text{-}1}) + \beta\ [p_{t\text{-}1} - \gamma\, p^{w}_{t\text{-}1}],$$

where p represents domestic prices; p_w world prices; τ the rate of protection, approximated by $(p\text{-}p_w)$; α, $\alpha < 0$, the coefficient of price insulation ranging from 0 for countries that do not insulate against the rise in world prices, to -1 for countries that adopt policies that fully insulate domestic markets; β, $\beta < 0$, the cost of being out of equilibrium or the speed with which policies achieve the target level of protection or policy makers move back toward this equilibrium after being forced away from it by a shock to world prices; γ determines the long-run relationship between a country's protection and the global level of agricultural protection; and $[p_{t-1} - \gamma \times p^{w}_{t-1}]$ is the deviation from the political economy equilibrium. It depends on factors like income levels, exportable/importable status, the elasticity of import demand, and the share of real income gains from higher protection that will accrue to politically organized producers (Anderson 1995; Grossman and Helpman 1994).

The database on Distortions to Agricultural Incentives (Anderson and Valenzuela 2008; Anderson and Nelgen 2013) is the main data source for estimating the ECM model. It includes estimates of domestic and world price levels, which also determine the level of protection. The price data used in the model capture natural shocks (oil prices, weather events) as well as the impact of trade policy interventions, the separate impacts of which are not possible to disentangle. The model is estimated for eight food commodities, with data for 82 countries, of which 26 are advanced economies, 44 emerging market and developing economies, and 12 low-income countries.

Measuring the extent of trade policy interventions

The approach to quantifying the extent of trade policy interventions builds on that used in Anderson, Ivanic, and Martin (2014). It is assumed that a primary shock, such as weather shock, generates an initial change in domestic and world prices. In attempting to insulate consumers and producers from price increases, governments make offsetting changes in protection measures, such as the introduction of export bans or reduction in import duties. These measures, in turn, reinforce the original shock to world prices. When a country imposes an export restriction, the availability of food to the rest of the world is reduced, and this tends to push up the world price. Similarly, when an importing country reduces its import tariffs, it increases the demand for imports and hence puts upward pressure on the world price.

The impact of the changes in trade policies can be distinguished from those of the primary shocks in the following equation:

$$\sum_i S_i(p_i) + v_i = \sum_i D_i(p_i),$$

where S_i is supply in region i; D_i is demand in region i; $p_i = p^*(1+t_i)$ is the domestic price; p^* is the world price; t_i is a country-specific trade barrier, such as a proportional tariff; and v_i is a random production shift variable for region i. Totally differentiating the equation above, rearranging, and expressing the results in percentage changes yields an expression of the impact of a set of changes in trade distortions on the world price:

$$\hat{p}^* = \frac{\Sigma_i H_i \hat{v}_i + \Sigma_i (H_i \gamma_i - G_i \eta_i)\hat{T}_i}{\Sigma_i (G_i \eta_i - H_i \gamma_i)}$$

where $\hat{p}^*$ is the proportional change in the international price; $\hat{v}_i$ is an exogenous output shock such as might result from good or bad seasonal conditions; η_i is the elasticity of demand in market i; γ_i is the elasticity of supply in market i; G_i is the share at world prices of country i in global demand; H_i is the share of country i in global production, and $\hat{T}_i = (1 + t_i)$.

In other words, the impact on the world price of a change in trade policies in country i is given as a weighted average of the changes in trade distortions in different markets, with the weight on region i depending on the importance of that country in global supply and demand, as well as the responsiveness of its production and consumption to price changes in the country, as represented by γ_i and η_i.

It is thus assumed that elasticities of demand are equal between countries, that is, that imported and domestic goods are perfect substitutes, and that there are no supply responses. Alternatively, the model could allow for differentiation between imported and domestic products, as well as a limited supply response (Jensen and Anderson 2017). The result would be an expression with weights that depend on, for instance, the shares of imports in consumption in each market. However, the overall result is similar in expressing the change in world prices as a weighted sum of changes in trade distortions.

To avoid having to deal with difficult-to-interpret interaction terms, all proportional changes are converted into log changes in T_i, p_i's, and p as:

$$\hat{p}_i = \hat{p} + \hat{T}_i$$

Changes in relative prices are measured as in the Agricultural Incentives database and capture a wide range of policy measures used to assess agricultural trade distortions—including tariffs, export subsidies, export taxes, export bans, and import subsidies.

If products are homogeneous, and a country is small, the change in Δt represents the change in the domestic price of the good. Additionally, if $\hat{T}_i$ is negative in a period of rising world prices, countries are seeking to insulate their markets from the increase in prices. If it is positive, policy makers are compounding the increase in world prices with an increase in protection. This may be due to the correction of past "errors." This might occur if domestic prices fall below policy makers' desired long-run level, or if policy insulated the domestic market from world markets and an exogenous shock—such as a harvest shortfall—has caused the domestic price to rise relative to the world price. Such insulation patterns have been observed in the maize markets in many African countries (Chapoto and Jayne 2009).

The MIRAGRODEP model

The analytical framework to measure the poverty implications of the 2010-11 food price spike relies on the MIRAGRODEP model (Laborde, Robichaud, and Tokgoz 2013), complemented with household surveys for more than 31 countries and 285,000 representative households. MIRAGRODEP is a dynamic, multicountry, and multisector computable general equilibrium (CGE) model. The model relies on the Global Trade Analysis Project (GTAP) 9, a global database for 2011. The GTAP database includes input-output tables linked by bilateral trade flows for 140 regions (countries or country aggregates) and 57 sectors. For the purposes of the simulations, these countries and sectors were aggregated into 31 countries/regions and 15 sectors among which rice, wheat, and maize are represented separately.

On the supply side, the production function is a Leontief function of value added and intermediate inputs. The intermediate inputs are represented by a nested, two-level constant elasticity of substitution (CES) function of all goods.

Based on this, substitutability exists between intermediate goods, but these are more substitutable when they are in the same category (such as agricultural inputs or services inputs). Value added is also represented by a nested structure of CES functions of unskilled labor, land, natural resources, skilled labor, and capital. This nesting allows the modeler to incorporate some intermediate goods that are substitutes of factors, such as energy or fertilizers.

On the demand side, a representative consumer is assumed to have a constant propensity to save. The remaining national income is used for the purchase of final consumption goods. Consumers' preferences are represented by a linear expenditure system–CES function, calibrated based on the U.S. Department of Agriculture Economic Research Service income and price elasticities to reflect nonhomothetic demand patterns with changes in revenue. Given an increase in the price staple foods, such as rice, wheat, or maize, consumers substitute away to consume other food products. Armington elasticities, which measure the elasticity of substitution between products of different countries, are drawn from the GTAP database and are assumed to be the same across regions.

Factor endowments are assumed to be fully employed. The supply of capital goods is modified each year because of depreciation and investment. New capital is allocated among sectors according to an investment function. Growth rates of labor supply are fixed exogenously. Land supply is endogenous and depends on the real remuneration of land. Skilled labor is the only factor that is perfectly mobile; unskilled labor is imperfectly mobile between agriculture and nonagriculture sectors according to a constant elasticity of transformation function. Unskilled labor's remuneration in agricultural activities is different from that of nonagricultural activities. The only factor whose supply is constant is the natural resources factor. However, it is possible to change the factor endowment endogenously in the baseline to reflect long-term depletion of resources with respect to a price trajectory.

The poverty impact is captured through a top-down approach using a data set of household surveys for more than 31 countries and 285,000 representative households. The impact of a policy shock on poverty depends on price changes, the relative reliance of households on the consumption of individual staple foods, and the net food-buying status of households in different segments of the distribution (Deaton 1989).

Beyond the standard features of a global dynamic CGE model, the MIRAGRODEP model includes several improvements: subnational land markets (agroecological zones or administrative districts) and endogenous land supply; poverty analysis through a top-down approach for global coverage or a bottom-up approach (for a subset of countries); the dual-dual approach for formal/informal and rural/urban labor markets (Stifel and Thorbecke 2003); a consistent aggregator for trade policies (Laborde, Martin, and van der Mensbrugghe 2017); differentiated data sets on actual trade and farm policies and existing policy space for scenario design and endogenous policy responses; a macro nutrient (calories, fats, and proteins) accounting system based on FAOSTAT food balance sheets and a global input-output matrix; and a sensitivity analysis framework based on Monte Carlo simulations.

Although the elasticities of substitution for rice, wheat, and maize used in this model are higher than for manufactured goods, they are not infinite, as is assumed using the perfect substitutes model (Thursby, Johnson, and Grennes 1986). This specification has important implications for the economy-wide analysis and at the household level. Given these assumptions, an increase in the price of an imported good has a muted impact on the domestic consumer price of that good. Since with the Armington assumption—imported goods differentiated based on their country of origin—the composite price of the consumer good is weighted by the shares of domestic and imported goods, the impact of a unit change in the world price, or in trade policy, is given by the share of imports in total consumption. Because the share of imports in total consumption of staple foods is typically small, the impact of trade policy on consumer prices is much more muted than under the assumption of perfect substitution used in Anderson, Ivanic, and Martin (2014). On the production side, the assumption that each country's export product is the same as the products sold domestically means that changes in export trade policies will have a more direct impact on producer prices if the country is an exporter and not too large in the markets it supplies.

References

Akiyama, T., J. Baffes, D. F. Larson, and P. Varangis. 2001. *Commodity Market Reforms: Lessons of Two Decades*. Washington, DC: World Bank.

Aksoy, M. A., and J. C. Beghin. 2004. *Global Agricultural Trade and Developing Countries*. Washington, DC: World Bank.

Aksoy, M. A., and B. Hoekman. 2010. *Food Prices and Rural Poverty*. Washington, DC: World Bank.

Al-Mamun, A., A. Chapoto, B. Chisanga, W. Martin, and P. Samboko. 2017. "El Niño Impacts and Trade Policy Responses on Grain Markets and Trade in Eastern and Southern Africa." International Food Policy Research Institute, Washington, DC.

Anderson, K. 1995. "Lobbying Incentives and the Pattern of Protection in Rich and Poor Countries." *Economic Development and Cultural Change* 43 (2): 401-23.

Anderson, K., M. Ivanic, and W. Martin. 2014. "Food Price Spikes, Price Insulation and Poverty." In *The Economics of Food Price Volatility,* edited by J. P. Chavas, D. Hummels, and Wright. Chicago: University of Chicago Press.

Anderson, K., W. Martin, and M. Ivanic. 2017. "Food Price Changes, Domestic Price Insulation and Poverty (When All Policy Makers Want to Be Above-Average)." In *Agriculture and Rural Development in a Transforming World,* edited by P. Pingali and G. Feder. London: Routledge.

Anderson, K., and S. Nelgen. 2011. "Trade Barrier Volatility and Agricultural Price Stabilization." *World Development* 40 (1): 36-48.

———. 2013. "Updated National and Global Estimates of Distortions to Agricultural Incentives, 1955 to 2011." World Bank, Washington, DC.

Anderson, K., and E. Valenzuela. 2008. "Estimates of Global Distortions to Agricultural Incentives, 1955 to 2007." World Bank, Washington, DC.

Barrett, C. 2013. *Food Security and Sociopolitical Stability.* Oxford: Oxford University Press.

Becker, T., and P. Mauro. 2006. "Output Drops and the Shocks That Matter." IMF Working Paper 06/172, International Monetary Fund, Washington, DC.

Chapoto, A., and T. S. Jayne. 2009. "Effects of Maize Marketing and Trade Policy on Price Unpredictability in Zambia." Food Security Collaborative Working Paper 54499, Department of Agricultural, Food, and Resource Economics, Michigan State University, East Lansing, MI.

Childs, N. W., and J. Kiawu. 2009. "Factors behind the Rise in Global Rice Prices in 2008." U.S. Department of Agriculture, Economic Research Service, Washington, DC.

Deaton, A. 1989. "Rice Prices and Income Distribution in Thailand: A Non-Parametric Analysis." *Economic Journal* 99 (395): 1-37.

Easterly, W., and S. Fischer. 2001. "Inflation and the Poor." *Journal of Money, Credit and Banking* 33 (2): 160-78.

FAO, IFAD, UNICEF, WFP, and WHO (Food and Agriculture Organization, International Fund for Agricultural Development, United Nations Children's Emergency Fund, World Food Programme, and World Health Organization). 2018. *The State of Food Security and Nutrition in the World 2018: Building Climate Resilience for Food Security and Nutrition.* Rome: FAO.

Freund, C., and C. Ozden. 2008. "Trade Policy and Loss Aversion." *American Economic Review* 98 (4): 1675-91.

Fukase, E., and W. Martin. 2017. "Agro-Processing and Horticultural Exports from Africa." International Food Policy Research Institute, Washington, DC.

Gillson, I., and A. Fouad. 2014. *Trade Policy and Food Security: Improving Access to Food in Developing Countries in the Wake of High World Prices.* Washington, DC: World Bank.

Giordani, P., N. Rocha, and M. Ruta. 2016. "Food Prices and the Multiplier Effect of Trade Policy." *Journal of International Economics* 101 (1): 102-22.

Gouel, C., M. Gautam, and W. Martin. 2016. "Managing Food Price Volatility in a Large Open Country: The Case of Wheat in India." *Oxford Economic Papers* 68 (3): 811-35.

Gouel, C., and S. Jean. 2015. "Optimal Food Price Stabilization in a Small Open Developing Country." *World Bank Economic Review* 29 (1): 74-101.

Grossman, G., and E. Helpman. 1994. "Protection for Sale." *American Economic Review* 84 (4): 833-50.

Headey, D., and W. Martin. 2016. "The Impact of Food Prices on Poverty and Food Security." *Annual Review of Resource Economics* 8 (1): 329-51.

IMF (International Monetary Fund). 2011. "Managing Volatility: A Vulnerability Exercise for Low-Income Countries." International Monetary Fund, Washington, DC.

Ivanic, M., and W. Martin. 2008. "Implications of Higher Global Food Prices for Poverty in Low-Income Countries." Policy Research Working Paper 4594, World Bank, Washington, DC.

———. 2014a. "Implications of Domestic Price Insulation for Global Food Price Behavior." *Journal of International Money and Finance* 42 (1): 272-88.

———. 2014b. "Short- and Long-Run Impacts of Food Price Changes on Poverty." Policy Research Working Paper 7011, World Bank, Washington, DC.

Jacoby, H. 2016. "Food Prices, Wages, and Welfare in Rural India." *Economic Inquiry* 54 (1): 159-76.

Jensen, H. G., and K. Anderson. 2017. "Grain Price Spikes and Beggar-Thy-Neighbor Policy Responses: A Global Economywide Analysis." *World Bank Economic Review* 31 (1): 158-75.

Kose, A., S. Kurlat, F. Ohnsorge, and N. Sugawara. 2017. "A Cross-Country Database of Fiscal Space." Policy Research Working Paper 8157, World Bank, Washington, DC.

Laborde, D., W. Martin, and D. van der Mensbrugghe. 2017. "Measuring the Impacts of Global Trade Reform with Optimal Aggregators of Distortions." *Review of International Economics* 25 (2): 403-25.

Laborde, D., V. Robichaud, and S. Tokgoz. 2013. "MIRAGRODEP 1.0: Documentation." AGRODEP Technical Note, International Food Policy Research Institute, Washington, DC.

Lustig, N. 2009. "Coping with Rising Food Prices: Policy Dilemmas in the Developing World." Institute for International Economic Policy, George Washington University, Washington, DC.

Martin, W., and K. Anderson. 2012. "Export Restrictions and Price Insulation during Commodity Price Booms." *American Journal of Agricultural Economics* 94 (2): 422-27.

Negassa, A., and T. S. Jayne. 1997. "The Response of Ethiopian Grain Markets to Liberalization." Food Security Collaborative Working Paper 55595, Department of Agricultural, Food, and Resource Economics, Michigan State University, East Lansing, MI.

Nickell, S. 1985. "Error Correction, Partial Adjustment and All That: An Expository Note." *Oxford Bulletin of Economics and Statistics* 47 (2): 119-29.

Stifel, D. C., and E. Thorbecke. 2003. "A Dual-Dual CGE Model of an Archetype African Economy: Trade Reform, Migration and Poverty." *Journal of Policy Modeling* 25 (3): 207-35.

Thursby, M., P. Johnson, and T. Grennes. 1986. "The Law of One Price and the Modelling of Disaggregated Trade Flows." *Economic Modelling* 3 (4): 293-302.

Tschirley, D., and T. Jayne. 2010. "Exploring the Logic behind Southern Africa's Food Crises." *World Development* 38 (1): 76-87.

Wakeyo, M., and B. Lanos. 2014. "Analysis of Price Incentives for Wheat in Ethiopia." Food and Agriculture Organization of the United Nations, Rome.

World Bank. 2009. *Global Economic Prospects: Commodities at the Crossroads.* January. Washington, DC: World Bank.

———. 2010. "Commodity Market Outlook." December. World Bank, Washington, DC.

———. 2011. "Responding to Global Food Price Volatility and Its Impact on Food Security." World Bank, Washington, DC.

Wright, B. 2014. "Global Biofuels: Key to the Puzzle of Grain Market Behavior." *Journal of Economic Perspectives* 28 (1): 73-98

APPENDIX

Cross-Country Database of Inflation and Country Characteristics

The database contains a wide range of inflation measures and key country characteristics, including macroeconomic and structural variables, for up to 175 countries for 1970-2018. This appendix describes the data sources and definitions of the variables and their construction in detail.

Measures of inflation

Measures. Data are available for six measures of inflation: headline, food, energy, and core consumer price index (CPI) inflation; producer price index (PPI) inflation; and gross domestic product (GDP) deflator changes. The database also includes headline CPI inflation expectations. Data sources include Haver Analytics, ILOSTAT, the International Monetary Fund's (IMF's) International Financial Statistics and World Economic Outlook database, OECDstat, UNdata, and the World Bank's Development Prospects Group internal databases.[1]

Country coverage. Headline inflation data are available for 175 countries, including 34 advanced economies and 141 emerging market and developing economies (EMDEs), including 31 low-income countries (LICs). A complete (balanced) data set of annual data for all six inflation measures is available for 25 countries for 1970-2017, including 20 advanced economies and 5 non-LIC EMDEs. One- or two-year data gaps are completed through interpolation. Quarterly data for headline CPI inflation are available for up to 34 advanced economies and 78 EMDEs, including 5 LICs for 1971:1-2018:2 (of which all but 7 non-LIC EMDEs have updated data to 2018). A balanced sample with quarterly data available for 1971:1-2018:2 includes 24 advanced economies and 22 non-LIC EMDEs. Table A.1 provides a breakdown of the number of countries with data available for every year of the period indicated in the column title.

Headline inflation. Data are drawn primarily from three databases: Haver Analytics, OECDstat, and the IMF's World Economic Outlook. The IMF Consumer Price Index database has data for its member countries for long time periods, but with gaps. The ILOSTAT database has coverage of most countries through 2011, but with some gaps.

[1] ILOSTAT is a database maintained by the International Labour Organization. OECDstat includes data and metadata for countries in the Organisation for Economic Co-operation and Development and select nonmember economies. UNdata is a database provided by the United Nations.

Food inflation. Data are drawn from four data sets. The ILOSTAT database on CPI components is the main source as it has the most comprehensive coverage. Data for some years are missing and coverage ends in 2011. The IMF Consumer Price Index database is used to fill data gaps. Haver Analytics provides coverage for some remaining data gaps. OECDstat covers data for Organisation for Economic Co-operation and Development (OECD) members and some nonmembers starting in 1970.

Energy, core, and PPI inflation. Data are primarily drawn from Haver Analytics (energy, core, and PPI inflation), ILOSTAT (energy), UNdata (energy), and OECDstat (energy, core, and PPI inflation). Data from these sources are merged only if there are no large discrepancies in values between the databases. Official core inflation data are available for 70 countries, including 36 non-LIC EMDEs and 2 LICs. For the other countries, missing core inflation series are constructed using CPI weights and inflation in CPI components (Table A.2).

Calculation of core inflation. For the countries for which official measures of core inflation are unavailable, core inflation series are obtained by subtracting the contribution of volatile components of CPI (food and energy) from headline inflation.

For most EMDEs and LICs, monthly energy inflation series are not available. For these countries, the calculation of core inflation uses the housing, water, electricity, gas, and other fuels category of the CPI as a proxy for energy inflation. The following formula is used to calculate core inflation in each period:

$$\text{Core inflation} = \frac{\left[\pi - \omega_F \pi_F - \omega_E \pi_E\right]}{1 - \omega_F \pi_F - \omega_E \pi_E}$$

where π, π_F, and π_E are the monthly inflation rates for headline, food, and energy, respectively, and ω_F and ω_E are the weights for food and energy, respectively. The weights of the sub-indexes in the total index are obtained from the IMF Consumer Price Index database as well as OECDstat and Haver Analytics. The information for the following categories is obtained for 66 countries: food and non-alcoholic beverages; alcoholic beverages, tobacco, and narcotics; clothing and footwear; housing, water, electricity, gas, and other fuels; furnishings, household equipment, and routine household maintenance; health; transport; communication; recreation and culture; education; restaurants and hotels; and miscellaneous goods and services.

Cyclical and trend inflation. Cyclical and trend inflation series are produced using the methodology in Stock and Watson (2016). Trend inflation is defined as the part of inflation that follows a permanent stochastic trend. Cyclical inflation is a serially uncorrelated transitory component of inflation.

GDP deflator. For 1970-2017, data are drawn from Haver Analytics, OECDstat, and the World Economic Outlook database. Quarterly data, defined as quarter-on-quarter percent change, seasonally adjusted, are available for 95 countries. Annual data are available for 175 countries.

Inflation expectations. Inflation expectations are from two sources. First, the survey of professional forecasters on medium- to long-term expectations is conducted by Consensus Economics multiple times each year. It provides forecasts for annual average CPI inflation over the next 5-10 years for 46 countries (including in the Euro Area) since 1989. The exceptions are the Russian Federation and Latin American countries. Their inflation forecasts are surveyed on an end-of-period (December-to-December) basis. Historical long-

TABLE A.1 Number of countries with available inflation data

	Number of countries with data available				
	Any year during 1970-2017	Every year since			
		1970	1980	1990	2000
Headline inflation					
Annual	175	153	154	161	175
Quarterly	172	45	51	64	81
Monthly	163	33	51	63	92
Food inflation					
Annual	171	101	105	124	139
Quarterly	163	21	25	31	52
Monthly	164	19	25	30	67
Energy inflation					
Annual	167	47	55	70	101
Quarterly	92	18	24	28	51
Monthly	157	13	23	27	61
PPI inflation					
Annual	103	45	49	54	74
Quarterly	104	8	35	46	70
Monthly	66	7	14	20	41
Core inflation					
Annual	146	44	54	68	96
Quarterly	142	20	28	29	60
Monthly	144	8	24	26	58
GDP deflator					
Annual	175	135	137	142	172
Quarterly	96	8	15	24	67
Monthly	...	...	...	...	...

Note: ... = data are not available for the full sample period; GDP = gross domestic product; PPI = producer price index.

TABLE A.2 Number of countries with estimates of core inflation

	Advanced economies		EMDEs		LICs		All countries	
Frequency	A	M	A	M	A	M	A	M
From 1970	25	8	16	0	3	0	44	8
From 1980	26	20	23	2	3	0	52	22
From 1990	28	22	34	3	4	0	66	25
From 2000	32	30	52	23	10	5	94	58
From 2010	33	31	77	58	14	12	124	101

Note: Each entry refers to the number of countries in the respective group for which core inflation data are available for every year in the period indicated. In addition to countries in the table, official core inflation data are available for 52 countries, including 29 countries from OECDstat and 23 countries from Haver Analytics. The former includes Australia, Belgium, Colombia, Denmark, Estonia, Finland, France, Germany, Greece, Hungary, Iceland, Ireland, Israel, Italy, Japan, Luxembourg, Latvia, Mexico, New Zealand, Norway, Poland, the Slovak Republic, Slovenia, Spain, Sweden, Switzerland, Turkey, the United Kingdom, and the United States. The latter includes Belarus, Brazil, Canada, Chile, China, Costa Rica, the Dominican Republic, El Salvador, Indonesia, Jordan, Kazakhstan, the Republic of Korea, Malaysia, Nicaragua, Paraguay, Peru, the Russian Federation, Singapore, South Africa, Tanzania, Thailand, Trinidad and Tobago, and Uganda. A = annual data; EMDEs = emerging market and developing economies; LICs = low-income countries; M = monthly data.

term consensus forecasts are available from October 1989 for the Group of Seven and six Western European economies. The data set contains long-term consensus forecasts for 7 Latin American countries since 1993, and for 12 East Asia and Pacific countries (excluding Japan) and 14 Eastern European countries since 1998. Second, the IMF World Economic Outlook database provides five-year-ahead annual average headline CPI inflation forecasts on a biannual basis for 47 countries for 1990-2017.

Global commodity price indexes. Global commodity prices and indexes are available from 1960 from the World Bank's Pink Sheet of commodity price data. The following global price indexes are available at monthly, quarterly, and annual frequencies: agricultural commodity; energy commodity; non-energy commodity; and food commodity. All indexes are in nominal U.S. dollars, scaled to 2010 equal to 100.

Measures of country characteristics

This section describes measures of country characteristics available in the database: macroeconomic variables; monetary policy-related variables; variables related to global integration; exchange rate variables; and structural variables. The section also describes the classification of countries. Table A.3 provides detailed information on each variable, including those related to inflation discussed in the previous section.

Macroeconomic variables

Gross domestic product (GDP). Annual and quarterly data (quarter-on-quarter, seasonally adjusted percent change) are available from Haver Analytics and OECDstat.

Industrial production. Unadjusted and seasonally adjusted series of industrial production are available from Haver Analytics and OECDstat for 63 countries at monthly frequency for 1970-2018. Country-specific indexes are rebased to 2010 equal to 100.

Savings. Gross national savings (as a percent of GDP) are computed as gross disposable income less final consumption expenditures after taking into account an adjustment for pension funds, when possible. These series are available from the IMF's World Economic Outlook database for around 170 countries for 1980-2017.

Investment. Investment is expressed as a percent of GDP. Investment or gross capital formation is measured by the total value of gross fixed capital formation and changes in inventories and acquisitions less disposals of valuables. It is available from the IMF's World Economic Outlook database for 173 countries for 1980-2017.

Gross public debt. This measure is defined as gross public debt as a percentage of GDP. It uses four data sources for constructing debt-to-GDP ratios. Mauro et al. (2015) provide a historical data set of government debt for 55 countries for 1800-2011. Abbas et al. (2011) provide a comprehensive database of gross central government debt-to-GDP ratios, covering 174 countries for 1700-2012. Data are updated to 2017 using the IMF Historical Public Debt Database and World Economic Outlook database.

Fiscal rules. A fiscal rule imposes a long-lasting constraint on fiscal policy through numerical limits on budgetary aggregates. The IMF Fiscal Rules Dataset 1985-2015 (Schaechter et al. 2012) provides systematic information on the use and design of fiscal rules covering national and supranational fiscal rules in 96 countries from 1985 to 2015. The data set covers four types of rules: budget balance rules, debt rules, expenditure rules, and revenue rules, applying to the central or general government or the public sector. It also presents details on various characteristics of rules, such as their legal basis, coverage, escape clauses, as well as enforcement procedures, and takes stock of key supporting features that are in place, including independent monitoring bodies and fiscal responsibility laws.

Monetary policy–related variables

Monetary policy framework. This variable classifies the monetary policy regimes into those with exchange rate anchors, monetary aggregate targets, inflation targeting frameworks, and other (hybrid) regimes. It is available for 197 countries from 1990. The main sources are the IMF Quarterly Report on Exchange Arrangements and the IMF *Annual Report on Exchange Arrangements* *and Exchange Restrictions* (AREAER). The database includes the following categories:

- Monetary aggregate targeting
- Inflation targeting regimes
- Free floating without inflation targeting regimes (including all Euro Area countries)
- Exchange rate anchor, U.S. dollar (including the Eastern Caribbean Currency Union)
- Exchange rate anchor, euro (including the West African Economic and Monetary Union and Central African Economic and Monetary Community)
- Exchange rate anchor, composite
- Exchange rate anchor, other currency.

Inflation targeting framework. The IMF's AREAER provides country-specific information on inflation targeting frameworks starting from 2010. It describes the de jure monetary policy regime as declared by the national monetary authorities. An electronic version of the data is provided by Caceres, Carrière-Swallow, and Gruss (2016). For countries with inflation targets, the data set provides the month and year of adoption of the inflation targeting framework. Because AREAER (and its online version) only provides information on inflation targeting frameworks since 2010, information from Carare and Stone (2006) is used to determine the exact year each country adopted inflation targeting. This variable is available for up to 170 countries for 1990-2017 on a monthly, quarterly, and annual basis.

Inflation targets. Information on "inflation target" ranges is available on a monthly basis for 37 countries from 1990. The data include three variables: the midpoint as well as the upper and lower bounds of inflation target ranges. For ease of analysis, for those countries that target a midpoint and do not have an official upper and lower bound, a range adding ±1 is calculated as the target range. Similarly, for those countries that do not have a midpoint for their inflation target, and instead target only a range, the midpoint was assumed to be the average of the lower and upper bounds of the announced target range. The data sources include national central banks, the Central Bank News website, AREAER database, and other sources.

Central bank independence. The measure of central bank independence relies on two sources. Garriga (2016) includes annual data on de jure central bank independence for 182 countries for 1970-2012. The data set identifies statutory reforms affecting central bank independence and their impact. Dincer and Eichengreen (2014) measure transparency and independence for about 120 central banks spanning 1998-2014. The index ranges from 0 to 15. The Dincer-Eichengreen index is selected as the main measure of central bank independence because it is available over a long timeframe (1998-2014). To expand the sample, the index is extrapolated to 2015-17 using 2014 data and extrapolated to 1970-97 using 1998 data. For countries not included in the Dincer and Eichengreen (2014) data set, the fitted values from an ordinary least squares regression of the Dincer-Eichengreen index on the Garriga index are used.

Central bank head turnover. Central bank head turnover data are available from Dreher, Sturm, and de Haan (2010). This data set contains information on the term in office and month and year at which a central bank governor is replaced. It also provides the official term in office according to the central bank law for 159 countries covering 1970-2014. The turnover rate (number of changes in central bank heads before the end of his or her legal term in office) using a four-year rolling average preceding a central bank governor change is calculated (similar to Klomp and de Haan [2010]). The four-year window matches the average turnover rate of central bank governors.

Variables related to global integration

De jure financial openness. Three sources are used to measure financial openness. Quinn and Toyoda (2008) have a capital controls index database of de jure measures of capital account and financial current account openness for 94 countries over 1980-2014. Fernandez et al. (2016) have a capital control measures data set of restrictions on capital account inflows and outflows for 10 categories of assets for 100 countries between 1995 and 2013. Chinn and Ito (2006) provide a de jure measure of capital account openness for 182 countries between 1970 and 2016. The annual and quarterly data sets contain all three measures of financial openness. To obtain the widest possible coverage, the primary source of financial openness is the Chinn-Ito index.

De facto financial openness. International financial integration provides a proxy for de facto financial openness. It is measured as the sum of foreign assets and liabilities as a percentage of GDP in current U.S. dollars. The External Wealth of Nations Mark II database (Lane and Milesi-Ferretti 2007) is the main source of financial integration data through 2014. Data from the IMF's Balance of Payments and International Investment Position Statistics are used to expand cross-country coverage. Data are available for 128 countries for the period since 1976.

Participation in global value chains (GVCs). Three measures of GVC participation are provided: backward and forward participation and the intermediate trade share of GDP. Backward participation in GVCs measures the foreign value added embodied in a country's exports, as a percentage of total gross exports. Forward participation in GVCs measures a country's value added embodied in foreign exports, as a percentage of total gross exports. Both data series are available from the OECD–World Trade Organization Trade in Value Added database for 58 countries for 1995, 2000, 2005, and 2008-11. The series of intermediate trade share of GDP are defined as the sum of intermediate imports and exports, as a percentage of GDP. Data are available for up to 166 countries, but with uneven year coverage. For 1988-2016, the series are available for 137 countries. Data are taken from the World Bank's World Integrated Trade Solution (WITS) and World Development Indicators. These three data series are used to construct a dummy variable indicating high participation in GVCs. A country is classified as highly integrated into GVCs (the dummy is assigned the value 1) if one of two conditions is met: the sum of backward and forward participation in GVCs is greater than the median of the sample in a particular year, or the intermediate trade ratio is greater than the median of the sample in a particular year.

Trade openness. The indicator for trade openness is defined as the sum of exports and imports of goods and services as a percentage of GDP. Data are available for 170 countries for 1970-2017, taken from the World Bank World Development Indicators. Data gaps are filled with data on exports, imports, and GDP obtained from the IMF's World Economic Outlook database.

Average effective tariff. This measure is the average rate of effectively applied tariffs, weighted by the product import shares corresponding to each partner country. Data are classified using the UN Harmonized System of trade at the six- or eight-digit level. This variable is available from the WITS website for a maximum of 149 countries, but with uneven year coverage; it is available for 109 countries for 2000-16.

Exchange rate variables

Bilateral exchange rate against the U.S. dollar. The IMF's International Financial Statistics database provides exchange rates in national currencies per U.S. dollar. Exchange rates in the database are classified into three broad categories, reflecting the role of the authorities in determining the rates and/or the multiplicity of the exchange rates in a country. The three categories are the market rate, describing an exchange rate determined largely by market forces; the official rate, describing an exchange rate determined by the authorities—sometimes in a flexible manner; and the principal, secondary, or tertiary rate, for countries maintaining multiple exchange arrangements. Data for the market exchange rate against the U.S. dollar are available for 34 advanced economies and 137 EMDEs, including 30 LICs, for 1970-2018.

Nominal and real effective exchange rates. The nominal and real effective exchange rates rely primarily on Darvas (2012). The database includes annual and monthly data for 178 countries, considerably more than in any other publicly available database. The series are available through mid-2017. The annual database covers 171 countries over 1960-2017, and the monthly database includes data for 165 countries over 1970-2017.

De facto exchange rate regime. The exchange rate regime classification of Shambaugh (2004) is used to determine whether a country has a pegged or flexible exchange rate. The original classification has four categories: "1" reflects no fluctuation at all; "2" indicates movements within 1 percent bands; "3" indicates movements within 2 percent bands; and "4" indicates a one-time devaluation with no change in the remaining 11 months of the year. Shambaugh (2004) assesses these movements against relevant base currencies. The constructed dummy variable indicating a pegged exchange rate regime is defined to equal 1 for countries classified as 1, 2, 3, or 4. A value of 0 is assigned to flexible exchange rates—that is, exchange rates that routinely fluctuate outside a 2 percent band. The indicator is available on an annual basis for 176 countries for 1960-2014.

De jure exchange rate regime. An alternative measure of the exchange rate regime is taken from Ilzetzki, Reinhart, and Rogoff (2017). They present annual and monthly data for 194 countries for 1946-2016. The classification includes the following categories:

1. No separate legal tender or currency union
2. Pre-announced peg or currency board arrangement
3. Pre-announced horizontal band that is narrower than or equal to ± 2 percent
4. De facto peg
5. Pre-announced crawling peg; de facto moving band narrower than or equal to ± 1 percent
6. Pre-announced crawling band that is narrower than or equal to ± 2 percent or de facto horizontal band that is narrower than or equal to ± 2 percent
7. De facto crawling peg
8. De facto crawling band that is narrower than or equal to ± 2 percent
9. Pre-announced crawling band that is wider than or equal to ± 2 percent
10. De facto crawling band that is narrower than or equal to ± 5 percent

11. Moving band that is narrower than or equal to ±2 percent (that is, allows for appreciation and depreciation over time)

12. De facto moving band ± 5 percent / managed floating

13. Freely floating

14. Freely falling

15. Dual market in which parallel market data are missing.

All countries with classification categories 1 to 11 are considered fixed exchange rate regimes and assigned a value of 1. Categories 12 to 15 are treated as flexible exchange rate regimes and assigned a value of 0.

Structural variables

Demographic variables. Population growth is the average annual growth of midyear population. It is available for 209 countries for 1970-2017 and obtained from the World Bank World Development Indicators. The old-age dependency ratio measures the ratio of people older than 64 years as a percent age of the working-age population (ages 15 to 64 years). The young-age dependency ratio is the share of people younger than 15 years as a percentage of the working-age population. The dependency ratios are also collected from the World Bank World Development Indicators and are available for 189 countries for 1970-2017.

Labor market flexibility. The labor market flexibility indicator uses the Fraser Institute's Economic Freedom of the World database. The labor market flexibility index uses survey responses to construct labor market flexibility indicators in four areas: minimum wage, hiring and firing practices, collective bargaining, and unemployment benefits. The survey asks respondents to answer questions on a scale from 1 (disagree) to 7 (agree), where 7 indicates strongest agreement. The index is standardized on a 0-10 scale. A higher value represents a more flexible labor market. Data are available for 152 countries for every five-year period between 1980 and 2000, and annually for 2001-14 (Gwartney, Lawson, and Hall 2017).

Collective bargaining coverage rate. The collective bargaining coverage rate is an indicator of the degree to which wages and working conditions are regulated by collective agreements. It measures the number of workers in employment whose pay and/or conditions of employment are determined by one or more collective agreements as a proportion of all those who are eligible to conclude a collective agreement. The collective bargaining coverage rate is available from ILOSTAT for 62 countries from 2001 to 2013.

Trade union density rate. Trade union membership, defined as the total number of workers who belong to a trade union, can be an indicator of trade union strength. The trade union density rate expresses union membership as a proportion of the eligible workforce and can be used as an indicator of the degree to which workers are organized. Data for this measure are available from ILOSTAT for 49 countries for 2000-13.

Rainfall. Rainfall data, defined as precipitation in millimeters per month, come from the Climate Change Knowledge Portal. The data set is produced by the Climatic Research Unit of the University of East Anglia and reformatted by the International Water Management Institute. It contains historical precipitation data aggregated from 2-degree gridded data to the country and basin levels. It is derived from observational data and provides quality-controlled temperature and rainfall values from thousands of weather stations worldwide, as well as derivative products, including monthly climatologies and long-term historical climatologies. The data cover more than 180 countries for 1901-2017.

Country classification

Country groups. Advanced economies include Australia; Austria; Belgium; Canada; Cyprus; the Czech Republic; Denmark; Estonia; Finland; France; Germany; Greece; Hong Kong SAR, China; Iceland; Ireland; Israel; Italy; Japan; the Republic of Korea; Latvia; Lithuania; Luxembourg; Malta; the Netherlands; New Zealand; Norway; Portugal; Singapore; the Slovak Republic; Slovenia; Spain; Sweden; Switzerland; the United Kingdom; and the United States.

Emerging market and developing economies (excluding low-income countries) include Albania; Algeria; Angola; Antigua and Barbuda; Argentina; Armenia; Azerbaijan; The Bahamas; Bahrain; Bangladesh; Barbados; Belarus; Belize; Bhutan; Bolivia; Bosnia and Herzegovina; Botswana; Brazil; Brunei Darussalam; Bulgaria; Cabo Verde; Cambodia; Cameroon; Chile; China; Colombia; the Republic of Congo; Costa Rica; Côte d'Ivoire; Croatia; Djibouti; Dominica; the Dominican Republic; Ecuador; the Arab Republic of Egypt; El Salvador; Equatorial Guinea; Eswatini; Fiji; Gabon; Georgia; Ghana; Grenada; Guatemala; Guyana; Honduras; Hungary; India; Indonesia; the Islamic Republic of Iran; Iraq; Jamaica; Jordan; Kazakhstan; Kenya; Kiribati; Kuwait; the Kyrgyz Republic; the Lao People's Democratic Republic; Lebanon; Lesotho; Libya; the former Yugoslav Republic of Macedonia; Malaysia; Maldives; the Marshall Islands; Mauritania; Mauritius; Mexico; the Federated States of Micronesia; Moldova; Mongolia; Montenegro; Morocco; Myanmar; Namibia; Nauru; Nicaragua; Nigeria; Oman; Pakistan; Palau; Panama; Papua New Guinea; Paraguay; Peru; the Philippines; Poland; Qatar; Romania; the Russian Federation; Samoa; São Tomé and Príncipe; Saudi Arabia; Serbia; the Seychelles; the Solomon Islands; South Africa; Sri Lanka; St. Kitts and Nevis; St.

Lucia; St. Vincent and the Grenadines; Sudan; Suriname; Thailand; Tonga; Trinidad and Tobago; Tunisia; Turkey; Turkmenistan; Tuvalu; Ukraine; the United Arab Emirates; Uruguay; Uzbekistan; Vanuatu; República Bolivariana de Venezuela; Vietnam; and Zambia.

Low-income countries include Afghanistan; Benin; Burkina Faso; Burundi; the Central African Republic; Chad; the Comoros; the Democratic Republic of Congo; Eritrea; Ethiopia; The Gambia; Guinea; Guinea-Bissau; Haiti; the Democratic People's Republic of Korea; Liberia; Madagascar; Malawi; Mali; Mozambique; Nepal; Niger; Rwanda; Senegal; Sierra Leone; Somalia; South Sudan; the Syrian Arab Republic; Tajikistan; Tanzania; Togo; Uganda; the Republic of Yemen; and Zimbabwe. The classification of LICs is based on the World Bank Group classification as of June 2018.

Commodity exporter status. A country is classified as a "commodity exporter" if one of the following two conditions was met during 2012-14: on average, commodity exports accounted for 30 percent or more of total goods exports, or exports of any single commodity accounted for 20 percent or more of total goods exports. Economies for which these thresholds were met because of re-exports were excluded. When data were not available, judgment was used. This taxonomy results in the classification of some well-diversified economies as importers, even if they are exporters of certain commodities (for example, Mexico). Commodity importers are all economies that are not classified as commodity exporters.

Regions. Regional dummy variables for East Asia and Pacific, Europe and Central Asia, Latin America and the Caribbean, Middle East and North Africa, South Asia, and Sub-Saharan Africa follow the World Bank Group classification.

Net food importer status. Net food importers are classified based on net food imports (food imports minus food exports) as a percentage of GDP. Food comprises the commodities in sections 0 (food and live animals), 1 (beverages and tobacco), and 4 (animal and vegetable oils and fats), as well as division 22 (oil seeds, oil nuts, and oil kernels) in the UN Standard International Trade Classification. A country is classified as a net food importer (the dummy is assigned the value 1) if its net food imports as a percentage of GDP are above the median of net food imports across countries in a given year.

Net energy importer status. Net energy importers are classified based on net fuel imports (fuel imports minus fuel exports) as a percentage of GDP. A country is classified as a net energy importer (the dummy is assigned the value 1) if its net fuel imports as a percentage of GDP are above the median of net fuel imports across countries in a given year.

TABLE A.3 Database

Variable name in database	Description	Units	Country coverage	Year coverage	Source
inflation	Consumer price inflation	Percent	175	From 1970	Central bank websites; IMF IFS; Haver Analytics; OECDstat
ppi	Producer price inflation	Percent	103	From 1970	Central bank websites; IFS; Haver Analytics; OECDstat
core_inf	Core consumer price inflation	Percent	145	From 1970	Central bank websites; IFS; ILOSTAT; Haver Analytics; OECDstat
deflator_gdp	GDP deflator change	Percent	175	From 1970	Central bank websites; IFS; Haver Analytics; OECDstat
food_inf	Food and non-alcoholic beverages consumer price inflation	Percent	171	From 1970	ILOSTAT database on CPI Components; IMF Consumer Price Index database; Haver Analytics; OECDstat
energy	Energy consumer price inflation	Percent	167	From 1970	Central bank websites; Haver Analytics; ILOSTAT; OECDstat
co_energy	Global energy commodity price inflation	Percent	175	From 1970	World Bank Pink Sheet commodity price data
co_non_energy	Global non-energy commodity price inflation	Percent	175	From 1970	World Bank Pink Sheet commodity price data
co_food	Food commodity price inflation	Percent	175	From 1970	World Bank Pink Sheet commodity price data
pegtype_bi	De facto exchange rate regime	Dummy variable; 1=fixed, 0=flexible	168	From 1970	Shambaugh (2004); IMF AREAER
xr_regime	De jure exchange rate regime	Dummy variable; 1=fixed, 0=flexible	169	From 1970	Ilzetzki, Reinhart, and Rogoff (2017)
cbi_trans	Central bank transparency	Index; 0=least transparent; 15=most transparent	108	1998-2014	Dincer and Eichengreen (2014)
cbi_trans_fit	Central bank transparency, extended sample	Index; 0=least transparent; 15=most transparent	165	From 1970	cbi_trans extended using Garriga (2016)
saving_wdi	Gross national savings	Percent of GDP	169	From 1980	IMF World Economic Outlook

Note: Country coverage indicates the number of countries with data available in any year during 1970-2017. AREAER = Annual Report on Exchange Arrangements and Exchange Restrictions; CPI = consumer price index; GDP = gross domestic product; IFS = International Financial Statistics; IMF = International Monetary Fund.

TABLE A.3 Database *(continued)*

Variable name in database	Description	Units	Country coverage	Year coverage	Source
mon_policy	Monetary policy framework	Dummy variable: 2=Monetary aggregate targeting 3=Inflation targeting regimes 4=Free floating without inflation targeting regimes (including all Euro Area countries) 11= Exchange rate anchor, U.S. dollar (including ECCU) 12= Exchange rate anchor, euro (including WAEMU and CEMAC) 13= Exchange rate anchor, composite 14=Exchange rate anchor, other currency	175	From 1990	IMF AREAER
IT	Presence of inflation targeting framework	Dummy variable; 1=inflation targeting; 0=not inflation targeting	175	From 1970	IMF AREAER; Carare and Stone (2006); Caceres, Carriere-Swallow, and Gruss (2016)
TOR_i	Central bank head turnover	Number of changes in central bank heads before the end of his or her legal term in office	143	From 970	Dreher, Sturm, and de Haan (2010)
CMA, CXA	Commodity importer and exporter status	Dummy variables; CMA of 1=commodity importers; CMA of 0=otherwise; CXA of 1=commodity exporter; CXA of 0=otherwise	175	From 1970	World Bank Global Economic Prospects reports
region	EMDE regions	EAP=East Asia and Pacific; ECA=Europe and Central Asia; LAC=Latin America and the Caribbean; MNA=Middle East and North Africa; SAR=South Asia; SSA=Sub-Saharan Africa	175	From 1970	World Bank Group classification
incomegro up	Income groups AEs (31), EMDEs (110), LICs (31)	AE=advanced economies; EMDE=non-LIC EMDEs; LIC=low-income countries	175	From 1970	World Bank and IMF classification
saving_wdi	Gross national savings	Percent of GDP	169	From 1980	IMF World Economic Outlook

Note: Country coverage indicates the number of countries with data available in any year during 1970-2017. AEs = advanced economies; AREAER = Annual Report on Exchange Arrangements and Exchange Restrictions; CEMAC = Central African Economic and Monetary Community; ECCU = Eastern Caribbean Currency Union; EMDEs = emerging market and developing economies; GDP = gross domestic product; LICs = low-income countries; WAEMU = West African Economic and Monetary Union.

TABLE A.3 Database *(continued)*

Variable name in database	Description	Units	Country coverage	Year coverage	Source
it, it_lower, it_upper	"it" refers to Inflation target, mid-point target, or average of target range; "it_upper" refers to upper bound of target range; and "it_lower" refers to lower bound of target range	Percent	38	From 1990	National central bank websites; Central Bank News website; IMF AREAER; other documents
cap100_new	De jure financial openness (Quinn-Toyoda Index)	Index; 0=least open; 100=most open	122	From 1970	Quinn and Toyoda (2008)
ka_open_new	De jure financial openness (Chinn-Ito Index)	Index; 0=least open; 1=most open	173	From 1970	Chinn and Ito (2006)
ka_new	De Jure Financial Openness Capital Control Measures data set of restrictions on capital account inflows and outflows for 10 categories of assets for 100 countries between 1995 and 2013	Index; 0=least open; 1=most open	99	From 1995	Fernandez et al. (2016)
fin_int	De facto financial openness, defined as the sum of international assets and liabilities in percent of GDP	Percent of GDP	175	From 1970	Lane and Milesi-Ferretti 2007; IMF Balance of Payments and International Investment Position Statistics
back_gvc	Backward participation in GVCs, defined as foreign value added in domestic exports in percent of total domestic exports	Percent	58	1995, 2000, 2005, and 2008-11	OECD-WTO TiVA
for_gvc	Forward participation in GVCs, defined as domestic value added embodied in foreign exporters, as percent of foreign exports	Percent	58	1995, 2000, 2005, and 2008-11	OECD-WTO TiVA

Note: Country coverage indicates the number of countries with data available in any year during 1970-2017. AREAER = Annual Report on Exchange Arrangements and Exchange Restrictions; GDP = gross domestic product; GVCs = global value chains; IMF = International Monetary Fund; OECD = Organisation for Economic Co-operation and Development; TiVA = Trade in Value Added; WTO = World Trade Organization.

TABLE A.3 Database *(continued)*

Variable name in database	Description	Units	Country coverage	Year coverage	Source
gvc_total	Sum of intermediate exports and imports as percent of GDP	Percent of GDP	58	1995, 2000, 2005, and 2008-11	WITS; World Development Indicators
gvc_dummy	High integration into global value chains, defined as one of two conditions being met: the sum of backward and forward participation in global value chains is greater than the median of the sample in a particular year, or the intermediate trade ratio is greater than the median of the sample in a particular year	Dummy variable; 1=highly integrated ; 0=not highly integrated	175	From 1970	Constructed from back_gvc, for_gvc, and gvc_total
trade_open	Sum of exports and imports of goods and services as percent of GDP	Percent of GDP	175	From 1970	World Development Indicators; IMF World Economic Outlook
tariff	Average effective tariff, weighted by product-level import share from each partner country	Percent	166	1988-2016	WITS
debt_gdp	Gross public debt as percent of GDP	Percent of GDP	175	From 1970	Abbas et al. (2011); Mauro et al. (2015); IMF Historical Public Debt Database; IMF World Economic Outlook
neer	Nominal effective exchange rate	Index, various base years	171	From 1970	Darvas (2012)
neer_index	Nominal effective exchange rate, rebased to 2007	Index, 2007=100	171	From 1970	Darvas (2012)
pop_growth	Average annual growth of midyear population	Percent	173	From 1970	World Development Indicators
old_dep	Old-age dependency ratio, defined as number of people older than 64 as percent of the working-age population (ages 15 to 64 years)	Percent of working-age population	171	From 1970	World Development Indicators
flexibility	Labor market flexibility	Index; 0=least flexible; 10=most flexible	152	2001-14	Fraser Institute Economic Freedom of the World

Note: Country coverage indicates the number of countries with data available in any year during 1970-2017. GDP = gross domestic product; IMF = International Monetary Fund; WITS = World Integrated Trade Solution.

TABLE A.3 Database *(continued)*

Variable name in database	Description	Units	Country coverage	Year coverage	Source
foodnet	Net food imports, defined as food imports minus food exports as percent of GDP. Food comprises the commodities in SITC sections 0 (food and live animals), 1 (beverages and tobacco), and 4 (animal and vegetable oils, and fats), as well as SITC division 22 (oil seeds, oil nuts, and oil kernels).	Percent of GDP	167	From 1970	World Development Indicators
foodnet_dum	High net food importer status defined as net food imports as percent of GDP above the median of net food imports across countries in a given year	Dummy variable; 0=net food imports below cross-country median; 1=net food imports above cross-country median	140	From 1970	Constructed from foodnet
energynet	Net fuel imports, defined as fuel imports minus fuel exports as percent of GDP	Percent of GDP	167	From 1970	World Development Indicators
energynet_dum	High net energy importer status defined as net fuel imports in percent of GDP above the median of net fuel imports across countries in a given year	Dummy variable; 0=net fuel imports below cross-country median; 1=net fuel imports above cross-country median	140	From 1970	Constructed from energynet
young_dep	Young dependency ratio, defined as number of people younger than 15 as percent of the working-age population (ages 15 to 64 years)	Percent of working-age population	171	From 1970	World Development Indicators
bargaining	Collective bargaining coverage, defined as the number of workers in employment whose pay and/or conditions of employment are determined by one or more collective agreements as a proportion of all those who are eligible to conclude a collective agreement	Percent of workers eligible to conclude a collective agreement	62	2001-13	ILOSTAT
inv	Gross capital formation	Percent of GDP	162	From 1980	IMF World Economic Outlook
fiscal_rule	Adoption of a fiscal rule	Dummy variable; Yes=fiscal rule has been adopted; No=no fiscal rule has been adopted	92	1985-2015	Schaechter et al. (2012)

Note: Country coverage indicates the number of countries with data available in any year during 1970-2017. GDP = gross domestic product; IMF = International Monetary Fund; SITC = Standard International Trade Classification.

TABLE A.3 Database *(continued)*

Variable name in database	Description	Units	Country coverage	Year coverage	Source
ener_weight	Weight of energy in the consumer price index; when unavailable, weight of housing, water, electricity, and gas	Percent	143	From 1970	OECDstat; Haver Analytics; IMF International Financial Statistics
food_weight	Weight of food and non-alcoholic beverages in the consumer price index	Percent	145	From 1970	OECDstat; Haver Analytics; IMF International Financial Statistics
crude_petro	Crude oil price (unweighted average of Dubai, Brent, and WTI prices)	U.S. dollars per barrel	170	From 1970	World Bank Pink Sheet commodity price data
kcrude_petro	Crude oil price (unweighted average of Dubai, Brent, and WTI prices) at constant 2005 U.S. dollars	U.S. dollars per barrel	170	From 1970	World Bank Pink Sheet commodity price data
gdp_weo	GDP in billions of U.S. dollars	Billions of U.S. dollars	169	From 1980	IMF World Economic Outlook
gdp_growthweo	Real GDP growth	Percent	174	From 1981	IMF World Economic Outlook
pppgdp_weo	PPP valuation of country GDP, in billions of U.S. dollars	Billions of U.S. dollars	169	From 1980	IMF World Economic Outlook
union	Trade union density rate, defined as union membership as a proportion of the eligible workforce	Percent of the eligible workforce	75	2000-13	ILOSTAT
trend	Trend component of inflation, estimated as in Stock and Watson (2016)	Percent	148	From 1970	World Bank estimates

Note: Country coverage indicates the number of countries with data available in any year during 1970-2017. GDP = gross domestic product; IMF = International Monetary Fund; WTI = West Texas Intermediate.

TABLE A.3 Database *(continued)*

Variable name in database	Description	Units	Country coverage	Year coverage	Source
cycle	Cyclical component of inflation, estimated as in Stock and Watson (2016)	Percent	148	From 1970	World Bank estimates
var_trend	Variance of trend component of inflation, estimated as in Stock and Watson (2016)	Percent	148	From 1970	World Bank estimates
var_cycle	Variance of cyclical component of inflation, estimated as in Stock and Watson (2016)	Percent	148	From 1970	World Bank estimates
inflation_qoq	Quarter-on-quarter, seasonally adjusted, annualized CPI inflation	Percent	111	From 1970	Haver Analytics; OECDstat; IMF International Financial Statistics
inflation_q	Year-on-year, CPI inflation	Percent	172	From 1970	Haver Analytics; OECDstat; IMF International Financial Statistics
food_qoq	Quarter-on-quarter, seasonally adjusted, annualized food CPI inflation	Percent	163	From 1970	ILOSTAT database on CPI Components; IMF Consumer Price Index database; Haver Analytics; OECDstat
energy_qoq	Quarter-on-quarter, seasonally adjusted, annualized energy CPI inflation	Percent	92	From 1970	Haver Analytics; ILOSTAT; UNdata; OECDstat.
ppi_qoq	Quarter-on-quarter, seasonally adjusted, annualized PPI inflation	Percent	103	From 1970	Haver Analytics; OECDstat
core_qoq	Quarter-on-quarter, seasonally adjusted, annualized core CPI inflation	Percent	142	From 1970	Haver Analytics; OECDstat; IMF International Financial Statistics
deflator	Quarter-on-quarter, seasonally adjusted, GDP deflator	Percent	96	From 1970	Haver Analytics; OECDstat
headline	Consumer price index, month-on-month inflation rate	Percent	170	From 1970	Haver Analytics
food	Food and non-alcoholic beverages price index, month-on-month inflation rate	Percent	169	From 1970	ILOSTAT database on CPI Components; IMF Consumer Price Index database; Haver Analytics; OECDstat

Note: Country coverage indicates the number of countries with data available in any year during 1970-2017. CPI = consumer price index; GDP = gross domestic product; IMF = International Monetary Fund; PPI = producer price index.

TABLE A.3 Database *(continued)*

Variable name in database	Description	Units	Country coverage	Year coverage	Source
Core	Core inflation, month-on-month inflation rate	Percent	112	From 1970	Haver Analytics; OECDstat; IMF International Financial Statistics; calculated
core_inflation	Official core inflation	Percent	56	From 1970	OECDstat; Haver Analytics; IMF International Financial Statistics
g_energy	Global energy commodity prices (nominal U.S. dollars)	Index, 2010=100	181	From 1970	World Bank Pink Sheet commodity price data
g_non_energy	Global non-energy commodity prices (nominal U.S. dollars)	Index, 2010=100	169	From 1970	World Bank Pink Sheet commodity price data
g_food	Global food commodity prices (nominal U.S. dollars)	Index, 2010=100	169	From 1970	World Bank Pink Sheet commodity price data
rainfall	Rainfall	Precipitation in millimeters per month	167	1990-2016	Climate Change Knowledge Portal
ind_pro	Industrial production	Index, 2010=100	60	From 1970	Haver Analytics; OECDstat; IMF International Financial Statistics
ind_pro_sa	Industrial production, seasonally adjusted	Index, 2010=100	34	From 1970	Haver Analytics; OECDstat; IMF International Financial Statistics
m3	Money supply M3	Local currency units	74	From 1980	Haver Analytics; OECDstat; IMF International Financial Statistics
base_money	Base money, local currency	Local currency units	42	From 1980	Haver Analytics; OECDstat; IMF International Financial Statistics
broad_money	Broad money, local currency	Local currency units	126	2001-17	Haver Analytics; OECDstat; IMF International Financial Statistics

Note: Country coverage indicates the number of countries with data available in any year during 1970-2017.

References

Abbas, S. M. A., N. Belhocine, A. El-Ganainy, and M. Horton. 2011. "Historical Patterns and Dynamics of Public Debt—Evidence from a New Database." *IMF Economic Review* 59 (4): 717-42.

Caceres, C., Y. Carrière-Swallow, and B. Gruss. 2016. "Global Financial Conditions and Monetary Policy Autonomy." IMF Working Paper 16/108, International Monetary Fund, Washington, DC.

Carare, A., and M. R. Stone. 2006. "Inflation Targeting Regimes." *European Economic Review* 50 (5): 1297-315.

Chinn, M. D., and H. Ito. 2006. "What Matters for Financial Development? Capital Controls, Institutions, and Interactions." *Journal of Development Economics* 81(1): 163-92.

Darvas, Z. 2012. "Real Effective Exchange Rates for 178 Countries: A New Database." Bruegel Working Paper 2012/06, Bruegel, Brussels.

Dincer, N. N., and B. Eichengreen. 2014. "Central Bank Transparency and Independence: Updates and New Measures." *International Journal of Central Banking* 10 (1): 189-253.

Dreher, A., J.-E. Sturm, and J. de Haan. 2010. "When Is a Central Bank Governor Replaced? Evidence Based on a New Data Set." *Journal of Macroeconomics* 32 (3): 766-81.

Fernández, A., M. W. Klein, A. Rebucci, M. Schindler, and M. Uribe. 2016. "Capital Control Measures: A New Dataset." *IMF Economic Review* 64 (3): 548-74.

Garriga, A. C. 2016. "Central Bank Independence in the World: A New Dataset." *International Interactions* 42 (5): 849-68.

Gwartney, J., R. Lawson, and J. Hall. 2017. *Economic Freedom of the World: 2017 Annual Report.* Vancouver: Fraser Institute.

Ilzetzki, E., C. Reinhart, and K. S. Rogoff. 2017. "Exchange Arrangements Entering the 21st Century: Which Anchor Will Hold?" NBER Working Paper 23134, National Bureau of Economic Research, Cambridge, MA.

Klomp, J., and J. de Haan. 2010. "Central Bank Independence and Inflation Revisited." *Public Choice* 144 (3-4): 445-57.

Lane, P. R., and G. M. Milesi-Ferretti. 2007. "The External Wealth of Nations Mark II: Revised and Extended Estimates of Foreign Assets and Liabilities,1970-2004." *Journal of International Economics* 73 (2): 223-50.

Mauro, P., R. Romeu, A. Binder, and A. Zaman. 2015. "A Modern History of Fiscal Prudence and Profligacy." *Journal of Monetary Economics* 76: 55-70.

Quinn, D. P., and A. M. Toyoda. 2008. "Does Capital Account Liberalization Lead to Growth?" *Review of Financial Studies* 21 (3): 1403-49.

Schaechter, A., T. Kinda, N. Budina, A. Weber. 2012. "Fiscal Rules in Response to the Crisis—Toward the 'Next-Generation' Rules: A New Dataset." IMF Working Paper 12/187, International Monetary Fund, Washington, DC.

Shambaugh, J. C. 2004. "The Effect of Fixed Exchange Rates on Monetary Policy." *Quarterly Journal of Economics* 119 (1): 301-52.

Stock, J. H., and M. W. Watson. 2016. "Core Inflation and Trend Inflation." *Review of Economics and Statistics* 98 (4): 770-84.

INDEX

N

O

P

R

S

T

U

V

W